Neurobiology
of Learning
and Memory

Neurobiology of Learning and Memory

Edited by

JOE L. MARTINEZ, JR.

Division of Life Sciences
The University of Texas at San Antonio
San Antonio, Texas 78249

RAYMOND P. KESNER

Department of Psychology
University of Utah
Salt Lake City, Utah 84112

Academic Press

San Diego   London   Boston   New York   Sydney   Tokyo   Toronto

147280

This book is printed on acid-free paper.

Copyright © 1998 by ACADEMIC PRESS

Academic Press
a division of Harcourt Brace & Company
525 B Street, Suite 1900, San Diego, California 92101-4495, USA
http://www.apnet.com

Academic Press Limited
24-28 Oval Road, London NW1 7DX, UK
http://www.hbuk.co.uk/ap/

Library of Congress Catalog Card Number: 98-84370

International Standard Book Number: 0-12-475655-7

PRINTED IN THE UNITED STATES OF AMERICA
98 99 00 01 02 03 EB 9 8 7 6 5 4 3 2 1

This book is dedicated, as always, to our wives,
Drs. Kimberly Smith-Martinez and Laya Kesner.

We also acknowledge the passing and the work of
David Olton, Ph.D., a contributor to our previous book,
Learning and Memory: A Biological View, and a person
who was admired for his research and clear thinking.

Contents

1   *Historical Perspectives on the Development of the Biology of Learning and Memory*

Mark R. Rosenzweig

9 *The Neuropsychology of Human Learning and Memory*

Felicia B. Gershberg and Arthur P. Shimamura

10 *Neurobiological Views of Memory*

Raymond P. Kesner

11 *Psychobiological Models of Hippocampal Function in Learning and Memory*

Mark A. Gluck and Catherine E. Myers

Contributors

Numbers in parentheses indicate the pages on which the authors' contributions begin.

Edwin J. Barea-Rodriguez (211)
Division of Life Sciences
The University of Texas
San Antonio, Texas 78249

C. A. Barnes (247)
Departments of Psychology and Neurology
and Arizona Research Laboratories
Division of Neural Systems, Memory and
Aging
University of Arizona
Tucson, Arizona 85724

James E. Black (55)
Departments of Psychology and Psychiatry
Neuroscience Program and Beckman
Institute
Urbana, Illinois 61801

Terry Crow (177)
Department of Neurobiology and Anatomy
University of Texas Medical School
Houston, Texas 77225

Brian E. Derrick (211)
Division of Life Sciences
The University of Texas
San Antonio, Texas 78249

Felicia B. Gershberg (333)
Memory Disorders Research Center
Boston University School of Medicine
Boston, Massachusetts 02130

Karl Peter Giese (89)
Cold Spring Harbor Laboratory
Cold Spring Harbor, New York 11724

Mark A. Gluck (417)
Center for Molecular and Behavioral
Neuroscience
Rutgers University
Newark, New Jersey 07102

William T. Greenough (55)
Departments of Psychology, Psychiatry, and
Cell and Structural Biology
Neuroscience Program and Beckman
Institute
University of Illinois
Urbana, Illinois 61801

Fay A. Guarraci (289)
Department of Psychology
The University of Vermont
Burlington, Vermont 05405

Bruce S. Kapp (289)
Department of Psychology
The University of Vermont
Burlington, Vermont 05405

Raymond P. Kesner (361)
Department of Psychology
University of Utah
Salt Lake City, Utah 84112

Joe L. Martinez, Jr. (211)
Division of Life Sciences
The University of Texas
San Antonio, Texas 78249

Catherine E. Myers (417)
Center for Molecular and Behavioral
    Neuroscience
Rutgers University
Newark, New Jersey 07102

Mark R. Rosenzweig (1)
Department of Psychology
University of California
Berkeley, California 94720

Christine Sahley (177)
Department of Biological Sciences
Purdue University
West Lafayette, Indiana 47907

Juan A. Salinas (143)
Department of Psychology
University of Virginia
Charlottesville, Virginia 22903

Arthur P. Shimamura (333)
Department of Psychology
University of California
Berkeley, California 94720

Alcina J. Silva (89)
Cold Spring Harbor Laboratory
Cold Spring Harbor, New York 11724

Amy J. Silvestri (289)
Department of Psychology
The University of Vermont
Burlington, Vermont 05405

Norman M. White (143)
Department of Psychology
McGill University
Montreal, Quebec H3A 1B1
Canada

Preface

Memory is a thing in a place in a brain. If one learns something and that learning lasts a long time, perhaps a lifetime, then something changes in the brain to represent that memory. What are these changes? We call the study of these changes the *Neurobiology of Learning and Memory,* which is the title of this book. The chapters in this book, contributed by expert researchers in the field, examine the stuff of memory from many perspectives.

Because the research in the area of learning and memory advances rapidly and new areas are emerging, we felt it necessary to develop a new edited book that includes the latest advances in our understanding. Each author was asked to present a historical introduction and an overview of the critical studies and ideas in his or her area of expertise. The topics were selected to examine different levels of analysis, theoretical views, and subject populations from invertebrates to humans. A new historical chapter that explores the major developments in the field from the time of William James is presented by Mark Rosenzweig.

James Black and William Greenough explore anatomical mechanisms that could mediate learning, plasticity, and memory storage in adult animals. Alcino Silva and Karl Peter Giese review the use of transgenic animals to eliminate a specific gene to study that gene's role in learning and long-term potentiation. Norman White and Juan Salinas show how perturbations of particular neurotransmitter systems in defined brain areas with pharmacological agents reveal how neurotransmitters systems function in memory storage. Christine Sahley and Terry Crow examine how the use of invertebrates with simpler nervous systems than mammals has revealed a great deal about how nervous systems in general learn at the cellular level. Joe Martinez, Jr., Edwin Barea-Rodriguez, and Brian Derrick inquire into how either increases or decreases in synaptic strength, known as long-term potentiation or long-term depression, may function in networks of neurons to form the basis of memories. Carol Barnes studies and reviews how a brain changes with age, how this affects memory storage, and how drug therapies to improve declining memory, such as that observed in Alzheimer's disease, may be developed. Bruce Kapp, Amy Silvestri, and Fay Guarraci review how the study of simple memories, such as seen in conditioned reflexes in mammals, promises to reveal the first engram or complete memory trace in a brain. Felicia Gershberg and Art Shimamura explore memory systems in humans and how damage to certain areas of the brain reveals the structure and kinds of memory. Raymond Kesner presents a comprehensive attribute theory of memory and reviews experiments that reveal which brain areas participate in each memory attribute. Finally, Mark Gluck and Catherine Myers analyze theories of how the brain stores information from a neuro-computational perspective.

This book will be of use to those who want to understand the neurobiology of learning and memory. The book assumes that the reader has a basic knowledge of psychology and biology. Previous versions of this book were used to teach advanced undergraduate and graduate students about the neurobiology of learning and memory. We expect that this book will serve the same purpose.

Joe L. Martinez, Jr.
Raymond P. Kesner

Historical Perspectives on the Development of the Biology of Learning and Memory

Mark R. Rosenzweig

Department of Psychology, University of California, Berkeley, California 94720

I. INTRODUCTION

This chapter presents a broad survey of more than a century of research on learning and memory and their biological mechanisms. The succeeding chapters focus on recent research in different main areas within this broad topic. Examining the history of research on learning and memory and their biological mechanisms reveals many intriguing anticipations of current thinking and also many sidetracks and errors. Such a survey provides insights about factors that favor discovery and also pitfalls that lie in the path of research. A historical review, especially a brief one, is necessarily selective; to help avoid selection that is either arbitrary or made to justify the present, this chapter will draw upon some major reviews made at key points in time.

II. HISTORY IN 50-YEAR SPANS

Let us concentrate on three time points to evaluate and consider the growth of knowledge about memory and its biological bases. The first is 1890 when William

James published his monumental *Principles of Psychology,* soon after the start of formal research on memory. What could James tell his readers about habit, memory, and their biological bases? The second time point is 1940 when Hilgard and Marquis published *Conditioning and Learning.* How does their account compare with that of James, to whom they refer briefly? What changes in topics occurred in the 50 years since James' book, and what new techniques had become available? Finally, we can use the present volume to survey briefly the status of the field in the 1990s.

III. WILLIAM JAMES (1890) ON THE PHYSICAL BASIS OF HABIT AND MEMORY

In his major textbook, *Principles of Psychology* (1890), James devoted separate chapters to habit, association, and memory. Before considering his positions on these subjects, let us note briefly some of the context in which James wrote.

A. Background for James' Account

At the time James wrote, psychology was becoming established as an independent academic discipline and as a laboratory science in Europe and North America. Wilhelm Wundt, a professor of philosophy with a doctorate in medicine, had founded the first formal laboratory of psychology at the University of Leipzig in 1879. James, also a professor of philosophy with a medical degree, began teaching physiological psychology at Harvard University in 1875, and he had an informal laboratory of psychology.

The decade of the 1880s saw several major advances in research on learning and memory. French psychologist Théodule Ribot published an important book, *Diseases of Memory* (1881). In presenting descriptions of impairments of memory as consequences of brain lesions and brain diseases, Ribot wrote that he regretted that it was not possible to state such impairments in quantitative terms. Only a few years later, German psychologist Hermann Ebbinghaus showed how memory could be measured in his pathbreaking book *On Memory* (1885). This book inaugurated the experimental investigation of learning and memory. In another important contribution of the 1880s, S. S. Korsakoff (1887) published a study of the syndrome that now bears his name.

B. James on Habit and Memory

In the *Principles of Psychology,* James often asserts that habit, memory, and other aspects of behavior are based on physiological properties of the brain, even when he cannot specify these properties very clearly. Thus James states that the cerebral hemispheres seem to be the chief seat of memory (p. 98). James devoted Chapter 4 to habit and Chapter 16 to memory; a related chapter, Chapter 14, was devoted to association. The separation of the chapters on habit and on memory can be seen as a precursor to the distinction made in the 1980s between nondeclarative and declarative memories. Habits, according to James, reflect the plasticity of the organic material [of the nervous system] (p. 105). Neural activity can either "deepen old paths or . . . make new ones" (p. 107). James admitted that it was not yet possible to define in a detailed way what happens in the nervous system when habits are formed or changed, but he was confident that scientific research would find the answers:

> . . . our usual scientific custom of interpreting hidden molecular events after the analogy of visible massive ones enables us to frame easily an abstract and general scheme of processes which the physical changes in question *may* be like. And when once the possibility of *some* kind of mechanical[1] interpretation is established, Mechanical Science, in her present mood, will not hesitate to set her brand of ownership upon the matter, feeling sure that it is only a question of time when the exact mechanical explanation of the case shall be found out. (p. 107)

James gave lessons on how to form habits effectively. Furthermore, he drew an ethical lesson, with a molecular basis:

> Could the young but realize how soon they will become mere walking bundles of habits, they would give more heed to their conduct while in the plastic state. . . . Every smallest stroke of virtue or vice leaves its never so little scar. The drunken Rip Van Winkle, in Jefferson's play, excuses himself for every fresh dereliction by saying, "I won't count this time!" Well! he may not count it, and a kind Heaven may not count it; but it is being counted none the less. Down among his nerve cells and fibres the molecules are counting it, registering and storing it up to be used against him when the next temptation comes. (p. 127)

James distinguished between what later came to be called short-term and long-term memories, referring to them as "primary" and "secondary" memories (p. 638).

Concerning the tendency of emotionally exciting experiences to be remembered well, James wrote, "An impression may be so exciting emotionally as to almost leave a *scar* on the cerebral tissues" (p. 670).

James devoted three pages (pp. 676-678) to the experiments of Ebbinghaus (1885) under the heading "Exact Measurements of Memory." Considering Ebbinghaus' curve of forgetting, James commented, "The nature of this result might have been anticipated, but hardly its numerical proportions" (p. 677). James praised Ebbinghaus especially for his novel and successful attempt to test experimentally between two opposed hypotheses: this referred to Ebbinghaus' evidence that serial learning involves not only direct associations between adjacent items but also the formation of remote associations between nonadjacent items. James commented

---

[1]James used "mechanical" here in the sense of mechanistic, that is, interpreting and explaining phenomena by referring to causally determined material forces.

that the fact of these remote associations ". . . ought to make us careful, when we speak of nervous 'paths,' to use the word in no restricted sense. They add one more fact to the set of facts which prove that association is subtler than consciousness, and that a nerve-process may, without producing consciousness, be effective in the same way in which consciousness would have seemed to be effective if it had been there" (p. 678).

As of 1890 there were few techniques available to study neural processes that might occur during learning and memory formation or ways of studying possible effects of memory on brain anatomy or neurochemistry. The development and use of such techniques characterize the research of the twentieth century.

IV. ADVANCES MADE AROUND THE END OF THE NINETEENTH CENTURY

Following Ebbinghaus' book of 1885, the field of research on memory expanded rapidly. Investigators also proposed hypotheses for the neural mechanisms of memory formation. Experiments on learning in animals began at the end of the nineteenth century. The next sections take up each of these topics.

A. Research on Human Learning and Memory

Contemporaries and immediate successors of Ebbinghaus soon expanded the work he had started, emphasizing controlled research on memory in a laboratory setting. Although Ebbinghaus' research obviously encouraged others, Postman (1985, p. 127) reported that his "survey shows clearly that Ebbinghaus' paradigm did not dominate or constrain the development of the field in its early years. Not only were many new methods of measurement and types of materials introduced in rapid succession, but the kinds of questions that were asked about memory soon began to move in different directions."

An important book on studies of verbal memory was published by Müller and Pilzecker (1900). In this work they put forth the "perseveration–consolidation hypothesis" which has engendered much research. They hypothesized that neural activity initiated by a learning trial continues and recurs for some time after the original stimulation has ceased and that this perseveration aids the consolidation of a stable memory trace. In reviewing this book, William McDougall (1901) pointed out that the perseveration–consolidation hypothesis could be used to account for retrograde amnesia following head injury.

B. Neural Junctions as Sites of Change in Learning

In the 1890s, several scientists speculated that changes at neural junctions might account for memory. This was anticipated, as Finger (1994a) points out, by associationist philosopher Alexander Bain (1872), who suggested that memory formation involves growth of what we now call synaptic junctions:

> For every act of memory, every exercise of bodily aptitude, every habit, recollection, train of ideas, there is a specific grouping or coordination of sensations and movements, by virtue of specific growths in the cell junctions. (p. 91)

Such speculations were put on a firmer basis in 1891 when neuroanatomist Wilhelm von Waldeyer enunciated the neuron doctrine, largely based on the research of Santiago Ramon y Cajal. Neurologist Eugenio Tanzi (1893) proposed the hypothesis that the plastic changes involved in learning probably take place at the junctions between neurons. He expressed confidence that investigators would soon be able to test by direct inspection the junctional changes he hypothesized to occur with development and training. About 80 years was to elapse, however, before the first results of this sort were announced (e.g., Cragg, 1967; Diamond, Lindner, Johnson, Bennett, & Rosenzweig, 1975; Globus, Rosenzweig, Bennett, & Diamond, 1973; West & Greenough, 1972).

Ramon y Cajal, apparently independently of Tanzi, went somewhat further in his Croonian lecture to the Royal Society of London (Cajal, 1894). He stated that the higher one looked in the vertebrate scale, the more the neural terminals and collaterals ramified. During development of the individual, neural branching increased, probably up to adulthood. Moreover he held it likely that mental exercise also leads to greater growth of neural branches, as he stated with a colorful set of analogies:

> The theory of free arborization of cellular branches capable of growing seems not only to be very probable but also most encouraging. A continuous pre-established network—a sort of system of telegraphic wires with no possibility for new stations or new lines—is something rigid and unmodifiable that clashes with our impression that the organ of thought is, within certain limits, malleable and perfectible by well-directed mental exercise, especially during the developmental period. If we are not worried about putting forth analogies, we could say that the cerebral cortex is like a garden planted with innumerable trees—the pyramidal cells—which, thanks to intelligent cultivation, can multiply their branches and sink their roots deeper, producing fruits and flowers of ever greater variety and quality. (pp. 467-468)

Ramon y Cajal then considered an obvious objection to his hypothesis:

> You may well ask how the volume of the brain can remain constant if there is a greater branching and even formation of new terminals of the neurons. To meet this objection we may hypothesize either a reciprocal diminution of the cell bodies or a shrinkage of other areas of the brain whose function is not directly related to intelligence. (p. 467)

We will return later to this assumption of constancy of brain volume and Ramon y Cajal's hypotheses to permit constancy in the face of increased neuronal ramification.

The neural junctions did not have a specific name when Tanzi and Ramon y Cajal wrote early in the 1890s, but a few years later neurophysiologist Charles Sherrington

(Foster & Sherrington, 1897) gave them the name "synapse." Sherrington also stated that the synapse was likely to be strategic for learning, putting it in this picturesque way:

> Shut off from all opportunities of reproducing itself and adding to its number by mitosis or otherwise, the nerve cell directs its pent-up energy towards amplifying its connections with its fellows, in response to the events which stir it up. Hence, it is capable of an education unknown to other tissues. (p. 1117)

From time to time since scientists of the 1890s proposed that development of the nervous system and memory formation share many processes and mechanisms, others have been struck by the same insight, often without knowledge (or at least without acknowledgment) of their predecessors. However, it has not yet proved possible to demonstrate that memory formation is necessarily based on and restricted to the processes involved in neural development. We will return to this question in Section IX.

During the first half of the twentieth century, psychologists and other scientists proposed memory hypotheses involving either the growth of neural fibrils toward one another to narrow the synaptic gap or more subtle chemical changes at synapses (see review in Finger, 1994a). However, the techniques then available allowed little progress on this issue.

C. Introduction of Research on Learning of Animal Subjects

Research on learning and memory was extended to animal subjects independently by the psychologist Edward L. Thorndike and the physiologist Ivan P. Pavlov. Thorndike demonstrated in his doctoral thesis (1898), conducted under William James, how learning and memory can be measured in animal subjects, using cats, dogs, and chicks. This research led to the concept of trial-and-error learning and, later, to the "law of effect" (Thorndike, 1911). The field Thorndike opened with this research was quickly entered by others (Hilgard & Marquis, 1940, p. 6).

In contrast to Thorndike's planned study of animal learning, Pavlov came upon the concept of conditioning from observations on salivary responses, made during his Nobel Prize winning research on secretions of the alimentary tract. His initial contribution to the study of learning has been dated anywhere from 1897 to 1904 or even 1906. The *American Psychologist* (1997, *52*(9)) and the *European Psychologist* (1997, *2*(2)) published parallel sections in 1997 to commemorate the centenary of Pavlov's book, in Russian, *Lectures on the Work of the Principal Digestive Glands* (Pavlov, 1897). Pavlov's book included observations on "psychic secretion" which foreshadowed his later research on conditioning. The first published use of the term "conditioned reflex" (actually "conditional reflex") was in a report by I. F. Tolotschinoff (Tolochinov), one of Pavlov's associates, at the Congress of Natural

Sciences in Helsinki in 1902. Pavlov discussed conditioning in his Nobel Prize lecture in 1904, although the main subject of the lecture was the research on the digestive glands, for which the Nobel Prize was awarded. Pavlov's first paper in English on salivary conditioning was his 1906 Huxley lecture, "The scientific investigation of the psychical faculties or processes in the higher animals," which was published in both *The Lancet* and *Science*. Even this review did not, however, "lead to any immediate repetitions of Pavlov's work in America, so far as published records reveal" (Hilgard & Marquis, 1940, p. 10). In introducing the commemorative articles in the *American Psychologist,* Dewsbury (1997) noted that one might argue that psychologists should hold off until 2006 to commemorate Pavlov but wrote that the editors saw no reason to wait to celebrate a scientist of Pavlov's stature and a book of the importance of *Lectures on the Work of the Principal Digestive Glands.*

In 1902, American psychologist Shepard I. Franz opened a further line in animal research on learning and memory: He sought to determine the site of learning in the brain by combining Thorndike's methods of training and testing animals with the technique of localized brain lesions. Franz later recruited Karl S. Lashley, and through Lashley many others, to research on this topic.

Conditioning is now such a widely used technique—it is used in the research reviewed in several chapters in this volume—that it is interesting to note that it did not gain acceptance rapidly. Only after the presidential address of John B. Watson to the American Psychological Association in 1915, "The place of the conditioned reflex in psychology" (1916), did conditioning begin to have a prominent place in textbooks, and its place in the laboratory lagged still further behind. The publication in 1927 and 1928 of translations of books by Pavlov, revealing the wealth of facts discovered by Pavlov and his colleagues during more than a quarter of a century of research on salivary conditioning in dogs, stimulated a series of replications and extensions to conditioning in other species.

Earlier Observations of "Psychical Secretion"

In evaluating Pavlov's contributions, it is important to note that Pavlov, as he stated in his 1904 Nobel Prize lecture, was not the first to observe that secretions of the salivary and gastric glands can be evoked by "psychic" (i.e., nongustatory) stimuli. Although Pavlov did not feel it necessary to name his predecessors in this respect, several medical or physiological investigators recorded such observations in the eighteenth and nineteenth centuries, and many more must have seen this phenomenon. One of the earliest such reports I have seen is that of Robert Whytt in his book *An Essay on the Vital and Other Involuntary Motions of Animals* (1763, p. 280):

> We consider, that not only an irritation of the muscles of animals, or parts nearly connected with them, is followed by convulsive motions; but that the remembrance or *idea* of substances, formerly applied to different parts of the body, produces almost the same effect, as if these substances were really present. Thus the sight, or even the recalled

idea of grateful food causes an uncommon flow of spittle into the mouth of a hungry person; and the seeing of a lemon cut produces the same effect in many people. . . . The sight of a medicine that has often provocked [*sic*] vomiting, nay, the very mention of its name, will in many delicate persons raise a nausea.

Note that in the last sentence Whytt also anticipated Garcia's (1990) "bait-shyness" learning. Further descriptions of salivary responses presumably elicited by learned stimuli were made by Erasmus Darwin (the grandfather of Charles Darwin) in 1796, French physiologist C.-L. Dumas (1803), Claude Bernard (1872), and others, as I have documented elsewhere (Rosenzweig, 1959, 1960).

Pavlov's contribution was not to note this phenomenon but to investigate it. He was the first to demonstrate that salivation could be evoked by a previously neutral stimulus after this had been paired with an effective stimulus. Moreover, he investigated carefully and skillfully both the conditions under which such acquisition occurs and conditions that do not lead to acquisition even though stimuli have been paired. This is one of many instances in the history of the field in which a casual observation has been exploited to lead to an important advance in knowledge.

V. THE STATUS OF THE FIELD IN 1940

By 1940 much information had been acquired about behavioral aspects of conditioning and learning but only little about their biological mechanisms. Hilgard and Marquis (1940) devoted the first nine chapters of *Conditioning and Learning* to research on conditioning and learning but only their last chapter (Chapter 13) to the neurophysiological mechanism of conditioning. The earlier chapters took up such topics as classical conditioning experiments, instrumental conditioning experiments, the nature of reinforcement, the nature of extinction, factors that determine the strength of conditioning, gradients of reinforcement, generalization and discrimination, and serial learning. The last chapter criticized Pavlov's theory of cortical function in conditioning, reviewed research on anatomical localization of conditioning, considered functional components of the conditioning mechanism, and reviewed speculations about the nature of synaptic modification.

As Hilgard and Marquis summarized, the fundamental concepts in Pavlov's physiological theory were excitation and inhibition, conceived as states or processes located in the cerebral cortex. Afferent stimulation by an originally neutral stimulus caused an excitatory process to be initiated at a particular point A on the cortex whence it spread or irradiated over the cortex. The irradiating excitation "will be concentrated at any other focus of excitation such as that aroused by an unconditioned stimulus. After a number of repetitions of the two stimuli, the excitation aroused by the neutral stimulus is drawn to the locus of the unconditioned stimulus in sufficient intensity to elicit the unconditioned response. The direction of the drainage of excitation is from the weaker to the stronger or more dominant focus of excitation" (Hilgard & Marquis, 1940, p. 310). These concepts were elaborated by Pavlov to account for such phenomena as generalization, extinction, sleep, hypnosis, and neurosis.

According to Hilgard and Marquis (pp. 311-313), in spite of the tempting simplicity and scope of Pavlov's conception of cortical physiology, it did not meet with any wide degree of acceptance. Some of the primary objections they summarized are these:

1. Concepts of cortical physiology should be based on direct measures of cortical function, but Pavlov's "excitation" and "inhibition" are purely inferential concepts based on overt movements or amounts of saliva secreted. "The concept of drainage is merely a figure of speech without any accepted neurophysiological basis." (p. 312)

2. "The temporal characteristic of irradiation, one of the most fundamental points in Pavlov's systematization, does not rest upon adequate experimental verification." (p. 312)

3. "Pavlov's physiological conceptions are explicitly based on the premise that conditioning is exclusively a cortical function. Recent experimentation . . . demonstrates, however, that conditioning is possible at a subcortical level. . . . The two-dimensional character in Pavlov's irradiation concept does not easily permit extension of the theory to embrace the integrated functioning of cortical and subcortical centers." (p. 313)

A. Where Does Conditioning Occur?

From the beginning of the twentieth century, many investigators have sought to find where in the nervous system conditioning occurs, and we will see a variety of conclusions. Hilgard and Marquis reviewed research to 1940 that attempted to find the brain locus of conditioning. These studies, which expanded on the pioneering work of Franz mentioned earlier, used mainly his technique of combining training with localized lesions, although in some cases (e.g., Culler, 1938) this was combined with localized electrical stimulation of the brain. Clearly, neurophysiological techniques available for research in this area had not progressed much since the early years of the 20th century. Concerning the brain locus of conditioning, Hilgard and Marquis offered this conclusion:

> The available evidence, although not conclusive, indicates that the locus of the conditioned association lies outside the regular pathways of the conditioned stimulus, the unconditioned stimulus, and the unconditioned response. . . . This does not, of course, imply the existence of an "association center" in the brain. Anatomical evidence reviewed earlier rules out the possibility of a single region in which associations are formed, but does not conflict with the conception of an association pathway which is different for each combination of stimuli involved in the conditioning. (pp. 324–325)

B. Speculations about the Nature of Synaptic Modification in Conditioning

Hilgard and Marquis reviewed in detail some of the attempts to account for changes that presumably occur at the synapses during conditioning, but it was too early to draw firm conclusions:

> Speculations regarding the nature of synaptic modification include anatomical growth of axons and dendrites, changes in the physico-chemical properties of the nerve cell, continued activity in closed neural chains, and the influence of bioelectric fields. Evidence is lacking for any of the proposed explanations, and at best the speculations serve only to account for stimulus-substitution which has been shown to be but one of the several forms which conditioning takes. (p. 335)

C. The Status of Learning Theory in the 1930s–1940s

In the United States, the development of theories of learning followed mainly from Thorndike's, and to a lesser extent, Watson's influence, as summarized by Donegan and Thompson (1991, pp. 6–7) in the second edition of this book. The main theories were the systematic and mechanistic system of Clark Hull (1943), emphasizing reinforcement through drive reduction as the mechanism for learning; Guthrie's (1935) notion of elemental stimulus–response (S–R) associations established through contiguity; Skinner's (1938) focus on the law of effect, and the effects of various schedules of reward and punishment on operant behaviors; and Tolman's development of a form of behaviorism that emphasized the cognitive nature of animal behavior. The approaches of Hull, Guthrie, and Tolman explained learning in terms of abstract associative principles arrived at through behavioral analysis, as opposed to physiological mechanisms, although Hull initially tried to cast his postulates in physiological terms.

It is worth noting that most of these theorists attempted to explain learning by a single set of rules. Tolman (1949), however, was convinced that there is more than one kind of learning and that different kinds might follow different laws.

As Nilsson (1992) points out, the approaches followed by American psychologists in the first half of the twentieth century could be seen as a continuation of the Ebbinghaus tradition. Alternative approaches in Europe included those of Bartlett in Great Britain and of the Gestalt psychologists.

VI. PESSIMISM AND THEN RAPID GAINS DURING THE LAST HALF CENTURY

For a decade after the publication of Hilgard and Marquis' book in 1940, there seemed to be little advance in the field. During graduate studies at Harvard in the late 1940s, I heard conflicting points of view about prospects for the field. Karl S. Lashley published a pessimistic review in 1950. When he surveyed the literature on possible synaptic changes as a result of training, he concluded that there was no solid evidence to support any of the "growth" theories. Specifically Lashley offered these criticisms: (a) Neural cell growth appears to be too slow to account for the rapidity with which some learning can take place; we will return to this point later. (b) Because he was unable to localize the memory trace, Lashley held there was no warrant to look for localized changes. A few years later, Hans–Lukas Teuber stated in an *Annual Review of Psychology* chapter on physiological psychology that ". . . the absence of any convincing physiological correlate of learning is the greatest gap in physiological psychology. Apparently, the best we can do with learning is to prevent it from occurring, by intercurrent stimulation through implanted electrodes . . . , by cerebral ablation . . . , or by depriving otherwise intact organisms, early in life, of normal sensory influx . . ." (Teuber, 1955, p. 267). Edwin G. Boring, the historian of psychology, with whom I studied in the latter 1940s, also testified in 1950 to the lack of progress in this area:

> Where or how does the brain store its memories? That is the great mystery. . . . The physiology of memory has been so baffling a problem that most psychologists in facing it have gone positivistic, being content with hypothesized intervening variables or with empty correlations. (Boring, 1950, p. 670)

At the end of his chapter on the history of research on brain functions, Boring gave his view about what was needed for further progress:

> In general it seems safe to say that progress in this field is held back, not by lack of interest, ability or industry, but by the absence of some one of the other essentials for scientific progress. Knowledge of the nature of the nerve impulse waited upon the discovery of electric currents and galvanometers of several kinds. Knowledge in psychoacoustics seemed to get nowhere until electronics developed. The truth about how the brain functions may eventually yield to a technique that comes from some new field remote from either physiology or psychology. Genius waits on insight, but insight may wait on the discovery of new concrete factual knowledge. (Boring, 1950, p. 688)

In fact, some major advances were beginning to occur in research on the neural mechanisms of learning and memory. Some of these resulted from application of recently developed techniques such as single-cell electrophysiological recording, electron microscopy, and use of new neurochemical methods, as we will review later. Another major influence encouraging research on neural mechanisms of learning and memory was Donald O. Hebb's 1949 monograph, *The Organization of Behavior*. I had the good fortune to be exposed to Hebb's optimistic perspective in a seminar he gave at Harvard in the summer of 1947, using as a text a mimeographed version of his book that was published in 1949.

Hebb (1949) was more positive about possible synaptic changes in learning than his colleague Lashley. Hebb noted some evidence for neural changes and did not let the absence of conclusive evidence deter him from reviving hypotheses about the conditions that could lead to formation of new synaptic junctions and underlie memory. In essence, Hebb's hypothesis of synaptic change underlying learning resembled James' formulation (as did the formulation of Hebb's contemporary Ralph W. Gerard, 1949): "When two elementary brain-processes have been active together or in immediate succession, one of them, on recurring, tends to propagate its excitement into the other" (James, 1890, p. 566). Hebb's dual-trace hypothesis also resembles the consolidation–perseveration hypothesis of Müller and Pilzecker. Much current neuroscience research concerns properties of what are now known as Hebbian synapses. Hebb was wryly amused that his name was connected to this resurrected hypothesis rather than to concepts he considered original (Milner, 1993, p. 127). The emphasis on the synaptic hypothesis reflects the fact, noted by Gallistel (1990, p. 570) that most neuroscientists have been more concerned with how synaptic changes can store information than with how neural networks can compute memories. By the 1990s the idea that correlated activity could lead to new neural connections was so well accepted that it could be epitomized in six words: neurons that fire together wire together (Löwel & Singer, 1992, p. 211).

VII. ELECTROPHYSIOLOGICAL STUDIES OF LEARNING AND MEMORY

Soon after Hilgard and Marquis' review, the first electrophysiological observations of training were made by accident during research with a human subject. The French neurophysiologists Gustav Durup and Alfred Fessard (1935) were studying how the alpha rhythm is blocked when a person's field of vision is illuminated. After switching on the light several times one day and seeing the subject's alpha rhythm disappear from the record each time, the experimenter again threw the light switch, but the bulb failed and the room remained dark—nevertheless the alpha rhythm again disappeared! Seeking to explain this puzzling occurrence, the investigators hypothesized that the sound of the switch became a conditioned stimulus predicting the appearance of light and thus caused the EEG to respond as if light were present. Tests with other subjects soon demonstrated that the sound of the switch did not block the alpha rhythm in naive subjects but came to do so after pairings of sound and light.

As this research became more widely known after the end of World War II, many investigators took up studies of EEG correlates of conditioning in the late 1940s and 1950s. However, precise localization of EEG activity in the human cortex is difficult, because of the overlying skull and tissue. Besides, the critical events might not be occurring in the cortex but in deeper brain structures. For these reasons, the focus of research shifted to recording from the brains of alert, behaving animal subjects, often with indwelling electrodes. We will soon review a program of such research to find the sites of plastic neural changes that accompany eyelid conditioning. With the invention of microelectrodes around 1950 it became possible to record the activity of single neurons during training. We will see this technique applied to investigating cellular activity during conditioning of a variety of animals, including relatively simple molluscs.

A. Sites of Synaptic Plasticity in the Nervous System of *Aplysia*

Observations on nonassociative learning in relatively simple invertebrates date back at least to the first decade of the twentieth century (e.g., Jennings, 1906). The relative simplicity of the central nervous systems of some invertebrates led several investigators to try to find in them the neural circuits necessary and sufficient for learning, with the goal of studying plastic synaptic changes in these circuits. Invertebrate preparations, such as the large sea slug *Aplysia,* appeared to offer the following advantages for this research, although we will see later that some of these were overestimated:

1. The number of nerve cells in an *Aplysia* ganglion is relatively small compared to that in a mammalian brain or even a brain region, although the number in the *Aplysia* ganglion is still on the order of 1000.

2. In the ganglia of molluscs such as *Aplysia,* the cell bodies form the outside and the dendritic processes are on the inside. This arrangement, the opposite of that in the mammal, makes it easy to identify and record from cells of such invertebrates.

3. Many individual cells in molluscan ganglia can be recognized both because of their shapes and sizes and because the cellular structure of the ganglion is uniform from individual to individual. Thus it is possible to identify certain cells and to trace their sensory and motor connections. The neurotransmitters in some of the large identifiable cells are also known.

Because of such advantages, J. W. Davis (1986, p. 268) stated in the first edition of this book that ". . . invertebrates offer the promise of immediate and comprehensive understanding of the physiological processes underlying associative learning, which may in turn provide insights into mammalian learning." However, research in the decade since 1986 showed Davis' prediction was overoptimistic.

A well-known example of such research is the program initiated by Eric Kandel that has investigated sites and mechanisms of plasticity for both nonassociative and associative learning in *Aplysia* (e.g., Kandel, Schacher, Castellucci, & Goelet, 1987; Kandel, Schwartz, & Jessell, 1995). Kandel's research indicated that conditioning of the gill-withdrawal reflex takes place within a straight-through sensory–motor chain that controls the behavior being studied. Many interesting results have been reported from this program, although some investigators have voiced reservations about the methods and findings.

Although Kandel concluded the gill-withdrawal response is a simple unitary reflex and is controlled only by cells in the abdominal ganglion, other investigators have shown that neither of these conclusions is accurate. In fact, the gill-withdrawal response occurs even when the central nervous system of *Aplysia* has been inactivated or removed.

Colebrook and Lukowiak (1988) further pointed out that in experiments on conditioning *Aplysia* no one had recorded both the electrical activity of the motor neurons and the gill responses in the *same* animals. When they carried out such an experiment, they found that, although both the neural responses and the gill-withdrawal amplitudes to the CS showed mean increases as a result of conditioning, over one-third of the animals showed an increase in one but not in the other measure! That is, the behavioral response and its supposed neural cause did not necessarily act in the same way. Colebrook and Lukowiak (1988) concluded that many loci and neural mechanisms are likely to be involved in conditioning of the gill-withdrawal response, with both the ganglia and peripheral sites combining their effects.

Kandel and his associates then began to move in this direction, using a reduced preparation for simultaneous behavioral and cellular studies of plasticity of the gill-withdrawal response. They published preliminary reports on nonassociative learning with this preparation (Cohen, Henzi, Kandel, & Hawkins, 1991; Hawkins, Cohen, & Kandel, 1992) but do not appear to have published full reports on this work. To investigate the role of different motor neurons in the ganglion, they inactivated one or another neuron by hyperpolarization; they reported that one motor neuron is responsible for about 70% of the gill-withdrawal response. They then recorded responses of this neuron during habituation, dishabituation, and sensitization. The "results suggest that habituation in this preparation is largely due to depression at central synapses, whereas dishabituation and sensitization are due to central and peripheral facilitation with different time courses" (Hawkins, Cohen, & Kandel, 1992). Further work on the sites involved in conditioning has not yet appeared, but it is likely that conditioning as well as sensitization involves the peripheral as well as the central nervous system of *Aplysia*.

Thus the results of more recent research challenge the earlier conclusions that plasticity is located exclusively in the ganglia of *Aplysia*. However, there seems to be no reason to question that synaptic mechanisms of plasticity occur at some large neurons in the abdominal ganglion.

Nevertheless, support for Kandel's neurochemical hypotheses comes from research with *Drosophila* mutants that are impaired in learning and memory, as pointed out in a review by Kandel and associates (Kandel et al., 1987, p. 26). These mutants were found to have deficiencies in some of the neurochemical steps identified by Kandel and his associates as being important for learning, and this provides independent support for generality of their hypotheses.

However, even in the ganglion the story is far from complete, because a single touch to the siphon can activate electrical responses in about 150 different neurons (Zecevic et al., 1989), and many of these probably play roles in the complex gill movements. Other investigators have reported that approximately 200 abdominal ganglion neurons are involved in the gill-withdrawal response, and most of them are also involved in respiratory movements (Wu, Cohen, & Falk, 1994). Study of the different kinds of responses mediated by these neurons suggests that the different behaviors are generated by altered activities of a single, large distributed network rather than by separate small networks, each dedicated to a particular response. Wu et al. (1994) report that the large motor neurons probably contribute less than 10% to the gill-withdrawal response. Beyond these problems at the *central* sites, the mechanisms of plasticity at *peripheral* neural sites in *Aplysia* have not yet been studied, so there is still much to learn about the mechanisms of learning even in what some investigators hoped would be a "simple" kind of learning in a "simple" organism.

B. Conditioning in *Hermissenda*

Another marine mollusc, *Hermissenda,* is the subject of extensive research on mechanisms of conditioning by Daniel Alkon and his colleagues (e.g., Alkon, 1975, 1989, 1992; Farley & Alkon, 1985). In the laboratory, pairing light with rotation on a turntable causes conditioned suppression of the tendency to approach the light. The plasticity in this system occurs in the eyes of *Hermissenda,* which contain only five photoreceptor cells.

The work with *Hermissenda,* which finds the important changes with training to occur in the neuronal membrane, affords quite a different picture of basic mechanisms of conditioning from that furnished by the research with *Aplysia,* which focuses on changes that occur at the presynaptic side of the synaptic junction. Both similarities and differences of the neurochemical mechanisms of learning in *Aplysia* and *Hermissenda* emerge from a comparison by Clark and Schuman (1992). After noting important similarities, they point out some distinctions: "Compared with plasticity in *Aplysia* siphon sensory cells, plasticity in *Hermissenda* Type B photoreceptors involves a different sensory modality (light rather than touch), different types of potassium conductances (I_A and I_{K-Ca}, rather than I_S), primarily a different second-messenger system (protein kinase C, rather than CAMP-dependent kinase), and an inhibitory rather than an excitatory synaptic potential, among other differences. These are meaningful distinctions, and their existence suggests that each preparation will provide unique insights into cellular mechanisms of learning" (Clark & Schuman, 1992, p. 598). Research in the coming years should demonstrate how well either or both of these pictures will be validated by further investigation in the two species. Similar research with other species of invertebrates and vertebrates will show whether these are only two of a wide variety of possible mechanisms of learning or whether either proves to be general over a number of species.

C. The Mammalian Cerebellum Houses the Brain Circuit for a Simple Conditioned Reflex

While many investigators studied learning in the apparently simpler nervous systems of invertebrates, others tried to define a circuit for learning in intact mammals.

Thus, psychologist Richard F. Thompson and his colleagues have been studying the neural circuitry of eyelid conditioning since the 1970s (Lavond, Kim, & Thompson, 1993; Thompson, 1990). Prior behavioral research had produced a great deal of knowledge about how the eye-blink reflex of the rabbit becomes conditioned when a puff of air to the cornea (US) follows an acoustic tone (CS). A stable conditioned response (CR) develops rather rapidly, and this is similar to eyelid conditioning in humans. The basic circuit of the eye-blink reflex is simple, involving two cranial nerves and some interneurons that connect their nuclei.

Early in their work, Thompson and colleagues found that during conditioning the hippocampus develops neural responses whose temporal patterns resemble closely those of the eyelid responses. Although the hippocampal activity closely parallels the course of conditioning and does so better than the activity of other limbic structures, this result does not prove that the hippocampus is required for conditioning to occur. In fact, destruction of the hippocampus has little effect on acquisition or retention of the conditioned eyelid response in rabbits (Lockhart & Moore, 1975). Therefore the hippocampus is not *required* for this conditioning. It may, however, participate in the conditioning, as indicated by the finding that abnormal hippocampal activity can disrupt the acquisition of conditioning.

Thompson and co-workers then searched further, mapping in detail the brain structures where neurons are active electrically during conditioning. They found that learning-related increases in activity of individual neurons are prominent in the cerebellum, in both its cortex and deep nuclei, and in certain nuclei in the pons.

In the cerebellum, there are only negligible responses to CS and US before the stimuli are paired, but a neuronal replica of the learned behavioral response emerges during conditioning. These responses, which precede the behavioral eye-blink responses by 50 msec or more, are found in the deep cerebellar nuclei ipsilateral to the eye that is trained. The interpositus nucleus appears to be particularly involved (McCormick & Thompson, 1984). Lesion experiments were then undertaken to find whether the cerebellar responses were required for conditioning or whether, like the hippocampal responses, they only correlated with the CRs. In an animal that had already been conditioned, destruction of the ipsilateral interpositus nucleus abolished the CR. The CR could not be relearned on the ipsilateral side, but the contralateral eye could still be conditioned normally. In a naive animal, prior destruction of the interpositus nucleus on one side prevented conditioning on that side. The effect of the cerebellar lesions could not be attributed to interference with sensory or motor tracts because the animal still showed a normal unconditioned blink when a puff of air was delivered to its eye.

The circuit of the conditioned reflex was then mapped in further detail using a combination of methods: electrophysiological recording, localized lesions, localized stimulation of neurons, localized infusion of small amounts of drugs, and tracing of fiber pathways (Krupa, Thompson, & Thompson, 1993). On the basis of these experiments, Thompson proposed a schematic circuit for the conditioned eye blink response, the latest version of which is reported in Thompson and Krupa (1994, p. 536, Fig. 1).

Since the main input to the deep cerebellar nuclei comes from the cerebellar cortex, lesions of the cortex would be expected to abolish the eyelid CR just as lesions of the deep nuclei do. Such a finding has been reported by a group working in England (Yeo, Hardiman, & Glickstein, 1985). Thompson and his associates, however, have not found lesions of the cerebellar cortex to interfere with the CR unless the lesions are very large. Perrett, Ruiz, and Mauk (1993) report that lesions of the anterior cerebellar cortex prevent rabbits from acquiring accurate timing of the CR. They propose that motor learning involves two sites of plasticity in the cerebellum: the CS–US association occurs at synapses between the mossy fibers and the deep cerebellar nuclei, whereas temporal discrimination is mediated by synapses between granule cells and Purkinje cells in the cerebellar cortex. The question of involvement of the cerebellar cortex remains under active study.

The role of the cerebellum in conditioning is not restricted to eye-blink conditioning. The cerebellum is also needed for conditioning of leg flexion; in this task, an animal learns to withdraw its leg when a tone sounds to avoid a shock to the paw (Donegan, Foy, & Thompson, 1983; Voneida, 1990). On the other hand, the cerebellum is not required for all forms of conditioning of skeletal muscular responses: Thompson and colleagues have found that cerebellar lesions do not prevent operant conditioning of a treadle press response in the rabbit (Holt, Mauk, & Thompson, unpublished, cited in Lavond et. al., 1993, p. 328).

Studies with human subjects are consistent with the animal research. Patients with unilateral cerebellar lesions (usually caused by a stroke) show normal eye-blink reflexes with both eyes, but they can acquire a conditioned eye-blink response only on the side where the cerebellum is intact (Papka, Ivry, & Woodruff-Pak, 1994). A recent PET study found that when humans received paired tone–airpuff training, several regions of the cerebellum and other brain structures showed increased glucose metabolism (Logan & Grafton, 1995). During the first, control session of the experiment, PET scans were taken while subjects received unpaired tone and right-eye airpuff stimuli. In the second session, 1–6 days later, subjects were given paired tone–airpuff trials. In the third session, 2–7 days after the first, PET scans were made while the subjects received paired trials. Comparison of the scans showed increased session-three activity in several regions of the cerebellum and also in other brain regions: right inferior thalamus/red nucleus, right hippocampal formation, right and left ventral striatum, right cortical middle temporal gyrus, and left cortex occipitotemporal fissure. Thus the neural network involved in human eyelid conditioning includes not only the cerebellar and brainstem regions found by Thompson and colleagues but also the hippocampus, the ventral striatum, and regions of the cerebral cortex.

D. Sleep and Memory Consolidation

After electrical recording helped to define the stages of sleep, beginning with the report of Aserinsky and Kleitman (1953), some investigators began to study the relation of stages of sleep to memory consolidation. Despite considerable research and a variety of findings, the field remains unsettled. Leconte and Bloch (1970) found that depriving rats of rapid eye movement (REM) sleep in the hours after learning impaired retention for avoidance conditioning. In a related experiment, the percentage of REM sleep to total sleep increased after a session of avoidance conditioning (Leconte, Hennevin, & Bloch, 1973). These results suggested that processing of newly acquired information continues during sleep as well as during waking. In this regard, Bloch (1976) referred to the perseveration–consolidation hypothesis of Müller and Pilzecker (1900) which we cited in Section IV.B. Some of Müller and Pilzecker's subjects in verbal learning experiments reported that, although instructed not to rehearse material between experimental sessions scheduled days apart, they found the material coming back to mind without their trying to recall it.

Attempts to relate learning in humans to REM sleep have usually yielded negative results, according to a review by sleep researcher Peretz Lavie (1996, p. 140). He does, however, note some positive findings: During intensive learning of a new language, young people show increases in REM sleep, and so do people who recover language after becoming aphasic because of brain damage. Most significant, however, was the discovery by Lavie and colleagues of a young man who showed virtually no REM sleep—on some nights this man showed no REM and overall only 2–5% of his total sleep was spent in REM, whereas healthy people of his age have 20–25% REM sleep (Lavie, Pratt, Scharf, Peled, & Brown, 1984). The patient had been injured by fragments of a shell in his brain; one splinter was lodged in the pons in the region believed to control activation of REM sleep. After recovery from the main effects of his injuries, this man completed high school and then law school, so the great reduction in REM sleep had not impaired his learning or memory.

Indications that brain activity during sleep is related to memory formation keep recurring. By monitoring the electrical activity of neurons in the hippocampus during sleep, Bruce McNaughton and colleagues may have observed such consolidation in process. The neurons in question appear to be "place cells," that is, while a rat learns its way in a maze, certain hippocampal cells come to favor firing when the rat is in a particular place in the maze, some cells firing when the rat is in one place and other cells firing more commonly when it is in another place. In such studies large, prominent landmarks are placed around the room containing the maze so that the rat can use them to keep track of its position. The firing of a particular hippocampal cell indicates not where the rat actually is, but the rat's perceived location in the maze.

Wilson and McNaughton (1994) simultaneously recorded the activity of many (>50) hippocampal cells before, during, and after rats learned a new maze. The activity of two cells that developed very different place preferences when the rats were learning the maze was uncorrelated throughout the experiment. However, hippocampal cells that developed place preferences for neighboring portions of the maze came to fire together. Thus, although the activity of these cells was uncorre-lated before the rats learned the maze, their firing was positively correlated by the end of the task. When the scientists examined the records made before the maze was learned, they found, as expected, that the activity of the cell pairs that was uncorrelated before maze learning during waking was also uncorrelated during prior sleep episodes. However, after the maze was learned and the hippocampal neurons developed a correlation in their discharge, that correlated discharge was also seen during slow-wave sleep. Wilson and McNaughton were able to find such neuron pairs (with uncorrelated discharge before learning and correlated discharge after learning) only by monitoring many neurons at once. Although these results are intriguing, it is not clear how to integrate them with results of other studies, most of which relate memory formation to rapid eye movement sleep rather than to slow-wave sleep. However, the fact that hippocampal neurons were active during sleep in these rats and the observation that the postlearning sleep activity reflected the modified discharge learned in the maze indicate that some active process is going on. It is almost as if the postlearning sleep reinforces the new relationships between the cells in their firing. A recent update (Skaggs & McNaughton, 1996) reports that even the order in which various hippocampal cells fired during the training session is reflected in the order in which they fire during sleep afterward. Whether this electrical activity during the posttraining sleep period in fact helps the rats remember the maze in subsequent trials remains to be seen. Because posttrain-ing sleep has been shown to improve memory retention and because the hippocam-pus seems to be important for at least some kinds of memory formation, these observations of neuronal activity seem tantalizingly like sleep consolidation of memory in action.

VIII. NEUROCHEMICAL AND NEUROANATOMICAL EFFECTS OF TRAINING AND EXPERIENCE

Ten years after Hebb's 1949 book was published, his postulate of use-dependent neural plasticity had still not been demonstrated experimentally. It seemed to many that it would not be possible, with available techniques, to find changes in the brain induced by training or experience. Thus, some neurobiologists spoke of a Catch 22 in trying to find neurochemical changes as a result of training in an extract of whole brain: if a change is detected, it can probably be ruled out as being a result of training—any changes observed can more reasonably be attributed to grosser and less specific concomitants of learning such as stress, attentiveness, and so on (Agranoff, Burrell, Dokas, & Springer, 1978, p. 628). At a symposium in 1957 my colleagues and I proposed that an approach to this problem would be to make neurochemical analyses of specific regions of trained and untrained brains. This might be able to integrate and permit measurement of small changes taking place over many thousands of neural units. If such changes were found within a region, then subsequent analyses might be able to focus down more closely (Rosenzweig, Krech, & Bennett, 1958, p. 338). In the early 1960s two experimental programs announced findings demonstrating that the brain can be altered measurably by training or differential experience. First was the demonstration by our group at Berkeley that both formal training and informal experience in varied environments led to measurable changes in neurochemistry and neuroanatomy of the rodent brain (Krech, Rosenzweig, & Bennett, 1960; Rosenzweig, Krech, & Bennett, 1961; Rosenzweig, Krech, Bennett, & Diamond, 1962). Soon after came the report of Hubel and Wiesel that occluding one eye of a kitten led to reduction in the number of cortical cells responding to that eye (Hubel & Wiesel, 1965; Wiesel & Hubel, 1963, 1965).

The original clues for the discovery of the Berkeley group came from data on rats given formal training in a variety of problems in order to examine possible relations between individual differences in brain chemistry and problem-solving ability. We did obtain significant correlations between levels of activity of the enzyme acetylcholinesterase (AChE) in the cerebral cortex and ability to solve spatial problems (e.g., Krech, Rosenzweig, & Bennett, 1956; Rosenzweig et al., 1958). When we tested the generality of this finding over six different behavioral tests, we found a surprise: As we reported at a 1959 symposium, total AChE activity was higher in the cerebral cortex of groups that had been trained and tested on more difficult problems than in those given easier problems, and all the tested groups measured higher in total cortical AChE activity than groups given no training and testing (Rosenzweig et al., 1961, p. 102 and Fig. 4). It appeared that training could alter the AChE activity of the cortex! To test this further, we conducted an experiment in which littermates were either trained on a difficult problem or left untrained; the trained rats developed significantly higher cortical AChE activity than their untrained littermates (Rosenzweig et al., 1961, p. 103). Control experiments showed that the results could not be attributed to the fact that the trained rats were underfed to increase their motivation or were handled.

Instead of continuing to train rats in problem-solving tests, a time-consuming and expensive procedure, we decided to house the animals in different environments that provided differential opportunities for informal learning. Measures made at the end of the experiment showed that informal enriched experience led to increased cortical AChE activity (Krech et al., 1960). The discovery that formal training or differential experience caused changes in cortical chemistry was soon followed by the even more surprising finding that enriched experience increased the *weights* of regions of the neocortex (Rosenzweig et al., 1962).

Work by students of Hebb (e.g., Forgays & Forgays, 1952) provided the models for the environments used in these experiments. Typically, we assigned littermates of the same sex by a random procedure among various laboratory environments, the three most common being the following: (a) a large cage containing a group of 10–12 animals and a variety of stimulus objects, which were changed daily (this was called the enriched condition (EC) because it provided greater opportunities for informal learning than did the other conditions); (b) the standard colony with three animals in a standard laboratory cage (this was called the social condition (SC)); and (c) SC-size cages housing single animals (this was called the impoverished condition or isolated condition (IC)). All three conditions provided food and water ad libitum.

Over the next several years, replications and extensions by us (e.g., Bennett, Diamond, Krech, & Rosenzweig, 1964) and by others (e.g., Altman & Das, 1964; Geller, Yuweiler, & Zolman, 1965; Greenough & Volkmar, 1973) added to the evidence that training or differential experience could produce measurable changes in the brain. Control experiments demonstrated that the cerebral differences could not be attributed to differential handling, locomotor activity, or diet. The brain weight differences caused by differential experience were extremely reliable, although small in percentage terms. Moreover, these differences were not uniformly distributed throughout the cerebral cortex: They were almost invariably largest in the occipital cortex and smallest in the adjacent somesthetic cortex; the rest of the brain outside the cerebral cortex tended to show very little effect (Bennett et al., 1964; Bennett, Krech, & Rosenzweig, 1964). Thus the experience caused changes in specific cortical regions and not undifferentiated growth of the brain. Later work also showed effects of differential experience in other parts of the brain that have been implicated in learning and formation of memory—the cerebellar cortex (Pysh & Weiss, 1979) and the hippocampal dentate gyrus (Juraska, Fitch, Henderson, & Rivers, 1985; Juraska, Fitch, & Washburne, 1989).

Further early studies revealed experience-induced changes in other measures, especially in the occipital cortex: these measures included cortical thickness (Diamond, Krech, & Rosenzweig, 1964), sizes of neuronal cell bodies and nuclei (Diamond, 1967), size of synaptic contact areas (West & Greenough, 1972), an increase of 10% in numbers of dendritic spines per unit of length of basal dendrites (Globus et al., 1973), an increase in extent and branching of dendrites (Holloway, 1966) amounting to 25% or more (Greenough & Volkmar, 1973), and a parallel increase in numbers of synapses per neuron (Turner & Greenough, 1985); mainly because of the increase in dendritic branching, the neuronal cell bodies are spaced farther apart in the cortex of EC than IC rats. These effects indicate substantial increases in cortical volume and intracortical connections; they suggest greater processing capacity of the cortical region concerned. They contradict the speculation of Ramon y Cajal (Cajal, 1894), noted earlier, that with training, neural cell bodies would shrink to allow neural arborizations to grow, thus allowing brain volume to remain constant. Instead, increased arborization requires *larger* cell bodies to maintain them, and the volume of the cortex increases as cell bodies and dendrites grow.

These experimental reports indicated growth of number and/or size of synaptic connections as results of training or enriched experience. Some workers declared for one or the other of these possibilities, as when neurophysiologist John C. Eccles (1965, p. 97) stated his belief that learning and memory storage involve "growth just of bigger and better synapses that are already there, not growth of new connections." Rosenzweig, Diamond, Bennett, and Mollgaard (1972), however, reviewed findings and theoretical discussions suggesting that negative as well as positive synaptic changes may store memory. Depending upon where one measures and the kind of training or differential experience, one may find an increase in the number of synapses, an increase in their size, a decrease in their number, or decrease in their size.

Did the discovery of neurochemical and neuroanatomical effects of training or experience require novel experimental techniques? Yes and no. Accurate measurement of AChE activity in large numbers of tissue samples became practical only in the early 1950s when we began our research. We first used a newly devised "pHstat" to titrate automatically the rate of hydrolysis and liberation of acid catalyzed by AChE. Then, when the Beckman UV spectrophotometer became available, we used it. On the other hand, most of the neuroanatomical effects of training or experience could have been discovered decades earlier, if anyone had had a reason to look for them; these were not findings that required technical advances for their discovery.

Skepticism and frank disbelief were the initial reactions to our reports that significant changes in the brain were caused by relatively simple and benign exposure of animals to differential experience. By the early 1970s some neurobiologists began to accept these results. Thus neurobiologist B. G. Cragg (1972, p. 42) wrote, "Initial incredulity that such differences in social and psychological conditions could give rise to significant differences in brain weight, cortical thickness, and glial numbers seems to have been overcome by the continued series of papers from Berkeley reporting consistent results. Some independent confirmation by workers elsewhere has also been obtained." Other neurobiologists continued into the 1980s to believe that neural connections in the adult brain remained fixed, as we will discuss further in Section IX.A.

Soon after the early publications of neurochemical and anatomical plasticity came another kind of evidence of cortical plasticity—the announcement by Hubel and Wiesel that depriving one eye of light in a young animal, starting at the age at which the eyes open, reduced the number of cortical cells responding to stimulation of that eye (Hubel & Wiesel, 1965, Wiesel & Hubel, 1963, 1965). Depriving an eye of light is a rather severe and pathological condition. In contrast, giving animals different amounts of experience without depriving them of any sensory modality is a rather mild and natural treatment, yet it leads to measurable changes of neurochemistry and neuroanatomy, and it has significant effects on problem-solving ability. The report of Wiesel and Hubel (1965) that changes can be induced in the visual system only during a critical period early in the life of the kitten served to solidify the belief of many neurobiologists that neural connections in the adult brain are fixed and do not vary as a result of training.

Black and Greenough (1986 and Chapter 2 in this volume) follow Piaget (1980) in distinguishing between two kinds of information acquired from the environment: (1) general information acquired by all members of a species from common features

of their environments (i.e., "expected" information) and (2) idiosyncratic information which the individual uses to adapt to its unique environment (i.e., "unexpected" information). As Black and Greenough (Chapter 2) point out, exposure
to light and visual pattern stimulation provides general, "expected" information,
whereas exposure to a complex environment provides idiosyncratic information.
Exposure to "expected" stimulation usually occurs early in development, and it
may be important in preparing the animal to respond adequately to idiosyncratic
information.

A. Differential Experience Produces Cerebral Changes throughout the Life Span, and Rather Rapidly

Further experiments revealed that significant cerebral effects of enriched versus
impoverished experience could be induced at any part of the life span and with
relatively short periods of exposure. In contrast, Hubel and Wiesel reported that
depriving an eye of light altered cortical responses only if the eye was occluded
during a critical period early in life. Later, however, investigators found that modifying sensory experience in adult animals—especially in the modalities of touch
and hearing—could alter both receptive fields of cells and cortical maps, as reviewed
by Kaas (1991) and Weinberger (1995).

Initially, we supposed that cerebral plasticity might be restricted to the early part
of the life span, so we assigned animals to differential environments at weaning
(about 25 days of age) and kept them there for 80 days. Later, members of our group
obtained similar effects in rats assigned to the differential environments for 30 days
as juveniles at 50 days of age (Zolman & Morimoto, 1962) and as young adults at
105 days of age (Bennett, Diamond, Krech, & Rosenzweig, 1964; Rosenzweig,
Bennett, & Krech, 1964). Riege (1971) in our laboratory found that similar effects
occurred in rats assigned to the differential environments at 285 days of age and kept
there for periods of 30, 60, or 90 days. Two hours per day in the differential
environments for a period of 30 or 54 days produced cerebral effects similar to
those found after 24-hr exposure for the same periods (Rosenzweig, Love, &
Bennett, 1968). Four days of differential housing produced clear effects on cortical
weights (Bennett, Rosenzweig, & Diamond, 1970) and on dendritic branching
(Kilman, Wallace, Withers, & Greenough, 1988); Ferchmin and Eterovic (1986)
reported that four 10-min daily sessions in EC significantly altered cortical RNA
concentrations.

The fact that differential experience can cause cerebral changes throughout the
life span, and relatively rapidly, was consistent with our interpretation of these effects
as due to learning. Recall also that our original observation of differences in cortical neurochemistry came from experiments on formal training. Later Chang and
Greenough (1982) reported that formal visual training confined to one eye of rats
caused increased dendritic branching in the visual cortex contralateral to the open

eye. Lowndes and Stewart (1994) found single-trial peck-avoidance training in chicks results in changes in density of dendritic spines.

Although the capacity for these plastic changes of the nervous system, and for learning, remain in older subjects, the cerebral effects of differential environmental experience develop somewhat more rapidly in younger than in older animals, and the magnitude of the effects is often larger in the younger animals. Also, continuing plasticity does not hold for all brain systems and types of experience. As noted earlier, changes in responses of cortical cells to an occluded eye are normally restricted to early development, as Wiesel and Hubel (1963) found. However, this restriction may itself be modifiable: Baer and Singer (1986) reported that plasticity of the adult visual cortex could be restored by infusing acetylcholine and noradrenaline. Further work showed that the plastic response of the young kitten brain to occlusion of one eye also depends upon glutamate transmission, because treating the striate cortex with an inhibitor of the glutamate NMDA receptor prevented the changes (Kleinschmidt, Baer, & Singer, 1987). Thus, the extent to which the brain shows plastic changes in response to a particular kind of experience depends on the age of the subject, the brain region, the kind of experience, and also the special circumstances or treatments that enhance or impair plasticity. The factor of age is reviewed by Barnes in Chapter 7.

B. Enriched Experience Improves Ability to Learn and Solve Problems

Hebb (1949, pp. 298–299) reported briefly that when he allowed laboratory rats to explore his home for some weeks as pets of his children and then returned the rats to the laboratory, they showed better problem-solving ability than rats that had remained in the laboratory throughout. Furthermore, they maintained their superiority or even increased it during a series of tests. Hebb concluded that "*the richer experience of the pet group during development made them better able to profit by new experience at maturity*—one of the characteristics of the 'intelligent' human being" (pp. 298–299, italics in the original). Moreover the results seemed to show a *permanent* effect of early experience on problem-solving at maturity.

We and others have found that experience in an enriched laboratory environment improves learning and problem-solving ability on a wide variety of tests, although such differences have not been found invariably. One general finding is that the more complex the task, the more likely it is that animals with EC experience will perform better than animals from SC or IC groups (see review and different explanations offered for this effect: Renner & Rosenzweig, 1987, pp. 46–48).

We were unable, however, to replicate an important aspect of Hebb's report— that over a series of tests, EC rats maintain or increase their superiority over IC rats. On the contrary, we found that IC rats tend to catch up with EC rats over a series of trials; this occurred with each of three different tests, including the Hebb–

Williams mazes (Rosenzweig, 1971, p. 321). Thus we did not find that early deprivation of experience caused a permanent deficit, at least for rats tested on spatial problems. Also, decreases in cortical weights induced by 300 days in the IC (versus the EC) environment could be overcome by a few weeks of training and testing in the Hebb–Williams maze (Cummins, Walsh, Budtz-Olsen, Konstantinos, & Horsfal, 1973). Later we will see a similar effect in birds.

C. Similar Neuroanatomical Effects of Training and Experience Occur in All Species Tested to Date

Experiments with several strains of rats showed similar effects of EC versus IC experience on both brain values and problem-solving behavior, as reviewed by Renner and Rosenzweig (1987, pp. 53–54). Similar effects on brain measures have been found in several species of mammals—mice, gerbils, ground squirrels, cats, and monkeys (reviewed by Renner & Rosenzweig, 1987, pp. 54–59)—and effects of training on brain values of birds have also been found. Thus the cerebral effects of experience that were surprising when first found in rats have now been generalized to several mammalian and avian species. Anatomical effects of training or differential experience have been measured in specific brain regions of *Drosophila* (R. Davis, 1993; Heisenberg, Heusipp, & Wanke, 1995). Synaptic changes with training have also been found in the nervous systems of the molluscs *Aplysia* and *Hermissenda,* as reviewed by Krasne and Glanzman (1995). In *Aplysia,* long-term habituation led to decreased numbers of synaptic sites, whereas long-term sensitization led to an increase (Bailey & Chen, 1983); this is a case where either a decrease or an increase in synaptic numbers stores memory. Thus, as noted by Greenough, Withers, and Wallace (1990, p. 164), "experience-dependent synaptic plasticity is more widely reported, in terms of species, than any other putative memory mechanisms."

D. Experience May Be Necessary for Full Growth of Brain and of Behavioral Potential

Sufficiently rich experience may be necessary for full growth of species-specific brain characteristics and behavioral potential. This is seen in recent research on differential experience conducted with different species of the crow family. Species that cache food in a variety of locations for future use are found to have significantly larger hippocampal formations than related species that do not cache food (Krebs, Sherry, Healy, Perry, & Vaccarino, 1989; Sherry, Vaccarino, Buckenham, & Herz, 1989). However, the difference in hippocampal size is not found in young birds that are still in the nest; it appears only after food storing has started, a few weeks after the birds have left the nest (Healy & Krebs, 1993). Even more interesting is the finding that this species-typical difference in hippocampal size depends on experience; it does not appear in birds that have not had the opportunity to cache food (Clayton & Krebs, 1994). Different groups of hand-raised birds were given experience in storing food at three different ages: 35–59, 60–83, and 115–138 days posthatch. Experience at each of these periods led to increased hippocampal size, much as we had found for measures of the occipital cortex in the rat. Thus, both birds and rats appear to retain considerable potential for experience-induced brain growth if it does not occur at the usual early age.

IX. ARE THE NEURAL MECHANISMS OF LEARNING AND DEVELOPMENT THE SAME?

A. Some Historical Background

Various relations between learning and development of the nervous system are treated in different chapters of this book. Here we consider the hypothesis that the mechanisms of learning and development are the same; this hypothesis was proposed separately by Tanzi and Ramon y Cajal in the 1890s, as we saw earlier. This hypothesis is undergoing a current wave of popularity as more is being learned about the mechanisms of both learning and development. Some of the current investigators recognize that this is an old hypothesis. Thus, Marcus, Emptage, Marois, and Carew (1994, p. 179) start their article in the following way: "At the turn of the century, Ramon y Cajal [Cajal] (1911) articulated the hypothesis that growth processes involved in the development of the nervous system persist into the adult where they subserve learning and memory." Others treat this hypothesis as being much more recent. Thus, Kandel and O'Dell (1992, p. 243) start the second paragraph of their article with the following statement:

> Perhaps the most interesting clues to shared mechanisms [of learning and development] are evidenced in the current revisions in our thinking about how connections in the vertebrate brain are formed in development. Until 10 or 15 years ago, most neurobiologists believed, as Roger Sperry proposed for cold-blooded vertebrates, that connections in the brain are formed independently of activity or experience and are programmed by a set of recognition molecules on each pre- and postsynaptic neuron of the synapse [Sperry, 1963].

This statement requires comments in two respects. First, how is it that "most neurobiologists" took until the later 1970s or early 1980s to recognize that activity and experience affect connections in the brain? Certainly accounts of the effects of experience on brain measures appeared in many neurobiological as well as psychological journals in the 1960s and early 1970s. This research was also reported in a cover article in the February 1972 *Scientific American* that discussed effects of experience on dendritic spine numbers and synaptic sizes, as well as other neural measures (Rosenzweig, Bennett, & Diamond, 1972). Some neurobiologists, such as

Cragg (1972), cited earlier, overcame their initial skepticism and accepted these reports by the early 1970s.

Second, although mentioning Sperry's conclusion about predetermined connections, Kandel and O'Dell ignore the fact that Sperry limited this inflexibility to the basic neural projection systems and believed that learning could alter connections in higher brain regions. In a presentation and discussion of his results and those of others, Sperry (1951, p. 237) tried to partial out the extent to which neural connections are "(1) preformed directly by processes of growth and cell differentiation and (2) patterned by functional regulation through experience and training." After concluding that the basic patterns of connections "are organized for the most part by intrinsic forces of development without the aid of learning," Sperry asked where effects of learning could be found. "By process of elimination the interneuronal relations patterned by learning would seem to be relegated to those circuits farthest removed from the conduction pathways which, in the mammal, would be confined mainly to the cerebral cortex." It is true that Sperry's evidence that the connections in the lower parts of the nervous systems of amphibians are preformed attracted more attention than his complementary conclusion of plasticity in the higher parts of the nervous system, but to ignore the latter conclusion does not do justice to the breadth of his views.

Accepting evidence that the adult brain can change neural connections throughout the life span was a paradigm shift, and such shifts are usually resisted strongly. It was more comfortable to accept Sperry's evidence of fixity of connections in the lower parts of the nervous system than to consider his conclusion that plasticity underlying learning must occur in upper regions of the brain. Hubel and Wiesel's evidence for plasticity in the cortex could be accepted, since it was restricted to an early critical period of life. Perhaps some neurobiologists were reluctant to accept evidence of lifelong neural plasticity because some of the investigators who discovered such effects were psychologists.

B. Tests of the Hypothesis That the Neural Mechanisms of Learning and Development Are the Same

The main method used so far to investigate the hypothesized identity between neural mechanisms of development and of learning has been to compile lists of mechanisms that are involved in both. However, as Marcus et al. (1994, p. 179) point out, " . . . to date no single experimental system has been extensively studied from both a developmental and a learning perspective. For this reason, comparisons between the mechanisms of learning and development often resort to analogies and inferences drawn across diverse systems." They therefore focus attention on research with *Aplysia,* using the growing "understanding of the cellular and molecular mechanism of learning in *Aplysia* as a basis for comparison with the three principle [*sic*] stages of neuronal development: differentiation, neurite outgrowth and synapse formation" (p. 180). Specific points of similarity between learning and development in *Aplysia* include the following: "(i) the role of serotonergic axosomatic contacts; (ii) the activation of transcription factors including immediate early genes and perhaps differentiation-inducing genes; (iii) the necessity of an appropriate post-synaptic target; (iv) the role of CAMP as a second messenger in the signal transcription cascade; and (v) the common role of cell adhesion molecules and other growth related proteins. During development, activation of these pathways leads to differentiation and neurite outgrowth; in adult learning, reactivation of these same pathways results in a growth-mediated increase in synaptic strength" (p. 181).

Beyond identifying similar processes involved in development and learning, Marcus et al. (1994, p. 186) point out that ". . . the real test of the relationship between development and learning will ultimately come from studies that ask whether the same process is *required* for both neuronal development and synaptic plasticity." They see hope for such tests in studies that can now be made with genetic manipulation in both vertebrates and invertebrates. For example, investigators are using homologous recombination technology in mice where knocking out the gene for a specific kinase produces both developmental abnormalities in the nervous system and a deficiency in long-term synaptic plasticity in the adult. In this regard Marcus et al. cite both Grant et al. (1992) and Silva, Stevens, Tonegawa, and Wang (1992). Kandel and O'Dell cite the same authors. Although knocking out a gene can impair some kinds of learning, it does not completely prevent the learning, raising questions about the necessity of the mechanism and the possibility of alternative mechanisms. Fortunately, in Chapter 3 Silva and Giese bring us up-to-date on this line of research.

X. NEUROCHEMICAL MECHANISMS OF LEARNING AND MEMORY

Research on neurochemical mechanisms of learning and memory has become a prominent line of investigation since the 1960s. Part of this stemmed from research on effects of enriched experience and formal training on the brain. Another source of this research was interest in mechanisms of consolidation of memory.

A. Tests of the Hypothesis That Protein Synthesis Is Required for Memory Storage

By what processes do enriched experience or formal training lead to plastic changes in cerebral neurochemistry and neuroanatomy? We found early on that enriched experience causes increased rates of protein synthesis and increased amounts of protein in the cortex (Bennett, Diamond, Krech, & Rosenzweig, 1964). Later, training (imprinting) was reported to increase the rates of incorporation of precursors into RNA and protein in the forebrain of the chick (Haywood, Rose, & Bateson, 1970), and enriched experience in rats was found to lead to increased amounts of RNA (Bennett, 1976; Ferchmin, Eterovic, & Caputto, 1970) and increased expression of RNA in the rat brain (Grouse, Schrier, Bennett, Rosenzweig, & Nelson, 1978). Maze training led to increased ratios of RNA to DNA in the rat cortex (Bennett, Rosenzweig, Morimoto, & Hebert, 1979). We viewed these findings in the light of the hypothesis, perhaps first enunciated by Katz and Halstead (1950), that protein synthesis is required for memory storage.

Tests of the protein-synthesis hypothesis of memory formation were initiated by Flexner and associates in the early 1960s (e.g., Flexner, Flexner, de la Haba, & Roberts, 1965; Flexner, Flexner, Stellar, de la Haba & Roberts, 1962), and much research followed their design: (1) giving animal subjects brief training that, without further treatment, would yield evidence of retention at a test a few days later; (2) administering to experimental subjects an inhibitor of protein synthesis at various times close to training, while control subjects received an inactive substance; and (3) comparing test performance of experimental and control subjects. By the early 1970s considerable evidence indicated that protein synthesis during or soon after training is necessary for formation of long-term memory (LTM), but the interpretation of the findings was clouded by serious problems such as the following: (1) The inhibitors of protein synthesis then available for research (such as puromycin and cycloheximide) were rather toxic, which impeded experiments and complicated interpretation. (2) It appeared that inhibition of protein synthesis could prevent memory formation after weak training but not after strong training (e.g., Barondes, 1970).

A new protein-synthesis inhibitor, anisomycin (ANI), helped to overcome these problems. Schwartz, Castellucci, and Kandel (1971) reported that ANI did not prevent an electrophysiological correlate of short-term habituation or sensitization in an isolated ganglion of *Aplysia,* but they did not investigate whether ANI can prevent long-term effects. The discovery by Bennett, Orme, and Hebert (1972) that ANI is an effective amnestic agent in rodents opened the way to resolving the main challenges to the protein-synthesis hypothesis of formation of LTM. ANI is much less toxic than other protein-synthesis inhibitors, and giving doses repeatedly at 2-hr intervals can prolong the duration of cerebral inhibition at amnestic levels. By varying the duration of amnestic levels of inhibition in this way, we found that the stronger the training, the longer the protein synthesis had to be maintained to prevent formation of LTM (Flood, Bennett, Orme, & Rosenzweig, 1975; Flood, Bennett, Rosenzweig, & Orme, 1973). We also found that protein must be synthesized in the cortex soon after training if LTM is to be formed; short-term memory (STM) or intermediate-term memory (ITM) do not require protein synthesis (e.g., Bennett et al., 1972; Mizumori, Rosenzweig, & Bennett, 1985; Mizumori, Sakai, Rosenzweig, Bennett, & Wittreich, 1987).

The terms "short-term memory" and "long-term memory" began to appear in research and theoretical articles in the 1950s (e.g., Broadbent, 1958; Bromley,

1958; Neumann & Ammons, 1957; Welford, 1952). "Intermediate-term memory" was first proposed by McGaugh (1966) and was soon taken up by others (e.g., Oléron, 1968).

B. Neurochemistry of Short-Term and Intermediate-Term Memories

Further studies were designed to find the neurochemical processes that underlie formation of STM and ITM. Lashley's concern, mentioned earlier, that some kinds of memory appear to be formed too quickly to allow growth of neural connections, ignored the distinction between STM and LTM, even though William James (1890) had already distinguished between these stores (although under different names). Observing this distinction was necessary if one was to look for different mechanisms of the two kinds of memory traces that Hebb distinguished: transient, labile memory traces, on the one hand, and stable, structural traces, on the other.

Much research on the neurochemistry of STM and ITM has been done with chicks, which have several advantages for this research, including the following: Chicks can be trained rapidly in a one-trial peck-avoidance paradigm and can be tested within seconds after training, or hours or days later. Large numbers of chicks can be studied in a single run, so one can compare different agents, doses, and times of administration within the same batch of subjects. Unlike invertebrate preparations, the chick system can be used to study the roles of different vertebrate brain structures and to investigate questions of cerebral asymmetry in learning and memory. The chick system permits study of learning and memory in the intact animal. The successive neurochemical stages occur more slowly in the chick than in the rat, thus allowing them to be separated more clearly. Further advantages have been stated elsewhere (e.g., Rosenzweig, 1990; Rosenzweig et al., 1992).

Although some amnestic agents, such as ANI, diffuse readily throughout the brain, others affect only a restricted volume of tissue at amnestic concentrations (Patterson, Alvarado, Warner, Rosenzweig, & Bennett, 1986). Such agents can be used to reveal the roles of different brain structures in different stages of memory formation (e.g., Patterson et al., 1986; Serrano, Rodriguez, Bennett, & Rosenzweig, 1995).

C. Both Enriched Experience and Formal Training Evoke Similar Cascades of Neurochemical Events That Cause Plastic Changes in the Brain

Using the chick system, several investigators have traced parts of a cascade of neurochemical events from initial stimulation to synthesis of protein and structural changes (e.g., Gibbs & Ng, 1977; Ng & Gibbs, 1991; Rose, 1992a,b; Rosenzweig et al., 1992). At some if not all stages, parallel processes occur. Briefly, here are some of the stages: The cascade is initiated when sensory stimulation activates receptor organs that stimulate afferent neurons by using various synaptic transmitter agents such as acetylcholine (ACh) and glutamate. Inhibitors of ACh synaptic activity, such as scopolamine and pirenzepine, can prevent STM, as can inhibitors of glutamate receptors, including both the NMDA and AMPA receptors. Alteration of regulation of ion channels in the neuronal membrane can inhibit STM formation, as seen in effects of lanthanum chloride on calcium channels and of ouabain on sodium and potassium channels. Inhibition of second messengers is also amnestic, for example inhibition of adenylate cyclase by forskolin or of diacylglycerol by bradykinin. These second messengers can activate protein kinases—enzymes that catalyze addition of phosphate molecules to proteins. We found that two kinds of protein kinases are important in formation, respectively, of ITM or LTM. Agents that inhibit calcium-calmodulin protein kinases (CaM kinases) prevent formation of ITM, whereas agents that do *not* inhibit CaM kinases but *do* inhibit protein kinase A (PKA) or protein kinase C (PKC) prevent formation of LTM (Rosenzweig et al., 1992; Serrano et al., 1994). From this research, Serrano et al. (1995) were able to predict for a newly available inhibitor of PKC its effective amnestic dose and how long after training it would cause memory to decline. One-trial training leads to an increase of immediate-early gene messenger RNA in the chick forebrain (Anokhin & Rose, 1991) and to an increase in the density of dendritic spines (Lowndes & Stewart, 1994). Many of these effects occur only in the left hemisphere of the chick or are more prominent in the left than in the right hemisphere. Thus, learning in the chick system permits study of many steps that lead from sensory stimulation to formation of neuronal structures involved in memory.

The neurochemical cascade involved in formation of memory in the chick is similar to the cascade involved in long-term potentiation (LTP) in the mammalian brain (e.g., Colley & Routtenberg, 1993) and in the nervous systems of invertebrates (e.g., Krasne & Glanzman, 1995).

Many of the steps in formation of memory in the chick can also be modulated by opioids and other substances. Opioid agonists tend to impair, and opioid antagonists to enhance, memory formation. Different opioids appear to modulate formation of different stages of memory (e.g., Colombo, Martinez, Bennett, & Rosenzweig, 1992; Colombo, Thompson, Martinez, Bennett, & Rosenzweig, 1993; Patterson et al., 1989; Rosenzweig et al., 1992).

Several groups of investigators have sought to determine which proteins must be synthesized to hold LTP or LTM. In general, this research has found effects such as alteration or activation of cellular kinases and phosphatases, activation of immediate-early genes, modulation of transcription factors, and activation of cell adhesion molecules. All of these may be steps leading to structural growth or alteration of synaptic transmitter processes, but complete cascades remain to be worked out.

D. Can Parts of the Neurochemical Cascade Be Related to Different Stages of Memory Formation?

Some of the difficulty in attempting to relate parts of the neurochemical cascade to different stages of memory formation comes from problems of defining stages of memory, as discussed more fully elsewhere (Rosenzweig, Bennett, Colombo, Lee, & Serrano, 1993). Consider, for example, some very different attempts to state the duration of STM. Early investigators of human STM (Brown, 1958; Peterson & Peterson, 1959) reported that it lasts only about 30 sec if rehearsal is prevented. Agranoff, Davis, & Brink (1966) reported that in goldfish, if formation of LTM is prevented by an inhibitor of protein synthesis, STM can last up to 3 days, although normally LTM forms within an hour after training. Kandel et al. (1987) wrote that in *Aplysia,* "A single training trial produces short-term sensitization that lasts from minutes to hours" (p. 17) and that long-term memory is "memory that lasts more than one day" (p. 35). Rose (1995) suggests that, in the chick, memories that persist only a few hours involve a first wave of glycoprotein synthesis, whereas "true long-term memory" requires a second wave of glycoprotein synthesis, occurring about 6 hr after training.

Instead of considering that STM can last several hours or even a day or more, it is useful to posit one or more intermediate-term memory (ITM) stages occurring between STM and LTM, as some theorists have done since the 1960s (e.g., McGaugh 1966, 1968). Thus, Gibbs and Ng (1977) referred to a "labile" stage occurring between STM and LTM and later (e.g., Gibbs & Ng, 1984; Ng & Gibbs, 1991) called this intermediate-term memory. My co-workers and I have discussed mechanisms of STM, ITM, and LTM in a series of papers (e.g., Mizumori et al., 1987; Patterson, Alvarado, Rosenzweig, & Bennett, 1988; Rosenzweig & Bennett, 1984; Rosenzweig et al., 1992, 1993). In investigating effects of protein kinase inhibitors (PKIs) on memory formation in chicks, we reported that those agents that inhibit CaM kinase activity disrupt formation of what some workers with chicks identify as ITM (lasting from about 15 min to about 60 min posttraining); those agents that inhibit PKC, PKA, or PKG, but do not inhibit CaM kinase, disrupt the formation of LTM (Rosenzweig et al., 1992; Serrano et al., 1994). Other investigators prefer to refer to different phases or stages of LTM rather than use the expression ITM. Thus, studying the LTP analog to memory in slices of rat hippocampus, Huang and Kandel (1994) reported findings similar to those of Rosenzweig et al. (1992) and Serrano et al. (1994) with regard to the roles of two classes of protein kinases: inhibitors of CaM kinase activity disrupted what Huang and Kandel called a transient, early phase of LTP (E-LTP), evoked by moderately strong stimuli and lasting from 1 hr to less than 3 hr after induction of LTP; agents that inhibit PKA, but do not inhibit CaM kinase, disrupt the formation of what they called a later, more enduring phase of LTP (L-LTP), evoked by strong stimulation and lasting at least 6–10 hr. Weak stimuli evoke only short-term potentiation (STP), lasting only 20–30 min. As mentioned earlier, Rose (1995) suggests that, in the chick, a kind of LTM that lasts a few hours involves a first wave of glycoprotein synthesis, whereas "true long-term memory" requires a second wave of glycoprotein synthesis, occurring about 6 hr after training. Rather than call the memory associated with Rose's first 6-hr-long wave a form of LTM, it may be better to think of it as ITM and to note that there is an earlier STM, lasting only a few minutes, as has been shown in many experiments with the chick.

These and other findings support the hypothesis of at least three sequentially dependent stages of memory formation, each dependent on different neurochemical processes. These results are important, not only for investigators of the neurochemistry of memory but also for neuropsychologists and others who work with patients who suffer from memory disorders. A review by Kopelman (1992, pp. 136–138) finds mixed results in attempts to distinguish losses of ITM and LTM in Korsakoff's and Alzheimer's patients. If it becomes possible to distinguish patients with disorders of ITM from those with impairment of STM or LTM, then perhaps their deficits can be traced to different disorders of the nervous system. If we can identify the neurochemical processes underlying each stage of memory formation, this could lead to attempts at rational pharmacological treatments. If investigators could then understand the genetics involved, they might eventually find genetic treatments for some memory defects.

E. Evidence That Certain Learning-Induced Neurochemical Processes and Neuroanatomical Plasticity Are Necessary for Memory

1. What Neurochemical Processes Are Necessary and Sufficient to Store Memories of Various Durations?

As evidence accumulated that learning and experience induce chemical changes in the brain and that inhibiting some chemical processes around the time of learning blocks formation of memory, some investigators tried to devise guidelines and criteria to judge whether such changes and processes are necessary and sufficient for formation of memory. Of course, reports of many studies stated one or more criteria against which to test their findings, but Entingh, Dunn, Wilson, Glassman, and Hogan (1975) and Rose (1981) tried to list several guidelines or criteria that would be applicable to a variety of studies. Some examples of the criteria are the following: (a) There must be changes in the quantity of the system or substance, or its rate of production or turnover, in some localized region of the brain during memory formation. (b) The amount of change should be related to the strength or amount of training, up to a limit. (c) Stress, motor activity, or other processes that accompany learning must not, in the absence of memory formation, result in the structural or biochemical changes. (d) If the cellular or biochemical changes are inhibited during the period over which memory formation would normally occur, then memory formation should be prevented and the animal should be amnesic. (However, Flood et al. [1973] found cases in which the protein synthesis required for LTM formation was only postponed by inhibition of protein synthesis and occurred later than usual, after the inhibition wore off.) Research on learning and memory, chiefly with chicks, has shown that some neurochemical processes appear to fulfill all the stated criteria, as I have discussed elsewhere (Rosenzweig, 1996, pp. 18–19).

Martinez, Barea-Rodriguez, and Derrick discuss in Chapter 6 whether LTP and long-term depression (LTD)—which involve neurochemical, electrophysiological, and neuroanatomical changes—are memory mechanisms. Most of the research on LTP has been done on rodent hippocampal preparations. It is generally believed that the hippocampus does not store memories for the long-term, because ablation of the hippocampus does not destroy long-term memories; rather, the hippocampus helps to process information for long-term storage elsewhere in the brain. Experiments in which hippocampal lesions were made at different numbers of days after training in rodents showed that memory was not impaired if the lesions were made more than 2 or 3 days after training (Kim & Fanselow, 1992; Winocur, 1990). Because of such findings, it is not clear what purpose would be served by a hippocampal mechanism for holding memory more than a few days in the rodent. Thus, some theorists consider the hippocampus to be a "temporary memory store" (Rawlins, 1985) or an "intermediate-term buffer store" (Treves & Rolls, 1994).

While conceding that convincing proof does not exist that LTP and LTD are involved in learning and memory, Martinez, Barea-Rodriguez, and Derrick (Chapter 6) believe that after many years of research dating back to the initial discovery of LTP by Bliss and Lomo (1973), "LTP and LTD remain the best candidates for a cellular process of synaptic change that underlies learning and memory in the vertebrate brain" (Chapter 6). They review findings of a cascade of neurochemical events underlying LTP that is similar to those found in research on memory formation.

2. Is Learning-Induced Neuroanatomical Plasticity Necessary for Storage of Long-Term Memory?

Whether learning-induced anatomical changes in the nervous system are necessary for storage of long-term memory has been discussed by several authors, including Morris (1989), Greenough, Withers, and Wallace (1990), Martinez and Derrick (1996), Black and Greenough (Chapter 2), and Martinez, Barea-Rodriguez, and Derrick (Chapter 6). Greenough et al. (1990, pp. 162–165) note several observations that relate number of synapses and degree of dendritic branching to the amount and sites of learning or experience; in some cases I augment the statements of Greenough, et al.: (a) The amount of dendrite per neuron in the occipital cortex of the rat reflects the amount of stimulation or complexity in the environment; for example, the measures are greatest in EC rats, least in those from IC, and intermediate in those from SC. (b) Similar effects of training or experience occur in young, adult, and old rats. (c) Changes in brain measures occur rapidly in the rat with 4 days of experience (Kilman et al., 1988) and in the chick after a single training trial (Lowndes & Stewart, 1994). (d) The changes in dendritic branching are paralleled by changes in numbers of synapses per neuron. (e) The synaptic and dendritic changes occur not only in rodents but also in cats and monkeys. (f) The synaptic and dendritic changes caused by enriched experience are similar to those induced by traditional learning tasks. (g) Learning-based morphological changes are greater than and different from changes induced by locomotor activity (Greenough et al., 1990, pp. 174–176). (h) Also, the changes occur in brain regions involved in the learned tasks; if learning is confined to one side of the brain, the synaptic and dendritic changes are also confined to that side. Note that some of the points on this list correspond to some given earlier for neurochemical processes.

The fact that training and experience usually lead to increased spacing of cortical neurons should be taken into account in interpreting some other findings, such as a report by Witelson, Glezer, and Kigar (1995) that received considerable coverage in the news media. They reported, based on a small number of cases, that women have a larger number of neurons in a region of the cortex related to language than do men and speculated that this might be related to women's greater proficiency in language. Actually, the measure was not the total number of neurons in the region but *neurons per unit of volume of cortex*. This means closer spacing of neurons, which, interpreted in terms of the results reviewed here, could as well suggest simpler and less extensive connections of neurons in this region of women's brains, perhaps reflecting less verbal training and experience. At the least, it does not seem compelling to interpret closer packing of neurons as evidence for greater cognitive proficiency.

XI. CEREBRAL LOCALIZATION OF LEARNING AND MEMORY PROCESSES USING DISSOCIATION DESIGNS

Findings of cerebral localization of motor and sensory processes developed extensively in the second half of the nineteenth century, based on both ablation and electrical stimulation techniques; see the review by Finger (1994c). Perhaps the first investigator to combine the animal learning methods of Thorndike with cortical ablations to try to localize the processes of learning and memory was American psychologist Shepard I. Franz. He found that in cats (1902) and in monkeys (1906, 1907) lesions of the prefrontal cortex impaired memory for recently formed puzzle-box habits while not affecting memory for older habits. Cortical lesions that left the prefrontal areas intact did not affect the habit. However, the tasks could be relearned following prefrontal lesions, so Franz concluded whereas the prefrontal region might normally contribute to memory, it was not essential for learning or memory. Karl S. Lashley joined Franz in extensions of these studies to rats (Franz & Lashley,

1917; Lashley & Franz, 1917), and Lashley went on to devote most of his career to related work. Kesner offers further review of this work in Chapter 10.

Lashley (1952) criticized ablation studies that purported to show localization even of sensory function. He pointed out that failure of an animal to continue to make a trained visual object discrimination after lesion of a temporal cortical area might instead mean impairment of comparison behavior or of comprehension of the training situation. This might be overcome, he suggested, by testing whether the lesion left intact ability to discriminate in another modality, such as somesthesis. In an important review, Hans-Lukas Teuber (1955, p. 283) countered that more was needed to resolve this question than simply to show that the lesion did not impair discrimination in another modality. Such a "simple dissociation" might only mean that visual discrimination is more vulnerable to temporal cortical lesions than is tactile discrimination. What is needed for conclusive proof, Teuber argued, is "double dissociation," that is, evidence that lesion of one cortical area impairs visual object discriminations without loss on comparable tactile tasks, while lesion of another cortical area impairs tactile discriminations without loss on the visual tasks, and that the impairments in the two tasks are comparable in severity. Subsequent investigators took up the challenge of finding double dissociations and also extended it to studies of localization of brain regions involved in learning and memory. At the same time, investigators devised learning tasks intended to involve rather specific processes, and they abandoned earlier rather nonspecific learning paradigms, such as Thorndike's puzzle boxes and Lashley's mazes, that could be solved in a variety of ways.

Knowlton, Mangels, and Squire (1996) start their review article by stating, "Students of brain and behavior have long recognized that double dissociations [references to Teuber (1955) and later authors] provide the strongest evidence for separating the functions of brain systems" (p. 1399). They present evidence for a double dissociation between human brain regions and kinds of memory: amnesic patients, with damage to the limbic-diencephalic regions, show impaired formation of declarative but not of nondeclarative memories, whereas patients with Parkinson's disease, who have damage to the neostriatum (caudate nucleus and putamen), show impaired formation of habits but not of declarative memories. Kesner, in a series of studies summarized in Chapter 10, has found evidence of double and triple dissociations between brain regions involved in working memory for different attributes of the learning situation. A similar research project in another laboratory also found a triple dissociation, using three different problems, all run in the radial maze: (1) a neural system that includes the hippocampus acquires information about relationships among stimuli and events (declarative memories); (2) a different system that includes the dorsal striatum (mainly the caudate nucleus) mediates the formation of reinforced stimulus–response associations (habits, or nondeclarative memories); (3) a third system that includes the amygdala mediates rapid acquisition of behaviors based on biologically significant events with affective properties (McDonald & White, 1993).

XII. GENETIC STUDIES OF LEARNING ABILITY: FROM SELECTION TO MUTATIONS TO MOLECULAR BIOLOGY

To what extent are abilities to learn and remember inherited? This is a question that has intrigued psychologists and those in related fields since the late nineteenth century. Successive techniques have been introduced, starting with experiments on selective breeding for learning ability, progressing to induction of mutations in *Drosophila* and identification of genes that affect learning and memory, and culminating in molecular biological manipulations of genes. Among the recent techniques are the following: (a) inducing the expression of genes by training and then identifying them, (b) the genetic "knock-out" approach described in Chapter 3 of this volume by Silva and Giese; (c) research with transgenic animals (animals with genes transferred from other species), and (d) modifying genes by mutation or otherwise. Thus, genes can now be turned on, knocked out, popped in, or made over. These complementary techniques continue to add to the topic, and their results can be appreciated in terms of the context of earlier work. In our brief review of research on this question, we will limit ourselves to research with animal subjects.

A. Selection for Learning Ability

Francis Galton was convinced that intelligence and learning ability are inherited, and in the late 1800s he had thought of breeding dogs for intelligence, as he reported later: ". . . it would be a most interesting occupation . . . to pick the cleverest dogs [one] could hear of, and mate them together, generation after generation—breeding purely for intellectual power. . . " (Galton, 1909, p. 319). Although he believed that the costs of such an experiment could largely be covered by selling the superior animals that would result, Galton never undertook this project nor was able to persuade others to do so. I believe the first experiment to breed animals for learning ability was that conducted by Edward C. Tolman (1924) with rats. This successful preliminary work was then extended by Tolman's former student Robert C. Tryon (1940, 1942), using a 17-unit automatic maze developed by Tolman, Tryon, and Jeffress (1929). Tryon started by testing a large number of male and female rats of heterogeneous stocks. Males and females with low error scores were then bred together, and so were males and females with high error scores. Among the offspring of the low-error parents, those who themselves made few errors were kept for breeding. Similarly, in the other group, those who made many errors were mated. By the seventh generation, there was very little overlap of scores between the "bright" and "dull" lines. Further selective breeding did not increase the separation.

Why did experimental selection for learning ability wait for the 1920s when Galton had conceived of such an experiment by the end of the nineteenth century? Factors that made the experiment feasible by the 1920s, but not when Galton originally conceived of it, include the following: Choice of the laboratory rat, rather than the dog, as the main subject for experiments on learning made such selection experiments economically feasible. This was especially the case for an experiment of selective breeding, since the generation time for rats is considerably shorter than for dogs. Also, by the 1920s there were animal laboratories in university departments of psychology supported by academic budgets. Galton would have had to undertake such an experiment with his own means, and even though he thought that eventually some of the costs could be recouped by sale of intelligent dogs, there would have been important start-up costs. Beyond the question of economics, there is also the conceptual question of measuring intelligence. Galton did not indicate how he would measure intelligence of dogs other than by observation and rating. By the 1920s there was a considerable background of experience and theory for testing learning ability of animals. The growing field of animal psychology soon made contact with the discipline of genetics that had emerged and gained its name in the first decade of the twentieth century.

About 1940, Tryon sought to test the possibility that motivational differences between the strains might account for the difference in their error scores in the maze. He therefore ran an experiment with animals of the 22nd generation, using the following groups: (a) 71 maze-bright rats with "normal" hunger motivation, that is, given the standard ration throughout the experiment, (b) 43 maze-bright rats that had been satiated with extra rations, (c) 71 maze-dulls with "normal" hunger motivation, and (d) 57 maze-dulls whose motivation was heightened by reduced rations. The results showed that the level of hunger motivation affected running speed but did not affect mean error scores of the groups: whether normally hungry or satiated, the maze-brights made only about a third as many errors as the normally hungry or strongly hungry maze-dulls. Tryon never published these results but about 20 years later gave them to me to include in a paper on effects of heredity and environment on brain measures and learning ability in the rat (Rosenzweig, 1964).

At about the same time that Tryon tested the effects of motivation on performance of the maze-bright and maze-dull rats in his multiunit maze, Tryon's student Lloyd V. Searle (1941, 1949) attempted to determine whether Tryon's maze-bright rats were generally superior in learning to the maze-dulls or whether their superiority was confined to the test employed in the selection program. He used 10 maze-bright, 10 maze-dull, and 15 animals of a crossed line, giving them a variety of tests of learning, activity, and emotional behavior. Searle (1949, p. 323) concluded:

> No evidence was found that a difference exists between the Brights and Dulls in the learning capacity *per se*. A detailed study of the behavior profiles indicated that the Brights are characteristically food-driven, economical of distance, . . . and timid in response to open space. Dulls are disinterested in food, . . . and timid of mechanical apparatus features.

It is concluded that brightness and dullness in the original Tryon Maze may be accounted for in large part by such motivational and emotional patterns. Although indications exist that the two strains may be differentiated with reference to certain basic 'cognitive' tendencies, the procedures followed in this experiment were not sufficiently analytical to indicate their nature.

Tryon's experiment in which food motivation was varied was done at almost the same time as Searle's, but Tryon employed much larger groups of animals. Tryon concluded, unlike Searle, that error scores were practically independent of food motivation in both strains. Searle's results, having been published, convinced many readers, however, that Tryon had selected for motivation and emotion rather than for learning ability. In the 1960s, my colleagues and I found that descendants of the maze-bright rats made significantly fewer errors than descendants of the maze-dulls on the Hebb–Williams maze, the Dashiell checkerboard maze, and the Lashley III maze (Rosenzweig, 1964), thus indicating some generality for Tryon's conclusions.

B. Effects of Mutations on Learning Ability

Geneticists have employed the fruit fly, *Drosophila melanogaster,* as a favorite subject since the early 1900s. Modern neurogenetic dissection of *Drosophila* behavior was pioneered by Seymour Benzer (1967, 1973). The application of this approach to study of mechanisms of learning and memory became possible only after Benzer and his colleagues demonstrated that *Drosophila* can learn (Quinn, Sziber, & Booker, 1979). As reviewed by Dudai (1989) two methods were then employed to isolate mutations that affect learning or memory specifically, without affecting other factors such as perception or motivation. In the first, mutants previously isolated by a variety of criteria—morphological, developmental, biochemical, or physiological— are subjected to tests of learning and memory. Because these mutants have salient abnormalities, the specificity of any defect in learning or memory must be tested with special care. Several previously identified mutants have been reported to show relatively specific impairments in learning (e.g., Cowan & Siegel, 1986; Heisenberg, Borst, Wagner, & Byers, 1985; Tempel, Livingstone, & Quinn, 1984).

The second method is more straightforward. Here one treats flies with a mutagen and screens the progeny for defects in learning and/or memory. If such effects are found, the mutants must also be tested for defects in factors such as perception or motivation that might account for impaired performance on tests of learning or memory. Most mutants for learning have been isolated in this way (e.g., Aceves-Pina et al., 1983; Dudai, Jan, Byers, Quinn, & Benzer, 1976; Quinn et al., 1979).

C. Molecular Biological Studies of Learning Ability

In addition to studying mutations, methods of molecular biology have made it possible to affect genes in a number of ways that have been applied to research on mechanisms of learning and memory. Chapter 3 discusses in detail the main methods and the results obtained to date with them. As noted in Chapter 3, mutations and gene knock-outs are genetic lesions, and the results of such treatments are subject to the problems and criticisms that beset lesion techniques in general. Moreover, most genetic techniques to date are rather blunt instruments with which to perform lesions. That is, they are not restricted in time or location—they affect animals throughout their development and throughout the body. Fortunately, techniques are now being developed to restrict the changes to specific times and to certain brain regions. Moreover, it may become possible to reverse the effects of gene alterations, and this will permit more powerful experimental designs.

The importance of the gene-modification techniques for research in learning and memory is reflected by the fact that Martinez, Barea-Rodriguez, and Derrick (Chapter 6) devote two substantial sections of their chapter to "Knockout mutants, LTP, and hippocampally dependent learning" and "Knockout mutants, LTD, and cerebellar dependent learning."

An example of genetic research related to learning but outside the purview of Chapter 3 is work with transgenic mouse strains proposed as models of Alzheimer's disease (AD). A recent report of this sort attracted much attention (Hsiao et al., 1996). The mice in this study overexpressed an amyloid precursor protein because they were given mutated genes obtained from a human family with early-onset AD. Mice of this strain showed normal spatial learning and memory at 3 or 6 months of age but were impaired on such tests at 9–10 months. Their brains also showed abnormal amounts of classic "senile" plaques at the older ages. Thus the appearance of behavioral deficits occurred at the same time as that of pathological neuroanatomy. The investigators hope that studies of developing mice of this strain will help to test drugs that may get at the basic disease process.

XIII. STUDIES USING NONINVASIVE BRAIN IMAGING

Neuroimaging techniques have recently been used to study cognitive processes, and since the early 1990s they have been used to study brain processes in learning and memory. This is a field of research on learning and memory that clearly could not have taken place without the discovery of brain-imaging techniques. An early review of this area was that of McCarthy (1995); it included material on 14 brain-imaging studies using working memory tasks and six studies investigating processes involved in long-term memory. Another review focused on hemispheric asymmetry in encoding and retrieval (Nyberg, Cabeza, & Tulving, 1996). It showed that encoding involves especially activation of the left prefrontal cortex, whereas retrieval involves especially activation of the right prefrontal cortex. More reports are continuing to appear, and the next edition of this book may very well include a chapter devoted to such studies.

As McCarthy notes, the majority of neuroimaging studies concerned with cognitive processes have been conducted with positron emission tomography (PET) using radioactive tracers such as $H_2^{15}O$ to measure blood flow or fluorodeoxyglucose to measure glucose metabolism. Images are usually recorded under two or more task conditions presumed to differ in the operation of a single cognitive process. As explained by Posner and Raichle (1994), subtraction of images taken in the two conditions reveals activity associated with the distinctive process.

The appearance of Posner and Raichle's *Images of Mind* (1994) evoked multiple book reviews with commentaries by 27 authors or pairs of authors (Posner & Raichle, 1995). Most commentaries were positive, but seven stated concerns or problems about use or interpretation of the subtraction procedure with regard to PET images. For example, some raised the problem of choice of an appropriate baseline from which to measure effects. Thus, Halgren (1995, p. 358) states that the subtraction procedure is biased against detection of areas that are activated in virtually all cognitive tasks (including control tasks). Horwitz (1995, p. 360) argues that Posner and Raichle put too much emphasis on localization in discrete neural areas and insufficient emphasis on interaction within networks of widely distributed systems. The poor temporal resolution of PET does not permit visualization of such interactions occurring within a few hundred milliseconds. For this reason, Posner, Raichle, and associates (Snyder, Abdullaev, Posner, & Raichle, 1995) have begun to combine the evoked-potential method, with its excellent temporal resolution, with PET to investigate the succession of processes in generating responses to visually presented nouns.

Dehaene (1996) has extended the subtraction technique to show how the additive-factors method can be employed in an experiment recording event-related potentials. During a task in which subjects responded as rapidly as possible to record their comparisons between numbers presented visually, the potentials indicated six successive processing activations occurring in different brain regions, the whole sequence taking place within 500 msec. I am not aware that the additive-factors method has yet been employed in brain-imaging studies.

In many reports, difference images from individual subjects are normalized to a common stereotaxic coordinate system. Comparison of subtraction images from individual subjects is sometimes used to advantage, however, as in the Logan & Grafton (1995) study of conditioning the eye-blink response in human subjects, mentioned earlier in another context. Logan and Grafton found that, in certain brain regions, the relative metabolic change in PET responses correlated significantly with learning performance.

Investigators have also begun to apply the technique of functional magnetic resonance imaging (FMRI) to studies of cognitive processing. This technique exploits the fact that local changes in blood flow related to neural activity alter the concentration of deoxyhemoglobin and the corresponding magnetic resonance signal. With specialized image acquisition techniques, repeated images of the same brain region can be obtained in less than 1 sec, permitting temporal studies of task-dependent activation. "Because FMRI is fast, noninvasive, and does not use ionizing radiation, subjects can be run repeatedly, allowing for more elaborate experimental designs" (McCarthy, 1995, p. 155).

Black and Greenough in Chapter 2 cite FRMI studies that demonstrate structural changes in the human brain caused by learning, changes that may reflect synaptogenesis. Gershberg and Shimamura in Chapter 9 cite findings from imaging studies in their review of roles of different brain regions in different memory processes.

XIV. CONCLUSIONS

1. Formal research on learning and memory extends back more than a century. Early work has often been neglected, and older ideas have sometimes later been presented as new.

2. Hermann Ebbinghaus' 1885 book initiated empirical research on human learning and memory. Psychology was ready for this, as shown by the fact that other investigators soon joined this field, using a variety of methods and materials.

3. Laboratory research on learning in animal subjects was begun independently by Edward L. Thorndike (1898), on the basis of planned experiments, and Ivan P. Pavlov (1897–1906), on the basis of unexpected observations during research on alimentary secretions. Thorndike's research was followed up rapidly by others. Although Pavlov conducted an extensive program of research on conditioning, few laboratories took up this research until the later 1920s.

4. Electrophysiological research on learning and memory began in the 1940s. Although changes in the EEG are found with training, this technique did not allow investigators to localize the processes precisely in the brain.

5. Use of indwelling electrodes and microelectrodes enabled investigators to pinpoint sites of learning-related changes to synapses in certain invertebrate and vertebrate preparations.

6. Training and differential experience were demonstrated by the early 1960s to cause measurable changes in neurochemistry and neuroanatomy of weanling rats (e.g., Krech et al., 1960; Rosenzweig et al., 1962). Similar results were later shown in adult animals. These sites were then examined in later research using pharmacological and neurochemical techniques.

7. Depriving one eye of visual experience in young kittens was found to cause changes in the electrical responses of cells in the visual cortex (Wiesel & Hubel, 1963). Wiesel and Hubel reported that such effects could not be induced in kittens more than a few months of age, but later workers found changes in cortical responses of adult animals as a result of experience.

8. Formation of long-term memory was demonstrated in the early 1970s to require synthesis of proteins in the hours following training (e.g., Bennett et al., 1972; Flood et al., 1973).

9. Formation of short-term, intermediate-term, and long-term memories has been found to require a cascade of neurochemical events, and the sequences are rather similar in birds, mammals, and invertebrates.

10. Different kinds of learning and memory follow different rules, involve different brain sites, and require somewhat different cascades of neurochemical events. Because of these differences, generalizing about learning and memory and their biological mechanisms must be done with great care.

11. Neural mechanisms of learning resemble in many ways neural mechanisms of development of the nervous system, although it is only recently that investigators have tried to determine experimentally whether the mechanisms of learning and development are necessarily the same.

12. Newer biomedical and behavioral techniques are adding to knowledge of the neural mechanisms of learning and memory. The biomedical techniques include noninvasive brain imaging and molecular biological approaches. The behavioral techniques include tests for implicit as well as explicit memory and tests for various kinds of declarative and nondeclarative memories. Both biomedical and behavioral investigators use computational models.

13. Double dissociation of brain regions and cognitive processes is a strong method of localizing regions particularly involved in specific cognitive processes.

14. Although it may be simpler to conduct behavioral tests on one set of subjects and neurobiological tests on others, more powerful experimental designs perform both behavioral and neurobiological measures on the same set of subjects.

15. Increasingly, investigators are using multiple tests of hypotheses and seeking converging evidence to establish conclusions.

REFERENCES

Aceves-Pina, E. O., Booker, R., Duerr, J. S., Livingstone, M. S., Quinn, W. G., Smith, R. F., Sziber, P. P., Tempel, B. L., & Tully, T. P. (1983). Learning and memory in *Drosophila*, studied with mutants. *Cold Spring Harbor Symposium in Quantitative Biology, 48,* 831–840.

Agranoff, B. W., Burrell, H. R., Dokas, L. A., & Springer, A. D. (1978). Progress in biochemical approaches to learning and memory. In M. A. Lipton, A. DiMascio, & K. F. Killam (Eds.), *Psychopharmacology: A generation of progress* (pp. 623–635). New York: Raven.

Agranoff, B. W., Davis, R. E., & Brink, J. J. (1966). Chemical studies on memory fixation in goldfish. *Brain Research, 1,* 303–309.

Alkon, D. L. (1975). Neural correlates of associative training in *Hermissenda. Journal of General Physiology, 65,* 46–56.

Alkon, D. L. (1989). Memory storage and neural systems. *Scientific American, 260,* 42–50.

Alkon, D. L. (1992). *Memory's voice: Deciphering the mind-brain code.* New York: Harper Collins.

Altman, J., & Das, G. D. (1964). Autoradiographic examination of the effects of enriched environment on the rate of glial multiplication in the adult rat brain. *Nature, 204,* 1161–1163.

Anokhin, K. V., & Rose, S. P. R. (1991). Learning-induced increase of early immediate gene messenger RNA in the chick forebrain. *European Journal of Neuroscience, 3,* 162–167.

Aserinsky, E., & Kleitman, N. (1953). Regularly occurring periods of eye motility, and concomitant phenomena during sleep. *Science, 118,* 273–274.

Baer, M. F., & Singer, W. (1986). Modulation of visual cortical plasticity by acetylcholine and noradrenaline. *Nature, 320,* 172–176.

Bailey, C. H., & Chen, M. (1983). Morphological basis of long-term habituation and sensitization in *Aplysia. Science, 220,* 91–93.

Bain, A. (1872). *Mind and body: The theories of their relation.* London: Henry S. King.

Barondes, S. H. (1970). Some critical variables in studies of the effect of inhibitors of protein synthesis on memory. In W. L. Byrne (Ed.) *Molecular approaches to learning and memory* (pp. 27–34). New York: Academic Press.

Bennett, E. L. (1976). Cerebral effects of differential experience and training. In M. R. Rosenzweig & E. L. Bennett (Eds.), *Neural mechanisms of learning and memory* (pp. 279–287). Cambridge, MA: MIT Press.

Bennett, E. L., Diamond, M. C., Krech, D., & Rosenzweig, M. R. (1964). Chemical and anatomical plasticity of brain. *Science, 146,* 610–619.

Bennett, E. L., Krech, D., & Rosenzweig, M. R. (1964). Reliability and regional specificity of cerebral effects of environmental complexity and training. *Journal of Comparative and Physiological Psychology, 57,* 440–441.

Bennett, E. L., Orme, A. E., & Hebert, M. (1972). Cerebral protein synthesis inhibition and amnesia produced by scopolamine, cycloheximide, streptovitacin A, anisomycin, and emetine in rat. *Federation Proceedings, 31,* 838.

Bennett, E. L., Rosenzweig, M. R., & Diamond, M. C. (1970). Time courses of effects on differential experience on brain measures and behavior of rats. In W. L. Byrne (Ed.), *Molecular approaches to learning and memory* (pp. 69–85). New York: Academic Press.

Bennett, E. L., Rosenzweig, M. R., Morimoto, H., & Hebert, M. (1979). Maze training alters brain anatomy and cortical RNA/DNA ratios. *Behavioral and Neural Biology, 26,* 1–22.

Benzer, S. (1967). Behavioral mutants of *Drosophila* isolated by countercurrent distribution. *Proceedings of the National Academy of Sciences U.S.A., 58,* 1112–1119.

Benzer, S. (1973). Genetic dissection of behavior. *Scientific American, 229*(12), 24–37.

Black, J. E., & Greenough, W. T. (1986). Induction of pattern in neural structure by experience: Implications for cognitive development. In M. E. Lamb, A. L. Brown, & B. Rogoff (Eds.), *Advances in developmental psychology* (Vol. 4, pp. 1–50). Hillsdale, NJ: Lawrence Erlbaum Associates.

Bliss, T. V., & Lomo, T. (1973). Long-lasting potentiation of synaptic transmission in the dentate area of the anaesthetized rabbit following stimulation of the perforant path. *Journal of Physiology (London), 232,* 331–356.

Bloch, V. (1976). Brain activation and memory consolidation. In M. R. Rosenzweig & E. L. Bennett (Eds.), *Neural mechanisms of learning and memory* (pp. 583–590). Cambridge, MA: MIT Press.

Boring, E. G. (1950). *A history of experimental psychology* (2nd ed.). New York: Appleton-Century-Crofts.

Broadbent, D. E. (1958). *Perception and communication.* London: Pergamon Press.

Bromley, D. B. (1958). Some effects of age on short-term learning and retention. *Journal of Gerontology, 13,* 398–406.

Brown, J. (1958). Some tests of the decay theory of immediate memory. *Quarterly Journal of Experimental Psychology, 10,* 12–21.

Cajal, R. S. (1894). La fine structure des centres nerveux. *Proceedings of the Royal Society, London, 55,* 444–468.

Cajal, R. S. (1911). *Histologie du système nerveux de l'homme et des vertébrés.* Paris: A. Maloine.

Chang, F.-L. F., & Greenough, W. T. (1982). Lateralized effects of monocular training on dendritic branching in adult split-brain rats. *Brain Research, 232,* 283–292

Clark, G. C., & Schuman, E. M. (1992). Snails' tales: Initial comparisons of synaptic plasticity underlying learning in *Hermissenda* and *Aplysia.* In L. R. Squire & N. Butters (Eds.), *Neuropsychology of learning and memory* (pp. 588–602). New York: Guilford.

Clayton, N. S., & Krebs, J. R. (1994). Hippocampal growth and attrition in birds affected by experience. *Proceedings of the National Academy of Sciences U.S.A., 91,* 7410–7414.

Cohen, T. E., Henzi, V., Kandel, E. R., & Hawkins, R. D. (1991). Further behavioral and cellular studies of dishabituation and sensitization in *Aplysia*. *Society for Neuroscience Abstracts, 17,* 1302.

Colebrook, E., & Lukowiak, K. (1988). Learning by the *Aplysia* model system: Lack of correspondence between gill and gill motor neuron responses. *Journal of Experimental Biology, 135,* 411–429.

Colley, P. A., & Routtenberg, A. (1993). Long-term potentiation as synaptic dialogue. *Brain Research Reviews, 18,* 115–122.

Colombo, P. J., Martinez, J. L., Bennett, E. L., & Rosenzweig, M. R. (1992). Kappa opioid receptor activity modulates memory for peck-avoidance training in the 2-day-old chick. *Psychopharmacology, 108,* 235–240.

Colombo, P. J., Thompson, K. R., Martinez, J. L., Jr., Bennett, E. L., & Rosenzweig, M. R. (1993). Dynorphin (1-13) impairs memory formation for aversive and appetitive learning in chicks. *Peptides, 14,* 1165–1170.

Cowan, T. M., & Siegel, R. W. (1986). *Drosophila* mutations that alter ionic conduction disrupt acquisition and retention of a conditioned odor avoidance response. *Journal of Neurogenetics, 3,* 187–201.

Cragg, B. G. (1967). Changes in visual cortex on first exposure of rats to light. *Nature, 215,* 251–253.

Cragg, B. G. (1972). Plasticity of synapses. In G. H. Bourne (Ed.), *The structure and function of nervous tissue* (Vol. 4, pp. 2–60). New York: Academic Press.

Culler, E. (1938). Observations on direct cortical stimulation in the dog. *Psychological Bulletin, 35,* 687–688.

Cummins, R. A., Walsh, R. N., Budtz-Olsen, O. E., Konstantinos, T., & Horsfall, C. R. (1973). Environmentally-induced changes in the brains of elderly rats. *Nature, 243,* 516–518.

Davis, J. W. (1986). Invertebrate model systems. In J. L. Martinez, Jr., & R. P. Kesner (Eds.), *Learning and memory: A biological view.* Orlando, FL: Academic Press.

Davis, R. (1993). Mushroom bodies and *Drosophila* learning. *Neuron, 11,* 1–14.

Dehaene, S. (1996). The organization of brain activations in number comparison: Event-related potentials and the additive-factors method. *Journal of Cognitive Neuroscience, 8,* 47–68.

Dewsbury, D. A. (1997). In celebration of the centennial of Ivan P. Pavlov's *The work of the digestive glands. American Psychologist, 52,* 933–935.

Diamond, M. C. (1967). Extensive cortical depth measurements and neuron size increases in the cortex of environmentally enriched rats. *Journal of Comparative Neurology, 131,* 357–364.

Diamond, M. C., Krech, D., & Rosenzweig, M. R. (1964). The effects of an enriched environment on the histology of the rat cerebral cortex. *Journal of Comparative Neurology, 123,* 111–119.

Diamond, M. C., Lindner, B., Johnson, R., Bennett, E. L., Rosenzweig, M. R. (1975). Differences in occipital cortical synapses from environmentally enriched, impoverished, and standard colony rats. *Journal of Neuroscience Research, 1,* 109–119.

Donegan, N. H., Foy, M. R., & Thompson, R. F. (1983). Neuronal responses of the rabbit cerebellar cortex during performance of the classically conditioned eyelid response. *Society for Neuroscience Abstracts, 11,* 835.

Donegan, N. H., & Thompson, R. F. (1991). The search for the engram. In J. L. Martinez, Jr., & R. P. Kesner (Eds.), *Learning and memory: A biological view* (2nd ed., pp. 3–58). San Diego: Academic Press.

Dudai, Y. (1989). *The neurobiology of memory.* Oxford: Oxford University Press.

Dudai, Y., Jan, Y.-N., Byers, D., Quinn, W. G., & Benzer, S. (1976). *dunce,* a mutant of *Drosophila* deficient in learning. *Proceedings of the National Academy of Sciences U.S.A., 73,* 1684–1688.

Durup, G., & Fessard, A. (1935). L'électroencéphalogramme de l'homme. *L'Année Psychologique, 36,* 1–32.

Ebbinghaus, H. (1885). *Ueber das Gedächtnis* [On memory]. Leipzig: Dunker and Humbolt.

Eccles, J. C. (1965). Comment. In D. P. Kimble (Ed.), *The anatomy of memory* (p. 97). Palo Alto, CA: Science and Behavior Books.

Entingh, D., Dunn, A., Wilson, J. E., Glassman, E., & Hogan, E. (1975). Biochemical approaches to the biological basis of memory. In M. S. Gazzaniga & C. Blakemore (Eds.), *Handbook of Psychobiology* (pp. 201–238). New York: Academic Press.

Farley, J., & Alkon, D. L. (1985). Cellular mechanisms of learning, memory, and information storage. *Annual Review of Psychology, 36,* 419–494.

Ferchmin, P., & Eterovic, V. (1986). Forty minutes of experience increase the weight and RNA content of cerebral cortex in periadolescent rats. *Developmental Psychobiology, 19,* 511–519.

Ferchmin, P., Eterovic, V., & Caputto, R., (1970). Studies of brain weight and RNA content after short periods of exposure to environmental complexity. *Brain Research, 20,* 49–57.

Finger, S. (1994a). The nature of the memory trace (pp. 332–348). *Origins of neuroscience: A history of explorations into brain function.* New York: Oxford University Press.

Finger, S. (1994b). The neuropathology of memory (pp. 349–368). *Origins of neuroscience: A history of explorations into brain function.* New York: Oxford University Press.

Finger, S. (1994c). The era of cerebral localization (pp. 32–50). *Origins of neuroscience. A history of explorations into brain function.* New York, Oxford University Press.

Flexner, J. B., Flexner, L. B., Stellar, E., de la Haba, G., & Roberts, R. B. (1962). Inhibition of protein synthesis in brain and learning and memory following puromycin. *Journal of Neurochemistry, 9,* 595–605.

Flexner, J. B., Flexner, L. B., de la Haba, G., & Roberts R. B. (1965). Loss of memory as related to inhibition of cerebral protein synthesis. *Journal of Neurochemistry, 12,* 535–541.

Flood, J. F., Bennett, E. L., Orme, A. E., & Rosenzweig, M. R. (1975). Relation of memory formation to controlled amounts of brain protein synthesis. *Physiology and Behavior, 15,* 97–102.

Flood, J. F., Bennett, E. L., Rosenzweig, M. R., & Orme, A. E. (1973). The influence of duration of protein synthesis inhibition on memory. *Physiology and Behavior, 10,* 555–562.

Forgays, D. G., & Forgays, J. W. (1952). The nature of the effect of free-environmental experience on the rat. *Journal of Comparative and Physiological Psychology, 45,* 747–750.

Foster, M., & Sherrington, C. S. (1897). *A text book of physiology. Part III. The central nervous system.* London: Macmillan.

Franz, S. I. (1902). On the functions of the cerebrum. I. The frontal lobes in the production and retention of simple sensory-motor habits. *American Journal of Physiology, 8,* 1–22.

Franz, S. I. (1906). Observations on the functions of the association areas (cerebrum) in monkeys. *Journal of the American Medical Association, 47,* 1464–1467.

Franz, S. I. (1907). On the functions of the cerebrum: The frontal lobes. *Archives of Psychology, 2,* 1–64.

Franz, S. I., & Lashley, K. S. (1917). The retention of habits by the rat after destruction of the frontal part of the cerebrum. *Psychobiology, 1,* 3–18.

Gallistel, C. R. (1990). *The organization of learning.* Cambridge, MA: MIT Press.

Galton, F. (1909). *Memories of my life* (3rd ed.). London: Methuen.

Garcia, J. (1990). Learning without memory. *Journal of Cognitive Neuroscience, 2,* 287–305.

Geller, E., Yuweiler, A., & Zolman, J. F. (1965). Effects of environmental complexity on constituents of brain and liver. *Journal of Neurochemistry, 12,* 949–955.

Gerard, R. W. (1949). Physiology and psychiatry. *American Journal of Psychiatry, 105,* 161–173.

Gibbs, M. E., & Ng, K. T. (1977). Psychobiology of memory: Towards a model of memory formation. *Biobehavioral Reviews, 1,* 13–36.

Gibbs, M. E., & Ng, K. T. (1984). Diphenylhydantoin extension of short-term and intermediate stages of memory. *Behavioural Brain Research, 11,* 103–108.

Globus, A., Rosenzweig, M. R., Bennett, E. L., & Diamond, M. C. (1973). Effects of differential experience on dendritic spine counts in rat cerebral cortex. *Journal of Comparative and Physiological Psychology, 82,* 175–181.

Grant, S. G., O'Dell, T. J., Karl, K. A., Stein, P. L., Soriano, P., & Kandel, E. R. (1992). Impaired long-term potentiation, spatial learning, and hippocampal development in *fyn* mutant mice. *Science, 258,* 1903–1910.

Greenough, W. T., & Volkmar, F. R. (1973). Pattern of dendritic branching in occipital cortex of rats reared in complex environments. *Experimental Neurology, 40,* 491–504.

Greenough, W. T., Withers, G. S., & Wallace, C. S. (1990). Morphological changes in the nervous system arising from behavioral experience: What is the evidence they are involved in learning and memory? In L. R. Squire & E. Lindenlaub (Eds.), *The Biology of Memory* (pp. 159–185). Stuttgart: F. K. Schattauer Verlag

Grouse, L. D., Schrier, B. K., Bennett, E. L., Rosenzweig, M. R., & Nelson, P. G. (1978). Sequence diversity studies of rat brain RNA: Effects of environmental complexity on rat brain RNA diversity. *Journal of Neurochemistry, 30,* 191–203.

Halgren, E. (1995). PET may image the gates of awareness, not its center. *Behavioral and Brain Sciences, 18,* 358–359.

Hawkins, R. D., Cohen, T. E., & Kandel, E. R. (1992). Motor neuron correlates of dishabituation and sensitization of the gill-withdrawal reflex in *Aplysia. Society for Neuroscience Abstracts, 18,* 360.

Haywood, J., Rose, S. P. R., & Bateson, P. P. G. (1970). Effects of an imprinting procedure on RNA polymerase activity in the chick brain. *Nature, 288,* 373–374.

Healy, S. D., & Krebs, J. R. (1993). Development of hippocampal specialisation in a food-storing bird. *Behavioural Brain Research, 53,* 127–130.

Hebb, D. O. (1949). *The organization of behavior: A neuropsychological theory.* New York: Wiley.

Heisenberg, M., Borst, A., Wagner, S., & Byers, D. (1985). *Drosophila* mushroom body mutants are deficient in olfactory learning. *Journal of Neurogenetics, 2,* 1–30,

Heisenberg, M., Heusipp, M., & Wanke, C. (1995). Structural plasticity in the *Drosophila* brain. *Journal of Neuroscience, 15,* 1951–1960.

Hilgard, E. R., & Marquis, D. G. (1940). *Conditioning and learning.* New York: Appleton-Century.

Holloway, R. L. (1966). Dendritic branching: Some preliminary results of training and complexity in rat visual cortex. *Brain Research, 2,* 393–396.

Horwitz, B. (1995). Regions, networks: Interpreting functional neuroimaging data. *Behavioral and Brain Sciences, 18,* 360.

Hsiao, K., Chapman, P., Nilsen, S., Eckman, C., Harigaya, Y., Younkin, S., Yang, F., & Cole, G. (1996). Correlative memory deficits, Aβ elevation, and amyloid plaques in transgenic mice. *Science, 274,* 99–102.

Huang, Y. Y., & Kandel, E. R. (1994). Recruitment of long-lasting and protein kinase A-dependent long-term potentiation in the CA1 region of hippocampus requires repeated tetanization. *Learning and Memory, 1,* 74–82.

Hubel, D. H., & Wiesel, T. N. (1965). Binocular interaction in striate cortex of kittens reared with artificial squint. *Journal of Neurophysiology, 28,* 1041–1059.

James, W. (1890). *Principles of psychology.* New York: Henry Holt.

Jennings, H. S. (1906). *Behavior of the lower organisms.* New York: Columbia University Press.

Juraska, J. M., Fitch, J. M., Henderson, C., & Rivers, N. (1985). Sex differences in dendritic branching of dentate granule cells following differential experience. *Brain Research, 333,* 73–80.

Juraska, J. M., Fitch, J. M., & Washburne, D. L. (1989). The dendritic morphology of neurons in the rat hippocampus CA3 area. II. Effects of gender and the environment. *Brain Research, 479,* 115–119.

Kaas, J. H. (1991). Plasticity of sensory and motor maps in adult animals. *Annual Review of Neuroscience, 14,* 137–167.

Kandel, E. R., & O'Dell, T. J. (1992). Are adult learning mechanisms also used for development? *Science, 258,* 243–245.

Kandel, E. R., Schacher, S., Castellucci, V. F., & Goelet, P. (1987). The long and short of memory in *Aplysia:* A molecular perspective. In *Fidia Research Foundation Neuroscience Award Lectures.* Padova: Liviana Press.

Kandel, E. R., Schwartz, J. H., & Jessell, T. M. (1995). *Essentials of neural science.* Norwalk, CT: Appleton & Lange.

Katz, J. J., & Halstead, W. G. (1950). Protein organization and mental function. *Comparative Psychology Monographs, 20,* 1–38.

Kesner, R. P. Neurobiological views of memory. Chapter 10, this volume.

Kilman, V. L., Wallace, C. S., Withers, G. S., & Greenough, W. T. (1988). 4 days of differential housing alters dendritic morphology of weanling rats. *Society for Neuroscience Abstracts, 14,* 1135.

Kim, J. J., & Fanselow, M. S. (1992). Modality-specific retrograde amnesia of fear. *Science, 256,* 675–677.

Kleinschmidt, A., Baer, M. F., & Singer, W. (1987). Blockade of NMDA receptors disrupts experience-dependent plasticity of kitten striate cortex. *Science, 238,* 355–358.

Knowlton, B. J., Mangels, J. A., & Squire, L. R. (1996). A neostriatal habit learning system in humans. *Science, 273,* 1399–1402.

Kopelman, M. D. (1992). The "new" and the "old": Components of the anterograde and retrograde memory loss in Korsakoff and Alzheimer patients. In L. R. Squire & N. Butters (Eds.), *Neuropsychology of memory* (2nd ed., pp. 130–46). New York: Guilford

Korsakoff, S. S. (1887). Disturbance of psychic functions in alcoholic paralysis and its relation to the disturbance of the psychic sphere in multiple neuritis of non-alcoholic origin. *Vestnik Psichiatrii, 4,* Fasc. 2.

Krasne, F. B., & Glanzman, D. L. (1995). What we can learn from invertebrate learning. *Annual Review of Psychology, 46,* 585–624.

Krebs, J. R., Sherry, D. F., Healy, S. D., Perry, V. H., & Vaccarino, A. L. (1989). Hippocampal specialisation of food-storing birds. *Proceedings of the National Academy of Sciences U.S.A., 86,* 1388–1392.

Krech, D., Rosenzweig, M. R., & Bennett, E. L. (1956). Dimensions of discrimination and level of cholinesterase activity in the cerebral cortex of the rat. *Journal of Comparative and Physiological Psychology, 82,* 261–268.

Krech, D., Rosenzweig, M. R., & Bennett, E. L. (1960). Effects of environmental complexity and training on brain chemistry. *Journal of Comparative and Physiological Psychology, 53,* 509–519.

Krupa, D. J., Thompson, J. K., & Thompson, R. F. (1993). Localization of a memory trace in the mammalian brain. *Science, 260,* 989–991.

Lashley, K. S. (1950). In search of the engram. *Symposia of the Society for Experimental Biology, 4,* 454–482.

Lashley, K. S., (1952). Functional interpretation of anatomic patterns. *Research Publications of the Association for Nervous and Mental Disease, 30,* 529–547.

Lashley, K. S., & Franz, S. I. (1917). The effects of cerebral destruction upon habit-formation and retention in the albino rat. *Psychobiology, 1,* 71–139.

Lavie, P. (1996). *The enchanted world of sleep.* New Haven: Yale University Press.

Lavie, P., Pratt, H., Scharf, B., Peled, R., & Brown, J. (1984). Localized pontine lesion: Nearly total absence of REM sleep. *Neurology, 34,* 118–120.

Lavond, D., Kim, J. J., & Thompson, R. F. (1993). Mammalian brain substrates of aversive conditioning. *Annual Review of Psychology, 44,* 317–342.

Leconte, P., & Bloch, V. (1970). Déficit de la rétention d'un conditionnement après privation de sommeil paradoxal chez le rat [Impairment in retention for conditioning after deprivation of paradoxical sleep in the rat]. *Comptes Rendus de l'Académie des Sciences (Paris), 271D,* 226–229.

Leconte, P., Hennevin, E., & Bloch, V. (1973). Analyse des effets d'un apprentissage et de son niveau d'acquisition sur le sommeil paradoxal consécutif [Analysis of the effects of learning and its strength on the paradoxical sleep that follows]. *Brain Research, 49,* 367–379.

Lockhart, M., & Moore, J. W. (1975). Classical differential and operant conditioning in rabbits (*Orycytolagus cuniculus*) with septal lesions. *Journal of Comparative and Physiological Psychology, 88,* 147–154.

Logan, C. G., & Grafton, S. T. (1995). Functional anatomy of human eye-blink conditioning determined with regional cerebral glucose metabolism and positron emission tomography. *Proceedings of the National Academy of Sciences U.S.A., 92,* 7500–7504.

Löwel, S., & Singer, W. (1992). Selection of intrinsic horizontal connections in the visual cortex by correlated neuronal activity. *Science, 255,* 209–212.

Lowndes, M., & Stewart, M. G. (1994). Dendritic spine density in the lobus parolfactorius of the domestic chick is increased 24 h after one-trial passive avoidance training. *Brain Research, 654,* 129–136.

Marcus, E. A., Emptage, N. J., Marois, R., & Carew, T. J. (1994). A comparison of the mechanistic relationships between development and learning in *Aplysia*. *Progress in Brain Research, 100*, 179–188.

Martinez, J. L., & Derrick, B. E. (1996). Long-term potentiation and learning. *Annual Review of Psychology, 47*, 173–203.

McCarthy, G. (1995). Functional neuroimaging of memory. *The Neuroscientist, 1*(3), 155–163.

McCormick, D. A., & Thompson, R. F. (1984). Cerebellum: Essential involvement in the classically conditioned eyelid response. *Science, 223*, 296–299.

McDonald, R. J., & White, N. M. (1993). A triple dissociation of memory systems: Hippocampus, amygdala, and dorsal striatum. *Behavioral Neuroscience, 107*, 3–22.

McDougall, W. (1901). Experimentelle Beiträge zur Lehre vom Gedächtnis, by G. E. Müller and A. Pilzecker [Review of "Experimental research on memory," by G. E. Müller and A. Pilzecker]. *Mind, 10*, 388–394.

McGaugh, J. L. (1966). Time-dependent processes in memory storage. *Science, 153*, 1351–1358.

McGaugh, J. L. (1968). A multi-trace view of memory storage processes. In D. Bouet, F. Bouet-Nitti, & A. Oliverir (Eds.), *Attuali orientamenti della ricerca sull'apprendimento e la memoria* (pp. 13–24). Accademia Nazionale dei Lincei, Rome.

McNaughton, B. L., Morris, R. G. M. (1987). Hippocampal synaptic enhancement and information storage within a distributed memory system. *Trends in Neurosciences, 10*, 408–415.

Meberg, P. J., Valcourt, E. G., & Routtenberg, A. (1995). Protein F1 / GAP–43 and PKC gene expression patterns in hippocampus are altered 1–2 h after LTP. *Brain Research. Molecular Brain Research, 34*, 343–346.

Milner, P. M. (1993). The mind and Donald O. Hebb. *Scientific American, 268*(1), 124–129.

Mizumori, S. J. Y., Rosenzweig, M. R., & Bennett, E. L. (1985). Long-term working memory in the rat: Effects of hippocampally applied anisomycin. *Behavioral Neuroscience, 99*, 220–232.

Mizumori, S. J. Y., Sakai, D. H., Rosenzweig, M. R., Bennett, E. L., & Wittreich, P. (1987). Investigations into the neuropharmacological basis of temporal stages of memory formation in mice trained in an active avoidance task. *Behavioural Brain Research, 23*, 239–250.

Morris, R. G. M. (1989). Does synaptic plasticity play a role in learning in the vertebrate brain? In R. G. M. Morris (Ed.), *Parallel distributed processing: Implications for psychology and neurobiology*. Oxford: Clarendon Press.

Müller, G. E., & Pilzecker, A. (1900). Experimentelle Beiträge zur Lehre vom Gedächtnis [Experimental research on memory]. *Zeitschrift für Psychologie* (Suppl.), 1–288.

Neumann, E., & Ammons, R. B. (1957). Acquisition and long-term retention of a simple perceptual-motor skill. *Journal of Experimental Psychology, 53*, 159–161.

Ng, K. T., & Gibbs, M. E. (1991). Stages in memory formation: A review. In R. J. Andrew (Ed.), *Neural and behavioural plasticity: The use of the domestic chick as a model* (pp. 351–369). Oxford: Oxford University Press.

Nilsson, L.-G. (1992). Human learning and memory: A cognitive perspective. In M. R. Rosenzweig (Ed.), *International psychological science: Progress, problems, and prospects*. Washington, DC: American Psychological Association.

Nyberg, L., Cabeza, R., & Tulving, E. (1996). PET studies of encoding and retrieval: The HERA model. *Psychonomic Bulletin & Review, 3*, 135–148.

Oléron, G. (1968). Influence of data structuration on short and medium term memory. *Année Psychologique, 68*, 83–95.

Papka, M., Ivry, R., & Woodruff-Pak, D. S. (1994). Eyeblink classical conditioning and time production in patients with cerebellar damage. *Society for Neuroscience Abstracts, 20*, 360.

Patterson, T. A., Alvarado, M. C., Rosenzweig, M. R., & Bennett, E. L. (1988). Time courses of amnesia development in two areas of the chick forebrain. *Neurochemical Research, 13*, 643–647.

Patterson, T. A., Alvarado, M. C., Warner, I. T., Rosenzweig, M. R., & Bennett, E. L. (1986). Memory stages and brain asymmetry in chick learning. *Behavioral Neuroscience, 100*, 856–865.

Patterson, T. A., Schulteis, G., Alvarado, M. C., Martinez, J. L., Bennett, E. L., Rosenzweig, M. R., & Hruby, V. J. (1989). Influence of opioid peptides on learning and memory processes in the chick. *Behavioral Neuroscience, 103,* 429–437.

Pavlov, I. P. (1897). *Lekstii o rabote glavnykh pishchevaritel'nykh zhelez* [Lectures on the work of the principal digestive glands]. St. Petersburg, Russia: Typographiia Ministerstva Putei Soobsheniia.

Pavlov, I. P. (1904). Physiology of digestion. In Nobel Foundation (Ed.), *Nobel lectures: Physiology or medicine, 1901–1921* (pp. 141–155). New York: Elsevier, 1967.

Pavlov, I. P. (1906). The scientific investigation of the psychical faculties or processes in the higher animals. *Science, 24,* 613–619. (Also in *The Lancet, 2,* 911–915.)

Pavlov, I. P. (1927). *Conditioned reflexes* (G. V. Anrep, Trans.). London: Oxford University Press.

Pavlov, I. P. (1928). *Lectures on conditioned reflexes* (W. H. Gantt, Trans.). New York: International.

Perrett, S. P., Ruiz, B. P., & Mauk, M. D. (1993). Cerebellar cortex lesions disrupt learning-dependent timing of conditioned eyelid responses. *Journal of Neuroscience, 13,* 1708–1718.

Peterson, L., & Peterson, M. J. (1959). Short-term retention of individual verbal items. *Journal of Experimental Psychology, 58,* 193–198.

Piaget, J. (1980). *Adaptation and intelligence: Organic selection and phenocopy.* (S. S. Eames, trans.). Chicago: University of Chicago Press.

Posner, M. I., & Raichle, M. E. (1994). *Images of mind.* New York: Scientific American Library.

Posner, M. I., & Raichle, M. E. (1995). Précis of *Images of mind,* and commentaries. *Behavioral and Brain Sciences, 18,* 327–383.

Postman, L. (1985). Human learning and memory. In G. Kimble & K. Schlessinger (Eds.), *Topics in the history of psychology.* Hillsdale, NJ: Lawrence Erlbaum Associates.

Pysh, J. J., & Weiss, M. (1979). Exercise during development induces an increase in Purkinje cell dendritic tree size. *Science, 206,* 230–232.

Quinn, W. G., Sziber, P. P., & Booker, R. (1979). The *Drosophila* memory mutant *amnesiac. Nature, 277,* 212–214.

Rawlins, J. N. (1985). Associations across time: The hippocampus as a temporary memory store. *Behavioral and Brain Sciences, 8,* 479–528.

Renner, M. J., & Rosenzweig, M. R. (1987). *Enriched and impoverished environments: Effects on brain and behavior.* New York: Springer-Verlag.

Ribot, T. (1881). *Les maladies de la mémoire.* Paris: J. B. Ballière [J. Fitzgerald (Trans.). (1883). *The diseases of memory* (Vol. 46, pp. 453–500). New York: Humboldt Library of Popular Science Literature].

Richardson-Klavehn, A., & Bjork, R. A. (1988). Measures of memory. *Annual Review of Psychology, 39,* 475–544.

Riege, W. H. (1971). Environmental influences on brain and behavior of old rats. *Developmental Psychobiology, 4,* 157–167.

Rose, S. P. R. (1981). What should a biochemistry of learning and memory be about? *Neuroscience, 6,* 811–821.

Rose, S. [P. R.] (1992a). *The making of memory.* New York: Doubleday.

Rose, S. P. R. (1992b). Of chicks and Rosetta stones. In L. R. Squire and N. Butters (Eds.), *Neuropsychology of memory* (2nd ed., pp. 547–556). New York: Guilford.

Rose, S. P. R. (1995). Glycoproteins and memory formation. *Behavioural Brain Research, 66,* 73–78.

Rosenzweig, M. R. (1959). Salivary conditioning before Pavlov. *American Journal of Psychology, 72,* 628–633.

Rosenzweig, M. R. (1960). Pavlov, Bechterev, and Twitmeyer on conditioning. *American Journal of Psychology, 73,* 312–316.

Rosenzweig, M. R. (1964). Effects of heredity and environment on brain chemistry, brain anatomy, and learning ability in the rat. *Kansas Studies in Education, 14*(3), 3–34.

Rosenzweig, M. R. (1971). Effects of environment on development of brain and behavior. In E. Tobach (Ed.), *Biopsychology of development* (pp. 303–342). New York: Academic Press.

Rosenzweig, M. R. (1990). The chick as a model system for studying neural processes in learning and memory. In L. Erinoff (Ed.), *Behavior as an indicator of neuropharmacological events: Learning and memory* (pp. 1–20). Washington, DC: NIDA Research Monographs.

Rosenzweig, M. R. (1992). Research on the neural bases of learning and memory. In M. R. Rosenzweig (Ed.), *International psychological science: Progress, problems, and prospects* (pp. 103–136). Washington, DC: American Psychological Association.

Rosenzweig, M. R. (1996). Aspects of the search for neural mechanisms of memory. *Annual Review of Psychology, 47,* 1–32.

Rosenzweig, M. R., & Bennett, E. L. (1984). Studying memory formation with chicks and mice. In N. Butters & L. R. Squire (Eds.), *The neuropsychology of memory* (pp. 555–565). New York: Guilford.

Rosenzweig, M. R., Bennett, E. L., Colombo, P. J., Lee, D. W., & Serrano, P. A. (1993). Short-term, intermediate-term, and long-term memories. *Behavioural Brain Research, 57,* 193–198.

Rosenzweig, M. R., Bennett, E. L., & Diamond, M. C. (1972). Brain changes in response to experience. *Scientific American, 226:2,* 22–29.

Rosenzweig, M. R., Bennett, E. L., & Krech, D. (1964). Cerebral effects of environmental complexity and training among adult rats. *Journal of Comparative and Physiological Psychology, 57,* 438–439.

Rosenzweig, M. R., Bennett, E. L., Martinez, J. L., Jr., Colombo, P. J., Lee, D. W., & Serrano, P. A. (1992). Studying stages of memory formation with chicks. In L. R. Squire & N. Butters (Eds.), *Neuropsychology of memory* (2nd ed., pp. 533–546). New York: Guilford.

Rosenzweig, M. R., Diamond, M. C., Bennett, E. L., & Mollgaard, K. (1972). Negative as well as positive synaptic changes may store memory. *Psychological Review, 79,* 93–96.

Rosenzweig, M. R., Krech, D., & Bennett, E. L. (1958). Brain chemistry and adaptive behavior. In H. F. Harlow & C. N. Woolsey (Eds.), *Biological and biochemical bases of behavior* (pp. 367–400). Madison, WI: Wisconsin University Press.

Rosenzweig, M. R., Krech, D., & Bennett, E. L. (1961). Heredity, environment, brain biochemistry, and learning. In *Current trends in psychological theory* (pp. 87–110). Pittsburgh: University of Pittsburgh Press.

Rosenzweig, M. R., Krech, D., Bennett, E. L., & Diamond, M. C. (1962). Effects of environmental complexity and training on brain chemistry and anatomy: A replication and extension. *Journal of Comparative and Physiological Psychology, 55,* 429–437.

Rosenzweig, M. R., Love, W., & Bennett, E. L. (1968). Effects of a few hours of enriched experience on brain chemistry and brain weights. *Physiology and Behavior, 3,* 819–825.

Rozin, P. (1976). The psychobiological approach to human memory. In M. R. Rosenzweig & E. L. Bennett (Eds.), *Neural mechanisms of learning and memory* (pp. 3–46). Cambridge, MA: MIT Press.

Schwartz, J. H., Castellucci, V. F., & Kandel, E. R. (1971). Functioning of identified neurons and synapses in abdominal ganglia of *Aplysia* in absence of protein synthesis. *Journal of Neurophysiology, 34,* 939–963.

Searle, L. V. (1941). A study of the generality of inherited maze-brightness and maze-dullness. *Psychological Bulletin, 38,* 742.

Searle, L. V. (1949). The organization of hereditary maze-brightness and maze-dullness. *Genetic Psychology Monographs, 39,* 279–325.

Serrano, P. A., Beniston, D. S., Oxonian, M. G., Rodriguez, W. A., Rosenzweig, M. R., & Bennett, E. L. (1994). Differential effects of protein kinase inhibitors and activators on memory formation in the 2-day-old chick. *Behavioral and Neural Biology, 61,* 60–72.

Serrano, P. A., Rodriguez, W. A., Bennett, E. L., & Rosenzweig, M. R. (1995). Protein kinase inhibitors disrupt memory formation in two chick brain regions. *Pharmacology, Biochemistry and Behavior, 52,* 547–554.

Sherry, D. F., Vaccarino, A. L., Buckenham, K., & Herz, R. S. (1989). The hippocampal complex of food-storing birds. *Brain, Behavior and Evolution, 34,* 308–317.

Silva, A. J., Stevens, C. F., Tonegawa, S., & Wang, Y. (1992). Deficient hippocampal long-term potentiation in alpha-calcium-calmodulin kinase II mutant mice. *Science, 257,* 201–206.

Skaggs, W. E., & McNaughton, B. L. (1996). Replay of neuronal firing sequences in rat hippocampus during sleep following spatial experience. *Science, 271,* 1870–1873.

Snyder, A. Z., Abdullaev, Y. G., Posner, M. I., & Raichle, M. E. (1995). Scalp electrical potentials reflect regional cerebral blood flow responses during processing of written words. *Proceedings of the National Academy of Sciences U.S.A., 92,* 1689–1693.

Sperry, R. W. (1951). Mechanisms of neural maturation. In S. S. Stevens (Ed.), *Handbook of experimental psychology* (pp. 236–280). New York: Wiley.

Sperry, R. W. (1963). Chemoaffinity in the orderly growth of nerve fiber patterns and connections. *Proceedings of the National Academy of Sciences U.S.A., 50,* 703–710.

Tanzi, E. (1893). I fatti e le induzioni nell'odierna isologia del sistema nervoso. *Revista Sperimentale di Freniatria e di Medicina Legale, 19,* 419–472.

Tempel, B. L., Livingstone, M. S., & Quinn, W. G. (1984). Mutations on the dopa decarboxylase gene affect learning in *Drosophila. Proceedings of the National Academy of Sciences U.S.A., 81,* 3577–3581.

Teuber, H.-L. (1955). Physiological psychology. *Annual Review of Psychology, 6,* 267–296.

Thompson, R. F. (1990). Neural mechanisms of classical conditioning in mammals. *Philosophical Transactions of the Royal Society, London, Series B, 329,* 161–170.

Thompson, R. F., & Krupa, D. J. (1994). Organization of memory traces in the mammalian brain. *Annual Review of Neuroscience, 17,* 519–549.

Thorndike, E. L. (1898). Animal intelligence: An experimental study of the associative processes in animals. *Psychological Monographs, No. 8,* 1–109.

Thorndike, E. L. (1911). *Animal intelligence: Experimental studies.* New York: Macmillan.

Tolman, E. C. (1924). The inheritance of maze-learning ability in rats. *Journal of Comparative Psychology, 4,* 1–18.

Tolman, E. C. (1949). There is more than one kind of learning. *Psychological Review, 56,* 144–155.

Tolman, E. C., Tryon, R. C., & Jeffress, L. A. (1929). A self-recording maze with an automatic-delivery table. *University of California Publications in Psychology, 4,* 99–112.

Tolotschinoff, I. F. (1902). Contribution à l'étude de la physiologie et de la psychologie des glandes salivaires [Contribution to the study of the physiology and psychology of the salivary glands]. *Forhandlinga vid Nordiska naturforskare och lakermotet,* (pp. 42–46). Helsinki, Finland.

Treves, A., & Rolls, E. T. (1994). Computational analysis of the role of the hippocampus in memory. *Hippocampus, 4,* 374–391.

Tryon, R. C. (1940). Genetic differences in maze learning ability in rats. *Yearbook of the National Society for Studies in Education, 39* (Part I), 111–119.

Tryon, R. C. (1942). Individual differences. In F. A. Moss (Ed.), *Comparative psychology* (revised ed., pp. 330–365). New York: Prentice Hall.

Turner, A. M., & Greenough, W. T. (1985). Differential rearing effects on rat visual cortex synapses. I. Synaptic and neuronal density and synapses per neuron. *Brain Research, 329,* 195–203.

Voneida, T. J. (1990). The effect of rubrospinal tractotomy on a conditioned limb response in the cat. *Society for Neuroscience Abstracts, 16,* 279.

Waldeyer-Hartz, W. von (1891). Ueber einige neuere Forschungen im Gebiete der Anatomie des Centralnervensystems. *Deutsche Medizinische Wochenschrift, 17,* 1213–1218, 1244–1246, 1267–1269, 1287–1289, 1331–1332, 1352–1356.

Watson, J. B. (1916). The place of the conditioned reflex in psychology. *Psychological Review, 23,* 89–116.

Welford, A. T. (1952). An apparatus for use in studying serial performance. *American Journal of Psychology, 65,* 91–97.

Weinberger, N. M. (1995). Dynamic regulation of receptive fields and maps in the adult sensory cortex. *Annual Review of Neuroscience, 18,* 129–158.

West, R. W., & Greenough, W. T. (1972). Effects of environmental complexity on cortical synapses of rats: Preliminary results. *Behavioral Biology, 7,* 279–284.

Whytt, R. (1763). *An essay on the vital and other involuntary motions of animals* (2nd ed.). Edinburgh: John Balfour.

Wiesel, T. N., & Hubel, D. H. (1963). Single-cell responses in striate cortex of kittens deprived of vision in one eye. *Journal of Neurophysiology, 26,* 1003–1017.

Wiesel, T. N., & Hubel, D. H. (1965). Comparison of the effects of unilateral and bilateral eye closure on cortical unit responses in kittens. *Journal of Neurophysiology, 28,* 1029–1040.

Wilson, M. A., & McNaughton, B. L. (1994). Reactivation of hippocampal ensemble memories during sleep. *Science, 265,* 676–679.

Winocur, G. (1990). Anterograde and retrograde amnesia in rats with dorsal hippocampal or dorsomedial thalamic lesions. *Behavioural Brain Research, 38,* 145–154.

Witelson, S. F., Glezer, I. I., & Kigar, D. L. (1995). Women have greater density of neurons in posterior temporal cortex. *Journal of Neuroscience, 15,* 3418–3428.

Wu, J. Y., Cohen, L. B., & Falk, C. X. (1994). Neuronal activity during different behaviors in *Aplysia:* A distributed organization? *Science, 263,* 820–823.

Yeo, C. H., Hardiman, M. J., & Glickstein, M. (1985). Classical conditioning of the nictitating membrane response of the rabbit. II. Lesions of the cerebellar cortex. *Experimental Brain Research, 60,* 99–113.

Zecevic, D., Wu, J. Y., Cohen, L. B., London, J. A., Hopp, H. P., & Falk, C. X. (1989). Hundreds of neurons in the *Aplysia* abdominal ganglion are active during the gill-withdrawal reflex. *Journal of Neuroscience, 9,* 3681–3689.

Zolman, J. F., & Morimoto, H. (1962). Effects of age of training on cholinesterase activity in the brains of maze-bright rats. *Journal of Comparative and Physiological Psychology, 55,* 794–800.

CHAPTER 2

Developmental Approaches to the Memory Process

James E. Black* and William T. Greenough†

Departments of *,†Psychology, *,†Psychiatry, and †Cell and Structural Biology, *,†Neuroscience Program, and *,†Beckman Institute, Urbana, Illinois 61801

Tinbergen (1951), one of the first students of animal behavior, suggested that the question "Why does this animal behave this way?" requires four related answers: (1) the immediate causal control of the behavior, (2) the animal's developmental history, (3) the behavior's contribution to the individual's survival, and (4) the evolutionary history of the species trait. In asking "Why does the animal learn and remember?", many scientists have concentrated primarily on the first answer: the immediate biological and psychological causes. In contrast, this chapter focuses more on the developmental perspective, set in the context of some ethological and evolutionary concerns.

I. SOME HISTORICAL ASPECTS OF MEMORY ONTOGENY RESEARCH

In the last half of the nineteenth century, scientists in fields ranging from histology to psychiatry were proposing that memory and development were intimately linked to subtle movements of neurons. Because synaptic connections between neurons were not visible with the existing technology, synapses became the focus of much speculation. Ramon y Cajal (1893), for example, suggested that learning might involve the formation of new synaptic connections between neurons. Tanzi (1893), noting that the resistance to transmission between neurons might vary with the size of the connection, proposed that frequent use of a synapse might cause them to grow larger, similar to the hypertrophy produced by exercising a muscle, and thereby strengthen pre-existing connections. These two perspectives, that memory results from making new connections or by modifying existing ones, remain an active area of study today and one we revisit at several points. Both theories presumed that the structural plasticity seen in development was basically the same as that of adulthood, a concept that has been partially borne out by recent research.

Little theoretical or empirical progress was made along this line for half a century, until Hebb (1949) suggested how experience could be represented in new or modified neural organizations. Rejecting the "one memory–one neuron" concept and anticipating modern neural network theories, Hebb proposed that memory involved large structures of interconnected neurons, termed "cell assemblies." These were hierarchically organized into larger systems called "phase sequences" controlling the activation of cell assemblies, a concept resembling that of a computer program which coordinates the use of simpler subroutines. Memory thus became a process more than a place, since encoding and retrieval depended on the cooperation of large sets of neurons rather than independent cells. Hebb, who also felt that developmental plasticity and adult memory might share mechanisms, proposed what is now termed the *Hebb synapse,* a model synapse with a rule that simultaneous pre- and postsynaptic activity increases synaptic efficacy. This basic concept of a cooperative set of modifiable connections as the basis of learning and memory, along with the Hebb synapse, continues to have substantial influence on neural network theory (e.g., McClelland & Rumelhart, 1986). For example, the Hebb synapse concept has been used to explain neural plasticity observed with N-methyl-D-aspartate- (NMDA) and voltage-regulated calcium channels found at some synapses (see Chapter 6).

Another line of interest in memory ontogeny and evolution began with the neural maturationist group. For example, Fleschsig (1927) observed that the myelin that wraps and insulates mature axons apparently develops in the order of a structure's phylogenetic appearance, suggesting that the human brain, for example, would have a progression of myelination patterns similar to the neural systems of a fish, a reptile, and so on up the "evolutionary ladder." The theory may now seem hopelessly outdated, but elements of it are still useful: it helps us focus on the evolutionary history of different neural systems (as Tinbergen recommended) and on how neural plasticity may have contributed to the survival of early ancestors. Mammalian brains did not arise *de novo,* designed for efficiency or esthetics, but are rather the product of old brain parts cobbled together and modified over a long history.

Another useful aspect of the maturationist approach is the concept of a "memory organ," a neural component that evolution shaped to be an information storage device, only needing to ripen on a phylogenetically determined schedule to take on its specialized role. To expand on that point, it seems likely that different parts of the brain have evolved to take on similar roles, such that multiple memory systems may be interacting in the mammalian brain, each playing different adaptive roles. For example, the peptide CCK is released when food is eaten and improves retention of information, and in what appears to be a phylogenetically older system, its influence is transferred via the vagus nerve to the amygdala and from there to other regions (Flood, Smith, & Morley, 1987). In other cases, older memory systems may have been co-opted for a new purpose of storing information, for example the relatively sudden emergence of lateralized language areas in humans, as if it had been "borrowed" from the sensory and motor regions other primates use for other purposes. This area of human cortex is species-specific and probably has genetically determined features, but the vast amount of linguistic information stored there during the first years of development certainly requires neural plasticity as a core function (see Locke, 1992).

The effects of early experience had a fundamental role in psychoanalytic theory, which has always had a substantial interest in memory ontogeny. Freud (1969) suggested that early childhood memories are often retained by the adult, still powerful but repressed from consciousness. Schactel (1947) reviewed studies of childhood memory and concluded that very few memories from early childhood could be recalled. In general, investigators had tried to explain this *infantile amnesia* in cognitive, neural, or psychoanalytic terms: (1) children process information too differently to access it as adults, (2) some area of the child's brain is too immature to consolidate memory or developmental processes later disrupt what was previously learned, and (3) the adult represses information that is distressing to recall (Allport, 1937). The first two explanations are still actively studied in memory research, and the last has taken on special significance in recent years due to controversy about repressed memories of psychological trauma (see Schacter, 1995, for a broad perspective).

Early animal studies of this issue, such as that of Campbell and Campbell (1962), suggested that infantile amnesia was a global phenomenon that would disrupt all kinds of learning equally. This result would be compatible with the kind of neural maturation process proposed by Flechsig, much as one destroys old information on a videotape when new images are recorded on it, but recent research has demonstrated that this issue is far more complex. Although adults can consciously recall little information about specific events in childhood, it is now very clear that children do remember many other things for a long time, such as the details of one's language, physical relationships, and social order (Thelen & Smith, 1994). Continued practice may preserve some memories (e.g., the memory for walking), while developmental changes in processing may selectively disrupt other kinds of memory (e.g., the transition from nonverbal to verbal coding of information), and other types of learning can be modified over time (e.g., the child's perception of "motherese" speech progressing to adult phoneme recognition). Some types of memories have obvious adaptive value to newborns, and they may be installed quite early without conscious awareness (e.g., taste aversions learned in utero; Stickrod, Kimble, & Smotherman, 1982).

Recent work by developmentalists (e.g., Thelen & Smith, 1994; Karmiloff-Smith, 1992) has emphasized that the brain can self-organize much of its structure, starting with genetically determined restrictions (e.g., the initial cortical architecture), and then develop *dynamically*, with environmental information interacting with existing neural structures to further organize and refine neural connections. We do not want to minimize the amount of genetic information used to build a brain (some tens of thousands of genes are uniquely expressed in brain development of the rat; Chaudhari & Hahn, 1983; Milner & Sutcliffe, 1983). Likewise, we do not want to fall into the maturationist trap, suggesting that memory systems will develop on a rigid developmental timetable. From the dynamic systems perspective, the interaction of genetic constraints and environmental information can *self-organize* highly complex systems, with each organism following potentially unique developmental paths of brain assembly to the extent that they have unique experiences.

The history of work in memory ontogeny demonstrates the importance of an integrated, interdisciplinary approach to studying memory. Tinbergen's "answers" are still useful to us after a century of memory research: describe the immediate psychobiological processes of memory, the development of memory systems, the adaptive value of such systems, and their phylogenetic history. In this chapter we will argue that (1) adult memory processes are related to, yet different from, neural plasticity during development; (2) some aspects of neural plasticity have remained stable during the evolution of the brain; (3) multiple memory systems have evolved and work in cooperation; and (4) specialized support systems have evolved to meet the regulatory or metabolic needs of memory.

II. EXPERIENCE-EXPECTANT AND EXPERIENCE-DEPENDENT NEURAL PLASTICITY

Piaget (1980) stressed that information storage depends on both the amount of information available in experience (termed *contrast* here) and the quality of it (termed *coherence* here). Contrast is not simply an external environmental quality, but is based rather on the organism's access to complex environmental information. For example, increasing the complexity of the environment clearly makes more information available to a kitten, provided that it is developed enough to extract it and make sense of it. Similarly, a kitten's mastery of locomotion can greatly increase contrast while the environment itself does not change. Coherence is also an organism-centered quality, reflecting the stability and reliability of experience. For example, the clumsy movements of a human infant initially provide relatively incoherent and inconsistent feedback from reaching for an object. After basic sensory-motor skills are established, experience then becomes more coherent as consistent relationships between movement and perception are established.

Piaget also argued from an ethological perspective that two types of information were acquired by young animals from their environment: (1) general information acquired by all species members from common features of their environments (i.e., "expected" information) and (2) idiosyncratic information which the individual uses to adapt to its own unique environment (i.e., "unexpected" information). We have formalized these concepts as proposed types of brain information storage, and we have asked whether different processes govern them in the brain (Black & Greenough, 1986). The first type of information storage, *experience-expectant,* allows a simplification and reduction in the information the genome must carry. For example, if the developmental mechanisms can expect visual stimuli of all orientations to be in the environment, then this information can be used to fine-tune genetically predisposed edge detectors in the visual system. That is, the information necessary to specify edge detectors need not be entirely provided by genes if it can be expected in the normal environment of all species members. (Chickens and other precocial animals that must use vision immediately after hatching may have to establish visual systems less sensitive to experience, possibly at some cost in operating precision.) Experience-expectant information storage typically involves a brief time span, often termed a *critical period* or *sensitive period,* when the organism is maximally ready (i.e., developmentally expects) to receive the appropriate information.

The second type of information storage, *experience-dependent,* optimizes individual adaptation to specific and sometimes unique features of the individual organism's environment and includes what we typically mean by "learning and memory." Experience-dependent information storage does not involve sensitive periods, although there may be sequential dependencies (e.g., the need to learn the alphabet before recognizing printed words). Even though experience-expectant and experience-dependent information storage may share neural mechanisms, memory recall for these two may differ in the adult. We would argue that humans, in particular, have modified cerebral cortex and associated regions to form a massive "memory organ," one capable of incorporating in its synaptic connections the complexity of language, culture, and even the content of college textbooks.

We will discuss what is known about these two types of mechanisms following a brief description of the neuroscience methods used in this area of research.

III. QUANTITATIVE METHODS IN DEVELOPMENTAL NEUROBIOLOGY

Nerve cell bodies, neural processes, glial cells, vasculature, etc. are tightly packed and intertwined in all brain regions. Figure 1A is a drawing of a thin section of rat visual cortex in which all tissue components were stained. Whereas larger dendrites, axons, cell bodies, and some other coarse features can be observed with standard

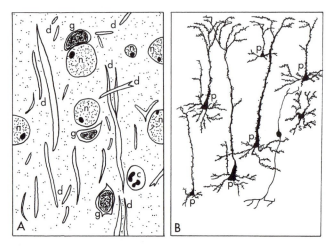

FIGURE 1   (A) Drawing of a cortical section stained with toluidine blue. Note the tangled packing of glial somata (g), neuronal somata (n), dendrites (d), and capillaries (c). The density and size of the neuronal somata allow the cortex to be divided into six layers. (B) Drawing at lower magnification of a Golgi-stained cortical section. Fewer pyramidal (p) and stellate (s) neurons are stained, with complete dendrites reaching across cortical layers. Unstained tissue is relatively transparent.

light microscopy, the complex tangle of fine synapses, dendrites, axons, and glial processes (termed *neuropil*) cannot be traced back and associated with any particular cell. Some staining methods can help us differentiate layers of cerebral cortex, generally termed Layers I–VI and identifiable by the characteristic size, shape, and density of neurons in them. Stains such as that used in Fig. 1A are also useful for quantifying numbers of neurons, glial cells, blood vessels, etc., however, since all of them are rendered visible in the section. Other types of staining are increasingly being used in neuroscience, particularly immunocytochemistry that labels particular proteins (or other complex molecules, or even fragments of DNA) that help us understand how genes are expressed during information storage. Without going into much technical detail, we will mention later some ways that these methods have substantially helped us understand the molecular foundations of memory.

Figure 1B is a drawing from a much thicker section stained with the Golgi method, named after its inventor and turn-of-the-century anatomist Camillo Golgi. It uniquely stains only a few neurons in a region and leaves the remainder transparent, thus allowing their dendrites (and their axons to varying degrees) to be viewed unobscured. To obtain accurate light microscopic measurement of neuron morphology, the dendritic field must be traced completely without becoming lost in the tangle of other neural processes. A camera lucida can be used to collect data by superimposing the slide's image onto a two-dimensional drawing, or a computer-aided microscope can record the three-dimensional coordinates of points on the dendritic branches, storing a mathematical representation of the neuron.

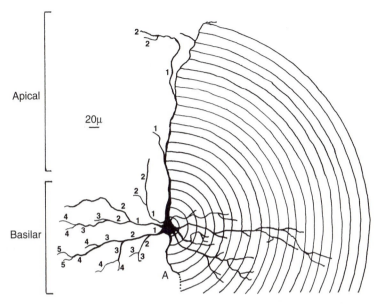

Apical

20μ

Basilar

A

FIGURE 2   The amount of dendritic material for cortical neurons can be analyzed in two ways: (1) The intersections between dendrites and a superimposed series of concentric rings are counted. Here then are six basilar intersections at the fourth ring on the right. (2) The number and length of dendrites at each order are measured. Here there are six basilar segments of third order on the left. The apical dendrite is that emanating from the top, or apex, of the pyramid-like cell body of a pyramidal neuron. Basilar dendrites radiate from its base.

Dendritic branches are commonly described in terms of order of bifurcation, as indicated in Fig. 2. A first-order segment is defined as originating from the soma (cell body), and a second-order segment has its root in the forked end of a first-order segment. Another method of measuring dendritic trees uses a two-dimensional transparent overlay of concentric rings (Sholl, 1956), or concentric spheres for three-dimensional computer-microscope data. The frequency of ring intersections indicates dendritic volume distribution. Golgi methods also allow analysis of dendritic spine density (numbers per unit length of dendrite) as well as spine sizes and shapes. Spines are small postsynaptic extensions on many kinds of neurons (see Figs. 1B and 3). The size and shape of spines may affect their conductive properties with regard to the effectiveness of transmission from one neuron to another, and hence the possible modification of spine structure by learning has been investigated in several studies (e.g., Coss, Brandon, & Globus, 1980).

Each of the neurons is surrounded by blood vessels and glial cells of various types (including astrocytes, mentioned later). The blood vessels supply nutrients to the high-metabolism neuropil, and their support can be improved by altering their size, installing new capillaries, or increasing blood flow. Memory processes have high

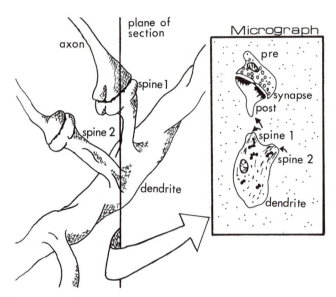

FIGURE 3   Drawings of a synapse before sectioning and the electron microscope image of the tissue at the plane of section. One can count and classify synapses from micrographs, as well as measure the synaptic cleft, postsynaptic thickening, and pre- or postsynaptic areas. Note how difficult it would be to identify which axon and dendrite a synapse belongs to.

metabolic rates and can be choked off by inadequate vascular support. Glial cells, long neglected by neuroscientists, are now known to have many important brain functions, including metabolic support, functional regulation of neurons, electrical insulation, immunological protection, and the blood–brain barrier that provides nutrients and shields the brain from potential toxins in the blood (Kimelberg, Jalonen, & Walz, 1993). Glia also conduct information, in the form of calcium-based potentials, and they respond to many neurotransmitters. In addition, there is good reason to suspect that glia play roles in the memory process itself.

Electron microscopic studies are useful for determining the number of very small structures like synapses as well as their size and other characteristics. Figure 3 illustrates the appearance of synapses in an electron micrograph. Since the thin electron microscopy section cuts randomly through synapses, specialized techniques must be used to compensate for variation in size and shape. Mathematically unbiased procedures termed *stereological methods* must be used to provide accurate estimates of synapse numbers. The result of these corrections, an accurate density estimate (e.g., number of synapses per unit volume), may still be misleading, since various manipulations may change the reference volume of a brain region such as the primary visual cortex. When the reference volume cannot be easily determined, another useful measure is the ratio of synapses-per-unit-volume to neurons-per-unit-volume, or synapses per neuron. The assumption is that the number of neurons is stable, as no new neurons are formed and there is no evidence for neuron death in most memory studies (interesting exceptions to this include birth defects or neuro-degenerative disorders that can affect both memory and neuron numbers; e.g., Fetal Alcohol Syndrome and Alzheimer's disease). Turner and Greenough (1983, 1985) and Sirevaag and Greenough (1987) found that electron microscopic estimates of the number of synapses per neuron corresponded well to estimates obtained from quantitative studies of Golgi material. They also reported changes in the structure of synapses as a consequence of behavioral experience, a widespread finding. In this chapter, we largely restrict our discussion to data indicating changes in number of synapses rather than their size or shape. Changes in structural characteristics of existing synapses that might also be involved in memory storage have been reviewed elsewhere (Greenough et al., 1994).

IV. NEUROBIOLOGICAL CORRELATES OF MEMORY DEVELOPMENT

Use of these techniques following early visual deprivation, general enrichment of the environment, and training tasks has provided evidence that changes in both numbers of synapses and structural characteristics of synapses are involved in the storage of experiential information. We also now have evidence that these changes are supported by corresponding changes in glia and vasculature. Remarkably similar but still distinct effects have been seen with manipulations directed at the experience-expectant and experience-dependent types of information storage, implying that some basic processes may have been phylogenetically conserved, while others were adapted for new needs.

A. Studies of Early Visual Deprivation

Early visual development appears to be a case of experience-expectant neural processes that are normally guided by visual stimulation. Behavioral and structural effects of early light and pattern deprivation have been reported in most mammalian species tested. The effects are most pronounced with monocular deprivation in species with binocularly overlapping visual systems where large parts of both eyes see the same visual field, such as cats or other predators, but significant effects also occur in largely nonoverlapping species such as rats. In fact, the studies of monocular deprivation in animals with binocularly overlapping visual systems constitute a special case and will be discussed separately.

1. Effects of Complete Visual Deprivation

Dark-reared animals are impaired in visual behavior. Walk and Walters (1973) showed that dark-reared animals have long-lasting deficits on a shallow visual cliff, where animals can unwisely choose to step off a small platform. Cats reared in darkness or unpatterned illumination are slower to learn complex discriminations, such as an X versus an N (Riesen, 1965). Tees (1968a) found that dark-reared rats learned simple pattern discriminations as well as normal rats but that dark-reared animals were slower in learning the more complex X–N task. However, the inherent difficulty of the task was not the primary determinant of poor performance of the dark-reared rats, as dark-reared animals could learn very difficult brightness discrimination tasks as well as normal rats (Tees, 1968b) and were still inferior at discriminating shapes and contours. Tees and Cartwright (1972) demonstrated that this learning deficit was related to effects on visual processing rather than some general learning disability. They found that dark-reared animals had no deficiency in associating two auditory stimuli but did have difficulty with an auditory–visual stimulus pair. These studies suggest that visual learning of adult animals is impaired if early visual experience has not established effective mechanisms of processing visual information; that is, early, normal visual experience is necessary for later normal visual perception.

Initial attempts to find neural correlates of visual deprivation were disappointing. Ramon y Cajal (1893) investigated whether neural junctions would grow closer together. He found no apparent differences between the optic lobes of amphibians raised in the light for 1 month and those raised in the dark. Later work suggests that amphibians were an unfortunate choice for this work. In general, it appears that mammals and birds are relatively unique in having devoted large portions of brain to neural plasticity that take advantage of expected experience. Some *invertebrate* species provide interesting exceptions, however, if their adaptive needs during evolution included a need to store information about their environment. For example, honeybees have evolved behavioral strategies that require learning spatial information about the location of flowers, the hive, etc. and communicating it to other bees in the hive. When a worker honeybee emerges from its hive, a developmentally programmed event, it rapidly learns this information and specialized sensory structures in the bee's brain called mushroom bodies undergo substantial morphological changes (Withers, Fahrbach, & Robinson, 1993).

Mammalian nervous system studies have been more consistent in revealing morphological effects of visual deprivation. Coleman and Riesen (1968) found smaller dendritic fields in primary visual cortex neurons of two of three dark-reared cats. Similarly, Valverde (1970) found reduced basilar dendritic branching of pyramidal neurons in the visual cortex of dark-reared mice. Borges and Berry (1976, 1978) found changes in the orientation, but not the number or length, of dendrites in a small sample of cells in rat visual cortex. Schwartz and Rothblat (1980) reared monocularly deprived rats in bright light, so that the retina of the sutured eye received unpatterned illumination at levels comparable to an open eye in normal light. They found that spine frequency on dendrites in the contralateral visual cortex was comparable in both cases, but behavioral measures of visual ability indicated a functional impairment of vision using the deprived eye. These results suggest that some spine density changes may require only a certain level of illumination, whereas neural organization underlying functional vision may require patterned visual experience. Aside from actual changes in the frequency of spines, another interesting possibility is that dark-rearing simply slows down their development. Freire (1978) examined the spines of apical dendrites in Layer IV of the occipital cortex of 19-day-old dark-reared and normal mice with serial-section electron microscopy. The three-dimensional reconstructions indicated that spine development progressed from small spines with no spine apparati and small heads to large spines with extensive spine apparati. Dark-reared mice had more of the small-type spines, whereas normally reared animals had more of the large-type spines. Freire suggested that the spine frequency differences observed by other investigators may reflect a maturational delay of spines in the dark-reared animals, since their relatively immature spines would be easy to miss in Golgi studies, distorting their frequency estimates. Since the maturational lag would eventually fade away as the dark-reared animals caught up, the smaller but persistent differences between older animals (Cragg, 1967; Valverde, 1971) probably reflect actual and long-lasting frequency changes.

Electron microscopy studies also suggest substantial changes in synaptic frequency after visual deprivation. Cragg (1975a) found that light-experienced kittens had about 40% more synapses per neuron than binocularly deprived kittens. These findings are compatible with the Golgi studies of Coleman and Riesen (1968), Rothblat and Schwartz (1979), and Valverde (1970), which suggest a reduction in the number of synapses per neuron with visual deprivation. It is possible in some cases that the formation of synapses is delayed and can later catch up. For example, Winfield (1981) showed that binocularly sutured cats eventually catch up with normally reared cats in synapses per neuron, although this study used few animals and they received some eyelid-filtered illumination. The molecular biology of visual deprivation is too complex to address in this chapter, but two examples of it are the important roles of serotonin receptors and second messenger systems (Gu & Singer, 1995) and NMDA receptors (Fox & Daw, 1993). NMDA receptors provide a biological implementation of the Hebb synapse discussed earlier. They respond selectively to simultaneous presynaptic neurotransmitter and postsynaptic depolarization, admitting calcium into the postsynaptic cell. Calcium can, in turn, trigger a variety of enzymatic "cascades" in the postsynaptic cell, some of which lead to structural changes in synapses. Early visual experience also alters the number of glial cell processes supporting synaptic changes in the visual cortex (Hawrylak & Greenough, 1995). These examples, selected from many, show our increasing understanding of the molecular biology of this particular neural plasticity process.

2. Selective Deprivation in Species with Stereoscopic Vision

For binocularly overlapping species such as cats, monkeys, and humans, the neurobiological effects of visual deprivation are clearly related to the behavioral effects.

Complete deprivation of both eyes leads to a loss in complex visuomotor learning and in the precision of neuronal response properties, but balance in eye dominance and basic perceptual skills are retained (e.g., Zablocka & Zernicki, 1990). In contrast, deprivation of *one* eye during the critical period leads to a drastic reduction in its control over visual cortex neurons or behavior, while the nondeprived eye correspondingly gains in control. The degree of recovery from deprivation depends on the species and the deprivation period's onset and duration.

One kind of selective deprivation in binocular species involves perceptual mismatch from both eyes, for example, when one eye is deviated outward (strabismus) during early development. If the two eyes are sending competing and conflicting signals to the visual cortex during the sensitive period, the brain effectively "shuts down" or becomes insensitive to the nondominant eye. In humans, the resulting perceptual disorder is termed *amblyopia* (or "lazy eye"), and it results in clear perceptual deficits if surgery does not correct this visual misalignment during the critical period. The strabismus-related deficit was the first and is still the best-established example of human neural plasticity (Crawford et al., 1993). Recent technology, such as a positron emission tomography (PET scans), has demonstrated that patients with uncorrected strabismus use different areas of the cortex for visual processing than do normal controls (e.g., Demer, 1993).

Monocular deprivation studies in animals with extensive binocular overlap of the visual fields have indicated involvement of competitive processes in establishing synaptic connections (LeVay, Wiesel, & Hubel, 1980). In monkeys, for example, binocular regions of the visual cortex receive input from the eyes in adjacent bands, also termed "columns," about 400 microns wide. After monocular deprivation, the functional blindness of the deprived eye is associated with a narrowing of its cortical columns, whereas the cortical columns of the nondeprived eye expand in width (LeVay et al., 1980). The establishment of the ocular dominance columns apparently involves regression of axon terminal branches. During development, axons associated with both eyes initially have more extensive, overlapping terminal fields in Layer IV, so that the cortical columns are indistinct, whereas the adult has columns with sharpened borders. If one eye is deprived early, the axon terminations in its ocular dominance columns regress excessively, while the axon terminations of the columns for the other eye do not regress to the normal degree. LeVay et al. (1980) attribute this shift in column width to competition between the axon terminal fields, with the more active connections winning out over the deprived. Correlates of this process are seen at the level of individual synapses. Tieman (1984) has shown that the average axon from a deprived eye has fewer synaptic terminals than that from an experienced eye. Correspondingly, Friedlander, Martin, and Wassenhove-McCarthy (1991) have shown that open-eye axons in monocularly deprived cats have larger presynaptic terminals with more postsynaptic contacts per terminal compared to axon terminals from the closed eye or those of nondeprived cats. This concept of axonal competition is also supported by the observation that a previously deprived eye can functionally recover if the other eye receives no visual input, but low-level, unpatterned stimulation of the other eye inhibits recovery (Smith & Loop, 1978).

In another type of selective visual deprivation, kittens exposed only to horizontal or vertical stripes with both eyes during development have visual cortex neurons that respond selectively to visual stimuli of the exposure orientation (Hirsch & Spinelli, 1970). To study anatomical correlates of this selective deprivation, Coleman, Flood, Whitehead, and Emerson (1981) raised six kittens in horizontally striped, vertically striped, and nonstriped cylinders. Layer IV stellate cells of the visual cortex from the horizontal- and vertical-stripe groups did not differ in dendritic length or number of branches, but the angular distributions of the distal dendritic segments were at approximately 90° from each other, just as their stimuli were at right angles. Tieman and Hirsch (1982) similarly reported that stripe-rearing modifies dendrite orientation of Layer III pyramidal cells of kitten visual cortex. They raised five cats viewing only vertical lines and three cats viewing only horizontal lines. The horizontal-stripe cats and vertical-stripe cats had approximately perpendicular distributions of dendritic orientation. The dendritic fields were generally perpendicular to the representation of the stripe stimuli in the cortex, suggesting a specific relationship between the morphology of Layer III pyramidal cells, their physiological orientation, and early experience.

Other types of selective visual deprivation also affect the behavior and neurophysiology of young animals. For example, rearing kittens in a strobe-illuminated environment (Marchand, Cremieux, & Amblard, 1990) provides them with plentiful visual detail but deprives them of any perception of movement (i.e., movement in the visual field would appear "jerky" or disconnected). In another example, Hendy and Riesen (1988) raised kittens wearing prism masks that laterally displaced the visual field. The kittens with the most severe displacement were later impaired on complex visual learning tasks. In an older but still elegant series of experiments (Held & Hein, 1963; Hein & Diamond, 1971), kittens rode in a gondola that allowed vision but restricted movement, wore large collars that allowed free movement but prevented visualization of their paws, or had surgery that prevented their eyes from tracking their paws in space. These kittens had normal amounts of visual and proprioceptive information, but the lack of perceptual integration in these modalities caused profound behavioral pathology. Note that all of the types of deprivation described here either interfere with contrast (less information; e.g., monocular deprivation, strobe-rearing, or stripe-rearing) or coherence (less consistency of input; e.g., strabismus, wearing prisms, or riding in gondolas).

We would use the term experience-expectant to describe all of these processes because the initial neural changes are produced in the "expectation" that normal visual experience will occur, allowing a fuzzy developmental system to be refined by experience into the more precise organization of maturity. Such experience has occurred reliably in the evolutionary history of cats and other binocular species. An important conclusion from this work is that the *pattern*, rather than the absolute number, of synaptic connections is the essential determinant of functional status.

Parallel work in the development of other sensory modalities suggests this is a correct conclusion. For example, Greenough and Chang (1988) studied the development of oriented dendritic fields in somatosensory cortex subserving whisker perception in mice (a sensory modality that is very refined in many rodents). In this region, each whisker is represented by a "barrel," the walls of which are neuronal cell bodies and the interior of which contains their dendrites and the axons from the whisker system. Dendritic fields of the neurons in the barrel walls are asymmetric in adults, with most of them projecting into the barrel center. In early development, their dendritic fields are pointing in all directions, with dendrites subsequently lost if they are pointing away from the barrel center, even as those pointing centrally continue to grow. Thus the development of these dendrites seems remarkably like those of the axons in the binocular visual systems. Similar findings of synaptic overproduction and pruning back have also been reported in other sensory systems (Clopton, 1986; Meisami, 1975; Woolsey & Wann, 1976).

3. Summary of Visual Deprivation Effects

These studies collectively indicate that early visual experience is used by experience-expectant plasticity as a programmed part of brain development. It is clear, however, that the role of experience-expectant mechanisms in brain development is complex, with early deprivation impairing later experience-dependent visual learning. Similarly, the simple presence of light can trigger simple maturational processes, but most mammalian species need coherent experience with a broad range of features and relationships for complete brain development. As suggested herein, these processes are not entirely independent. For example, the experience-expectant requirement for early coherent experience ultimately affects experience-dependent processes, since young animals deprived of it have impaired visual learning ability and thus will not be able to take full advantage of later experience.

Experience-expectant neural plasticity often (perhaps always) arises in a context of synapse overproduction. For example, Cragg (1975b) reported that the number of synapses per neuron in cat visual cortex reached a peak at about 5 weeks of age and then fell to lower levels in adulthood. Similarly, Boothe, Greenough, Lund, and Wrege (1979) reported that spine frequency on some types of monkey visual cortex neurons reached an early peak and later declined to adult values. The peak values are reached, in both cases, at about the time that sensitivity to gross manipulations of visual experience, such as monocular pattern deprivation, is also maximal. In both species, afferent axonal terminal fields overlap during early development, segregating through the elimination of overlapping synapses as development progresses (e.g., LeVay et al., 1980), and in both species, occlusion of one eye causes more of its connections to be lost and more of the open eye's connections to be preserved (LeVay et al., 1980; Tieman, 1984). Similar phenomena are seen in other developing sensory projection systems, and entire dendritic or axonal branches regress in some cases (e.g., Falls & Gobel, 1979; Feng & Rogowski, 1980; Mariani & Changeaux, 1981; Greenough and Chang, 1988).

It thus appears that the nervous system may become ready for expected experience by overproducing connections on a sensory-system-wide basis, such that experience-related neural activity can select a functionally appropriate subset of them. The proposals of Changeaux and Danchin (1977), Greenough (1978), Levy and Steward (1979), and Purves and Lichtman (1980) presume that synaptic contacts are initially transient and require some type of confirmation, perhaps by use, for their survival. If not confirmed or stabilized, these synapses regress according to a developmental schedule and/or due to competition from confirmed synapses. Note that synapse overproduction and loss fits well with the neural maturationist ideas of Flechsig and others and that the pruning back could account for some aspects of infantile amnesia. Overproduction is not evident in development of some sensory systems or in some species (e.g., Valverde, 1971), but it is quite possible that if some synapses are being generated as others are being lost, then the process could be masked in quantitative studies (Greenough & Chang, 1988).

There is preliminary evidence that the local synthesis of protein at synapses may be involved in this synapse process. Protein is synthesized at synapses in response to neurotransmitter activation of receptors (Weiler & Greenough, 1991; 1993). One of the proteins synthesized at synapses is the fragile X mental retardation protein (Weiler et al., 1997), so named because its gene is on the X chromosome; if the gene is defective, it interferes with replication of the chromosome, and those with the defective gene, who can produce little or no fragile X protein, are mentally retarded. Recent studies of a mutant mouse in which the fragile X gene was "knocked out" indicate that its cortical synapses retain a developmentally immature synapse structure and that it has more dendritic spines than the normal "wild type" mouse (Comery et al., 1997). This suggests that the fragile X protein is required for the normal synapse maturation and elimination process and that fragile X mental retardation may occur, at least in part, because of a failure to achieve normal experience-expectant brain organization. The neural basis of experience-expectant information storage thus appears to be the overproduction of potentially permanent synaptic connections paired with selective survival of connections deemed valuable by use.

B. Manipulating Environmental Complexity

The effects of differential experience are not limited to early sensory development or to relatively extreme manipulations. Studies manipulating the complexity of the housing environment have indicated both microscopic and macroscopic experiential effects on brain structure. Most of the work has used three basic types of environments, although different research groups have sometimes defined them

FIGURE 4   Sketch of rats playing in a complex environment. Each rat has many opportunities to interact socially with other rats, explore novel arrangements of barriers and ramps, and play with toys that roll, make noises, smell, etc. (From Black and Greenough, 1986. Copyright 1986, Lawrence Erlbaum Associates. Reprinted by permission.)

differently. Environmental complexity (EC) involves housing rats in large groups in a large cage with various toys that are changed daily. This is depicted in Fig. 4. Individual cage (IC) animals are singly housed in standard laboratory cages. Social cage (SC) animals are housed as pairs in cages comparable to those of IC rats. The behavioral, synaptic, neuronal, and nonneuronal effects observed after manipulating experience appear largely to be driven by learning that occurs in the complex environment at any age, and hence this would be a model for experience-dependent information storage.

1. Behavioral Effects of Environmental Complexity

The behavioral effects of differential rearing are profound. One of the earliest studies was that of Hebb (1949), who reported that rats raised as pets at home were superior to laboratory rats in learning the Hebb–Williams maze. In general, rats raised in complex laboratory environments have been found superior to isolated or socially raised rats in complex, appetitively motivated learning tasks (reviewed in Greenough, 1976). The superior performance of EC animals is not simply due to greater visual experience, since Krech, Rosenzweig, and Bennett (1962) found blinded EC rats superior to blind IC rats in maze performance. Greenough, Wood, and Madden (1972) argued that the information-processing capability of EC mice was superior to that of IC or SC mice because they were uniquely capable of mastering the difficult Lashley III maze in a massed-trial situation. While learning a Hebb–Williams maze, EC rats make fewer errors than IC rats, but that superiority vanishes if the maze is rotated, effectively disrupting extramaze cues (Brown, 1968; Hymovitch, 1952). Ravizza and Herschberger (1966), however, found EC rats were better at maze learning even if extramaze cues were hidden by a curtain, suggesting that intramaze cues can also be better utilized by EC rats when they cannot use extramaze cues.

2. Effects of Differential Rearing on the Brain

While investigating neurochemical changes related to experience, a laboratory in Berkeley fortuitously found that EC rats had heavier brains than IC rats, one of the first findings that experience could affect brain anatomy (Bennett, Diamond, Krech, & Rosenzweig, 1964). In this important early report, Bennett et al. also disclosed that several regions of the dorsal neocortex were heavier and thicker in EC rats than IC rats, particularly the occipital cortex. Values in SC rats were intermediate but generally closer to those of IC rats.

Holloway (1966) first reported that ring analysis of Golgi-stained neurons in the visual cortex (see Fig. 2) indicated larger dendritic fields in rats reared in EC. Greenough and Volkmar (1973) placed rats in the EC, SC, and IC conditions at 23–25 days of age for 30 days. Pyramidal neurons from Layers II, IV, and V and Layer IV stellates in the visual cortex had more ring intersections in EC rats than IC rats. These effects were most pronounced in higher order branches—the outer part of the dendritic field. To confirm that these dendritic differences reflected synapse number differences, Turner and Greenough (1983, 1985) using electron microscopy found that EC rats exceeded IC rats in synapses per neuron in the upper visual cortex by roughly the amount predicted from the Golgi studies, with SC rats intermediate but somewhat closer to IC rats. This result is shown in Fig. 5. Thus quantitative Golgi procedures in the visual cortex appear to accurately reflect EC–IC differences in synapse numbers. Reports of EC–IC differences in rat hippocampus (see later paragraph on EC–IC sex differences), basal ganglia (Comery, Shah, & Greenough, 1995), brainstem (Fuchs, Montemayor, & Greenough, 1990), and monkey and rat cerebellar cortex (Floeter & Greenough, 1979; Pysh & Weiss, 1979) indicate that the experience-dependent EC effects are widespread, perhaps including phylogenetically older brain structures or their modified equivalents.

Changes in cortical thickness and dendritic branching can occur after just 4 days of enrichment (Wallace, Kilman, Withers, & Greenough, 1992). The glial changes described in the previous section also occur in EC animals after the usual 30 days

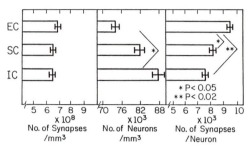

FIGURE 5   Numerical density of synapses and neuronal nuclei and ratio of synapses to neurons in the upper occipital cortex (Layers I–IV) of rats reared from 23 to 55 days of age in environmental complexity (EC), in pairs in social cages (SC), or in individual cages (IC). Synapses were counted in conventionally stained (osmium–uranyl–lead) electron micrographs and the counts corrected for differences in size using stereological formulae. Neuronal nuclei were estimated by point counting in toluidine blue stained light microscopic sections. Reduced neuronal density in more experienced animals reflects the greater volume of neuronal processes, glia, vasculature, neuronal somata, etc. that accompanies the new synapses. (Data from Turner and Greenough, 1985; figure reprinted from Greenough, copyright (1984) pp. 229–233, with permission from Elsevier Science.)

and glia continue to change over the next 30 days (Sirevaag & Greenough, 1991), but after just 4–10 days, the glial effects are restricted primarily to the cortical layer where most synaptic change is occurring, possibly in support of information storage (Jones, Hawrylak, & Greenough, 1996). NGFI-A, a gene transcription factor that regulates expression of other proteins possibly involved in synaptogenesis, is up-regulated in brain areas that subsequently exhibit synaptic change during the first days of exposure to EC (Wallace et al., 1995).

Patterned neural activity can cause the rapid formation of synapses in the adult brain, as suggested by studies of long-term potentiation (LTP) in the rat hippocampus. LTP is a long-lasting increase in the postsynaptic response evoked by one or a series of high-frequency stimuli delivered to the afferent fibers and is viewed as a possible memory mechanism. Lee, Schottler, Oliver, and Lynch (1980; Lee, Oliver, Schottler, & Lynch, 1981) have reported an increased frequency of certain synapse types in the hippocampus after LTP. Moreover, this synaptogenesis can be quite rapid. Chang and Greenough (1984) found synaptic number to increase within 10–15 min following electrical stimulation (possibly earlier as this was the shortest time studied). These results indicate that synapses form in response to neural activity on a time scale compatible with that of long-term memory and provide significant support for the idea that experience-dependent information storage could involve local, activity-dependent synaptogenesis.

Greenough, Volkmar, and Juraska (1973) found that EC rats also had more dendritic material than their IC counterparts in some types of neurons in the temporal (auditory) cortex but not in the frontolateral cortex. This suggests that the effects do not merely result from visual stimulation. The lack of frontolateral cortex effects suggests that general hormonal or metabolic factors, which would be expected to affect all cortical areas, do not play a significant role. The lateralized effects of training on the cortex discussed later also argue against general hormonal and metabolic effects. However, the fact that males and females differ in their responses to the complex environment in both the visual cortex and the hippocampus suggests at least a modulatory role for the presence of sex hormones at some point in the animal's life (Juraska, 1984; Juraska, Fitch, Henderson, & Rivers, 1985). In a parallel manner, a modulatory role for sex hormones in synaptogenesis is suggested by changes in synapse number of hippocampal neurons across the estrous cycle of rats (Woolley & McEwen, 1993) with corresponding effects on LTP (Warren, Humphreys, Juraska, & Greenough, 1995).

It has also been suggested that the EC–IC effects can be explained as general hormonal effects of stress (Thomas & Devenport, 1988), echoing a number of similar proposals in the past (e.g., Uphouse, 1980). Two current arguments are that (1) the patterns of cortical response to IC versus EC rearing and to adrenalectomy (removal of the stress-responsive adrenal glands) are similar and (2) some studies have reported greater adrenal weight in IC than in EC rats, suggesting that IC housing may evoke stress responses. However, Black, Sirevaag, Wallace, Savin, & Greenough (1989) have argued that adrenal reactions to stress, and reactions to stress in general, do not by themselves account for significant components of EC–SC–IC brain differences, based on the following findings:

1. In typical experiments in our laboratory, EC, SC, and IC rats do not exhibit adrenal weight differences or show other signs of chronic stress, and, in general, those experiments that reported higher adrenal weight in IC rats involved procedures, such as shipping the animals by air, that may have produced a stress reaction in the IC rats.

2. IC rats actually have faster peripheral body growth than EC rats, including the skull itself, at the same time that brain growth is greater in EC rats. Any general metabolic stimulus (except one that shifted resources from the periphery to the brain or vice versa) would not be expected to have the opposite effect upon the body's periphery and select brain regions.

3. In an experiment with adult rats, EC rats had heavier adrenals, probably reflecting stresses of adapting to a novel social group as adults, but they nonetheless exhibited typical brain effects of EC.

4. Typical EC–IC differences in brain morphology occurred in hypophysectomized rats, disrupting several endocrine systems, including the pituitary–adrenal system (Rosenzweig, Bennett, & Diamond, 1972).

5. Typical EC–IC differences in brain morphology occurred in rats that were also subjected to daily tumbling stress that increased adrenal weight of both EC and IC animals (Riege & Morimoto, 1970).

6. Sirevaag, Black, & Greenough (1991) reported that, although there was a correlation between individual adrenal weights in EC and IC rats and the density of

astrocytic processes (a possible indicant of stress-related brain damage) in the dentate gyrus, there was no EC–IC difference in either adrenal weight or the dentate measurement, which would have indicated treatment-induced differences in stress history.

The differences in synaptic and dendritic numbers are accompanied by differences in supportive tissue components such as glial cells and blood vessels. For example, Szeligo and Leblond (1977) have shown that subcortical white matter myelinization is greater in EC than in IC rats. Sirevaag and Greenough (1991) reported that EC rat visual cortex contained larger astrocytes with more processes than in SC or IC cortex. In a related study, Jones et al. (1996) used electron microscopy and unbiased stereolology methods to demonstrate that EC synapses in the visual cortex had closer contact with astrocyte processes. Astrocytes appear responsible for regulating the levels of some ions and neurotransmitters (e.g., Kimelberg et al., 1993), a function that might be upregulated in response to increased activity of neurons as well as increased synapse numbers in the EC rats. However, there is also the possibility that glial changes are involved in the initiation of synapse formation. This is suggested by both the rapid, coordinated glial process withdrawal and synapse formation that have been reported in the hypothalamus and in tissue cultures from the cerebellum (Tweedle & Hatton, 1984; Meshul, Seil, & Herndon, 1987). Increases in blood vessel density in the visual cortex of weanling EC rats could similarly be involved in supporting a more electrophysiologically active cortex (Black, Sirevaag, & Greenough, 1987). However, the production of new blood vessels may be substantially impaired in middle-aged rats, and this failure may restrict their capacity for storing information in the form of new synapses or for retrieving that information when they reach old age (Black, Polinsky, & Greenough, 1989).

3. Effects in Adult Animals

The neocortex retains considerable structural plasticity in response to such differential housing into adulthood. Riege and Morimoto (1970) reported cortical weight differences between groups placed in different environments at 1 year of age. Correspondingly, Uylings, Kuypers, and Veltman (1978) and Juraska, Greenough, Elliott, Mack, and Berkowitz (1980) found EC–IC branching differences of 10% or more in two of three visual cortex cell populations in adult rats, quite substantial differences, although smaller than those described in animals exposed as weanlings (Greenough & Volkmar, 1973). Green, Greenough, and Schlumpf (1983) reported somewhat larger EC–IC differences in middle-aged (450-day-old) rats. Increased numbers of synapses per neuron have also been reported in adult EC rats compared to IC rats (Hwang & Greenough, 1986). The environmental complexity studies in adult animals clearly suggest that experience alters the adult neocortex in a way similar to that seen in young animals, although some neuron types affected at weaning may not be affected later (Juraska et al., 1980).

4. Principal Conclusions from EC–IC Studies

The changes resulting from differential rearing complexity are probably not a simple extension of those found in the visual deprivation studies. Although the deprivation studies demonstrated that a drastic but simple manipulation of experience can modify connectivity and subsequent learning ability, visual experience is definitely "expected" during ontogeny. The types of visual experience of which the animals are deprived are normally quite uniform for all species members in their timing (i.e., after eye-opening) and quality (e.g., all visual angles present). Visual deprivation at later ages, once the animals have had experience, has minimal lasting effect. On the other hand, experience in the environmental complexity research has a character that is much less "expected" from the phylogenetic perspective. The timing and character of individual experience in the EC environment cannot be uniformly predicted for all species members. In fact, the EC condition resembles to some extent the "natural" environment rats evolved in, which is full of unexpected, idiosyncratic things to learn, for example the locations of warrens or food caches and how to evade predators.

The specific experiences of animals raised in EC differ from those of the ICs primarily in the complexity of experience available, so that self-initiation of experience (e.g., exploratory activity) is a key determinant of the timing and quality of experience. This feature is consistent with the dynamic systems perspective of development described by Thelen and Smith (1994) and Karmiloff-Smith (1992), in that the connectivity modifications observed in the EC animals appear more related to *how* neural activity is processed than *how much* is processed. For example, both EC and IC animals use approximately the same amount of light (average intensity on the retina) quite differently, one with self-initiated activity and its visual consequences, the other with dull routine. The importance of active involvement is particularly evident in the finding that there is essentially no brain effect of rearing rats within a small cage inside the EC environment (Ferchmin, Bennett, & Rosenzweig, 1975). Early exposure to EC may help the animal extract more information later on, as suggested by the studies showing improved learning ability in EC rats.

The distinction between visual deprivation and rearing complexity is further justified by the clear differences between their structural consequences. First, the differences in synapses per neuron appear to be considerably greater in EC/IC rats than in visually experienced/deprived rats. This may indicate that the complex environment paradigm approximates stimulation levels nearer the dynamic range of neural plasticity mechanisms. Alternatively, we propose that the sizes of the effects differ because early visual experience primarily affects experience-expectant neural mechanisms, whereas postweaning EC experience affects experience-dependent mechanisms. The following findings support this view:

1. The effects of environmental complexity are apparently more widespread in the brain. This has not been studied in detail in the visual deprivation paradigms, but where it has, visual deprivation (analogous to the IC condition) has resulted in

increases in measures related to synapses per neuron in the auditory cortex (Gyllensten, Malmfors, & Norrlin, 1966; Ryugo, Ryugo, Globus, & Killackey, 1975) and no effect in the somesthetic cortex, whereas the EC rats exceed IC rats in all three regions (Diamond, Rosenzweig, Bennett, Lindner, & Lyon, 1972; Greenough et al., 1973).

2. The effects of EC–IC housing are relatively independent of age, as we would expect for experience-dependent neural plasticity of the sort related to memory, whereas visual deprivation involves an experience-expectant period shortly after birth or eye-opening.

3. There is little evidence for systemwide overproduction and pruning back of synapses in these cases (although low-level and constant systemwide turnover cannot be ruled out; Sotelo & Palay, 1971; Greenough & Green, 1981).

We have argued that EC is an example of an experience-dependent process, using unexpected and idiosyncratic information, but sometimes developmental factors can play an important modulating role. This potentially blurs the distinction between experience-expectant and experience-dependent. For example, weanling rats are generally quite playful and active in comparison to adults, probably due to the same burst of playful activity we observe in kittens, puppies, and toddlers. The burst of playfulness may be developmentally programmed and generally useful to all members of a species (Ikemoto & Panksepp, 1992; Smith, 1982), and weanling rats show larger responses to EC than do adult rats. However, in contrast to information acquired during sensitive periods, information in EC varies in its timing and nature. It cannot be reliably "expected" for all members of the species, and there is no boundary defining a sensitive period. We believe that stronger response to EC during weaning reflects an indirect modulation of the EC response by developmental factors, rather than an experience-expectant process. Other modulatory factors during development might well include sex hormones, pheromones, and other endocrine signals. We will return to this hypothesis following a discussion of experiments directed more specifically at the importance of learning to the production of these morphological changes.

C. Structural Effects of Training

If the dendritic and synaptic alterations seen after EC experience are related to experience-dependent mechanisms such as learning, then we would expect similar structural changes after training on traditional psychological tasks. Greenough, Juraska, and Volkmar (1979) used the Hebb–Williams maze, which has movable barriers allowing a large variety of problems. Adult rats received extensive training for 25–26 days on a new problem plus several old problems each day for water reward. Littermate control rats were allowed to drink water several times daily while held by the investigator. Trained animals had more dendrite branches along distal

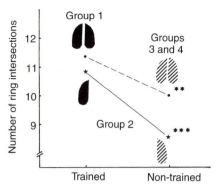

FIGURE 6   Number of apical dendrites intersecting distal spheres beyond 250 microns of the cell body in nerve cells from trained and untrained brain areas. **, $p < .025$; ***, $p < .01$ (after Chang & Greenough, 1982).

apical dendrites of Layer IV and Layer V pyramidal cells in the occipital cortex. Similarly, Bennett, Rosenzweig, Morimoto, and Hebert (1979) exposed rats to complex mazes in their cages which were changed daily for 30 days, while their littermates were kept in IC. The maze-reared animals had heavier visual cortices. The complexity of the environment is a factor in the effect, since rats housed with a single, simple maze for 30 days had brain weights between those of EC and IC rats. Cummins, Walsh, Budtz-Olsen, Konstantinos, and Horsfall (1973) similarly found that extensive Hebb–Williams maze training of 500-day-old rats otherwise kept in IC increased forebrain weight and cortical area relative to baseline groups remaining in the IC cages. However, littermates from an EC condition showed no effect of maze training, suggesting that additional training effects were small or were obscured by the already substantial effects of EC exposure.

To further examine the specificity of training effects, Chang and Greenough (1982) studied monocular maze training effects on the visual cortex of split-brain rats. Since about 90% of visual afferents in the rat cross to the contralateral cortex, use of an opaque contact lens over one eye of a split-brain rat can effectively direct visual input to just one occipital area. Split-brain littermate triplets were placed in one of four conditions: (1) the left and right eyes were occluded on alternate days during successive training periods, (2) the same eye was occluded during all training periods, (3) the left and right eyes were occluded on alternate days with no training, and (4) the same eye was occluded with no training. The occluders were worn for about 4 hrs daily during the training period. There was no effect of fixed versus alternating occluder position in the nontrained rats (Group 3 versus Group 4), indicating that occluder insertion alone did not affect the brain measures. Figure 6 summarizes the comparison of the distal region of the apical dendrites of Layer V pyramidal cells in the hemispheres receiving or not receiving visual input from maze training. The apical dendrites of cells in trained visual cortex were more extensive both within the fixed occluder rats (Group 2, comparing adjacent hemispheres) and between the alternating occluder and nontrained rats (Group 1 versus Groups 3 and 4, comparing two trained hemispheres to two nontrained). This indicates that the effects of training are relatively restricted to the side of the brain most involved in learning the task. Thus the effects appear to be related to where memory for the task may be stored rather than to general metabolic or other activity.

A similar interpretation arises from experiments in which rats are trained with one or both forepaws to reach into a tube for food (Greenough, Larson, & Withers, 1985; Withers & Greenough, 1989). Dendritic changes occurred in several neuronal populations in the sensory-motor cortex region that governs forelimb activity. Some of these changes were lateralized with respect to the particular forelimb that had been trained, whereas other dendritic changes occurred on both sides of the brain, even in unilaterally trained animals. We believe that all of the changes reflect memory-associated brain reorganization, with multiple brain regions cooperating for the task to be learned. However, this design confounds potential effects of repetitive motor movement (similar to muscle hypertrophy after exercise) with effects related to storing information and creating new synaptic connections.

Recent work in our laboratory has demonstrated that the effects of the motor and neural activity required during training appear to be separable from the effects of learning per se (Black, Isaacs, Anderson, Alcantara, & Greenough, 1990; Isaacs, Anderson, Alcantara, Black, & Greenough, 1992; Anderson et al., 1994). Adult female rats that had been socially housed previously were assigned to one of four conditions for 30 days: AC, an acrobatic condition in which they were required to traverse an increasingly difficult series of obstacles (e.g., narrow platforms, rope ladders, and seesaws); FX, a forced-exercise condition that required running on a treadmill for up to 60 min daily; VX, a voluntary exercise condition in which the animals had free access to a running wheel attached to the home cage; and IC, an inactive condition in which the animals had no opportunities for learning or physical exercise. Thus the AC rats had extensive learning with little exercise, the FX and VX rats had extensive exercise with little learning, and the IC rats had little of either. As Fig. 7 shows, the paramedian lobule of the cerebellum, an area driven largely by movements of the limbs and head, was significantly expanded in the AC group, and the density of synapses was maintained, indicating that substantial numbers of new synapses were formed in this region. On the other hand, the synaptic numbers in the paramedian lobule of the FX and VX groups were similar to that of the IC rats, indicating that extensive neural activity in this region without learning did not produce synaptogenesis. Interestingly, repetitive exercise-associated activity did influence another measure of brain function: there were more capillaries in the paramedian lobule of the FX and VX exercise groups.

In a similar study, AC rats had more synapses per neuron in the motor cortex (Kleim, Lussnig, Schwarz, Comery, & Greenough, 1996), indicating that synaptogenesis also occurs there as well as the cerebellum, suggesting that the motor skill learning of this task is cooperatively distributed across multiple brain regions. In this

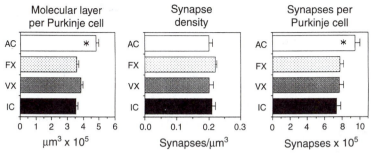

FIGURE 7   Data from the cerebellar cortex indicate that new patterns of neural activity associated with motor learning, rather than the stereotyped patterns associated with repetitive exercise, affect synaptic connectivity. The paramedian lobule of the cerebellar cortex was examined in four groups of adult rats: the AC group (acrobatic conditioning), which were trained to traverse a complicated elevated obstacle course that became progressively more difficult over the 30-day training period; the FX group (voluntary exercise), which had free access to a running wheel; the FX group (forced exercise), which were subjected to a treadmill exercise routine; and the IC group (individual condition), which were kept in standard cages without opportunity for additional exercise. In terms of distance traveled, the AC group covered much less distance than the two exercise groups, whereas in terms of opportunity for learning, the AC condition offered new skills to be acquired each day while the exercise conditions quickly became dull routine. Relative to the other three groups, the AC group had a lower density of Purkinje somata. Since the density of molecular layer synapses did not differ, the number of synapses per Purkinje neuron was substantially higher in the learning group than in the others (adapted from Black et al., 1990).

study, another immediate-early gene that regulates subsequent synthesis of other proteins, c-Fos, was expressed during the early stages of training, similar to NGFI-A in the EC rats described earlier. These results show promise for discerning molecular events that link learning to synapse formation.

All of these learning tasks produced localized effects on brain tissue that resembled (but were not identical to) those found in the EC–SC–IC rearing experiments. Since the effects were localized to the regions or hemisphere most involved in learning, it is not likely that they were the result of general hormonal or metabolic processes. Since the effects were not evident in groups with equivalent or greater amounts of overall neural activity but were evident in groups that had undergone significant amounts of learning, the overall pattern of the results strongly suggests that these changes in synaptic connections are involved in the storage of memory for the learning that took place.

These studies have also put an interesting twist on the issue of new synapse formation (Ramon y Cajal, 1893) versus the strengthening of previously existing synapses (Tanzi, 1893), discussed at the beginning of this chapter. We had generally assumed that the formation of new synapses could recruit new neurons into learning-associated circuitry, whereas synapse strengthening only changed the circuit of previously connected neurons. Federmeier, Kleim, and Greenough (in preparation) examined the cerebellar synapses in AC rats in more detail and found that many of the synapses were formed using the same presynaptic boutons, in parallel with pre-existing synapses between the same two neurons. Thus the formation of *new* synapses in this case merely increased the strength of the existing connection, similar to strengthening an existing synapse by increasing its size. Whether this is unique to the cerebellum or occurs in other brain regions remains to be determined, but it is of interest that multiple use of presynaptic and postsynaptic processes is also a common result in the EC–IC paradigm (Comery, Stamoudis, Irwin, & Greenough, 1996; Jones, Klintsova, Kilman, Sirevaag, & Greenough, in press).

Although it has not been possible to use any of the methods described in this chapter to demonstrate human neural plasticity, some indirect measures have recently been effective. Using functional magnetic resonance imaging (fMRI) to measure regional blood flow in the brain, Karni et al. (1995) demonstrated increased cortical involvement after training subjects in a finger-tapping sequence; Elbert, Pantev, Wienbruch, Rockstroh, and Taub (1995) showed similar expansion after extensive training to play the violin; and rehabilitation therapy after brain injury produced similar fMRI changes (Frackowiak, 1996). Nobody can yet show directly that humans produce new synapses when learning, but the foregoing fMRI changes are what we would expect if synaptogenesis were occurring.

V. IMPLICATIONS FOR THE NEUROBIOLOGICAL STUDY OF MEMORY

In describing information storage mechanisms, we have tried to define the similarities and differences between maturation, experience-sensitive development, and learning. Some aspects of experience (e.g., play in juvenile EC–IC rearing) may influence both experience-expectant and experience-dependent processes. In fact, these processes probably cannot be entirely isolated, since they have substantial interactive consequences for how the brain processes information and they share mechanisms at the cellular level.

The evidence that different species have different susceptibility to experience and that brain areas are differentially influenced by experience suggests that information storage mechanisms have not remained stable through evolution. We suggest that, as more complicated sensory, motor, and information processing schemes evolved, experience was utilized in two ways: (1) to shape common features of the nervous system through experiences common to members of the species and (2) to provide for storage of information about the unique environment of the individual. The underlying mechanisms may have diverged to meet these separate needs, such that systemwide overproduction at a specific maturational stage, followed by selection, subserves storage of common information, whereas local activity-dependent synaptogenesis, again followed by selection, subserves later storage of unique information.

The evidence presented here demonstrates that learning is associated with synaptogenesis in many brain regions of animals at nearly any age. Of course, other aspects of neural plasticity are likely to occur as well, for example, changes in synapse size, receptor density, glial support, or vascular support. In addition to these examples, changes in the size and structure of synapses have been observed in association with EC or training (e.g., West & Greenough, 1972; Greenough, West, & DeVoogd, 1978; Vrensen & Nunes-Cardozo, 1981). The fact that potentially independent structural effects are seen across a number of species, across many brain regions, and across diverse types of experience suggests that evolution did not establish just one simple mechanism for learning and memory. Rather, there may be a set of cellular mechanisms upon which the organism can draw for the incorporation of information from a wide variety of experiences, and it is likely that we have not yet discovered all of the types of changes involved in encoding experience. At this point, however, the most consistently reported effect of various experiences is upon the number, and presumably changes in the pattern, of synaptic connections.

Experience-expectant processes have been described here in terms of the species-wide reliability of some types of experience. We suggested that species survival may be facilitated by information storage processes anticipating an experience with identical timing and features for all juvenile members. A structural correlate of "expectation" may be a temporary overproduction of synapses during the sensitive period with a subsequent pruning back of inappropriate synapses. This experience-expectant blooming of new synapses is distributed more or less uniformly across the entire population of homologous cells. The neuromodulatory event that triggers this synapse overproduction may be under maturational control or may be activity dependent (as after eye-opening), but it is diffuse and pervasive. The expected experience produces patterned activity of neurons, effectively targeting which synapses will be selected, as illustrated for monocular deprivation in binocular species.

Experience-dependent mechanisms, on the other hand, may utilize synapse generation and preservation in different balance for a quite different effect. Because these neural plasticity mechanisms cannot anticipate the timing or the specific features of such idiosyncratic experience, the "sensitive period" is necessarily left wide open. Here synapses are generated locally, upon demand of some modulatory signal. The specific nature of modulation, which could be locally elicited by neural activity or by hormonal signals, remains an open question for future research. The organism's active participation is important in obtaining and stabilizing experience. For example, juvenile play or adult attention may serve to both extract new information (increase contrast) and help repeat it or stabilize it (increase coherence). This experience-dependent localized shaping of connectivity suggests that very multimodal and diverse experience (as in EC) would produce widespread increases in synaptic frequency but that relatively specific experience (as in training tasks) would produce more localized increases.

ACKNOWLEDGMENTS

This work was supported by Grants MH35321, AG43830, and AA0938, the National Association for Research on Schizophrenia & Affective Disorders, the Kiwanis Foundation, and the FRAXA Research Foundation.

REFERENCES

Allport, G. W. (1937). *Personality: A psychological interpretation.* New York: Holt.

Anderson, B. J., Li, X., Alcantara, A. A., Isaacs, K. R., Black, J. E., & Greenough, W. T. (1994). Glial hypertrophy is associated with synaptogenesis following motor skill learning, but not with angiogenesis following exercise. *Glia, 11,* 73–80.

Bennett, E. L., Diamond, M. C., Krech, D., & Rosenzweig, M. R. (1964). Chemical and anatomical plasticity of brain. *Science, 146,* 610–619.

Bennett, E. L., Rosenzweig, M. R., Morimoto, H., & Herbert, M. (1979). Maze training alters brain weights and cortical RNA / DNA ratios. *Behavioral and Neural Biology, 26,* 1–22.

Black, J. E., & Greenough, W. T. (1986). Induction of pattern in neural structure by experience: Implications for cognitive development. In M. E. Lamb, A. L. Brown, & B. Rogoff (Eds.), *Advances in developmental psychology* (vol. 4, pp. 1–50). Hillsdale, NJ: Lawrence Erlbaum Associates.

Black, J. E., Isaacs, K. R., Anderson, B. J., Alcantara, A. A., & Greenough, W. T. (1990). Learning causes synaptogenesis, whereas motor activity causes angiogenesis, in cerebellar cortex of adult rats. *Proceedings of the National Academy of Sciences U.S.A., 87,* 5568–5572.

Black, J. Polinsky, M., & Greenough, W. T. (1989). Progressive failure of cerebral angiogenesis supporting neural plasticity in aging rats. *Neurobiology of Aging, 10,* 353–358.

Black, J., Sirevaag, A. M., & Greenough, W. T. (1987). Complex experience promotes capillary formation in young visual cortex. *Neuroscience Letters, 83,* 351–355.

Black, J. E., Sirevaag, A. M., Wallace, C. S., Savin, M. H., & Greenough, W. T. (1989). Effects of complex experience on somatic growth and organ development in rats. *Developmental Psychobiology, 22,* 727–752.

Boothe, R. G., Greenough, W. T., Lund, J. S., & Wrege, K. (1979). A quantitative investigation of spine and dendritic development of neurons in visual cortex (Area 17) of *Macaca nemistrina* monkeys. *Journal of Comparative Neurology, 186,* 473–490.

Borges, S., & Berry, M. (1976). Preferential orientation of stellate cell dendrites in the visual cortex of the dark-reared rat. *Brain Research, 112,* 141–147.

Borges, S., & Berry, M. (1978). The effects of dark rearing on the development of the visual cortex of the rat. *Journal of Comparative Neurology, 180,* 277–300.

Brown, R. T. (1968). Early experience and problem solving ability. *Journal of Comparative and Physiological Psychology, 65,* 433–440.

Campbell, B. A., & Campbell, E. H. (1962). Retention and extinction of learned fear in infant and adult rats. *Journal of Comparative and Physiology Psychology, 55,* 1–8.

Chang, F.-L.F., & Greenough, W. T. (1982). Lateralized effects of monocular training on dendritic branching in adult split-brain rats. *Brain Research, 232,* 283–292.

Chang, F.-L. F., & Greenough, W. T. (1984). Transient and enduring morphological correlates of synaptic activity and efficacy changes in the rat hippocampal slice. *Brain Research, 309,* 35–46.

Changeaux, J.-P., & Danchin, A. (1977). Biochemical models for the selective stabilization of developing synapses. In G. A. Cottress & P. M. Usherwood (Eds.), *Synapses* (pp. 705–712). New York: Academic Press.

Chaudhari, N., & Hahn, W. E. (1983). Genetic expression in the developing brain. *Science, 220,* 924–928.

Clopton, B. M. (1986). Neural correlates of development and plasticity in the auditory, somatosensory, and olfactory systems. In W. T. Greenough & J. M. Juraska (Eds.), *Developmental neuropsychobiology* (pp. 363–386). New York: Academic Press.

Coleman, P. D., Flood, D. G., Whitehead, M. C., & Emerson, R. C. (1981). Spatial sampling by dendritic trees in visual cortex. *Brain Research, 214,* 1–21.

Coleman, P. D., & Riesen, A. H. (1968). Environmental effects on cortical dendritic fields. I. Rearing in the dark. *Journal of Anatomy, 102,* 363–374.

Comery, T. A., Harris, J. B., Willems, P. J., Oosta, B. A., Weiler, I. J., & Greenough, W. T. (1997). Abnormal dendritic spine morphology in Fragile X knockout mice: Maturation and pruning deficits. *Proceedings of the National Academy of Sciences U.S.A., 94,* 5401–5404.

Comery, T. A., Shah, R., & Greenough, W. T. (1995). Differential rearing alters spine density on medium size spiny neurons in the rat corpus striatum. *Neurobiology of Learning and Memory, 63,* 217–219.

Comery, T. A., Stamoudis, C. X., Irwin, S. A., & Greenough, W. T. (1996). Increased density of multi-head dendritic spines on medium-sized spiny neurons of the striatum in rats reared in a complex environment. *Neurobiology of Learning and Memory, 66,* 93–96.

Coss, R. G., Brandon, J. G., & Globus, A. (1980). Changes in morphology of dendritic spines on honeybee calycal interneurons associated with cumulative nursing and foraging experiences. *Brain Research, 192,* 49–54.

Cragg, B. G. (1967). Changes in visual cortex on first exposure of rats to light. Effect on synaptic dimensions. *Nature, 215,* 251–253.

Cragg, B. G. (1975a). The development of synapses in kitten visual cortex during visual deprivation. *Experimental Neurology, 46,* 445–451.

Cragg, B. G. (1975b). The development of synapses in the visual system of the cat. *Journal of Comparative Neurology, 160,* 147–166.

Crawford, M. L., Harwerth, R. S., Smith, E. L., & von Noorden, G. K. (1993). Keeping an eye on the brain: The role of experience in monkeys and children. *Journal of General Psychology, 120,* 7–19.

Cummins, R. A., Walsh, R. N., Budtz-Olsen, O. E., Konstantinos, T., & Horsfall, C. R. (1973). Environmentally-induced changes in the brains of elderly rats. *Nature, 243,* 516–518.

Demer, J. L. (1993). Positron emission tomographic studies of cortical function in human amblyopia. *Neuroscience & Biobehavioral Review, 17,* 469–476.

Diamond, M. C., Rosenzweig, M. R., Bennett, E. L., Lindner, B., & Lyon, L. (1972). Effects of environmental enrichment and impoverishment on rat cerebral cortex. *Journal of Neurobiology, 3,* 47–64.

Elbert, T., Pantev, C., Wienbruch, C., Rockstroh, B., & Taub, E. (1995). Increased cortical representation of the fingers of the left hand in string players. *Science, 270,* 305–307.

Falls, W., & Gobel, S. (1979). Golgi and EM studies of the formation of dendritic and axonal arbors: The interneurons of the substantia gelatinosa of Rolando in newborn kittens. *Journal of Comparative Neurology, 187,* 1–18.

Federmeier, K. D., Kleim, J. A., & Greenough, W. T. (in preparation). Multiple synapse formation in the cerebeller cortex after complex motor learning.

Feng, A. S., & Rogowski, B. A. (1980). Effects of monaural and binaural occlusion on the morphology of neurons in the medial superior olivary nucleus of the rat. *Brain Research, 189,* 530–534.

Ferchmin, P. A., Bennett, E. L., & Rosenzweig, M. R. (1975). Direct contact with enriched environments is required to alter cerebral weights in rats. *Journal of Comparative and Physiological Psychology, 8,* 360–367.

Flechsig, P. (1927). *Meine Myelogenetische Hirnlehre mit Biographischer Einleitung.* [My theory of brain myelinization with a biographical introduction.] Berlin: Springer.

Floeter, M. K., & Greenough, W. T. (1979). Cerebellar plasticity: Modification of Purkinje cell structure by differential rearing in monkeys. *Science, 206,* 227–229.

Flood, J. F., Smith, G. E., & Morley, J. E. (1987). Modulation of memory processes by cholecystokinin: Dependence on the vagus nerve. *Science, 236,* 832–834.

Fox, K., & Daw, N. W. (1993). Do NMDA receptors have a critical function in visual cortical plasticity? *Trends in Neurosciences, 16,* 116–122.

Frackowiak, R. S. J. (1996). Plasticity and the human brain: Insights from functional imaging. *The Neuroscientist, 2,* 353–362.

Freire, M. (1978). Effects of dark rearing on dendritic spines in Layer IV of the mouse visual cortex. A quantitative electron microscopical study. *Journal of Anatomy, 126,* 193–201.

Freud, S. (1969). *An outline of psychoanalysis* (J. Strachey, Trans.). New York: W. W. Norton. (Original work published 1933)

Friedlander, M. J., Martin, K. A., Wassenhove-McCarthy, D. (1991). Effects of monocular deprivation on geniculocortical innervation of area 18 in cat. *Journal of Neuroscience, 11,* 3268–3288.

Fuchs, J. L., Montemayor, M., & Greenough, W. T. (1990). Effect on environmental complexity on size of the superior colliculus. *Behavioral and Neural Biology, 54,* 198–203.

Green, E. J., Greenough, W. T., & Schlumpf, B. E. (1983). Effects of complex or isolated environments on cortical dendrites of middle-aged rats. *Brain Research, 264,* 233–240.

Greenough, W. T. (1976). Enduring brain effects of differential experience and training. In M. R. Rosenzweig and E. L. Bennett (Eds.), *Neural mechanisms of learning and memory* (pp. 255–278). Cambridge, MA: MIT Press.

Greenough, W. T. (1978). Development and memory: The synaptic connection. In T. Teyler (Ed.), *Brain and learning* (pp. 127–145). Stamford, CT: Greylock Publishers.

Greenough, W. T. (1984). Possible structural substrates of plastic neural phenomena. In G. Lynch, J. L. McGaugh, & N. M. Weinberger (Eds.), *Neurobiology of Learning and Memory* (pp. 470–478). New York: Guilford Press.

Greenough, W. T., Armstrong, K. E., Comery, T. A., Hawrylak, N., Humphreys, A. G., Kleim, J., Swain, R. A., & Wang, X. (1994). Plasticity-related changes in synapse morphology. In A. I. Selverston & P. Ascher (Eds.), *Cellular and molecular mechanisms underlying higher neural functions* (pp. 211–220). Chichester: John Wiley & Sons, Ltd.

Greenough, W. T., & Chang, F.-L. F. (1988). Plasticity of synapse structure and pattern in the cerebral cortex. In A. Peters & E. G. Jones (Eds.), *Cerebral cortex* (Vol. 7, pp. 391–440). New York: Plenum Publishing.

Greenough, W. T., & Green, E. J. (1981). Experience and the changing brain. In J. L. McGaugh, J. G. March, & S. B. Kiesler (Eds.), *Aging: Biology and behavior* (pp. 159–200). New York: Academic Press.

Greenough, W. T., Juraska, J. M., & Volkmar, F. R. (1979). Maze training effects on dendritic branching in occipital cortex of adult rats. *Behavioral and Neural Biology, 26,* 287–297.

Greenough, W. T., Larson, J. R., & Withers, G. S. (1985). Effects of unilateral and bilateral training in a reaching task on dendritic branching of neurons in the rat motor-sensory forelimb cortex. *Behavioral and Neural Biology, 44,* 301–314.

Greenough, W. T., & Volkmar, F. R. (1973). Pattern of dendritic branching in occipital cortex of rats reared in complex environments. *Experimental Neurology, 40,* 491–504.

Greenough, W. T., Volkmar, F. R., & Juraska, J. M. (1973). Effects of rearing complexity on dendritic branching in frontolateral and temporal cortex of the rat. *Experimental Neurology, 41,* 371–378.

Greenough, W. T., West, R. W., & DeVoogd, T. J. (1978). Sybsynaptic plate perforations: Changes with age and experience in the rat. *Science, 202,* 1096–1098.

Greenough, W. T., Wood, W. E., & Madden, T. C. (1972). Possible memory storage differences among mice reared in environments varying in complexity. *Behavioral Biology, 7,* 717–722.

Gu, Q., & Singer, W. (1995). Involvement of serotonin in developmental plasticity of kitten visual cortex. *European Journal of Neuroscience, 7,* 1146–1161.

Gyllensten, L., Malmfors, T., Norrlin, M.-L. (1966). Growth alteration in the auditory cortex of visually deprived mice. *Journal of Comparative Neurology, 26,* 463–470.

Hawrylak, N., & Greenough, W. T. (1995). Monocular deprivation alters the morphology of glial fibrillary acidic protein-reactive astrocytes in rat visual cortex. *Brain Research, 683,* 187–199.

Hebb, D. O. (1949). *The organization of behavior.* New York: Wiley.

Hein, A., & Diamond, R. (1971). Contributions of eye movements to the representation of space. In A. Hein & M. Jeannerod (Eds.), *Spatially oriented behavior* (pp. 119–134). New York: Springer.

Held, R., & Hein, A. (1963). Development and segmentation of visually controlled movement by selective exposure during rearing. *Journal of Comparative and Phsyiological Psychology, 73,* 181–187.

Hendy, H. M., & Riesen, A. H. (1988). Effects of lateral displacement of the visual field on the development of visual-motor abilities in cats. *Developmental Psychobiology, 21,* 635–650.

Hirsch, H. V. B., & Spinelli, D. N. (1970). Visual experience modifies distribution of horizontally and vertically oriented receptive fields in cats. *Science, 168,* 869–871.

Holloway, R. L. (1966). Dendritic branching: Some preliminary results of training and complexity in rat visual cortex. *Brain Research, 2,* 393–396.

Hwang, H.-M., & Greenough, W. T. (1986). Synaptic plasticity in adult rat occipital cortex following short-term, long-term, and reversal of differential housing environmental complexity. *Society for Neuroscience Abstracts, 12,* 1284.

Hymovitch, B. (1952). The effects of experimental variations on problem solving in the rat. *Journal of Comparative and Physiological Psychology, 5,* 313–321.

Ikemoto, S., & Panksepp, J. (1992). The effects of early social isolation on the motivation for social play in juvenile rats. *Developmental Psychobiology, 25,* 261–274.

Isaacs, K. R., Anderson, B. J., Alcantara, A. A., Black, J. E., & Greenough, W. T. (1992). Exercises for the brain: Angiogenesis in the adult rat cerebellum after vigorous physical activity and motor skill learning. *Journal of Cerebral Blood Flow and Metabolism, 12,* 110–119.

Jones, T. A., Hawrylak, N., & Greenough, W. T. (1996). Rapid laminar-dependent changes in GFAP immunoreactive astrocytes in visual cortex of rats reared in a complex environment. *Psychoneuroendocrinology, 21,* 189–201.

Jones, T. A., Klintsova, A. Y., Kilman, V. L., Sirevaag, A. M., & Greenough, W. T. (in press). Induction of multiple synapses by experience in the visual cortex of adult rats. *Learning and Memory.*

Juraska, J. M. (1984). Sex differences in dendritic response to differential experience in the rat visual cortex. *Brain Research, 295,* 27–34.

Juraska, J. M., Fitch, J. M., Henderson, C., & Rivers, N. (1985). Sex differences in dendritic branching of dentate granule cells following differential experience. *Brain Research, 333,* 73–80.

Juraska, J. M., Greenough, W. T., Elliott, C., Mack, K. J., & Berkowitz, R. (1980). Plasticity in adult rat visual cortex: An examination of several cell populations after differential rearing. *Behavioral and Neural Biology, 29,* 157–167.

Karmiloff-Smith, A. (1992). *Beyond modularity: A developmental perspective on cognitive science.* Cambridge, MA: MIT Press.

Karni, A., Meyer, G., Jezzard, P., Adams, M. M., Turner, R., & Ungerleider, L. G. (1995). Functional MRI evidence for adult motor cortex plasticity during motor skill learning. *Nature, 377,* 155–158.

Kimelberg, H. K., Jalonen, T., & Walz, W. (1993). Regulation of the brain microenvironment: Transmitters and ions. In S. Murphy (Ed.), *Astrocytes: Pharmacology & function* (pp. 193–218). San Diego: Academic Press.

Kleim, J. A., Lussnig, E., Schwarz, E. R., Comery, T. A., & Greenough, W. T. (1996). Synaptogenesis and Fos expression in the motor cortex of the adult rat after motor skill learning. *Journal of Neuroscience, 16,* 4529–4535.

Krech, D., Rosenzweig, M. R., & Bennett, E. L. (1962). Relations between brain chemistry and problem-solving among rats raised in enriched and impoverished environments. *Journal of Comparative and Physiological Psychology, 55,* 801–807.

Lee, K. S., Oliver, M., Schottler, F., & Lynch, G. (1981). Electron microscopic studies of brain slices: The effects of high-frequency stimulation on dendritic ultrastructure. In G. A. Kerkut and H. V. Wheal (Eds.). *Electrophysiology of isolated mammalian CNS preparations* (pp. 189–211). New York: Academic Press.

Lee, K. S., Schottler, F., Oliver, M., & Lynch, G. (1980). Brief bursts of high-frequency stimulation produce two types of structural change in rat hippocampus. *Journal of Neurophysiology, 44,* 247–258.

LeVay, S., Wiesel, T. N., & Hubel, D. H. (1980). The development of ocular dominance columns in normal and visually deprived monkeys. *Journal of Comparative Neurology, 191,* 1–51.

Levy, W. B., & Steward, O. (1979). Synapses as associative memory elements in the hippocampal formation. *Brain Research, 175,* 233–245.

Locke, J. L. (1992). Thirty years of research on developmental neurolinguistics. *Pediatric Neurology, 8,* 245–250.

Marchand, A. R., Cremieux, J., & Amblard, B. (1990). Early sensory determinants of locomotor speed in adult cats: II. Effects of strobe rearing on vestibular functions. *Behavioral Brain Research, 37,* 227–235.

Mariani, J., & Changeaux, J.-P. (1981). Ontogenesis of olivocerebellar relationships. I. Studies by intracellular recording of the multiple innervation of Purkinje cells by climbing fibers in the developing rat. *Journal of Neuroscience, 1,* 696–702.

McClelland, J. L., & Rumelhart, D. E. (1986). *Parallel distributed processing. Explorations in the microstructure of cognition: Vol. 2. Psychological and biological models.* Cambridge, MA: MIT Press.

Meisami, E. (1975). Early sensory influences on regional activity of brain ATPases in developing rats. In M. A. B. Brazier (Ed.), *Growth and development of the brain* (pp. 51–74). New York: Raven Press.

Meshul, C. K., Seil, F. J., & Herndon, R. M. (1987). Astrocytes play a role in regulation of synaptic density. *Brain Research, 402,* 139–145.

Milner, R. J., & Sutcliffe, J. G. (1983). Gene expression in the rat brain. *Nucleic Acids Research, 11,* 5497–5520.

Piaget, J. (1980). *Adaptation and intelligence: Organic selection and phenocopy* (S. S. Eames, Trans.). Chicago: University of Chicago Press. (Original work published 1974)

Purves, D., & Lichtman, J. W. (1980). Elimination of synapses in the developing nervous system. *Science, 210,* 153–157.

Pysh, J. J., & Weiss, M. (1979). Exercise during development induces an increase in Purkinje cell dendritic tree size. *Science, 206,* 230–232.

Ramon y Cajal, S. (1893). Neue Darstellung vom histologischen Bau des Centralnervensystem [New findings about the histological structure of the central nervous system]. *Archiv für Anatomie und Physiologie (Anatomie), 17,* 319–428.

Ravizza, R. J., & Herschberger, A. C. (1966). The effect of prolonged motor restriction upon later behavior of the rat. *Psychological Record, 16,* 73–80.

Riege, W. H., & Morimoto, H. (1970). Effects of chronic stress and differential environments upon brain weights and biogenic amine levels in rats. *Journal of Comparative and Phsyiological Psychology, 71,* 396–404.

Riesen, A. H. (1965). Effects of visual deprivation on perceptual function and the neural substrate. In J. DeAjuriaguerra (Ed.), *Symposium Bel Air II, Desafferentation Experimentale et Clinique* (pp. 47–66). Geneva: George & Cie.

Rosenzweig, M. R., Bennett, E. L., & Diamond, M. C. (1972). Cerebral effects of differential experience in hypophysectomized rats. *Journal of Comparative and Physiological Psychology, 79,* 56–66.

Rothblat, L. A., & Schwartz, M. L. (1979). The effect of monocular deprivation on dendritic spines in visual cortex of young and adult albino rats: Evidence for a sensitive period. *Brain Research, 161,* 156–161.

Ryugo, D. K., Ryugo, R., Globus, A., & Killackey, H. P. (1975). Increased spine density in auditory cortex following visual or somatic deafferentation. *Brain Research, 90,* 143–146.

Schactel, E. G. (1947). On memory and childhood amnesia. *Psychiatry, 10,* 1–26.

Schacter, D. L. (Ed.). (1995). *Memory distortion: How minds, brains, and societies reconstruct the past.* Cambridge, MA: Harvard University Press.

Schwartz, M. L., & Rothblat, L. A. (1980). Behavioral and dendritic spine deficits in monocularly deprived rats: The role of reduced photic stimulation. *Society for Neuroscience Abstracts, 6,* 635.

Sholl, D. A. (1956). *Organization of the cerebral cortex.* London: Methuen.

Sirevaag, A. M., Black, J. E., & Greenough, W. T. (1991). Astrocyte hypertrophy in dentate gyrus of young male rats is modulated by individual stress rather than group environment manipulations. *Experimental Neurology, 111,* 74–79.

Sirevaag, A. M., & Greenough, W. T. (1987). A multivariate statistical summary of synaptic plasticity measures in rats exposed to complex, social and individual environments. *Brain Research, 441,* 320–332.

Sirevaag, A. M., & Greenough, W. T. (1991). Plasticity of GFAP-immunoreactive astrocytes size and number in visual cortex of rats reared in complex environments. *Brain Research, 540,* 273–278.

Smith, D. C., & Loop, M. S. (1978). Rapid restoration of visual abilities in the monocularly deprived adult cat. *Investigative Ophthalmology and Visual Science, 17* (Suppl.), 294.

Smith, P. K. (1982). Does play matter? Functional and evolutionary aspects of animal and human play. *Behavioral and Brain Sciences, 5,* 139–184.

Sotelo, C. & Palay, S. L. (1971). Altered axons and axon terminals in the lateral geniculate nucleus of the rat. Possible example of axonal remodeling. *Laboratory Investigation, 15,* 653–671.

Stickrod, G., Kimble, D. P., & Smotherman, W. P. (1982). In utero taste/odor aversion conditioning in the rat. *Physiology and Behavior, 28,* 5–7.

Szeligo, F., & Leblond, C. P. (1977). Response of the three main types of glial cells of cortex and corpus callosum in rats handled during suckling or exposed to enriched control and impoverished environments following weaning. *Journal of Comparative Neurology, 172,* 247–264.

Tanzi, E. (1893). I fatti e le induzioni nell'odierna istologia del sistema nervoso. [The facts and the inductions in current histology of the nervous system]. *Rivista Sperimentale di Freniatria e Medicina Legale delle Mentali Alienazioni, 19,* 419–472.

Tees, R. C. (1968a). Effect of early restriction on later form discrimination in the rat. *Canadian Journal of Psychology, 22,* 294–298.

Tees, R. C. (1968b). Effect of early visual restriction on later visual intensity discrimination in rats. *Journal of Comparative and Physiological Psychology, 66,* 224–227.

Tees, R. C., & Cartwright, J. (1972). Sensory preconditioning in rats following early visual deprivation. *Journal of Comparative and Physiological Psychology, 81,* 12–20.

Thelen, E., & Smith, L. B. (1994). *A dynamic systems approach to the development of cognition and action.* Cambridge, MA: MIT Press.

Thomas, T. L., & Davenport, L. D. (1988). Site specificity of adrenalectomy-induced brain growth. *Experimental Neurology, 102,* 340–345.

Tieman, S. B. (1984). Effects of monocular deprivation on geniculocortical synapses in the cat. *Journal of Comparative Neurology, 222,* 166–176.

Tieman, S. B., & Hirsch, H. V. B. (1982). Exposure to lines of only one orientation modifies dendritic morphology of cells in the visual cortex of the cat. *Journal of Comparative Neurology, 211,* 353–362.

Tinbergen, N. (1951). *The study of instinct.* London: Oxford University Press.

Turner, A. M., & Greenough, W. T. (1983). Synapses per neuron and synaptic dimensions in occipital cortex of rats reared in complex, social, or isolation housing. *Acta Stereologica, 2* (Suppl. I), 239–244.

Turner, A. M., & Greenough, W. T. (1985). Differential rearing effects on rat visual cortex synapses. I. Synaptic and neuronal density and synapses per neuron. *Brain Research, 329,* 195–203.

Tweedle, C. D., & Hatton, G. I. (1984). Synapse formation and disappearance in adult rat supraoptic nucleus during different hydration states. *Brain Research, 309,* 373–376.

Uphouse, L. (1980). Reevaluation of mechanisms that mediate brain difference between enriched and impoverished animals. *Psychological Bulletin, 88,* 215–232.

Uylings, H. B. M., Kuypers, K., & Veltman, W. A. M. (1978). Environmental influences on neocortex in later life. *Progress in Brain Research, 48,* 261–274.

Valverde, F. (1970). The Golgi method: A tool for comparative structural analyses. In W. J. H. Nauta & S. O. E. Ebbesson (Eds.), *Contemporary research methods in neuroanatomy* (pp. 12–31). New York: Springer-Verlag.

Valverde, F. (1971). Rate and extent of recovery from dark rearing in the mouse. *Brain Research, 33,* 1–11.

Vrensen, G., & Nunes-Cardozo, J. N. (1981). Changes in size and shape of synaptic connections after visual training: An ultrastructural approach of synaptic plasticity. *Brain Research, 218,* 79–97.

Walk, R. D., & Walters, C. P. (1973). Effect of visual deprivation on depth discrimination of hooded rats. *Journal of Comparative and Phsyiological Psychology, 85,* 559–563.

Wallace, C. S., Kilman, V. L., Withers, G. S., & Greenough, W. T. (1992). Increases in dendritic length in occipital cortex after four days of differential housing in weanling rats. *Behavioral and Neural Biology, 58,* 64–68.

Wallace, C. S., Withers, G. S., Weiler, I. J., George, J. M., Clayton, D. F., & Greenough, W. T. (1995). Correspondence between sites of NGFI-A induction and sites of morphological plasticity following exposure to environmental complexity. *Molecular Brain Research, 32,* 211–220.

Warren, S. G., Humphreys, A. G., Juraska, J. M., & Greenough, W. T. (1995). LTP varies across the estrous cycle: Enhanced synaptic plasticity in proestrous rats. *Brain Research, 703,* 26–30.

Weiler, I. J., & Greenough, W. T. (1993). Metabotropic glutamate receptors trigger postsynaptic protein synthesis. *Proceedings of the National Academy of Sciences U.S.A., 90,* 7168–7171.

Weiler, I. J., & Greenough, W. T. (1991). Potassium ion stimulation triggers protein translation in synaptoneurosomal polyribosomes. *Molecular and Cellular Neurosciences, 2,* 305–314.

Weiler, I. J., Irwin, S. A., Lintsova, A. Y., Spencer, C. M., Brazelton, A. D., Miyashiro, K., Comery, T. A., Patel, B., Eberwine, J., & Greenough, W. T. (1997). Fragile X mental retardation protein is translated near synapses in response to neurotransmitter activation. *Proceedings of the National Academy of Sciences U.S.A., 94,* 5395–5400.

West, R. W., & Greenough, W. T. (1972). Effect of environmental complexity on cortical synapses of rats: Preliminary results: *Behavioral Biology, 7,* 279–284.

Winfield, D. A. (1981). The postnatal development of synapses in the visual cortex of the cat and the effects of eyelid closure. *Brain Research, 206,* 166–171.

Withers, G. S., Fahrbach, S. E., & Robinson, G. E. (1993). Selective neuroanatomical plasticity and division of labour in the honeybee. *Nature, 364,* 238–240.

Withers, G. S., & Greenough, W. T. (1989). Reach training selectively alters dendritic branching in subpopulations of layer II–III pyramids in rat motor-somatosensory forelimb cortex. *Neuropsychologia, 27,* 61–69.

Woolley, C. S., & McEwen, B. S. (1993). Roles of estradiol and progesterone in regulation of hippocampal dendritic spine density during the estrous cycle in the rat. *Journal of Comparative Neurology, 336,* 293–306.

Woolsey, T., & Wann, J. (1976). Areal change in mouse cortical barrels following vibrissal damage at different postnatal ages. *Journal of Comparative Neurology, 170,* 53–56.

Zablocka, T., & Zernicki, B. (1990). Partition between stimuli slows down greatly discrimination learning in binocularly deprived cats. *Behavioral Brain Research, 36,* 13–19.

CHAPTER 3

Gene Targeting: A Novel Window into the Biology of Learning and Memory

Alcino J. Silva and Karl Peter Giese

Cold Spring Harbor Laboratory, Cold Spring Harbor, New York 11724

I. INTRODUCTION

A number of techniques have been developed to manipulate the mouse genome: Genes can be added, deleted, or altered, and mice can be derived with mutations as subtle as single nucleotide changes. Additionally, other genetic techniques currently being developed will allow the restriction of these mutations to certain brain regions and to specific times. The ability to manipulate genomes has had a powerful impact on almost every area of biological research and undoubtedly will influence the way we study the brain. The powerful arsenal of genetic techniques developed has already been used successfully in the study of mammalian learning and memory. The studies done so far demonstrate that it is possible to derive mice with very restricted molecular, cellular, neuroanatomical, and behavioral phenotypes. Despite their complexity, these results have been easily integrated with findings from neuroanatomical and pharmacological lesion studies. The general goal of genetic studies of learning and memory is to develop and test theories that explain the animal's behavior in neuroanatomical, neurophysiological, cellular, and molecular terms. The purpose of this chapter is to outline the main features of these studies, not as a general comprehensive survey of the literature, but as a personal account of the development of this young field, of its promise and advantages, but also of its caveats and limitations. Although the focus of this chapter will be on studies of hippocampal function, there are also elegant gene-targeting studies of cerebellum-mediated learning (Aiba et al., 1994; Chen et al., 1995; Shibuki et al., 1996). Furthermore, genetic engineering can be used to create models of human diseases associated with learning and memory disabilities (for review, see Bedell, Largaespada, Jenkins, & Copeland, 1997). For example, mouse models for Alzheimer's disease, for the fragile X syndrome, and for neurofibromatosis type 1 have been generated (e.g., Bakker et al., 1994; Hsiao et al., 1996; Silva et al., 1997).

II. THE ROLE OF GENETICS

Decades of studies on how and what organisms learn and remember have given neuroscience a rich foundation in which to build theoretical and experimental investigations of learning and memory. For the geneticist, as well as for other neuroscientists, knowledge and insight into behavior are essential, since the design and interpretation of their experiments will depend on the clarity of the behavioral concepts that are being studied. Consequently, insights into animal behavior have had and will continue to have a central place in neuroscience. Why are some forms of learning hippocampal dependent? What are the conditions that recruit hippocampal function? Is it spatial or configural demands, is it the level of ambiguity, or is it simply complexity? Answers to questions such as these will come most probably from careful and insightful behavioral analysis, and they will be crucial for neuroscience studies of hippocampal function (for review, see Eichenbaum, 1996; McClelland, McNaughton, & O'Reilly, 1995).

Beyond behavioral analysis, studies of learning and memory must also include information about the neuroanatomy of the brain regions required for the particular behaviors studied. Neuroanatomical results have often provided hints about the kinds of computations that a specific brain region could support. For example, the interconnective pattern of CA3 suggests that it can be used as an association matrix. Neuroanatomy has placed Purkinje cells in the central stage of cerebellar computational models, because these cells not only receive inputs from prominent pathways in the cerebellum but their axons are also the principal outputs of this structure (for review, see Raymond, Lisberger, & Mark, 1996). Insights into the neuroanatomical structure of a brain region can also be extremely important in guiding physiological studies. For example, modeling considerations led to the discovery of LTD in the cerebellum and to intensive study of LTP in the hippocampus.

Armed with a plethora of technologies, the reductionist ladder can take us from behaviors of interest, to the regions mediating these behaviors, to models concerning how information is processed and/or stored there, to the very circuit mechanisms involved. One view proposes that useful reductionism stops there, that all relevant information will come from approaches that focus on the structural and computational aspects of the problem, and that very little will be gained from molecular and cellular insights. According to this perspective, molecular and cellular biology is to learning and memory what particle physics is to cell biology: related at a very infinitesimally reduced level, but essentially irrelevant.

We propose an alternative view, that information about molecular and cellular processes in the brain will complement and synergize with system-level information, because the richness of the mechanisms discovered will both constrain and guide higher order models. Additionally, in some cases the computational unit may not be the neuron or even the dendrite, but a group of proteins somewhere in the neuron. Computations performed by these protein clusters may not be entirely orchestrated by the cell they reside in but could instead transcend that cell's output and be a part of a larger system that incorporates different biochemical compartments of different cells. The existence of chemical messengers, such as NO (for review, see Garthwaite & Boulton, 1995), that freely cross cell membranes is just one of several examples of how biochemical processes transcend the very cells they reside in. In summary: even taking the restricted view of computational approaches, it is unwise to ignore subcellular mechanisms because it is impossible to predict exactly what and where are the relevant computational units.

Genetic manipulations, such as gene targeting, affect the very components that mediate these biochemical processes. However, its uses are not limited to the study of molecular phenomena. The magic of genetic manipulations is that they involve living animals with very specific changes in biochemistry, electrophysiology, and behavior (Fig. 1). At each of these levels the mutations affect only a restricted subset of phenomena, leaving others relatively unaffected. This specificity allows us to follow the effects of the mutation from level to level up the reductionist ladder all the way to behavior. Studies of mutant animals are forging connections between phenomena from different levels of hierarchical complexity, thus providing one of the most crucial steps in developing and testing theories of learning and memory.

In modern biology, genetics has been successful at uncovering simple principles from very complex biological phenomena. As a consequence, genetics has played a key role in almost every field of biological research, not necessarily by identifying genes related to complex biological processes but by identifying mutants that yield insights into a seemingly intractable complexity. Homeotic mutants are a very good example of this: the monstrously deformed *Drosophila* of Edward Lewis triggered a revolution in our understanding of developmental principles and resulted in an elegant framework of how networks of transcription cascades can mastermind the development of a segmental body plan (for review, see Roush, 1995). The phenotypes of mutants force us to see what we would otherwise ignore, revealing rich contrasts with patterns that unravel important principles. This is in essence the role that genetics is beginning to play and will continue to play in learning and memory: it will provide a fresh perspective into the problem, serving as a novel window into the fundamental processes of learning and memory.

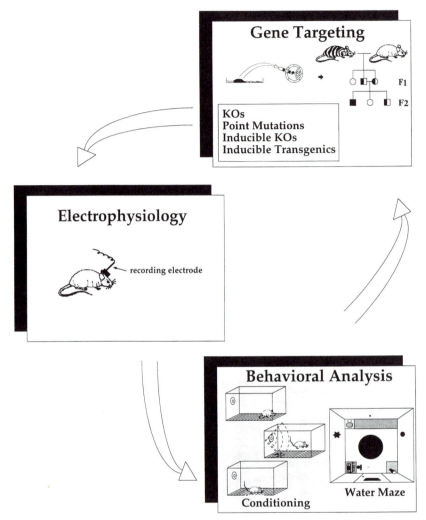

FIGURE 1   Scheme of different approaches used in the genetic study of learning and memory. Via gene targeting a mouse mutant is generated. The electrophysiological phenotype of the mutant is studied. The following behavioral analysis of the mutant leads to correlations between electrophysiological changes and the behavioral phenotype. From these results the generation of new mutants becomes apparent and the circle is repeated. In this way the mechanisms underlying learning and memory could be elucidated. Modeling will play a key role in this process.

III.   WHAT IS GENE TARGETING?

Gene targeting is a technique designed to derive mice with specific mutations in any cloned gene (Fig. 2) (for review, see Capecchi, 1989). The desired mutation is

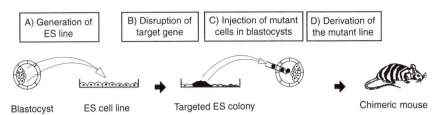

FIGURE 2   Illustration of the gene-targeting approach. The inner cell mass of a blastocyst is used for the generation of an ES cell line (A). Many ES cell lines have been established and are available, making it unnecessary for each laboratory to generate a new ES cell line. The ES cell line is transfected with the KO vector (B). This vector integrates mostly randomly, but in some cells it replaces the corresponding part of the target gene. ES cells grow in colonies and therefore it is possible to isolate clones after the selection has taken place. These clones are screened for the desired mutation. Cells from clones with the desired mutation (due to homologous recombination) are then injected into blastocysts (C). The blastocysts are transferred into a host mother (D) and resulting offspring are chimeras (mice deriving from the blastocysts used for injection and from the manipulated ES cells). Breeding of the chimeras generates a mutant line that can be bred indefinitely.

engineered within the cloned gene, and this mutant DNA is introduced into embryonic stem (ES) cells. These cells can be used to derive mice with the mutation. When returned to embryos, ES cells can participate in normal development. Some of them become part of the germ line, which enables the transmission and propagation of the mutant genotype. Thus, ES cells are injected into early embryos (blastocysts), and these blastocysts are transferred into host mothers. The resulting chimeric (having mutant and normal cells) offspring are then mated to obtain mutant mice. The generation of chimeras can also be done by simply joining normal morulae with ES cells (Nagy, Rossant, Nagy, Abramow-Newerly, & Roder, 1993). This approach may be more efficient and easier than injections into blastocysts. Nevertheless, in both cases the idea is the same: to add the mutant cells to a carrier embryo that will allow the generation of the mutant mouse line.

A. Knock Outs

In most gene-targeting experiments to date, the gene is "knocked out" (KO) by insertion of a bacterial gene. The first step in this procedure is designing a KO targeting vector. These KO vectors include the gene of interest mutated by the insertion of a bacterial gene, such as the neomycin resistant (neo) gene. The neo gene is also used for selecting those ES cell colonies that incorporated the targeting vector, since during the transfection process not all cells acquire the mutant DNA. Cells without the neo gene are killed by neomycin. The neo gene confers resistance to neomycin, an aminoglycoside that blocks protein synthesis. The insertion of the neo gene may lead to the premature stop of the transcription of the targeted gene,

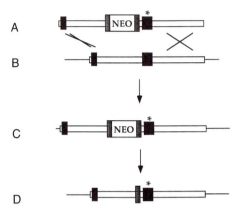

FIGURE 3   The Pointlox strategy to introduce a point mutation into the target gene. The gene-targeting vector (A) is engineered with the desired point mutation leading to an amino acid substitution (asterisk). Furthermore, a neo gene is inserted into an intron (exons are shown as black boxes; the white boxes indicate the region of homology between gene-targeting vector and target gene). The neo gene is used for selection and it is flanked by loxP sites. After homologous recombination, part of the target gene (shown in B) is substituted (C). Since the neo gene can interfere with the expression of the target gene, it is removed by the Cre recombinase (D). After the removal of the neo gene, one loxP site is left behind in the intron. The presence of this loxP site may not interfere with splicing of the target gene.

to a shift of the translation frame, or if incorporated into the mutant protein, to the disruption of the structure of the protein of interest.

B. Adding and Deleting Functional Domains

An alternative to disrupting the gene by inserting neo is to use KO vector designs that promote a deletion of a critical region. With this process it is also possible to add or replace domains in proteins. In this case, it is important to place the neo gene (the selectable marker) in a noncoding region and to remove it by Cre recombinase (vide infra) before the ES cells are injected into blastocysts.

C. Amino Acid Substitutions

In addition to adding and removing genes or domains within genes, it is also possible to change single amino acids in a region of interest (Pointlox procedure; Fig. 3). To do this a DNA is engineered with a specific amino acid mutation, and the neo gene is positioned in a noncoding region. Before the ES cells are injected into blastocysts, this neo gene is removed by the Cre recombinase (vide infra).

The ability to make single amino acid changes in genes of interest is a crucial technique because it allows the testing of hypotheses involving specific functional models. For example, two models have been proposed for the role of the autophosphorylation at threonine 286 of αCaMKII in long-term potentiation (LTP). The first model suggested that this autophosphorylation event occurs in the postsynapse during or immediately after a tetanic stimulation leading to a constitutively active kinase. The autophosphorylated kinase would then continuously phosphorylate a substrate, resulting in the maintenance of LTP (Lisman, 1994). The second model is based on trapping of calmodulin by the autophosphorylation at threonine 286 of αCaMKII (for review, see Hanson & Schulman, 1992). The model suggests that this autophosphorylation determines the level of free calmodulin in the postsynapse during a tetanus and that this affects the balance between LTP and long-term depression (LTD) (Mayford, Wang, Kandel, & O'Dell, 1995).

These models were tested by substituting the αCaMKII threonine 286 by alanine in mice (Giese, Fedorov, Filipkowski, & Silva, 1998). This mutant kinase functions normally under conditions not requiring autophosphorylation of this residue. One of the important features of this type of experiments is that regardless of the electrophysiological phenotype of the point mutations they will be valuable in elucidating how the biochemistry of key proteins affects neuronal physiology and how the changes in physiology affect behavior.

IV. GENES AND ORGANISMS

Before we review the key features of gene-targeting studies of learning and memory, we will discuss the crucial relation between single genes and behavior. Misunderstanding of this central issue leads to misleading preconceptions and to avoidable confusion.

It is clear that mutations of specific genes have an enormous impact on behavior. For example, in neurofibromatosis type I (NF1), the mutation of a GTPase activating protein (NF1-GAP) leads to learning disabilities in as many as 1 out of 5000 children worldwide (for review, see Gutmann & Collins, 1995). The loss of the α-calcium-calmodulin kinase II (αCaMKII) leads to profound behavioral changes in mice, which range from alterations in social responses to profound deficits in learning tasks (Silva, Paylor, Wehner, & Tonegawa, 1992; Chen, Rainnie, Greene, & Tonegawa, 1994). However, the extensive evidence that the mutation of genes can cause specific behavioral disruptions cannot be used to conclude that single genes have behavioral functions or that it is possible to predict behavioral performance from genotype. Nevertheless, the problem of lesion studies in general is that it is irresistible to assume that the functional loss caused by the lesion is directly and almost exclusively attributable to the component damaged. Despite endless functional analogies that show the naiveté of such conclusions (for example, we would not claim that just because the loss of the wheels keeps a car from moving, what drives the car is its wheels), they are irresistible because in many cases they are useful simplifications.

Mutations are genetic lesions, and consequently, even though single gene muta-tions can often result in selective behavioral, electrophysiological, and cellular alter-ations, it is dangerous to assign these lost functions to the genes mutated. Outside of the confines of biochemical reactions, and other cellular events, gene products may not have easily attributable functions. The major reason for this is that biolog-ical systems are highly dynamic at all levels of organization. Thus, when a single protein is lost, the cell adjusts, and this process could involve many proteins. The functional output of a cell or cells involves thousands of proteins working together, and as outputs are integrated across many interacting systems, the complexity of the emerging output confounds the contribution of a single protein.

The consequences of mutations and other lesions are never restricted to the components manipulated. These components are little more than iceberg tips in a sea of hidden secondary adaptive changes. Importantly, many, if not most, of these adaptive changes may transcend genetics and could involve other responses resulting from the accumulated history of the system or systems involved.

If it is not possible to make direct connections between genes and behavior, then what is the point of using mutants in studies of learning and memory? First, muta-tions are a means to manipulate the molecular, electrophysiological, neuroanatom-ical, and behavioral characteristics of an animal. By contrasting mutants with their littermates, it has been possible to discern functional patterns otherwise hidden from view. Often the abnormal, the unusual, serves to focus our attention to specific features of the overwhelming complexity of natural phenomena. Even in the rela-tively short time that mutant mice have been used in studies of learning and mem-ory, we have already collected an interesting array of mice with very intriguing and suggesting phenotypes. Hypotheses arising from these phenotypes can be tested by manipulating other genes or simply by changing the genetic background of the mutation. These manipulations can change aspects of the phenotype and thus create the opportunity to test physiological/behavioral correlations suggested by the initial studies. The point is that the derivation of a mutant is never an end, but a beginning, a means to uncover what is hidden, what had remained unnoticed. The following are a few representative examples of the gene-targeting studies done that are provid-ing biological insights into learning and memory.

V. PROBING HIPPOCAMPAL FUNCTION WITH GENE TARGETING

The hippocampus is a central processing station of information in the brain. Lesion work has suggested a key role for the hippocampus in memory, and neuroanatomi-cal analysis shows that it receives inputs from key neocortical and thalamic areas as well as from other limbic structures such as the amygdala. This kind of connectivity is suggestive of a structure that integrates high-order information processed elsewhere, functioning as a comparing device that single-unit studies suggest is constantly assessing and contrasting incoming signals. Although the rodent hippocampus seems to have a key role in spatial navigation, there are now overwhelming data that the hippocampus is involved in a variety of other complex behaviors (for review, see Eichenbaum, 1996). It seems that hippocampal lesions affect performance in most complex tasks requiring unique solutions and flexible handling of learned information. Nevertheless, despite these provocative functional sketches, little is known about how the loss of the hippocampus has such striking effects in the behavior of the animals and how the striking physiology of the hippocampus accounts for its putative behavioral functions.

Important connections between physiology and behavior were derived from studies of animals exposed to a variety of compounds with known physiological effects. For example, N-methyl-D-aspartate (NMDA) receptor antagonists delivered to the hippocampus block long-term potentiation and also impair some measures of hippocampal-dependent learning (Davis, Butcher, & Morris, 1992), reinforcing the suggestion that the Hebbian mechanisms of LTP might be required for learning. However, the involvement of this receptor in other electrophysiological mechanisms complicated the interpretation of these studies, and recent results show that under some conditions antagonists of this receptor do not seem to block hippocampal-dependent learning (Bannermann, Good, Butcher, Ramsay, & Morris, 1995; Cain, Saucier, Hall, Hargreaves, & Boon, 1996; Saucier, Hargreaves, Boon, Vanderwolf, & Cain, 1996).

Another important strategy to investigate neurophysiological models of behavior is to study directly the physiology of behaving animals (*in vivo* electrophysiology). For example, electrophysiological recordings of hippocampal neurons in rats during learning showed that they fire in ways known to be optimal for the induction of LTP *in vitro* (Larson & Lynch, 1986; Otto, Eichenbaum, Wiener, & Wible, 1991; Ranck, 1973; Vanderwolf, 1969). This finding considerably strengthened the connection between LTP and learning. However, the physiological complexity of a working brain can obscure the relevance of any single physiological phenomenon. For example, short-term exploratory modulation, or STEM, a correlate of learning, also is affected by increases in brain temperature during active exploration (Moser, Mathiesen, & Andersen, 1993). These concerns once again underscore the assertion that no single approach will suffice to unveil the exceedingly complex interactions between physiology and behavior.

The established history of neuroanatomical and pharmacological lesions has led naturally to the use of genetic lesions in neuroscience. Mice are an ideal system for these studies because of several factors, not the least of which is the availability of transgenic technologies capable of adding, replacing, and modifying a gene or even a single nucleotide within an interesting functional domain. The sophisticated electrophysiological and behavioral techniques used with rats have been applied to mice, thus dispelling early fears that mice were inadequate for serious electrophysiological or behavioral work.

A. KOs, LTP, and Learning

Most of the genetic work on the basis of hippocampal-dependent learning and memory has focused on long-lasting changes in synaptic efficacy (i.e., LTP and LTD). The underlying general hypothesis, with its many variations, has been the primary focus of most theoretical and experimental studies on the biological basis of learning and memory. The idea, as expanded upon in several chapters of this book, is that information can be stored in neural circuits by adjusting the synaptic weights of neurons activated by the learning experience. The changes in synaptic strengths are thought to leave an imprint that can be used later to partly re-create the original experience (i.e., memory). The concept that memories can be stored as patterns of synaptic weights has been implemented with surprising success by parallel-neuronal network models with every increasing power and sophistication. Structures such as the hippocampus, with an acknowledged participation in learning and memory, are capable of long-lasting changes in synaptic strength, which have the very properties thought to be crucial for memory formation (associativity, specificity, reversibility, and stability). Additionally, pharmacological blockers of these synaptic changes were shown in many cases to also disturb memory formation (but see Bannermann et al., 1995; Cain et al., 1996; Saucier et al., 1996). However, these are very complex phenomena with many alternative explanations and thus requiring additional experimental approaches. In the early nineties the time was ripe to apply genetics to probe the connection between these synaptic phenomena and learning and memory.

As an introduction to the genetic studies, it is useful to start with a very brief note on the biochemistry of LTP, undoubtedly the most extensively studied long-lasting change in synaptic function. The study of LTP is full of controversial findings, with many of its properties hotly debated between laboratories. Nevertheless, most researchers agree that the induction of LTP in the CA1 region involves the activation of NMDA receptors and a consequent postsynaptic increase in calcium (for review, see Bliss & Collingridge, 1993). This increase in calcium is known to activate a number of protein kinases and other enzymes (e.g., adenylate cyclase) that are thought to trigger the biochemical cascade of events that modulate synaptic strength.

Interestingly, genetic deletions of the NMDA receptor $\epsilon 1$ subunit (Sakimura et al., 1995), α–calcium-calmodulin kinase II (αCaMKII) (Silva, Paylor, Wehner, & Tonegawa, 1992; Silva, Stevens, Tonegawa, & Wang, 1992), Fyn tyrosine kinase (Grant et al., 1992), PKCγ (Abeliovich, Chen, et al., 1993; Abeliovich, Paylor, et al., 1993), type I adenylate cyclase (Wu et al., 1995), and mGluR5 (Lu et al., 1997)

TABLE I   Summary of the Mutants Having Impairments in LTP in the Hippocampal CA1 Region and Being Affected in Learning the Hidden-Platform Version of the Morris Water Maze (MWM)[a]

Mutant	CA1 LTP	MWM learning
αCaMKII$^{-/-}$	↓	↓
$fyn^{-/-}$	↓	↓
NMDAR $\epsilon1^{-/-}$	↓	↓
Type 1 adenylate cyclase$^{-/-}$	↓	↓
CREB$^{-/-}$	↓	↓
mGluR5$^{-/-}$	↓	↓
αCaMKII^{D286}	↓	↓

[a]These results support the hypothesis that changes in LTP in the CA1 region lead to spatial learning changes. Arrow down, impaired or decreased.

all affect to some extent LTP in the hippocampal CA1 region and hippocampal-dependent learning and memory (Table I). This is in remarkable consistency with the hypothesis that LTP is a learning mechanism. Therefore these experiments have added support to the hypothesis that LTP in the CA1 region plays a role in the cellular events encoding information in the hippocampus. The most we can say at this point is that disrupting mechanisms required for LTP disrupts, in some but not in all cases, processes that are needed for memory formation. If it were not for the considerable theoretical work done on Hebbian mechanisms and their possible relevance to learning and memory, we and others would not venture to add much more significance to these findings.

However, the LTP hypothesis has both reasonable and compelling theoretical arguments as well as a considerable body of pharmacological, electrophysiological, and genetic evidence that support it. Other competing ideas have failed to capture the interests and the imagination of neuroscientists to the extent that the Hebbian hypothesis and its derivatives have.

Nevertheless, many problems remain unsolved. These problems fall into at least two categories: First, there is the possibility that LTP is not involved in learning or memory but that it shares many biochemical components with the cellular mechanism(s) of learning and memory. To address this possibility it is worthwhile to reexamine the details of experiments associating LTP with learning, since one would expect to see dissocations, if subtle, between these two phenomena. Second, there is a fundamental theoretical problem with claiming that a single aspect of cellular physiology could be responsible for learning and memory in the hippocampus or in any other structure. Learning is a property of circuits and brains, and it is likely to involve a variety mechanisms. The gene-targeting studies that follow address these issues.

B. The Ablation of Synaptic Plasticity and Its Effects on Learning

The first gene-targeting study of LTP and learning used mice with a null mutation for the αCaMKII (Silva, Paylor, Wehner, & Tonegawa, 1992; Silva, Stevens, Tonegawa, & Wang, 1992). The αCaMKII is mostly expressed postnatally in forebrain structures, whereas the βCaMKII, another related kinase with similar properties, is expressed more uniformly throughout the brain and during embryonic development (Burgin et al., 1990). CaMKII can be in a number of activity states (Fig. 4) that depend mainly on the interaction with Ca^{2+}/calmodulin (Ca/CaM) and on autophosphorylation (for review, see Hanson & Schulman, 1992). The enzyme is most active when unphosphorylated and bound to Ca/CaM. The autophosphorylated enzyme traps Ca/CaM and is only partly active. These complex responses to Ca^{2+} are likely to be involved in the induction of LTP, because electrophysiological studies have shown that peptides designed to simulate the inhibitory domain of the enzyme, and thus inhibit its activity, can also block the induction of LTP in the CA1 region of the hippocampus (Malenka et al., 1989; Malinow, Schulman, & Tsien, 1989; but see Hvalby, et al., 1994).

The studies with the αCaMKII mutants showed that in the absence of this isoform, LTP and long-term depression (LTD) were severely imparied in the hippocampus and neocortex (Kirkwood, Silva, & Bear, 1994; Silva, Stevens, Tonegawa, & Wong, 1992; Stevens, Tonegawa, & Wang, 1994). Interestingly, however, field and whole-cell recordings did occasionally detect seemingly normal LTP in hippocampal slices from the mutant mice, suggesting that in the absence of αCaMKII, a rarer form of LTP can be induced in the hippocampus. A number of studies suggest that these LTP deficits are not due to gross developmental abnormalities: (1) Electron microscopic analysis in the CA1 region suggests that there are similar neuronal and synaptic numbers in these mutants and that the size and general structure organization of postsynaptic densities are unaltered by the mutation (Comery, Kleim, Silva, & Greenough, 1994). (2) Studies in the somatosensory and visual cortices demonstrated that the functional topography and general properties of these regions are normal in the mutants (Glazewski, Chen, Silva, & Fox, 1996; Gordon, Cioffi, Silva, & Stryker, 1996). (3) Extensive electrophysiological analysis showed that the mutants do not have a general loss in synaptic function (Chapman, Frenguelli, Smith, Chen, & Silva, 1995; Silva, Stevens, Tonegawa, & Wang, 1992; Stevens et al., 1994).

A number of behavioral studies attest to the specificity of the deficits observed in the αCaMKII mutants. Although the αCaMKII mutant mice were severely impaired in the hippocampal-dependent version of the water maze, they were able to learn the "visible-platform" version of this task, which is known not to depend on hippocampal function (Silva, Paylor, Wehner, & Tonegawa, 1992). These results illustrate that the αCaMKII mutants can learn that the platform is the only escape in the pool, that they have the motivation to escape the water and the motor

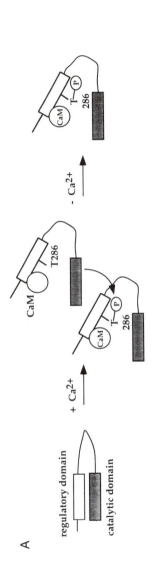

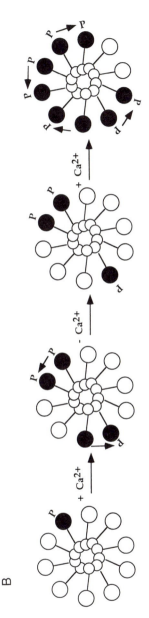

FIGURE 4 Multiple states of αCaMKII. (A) In the absence of CA²⁺/calmodulin (CaM) the inhibitory domain (part of the regulatory domain) blocks the catalytic domain. Binding of CaM results in a conformational change, so the catalytic domain is not blocked any longer. If two neighboring αCaMKII subunits in the holoenzyme are activated, one subunit can be phosphorylated at T286 by an intersubunit reaction. This phosphorylation leads to trapping of CaM (probably due to a further conformational change) and the enzyme can now be active in the absence of CaM. (B) Since the holoenzyme consists of 10 subunits, the trapping of CaM is a cooperative process during successive Ca²⁺ spikes. (Trapping is indicated by black circles.)

coordination and sensory perception required to efficiently swim to the escape platform, but that they are nevertheless unable to learn the spatial relationships required to guide them to the hidden platform. For example, at the end of training with the platform removed from the pool, the mutants search for it everywhere in the pool, whereas the searches of the control littermates are focused on the quadrant of the pool where the platform was located during training.

Surprisingly, despite this spatial learning deficit, the performance of the mutants appears to improve during training. To resolve this apparent paradox, the mice were tested in two other tests: The random platform task tested the hypothesis that trained controls would escape quickly to a randomly placed hidden platform only if it were in the same location as their training platform, whereas animals that had experience in the pool but no memory for a platform location would perform equally well on a task in which the platform is randomly placed in any of the four quadrants. The plus-maze required the animals to use extramaze cues for orientation but constrained them to "alleys" in which they were forced to swim, thus reducing the spatial components of the hidden-platform task to a decision to turn right or left. Mice homozygous for the αCaMKII mutation showed no deficit in the plus-maze and no evidence for any spatial learning in the random platform task, confirming that they are unable to learn spatial information but that they can learn other simpler tasks.

Further studies have shown that this mutation also seems to affect aggressive and defensive behaviors (Chen et al., 1994). The homozygous αCaMKII mice showed fewer fear responses and fewer defensive and aggressive behaviors than controls. Perhaps correlated with this decrease in aggression, cellular studies in the dorsal raphe of the mutants did find a reduction in serotonin release there. The specific question that emerges is whether there is a connection between the spatial learning deficits and the alterations in aggressive and defensive behaviors in these mutants. In this respect it is interesting that animals with hippocampal lesions are known to have increases in aggressive behaviors. Recent studies have outlined massive topographic connections between the hippocampus and the lateral septum (Risold & Swanson, 1996). Remarkably, the CA1-subiculum fields project specifically to the enkephalin-rich rostral region of the lateral septum, which projects to hypothalamic medial zone nuclei, a brain region thought to be involved in the expression of social behaviors. Thus, a component of the abnormal social behavior expressed by these mutants may originate in faulty processing in the hippocampus.

In vivo electrophysiological studies found that repetitive stimuli delivered to the amygdala cannot kindle the αCaMKII mice (A. J. Silva, unpublished data) and that their hippocampal and amygdala circuits are hyperexcitable (Butler et al., 1995). Perhaps, the same cellular mechanisms that are required for the induction of LTP are also involved in kindling. Both phenomena involve stable and long-lasting changes in synaptic function that are severely impaired in the αCaMKII mutants. Alternatively, the deficits in LTP and kindling may represent two independent consequences of the mutation. Therefore, either of these two abnormalities could impair learning in the αCaMKII homozygotes, thus confounding the interpretation of these results. This illustrates a common problem with studies of learning and memory: very often the manipulation used (genetics, pharmacology, neuroanatomical lesions, etc.) has side effects that add variables to the experiment. This problem emphasizes the need to test important physiological explanations of behavior with multiple experimental approaches. Finding a convergence of experimental results strengthens the involvement of LTP in learning.

C. Exploring the Molecular Basis for the Covariance Rule

The deletion of the αCaMKII gene affects LTP and learning. Interestingly, the addition of a constitutively active αCaMKII to the mouse also affects hippocampal LTP and learning (Bach, Hawkins, Osman, Kaudel, & Mayford, 1995; Mayford et al., 1995). Cloning of the promoter elements of this gene allowed the faithful expression of a mutant αCaMKII gene in transgenic mice. The artificial gene used included the substitution of a threonine for an aspartate (D) at position 286 of the protein. The aspartate mimics a phosphorylated threonine and consequently the mutant kinase (αCaMKII^{D286}) is fixed in a configuration that is active even in the absence of Ca^{2+}. This transgene was injected into zygotes and integrated randomly within one of the chromosomes. In this type of transgenic experiment there is always the danger of inadvertent disruption of an unrelated gene by the insertion of the transgene. To control for this possibility multiple transgenic lines are studied in parallel because the probability that the same gene is disrupted by the transgene in independently derived lines is extremely low. Comparison of the results obtained for independent lines with the same transgene is important to demonstrate that the phenotype observed is due to the gene added and not to inadvertently disrupted genes in the host genome.

Electrophysiological analysis of the αCaMKII^{D286} mice revealed that the range of tetanic frequencies at which hippocampal LTP or LTD takes place are changed by this mutant kinase (Mayford et al., 1995). High-frequency stimulation (100 Hz) induced LTP in both mutant and controls. However, a lower range of frequencies, which induced LTP in the controls, favored LTD in the mutants. This result indicates that CaMKII can shift the threshold for LTP and LTD in synapses. Second, it suggests that there is a biochemical continuity between LTP and LTD, a result consistent with the covariance rule. According to the covariance rule, the levels of LTP or LTD are determined by synaptic activity (frequency and duration) (e.g., Huang et al., 1992). In the αCaMKII^{D286} mice the whole frequency curve for LTP and LTD has been shifted to favor LTD.

Interestingly, the history of synaptic activity also seems to impact on the effect of the αCaMKII^{D286}, a phenomenon that has recently been named metaplasticity (for review, see Abraham & Bear, 1996). Stimulation at 5 Hz induces a small LTP in normal mice, but LTD in the mutants. However, 20 min after LTP induction with 100-Hz stimulation, which triggers similar levels of LTP in mutants and controls,

5-Hz stimulation induces a similar degree of LTD in mutants and controls. This result shows that the covariance rule changes with the history of the synapse, a result that implies that the underlying biochemistry must also be responding to the activation history of the synapse. Consistent with this idea, relatively naive synapses, which have greater levels of constitutively active CaMKII, also have higher levels of LTD. Behavioral studies with the Barnes maze suggested the αCaMKII[D286] mice have learning deficits (Bach et al., 1995).

Altogether, the gene targeting and the transgenic studies show that modifying the activity of the αCaMKII affects not only the synaptic physiology in the hippocampus but learning and memory as well.

D. Plasticity, Development, and Learning

Pharmacological studies indicate that tyrosine kinase activity is also required for the induction of LTP (O'Dell, Kandel, & Grant, 1991). Consistent with this, mice with a mutation in a cytoplasmic tyrosine kinase (Fyn) show a striking reduction in hippocampal LTP (Grant et al., 1992). In constrast, similar studies did not find LTP deficits in mice deficient for three other cytoplasmic tyrosine kinases expressed in the hippocampus (Abl, Src, and Yes), demonstrating the molecular specificity of the LTP deficits of the *fyn* mutants (Grant et al., 1992). Interestingly, either strong stimuli or direct postsynaptic depolarization is able to trigger LTP in the *fyn* mutants, suggesting that at least some of the postsynaptic mechanisms for the induction of LTP are not disrupted in the *fyn* mutation. Nevertheless, the LTP induced by strong tetanization in the *fyn* mutants can be blocked by inhibitors of tyrosine kinases, suggesting that other tyrosine kinases may have compensated for the Fyn deficiency. Furthermore, the ratio of NMDA to non-NMDA currents as well as PTP and PPF appeared to be normal in the *fyn* mutants (Grant et al., 1992).

Like the αCaMKII mutants, *fyn* mutants are also severely affected in the hidden- but not in the visible-platform version of the Morris water maze (Grant et al., 1992), suggesting that hippocampal function was especially affected by the mutation. However, a recent study showed that the *fyn* mutants have swimming abnormalities (Huerta, Scearce, Farris, Empson, & Prosky, 1996). By mechanical stimulation of the hind feet the *fyn* mutants were able to swim normally and to learn the hidden-platform version of the Morris water maze. This result is an eloquent demonstration of the complex nature of deficits in learning tasks, and it shows that abnormalities in sensory, motivational, or motor coordination systems can often appear to be impairments in learning.

Neuroanatomical analysis of the hippocampus in the *fyn* mutants revealed an interesting structural change in the dentate gyrus and CA3 region. It seems that a 25% increase in cell number forced the cells to form an undulated cell layer (Grant et al., 1992), presumably to accommodate the additional cells present. Likewise, similar undulations are also observed in the primate hippocampus and neocortex, presumably because of the same need to accommodate larger cell numbers. The final number of CA3 cells (but not CA1 cells) seems to be dependent on cell death. Interestingly, under certain conditions calcium triggers cell death in developing T-cells in a Fyn-dependent manner (Appleby et al., 1992; Stein, Lee, Rich, & Soriano, 1992). Thus, Fyn may be an important regulator of cell death in the development of both T-cells and hippocampal neurons.

Studies of another independently derived *fyn* mutant line found a 50% decrease in myelin in these mutants (Umemori, Sato, Yogi, Aizawa, & Yamamoto, 1994). It appears that Fyn expression in oligodendrocytes is required for the early stages of myelination. These structural deficits confound the interpretation of the electrophysiological and behavioral experiments with the *fyn* mutants. It is possible, for example, that the LTP deficits of these mutants are due to structural deficits or to incomplete myelination in the hippocampus. It is exciting that we currently have the technology required to test this possibility (vide infra). Curing the learning deficits of adult *fyn* mutants with an inducible *fyn* gene would test whether the developmental abnormalities of the *fyn* mutants are the primary cause for their learning deficits. Remarkably, neither the structural abnormalities nor the myelination and LTP deficits seem to impair hippocampal-dependent learning in the mutants, since they show unambiguous evidence of spatial learning in the Morris water maze (Huerta et al., 1996).

E. History of Synaptic Activation Affects the Biochemistry of Plasticity

Besides Ca/CaM kinases and tyrosine kinases, calcium and phospholipid-dependent protein kinases (PKC) have also been involved in hippocampal LTP. Peptide inhibitors that block the activity of PKC interfere with the induction and even the maintenance of LTP (Malenka et al., 1989; Malinow et al., 1989; Reymann, Brödemann, Kase, & Matthies, 1988). Interestingly, a mouse mutant for the γ-isoform of PKC shows abnormal hippocampal LTP (Abeliovich, Chen, et al., 1993). The expression of PKCγ is restricted to the brain and starts late in the development of the postnatal hippocampus (for review, see Nishizuka et al., 1991). Despite abnormal LTP, the mutant mice show normal synaptic transmission and LTD (Abeliovich, Chen, et al., 1993).

Unexpectedly, after LTD induction, the mutant slices express normal levels of LTP (Abeliovich, Chen, et al., 1993). A simple explanation for these results is that LTP is saturated in mutant synapses and therefore it can only be induced if these synapses are first depressed. This does not seem to be the case, however, because there is no increase in basal synaptic function in the mutants, and there is no correlation between the size of the induced depression and the subsequent size of potentiation. If the LTP was saturated, then mutant hippocampal slices with greater LTD should have revealed greater LTP.

Even if NMDA receptors are blocked during LTD, which effectively blocks synaptic depression, mutants still reveal normal LTP. Thus, the low-frequency stimulation, even in the absence of the subsequent synaptic depression, is sufficient to prime these mutants for LTP induction. These results suggest that after low-frequency stimulation, the induction of LTP is not PKCγ dependent, even though LTP induced in unstimulated synapses is definitely PKCγ dependent. These results indicate that the history of activation of a synapse determines what biochemical mechanisms it uses for LTP induction. This biochemical flexibility may allow the synapse a great deal of control over the conditions that can trigger LTP. This biochemical regulation may be a means to implement computational rules for LTP induction that are contingent on relevant details of a synapse's history of activity. This may be of special significance for the hippocampus, a structure that integrates information coming from several brain centers, under many different behavioral conditions. This is an elegant example of the usefulness of genetics. Without this approach we may not have had this important insight on synaptic function.

This perspective on the regulation of LTP metaplasticity is consistent with the αCaMKII^{D286} results and with recent data from a very different set of experiments in the rat visual cortex. It appears that the thresholds for LTP induction in the visual cortex (but not in the hippocampus) are very different in dark-reared versus light-reared rats (Kirkwood, Rioult, & Bear, 1996). Stimulation frequencies that induce robust LTP in dark-reared rats fail to do so in light-reared animals, a result that eloquently demonstrates the idea that the complex processes underlying synaptic changes are very responsive to the activation history of a circuit. The findings discussed in this section also illustrate the complementarity between results of experiments done with very different approaches, each contributing to the elucidation of a new and potentially very important concept in the physiology of learning and memory. Without the PKCγ KOs, it may have been difficult to discover that a synapse's history of activation determines what biochemical pathways are used during LTP induction.

F. Transcription, Translation, and Memory

The foregoing mechanisms are likely to be involved in early stages of memory formation (i.e., during learning). However, little is known about the molecular and cellular processes required to support memory. Previous pharmacological studies showed that the synthesis of new proteins is a povital requirement of long-term memory (for reviews, see Davis & Squire, 1984; Matthies, 1989). A variety of inhibitors of protein and RNA synthesis have been shown to block effectively long-term but not short-term memory. Since these inhibitors have a general effect on all protein synthesis, they cannot be used to identify and study the specific components and mechanisms involved in triggering long-term memory.

Experiments with *Aplysia* demonstrate that serotonin applications activate cAMP-dependent signal transduction (for review, see Byrne, 1987). One of the important components of this pathway is the cAMP-dependent protein kinase A (PKA). Phosphorylation by this kinase is required for a number of processes in the cytoplasm and for the activation of transcription factors, such as CREB, in the nucleus (Dash, Hochner, & Kandel, 1990). To trigger transcription, CREB binds to a specific regulatory DNA sequence (TGACGTCA) in the promoter region of certain genes (Brindle & Montminy, 1992; Lee & Masson, 1993). This sequence is designated as the cAMP-responsive element, or CRE, because the transcription of CRE-containing genes is responsive to changes in the concentration of cytosolic cAMP.

Interestingly, oligonucleotides with CRE sequences injected into *Aplysia* sensory neurons in culture selectively block long-term but not short-term facilitation (Dash et al., 1990). Presumably, the CRE-oligos trap the CREB proteins needed for the transcriptional activation of genes involved in long-term facilitation (Alberini, Ghirardi, Metz, & Kandel, 1994; Kaang, Kandel, & Grant, 1993).

There is also ample evidence for the involvement of cAMP second-messenger pathways in *Drosophila* learning (for review, see Tully, 1991). Recently, work in *Drosophila* showed that a dominant-negative mutant form of *Drosophila* CREB can block long-term memory, without having a measurable effect in other memory stages, including anesthesia-resistant memory (Tully, Preat, Boynton, & Vecchio, 1994, Yin et al., 1994). These studies also showed that the memory phase disrupted by the CREB transgene appears to be identical to that affected by protein synthesis inhibitors. It is noteworthy that the striking long-term memory (LTM) loss observed in the CREB transgenic flies could not be attributed to developmental changes, since the mutant transgene was not expressed during development. In this case the mutant CREB was under the control of a promoter that is activated by higher temperatures but that remains otherwise silent. Only flies in which the transgene was induced by heat shock (prior to training) showed the long-term memory deficits. The transgene remained silent and without consequence in transgenic flies that were not subjected to heat induction prior to training.

Strikingly, induction of a transgenic CREB activator under a similar heat shock promoter triggered LTM with a single trial, whereas in control flies the induction of LTM required multiple spaced trials (Yin, Vecchio, Zhou, & Tully, 1995). Similarly, removing CREB repression with an antibody against a natural CREB blocker also avoids the requirement for multiple spaced serotonin applications in the induction of long-term synaptic facilitation in *Aplysia* (Bartsch et al., 1995). These results argue for a role of CREB in the induction of LTM and suggest that the requirement for spaced training during the induction of LTM in flies is related to the levels of CREB activator (Yin et al., 1995). Perhaps, CREB is a limiting factor in the nuclear events leading to LTM in flies. This result, however, does not show that all forms of memory could be facilitated by simply providing additional CREB. Instead, it illustrates eloquently the involvement of this factor in cellular processes required for memory formation.

Parallel studies in mice also demonstrated the requirement for CREB in memory formation (Bourtchuladze et al., 1994). Mice, lacking the α- and the δ-isoform of CREB, were generated by gene targeting (Hummler et al., 1994). Interestingly, the levels of another CREB-like transcription factor (CREM) were increased (2–4 times) in these mutants (Hummler et al., 1994; Blendy, Kaestner, Schmid, Gass, & Schütz, 1996). This compensatory increase in CREM is consistent with evidence that there is a close interaction between CREB and CREM in normal cells (Brindle & Montminy, 1992; Hai, Liu, Conkos, & Green, 1989; Hurst, Totty, & Jones, 1991; Liu, Thompson, Wagner, Greenberg, & Green, 1993; Masson, Hurst, & Lee, 1993). These results demonstrate that deleting or altering specific genes can trigger adaptive changes in other genes. Proteins are not static and rigid functional units, and they do not function in isolation. Instead, proteins form functional networks in cells that are highly dynamic and cooperative, responding and adapting to incoming signals.

That the CREB mutant mice appeared normal in most respects studied suggests that this mutation has a very specific impact on function. The CREB animals appear healthy and groomed, they show no hints of ataxia or of any other motor disorders, and they can mate. In contrast, fear-conditioning studies showed that long-term memory is impaired in these mice (Bourtchuladze et al., 1994).

Fear conditioning is a simple form of associative learning (Fanselow, 1980), in which animals learn to "fear" a previously neutral stimulus (conditioned stimulus, or CS) simply because of its temporal association with an aversive stimulus (unconditioned stimulus, or US), such as a foot shock. Conditioned animals, when exposed to the CS, tend to refrain from all but respiratory movement by "freezing" (Fanselow, 1986). Freezing responses can be triggered with two different types of CS, each with distinct neuroanatomical substrates (Kim, Rison, & Fanselow, 1993; Phillips & LeDoux, 1992). In "cued conditioning" the CS is simply a tone (i.e., 85 dB, 2800 Hz), and lesions of the amygdala (but not the hippocampus) appear to disrupt this type of conditioning (Kim et al., 1993; Phillips & LeDoux, 1992). Alternatively, rodents can be conditioned to the "context" in which they were exposed to the US. "Contextual conditioning" is thought to be dependent on both hippocampal and amygdala function (Kim et al., 1993; Phillips & LeDoux, 1992). Studies with anisomycin showed that 24-hr memory of contextual conditioning is protein synthesis dependent (Abel et al., 1997).

Remarkably, contextual conditioning is normal in CREB mice 30 min after training but not at 1 or 24 hr after training (Bourtchuladze et al., 1994). Importantly, the freezing responses observed 30 min after training were specific to the training context, since CREB mice tested on a novel context displayed little or no freezing. Similar results were also obtained for conditioning to a sound (cued conditioning). In contrast to contextual conditioning, cued conditioning produced nearly normal freezing responses in CREB mice tested 1 hr after training but not thereafter, demonstrating that the onset of the amnesia is different for these two forms of conditioning. Training in the water maze confirmed that these mutants have deficits in specific types of learning and memory, since the CREB mice were unable to learn this task with 1 trial per day for 15 days, even though controls learn to search selectively for the hidden platform after only 10 days of similar training (Bourtchuladze et al., 1994). However, performance in the visible-platform task is unaffected by the CREB mutation. Even though with the water maze it is impossible to separate learning from memory, it was important to show that two tasks sensitive to hippocampal lesions detected a deficit in the CREB mutants. The CREB mutants were also impaired in a third hippocampal-dependent test, the social transmission of food preference (Kogan et al., 1997). In this test a "demonstrator" mouse is given distinctively scented food. Afterward these demonstrator mice are allowed to interact with "observer" mice. Immediately or 24 hr after this interaction the observer mice are given a choice to eat either the same scented food as the demonstrator mice (cued) or food of a different scent (noncued). Mice prefer usually the cued food, presumably because they sensed the demonstrator mice. Twenty-four-hour memory of food preference is hippocampal dependent, whereas immediate memory is not (Bunsey & Eichenbaum, 1995). The CREB mutants were impaired in the test 24 hr after the interaction with demonstrator mice but not in the immediate testing (Kogan et al., 1997). Interestingly, spaced training of the CREB mutants allowed them to overcome the impairments in fear conditioning, in spatial learning, and in the social transmission of food preferences (Kogan et al., 1997). This indicates that CREB is an important determinant of the number of trials, as well as of the intertrial interval, required to commit information to long-term memory.

Protein synthesis not only is essential for LTM but also is required for late long-term potentiation (L-LTP) (Frey, Krug, Reymann, & Matthies, 1988; Matthies, 1989; Stanton & Sarvey, 1984). LTP was measured in hippocampal slices of adult mice (~3–4 months) by stimulating Schaffer collaterals and recording field potentials in the stratum radiatum. LTP induced by a train of 100 pulses (250-μsec pulse width) at 100 Hz was stable for at least 2 hr in controls. In contrast, LTP returned to baseline levels within 1.5 hr in CREB mutants (Bourtchaladze et al., 1994). Thus, both LTP and memory seem to be unstable in these mutants, even though the time courses for the loss of LTP and memory are different. Nevertheless, it would be naive to expect that these two very different events, measured in two distinct preparations, should be synchronous. First, memory formation is likely to involve many aspects of hippocampal physiology other than just LTP. Second, the time course of LTP decay is affected by the conditions of the experiment, such as temperature, the type of tetanic stimulation, and other variables. Similarly, the rate of amnesia is affected also by the training, the type of test, and other behavioral variables.

Previous studies found that cAMP inhibitors caused a drastic decrease in LTP between 45 and 90 min posttetanus and that addition of cAMP agonists induced a potentiation within the first 90 min, both suggesting that a cAMP-dependent mechanism can affect LTP as early as 90 min after the tetanus (Frey, Huang, &

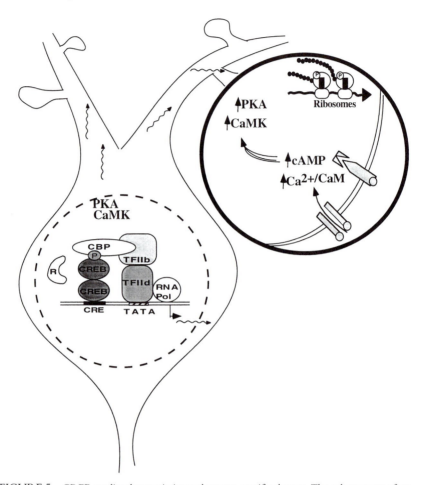

FIGURE 5   CREB-mediated transcription and synapse-specific changes. The enhancement of synaptic transmission leads to an increase in cAMP activating PKA and/or CaMK. In the nucleus, these kinases activate CREB by phosphorylation, resulting in the expression of genes containing Cre sites. These transcripts diffuse in the dendrites of the neuron but can only be translated in potentiated synapses. The very mechanisms that potentiate synapses may also activate the protein machinery needed to translate the mRNAs sent to the synapses (for review, see Silva & Giese, 1994; Steward & Banker, 1992).

Kandel, 1993). It is possible that this potentiation is protein synthesis dependent and that it requires CREB function (Fig. 5). Indeed, several studies have shown clear evidence of synthesis of new proteins as early as 20–30 min after tetanic stimulation (Feig & Lipton, 1993; Frey et al., 1993; Frey & Morris, 1997; Matthies, 1989). Furthermore, it has been shown that CRE-mediated transcription is induced after a tetanus evoking LTP (Deisseroth, Bito, & Tsien, 1996; Impey et al., 1996). These results are consistent with the hypothesis that the instability of LTP and the decay of memory in the mutants are dependent on the downregulation of a protein synthesis dependent phase of LTP and memory. The electrophysiological studies also showed that not all other aspects of synaptic function are affected in the mutants. For example, PPF and PTP do not appear to be changed by the CREB mutation (Bourtchuladze et al., 1994).

Curiously, at the offset of PTP (within 4 min of the tetanus), the level of synaptic potentiation in CREB mutants was lower than in the controls (Bourtchuladze et al., 1994). Nevertheless, CREB mutants show normal memory in the first 30 min posttraining. It is possible that in hippocampal pyramidal cells, CREB and the transcriptional machinery are often engaged in transcribing genes required for the later phases of LTP. Some of these proteins may be essential not only for the consolidation of long-term synaptic changes but also for earlier responses to tetanic stimulation. Thus, a chronic decrease in CREB may lead to the downregulation of the synaptic machinery that promotes and supports the later phases of LTP. Good molecular candidates for these processes are the components of the cAMP second-messenger system. For example, studies with antisense CREB oligonucleotides injected into the nucleus accumbens showed the expected decrease in CREB levels there but also a decrease in the levels of the catalytic subunits of PKA (Widnell et al., 1996). Interestingly, mutants lacking the βI catalytic subunit of PKA also show a late-phase deficit in LTP and lower synaptic responses immediately after the tetanus (Qi et al., 1996). Importantly, a weak tetanus that does not trigger the protein synthesis dependent phase of LTP induces responses of normal sizes in both the CREB (J. H. Kogan and A. J. Silva, unpublished data) and the PKA mutants (Qi et al., 1996). These results suggest that the mechanisms required for the late stages of LTP affect synaptic responses almost immediately after tetanic stimulation. The chronic decrease of CREB and PKA, presumably, affects the induction and maintenance of protein synthesis dependent LTP. Interestingly, transgenic mice expressing a mutant form of the regulatory subunit of PKA that inhibits PKA activity (R(AB)) also show long-term memory deficits (Abel et al., 1997). Short-term memory, however, is normal in these mutants. Consistent with the idea that LTP underlies memory, long-lasting LTP is specifically impaired in these transgenic mice (Abel et al., 1997).

It is noteworthy that studies in *Drosophila, Aplysia,* and mice—three widely divergent species—found evidence for a requirement for CREB in LTM processes. This strongly suggests that the insights into the molecular and electrophysiological mechanisms responsible for the LTM loss in CREB mutants might also be directly applicable to humans. Indeed, a dysfunction of CREB may account for the mental retardation observed in patients with Rubinstein–Taybi syndrome (Petrij et al., 1995).

It is important to stress that CREB is almost certainly not the only transcription factor modulating the induction of protein synthesis required for LTM, since CREB is known to function in association with other factors (for review, see Lee & Masson,

1993). Additionally, organismal memory cannot be explained purely in terms of transcriptional regulation. Instead, the CREB mutants have been valuable in unraveling the molecular cascade of events that are required to support memory formation. The chemistry of combustion is important to understand how a car engine works, but it does not explain the many complex engineering principles required for designing cars. The same is true for all of the molecular processes required to support learning and memory: they will be essential components of theories of learning and memory, but they will not in and of themselves explain these complex phenomena.

G. The Connection between LTP and Learning

The foregoing results indicate that second-messenger mechanisms involving cAMP and protein kinase A (PKA) are involved in learning and memory in a varietey of species, and they also indicate that they are involved in hippocampal plasticity. Gene-targeting experiments have generated mutants that lack either the β1 isoform of the catalytic subunit (CB1⁻) (Qi et al., 1996) or the β isoform of the inhibitory subunit (RIβ⁻) (Brandon et al., 1995). Surprisingly, both mutants lack CA3 LTP but have normal learning (Huang et al., 1995). An important consideration in interpreting these studies is that all LTP experiments were done *in vitro* in hippocampal slices.

Mossy fibers connect dentate gyrus granular cells with CA3 pyramidal neurons. These fibers are the output of the dentate gyrus within the hippocampal trisynaptic circuit, and consequently they have a prominent role in theories of hippocampal function (Treves and Rolls, 1994). LTP in this synapse is known to be NMDA receptor independent but seems to involve cAMP- and PKA-dependent intracellular signaling pathways (for reviews, see Martinez & Derrick, 1996; Nicoll & Malenka, 1995).

Electrophysiological analysis of the Schaffer collateral pathway into CA1 revealed normal 1-hr LTP in both of these PKA mutants (Brandon et al., 1995; Qi et al., 1996). However, in the Cβ1⁻ mutants LTP became unstable 1.5 hr after induction and appears to have decayed to near-baseline levels 3 hr later (Qi et al., 1996). In contrast, the LTP of controls as well as that of RIβ⁻ mice is stable for the duration of the experiments (200 min) (Brandon et al., 1995; Qi et al., 1996). The mutations did not affect all aspects of synaptic function, since basal synaptic transmission as well as PPF is normal in both mutants (Brandon et al., 1995; Qi et al., 1996).

The inability to find a learning or memory phenotype (despite a very extensive analysis) for these mutants is remarkable because the effects on hippocampal electrophysiology go beyond LTP. Both mutants also show a loss of LTD and LTP depotentiation in the CA1 region (Brandon et al., 1995; Qi et al., 1996). LTD triggered with 900 pulses (1 Hz) delivered to either naive or potentiated synapses, is severely impaired in these two mutants. Studies with RIβ⁻ mice found that LTD triggered with the same protocol is also blocked in the perforant path–dentate gyrus synapse

(Brandon et al., 1995). Additionally, mGluR2-deficient mice are impaired in mossy fiber LTD but have no learning impairments (Yokoi et al., 1996). The very theoretical reasons that make LTP a compelling learning mechanism also apply to LTD. LTD-like phenomena are thought to have an enormous impact on the storage capacity of neuronal networks and on fine-tuning synaptic weights during performance optimization.

Mice lacking the tissue plasminogen activator (tPA) are impaired in homosynaptic long-lasting LTP but are normal in hippocampal-dependent learning (Frey, Müller, & Kuhl, 1996; Huang et al., 1996). Under certain conditions, however, a GABA-dependent potentiation can compensate for the loss of long-lasting LTP (Frey et al., 1996), which may explain the normal hippocampal-dependent learning of the tPA-deficient mice.

These studies seriously question the model that long-term synaptic changes; (LTP/LTD) are central to learning and memory. However, it is important to emphasize that the measurements of LTP/LTD were done in hippocampal slices and that the mutations did not completely block LTP. Although tetanically induced CA3 LTP appears to be completely absent in both PKA mutants, agents that increase the levels of cAMP (forskolin and IBMX) in these synapses can induce an LTP-like potentiation (Huang et al., 1995). This potentiation has properties similar to LTP, and it can even occlude further induction of LTP. Curiously, these agents are thought to increase the concentration of cAMP, the activator of PKA, suggesting that biochemical events downstream of cAMP generation are not completely disrupted in the two PKA mutants. Perhaps the remaining isoforms of PKA in the mutants are less sensitive to cAMP. Since the deficit is not complete, certain conditions *in vivo* may be able to override the electrophysiological deficits of these two mutants, just as treatment with forskolin and IBMX seemed to override the LTP deficits in the mossy fiber of the mutants. This may explain why behavioral studies with the Morris water maze, Barnes maze, and contextual conditioning did not detect any deficits in either mutant.

Nevertheless, it is possible that similar LTP/LTD deficits are also observed *in vivo* and that these phenomena are not essential for learning. Perhaps consistent with this interpretation, mice mutant for a neuronal glycoprotein Thy-1 show abnormal dentate gyrus LTP (both *in vivo* and in slices) but normal learning in the water maze (Nosten-Bertrand et al., 1996). The LTP deficit seems to be due to abnormally high inhibition mediated by $GABA_A$ receptors. When this inhibition is removed by adding bicuculline, an antagonist of $GABA_A$ receptors, LTP can be induced normally in these mutants. The authors claim that this result shows that LTP in the dentate gyrus is not required for performance in the Morris water maze.

Alternatively, the increase in inhibition may not affect the naturally induced LTP the same way that it affects the artificially induced LTP. Septal inputs into the hippocampus are thought to drive oscillations in hippocampal inhibition (for review, see Bland, 1986). Natural LTP may be synchronized to the point in these oscillations where inhibition is lowest. Thus, the enhancement in inhibition in these mutants may not affect the natural potentiation that is thought to accompany learning, but it may completely block the induction of LTP *in vivo* or in slices.

The problems with the interpretation of these experiments illustrate the need to understand the circuit events that surround natural LTP induction. Without insight into these events, it will be very hard to interpret data concerning the relation between LTP lesions and learning. Additionally, the connection between LTP and learning will be strengthened not only by additional LTP–learning experiments but also by experiments designed to elucidate other aspects of hippocampal function that may also participate in the cellular and circuit events required for learning (see the following).

Results from gene-targeting experiments are not alone in questioning the tenuous association between LTP and learning. There are also several pharmacological experiments that have challenged this hypothesis. Ironically, the first and most elegant series of experiments that shed a great deal of doubt on the connection between LTP and learning is often quoted as the best support for the hypothesis. Rats were given a series of concentrations of a blocker of NMDA receptors (APV), and *in vivo* LTP experiments as well as behavioral tests were performed on the same animals (Davis et al., 1992). With increasing concentrations of the NMDA receptor blocker, the impairment of LTP and the learning deficit also became more exacerbated, a result that is generally thought to be consistent with the LTP–learning hypothesis.

However, at concentrations of APV sufficient to block all of the measurable LTP, the animals were still able to learn to search for the platform in a highly selective manner (Davis et al., 1992). In a probe trial at the end of training in the water maze, these animals without LTP (and presumably without LTD, since APV blocks both at the same concentrations) still search selectively for the platform. This is more remarkable considering that APV may have severe neurological effects. Under NMDA blockers animals can become uncoordinated, they tend to swim over and fall off the platform, and they have several other behavioral impairments which may include hyperactivity, ataxia, catalepsy, and stereotypy. Consistent with this interpretation, a recent study has shown that rats pretrained in the maze did not show the learning impairments associated with APV (Cain et al., 1996). The pretraining did not include spatial training and simply exposed the rats to the maze, supposedly ameliorating the sensory, emotional, and motor impairments caused by APV. An important caveat of these experiments is that NMDA receptor dependent LTP is only one of several forms of LTP present in the hippocampus, and consequently it is possible that other forms of LTP are unaffected by the APV treatments.

For each of the foregoing genetic and pharmacological experiments, there are important considerations that question whether the results really dissociate LTP from learning. Nevertheless, similar caveats also exist in experiments (some of which were reviewed here) that argue for a role of LTP in learning. The simplest form of the hypothesis, that learning is completely and solely mediated by changes in LTP that can be measured reliably in brain slices, is rejected by these results. But if changes in LTP are not responsible for learning and memory, then what is? How can we falsify an idea without having competing alternatives? These are a few of the many problems that a combination of genetic and pharmacological manipulations may resolve in the next few years.

H. SLP and Learning

Besides the use of genetics to test the widely held hypothesis that there is an important connection between LTP and learning, genetics can be used to uncover novel mechanisms. Such discoveries may reveal new possibilities that may enrich the range of physiologies included in theories of learning and memory. An example of this is short-lived plasticity.

Studies with a variety of organisms suggest that short-lived plasticity might endow circuits with the ability to adapt quickly to changing environments. For example, short-term decreases in synaptic efficacy seem to underlie habituation to repeated stimuli, such as habituation of the gill-withdrawal response in *Aplysia* (Castellucci, Pinsker, Kupfermann, & Kandel, 1970) and the habituation of escape responses in vertebrate and invertebrate species (Auerbach & Bennet, 1969; Zilber-Gachelin & Chariter, 1973; Zucker, 1972). Abnormal short-term plasticity was found in the neuromuscular junction of *Drosophila* learning mutants (Zhong & Wu, 1991). These results suggest the possibility that short-lived plasticity could play a role in learning even in the central nervous system.

Short-lived plasticity (SLP) has also been included in computational models of neuronal function (Buonomano and Merzenich, 1995; Little & Shaw, 1975). With elements of SLP, a continuous-time neuronal network model was able to discriminate different temporal patterns, suggesting that time-dependent synaptic properties may enable networks to transform temporal information into a spatial code, a critical element in many forms of learning (Buonomano and Merzenich, 1995). Taken together, these studies suggest that SLP is not simply a byproduct of the complex regulation of longer lasting changes in synaptic strength but that it may have a significant role of its own in information processing. The availability of mutants with normal long-term potentiation (LTP) but abnormal SLP allowed the testing of this hypothesis.

Mice heterozygous for a null mutation of the α-calcium-calmodulin kinase II (αCaMKII$^{+/-}$) (Chapman et al., 1995; Silva, Stevens, Tonegawa, & Wang, 1992), mice lacking synapsin II (SyII$^{-/-}$) (Rosahl et al., 1995), and synapsin I/II mutants (SyI/II$^{-/-}$) (Rosahl et al., 1995; Spillane, Rosahl, Südhof, & Malenka, 1995) have abnormal hippocampal PTP, although studies of LTP revealed no abnormalities in these mutants (Table II). Remarkably, all these mutants show marked impairments in hippocampal-dependent learning, as measured by contextual conditioning and the water maze (Silva et al., 1996). In contrast, the loss of only synapsin I (SyI$^{-/-}$) (Li et al., 1995; Rosahl et al., 1993, 1995), which affects PPF but not PTP, does not

TABLE II   Summary of the Analysis of Four Mouse Mutants Having No Impairments in Long-Term Synaptic Changes but Being Affected in Short-Term Synaptic Changes in the Hippocampal CA1 Region[a]

Mutant	PPF	PTP	LTD	LTP	Learning
αCaMKII$^{+/-}$	↓	↑	OK	OK	↓
Synapsin II$^{-/-}$	OK	↓	OK	OK	↓
Synapsin I/II$^{-/-}$	OK	↓	OK	OK	↓
Synapsin I$^{-/-}$	↑	OK	OK	OK	OK

[a]Comparing the changes in hippocampus-dependent learning with the changes in short-term plasticity, it can be suggested that changes in PTP lead to learning impairments. Arrow down, decreased or impaired; arrow up, increased.

affect learning in a number of tasks and conditions used (Silva et al., 1996). Taken together, these results suggest that hippocampal PTP is involved in learning.

These four kinds of mutant mice lack key presynaptic proteins that are known to affect the regulation of neurotransmitter release (Chapman et al., 1995; Greengard, Valtorta, Czernik, & Benfenati, 1993; Rosahl et al., 1993, 1995). It is noteworthy that the electrophysiological changes detected in the mutant mice were very specific and that hippocampal CA1 LTP seemed unaffected in all of these mutants. The loss of synapsin II also does not affect LTP in the mossy fiber pathway of the hippocampus even though it does disrupt PTP there (Spillane et al., 1995). Importantly, SyII$^{-/-}$, SyI/II$^{-/-}$, and αCaMKII$^{+/-}$ mutants with abnormal PTP show learning deficits, whereas the increase in PPF in SyI$^{-/-}$ mutants does not seem to affect learning.

The SyII$^{-/-}$ and the SyI/II$^{-/-}$ mice show a decrease in PTP, whereas the αCaMKII$^{+/-}$ mutants reveal an increase in PTP. In this respect, it is noteworthy that there are also differences between their performances in the learning tests: the αCaMKII$^{+/-}$ mutants show a fast decrease of freezing responses during cued and contextual conditioning, whereas the SyII$^{-/-}$ and the SyI/II$^{-/-}$ mice do not. Instead, the SyII$^{-/-}$ and the SyI/II$^{-/-}$ mice both show a gradual increase in contextual freezing throughout the 5 min of testing. This intriguing difference in behavior may parallel the opposite effects of the mutations on PTP.

Importantly, these mutants do not have general deficits in brain morphology and synaptic connectivity, have normal life expectancies, have normal nociception, and show no hints of ataxia (Comery et al., 1994; Li et al., 1995; Rosahl et al., 1993, 1995; Silva, Stevens, Tonegawa, & Wang, 1992). Some of the mutants can have seizures, and these may confound the interpretation of the learning results. However, a comparison between the seizure severity (Rosahl et al., 1995) and the learning deficits in these four mutants does not support the hypothesis that seizures are the cause for the learning deficits: First, SyI$^{-/-}$ and SyII$^{-/-}$ mutants have similar behavioral seizure frequencies (Rosahl et al., 1995), but only SyII$^{-/-}$ mutants show abnormal learning. Despite their increased neuronal excitability and seizure propensity (Li et al., 1995; Rosahl et al., 1995), the SyI$^{-/-}$ mice showed normal learning and memory in an extensive analysis of both fear conditioning and water maze tests. Furthermore, behavioral observations did not detect any seizures in the αCaMKII$^{+/-}$ mutant mice tested (Silva et al., 1996).

These studies open up the possibility that short-lived plasticities are involved in learning. These brief but highly dynamic changes in synaptic strength are extremely sensitive to a neuron's recent history of activation, to the architecture of circuits, and to brainwide modulatory mechanisms (Zucker, 1989). Thus, it is likely that SLP could have a role in information processing, modifying, filtering, and integrating information as it flows through neuronal networks. It is important to note that the potential involvement of SLP in learning does not exclude LTP. Indeed, these two mechanisms may have complementary functions, both contributing to the complex set of events that allow an animal to learn and remember.

VI. GENETICS: CONCERNS AND CRITIQUES

All methods have advantages and disadvantages, and certainly gene targeting and other genetic techniques are no exception. It is crucial to define the scientific questions that this technology will be able to address and the kinds of experiments that it will be useful for. Often some of the "disadvantages" of a particular technology or approach stem from experiments or interpretations that overstep its scope and applicability. For example, gene targeting may never be able to determine the behavioral function of specific genes because, as we pointed out, the idea that single proteins have a behavioral function may be meaningless.

Single mutations have effects (often very specific) on behavior, but this does not mean that single genes have specific behavioral functions. It is virtually impossible to separate, and unambiguously identify, the contributions of single proteins within the myriad of complex events involved in any one behavior. In contrast, it can be straightforward to identify deficits brought about by the loss of a single protein.

Despite the difficulty with assigning organismal function to genes, the history of modern biology has demonstrated repeatedly the usefulness of genetic approaches. Therefore, there is no reason to believe that neuroscientists will be any less adept at using this powerful experimental tool than developmental biologists, immunologists, plant biologists, etc. For all of its wonder, the brain is a biological organ with genes, proteins, cells, etc., and thus genetics should be useful in unraveling its mysteries, as recent data show.

The main advantages of this methodology are (i) any cloned gene can be deleted or modified, key functional domains may be targeted, and technology under development will allow temporal and regional control over the mutations; (ii) the mutations are defined precisely; (iii) the mutant animals only have to be derived once, and they can be easily shared with other investigators (the availability of the mutant mice can foster interdisciplinary studies, a crucial aspect of integrating information from different levels of hierarchical complexity; (iv) genetic analysis may complement pharmacological manipulations of biological function (convergent results are extremely persuasive); and finally (v) the study of mutants allows both system- and component-level analysis (the integration of these will be crucial for developing explanations of learning; for example, without understanding synaptic function, it may be impossible to determine whether Hebbian-like mechanisms are implemented during learning). Nevertheless there are several critical issues that if left unaddressed can seriously compromise the usefulness of this approach. The following is a discussion of key problems and criticisms as well as possible solutions.

A. Compensatory Effects by Other Genes

It is an incontestable fact that single mutations lead to an avalanche of compensatory effects by other genes, and thus it is impossible to connect the function of a single gene with any given phenotype observed. However, this is only a problem if the approach is misused. Genetics cannot be used to determine the behavioral function of a protein, but it can be used to determine the electrophysiological, neuroanatomical, and behavioral changes brought about by a mutation. Proteins function in highly dynamic networks of cells and tissues, and therefore it is difficult to make direct correlations between a protein and any higher order function in an organism. This is true for any methodology, not just gene targeting. Pharmacological interventions, for example, trigger an immediate cascade of changes, some of which are only indirectly connected with the component modified. Thus, it is difficult to assert, and perhaps meaningless, that the behavioral changes observed in the animal are due to the specific alteration in the function of the targeted component.

Proteins have biochemical functions that can be studied and characterized as individual biophysical entities. Thus, kinases add phosphate groups to molecules, phosphatases remove them, etc. The function of a protein is only accurately defined at the molecular level. The further the functional descriptions depart from the biochemistry involved, the more inaccurate they are likely to be. Once again, the reason is simple: molecular processes, cells, and organisms are highly complex, dynamic, and adaptive. This complexity creates webs of interrelated functions that make the role of each component ambiguous and hard to test.

Early genetic studies used the idea of organismal functions of single genes as a useful simplification. However, with the ever growing number of possible experimental manipulations, the complexity of these functions also grows, and it became obvious that the function of a single protein depends on the state of many other proteins working in the same cellular process. For this reason geneticists and pharmacologists alike learned always to do their experiments in the same strain of animals, since the genetic makeup of a strain can affect the impact of the pharmacological or genetic manipulation profoundly.

Despite these apparent "problems," it is clear that genetics has had an enormous impact in modern biology. This is becasue its role has not been to assign function to genes but to yield insights into the molecular processes underlying complex biological phenomena such as development. Nevertheless, simplifications are useful, and very often they represent faithfully the current relevant knowledge. As our knowledge base and techniques change, we should also change our models and simplifying assumptions.

This is the reason why the emphasis should not be placed on the function of particular genes and proteins. Instead, it may be more feasible to point to the functions of a process or a set of processes. Processes are carried out by groups of proteins, and they encompass a defined cellular function, such as synaptic plasticity, intrinsic excitability, transcriptional regulation, or some other function. Although different processes are closely interconnected in cells, they retain some degree of functional independence. For example, not all changes in synaptic function affect the intrinsic excitability of cells, or their transcription regulation, even though some synaptic mechanisms certainly do. Additionally, individual cellular processes only share a minority of their components with any one other process. This uniqueness is the reason for their relative functional independence within cells. Deleting or altering the function of a protein may completely disrupt one cellular process while leaving others relatively unaffected. Although distinct processes may share molecular components, the degree of redundancy for any one component may be different. Consequently, some components may be critical for a key cellular process, which could account for the varying severity of mutant phenotypes.

B. Genetic Background Effects

The effects of a mutation not only are the result of the mutated gene but also reflect other unknown mutations in the background. Proteins do not work alone but rather in large biochemical complexes and cascades, where the importance of each step is directly dependent on many other simultaneous molecular events. Many of the concepts reviewed in previous sections of this chapter also apply here. The fact that the impact of a mutation can be affected by other "silent" mutations elsewhere is a phenomenon well understood in genetics. There are even experiments that take advantage of this to manipulate the phenotype. As mentioned earlier, even pharmacological experiments have to control carefully for the genetic background of the animals used.

Thus, genetic background has to be carefully controlled as much as any other experimental variable. The simplest way to do this is to derive the mutation in a specific genetic background and maintain it there during breeding. This is common practice in most genetic studies with yeast, *Drosophila, C. elegans,* etc. By maintaining mutations in a homogeneous background, it is easier to study and cross-correlate different phenotypes, because the mutation is the only significant variable.

Heterogeneous genetic backgrounds introduce other genetic variables that are hard to control for. For example, two independent studies of mice deficient for the prion protein found different electrophysiological phenotypes (Collinge et al., 1994; Lledo, Tremblay, DeArmond, Prusiner, & Nicoll, 1996). This difference could be due to the genetic background of the animals studied.

The problem that was encountered in early gene-targeting studies of learning and memory is that the ES cells available were from the 129/Sv background. These cells were not derived specifically for behavioral studies, and unfortunately the 129/Sv mice just happen to perform poorly in hippocampal-dependent behavioral tasks. This forced researchers to transfer the mutations derived onto a background that performed normally in the behavioral tasks used.

Transferring a mutation to another strain by breeding is time-consuming, and it is not completely effective, since the region immediately around the targeted gene cannot easily be exchanged by sequences of the new line (Fig. 6) (Gerlai, 1996). Although the rest of the genome is freely exchanged during crosses into the other line, DNA around the targeted locus is not because the presence of the mutation is selected for. Inevitably, the region around the targeted locus is also carried along. The problem is that this region can be considerably large. Even after 12 crosses, which take more than 2 years to make, as many as 300–400 genes may be carried along with the targeted locus. Many of the random mutations in these genes may be simple substitutions for equivalent amino acids, but there may also be mutations that could affect the phenotype of the original mutants. This is a special problem because the control mice do not preserve this region, since it is not selected for during breeding.

Genetic background also affects the amount of variability among individuals of the population studied. Studying mutations in populations of clonal individuals (isogenic) reduces but does not eliminate variability. Technically, this would mean either that the mutant chimeras should be mated with mice of the same strain as that used to derive the embryonic stem (ES) cells or that the mutant mice should be continuously crossed with another appropriate inbred strain until the mutation is completely transferred to the new background.

However, the particular genetic background chosen (i.e., C57BL/6) may have a number of naturally occurring mutations that synergize with the targeted mutation, so that the phenotype of the mutant is primarily due to the particular interaction between the targeted mutation and the specific mutations in the genetic background of the animals used. This synergism may obscure the contribution of the targeted mutation to the phenotype and may result in a very distorted evaluation of the effects of a particular mutation.

Alternatively, the effects of the mutation can also be studied in a heterogeneous background. Since most mutations in inbred strains are known to be recessive, their effects can be avoided in mice that are first-generation (F1) offspring of parents from unrelated strains. These mice are heterozygous at all alleles, which results in the elimination of many of the recessive mutations segregating in either parent strain.

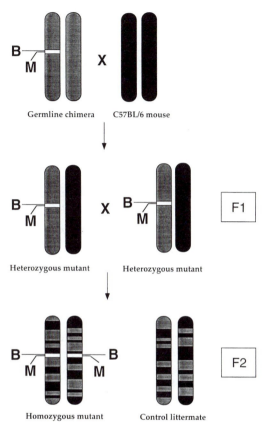

FIGURE 6   Genetic background. The most commonly used breeding strategy for obtaining homozygous mutants is illustrated in this figure. For simplicity just one pair of chromosomes is shown.
Germline chimeras having the desired mutation (M) in the 129/Sv background are mated with C57BL/6
mice to obtain heterozygous mutants (F1 generation). By intercrossing the heterozygous mutants, the
homozygous mutants and the control littermates are obtained (F2 generation). During this breeding step
recombination takes place, leading to a random exchange of chromosomal parts from the C57BL/6 and
the 129/Sv genomes. However, several genes in proximity to the mutation are linked with the mutation
(white band) and these are from the 129/Sv background. In contrast, in control littermates the corresponding genes are from the C57BL/6 background. It is known that 129/Sv mice have poor learning
behavior in comparison to C57BL/6 mice. One could assume that a mutation B, in the linked region,
is responsible for this difference in behavior. In this case, it could be that the observed behavioral
phenotype is actually due to the mutation B and not due to the desired mutation M. However, the
probability for such an event is extremely low.

The problem with this scheme is that it is difficult to generate homozygotes in
F1 crosses because this requires that the mutation be transferred into two inbred
lines. In summary, many laboratories are considering studying mutations in either

isogenic backgrounds or F1 mice that are the progeny between two strains, such as C57BL/6 and 129/Sv.

Genetic background can also be used as a tool, since it affects the phenotype of the mutation. Therefore, it may be used to test and extend the connections between cell physiology and systems function in the mutants. For example, studies of mice heterozygous for the αCaMKII (αCaMKII$^{+/-}$) in a BALBc/129 genetic background showed that these mice have the offensive postures and aggressiveness characteristic of resident males when placed in another male's home cage (Chen et al., 1994). In contrast, in their own home cage they are not any more aggressive to other male intruders than control mice. This could be due to a loss of fear responses in the mutants, since the intruder is normally intimidated in another male's territory. Interestingly, in this BALBc/129 genetic background these mice show no apparent fear responses (freezing) in either cued or contextual fear conditioning tasks.

However, in a C57BL/6 genetic background these same mutants show cued but not contextual fear conditioning (Silva et al., 1996), demonstrating that their inability to perform normally in contextual conditioning cannot be explained solely by a loss of fear responses, since they can be fear conditioned to a sound. Contextual, but not cued, conditioning requires hippocampal function. Studies in the water maze confirmed that these animals can perform well in the hippocampal-independent version of the task but not in the spatial, hippocampal-dependent version (Silva et al., 1996). These results suggest an alternative interpretation of the resident–intruder experiments summarized in the preceding paragraph: the αCaMKII$^{+/-}$ mice may not be able to distinguish between their own and another male's cage, therefore always assuming the offensive postures characteristic of host males. These results show that these mutants have learning impairments and that these learning impairments could be a factor in their abnormal aggressive behavior in another male's home cage.

Differences between genetic backgrounds can also be used to facilitate the analysis of the mutant mice. The loss of the α and δ CREB isoforms is lethal in the C57BL/6 background but not in a 129/C57BL/6 background (J. H. Kogan and A. J. Silva, unpublished observations). In some backgrounds the effects of a given mutation may not result in a lethal phenotype, but it may cause large behavioral and/or electrophsiological abnormalities that are hard to study because of their lack of specificity. This is the case with the loss of synapsin I in mutants, which with increasing number of crosses into the C57BL/6 background become more and more epileptic. In contrast, this mutation results in less epilepsy in the 129/C57BL/6 background.

It is now feasible to identify and clone the gene or genes in the genetic background that modify (genetic modifiers) the effects of a mutation of interest. The identification of these genes may yield important information on the biochemical and cellular processes affected by the mutation.

Despite the justifiable concerns with issues of genetic background, it has not been a problem in many of the studies to date because the mutation has been studied in different backgrounds and by independent manipulations. For example, the αCaMKII studies involved heterozygotes, homozygotes, and mice expressing a mutant form of the transgene. The results are also consistent with pharmacological studies that used peptide inhibitors. The key results of the CREB studies were confirmed with genetic and pharmacological studies in *Aplysia* and *Drosophila*. The complexity of nature and the inadequacy of most scientific methods are such that only strong theories and convergent evidence can help us to distinguish between experimental noise and natural phenomena.

C. The Impact of Unknown Effects

Unknown physiological or environmental effects and other miscellaneous factors could affect a mutant phenotype. Indeed, the complexity of the brain is such that it is extremely difficult to determine all possible consequences of any one manipulation on the many facets of brain function. Similarly, it is also very difficult to eliminate all possible sources of artifacts that plague every experimental method. The tools that we use in science are only partially specific, they are often incompletely effective, and very often they alter drastically the very phenomenon that we intend to study. For example, whole-cell patch recordings result in large holes in cells that dialyze cytoplasmic contents, pharmacological agents are never completely specific to the intended target, neuroanatomical lesions are notorious for their nonselective effects, *in vivo* recordings injure the very cell neighborhood being recorded from and are prone to a number of artifacts, behavioral observations are inextricably linked to biases related to the apparatus, the observer, and the history of the animal, etc. Nevertheless, we use these powerful approaches because they continue to give us valuable insights into the function of the nervous system and because we learn to work within their limitations. In this respect, genetics is no exception.

For any experiment in science there are obvious immediate variables that are controlled for and there is another, more difficult set of variables that is harder to control because their importance often goes unnoticed because of their apparent irrelevance to the experiment. This is true for gene targeting as well as for all other experimental approaches. In essence there is no general solution to this problem, other than the use of the utmost care in the design and interpretation of experiments. Much effort is being expended by many transgenic laboratories to make this methodology as specific and as controllable as possible. It is interesting that many of the problematic issues that have been suggested to possibly affect the interpretation of genetic studies of learning and memory are not specific to only this young field but are issues that are relevant to all of biology, if not to all of science. One of the many fortunate aspects of being in a new field is that the discussions and debates that are critical for its evaluation often force us to reflect not only on the power and problems of the approach but also on the very essence of science in general. With time the issues are resolved, the new approach finds its niche in the scientific community, the debate subsides, and very often the limitations and caveats are forgotten. This is unfortunate because the debate often fuels the change required to overcome some of the problems and limitations.

D. Developmental Effects

One of the problems of genetic studies of learning and memory is that many molecular components of adult brain function, such as the NMDA receptor, are also known to play critical roles during development (Li, Erzurumlu, Chen, Jhaveri, & Tonegawa, 1994; Forrest et al., 1994). Thus, disrupting or modifying these genes may produce changes in development that could confound studies of adult function. The study of the *fyn* mutants illustrates this problem (Grant et al., 1992). The *fyn* mutation seems to affect programmed cell death in certain tissues, including the dentate gyrus and pyramidal cell of CA3. As a result of the greater cell numbers, the *fyn* mutants have abnormally undulated hippocampal cell layers. This structural change complicates the interpretation of the LTP and learning deficits of these mutants. Reintroducing the missing gene product into adult *fyn* mutant slices (with a virus vector or with protein injections) could rescue the LTP deficit, thus excluding developmental changes as the cause for this deficit. For example, the hippocampal LTP deficits of mice deficient for the brain-derived neurotrophic factor (BDNF) were rescued either with recombinant protein or with a viral vector encoding this peptide (Korte et al., 1996; Patterson et al., 1996).

Since developmental and adult plasticity have many common features, insights into developmental processes may shed light into adult mechanisms. For example, there is a critical period after birth when neuronal activity shapes the connectivity of neurons in the visual cortex, just as experience is thought to change synaptic connections during learning. The recent characterization of plasticity in the mouse visual cortex (Gordon & Stryker, 1996) permits the use of mutant mice to investigate the cellular mechanisms underlying activity-dependent changes in the mouse visual cortex.

As calcium-dependent signaling pathways have been implicated in neuronal plasticity, αCaMKII homozygous and heterozygous mutants have been used in studies of neocortical plasticity (Gordon et al., 1996). In wild-type mice, brief occlusion of vision in one eye during a critical period (between 20 and 50 days postnatally) reduces responses in the visual cortex to stimuli presented to the deprived eye. These studies found that the homozygous mutants have reduced plasticity following monocular deprivation. Depriving one eye of visual input for 6 days strongly inhibits the responses in the visual cortex to inputs from this eye in controls but not in mutants. Interestingly, LTD and LTP are also strongly impaired in the visual cortex of homozygous αCaMKII mutants. In contrast with the homozygous mutants, heterozygous mutants with deficits in short-term plasticity and learning showed normal neocortical visual plasticity. It is important to note that despite impaired plasticity, the homozygous mice have normal visual receptive fields (size and location), ocular dominance, orientation selectivity, and single-unit response strength. Thus, the deficit in plasticity is not due to deficits in the organization, structure, or basic properties of the neocortex.

These αCaMKII mutants were also used in similar studies in the somatosensory cortex (Glazewski et al., 1996). The mammalian sensory cortex shows experience-dependent plasticity so that neurons modify their responses according to changes in sensory experience. Plasticity in adult mice can be induced by changes in the patterns of stimulation to the barrel neocortex. Unlike the visual cortex, where there is a narrow critical period for plasticity, the somatosensory cortex shows plasticity during the adult life of the animal. These plastic responses were found to be compromised in adult homozygotes (more than 3 months old) but, surprisingly, not in young homozygotes (less than 2 months old). In contrast, control animals of both age groups reveal robust plasticity. Once again, these studies showed that the general properties of the neocortex of the mutants (topography, responsiveness, etc.) were unchanged by the mutation.

Taken together, these results demonstrate that this kinase is required for adult neocortical plasticity and that similar mechanisms may underlie the learning and the neocortical (somatosensory and visual) plasticity deficits. Nevertheless, these results raise the possibility that the hippocampal deficits described for the homozygous mutants may be due to changes in the plasticity of the neocortex.

Fortunately, there are mutations that do not seem to affect developmental mechanisms but that do disrupt learning and memory. One such example is the heterozygous αCaMKII mutation, which has a profound effect on hippocampal-dependent learning but no measurable impact on neocortical plasticity.

Methods being developed might partly circumvent the developmental effects of these mutations by restricting them to adult animals. However, even these approaches might not entirely get around all of the potential complications. Unfortunately, even the most sophisticated research techniques interfere with the subject, and only theory distinguishes between experimental artifact and authentic natural phenomena. Clearly, gene disruptions are no exception, and extreme care must be taken in interpreting the complex effects of the mutations. Nevertheless, the study of the null mutants is only the first step in this genetic approach. Eventually, only a strong model can inject meaning into phenomena and thus transfigure the messy complexity of empirical observations into the aesthetically compelling simplicity of scientific "fact."

VII. THE NEAR FUTURE

In addition to adding and removing genes, domains, or even amino acids of interest, it is now feasible to restrict the mutations to particular tissues and to a particular time of choice. Advances in techniques must also be accompanied by advances in the analytical methods used to study the mice. Gene-targeting studies of learning and memory started with behavioral studies that were mostly restricted to the water maze. Now, a number of other tests have been used, including the Barnes maze, cued and contextual conditioning, social transmission of food preference, active and passive avoidance, and olfactory learning tests. As the repertoire of behavioral paradigms has expanded, so has the number of electrophysiological tests used in studies of mutant mice. Many of the initial studies were restricted to studies of synaptic plasticity in field and single-cell recordings from the CA1 region of hippocampal slices. However, recent studies have included all of the other major hippocampal synapses, including the interesting mossy fiber synapse, the amygdala, and the neocortex, as well as *in vivo* electrophysiological recordings.

Nevertheless there is a very large gulf between electrophysiological recordings and animal behavior. Finding important connections between those two levels will be crucial for neuroscience in general and for the development of this field in particular. Therefore, current work in the field has turned to the development of imaging techniques and to the use of single-unit studies in the analysis of mouse mutants. By determining the series of deficits caused by the mutation at each of these different levels of hierarchical complexity, it will be possible to start to connect these events into explanations of learning and memory. Perhaps this rich plethora of findings will motivate modelers to devise theoretical frameworks that can accommodate these findings. Very soon our ability to collect interesting data will far outstrip our ability to interpret it and to frame these observations into coherent theories of learning and memory. In this field, as in other fields of neuroscience, collaboration between theoretical and experimental neuroscientists is essential.

A. Inducible and Tissue-Specific KOs

It is clear that the ability to carefully control the time and place of a mutation would help to address many of the concerns some neuroscientists have with the use of genetics. This is not to say, however, that the experiments done so far are vitiated. This chapter has summarized many of the significant contributions that the techniques now in use have made to the understanding of learning and memory. Instead, new developments will allow novel manipulations that were not possible with the older methods.

Current methodologies cannot control for the onset of the mutation. Thus, in some cases there are developmental effects that complicate the interpretation of the experiments. In other cases the mutant animals cannot be derived because the mutation is lethal. For example, the complete loss of the NMDAR1 is lethal (Li et al., 1994; Forrest et al., 1994), so it is impossible to study the adult implication of this mutation. Conditional gene targeting can restrict genetic modifications to certain regions and cell types and to specific times chosen by the investigator

(Gu, Marth, Orban, Mossmann, & Rajewsky, 1994; Kühn, Schwenk, Aguet, & Rajewsky, 1995).

A strategy based on the bacteriophage P1 derived Cre/loxP recombination system has been developed for the restricted inactivation of genes in the mouse. The Cre recombinase recognizes loxP sites and specifically excises the loxP-flanked gene segment from the genome (for review, see Sauer, 1993). Thus, to delete a gene it would be sufficient to flank it with loxP sites. These sites are 34-base-pair sequences of DNA recognized by the Cre recombinase. The active Cre then deletes any DNA between the two loxP sites. The Cre system was first applied in the mouse to the manipulation of transgenes. For example, Cre expression regulated by the αCaMKII promoter was used to delete a stop sequence from a reporter gene (Tsien et al., 1996). Deletion of this sequence activated the reporter gene in specific brain regions. The activation of the reporter gene varied in different mouse lines due to position effects on the activity of the αCaMKII promoter. Interestingly, in some mouse lines the reporter gene was only activated in the CA1 region of the hippocampus. Taking advantage of a mouse line expressing Cre recombinase predominantly in the hippocampal CA1 region, Tsien, Huerta, and Tonegawa (1996) were able to delete the NMDAR1 gene in this area. These mutants lack CA1 LTP and have spatial learning deficits in the Morris water maze, enhancing the connection between LTP and spatial learning.

The Cre system ensures that only loxP-flanked genes are deleted, but it does not control the time of the deletion itself. To do that the activity of the Cre recombinase has to be regulated (Fig. 7). The function of Cre can be turned on and off if this recombinase is fused to the ligand-binding domain of steroid receptors (LBD) (Zhang et al., 1996). When the ligand is unavailable, the Cre is off, and it is turned on by the presence of the ligand. However, the widespread distribution of steroids in the brain complicates this strategy, because the natural steroids could activate the Cre at inappropriate times.

To avoid this complication, a mutant form of the ligand-binding domain was built that does not bind endogenous steroids. Instead, this mutant protein only binds certain ligands that can be injected in mice at chosen times. The activity of such a fusion between LBD and Cre is not regulated at the transcriptional level but via its intracellular location. In the absence of the hormone, the LBD/Cre protein is inactive because it is bound to heat-shock proteins that have a natural affinity to inactive steroid receptors. Ligand binding changes the conformation of the receptor, which frees it from heat-shock proteins and allows the fusion protein to enter the nucleus and promote the loxP-guided gene deletion.

The fusion of proteins with LBDs has been shown to efficiently regulate the activity of protein kinases and transcription factors, including Gal4 and VP16, in mammalian cells (for review, see Picard, 1993). In the presence of estradiol a fusion protein between a recombinase and the human estrogen receptor was shown to rapidly delete a loxP-flanked DNA segment integrated in the genome of a human cell line. No such deletion was found in the absence of hormone. Similar to natural

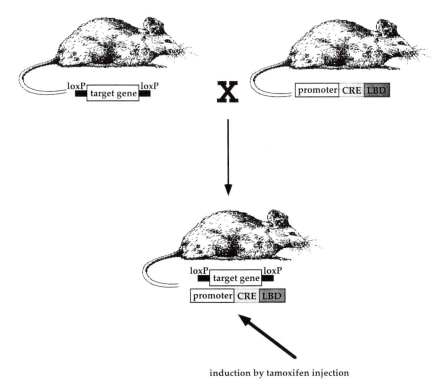

induction by tamoxifen injection

FIGURE 7   Inducible KO via the regulation of a fusion protein. A transgenic mouse expresses a fusion protein, consisting of Cre recombinase (CRE) and the ligand-binding domain (LBD) of a steroid receptor, under the control of a certain promoter. In the absence of an appropriate ligand, the Cre recombinase is not active. This transgenic mouse is mated with a mouse having the target gene flanked by loxP sites. The resulting mouse is an inducible KO mouse. In the cells where the transgene is expressed, the Cre recombinase can be activated after injection of the proper ligand, such as tamoxifen, into the mouse. The active Cre recombinase recognizes there the loxP sites surrounding the target gene and excises the target gene from the genome.

ligands, synthetic hormone antagonists, such as tamoxifen, can also free the steroid receptor LBDs from the heat-shock proteins. Estrogen and progesterone receptor mutants have been isolated that are unable to bind their natural ligands but instead are activated by other ligands, such as 4-hydroxytamoxifen (Danielian, White, Hoare, Fawell, & Parker, 1993; Vegeto et al., 1992). Thus, the LBDs of this mutant receptor, when fused with Cre, stimulate recombinase activity in human and mouse cell lines in response to 4-hydroxytamoxifen but not in the presence of estradiol (R. Kühn, personal communication). Tamoxifen, which is metabolized in the liver to 4-hydroxytamoxifen, is commonly used for breast cancer therapy in humans and is known to cross the blood–brain barrier in rats and mice (Etgen, 1979; Wade, Blaustein, Gray, & Meredith, 1993; Wilking, Applegren, Carlstrom, Pousette, &

Theve, 1982). In addition, fusion proteins with the LBDs of the estrogen receptor and transcription-activating domains of Gal4 and VP16 have been shown to act as hormone-dependent regulators of transcription (Braselmann, Graninger, & Busslinger, 1993; Wang, O'Malley, Tsai, & O'Malley, 1994).

Conditional, cell type specific inactivation of an endogenous gene has been done in nonneuronal tissues. For this a key segment of the DNA polymerase β gene was flanked with loxP sites (Gu et al., 1994). To establish an inducible gene-targeting system, Cre was placed under the control of the *Mx1* gene promoter. This promoter is off in healthy animals but can be activated in many tissues in response to interferon-α or -β (Kühn et al., 1995). In these mice there was 97% deletion of the polymerase β gene in the liver within 2 days of a single injection of an interferon inducer. After a second injection, deletion was complete. These studies demonstrated the feasibility of the Cre/loxP approach.

The Cre–LBD system is attractive because it involves only a single transgene and because it can be made cell type specific by using a cell type specific promoter for its expression, such as the αCaMKII promoter. In contrast, another system that uses a tetracycline-sensitive promoter requires the appropriate expression of two transgenes at independent integration sites (Fig. 8) and may require the screening of large numbers of transgenic lines to identify the right combination of strains.

Unlike the LBD system, the tetracycline-regulated (tet) system (Gossen et al., 1995) is designed to control the transcription of genes in mammalian cells. In this case the expression of Cre is regulated by tetracycline-sensitive promoters. There are two versions of this system: in one version tetracycline derivatives activate the expression of Cre; in the other they repress the expression of Cre. In either case this system requires the derivation of two different transgenic mice in addition to the mice with the loxP-flanked gene. The tet system has been shown to regulate the activity of a luciferase reporter gene in cultured human cells and in transgenic mice (Gossen et al., 1995).

B. Inducible Expression or Activation of Mutant Proteins

Inducible gene targeting can irreversibly delete a gene of interest. After the deletion of the gene, the protein remaining has to be naturally degraded before the mutant can be studied. Depending on the stability of the specific protein, this may take from a few days to a few weeks. In addition to gene-targeting approaches, it is also possible to study the functional impact of expressing mutant genes. In this case the gene is mutated and added to the genomes of mice. The resulting transgenic mice will have the normal complement of genes and the added mutant gene. This will be referred to as inducible transgenics.

Just as the expression of the Cre recombinase can be controlled by a variety of schemes as described earlier, the expression of the inducible transgenes can also be regulated in similar ways. For example, the tet system was used to inducibly suppress

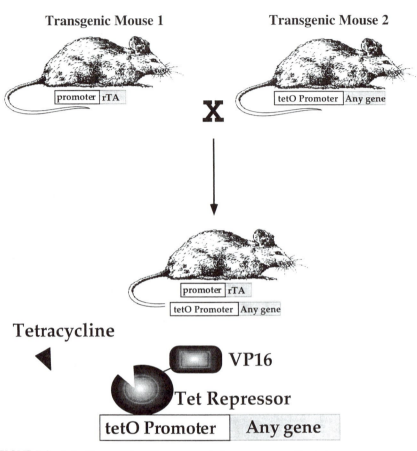

FIGURE 8 Inducible expression of a transgene via the reverse tetracycline (tet) system. To obtain an inducible expression of a desired gene (which could for example encode for Cre recombinase or for a dominant-negative protein) two different transgenic mouse lines have to be crossed. One transgenic line contains the desired gene under the control of a minimal promoter including the tet operon (transgenic mouse 2). In this transgenic mouse line the desired gene is not expressed. The other transgenic line contains a reverse transactivator (rTA) under the control of a specific promoter, such as the αCaMKII promoter (transgenic mouse 1). The reverse transactivator consists of the VP16 transactivation domain of Herpes simplex virus and of a mutated form of the tet repressor. In a mouse having both transgenes the expression of the desired gene can be turned on by tetracycline or by a tetracycline derivative, like doxycycline. Tetracycline (or doxycycline) activates the transactivator, which is bound to the tet operon, resulting in expression of the desired gene.

the expression of a transgene encoding a constitutively active form of CaMKII (Mayford et al., 1996). Before suppression of the transgene the mutants were impaired in CA1 LTP and in spatial learning as well as in fear conditioning. Interestingly, the inducible suppression of the transgene reversed the phenotype, suggesting no irreversible developmental abnormalities in the mutants. As an alternative for inducible transgenic systems, it would be possible to fuse the LBD to a repressor form of CREB, so that CREB transcription could be blocked upon induction of the repressor. A related strategy was used in *Drosophila* to interfere with CREB function. A repressor form of CREB was expressed under the regulation of a promoter that is activated by increases in temperature (heat-shock promoters). Unfortunately, strategies depending on promoters sensitive to temperature have not been successful in mammals. Unlike *Drosophila,* mammals have a sophisticated system to regulate body heat, and thus it is difficult to use temperature change as the inducing agent.

The advantage of using inducible transgenic approaches is that the effects of the mutated protein can be reversed by simply turning off the expression of the transgene (inducible KOs cannot). Furthermore, the time required for the induction and expression of the mutant protein can be very fast. In inducible KOs, where the gene is actually deleted from the genome, the expressed protein remaining has to be naturally degraded, which may take weeks. Inducible transgenics only involve a single line of mutant mice, whereas the inducible KOs require the derivation of at least two different lines of mice.

The disadvantage of the inducible transgenic method is that the normal protein is always there, competing with the mutant version, which may complicate the interpretation of the results. Transgenic constructs never faithfully reproduce the range of tissue and cellular expression of the native proteins. As a result the mutant proteins are expressed in inappropriate places, thus creating the potential for artificial and misleading results. In experiments designed to interfere with the function of native proteins, it is often difficult to express the right amount of the toxic protein. Too little may not have a measurable effect, and too much may result in nonspecific effects (i.e., an overexpressed kinase that phosphorylates inappropriate substrates). Nevertheless, it is a powerful tool that will have many valuable applications.

C. Single-Unit Recordings

Lesion studies have implicated the hippocampus in place learning (for reviews, see Eichenbaum, 1996; McClelland et al., 1995). Additionally, genetic and pharmacological studies have suggested a connection between hippocampal electrophysiology (LTP, LTD, and SLP) and learning mediated by this structure (as discussed previously). However, it is difficult to test connections between cellular electrophysiological properties of the hippocampus and animal behavior, because of the multisystem complexity of the brain. Changes in cellular function can be more directly connected with changes in circuit properties than with alterations in behavior. Similarly, the behavior of an animal may be more easily explained on the basis of circuit properties than with cellular biology. Therefore, the understanding of circuit properties may bridge cellular mechanisms with behavior.

One way to study the properties of circuits is to collect information about cell firing during behavior with techniques that allow simultaneous recording from multiple cells in a given circuit. For example, single-unit recordings in the hippocampus found that many cells seem to fire at higher frequencies when the animal is in a specific place (place cells), as if they were encoding a specific spatial location (for review, see O'Keefe & Nadel, 1978). Thus, multiple *in vivo* recordings of cell firing allow us to glimpse at the properties of cells in functioning neuronal ensembles.

Mutant mice are ideal tools to explore the connection between cellular physiology (LTP, LTD, and SLP), circuit properties, and behavior. So far, single-unit recordings have only been used in a few mutant studies. The first were neocortical single-unit recordings that were used to study the impact of the loss of the αCaMKII on neocortical plasticity (Gordon et al., 1996; Glazewski et al., 1996). Single-unit recordings were used to study responses to sensory stimulation before and after periods of deprivation. These studies implicated this kinase in neocortical plasticity, both in the somatosensory and in the visual cortex.

Single-unit recordings have also been used to study place cell activity in mice. For example, a CA1-specific deletion of the NMDAR1, which results in deficits in LTP and in spatial learning, also alters the properties of place cells in this region. The CA1-specific NMDAR1 knockout mice can establish place cells, but the place fields are enlarged, showing decreased spatial selectivity (McHugh, Blum, Tsien, Tonegawa, & Wilson, 1996). Perhaps because of their diffused place fields, the CA1-specific knockout mice show a decrease in the correlated firing of place cells. Furthermore, transgenic mice expressing a constitutively active form of CaMKII under the control of the αCaMKII promoter also have LTP and spatial learning abnormalities as well as abnormal place cell characteristics (Rotenberg, Mayford, Hawkins, Kandel, & Muller, 1996). The place cells in these mutants are less common, less precise, and less stable over independent trials. It is important to note that both mutants with place cell abnormalities are impaired in spatial learning (Mayford et al., 1995; Tsien, Huerta, & Tonegawa, 1996), suggesting that CA1 place cells are important for hippocampal-dependent spatial learning. The substitution of threonine 286 by alanine in the αCaMKII gene (with the Pointlox procedure) also results in impaired NMDAR-dependent LTP and unstable place cells (Cho, Giese, Tanila, Silva, & Eichenbaum, 1998; Giese, Federov, Filipkowski, & Silva, 1998). These studies are just the beginning of what will undoubtedly be a very active area of research.

Single-unit studies with mutant mice will enhance our understanding of hippocampal circuitry and will therefore improve our insight into hippocampal-dependent learning and memory.

VIII. CONCLUSIONS

The history of neuroscience eloquently demonstrates the difficulties of connecting findings from different levels of hierarchical complexity. New conceptual models are required to integrate the biochemical, electrophysiological, neuroanatomical, and behavioral analysis of the mutants, despite the many advances of transgenic technology. However, all other approaches for the integrative study of learning face similar difficulties, which simply stem from the dimensions of the problem and not just from limitations of any one of the approaches used.

Undoubtedly, the complexity of the problem will be partially overcome by convergence of data and approaches. Each approach provides a unique window into the seemingly inscrutable complexity of these problems. New research strategies often offer unique opportunities both to test key hypotheses and to enrich existing theories with new questions and new emphasis. Indeed, the work reviewed in this chapter combined these two aspects: not only were existing questions tested by genetics (i.e., is LTP required for learing?), but new models and avenues of research have been and will continue to be unveiled by this approach (i.e., is short-term plasticity involved in learning?).

The complex behavioral and electrophysiological phenotypes of these mice will hopefully raise more questions than they will immediately answer, since our understanding of the mechanism of behavior is so incomplete. The strength of genetics is that it often uncovers hidden processes, thus making them amenable for analysis. For example, homeotic mutations in *Drosophila* resulted in flies with duplicated thoracic or abdominal segments. Indeed, the changes caused by those mutations were extremely complex. However, the study of homeotic mutants has had a widespread and profound impact on our understanding of development. Analogously, in some cases mutations in synaptic proteins might result in grossly abnormal physiological and behavioral patterns that could nevertheless reshape our concepts of how organisms learn and remember information. Thus, the potential complexity of the mutant phenotypes is not a disadvantage of this approach, since genetic manipulations do not create complexity but simply reveal it.

One of the most important aspects of the results obtained with gene targeting is that the mutations studied have had such a specific effect on the electrophysiology and behavior of the mutant mice. This specificity is crucial for determining how changes in physiology affect behavior. Complex connections between cellular biology, circuit function, and behavior will not be established with individual mutant mice, but with a collection of genetic studies confirmed with results obtained with other methodologies. This process is well under way, and the hippocampal studies summarized here illustrate the feasibility of using this approach to derive explanations of learning and memory. Although the focus of this review is on hippocampal studies, similar results have also been obtained for other systems, including the cerebellum.

The beginning of a new field is marked by a period of excitement but also uncertainty, when key elements of the approach are being tested, criticisms examined, and misconceptions explained. For a new field, those that strongly oppose it with well-constructed intellectual arguments are just as important as those that enthusiastically support it. This dialectical process of critique, which sharpens the structure and direction of the field, has already helped genetic studies of learning and memory. First, it helped to question the notion that single genes have organismal function. This concept was a useful simplification that emerged from genetic and cell biological studies with genes. Certainly, proteins can have well-defined bio-chemical roles, and mutationis of single genes can also have exquisitely specific effects on cells and on organisms.

However, presently it is difficult to assign function to proteins beyond the exact confines of controlled biochemical reactions. The functional output of a protein summates, synergizes, antagonizes, and integrates with the functional outputs of a large number of other proteins in a variety of interacting neurons and glial cells. These cells form networks with many millions of other neurons which finally affect the behavioral output of the animal. To ascribe significance to the function of a single protein in behavioral terms is a difficult, if not meaningless, task. Neverthe-less, the studies described here and the many spectacular applications of genetics in biology show that the disruption of single genes can be a powerful way to under-stand important biological processes underlying complex organismal phenomena such as behavior.

The current development of inducible transgenic technologies was also partially fueled by the recurrent criticism that the interpretation of genetic studies of learning and memory is confounded by possible developmental effects of the mutations. These novel techniques will allow the control of the place and the time of the mutation. Reversibility will be another important facet of some of these techniques. These advantages will lead to new kinds of experiments that will go well beyond just eliminating developmental concerns. For example, these techniques will allow us to specifically disrupt key cellular processes at different stages of learning and memory and thus test hypotheses about the biochemical mechanisms required to support different stages of memory formation.

Despite all of the excitement surrounding their potential usefulness, mutant mice are simply tools. All that can be asked from a tool is specificity, flexibility, reliability, and reproducibility. The studies reviewed here have certainly shown that this ap-proach can have all of those properties, which suggests that it has been a fruitful addition to a number of other tools that might one day allow us to catch a glimpse of the first among all of scientific mysteries: the brain.

ACKNOWLEDGMENTS

We are grateful to Paul Frankland, Jeffrey Kogan, and Alan Smith for helpful discussions.

REFERENCES

Abel, T., Nguyen, P. V., Barad, M., Deuel, T. A. S., Kandel, E. R., & Bourtchouladze, R. (1997). Genetic demonstration of a role for PKA in the late phase of LTP and in hippocampal-based long-term memory. *Cell, 88,* 615–626.

Abeliovich, A., Chen, C., Goda, Y., Silva, A. J., Stevens, C. F., & Tonegawa, S. (1993). Modified hippocampal long-term potentiation in PKCγ-mutant mice. *Cell, 75,* 1253–1262.

Abeliovich, A., Paylor, R., Chen, C., Kim, J. J., Wehner, J. M., & Tonegawa, S. (1993). PKCγ mutant mice exhibit mild deficits in spatial and contextual learning. *Cell, 75,* 1263–1271.

Abraham, W. C., & Bear, M. F. (1996). Metaplasticity: The plasticity of synaptic plasticity. *Trends in Neurosciences, 19,* 126–130.

Aiba, A., Kano, M., Chen, C., Stanton, M. E., Fox, G. D., Herrup, K., Zwingman, T. A., & Tonegawa, S. (1994). Deficient cerebellar long-term depression and impaired motor learning in mGluR1 mutant mice. *Cell, 79,* 377–388.

Alberini, C. M., Ghirardi, M., Metz, R., & Kandel, E. R. (1994). C/EBP is an immediate-early gene required for the consolidation of long-term facilitation in *Aplysia. Cell, 76,* 1099–1114.

Appleby, M. W., Gross, J. A., Cooke, M. P., Levin, S. D., Qian, X., & Perlmutter, R. M. (1992). Defective T cell receptor signaling in mice lacking the thymic isoform of p59fyn. *Cell, 70,* 751–763.

Auerbach, A. A., & Bennet, M. V. L. (1969). Chemically mediated transmission at a giant fiber synapse in the central nervous system of a vertebrate. *Journal of General Physiology, 53,* 183–210.

Bach, M. E., Hawkins, R. D., Osman, M., Kandel, E. R., & Mayford, M. (1995). Impairment of spatial but not contextual memory in CaMKII mutant mice with a selective loss of hippocampal LTP in the range of the θ frequency. *Cell, 81,* 905–915.

Bakker, C. E., Verheij, C., Willemsen, R., van der Helm, R., Oerlemans, F., Vermey, M., Bygrave, A., Hoogeveen, A. T., Oostra, B. A., Reyniers, E., De Boulle, K., D'Hooge, R., Cras, P., van Velzen, D., Nagels, G., Martin, J.-J., De Deyn, P. P., Darby, J. K., & Willems, P. J. (1994). Fmr1 knockout mice: A model to study fragile X mental retardation. *Cell, 78,* 23–33.

Bannerman, D. M., Good, M. A., Butcher, S. P., Ramsay, M., & Morris, R. G. M. (1995). Distinct components of spatial learning revealed by prior and NMDA receptor blockade. *Nature, 378,* 182–186.

Bartsch, D., Ghirardi, M., Skehel, P. A., Karl, K. A., Herder, S. P., Chen, M., Bailey, C. H., & Kandel, E. R. (1995). *Aplysia* CREB2 represses long-term facilitation: Relief of repression converts transient facilitation into long-term functional and structural change. *Cell, 83,* 979–992.

Bedell, M. A., Largaespada, D. A., Jenkins, N. A., & Copeland, N. G. (1997). Mouse models of human disease. Part II: Recent progress and future directions. *Genes & Development, 11,* 11–43.

Bland, B. H. (1986). The physiology and pharmacology of hippocampal formation theta rhythms. *Progress in Neurobiology, 26,* 1–54.

Blendy, J. A., Kaestner, K. H., Schmid, W., Gass, P., & Schütz, G. (1996). Targeting of the CREB gene leads to up-regulation of a novel CREB mRNA isoform. *EMBO Journal, 15,* 1098–1106.

Bliss, T. V. P., & Collingridge, G. L. (1993). A synaptic model of memory: Long-term potientiation in the hippocampus. *Nature, 351,* 31–39.

Bourtchuladze, R., Frenguelli, B., Blendy, J., Cioffi, D., Schütz, G., & Silva, A. J. (1994). Deficient long-term memory in mice with a targeted disruption of the cAMP-responsive element-binding protein. *Cell, 29,* 59–68.

Brandon, E. P., Zhuo, M., Huang, Y.-Y., Qi, M., Gerhold, K. A., Burton, K. A., Kandel, E. R., McKnight, G. S., & Idzerda, R. L. (1995). Hippocampal long-term depression and depotentiation are defective in mice carrying a targeted disruption of the gene encoding the R1β subunit of cAMP-dependent protein kinase A. *Proceedings of the National Academy of Sciences U.S.A., 92,* 8851–8855.

Braselmann, S., Graninger, P., & Busslinger, M. (1993). A selective transcriptional induction system for mammalian cells based on Gal4-estrogen receptor fusion proteins. *Proceedings of the National Academy of Sciences U.S.A., 90,* 1657–1661.

Brindle, P. K., & Montminy, M. R. (1992). The CREB family of transcription activators. *Current Opinion in Genetics and Development, 2,* 199–204.

Bunsey, M., & Eichenbaum, H. (1995). Selective damage to the hippocampal region blocks long-term retention of a natural and nonspatial stimulus–stimulus association. *Hippocampus, 5,* 546–556.

Buonomano, D. V., & Merzenich, M. M. (1995). Temporal information transformed into a spatial code by a neural network with realistic properties. *Science, 267,* 1028–1030.

Burgin, K. E., Waxham, M. N., Rickling, S., Westgage, S. A., Mobley, W. C., & Kelly, P. T. (1990). In situ hybridization histochemistry of Ca^{2+}/calmodulin-dependent protein kinase in developing rat brain. *Journal of Neuroscience, 10,* 1788–1798.

Butler, L. S., Silva, A. J., Abeliovich, A., Watanabe, Y., Tonegawa, S., & McNamara, J. O. (1995). Limbic epilepsy in transgenic mice carrying a CA^{2+}/calmodulin-dependent kinase II α-subunit mutation. *Proceedings of the National Academy of Sciences U.S.A., 92,* 6852–6855.

Byrne, J. H. (1987). Cellular analysis of associative learning. *Physiological Reviews, 67,* 329–439.

Cain, D. P., Saucier, D., Hall, J., Hargreaves, E. L., & Boon, F. (1996). Detailed behavioral analysis of water maze acquisition under APV or CNQX: Contribution of sensorimotor disturbances to drug-induced acquisition deficits. *Behavioral Neuroscience, 110,* 86–102.

Capecchi, M. R. (1989). Altering the genome by homologous recombination. *Science, 244,* 1288–1292.

Castellucci, V., Pinsker, H., Kupfermann, I., & Kandel, E. R. (1970). Neuronal mechanisms of habituation and dishabituation of the gill-withdrawal reflex in Aplysia. *Science, 167,* 1745–1748.

Chapman, P. F., Frenguelli, B. G., Smith, A., Chen, C.-M., & Silva, A. J. (1995). The α-Ca^{2+}/calmodulin kinase II: A bidirectional modulator of presynaptic plasticity. *Neuron, 14,* 591–597.

Chen, C., Kano, M., Abeliovich, A., Chen, L., Bao, S., Kim, J. J., Hashimoto, K., Thompson, R. F., & Tonegawa, S. (1995). Impaired motor coordination correlates with persistent multiple climbing fiber innervation in PKCγ mutant mice. *Cell, 83,* 1233–1242.

Chen, C., Rainnie, D. G., Greene, R. W., & Tonegawa, S. (1994). Abnormal fear response and aggressive behavior in mutant mice deficient for α-calcium–calmodulin kinase II. *Science, 266,* 291–294.

Cho, Y. H., Giese, K. P., Tanila, H., Silva, A. J., & Eichenbaum, H. (1998). Abnormal hippocampal spatial representations in $\alpha CaMKII^{T286A}$ mutant and $CREB^{\alpha\delta-}$ mice. *Science,* in press.

Collinge, J., Whittington, M. A., Sidle, K. C. L., Smith, C. J., Palmer, M. S., Clarke, A. R., & Jefferys, J. G. R. (1994). Prion protein is necessary for normal synaptic function. *Nature, 370,* 295–297.

Comery, T. A., Kleim, J. A., Silva, A., & Greenough, W. T. (1994). Hippocampal anatomy and ultrastructural morphology of α-calcium calmodulin kinase II deletion mice. *Society for Neuroscience Abstracts, 24,* 1506.

Danielian, P. S., White, R., Hoare, S. A., Fawell, S. E., & Parker, M. G. (1993). Identification of residues in the estrogen receptor that confer differential sensitivity to estrogen and hydroxitamoxifen. *Molecular Endocrinology, 7,* 232–240.

Dash, P. K., Hochner, B., & Kandel, E. R. (1990). Injection of the cAMP-responsive element into the nucleus of Aplysia sensory neurons blocks long-term facilitation. *Nature, 345,* 718–721.

Davis, H. P., & Squire, L. R. (1984). Protein synthesis and memory. *Psychological Bulletin, 96,* 518–559.

Davis, S., Butcher, S. P., & Morris, R. G. M. (1992). The NMDA receptor antagonist D-2-amino-5-phosphonopentanoate (D-AP5) impairs spatial learning and LTP in vivo at intracerebral concentrations comparable to those that block LTP in vitro. *Journal of Neurosciences, 12,* 21–34.

Deisseroth, K., Bito, H., & Tsien, R. W. (1996). Signaling from synapse to nucleus: Postsynaptic CREB phosphorylation during multiple forms of hippocampal synaptic plasticity. *Neuron, 16,* 89–101.

Eichenbaum, H. (1996). Is the rodent hippocampus just for 'place.' *Current Opinion in Neurobiology, 6,* 187–195.

Etgen, A. M. (1979). Antiestrogen: Effects of tamoxifen, nafoxidine, and Cl-628 on sexual behavior, cytoplasmic receptors, and nuclear binding of estrogen. *Hormones and Behavior, 13,* 97–112.

Fanselow, M. S. (1980). Conditional and unconditional components of postshock freezing. *Pavlovian Journal of Biological Science, 15,* 177–182.

Fanselow, M. S. (1986). Associative versus topographical accounts of the immediate shock-freezing deficit in rats: Implications for the response selection rules governing species-specific defensive reactions. *Learning and Motivation, 17,* 16–39.

Feig, S., & Lipton, P. (1993). Pairing the cholinergic agonist carbachol with patterned Schaffer collateral stimulation initiates protein synthesis in hippocampal CA1 pyramidal cell dendrites via a muscarinic, NMDA-dependent mechanism. *Journal of Neuroscience, 13,* 1010–1021.

Forrest, D., Yuzaki, M., Soares, H. D., Ng, L., Luk, D. C., Sheng, M., Stewart, C. L., Morgan, J. I., Connor, J. A., & Curran, T. (1994). Targeted disruption of NMDA receptor 1 gene abolishes NMDA response and results in neonatal death. *Neuron, 13,* 325–338.

Frey, U., Huang, Y.-Y., & Kandel, E. R. (1993). Effects of cAMP stimulate a late stage of LTP in hippocampal CA1 neurons. *Science, 260,* 1661–1664.

Frey, U., Krug, M., Reymann, K. G., & Matthies, H. (1988). Anisomycin, an inhibitor of protein synthesis, blocks late phases of LTP phenomena in the hippocampal CA1 region in vitro. *Brain Research, 452,* 57–65.

Frey, U., & Morris, R. G. M. (1997). Synaptic tagging and long-term potentiation. *Nature, 385,* 533–536.

Frey, U., Müller, M., & Kuhl, D. (1996). A different form of long-lasting potentiation revealed in tissue plasminogen activator mutant mice. *Journal of Neurosciences, 16,* 2057–2063.

Garthwaite, J., & Boulton, C. L. (1995). Nitric oxide in the central nervous system. *Annual Review of Physiology, 57,* 683–706.

Gerlai, R. (1996). Gene-targeting studies of mammalian behavior: Is it the mutation or the background phenotype? *Trends in Neurosciences, 19,* 177–181.

Giese, K. P., Federov, N., Filipkowski, R., & Silva, A. J. (1998). Autophosphorylation at threonine 286 of the α calcium–calmodulin–kinase II is required for LTP and learning. *Science,* in press.

Glazewski, S., Chen, C.-M., Silva, A., & Fox, K. (1996). Requirement for α-CaMKII in experience-dependent plasticity of the barrel cortex. *Science, 272,* 421–423.

Gordon, J. A., Cioffi, D., Silva, A. J., & Stryker, M. P. (1996). Deficient plasticity in the primary visual cortex of α-calcium/calmodulin-dependent protein kinase II mutant mice. *Neuron, 17,* 491–499.

Gordon, J. A., & Stryker, M. P. (1996). Experience-dependent plasticity of binocular responses in the primary visual cortex in the mouse. *Journal of Neuroscience, 16,* 3274–3286.

Gossen, M., Freundlieb, S., Bender, G., Müller, G., Hillen, W., & Bujard, H. (1995). Transcriptional activation by tetracyclines in mammalian cells. *Science, 268,* 1766–1769.

Grant, S. G. N., O'Dell, J., Karl, K. A., Stein, P. L., Soriano, P., & Kandel, E. R. (1992). Impaired long-term potentiation, spatial learning, and hippocampal development in *fyn* mutant mice. *Science, 258,* 1903–1910.

Greengard, P., Valtorta, F., Czernik, A. J., & Benfenati, F. (1993). Synaptic vesicle phosphoproteins and regulation of synaptic function. *Science, 259,* 780–785.

Gu, H., Marth, J. D., Orban, P. C., Mossmann, H., & Rajewsky, K. (1994). Deletion of a DNA polymerase β gene segment in T cells using cell type-specific gene targeting. *Science, 265,* 103–106.

Gu, H., Zou, Y.-R., & Rajewsky, K. (1993). Independent control of immunoglobulin switch recombination at individual switch regions evidenced through Cre-loxP-mediated gene targeting. *Cell, 73,* 1155–1164.

Gutmann, D. H., & Collins, F. S. (1995). Von Recklinghausen neurofibromatosis. In *The metabolic and molecular bases of inherited disease* (7th ed.). New York: McGraw-Hill.

Hai, T., Liu, F., Coukos, W. J., & Green, M. R. (1989). Transcription factor ATF cDNA clones: An extensive family of leucine zipper proteins able to selectively form DNA-binding heterodimers. *Genes & Development, 3,* 2083–2090.

Hanson, P. I., & Schulman, H. (1992). Neuronal Ca^{2+}/calmodulin-dependent protein kinases: *Annual Review of Biochemistry, 61,* 559–601.

Hsiao, K., Chapman, P., Nilsen, S., Eckman, C., Harigaya, Y., Younkin, S., Yang, F., & Cole, G. (1996). Correlative memory deficits, Aβ elevation, and amyloid plaques in transgenic mice. *Science, 274,* 99–102.

Huang, Y.-Y., Bach, M. E., Lipp, H.-P., Zhuo, M., Wolfer, D. P., Hawkins, R. D., Schoonjans, L., Kandel, E. R., Godfraind, J.-M., Mulligan, R., Collen, D., & Carmeliet, P. (1996). Mice lacking the gene encoding tissue-type plasminogen activator show a selective interference with late-phase long-term potentiation in both Schaffer collateral and mossy fiber pathways. *Proceedings of the National Academy of Sciences U.S.A., 93,* 8699–8704.

Huang, Y., Colino, A., Selig, D. K., & Malenka, R. C. (1992). The influence of prior synaptic activity on the induction of long-term potentiation. *Science, 255,* 730–734.

Huang, Y.-Y., Kandel, E. R., Varshasky, L., Brandon, E. P., Qi, M., Idzerda, R. L., McKnight, G. S., & Bourtchuladze, R. (1995). A genetic test of the effects of mutations in PKA on mossy fiber LTP and its relation to spatial and contextual learning. *Cell, 83,* 1211–1222.

Huerta, P. T., Scearce, K. A., Farris, S. M., Empson, R. M., & Prosky, G. T. (1996). Preservation of spatial learning in *fyn* tyrosine kinase knock-out mice. *NeuroReport, 7,* 1685–1689.

Hummler, E., Cole, T. J., Blendy, J. A., Ganss, R., Aguzzi, A., Schmid, W., Beermann, F., & Schütz, G. (1994). Targeted mutation of the CREB gene: Compensation within the CREB/ATF family of transcription factors. *Proceedings of the National Academy of Sciences U.S.A., 91,* 5647–5651.

Hurst, H. C., Totty, N. F., & Jones, N. C. (1991). Identification and functional characterization of the cellular activating transcription factor 43 (ATF-43) protein. *Nucleic Acids Research, 19,* 4601–4609.

Hvalby, O., Hemmings, H. C., Paulsen, O., Czernik, A. J., Nairn, A. C., Godfraind, J.-M., Jensen, V., Raastad, M., Storm, J. F., Andersen, P., & Greengard, P. (1994). Specificity of protein kinase inhibitor peptides and induction of long-term potentiation. *Proceedings of the National Academy of Sciences U.S.A., 91,* 4761–4765.

Impey, S., Mark, M., Villacres, E. C., Poser, S., Chavkin, C., & Storm, D. R. (1996). Induction of CRE-mediated gene expression by stimuli that generate long-lasting LTP in area CA1 of the hippocampus. *Neuron, 16,* 973–982.

Kaang, B.-K., Kandel, E. R., & Grant, S. G. N. (1993). Activation of cAMP-responsive genes by stimuli that produce long-term facilitation in *Aplysia* sensory neurons. *Neuron, 10,* 427–435.

Kim, J. K., Rison, R. A., & Fanselow, M. S. (1993). Effects of amygdala, hippocampus, and periaqueductal gray lesions on short- and long-term contextual fear. *Behavioral Neuroscience, 107,* 1093–1098.

Kirkwood, A., Rioult, M. G., & Bear, M. F. (1996). Experience-dependent modification of synaptic plasticity in visual cortex. *Nature, 381,* 526–528.

Kirkwood, A., Silva, A., & Bear, M. F. (1994). Reduced synaptic plasticity in visual cortex slices of α-CaM-KII knockout transgenic mice. *Society for Neuroscience Abstracts, 24,* 1471.

Kogan, J. H., Frankland, P. W., Blendy, J. A., Coblentz, J., Marowitz, Z., Schütz, G., & Silva, A. J. (1997). Spaced training induces normal long-term memory in CREB mutant mice. *Current Biology, 7,* 1–11.

Korte, M., Griesbeck, O., Carroll, P., Staiger, V., Thoenen, H., & Bonhoeffer, T. (1996). Virus-mediated gene transfer into hippocampal CA1 region restores long-term potentiation in brain-derived neurotrophic factor mutant mice. *Proceedings of the National Academy of Sciences U.S.A., 93,* 12547–12552.

Kühn, R., Schwenk, F., Aguet, M., & Rajewsky, K. (1995). Inducible gene targeting in mice. *Science, 269,* 1427–1429.

Larson, J., & Lynch, G. (1986). Induction of synaptic potentiation in hippocampus by patterned stimulation involves two events. *Science, 232,* 985–988.

Lee, K. A., & Masson, N. (1993). Transcriptional regulation by CREB and its relatives. *Biochemica et Biophysica Acta, 1174,* 221–233.

Li, L., Chin, L.-S., Shupliakov, O., Brodin, L., Sihra, T. S., Hvalby, Ø., Jensen, V., Zheng, D., McNamara, J. O., Greengard, P., & Andersen, P. (1995). Impairment of synaptic vesicle clustering and of synaptic transmission, and increased seizure propensity, in synapsin I-deficient mice. *Proceedings of the National Academy of Sciences U.S.A., 92,* 9235–9239.

Li, Y., Erzurumlu, R. S., Chen, C., Jhaveri, S., & Tonegawa, S. (1994). Whisker-related neuronal patterns fail to develop in the trigeminal brainstem nuclei of NMDAR1 knockout mice. *Cell, 76,* 427–437.

Lisman, J. (1994). The CaM kinase II hypothesis for storage of synaptic memory. *Trends in Neurosciences, 17,* 406–412.

Little, W. A., & Shaw, G. L. (1975). A statistical theory of short and long-term memory. *Behavioral Biology, 14,* 115–133.

Liu, F., Thompson, M. A., Wagner, S., Greenberg, M. E., & Green, M. R. (1993). Activating transcription factor-1 can mediate Ca(2+)− and cAMP-inducible transcriptional activation. *Journal of Biological Chemistry, 268,* 6714−6720.

Lledo, P.-M., Tremblay, P., DeArmond, S. J., Prusiner, S. B., & Nicoll, R. A. (1996). Mice deficient for prion protein exhibit normal neuronal excitability and synaptic transmission in the hippocampus. *Proceedings of the National Academy of Sciences U.S.A., 93,* 2403−2407.

Lu, Y.-M., Jia, Z., Janus, C., Henderson, J. T., Gerlai, R., Wojtowicz, J. M., & Roder, J. C. (1997). Mice lacking metabotropic glutamate receptor 5 show impaired learning and reduced CA1 long-term potentiation (LTP), but normal CA3 LTP. *Journal of Neuroscience, 17,* 5196−5205.

Malenka, R. C., Kauer, J. A., Perkel, D. J., Mauk, M. D., Kelly, P. T., Nicoll, R. A., & Waxham, M. N. (1989). An essential role for postsynaptic calmodulin and protein kinase activity in long-term potentiation. *Nature, 340,* 554−557.

Malinow, R., Schulman, H., & Tsien, R. W. (1989). Inhibition of postsynaptic PKC or CaMKII blocks induction but not expression of LTP. *Science, 245,* 862−866.

Martinez, J. L., Jr., & Derrick, B. E. (1996). Long-term potentiation and learning. *Annual Review of Psychology, 47,* 173−203.

Masson, N., Hurst, H. C., & Lee, K. A. (1993). Identification of proteins that interact with CREB during differentiation of F9 embryonal carcinoma cells. *Nucleic Acids Research, 21,* 1163−1169.

Matthies, H. (1989). In search of cellular mechanisms of memory. *Progress in Neurobiology, 32,* 277−349.

Mayford, M., Bach, M. E., Huang, Y.-Y., Wang, L., Hawkins, R. D., & Kandel, E. R. (1996). Control of memory formation through regulated expression of a CaMKII transgene. *Science, 274,* 1678−1683.

Mayford, M., Wang, J., Kandel, E. R., & O'Dell, T. J. (1995). CaMKII regulates the frequency-response function of hippocampal synapses for the production of both LTD and LTP. *Cell, 81,* 891−904.

McClelland, J. L., McNaughton, B. L., & O'Reilly, R. C. (1995). Why there are complementary learning systems in the hippocampus and neocortex: Insights from the successes and failures of connectionist models of learning and memory. *Physiological Reviews, 102,* 419−457.

McHugh, T. J., Blum, K. I., Tsien, J. Z., Tonegawa, S., & Wilson, M. A. (1996). Impaired hippocampal representation of space in CA1-specific NMDAR1 knock-out mice. *Cell, 87,* 1339−1349.

Moser, E., Mathiesen, I., & Andersen, P. (1993). Association between brain temperature and dentate field potentials in exploring and swimming rats. *Science, 259,* 1324−1326.

Nagy, A., Rossant, J., Nagy, R., Abramow-Newerly, W., & Roder, J. C. (1993). Derivation of completely cell culture-derived mice from early-passage embryonic stem cells. *Proceedings of the National Academy of Sciences U.S.A., 90,* 8424−8428.

Nicoll, R. A., & Malenka, R. C. (1995). Contrasting properties of two forms of long-term potentiation in the hippocampus. *Nature, 377,* 115−118.

Nishizuka, Y., Shearman, M. S., Oda, T., Berry, N., Shinomura, T., Asaoka, Y., Ogita, K., Koide, H., Kikkawa, U., Kishimoto, A., Kose, A., Saito, N., & Tanaka, C. (1991). Protein kinase C family and nervous function. *Progress in Brain Research, 89,* 125−141.

Nosten-Bertrand, M., Errington, M. L., Murphy, K. P. S. J., Tokugawa, Y., Barboni, E., Kozlova, E., Michalovich, D., Morris, R. G. M., Silver, J., Stewart, C. L., Bliss, T. V. P., & Morris, R. J. (1996). Normal spatial learning despite regional inhibition of LTP in mice lacking Thy-1. *Nature, 379,* 826−829.

O'Dell, T. J., Kandel, E. R., & Grant, S. G. N. (1991). Long-term potentiation in the hippocampus is blocked by tyrosine kinase inhibitors. *Nature, 353,* 558−560.

O'Keefe, J., & Nadel, L. (1978). *The hippocampus as a cognitive map.* New York: Oxford University Press.

Otto, T., Eichenbaum, H., Wiener, S. I., & Wible, C. G. (1991). Learning-related patterns of CA1 spike trains parallel stimulation parameters optimal for inducing hippocampal long-term potentiation. *Hippocampus, 1,* 181−192.

Patterson, S., Abel, T., Deuel, T. A. S., Martin, K. C., Rose, J. C., & Kandel, E. R. (1996). Recombinant BDNF rescues deficits in basal synaptic transmission and hippocampal LTP in BDNF knock-out mice. *Neuron, 16,* 1137−1145.

Petrij, F., Giles, R. H., Dauwerse, H. G., Saris, J. J., Hennekam, R. C. M., Masuno, M., Tommerup, N., van Ommen, G.-J., B., Goodman, R. H., Peters, D. J. M., & Breuning, M. H. (1995). Rubinstein–Taybi syndrome caused by mutations in the transcriptional co-activator CBP. *Nature, 376,* 348–351.

Phillips, R. G., & LeDoux, J. E. (1992). Differential contributions of amygdala and hippocampus to cued and contextual fear conditioning. *Behavioral Neuroscience, 106,* 274–285.

Picard, D. (1993). Steroid-binding domains for regulating the functions of heterologous proteins in cis. *Trends in Cell Biology, 3,* 278–280.

Qi, M., Zhuo, M., Skalhegg, B. S., Brandon, E. P., Kandel, E. R., McKnight, G. S., & Idzerda, R. L. (1996). Impaired hippocampal plasticity in mice lacking the Cβ1 catalytic subunit of cAMP-dependent protein kinase. *Proceedings of the National Academy of Sciences U.S.A., 93,* 1571–1576.

Ranck, J. B., Jr. (1973). Studies on single neurons in dorsal hippocampal formation and septum in unrestrained rats. *Experimental Neurology, 41,* 462–531.

Raymond, J. L., Lisberger, S. G., & Mauk, M. D. (1996). The cerebellum: A neuronal learning machine? *Science, 272,* 1126–1131.

Reymann, K. G., Brödemann, R., Kase, H., & Matthies, H. (1988). Inhibitors of calmodulin and protein kinase C block different phases of long-term potentiation. *Brain Research, 461,* 388–392.

Risold, P. Y., & Swanson, L. W. (1996). Structural evidence for functional domains in the rat hippocampus. *Science, 272,* 1484–1486.

Rosahl, T. W., Geppert, M., Spillane, D., Herz, J., Hammer, R. E., Malenka, R. C., & Südhof, T. C. (1993). Short-term synaptic plasticity is altered in mice lacking synapsin I. *Cell, 75,* 661–670.

Rosahl, T. W., Spillane, D., Missler, M., Herz, J., Selig, D. K., Wolff, J. R., Hammer, R. E., Malenka, R. C., & Südhof, T. C. (1995). Essential functions of synapsins I and II in synaptic vesicle regulation. *Nature, 375,* 488–493.

Rotenberg, A., Mayford, M., Hawkins, R. D., Kandel, E. R., & Muller, R. U. (1996). Mice expressing activated CaMKII lack low frequency LTP and do not form stable place cells in the CA1 region of the hippocampus. *Cell, 87,* 1351–1361.

Roush, W. (1995). Nobel prizes: Fly development bears prize-winning fruit. *Science, 270,* 380–381.

Sakimura, K., Kutsuwada, T., Ito, I., Manabe, T., Takayama, C., Kushiya, E., Yagi, T., Aizawa, S., Inoue, Y., Sugiyama, H., & Mishina, M. (1995). Reduced hippocampal LTP and spatial learning in mice lacking NMDA receptor ϵ1 subunit. *Nature, 373,* 151–155.

Saucier, D., Hargreaves, E. L., Boon, F., Vanderwolf, C. H., & Cain, P. (1996). Detailed behavioral analysis of water maze acquisition under systemic NMDA or muscarinic antagonism: Nonspatial pretraining eliminates spatial learning deficits. *Behavioral Neuroscience, 110,* 103–116.

Sauer, B. (1993). Manipulation of transgenes by site-specific recombination: Use of Cre recombinase. *Methods in Enzymology, 225,* 890–900.

Shibuki, K., Gomi, H., Chen, L., Bao, S., Kim, J. J., Wakatsuki, H., Fujisaki, T., Ikeda, T., Chen, C., Thompson, R. F., & Itohara, S. (1996). Deficient cerebellar long-term depression, impaired eyeblink conditioning, and normal motor coordination in GFAP mutant mice. *Neuron, 16,* 587–599.

Silva, A. J., Frankland, P. W., Marowitz, Z., Friedman, E., Lazio, G., Cioffi, D., Jacks, T., & Bourtchuladze, R. (1997). A mouse model for the learning and memory deficits associated with neurofibromatosis type I. *Nature Genetics, 15,* 281–284.

Silva, A. J., & Giese, K. P. (1994). Plastic genes are in! *Current Opinion in Neurobiology, 4,* 413–420.

Silva, A. J., Paylor, R., Wehner, J. M., & Tonegawa, S. (1992). Impaired spatial learning in alpha-calcium calmodulin kinase II mutant mice. *Science, 257,* 206–211.

Silva, A. J., Rosahl, T. W., Chapman, P. F., Marowitz, Z., Friedman, E., Frankland, P. W., Cestari, V., Cioffi, D., Südhof, T. C., & Bourtchuladze, R. (1996). Impaired learning in mice with abnormal short-lived plasticity. *Current Biology, 6,* 1509–1518.

Silva, A. J., Stevens, C. F., Tonegawa, S., & Wang, Y. (1992). Deficient hippocampal long-term potentiation in alpha-calcium calmodulin kinase II mutant mice. *Science, 257,* 201–206.

Spillane, D. M., Rosahl, T. W., Südhof, T. C., & Malenka, R. C. (1995). Long term potentiation in mice lacking synapsins. *Neuropharmacology, 34,* 1573–1579.

Stanton, P., & Sarvey, J. (1984). Blockade of long-term potentiation in rat hippocampal CA1 region inhibitors of protein synthesis. *Journal of Neuroscience, 4,* 3080–3088.

Stein, P., Lee, H.-M., Rich, S., & Soriano, P. (1992). pp59fyn mutant mice display differential signaling in thymocytes and peripheral T cells. *Cell, 70,* 741–750.

Stevens, C. F., Tonegawa, S., & Wang, Y. (1994). The role of calcium–calmodulin kinase II in three forms of synaptic plasticity. *Current Biology, 4,* 687–693.

Steward, O., & Banker, G. A. (1992). Getting the message from the gene to the synapse: Sorting and intracellular transport of RNA in neurons. *Trends in Neurosciences, 15,* 180–186.

Treves, A., & Rolls, E. T. (1994). Computational analysis of the role of the hippocampus in memory. *Hippocampus, 4,* 374–391.

Tsien, J. Z., Chen, D. F., Gerber, D., Tom, C., Mercer, E. H., Anderson, D. J., Mayford, M., Kandel, E. R., & Tonegawa, S. (1996). Subregion- and cell type-restricted gene knock-out in mouse brain. *Cell, 87,* 1317–1326.

Tsien, J. Z., Huerta, P. T., & Tonegawa, S. (1996). The essential role of hippocampal CA1 NMDA receptor-dependent plasticity in spatial memory. *Cell, 87,* 1327–1338.

Tully, T. (1991). Physiology of mutations affecting learning and memory in *Drosophila*—The missing link between gene product and behavior. *Trends in Neuroscience, 14,* 163–164.

Tully, T., Preat, T., Boynton, S. C., & Vecchio, M. D. (1994). Genetic dissection of consolidated memory in *Drosophila*. *Cell, 9,* 35–47.

Umemori, H., Sato, S., Yagi, T., Aizawa, S., & Yamamoto, T. (1994). Initial events of myelination involve *fyn* tyrosine kinase signalling. *Nature, 367,* 572–576.

Vanderwolf, C. H. (1969). Hippocampal electrical activity and voluntary movement in the rat. *Electroencephalography and Clinical Neurophysiology, 26,* 407–418.

Vegeto, E., Allan, G. F., Schrader, W. T., Tsai, M. J., McDonnell, D. P., & O'Malley, B. W. (1992). The mechanism of RU486 antagonism is dependent on the conformation of the carboxy-terminal tail of the human progesterone receptor. *Cell, 69,* 703–713.

Wade, G. N., Blaustein, J. D., Gray, J. M., & Meredith, J. M. (1993). ICI 182,780: A pure antiestrogen that affects behavior and energy balance in rats without activity in the brain. *American Journal of Physiology, 265,* R1392–R1398.

Wang, Y., O'Malley, B. W. J., Tsai, S. Y., & O'Malley, B. W. (1994). A regulatory system for use in gene transfer. *Proceedings of the National Academy of Sciences U.S.A., 91,* 8180–8184.

Widnell, K. L., Self, D. W., Lane, S. B., Russell, D. S., Vaidya, V. A., Miserendino, M. J., Rubin, C. S., Duman, R. S., & Nestler, E. J. (1996). Regulation of CREB expression: In vivo evidence for a functional role in morphine action in the nucleus accumbens. *Journal of Pharmacology and Experimental Therapeutics, 276,* 306–315.

Wilking, N., Applegren, L. E., Carlstrom, K., Pousette, A., & Theve, N. O. (1982). The distribution and metabolism of ^{14}C-labelled tamoxifen in spayed female mice. *Acta Pharmacologica et Toxicologica, 50,* 161–168.

Wu, Z.-L., Thomas, S. A., Villacres, E. C., Xia, Z., Simmons, M. L., Chavkin, C., Palmiter, R. D., & Storm, D. R. (1995). Altered behavior and long-term potentiation in type I adenylyl cyclase mutant mice. *Proceedings of the National Academy of Sciences U.S.A., 92,* 220–224.

Yin, J., Vecchio, M. D., Zhou, H., & Tully, T. (1995). CREB as a memory modulator: Induced expression of a dCREB2 activator isoform enhances long-term memory in *Drosophila. Cell, 81,* 107–115.

Yin, J., Wallach, J. S., Vecchio, M. D., Wilder, E. L., Zhou, H., Quinn, W. G., & Tully, T. (1994). Induction of a dominant-negative CREB transgene specifically blocks long-term memory in *Drosophila melanogaster. Cell, 79,* 49–58.

Yokoi, M., Kobayashi, K., Manabe, T., Takahashi, T., Sakaguchi, I., Katsuura, G., Shigemoto, R., Ohishi, H., Nomura, S., Nakamura, K. Nakao, K., Katsuki, M., & Nakanishi, S. (1996). Impairment of hippocampal mossy fiber LTD in mice lacking mGluR2. *Science, 273,* 645–647.

Zhang, Y., Riesterer, C., Ayrall, A.-M., Sablitzky, F., Littlewood, T. D., & Reth, M. (1996). Inducible site-directed recombination in mouse embryonic stem cells. *Nucleic Acids Research, 24,* 543–548.

Zhong, Y., & Wu, C.-F. (1991). Altered synaptic plasticity in *Drosophila* memory mutants with a defective cyclic AMP cascade. *Science, 251,* 198–201.

Zilber-Gachelin, N. F., & Chartier, M. P. (1973). Modification of motor reflex responses due to repetition of the peripheral stimulus in the cockroach. I. Habituation at the level of an isolated abdominal ganglion. *Journal of Experimental Biology, 59,* 359–382.

Zucker, R. S. (1972). Crayfish escape behavior and central synapses. II. Physiological mechanisms underlying behavioral habituation. *Journal of Neurophysiology, 35,* 621–637.

Zucker, R. (1989). Short-term synaptic plasticity. *Annual Review of Neuroscience, 12,* 13–31.

CHAPTER 4

Pharmacological Approaches to the Study of Learning and Memory

Norman M. White and Juan A. Salinas

Department of Psychology, McGill University, Montreal, Quebec H3A 1B1, Canada

I. INTRODUCTION

A. Rationale

The pharmacological approach to the study of learning and memory is of interest for several reasons. First, on a purely scientific level, observing and understanding how drugs affect learning and memory functions can advance understanding of the neural and neurochemical processes that underlie these faculties. Second, the effects of drugs on behavior is a topic of great general as well as scientific interest. This interest is occasioned by the extent to which both legal and illegal drugs that affect behavior are used by the general public. The behavioral changes produced by such drugs are due to their interaction with the same neural systems that form the basis of learning and memory capacities. Accordingly, the study of the pharmacology of learning and memory provides a way of understanding (and ultimately controlling) the effects of drugs—including addictive drugs—on behavior.

Understanding the effects of drugs on behavior requires a brief review of basic concepts in two areas: the organization of memory functions in the brain, and psychopharmacology (the effect of drugs on behavior). Following this material, the application of these concepts to two "pharmacological systems" will be examined as examples of the application of these principles to the study of learning and memory processes. Insights into the neural basis of learning and memory functions derived from this work will be discussed.

B. History

Three main ideas form the basis of understanding the effects of drugs on learning and memory processes. The first of these originates with the Epicurean school of philosophy (Boring, 1950), which recognized the existence of rewarding and aversive experiences and suggested that they function to organize behavior. The basic idea of this philosophy is that individuals act to maximize pleasure and minimize pain. Much more recently, these ideas were restated and quantified by P. T. Young, who studied the influence of affective states on behavior, and demonstrated such phenomena as their algebraic summation (Young, 1959; Young & Christensen, 1962; Young & Shuford, 1955). This line of thought and experiment provides a basis for thinking about one way in which drugs influence behavior.

A second set of important ideas are those of Pavlov (1927), the famous digestive physiologist who recognized and formally described a form of automatic, unconscious learning called Pavlovian or classical conditioning. The findings and concepts of classical conditioning provide a basis for understanding how drugs can influence affective states which organize behavior when the drugs themselves are not present.

Finally, the idea that certain events indirectly influence behavior by "stamping in" patterns of behavior, as described by Thorndike (1911) in his "Law of Effect," provides the basis for understanding another effect of drugs on behavior. This concept is closely related to those of memory "consolidation," or "modulation" (both of which are discussed at length later), the idea that memories can be weakened or strengthened by events that are unrelated to the material that is actually remembered.

II. MEMORY

A. Neuropsychological Organization

1. Forms of Memory

a. Declarative versus Procedural

There is general agreement that there are several different types of memory, each of which is critically served by a different part of the brain (Moscovitch, 1994; Squire, Knowlton, & Musen, 1993; Squire & Zola-Morgan, 1991; Zola-Morgan &

Squire, 1993). Perhaps the best known of these dichotomies is between "declarative" and "procedural" memory (Cohen, 1984; Cohen & Squire, 1980). This distinction is based on the observation that people with neurological diseases primarily affecting the hippocampus (e.g., Alzheimer's disease) are unable to learn or remember ordinary events (declarative memory) but are normal or nearly normal at learning and remembering how to do things (procedural memory). In the original demonstration, neurological patients learned and remembered how to read complex words in a mirror as well as normal control subjects but were unable to recall the training sessions or the fact that they had acquired this skill (Cohen & Squire, 1980).

The fact that these people with hippocampal damage learned to perform a complex memory task normally suggests two things: (1) there are at least two different kinds of memory; (2) the hippocampus is critical for one of them (declarative), but the other kind of memory (procedural) must be mediated in some other part of the brain. Similar distinctions have been demonstrated in animals (McDonald & White, 1994; Packard, Hirsh, & White, 1989; Packard & White, 1991). These experiments suggest that the basal ganglia, primarily the dorsal striatum (caudate-putamen) may mediate procedural learning.

b. Classical Conditioning

A different line of research suggests the existence of yet another kind of memory that is distinct both behaviorally and anatomically from the declarative and procedural forms. This is Pavlovian conditioning (Pavlov, 1927). This form of learning is based on the tendency of certain naturally occurring events (sometimes called "reinforcers" or "incentive stimuli") to elicit responses with little or no previous experience. For example, in a hungry individual food may elicit salivation and an approach response, an attractive sexual partner may elicit arousal and an approach response, and a painful event may elicit a different pattern of arousal and a withdrawal or escape response. In Pavlovian terms, these naturally occurring events are the unconditioned stimuli (USs), and the patterns of responses they elicit are the unconditioned responses (URs).

As suggested by the examples just given, URs are not individual responses. Rather, URs are complex response patterns consisting of a number of individual components. These components can be divided into two types. One type is easily observable because it consists of overt behaviors including approach and escape responses. These are tendencies to move toward or away from the CSs that elicit them. The second type is relatively unobservable, consisting primarily of responses by the autonomic nervous system and neurotransmitter release in certain brain systems. Taken together, these covert response patterns are sometimes labeled as "affective arousal" and may form the basis of alterations in the subjective state of an individual who encounters a US. Accordingly, these internal states may be perceived as being good ("rewarding"), bad ("aversive"), or indifferent.

Normally, naturally occurring USs produce compatible patterns of URs. That is, a UR that elicits an overt approach response produces a pattern of covert responses labeled as reward, and a UR that produces an overt escape response produces a covert pattern labeled as aversive.

When a US elicits a pattern of responses, it is rarely if ever the only stimulus present in the situation. Other stimuli that do not normally elicit responses (except, perhaps, for initial orienting responses until the individual habituates to them) will also be present. By their mere presence when a US elicits a response pattern these "neutral" stimuli acquire the ability to elicit response patterns similar to the UR. This learning process proceeds automatically, with no control, voluntary participation, or (usually) even awareness on the part of the individual to whom it occurs. This is Pavlovian conditioning: the neutral stimuli are the conditioned stimuli (CS) and the learned response patterns they elicit are the conditioned response (CR).

There is considerable evidence from both human (Adolphs, Tranel, Damasio, & Damasio, 1995; Tranel & Hyman, 1990; Zola-Morgan, Squire, Alvarez-Royo, & Clower, 1991) and animal (Gallagher & Holland, 1994; LeDoux, 1993; McDonald & White, 1993; White & McDonald, 1993) studies that the amygdala is critical for the classical conditioning processes. Furthermore, this evidence suggests that the amygdala mediates expression of conditioned rewarding and approach behaviors as well as conditioned aversive and escape responses (including "freezing").

These conditioned response patterns and the classical conditioning process that produces them are critical to the effects of drugs on behavior. This is because drugs act (in ways that will be discussed in detail later) to produce response patterns similar to those produced by naturally occurring USs. In this sense, drugs are USs that produce URs. However, drugs differ from naturally occurring USs in important ways that are also discussed later.

B. Information Storage

1. Cell Assembly

As discussed in other chapters, the best currently accepted idea about how information is stored in the nervous system is based on the concept of the "cell assembly," originally described by D. O. Hebb (1949). This hypothetical construct starts with the idea that every perception evokes a unique pattern of neural activity. The activated neurons represent the percept. They are connected to each other in a closed loop (the cell assembly) that reactivates itself repeatedly (reverberatory activity). This recurrent connectivity and reverberatory activity keeps the cell assembly active, allowing a newly formed assembly to retain the information it represents for a period of minutes to hours.

Hebb suggested that this period of recurrent activation repeatedly activates the synapses connecting the neurons making up a cell assembly, causing the synapses to undergo permanent changes. These changes facilitate future activation of the synapse. The pattern of permanently facilitated synapses increases the probability that on future occasions activation of one part of the cell assembly will activate the rest of it, leading to recall of the information it represents. Hypotheses about the nature of these synaptic changes are discussed elsewhere in this book.

As already described, not all forms of memory involve representations of perceptions. However, the notion of changes in synapses resulting from the simultaneous (or near-simultaneous) activation of the neurons that form them is generally thought to be the basis of all changes in behavior due to experience, including those that involve procedural learning and classical conditioning. The central role of synaptic change in the learning and memory process provides a basis for the action of drugs on this process.

2. Consolidation

a. Concept and Evidence

Hebb's notion of the cell assembly was based on evidence suggesting that memory is a time-dependent process. This notion was first suggested by Muller and Pilzecker (1900), who observed that memory for a list of words became less subject to disruption by learning a second list of words with the mere passage of time after the first list had been learned. These investigators suggested that when first acquired, memories are stored in a labile state (represented by Hebb's recurrent activation phase) and are subject to disruption by external events. With the passage of time their storage becomes more permanent (represented by Hebb's synaptic change) and are less susceptible to disruption.

The process by which memories become permanent is called "consolidation." The interval during which the hypothesized process of synaptic change occurs is called the consolidation period. This is illustrated in Fig. 1.

Considerable evidence is consistent with these ideas. Humans experiencing trauma such as head injury (Russell & Nathan, 1946) or electroconvulsive shock (Zubin & Barrera, 1941) exhibit amnesia for events that occurred immediately before the trauma. Memory for events that occurred earlier is unaffected. This suggests that the most recently acquired memories were subject to disruption by the trauma. Older, consolidated memories were not affected.

In animal studies, electroconvulsive shock (Duncan, 1949) and other treatments (Bloch, 1970; McGaugh & Herz, 1972) have similar effects. Using groups of animals that receive the memory-disrupting event at different times after training, it has been possible to demonstrate a "consolidation gradient" in which the effectiveness of the memory-disrupting agent decreases as the posttraining time increases (Duncan, 1949). Figure 1 illustrates the temporal relationship of the consolidation period to the training and testing times in a typical experiment of this type. Treatments given during the consolidation period can affect the memory whereas

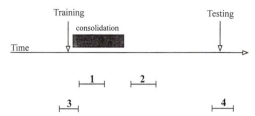

FIGURE 1   Effects of drugs on memory processes. The horizontal arrow represents the passage of time. Experience of an event (Training) is followed immediately by a period of consolidation of the information representing the experience (shaded area). Some time later, the stored information is retrieved and influences behavior (Testing). A drug administered during the immediate posttraining period (1) influences consolidation but has no direct effect on the acquisition of information during training or on the later recall and expression of the information during testing. Administration of the same drug after the end of the consolidation period but well before testing (2) should have no effect on training, testing, or memory. This is the standard control condition required to conclude that an effect of immediate posttraining administration is due to an interaction with a memory process. Drug administration prior to training (3) or prior to testing (4) can alter behavior due to direct effects of the drug on either acquisition or expression of the stored information. These effects may be indistinguishable from effects on the memory process itself.

treatments given after it have little or no effect. The influence on memory of treatments given during the posttraining consolidation period has been referred to as "memory modulation" (McGaugh & Gold, 1989b).

b. Enhancement

There is also evidence that certain posttraining treatments can modulate memory storage in ways that enhance retention. This phenomenon was first observed using stimulant drugs such as strychnine (in very low doses) (Hudspeth, 1964; McGaugh & Thomson, 1962) and amphetamine (Doty & Doty, 1966; Krivanek & McGaugh, 1969). It has since been demonstrated using other drugs (Breen & McGaugh, 1961; Evangelista, Gattoni, & Izquierdo, 1970; Garg & Holland, 1968; Gold & van Buskirk, 1975, 1976; Grossman, 1969; Stein et al., 1975), using electrical stimulation of the brain (Bloch, 1970; Coulombe & White, 1980; Huston, Mondadori, & Waser, 1974; Major & White, 1978), and with a number of commonly occurring substances such as caffeine (Castellano, 1976; Izquierdo, 1982) and sugar (Gold, 1995; Gold, Vogt, & Hall, 1986; Messier & Gagnon, 1996; Messier & White, 1984). Certain specific experimental controls are required to reach these conclusions. These are illustrated in Fig. 1 and explained in the following paragraphs.

In one such experiment (Carr & White, 1984), rats were trained on a conditioned emotional response (CER). They were water-deprived and placed into a test cage where they were allowed to drink for 15 min/day. After they had learned to drink in the cage, the rats heard a series of 10sec tones, each terminated with a brief

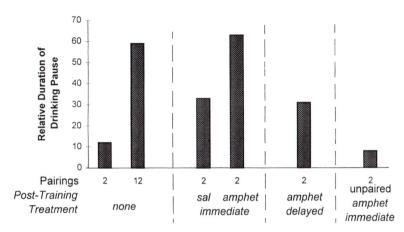

FIGURE 2   Modulation of conditioned emotional response (CER) by posttraining amphetamine. The bars show the relative pauses in drinking by thirsty rats produced by a tone that had been presented together (Paired) with a footshock the indicated number of times. The pairings were followed by different Posttraining Treatments in different groups of rats: sal = saline, amphet = amphetamine, delay = 2 hr. The duration of the pauses indicates the strength of the rats' memory for the association between the tone and the freezing response that produces the drinking pauses. Data from Carr and White (1984).

footshock. The shock caused the animals to stop moving completely ("freeze") and, after several such tone–shock pairings, they acquired a conditioned freezing response which lasted for several minutes each time the tone was presented. The next day they were placed into the drinking cage. When they began to drink, the tone came on. The animals froze, which caused them to stop drinking. The duration of this drinking pause was used as a measure of the rats' memory for the tone–freezing association. Not surprisingly, rats that experienced twelve tone–shock pairings froze for significantly longer than rats that experienced two pairings. These results are illustrated in Fig. 2.

Some groups of rats received drug injections during the period immediately following their experience of the tone–shock pairings. Rats that experienced two pairings followed by an injection of saline (the vehicle for the drug) froze for slightly longer than the rats that received no injection (Fig. 2). However, rats that experienced two pairings followed by an injection of d-amphetamine sulfate froze for about the same time as the rats that received twelve pairings (with no drug). Another group of rats experienced two pairings followed by an amphetamine injection 2 hr later. These rats froze for the same amount of time as the rats that received saline or no injection. These findings suggest that the immediate amphetamine injections improved the rats' memory for the tone–freezing association. The fact that the delayed injection had no effect is consistent with the idea that the memory was susceptible to modulation only during a consolidation period that lasted for less than 2 hr.

At least two other hypotheses about how the amphetamine injection could have caused the increase in freezing time are possible. The first of these is illustrated in Fig. 1. It is possible that the posttraining drug injection had a "proactive" effect; that is, that it directly affected the rats' performance on the test day, somehow causing the increased latencies. This hypothesis can be ruled out because the same drug was injected somewhat closer in time to the test in the delayed group but did not increase freezing time. It is therefore unlikely that the immediate posttraining injection increased freezing time for this reason.

The second alternative hypothesis is that some response produced by the drug (see later discussion of drug-produced responses) became associated with the tone and that this association and not that between the tone and freezing (produced by the shock) was the cause of the increased freezing time. This idea is ruled out by the "unpaired" control group. The rats in this group experienced two tones and two shocks presented at random times, followed by an injection of amphetamine. Since the tone did not occur at the same time as the shock in this arrangement, no tone–freezing association could have been learned. However, the relationship between the tone and any drug-produced responses was the same for this group as for the others, so any learning based on such associations should have occurred in the same way. As shown in Fig. 2, the freezing times for the rats that experienced unpaired presentations of tone and shock followed by immediate amphetamine were similar to those for the no drug and saline groups.

All of these findings are consistent with the hypothesis that the amphetamine modulated the memory of the tone–freezing association by acting during the consolidation period on some aspect of the memory trace itself. We now consider how a drug like amphetamine could have an effect like this.

III. PSYCHOPHARMACOLOGY

A. Pharmacodynamics

1. Peripheral Administration

The pharmacological investigation of memory requires the administration of drugs. The two major routes of administration are "peripheral," or systemic; and "central," or directly into the brain.

The logic of the systemic route is to deliver the drug to the circulatory system so that it is quickly transported to the target organ, for example, the brain or a specific brain structure. The obvious way to accomplish this is to inject the drug intravenously, directly into the bloodstream. However, this route is not always the best choice. Access to an appropriate vein is often difficult in a small animal such as a rat, and the procedure can disrupt normal ongoing behavior in any animal or person. Some drugs have properties (e.g., low pH) that make this route inappropriate. Accordingly, other routes of administration are often used. The most straightforward alternative, the oral route, also has a number of disadvantages. The digestive process in the stomach and intestines can alter the properties of ingested drugs, and once absorbed into the portal circulation, ingested drugs pass directly through the liver, the major organ for drug inactivation. For these reasons, the intraperitoneal (into the abdominal cavity, avoiding the stomach) and subcutaneous (under the skin) routes are most commonly used, especially with rats.

These routes depend mostly on a passive process of diffusion for the drugs to reach the circulatory system. They also bring the drugs into contact with various bodily tissues that may absorb them to some degree. Therefore, the physical and chemical properties of injected drugs (that may be unrelated to their desired pharmacological action) determine how quickly and in what amounts they reach the blood and, in turn, their target organ. These considerations are known as "pharmacodynamics" (Benet, Mitchell, & Sheiner, 1990a, 1990b). Each drug type has its own pharmacodynamic properties. These can be important considerations in experiments such as those on memory where temporal factors are critical.

In most experiments on memory the brain is the target organ. Access to the brain from the circulatory system is controlled by a system known as the "blood–brain barrier" (Goldstein & Betz, 1986). This barrier is made up of a layer of cells surrounding the capillaries that supply blood to the brain. The properties of these cells determine the degree to which substances in the blood can enter the brain. In general, fat-soluble substances (e.g., alcohol) enter more easily than water-soluble substances (e.g., most catecholamines). Drugs and hormones with large molecular weights are also generally excluded. A few substances, notably glucose and insulin, are actively transported into the brain. Obviously, the degree to which peripherally administered substances can penetrate the blood–brain barrier is a critical determinant of their effect on brain substrates of memory.

A final consideration with respect to systemic administration of drugs is the fact that they are carried by the circulatory system to all parts of the body. Therefore, their effects cannot be limited to the intended target organ (e.g., a specific part of the brain) and they often have effects on other substrates. These added actions of systemically injected drugs may be unrelated to any effects they have on memory functions. However, they may also interact in important ways either with the memory functions under study or with the subject's response to the learning situation.

The latter form of interference can easily lead to false conclusions about the memory-related actions of the drugs, and close attention to experimental design is required to prevent errors of this kind. The posttraining administration technique (see Fig. 1) suggested by the theory of memory consolidation is also recommended by these experimental design considerations. Since the drugs are given after training, the subjects are in a normal drug-free state during both the learning and testing sessions. The time at which the drug is administered means that it can only interact with memory consolidation processes.

2. Central Administration

Peripheral actions of drugs can often be avoided completely by injecting them directly into the brains of animal subjects. They can be injected into the ventricles of the brain or into specific brain sites. This is done using stereotaxic surgery to place permanent, minute guide shafts aimed at the ventricles or the brain area of interest. When the animals have recovered from the surgery, they can be trained normally, injected during the posttraining period, and tested normally. The injections, in microliter amounts, are made through cannulae inserted through the guide shafts.

Injections into the ventricles (sometimes called "intraventricular" or "intracerebroventricular" injections) avoid some of the disadvantages of systemic injections by placing the drugs on the brain side of the blood–brain barrier. Even if the drug can cross the barrier from brain to blood, the amounts injected are usually too small to have any action in the periphery. Therefore a central site of action is usually assumed when drugs are injected via this route, although the site of action within the brain cannot be determined with this method.

Although drug injections directly into brain tissue allow the determination of the specific brain area affected, this method of drug administration also has some problems. Injection of even very small volumes of liquid into the brain inevitably produces some damage; this is generally controlled for by injecting equivalent volumes of the vehicle in control subjects. In this regard, the acid–base properties of the injected substances are even more critical with central than with peripheral injections.

Although a known amount of drug can be injected into brain tissue, the amount or "effective dose" that actually reaches the synaptic target of interest is difficult or impossible to establish. A major determinant of the effective dose is the rate at which the injected substance diffuses away from the injection site. This is largely controlled by the fat solubility of the substance. Fat-soluble drugs diffuse farther faster, increasing the volume of tissue in which the drug is distributed and decreasing the effective dose at each affected synapse. Although direct determination of the effective area of action of an injected drug is virtually impossible, this can often be inferred from observations of ineffective injection sites adjacent to effective ones.

Finally, the specificity of action of injected drugs is always an important issue. In this case, specificity refers to the precise synaptic substrates on which a drug may act. Accurate information on this matter is obviously critical for the interpretation of any behavioral effects observed, but such information is often difficult or impossible to obtain.

B. Drug Action

1. How Drugs Act on Synapses

The fact that neurons communicate with each other at synapses using chemical neurotransmitters provides the basis for the ability of certain substances to affect the process of synaptic transmission. Drugs with chemical properties that correspond in some way to those of neurotransmitters can act on synapses to alter behavior and thought processes. Drugs that have these effects are said to be "psychotropic" and "psychoactive."

A number of different neurotransmitters exist in the mammalian brain. Most psychoactive drugs act on the synapses of a single neurotransmitter. However, these synapses may occur in a number of different, functionally unrelated neural systems, each of which controls a different behavior. Therefore, the psychological actions of a psychotropic drug can be quite complex.

Figure 3 presents a summary of the major processes involved in synaptic neurotransmission, together with an indication of the major ways in which drugs can alter these processes. In general, drugs that potentiate synaptic transmission are called "agonists"; drugs that impede synaptic transmission are called "antagonists." The following brief descriptions of how drugs can produce these effects correspond to the numbers on Fig. 3. More details about each of these processes are available from many sources (e.g., Cooper, Bloom, & Roth, 1982; Katz, 1966; Levitan & Kaczmarek, 1991).

1. Neurotransmitters are synthesized in neurons, stored in microscopic sacs called vesicles, and transported to the cell membrane at the nerve ending. Drugs can either increase or decrease synthesis and/or the rate of transport.

2. When they reach the cell membrane, the vesicles join with it, opening the membrane and releasing their contents (the neurotransmitter) into the synaptic cleft (the area between the two neurons). Drugs can promote or inhibit this process.

3 and 4. The neurotransmitter acts at "receptors" on both the presynaptic neuron ("autoreceptors") and postsynaptic neuron ("postsynaptic receptors"). Receptors are organs that trap, or "bind," molecules with specific configurations. Each neurotransmitter has its own unique molecular configuration and receptors that match or "recognize" the neurotransmitter.

Activation of autoreceptors (3) inhibits the further release of neurotransmitter from the neuron and may also inhibit synthesis and transport of the neurotransmitter. Activation of postsynaptic receptors (4) affects ion channels on the membrane, contributing to postsynaptic potentials. These effects can be either excitatory or inhibitory on the postsynaptic neuron.

Certain drugs have molecular configurations that allow them to bind to specific receptor types. Some drugs bind to receptors and mimic the action of the neurotransmitter. Others bind to the receptor, produce no activation, but block access by the neurotransmitter. Drugs often have detectable effects on autoreceptors at lower

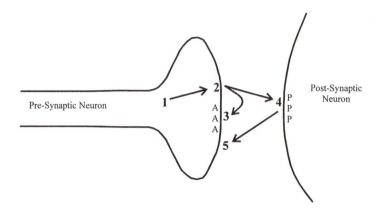

PROCESS	AGONIST	ANTAGONIST
1. synthesis	increase	decrease
2. release	promote	inhibit
3. autoreceptors (A)	block	activate
4. post-synaptic receptors (P)	activate	block
5. deactivation	block reuptake or degredation	

FIGURE 3   Effects of drugs on synaptic processes. Details about each numbered process can be found in the text.

doses than on postsynaptic receptors. Therefore, the same drug can have opposite effects at low and high doses.

5. Neurotransmitters are inactivated in two main ways. They can be degraded by enzymes found in the synaptic cleft or they can be reabsorbed by the presynaptic neuron ("reuptake"). Enzymatic degradation can be potentiated or inhibited by drugs. Reuptake can be blocked by drugs.

In addition to these major modes of drug action on synapses, there is some evidence for so-called modulatory effects (e.g., Libet, 1986; Smolders, De Klippel, Sarre, Ebinger, & Michotte, 1995). Some neurotransmitters have no effect on their own but may potentiate or inhibit the effect of another neurotransmitter. Other substances with effects of this nature may not come from neurons, but may be modulatory hormones, released at distant sites in the brain or periphery. Drugs can potentiate, inhibit, or otherwise interact with these functions.

2. How Drugs Act in the Periphery

There are three special points to consider with respect to the action of drugs in the periphery. First, drugs act at synapses in the periphery in the same way as they act at synapses in the central nervous system. For example, the neuromuscular junction uses acetylcholine as a neurotransmitter, and drugs that block acetylcholine receptors (e.g., curare) produce paralysis of skeletal muscles. Drugs can also act at synapses of the autonomic nervous system in this way.

Second, certain organs that are not part of the nervous system may contain receptors that can bind certain drugs. For example, the liver and adrenal medulla may contain receptors that can bind glucose molecules, and the liver may contain epinephrine receptors.

Finally, the role of the blood–brain barrier should be emphasized. Because of its existence, the action of certain drugs will be restricted to the periphery and will not affect central nervous system structures.

3. Drug-Induced Responses

The specific synaptic action of each psychotropic drug affects the behavioral and cognitive processes in which those synapses normally participate. It is useful to conceptualize the effects of these actions as "responses" elicited by the drugs. In this sense, drug-produced responses are similar to the responses (URs in Pavlovian terms) produced by naturally occurring incentive events such as food, water, or sexual partners. As already described, a systemically injected drug may act simultaneously at synapses that participate in a number of different functions both in the central nervous system and in the periphery. It is highly unlikely that the pattern of responses elicited by any drug would correspond to that produced by a naturally occurring event. Accordingly, each drug can be seen as producing a unique pattern of responses, or URs.

As with naturally occurring incentive stimuli, the responses elicited by drugs are of two types: internal (covert) and relatively unobservable, and overt. The covert response patterns elicited by drugs constitute affective states that can be perceived as rewarding or aversive. Moreover, there is evidence that experienced human drug users can discriminate among the internal states produced by several common drugs of abuse (Kliner & Pickens, 1982), suggesting that the internal state produced by each of these drugs is unique.

Comparing the overt responses produced by drugs to those produced by naturally occurring stimuli (approach or escape) is not so straightforward. Each natural incentive event involves an external object of some kind (food, sexual partner, etc.), which an individual can approach or escape from. However, drugs lack this external reference point for these behaviors. Therefore, if a drug activates synapses involved in approach responses, there is nothing for the animal to approach, and no way for an observer to detect this behavior. For example, it has been suggested that the high level of locomotor activity produced by moderate doses of amphetamine in rats is a reflection of the activation of an approach tendency by the drug (Carr, Phillips, & Fibiger, 1988). In the absence of an external reference object for the animal to approach, the response appears as random locomotion.

Thus, a drug may activate the neural substrate of an approach or escape response, but this response will not be obvious to an observer. However, if the activation of this substrate becomes a conditioned response to a neutral stimulus (see next section), then the neutral stimulus serves as the external reference point for the conditioned behavior and this behavior becomes observable and identifiable as an approach response.

Finally, recall that naturally occurring USs elicit patterns of URs with compatible components (i.e., approach responses with positive affective states, escape responses with aversive affective states). This compatibility does not necessarily apply to drugs. Because a systemically injected drug acts on synapses in patterns that are unrelated to the synaptic activity elicited by naturally occurring USs, it is possible to imagine a drug simultaneously activating synapses involved in producing an approach response and synapses that produce an aversive internal state. In fact, there is evidence that just such opposing patterns of activation are conditioned with certain drugs.

IV. CONDITIONING OF DRUG-INDUCED RESPONSES

A. Introduction

As is the case with responses elicited by naturally occurring incentive stimuli, drug-produced responses become conditioned to neutral cues that are present when the drugs have their effects. In this situation the drug corresponds to the US (recall the differences from natural USs) and the responses elicited by the drug correspond to the UR. Neutral environmental cues are the CSs, and the responses elicited by these cues on future occasions are the CRs.

1. Conditioned Cue Preference (CCP)

One of the most common methods of measuring the conditioned effects of drugs is with the conditioned cue preference (more commonly called the conditioned place preference). In this experimental paradigm animals are injected with a drug (i.e., exposed to a US) and placed into an environment containing a distinctive set of neutral cues. The same animals are also exposed to another set of neutral cues in the absence of the US. Subsequently, the animals are given a choice between the two sets of cues. If they approach and spend more time in the presence of the

US-paired cues than the nonpaired cues, the US is inferred to have produced a conditioned approach response and/or an internal conditioned reward state. If they approach and spend more time in the presence of the control-paired cues than the drug cues, the US is inferred to have produced a conditioned escape response and/or a conditioned aversive state. Conditioned cue preferences have been produced using food (Bechara & van der Kooy, 1992; White & McDonald, 1992b), sucrose solutions (Everitt, Morris, O'Brien, & Robbins, 1991; White & Carr), and sexual partners (Everitt, 1990; Mehrara & Baum, 1990) as the US.

2. Conditioned Taste Aversion (CTA)

Another conditioning method that has been extensively used with drugs involves taste cues as the CS. In these experiments animals are allowed to consume a substance with a taste they have not previously experienced and then injected with a drug. On subsequent tests, the animals often exhibit decreased consumption of the substance and this response is known as a conditioned taste aversion (CTA). CTAs are produced by substances that are known to make animals sick, such as lithium chloride (Nachman & Ashe, 1973; Revusky, Taukulis, & Peddle, 1979).

The fact that many drugs produce CTAs in this paradigm has led to the inference that they produce aversive affective states. In several cases the same drugs also produce CCPs, leading to the inference that they produce rewarding states. We now consider two drugs that have such paradoxical actions.

B. Amphetamine

Amphetamine produces a CCP (Phillips, Spyraki, & Fibiger, 1982; White, Messier, & Carr, 1987). A demonstration of this is illustrated in Fig. 4. This experiment utilized an apparatus with two large, distinctive compartments, connected by a small tunnel. Rats received different doses of the drug immediately before being placed into one of the large compartments and injections of the vehicle before being placed into the other one. Each of these treatments was repeated four times on consecutive days. Following these training trials, the rats were placed in the tunnel and allowed to move freely between the two compartments. Figure 4 shows the amounts of time they chose to spend in each. Note that the time spent in the drug-paired compartment and the difference between the time spent in the paired and unpaired compartments are both monotonic functions of dose.

In this example, the drug amphetamine is the US, and the responses elicited by the drug are the URs. Since the rats were placed into one of the distinctive large compartments immediately after receiving the drug, the responses it elicited occurred in the presence of the stimuli in that compartment. Accordingly, these stimuli became the CSs. On the test day, these stimuli elicited CRs that were similar to the URs produced by the drug. Since the rats approached and spent more time in

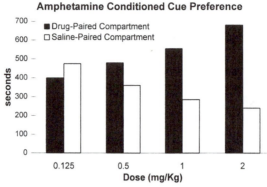

FIGURE 4   Amphetamine conditioned cue preference (CCP). The CCP apparatus consisted of two large, distinct chambers connected by a small tunnel. Each dose was tested with eight rats. In each group of eight, four rats received drug injections before being placed into one compartment and saline injections before being placed into the other compartment; the drug–compartment pairing was reversed for the other four rats. All rats received four pairings with each compartment over 8 days. On the ninth day each rat was placed into the tunnel and allowed to move freely through both compartments for 20 min. The graph shows the mean amounts of time the rats chose to spend in each compartment. The rats' preference for the drug-paired compartment increased steadily as a function of the dose of amphetamine. Data from White, Messier, and Carr, (1987).

the presence of the drug-paired stimuli, it is inferred that the CRs consist of a conditioned approach response and/or a conditioned rewarding internal state. Since these responses were originally produced by the drug, they are taken to reflect the properties of the drug.

When a taste is substituted for external cues as the CS, amphetamine produces a conditioned taste aversion rather than a conditioned place preference (LeBlanc & Cappell, 1974; Stolerman & D'Mello, 1978). In fact, both the CCP and CTA to amphetamine can be produced simultaneously (Reicher & Holman, 1977). In the latter experiment, water-deprived rats were injected with amphetamine and placed into one compartment of a CCP apparatus, where they were allowed to drink a novel flavored solution. On alternate days they received no injection and were placed into the other compartment, where they drank a different novel flavored solution. Cue and taste preferences were tested separately: the rats exhibited a conditioned preference for the amphetamine-paired compartment, but a conditioned aversion for the amphetamine-paired flavor.

In an investigation of this phenomenon (Carr & White, 1986), it was shown that microinjections of amphetamine into nucleus accumbens produced a CCP but no effect in a conditioned taste test; in contrast, microinjections into area postrema produced a CTA but no effect in a conditioned cue test. These findings suggest that amphetamine may act independently on substrates in nucleus accumbens and area postrema to produce responses that become conditioned to external cues and taste cues, respectively. Amphetamine promotes dopamine release in nucleus accumbens (Guix, Hurd, & Ungerstadt, 1992; Robinson & Camp, 1990) and this response is critical for both acquisition and expression of the amphetamine CCP (Hiroi & White, 1990, 1991). Dopamine release in nucleus accumbens has also been associated with locomotion (Kelly, 1991; Swerdlow, Amalric, & Koob, 1987), which may reflect approach responding in the absence of an external reference point.

There is also evidence that amphetamine can act in an area of the brainstem that includes the nucleus of the solitary tract and the dorsal motor nucleus of the vagus nerve to produce an aversive internal state that can become associated with taste cues, resulting in a CTA (Carr & White, 1986). Taken together with the CCP-producing action of amphetamine in nucleus accumbens, these findings provide a good example of how a drug can act simultaneously at different sites to produce different, even paradoxical, effects on behavior. The findings also show how experimental manipulations with drugs can elucidate mechanisms of naturally occurring learning and memory. In this case, the unnatural combination of responses produced by the drug led to the investigation of neural mechanisms that function independently to influence normal behavior.

C. Morphine

Morphine also produces both a CCP (Beach, 1957; Mucha, van der Kooy, O'Shaughnessy, & Bucenieks, 1982) and a CTA (LeBlanc & Cappell, 1974; Sherman, Pickman, Rice, Liebeskind, & Holman, 1974) when injected systemically and, as with amphetamine, both of these responses can be acquired simultaneously (White, Sklar, & Amit, 1977). This suggests that the peripherally injected drug is transported to and acts at several different sites to produce a number of different response patterns.

The morphine CCP is produced by central microinjections into nucleus accumbens (van der Kooy, Mucha, O'Shaugnessy, & Bucenieks, 1982), ventral tegmental area (Wise & Hoffman, 1992), or hippocampus (Corrigall & Linseman, 1988). Since the response patterns elicited by morphine at each of these sites of action are likely to be different, these findings suggest the possibility that morphine can produce a CCP by eliciting several different response patterns that are perceived as rewarding.

Investigation of the aversive action of morphine illustrates several concepts of drug action and the use of these actions to understand mechanisms. The discovery of opiate receptors in the brain (Pert, Kuhar, & Snyder, 1976; Pert, Pasternak, & Snyder, 1973) led to the identification of the endogenous opiate peptides ("endorphins") (Bloom et al., 1978; Holaday & Loh, 1979), substances found in the normal brain that are similar to drugs (morphine and heroin) that are derivatives of the opium poppy. Later, opiate receptors were also identified in smaller numbers on primary sensory neurons in the peripheral nervous system, including the gut

(Ninkovic, Hunt, & Gleave, 1982). Because central injections of morphine produce CCPs, Bechara and van der Kooy (1985) hypothesized that eliminating the normal action of endorphins at receptors in the brain might result in an aversive affective state. They confirmed this idea by showing that systemic (intraperitoneal or subcutaneous) injections of naltrexone, an opiate receptor blocker, produce conditioned cue aversions (CCAs). Although this systemically injected drug blocked opiate receptors in both the brain and the periphery, the investigators suggested that the smaller number of receptors in the periphery may have led to a net aversive effect due to blockade of the central receptors.

Bechara and van der Kooy (1985) also tested the hypothesis that blocking the action of endogenous opiates at receptors in the gut would produce a rewarding effect. This hypothesis was confirmed by the finding that systemic injections of methylnaltrexone, a form of the opiate receptor antagonist that does not cross the blood–brain barrier, produced a CCP. The peripheral location of the receptors mediating this aversive effect was confirmed in several further experiments. First, the effects of systemic injections of a dose of morphine (0.05 mg/kg) too low to allow an effective amount to be transported to the brain were tested. Intraperitoneal injections of this dose produced a CCA, whereas subcutaneous injections of the same dose had no effect, suggesting that the receptors mediating the aversion are located in the peritoneal cavity (gut). The aversive effect of these intraperitoneal morphine injections was blocked by cutting the vagus nerve, the probable afferent pathway activated by the peripheral opiate receptors. This finding is consistent with the idea that receptors mediating aversive effects of opiates are in the gut.

In a final experiment, these investigators showed that vagotomy also blocks the CTA produced by morphine, suggesting that the aversive effects observed in the CCA and CTA paradigms are probably due to the action of the drug on the same peripheral opiate receptors.

These experiments illustrate the use of the pharmacodynamic properties of drugs to investigate receptor and synaptic processes involved in both drug-related and normal behavioral processes.

V. DRUG-PRODUCED MODULATION OF MEMORY

A. Introduction

As already discussed, memory, including the memory that produces classically conditioned responses to drugs, is subject to modulation during the period immediately after it is formed. Drugs have been used in many experiments to affect the memory consolidation process. An example of an experiment of this type is the posttraining effect of amphetamine on retention of the CER response described in Section II.B.2.b. Recall the importance of administering drugs during the period immediately after training for concluding that their effects are due to an interaction with a memory process as opposed to some other kind of effect on behavior.

There are three different ways in which a drug such as amphetamine could act to modulate memory in this example. Two of these depend on the ability of the drug to reach brain structures. First, a drug in the brain can act directly on the synapses that form parts of cell assemblies that store information. Second, a drug can act on a modulatory mechanism, that is, at synapses that are part of a system with the normal function of modulating memory-related synapses. Evidence for both of these types of action is described later in this section.

Systemically administered drugs can also act on peripheral target organs that, in turn, can affect memory-related functions. There is evidence that drugs acting on the adrenal glands can cause the release of epinephrine and glucocorticoids that have memory-modulating effects. Some of these findings are also discussed in this section.

B. The U-Shaped Dose–Response Function

The dose–response curve is a standard tool in the pharmacological investigation of any drug effect. A dose–response curve is generated by giving increasing doses of a drug and measuring the amplitude of the behavioral effect at each dose. Not surprisingly, higher doses generally produce larger effects than smaller doses (e.g., the CCP illustrated in Fig. 4). Furthermore, there is usually some apparent minimum dose below which no effect is produced and some maximum dose above which the amplitude of the effect ceases to increase. In other words, most dose–response curves are monotonic.

The dose–response curve for the posttraining effect of drugs (and all other known treatments) on memory is not monotonic. These curves are U-shaped functions. Figure 5 illustrates two such functions for the effect of quinpirole (LY 171555; a dopamine D2/D3 receptor agonist) on win–stay learning in the radial maze. Both of these dose–response functions include low doses with no modulatory effects, intermediate doses with clear memory-enhancing actions, and higher doses with no apparent effect. The significance of the fact that a single drug produced separate U-shaped functions at different dose ranges is discussed in Section C.

The dose–response curves of all known instances of posttraining enhancement of memory have curves similar in shape to those illustrated in Fig. 5 (e.g., Flood, Jarvik, Bennett, Orme, & Rosenzweig, 1977; Huston, Mueller, & Mondadori, 1977; McGaugh, 1989; McGaugh & Petrinovitch, 1965). No generally accepted explanation for this phenomenon is available. One possibility is based on the concept already discussed, that memory modulation involves an action of drugs at synapses that have been repeatedly activated by reverberatory activity in the cell assembly that represents recent experience (Hebb, 1956). The training trial of a memory task would activate such a pattern of synapses. During the posttraining

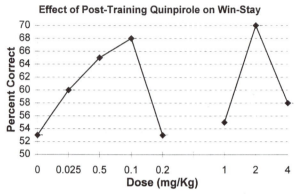

FIGURE 5   U-Shaped dose–response curves for effect of a dopamine agonist on memory. The curves show the effect of quinpirole (LY 171555), a dopamine D2/D3 receptor-specific agonist, on retention of win–stay behavior in the eight-arm radial maze. Rats learned to discriminate four lit arms containing food from four dark arms that were empty. They were given one trial per day for 5 days. After the fifth trial they received an injection of the indicated dose of quinpirole. The graph shows the mean percentage of correct responses on Day 6. The inverted U-curve on the left (from White, Packard, & Seamans, 1993) has an optimal dose of 0.1 mg/kg. The inverted U-curve on the right (from Packard & White, 1989) has an optimal dose of 2 mg/kg. Injections of 0.1 or 2.0 mg/kg given 2 hr after training on Day 5 had no effect on Day 6 performance.

period these most recently active synapses would be more susceptible than other synapses to the drug's action. Therefore, the low-dose ascending part of the U-shaped curve is the behavioral expression of a monotonic dose–response function for the enhancing action of the drug on those synapses. According to this hypothesis, at the optimal dose a very high proportion of the synapses representing the memory task have been enhanced by the drug; further increases in the dose cannot produce any further modulation of the behavior being measured by the experimenter. However, supraoptimal doses might act on additional synapses enhancing memories that represent thoughts and behaviors that are irrelevant to the memory task under study. These cognitions and behaviors could interfere with the performance of the memory task, producing an apparent decrease in the memory-enhancing action of the drug. This would result in the high-dose, descending limb of the U-shaped dose–response curve.

C. Amphetamine

A series of studies shows that posttraining injections of *d*-amphetamine improves memory in a variety of different learning situations (e.g., Doty & Doty, 1966; Krivanek & McGaugh, 1969; Packard & White, 1989). In the brain this drug promotes the release of monoamines (dopamine and noradrenaline) from the terminals of neurons that contain these neurotransmitters (Biel & Bopp, 1978; Romo, Cheramy, Godeheu, & Glowinski, 1986). In the periphery amphetamine promotes the release of noradrenaline from the adrenal medulla (Weiner, 1980) and may also activate autonomic afferents to the brain (Williams & Jensen, 1991). In this context, these drug actions can be regarded as effects on modulatory mechanisms.

Adrenal demedulation eliminates the posttraining, memory-enhancing action of systemically injected amphetamine on inhibitory avoidance (Martinez, Vasquez, et al., 1980), suggesting that the drug may produce this effect by way of a peripheral site of action. However, it has also been reported that systemic, posttraining amphetamine failed to improve memory for a CER in rats with dopamine-specific lesions of the nigro-neostriatal bundle (White, 1988), suggesting a central site of action. It is possible that both the central (dopamine-containing nigro-striatal neurons) and peripheral (adrenal medulla) structures must be intact for either treatment to affect memory; in other words, that the peripheral and central actions of amphetamine are synergistic. This possibility remains to be tested with the appropriate experiments.

4-Hydroxyamphetamine (4-OH-A) is a form of amphetamine in which the molecule is enlarged by the addition of a hydroxy radical, preventing it from crossing the blood–brain barrier. This does not affect the ability of the drug to interact with monoamine receptors in the periphery. Posttraining administration of 4-OH-A improves retention of inhibitory avoidance (Martinez et al., 1983) and win–shift behavior in the radial maze (Packard, Williams, & McGaugh, 1992). These findings suggest that the peripheral action of 4-OH-A is sufficient to enhance retention of these tasks. It is possible that this action could involve the drug-stimulated release of noradrenaline from the adrenal medulla, an action known to have memory-enhancing effects (Martinez, Jensen, et al., 1980a). These findings do not affect the possibility that the nigro-striatal dopamine system must be intact for 4-OH-A to enhance retention or the conclusion that a central action of amphetamine, which crosses the blood–brain barrier easily, may also enhance retention by acting directly in the brain (Williams, Packard, & McGaugh, 1994).

The latter possibility is supported by the observations that posttraining injections of amphetamine directly into the caudate nucleus improve retention of the CER (Carr & White, 1984; Viaud & White, 1987), and similar injections of a receptor-specific dopamine agonist (quinpirole) have the same effect (White & Viaud, 1991), implicating dopamine receptors. Posttraining injections of amphetamine into the dorsal striatum or the hippocampus also improve retention for different radial maze tasks (Packard & White, 1991). In this experiment, the dopamine-specific receptor agonists SKF 38393 and quinpirole had effects similar to those of amphetamine. The effect of these latter drugs implicates the dopamine systems terminating in dorsal striatum and hippocampus in these memory-improving actions of amphetamine.

Similar findings, dissociating the enhancement of learning of the location of a submerged platform in a water maze on the basis of either spatial or individual cues by posttraining microinjections of amphetamine into the hippocampus and caudate nucleus, respectively, have also been reported (Packard, Cahill, & McGaugh, 1993). Posttraining injections of amphetamine into the dorsomedial amygdala also improved retention of both of these water maze tasks, and the temporary inactivation of the amygdala with lidocaine on the test day did not affect the improved performance on either task. These findings suggest that, in addition to a direct action of amphetamine on dopamine-containing neurons in the hippocampus and caudate nucleus, the drug also acts on the amygdala to active a mechanism that can modulate memories that are mediated in the hippocampus and dorsal striatum (McGaugh & Gold, 1989b; McGaugh, Intnoini-Collison, & Nagahara, 1988).

Systemic injections of receptor-specific dopamine agonists (SKF 38393 or quinpirole) also improve retention on the win–shift and win–stay radial maze tasks (Packard & White, 1989; White, Packard, & Seamans, 1993). The data for the win–stay task are illustrated in Fig. 5. In one of these experiments (Packard & White, 1989), the effective doses were on the order of 2 mg/kg (higher and lower doses were ineffective); in the other (White et al., 1993), the effective doses were on the order of 0.5 mg/kg (higher and lower doses were ineffective). Thus, there appear to be two different U-shaped dose–response functions, each with its own optimal dose. This pattern suggests that each optimal dose activates a different substrate. There is considerable evidence suggesting that the higher dose range activates postsynaptic dopamine receptors (Conway & Uretsky, 1982; Jackson, Ross, & Larsson, 1989; Stahle & Ungerstedt, 1989) and that the lower dose range activates presynaptic dopamine receptors (Imperato & Di Chiara, 1988) (see Fig. 3). At present it is unknown if these two mechanisms are related to the central and peripheral actions of amphetamine described earlier.

In summary, the use of amphetamine to investigate memory modulation has revealed several mechanisms that may produce this phenomenon during normal memory functions. The data suggest the existence of a peripheral modulatory mechanism involving noradrenaline. There is also evidence for at least two direct actions of amphetamine on dopamine neurons that may include independent pre- and postsynaptic functions. Finally, findings with amphetamine suggest the existence of a modulatory mechanism involving part of the amygdala that can act on memories not actually mediated in this structure. The mechanisms revealed by these pharmacological investigations are thought to form the basis of normally occurring memory processes.

D. Opiates

The effect of opiate agonists in memory is controversial. Although there are several reports that posttraining injections of morphine have memory-improving effects in rats on a number of different memory tasks (Cavalheiro & Izquierdo, 1977; Classen & Mondadori, 1984; Staubli & Huston, 1980; White, Major, & Siegel, 1978), the drug has also been reported to impair memory function on several different tasks

(Castellano, 1975; Castellano, Cestari, Cabib, & Puglisi-Allegra, 1994; Izquierdo, 1979). The discrepant results could be due to task parameters (Classen & Mondadori, 1984) or to strain differences (Castellano, 1981). These factors could interact with actions of the drug on different memory systems increasing or decreasing its direct or indirect modulatory effects, leading to enhancement of performance or to interference with performance. The resolution of this controversy will have to await the appropriate experiments.

A much more consistent finding with respect to opioid drugs is the facilitation of acquisition by posttraining injection of naloxone and other opiate receptor antagonists (Castellano, 1981; Faust, Johnson, Stern, & Hirsch, 1978; Gallagher, King, & Young, 1983; Izquierdo, 1979), including inhibitory avoidance, active avoidance, habituation, discrimination learning, spatial learning, and Pavlovian latent inhibition (Gallagher, Fanelli, & Bostock, 1985; Gallagher et al., 1983; Izquierdo, 1979; McGaugh et al., 1988). These effects could be due to an action of opiate receptor antagonists in the amygdala (Gallagher & Kapp, 1978; Gallagher, Kapp, Pascoe, & Rapp, 1981), possibly on a modulatory mechanism that affects memories stored in other parts of the brain. The accumulated evidence for this idea starts with the investigation of a peripheral modulatory mechanism.

Adrenaline, an adrenal medullary hormone that is released into the bloodstream in response to stress and does not freely cross the blood–brain barrier, enhances memory of inhibitory avoidance (Gold & van Buskirk, 1975) and a number of other memory tasks (Introini-Collison & McGaugh, 1986; Sternberg, Isaacs, Gold, & McGaugh, 1985) when administered immediately after training. Presumably, adrenaline acts on receptors at some peripheral site that activate a neural signal that reaches the brain. Using inhibitory avoidance, Liang, Juler, and McGaugh (1986) found that pretraining intra-amygdala microinjections of the β-noradrenergic antagonist propranolol blocked the memory-enhancing effects of posttraining peripheral epinephrine. Since the systemic injections of propranolol were given before training (see Fig. 1), controls showing that the drug did not affect the animals' ability to learn the task at the doses used were included in this experiment. The finding demonstrates that the noradrenergic system of the amygdala is involved in the memory modulation of inhibitory avoidance by peripherally injected epinephrine. Intra-amygdala microinjections of norepinephrine or the β-noradrenergic agonist clenbuterol also enhanced retention of inhibitory avoidance (Introini-Collison, Miyazaki, & McGaugh, 1991; Liang, McGaugh, & Yao, 1990). This suggests that increased activity of β-noradrenergic synapses in the amygdala may be sufficient for enhancing retention of at least some forms of memory.

Propranolol also blocks the posttraining, memory-improving action of naloxone when injected systemically before training (McGaugh et al., 1988) or when mixed with naloxone and microinjected into the amygdala after training (Introini-Collison, Nagahara, & McGaugh, 1989). These findings suggest that the memory-enhancing function of the amygdala involves opiate and noradrenergically mediated mechanisms, in that order.

These findings show how drugs have been used to reveal the interaction between central and peripheral processes in memory modulation. They also show how the multiple actions of a single drug on synaptic mechanisms in different parts of the brain can produce different behavioral effects. This can make it very difficult to interpret the behavioral effects of such drugs correctly.

VI. CONCLUSION

A. Drug Addiction

A major application of the pharmacological approach to the study of learning and memory is to understand how drugs themselves influence behavior. Of particular interest is the influence of a class of drugs sometimes called "addictive" because they tend to promote their own self-administration, often to the extent of completely displacing virtually all other behaviors in afflicted individuals. Both amphetamine and morphine (and its derivative heroin) are highly addictive drugs. The information about their effects on learning and memory systems summarized in this chapter can be synthesized into an explanation for the powerful effects that these two drugs have on behavior (White, 1996). In fact, both amphetamine and morphine have several different effects on behavior that may independently promote their self-administration.

Drug self-administration is studied in animals by preparing them with intravenous or intracerebral cannulae. The cannulae are attached to a reservoir of the drug under study; the drug is injected in small unit doses by means of a pump. The pump is placed under the animal's control by connecting it to a manipulandum in the animal's cage. The animals learn to respond to the manipulandum to control the pump and self-administer the drug.

Amphetamine is intravenously self-administered by monkeys (Balster & Schuster, 1973; Wilson & Schuster, 1972) and rats (Yokel & Wise, 1975, 1978). Rats also self-administer amphetamine directly into nucleus accumbens (Hoebel et al., 1983). Dopamine-specific manipulations of nucleus accumbens have similar effects on amphetamine self-administration and on the amphetamine CCP (Lyness, Friedle, & Moore, 1979; White & Hiroi, 1993), suggesting the possibility that similar processes involving Pavlovian conditioning of approach responses and internal states may influence both behaviors.

The behavior-altering actions of amphetamine may also be promoted by its memory-modulating action in both the hippocampus and dorsal striatum and by the action of the drug on the amygdala-based modulation system. In the former structure, the drug may act to enhance declarative information about the internal states produced by the drug and about the behaviors required to obtain the drug to alter these states. In the dorsal striatum, amphetamine may act to reinforce drug-related stimulus–response sequences, or habits. All of these actions would tend to promote drug-related behaviors, including self-administration.

Morphine is self-administered intravenously (Smith, Guerin, Co, Barr, & Lane, 1985; Weeks, 1962), intraventricularly (Amit, Brown, & Sklar, 1976), and directly into the ventral tegmental area (Bozarth & Wise, 1988). The latter behavior is eliminated by naloxone, an opiate receptor blocker (Bozarth & Wise, 1988).

Lesions of the nucleus accumbens have relatively minor effects on morphine self-administration (Dworkin, Guerin, Goeders, & Smith, 1988; Smith et al., 1985), differentiating this behavior from that produced by amphetamine and suggesting that the two drugs do not produce the same classically conditioned responses. Morphine self-administration may be more dependent on hippocampus-based learning about internal states than is amphetamine self-administration.

Lesions of the caudate-putamen in rats decrease the dose of the drug required to initiate and maintain self-administration (Glick, Cox, & Crane, 1975). This finding suggests that the caudate putamen memory system does not participate in morphine self-administration but that some function of the structure could influence the development of self-administration by affecting the initial response to the drug.

The posttraining enhancement of memory by morphine in some situations could contribute to the drug's self-administration. The impairing action of morphine in other memory-related situations might be expected to retard the development of these behavioral processes.

It is important to note that the two drugs under consideration here do not have the same actions on the brain, so that the ways in which they promote their own self-administration are also different. This principle extends to all self-administered, addictive drugs. It is likely that they all have different actions, each of which promote self-administration in a different way.

B. Cognitive Enhancement

Cognitive enhancement refers to the idea that "mental performance" can be improved, usually by pharmacological treatments. An implicit assumption is that such treatments would act on a unitary memory substrate but, as we have seen, this is not the case for any systemically administered drug. The evidence cited showing that amphetamine and morphine/naloxone can improve retention falls into this category because memory is a critically important component of cognitive ability. There have been a few demonstrations of improved memory in humans who received posttraining injections of amphetamine (Soetens, Casaer, D'Hooge, & Hueting, 1995) but, for obvious reasons (see previous section on addiction), this drug is not a candidate for general distribution as a cognitive enhancer.

Interestingly, there is evidence that a number of other relatively safe and sometimes quite common substances have memory-enhancing effects and therefore qualify as cognitive enhancers. These include estrogen in menopausal women (Kampen

& Sherwin, 1994; Robinson, Friedman, Marcus, Tinklenberg, & Yesavage, 1994), ordinary sugar in normal (Benton, Owens, & Parker, 1994) and memory-impaired (Parsons & Gold, 1992; Gold, 1995) individuals, and caffeine (Jarvis, 1993). Each of these substances has also been shown to improve retention in rats when administered during the period immediately after training on a memory task (Dohanich, Fader, & Javorsky, 1994; Flood, Bennett, Orme, Rosenzweig, & Jarvik, 1978; Messier & White, 1984).

Although each of the experiments on humans cited in the previous paragraph reports a statistically significant improvement of recall following posttraining administration of the substance under study, the overall size of the effects is small, averaging on the order of about 10% improvement. This raises questions about their clinical significance. It remains an open question whether some new substance will be found that can produce larger effects. However, the cell assembly model of memory storage described in this chapter and elsewhere in this volume suggests that there is a finite substrate for the storage of any memory. This and the U-shaped dose–response curve for the memory-enhancing action of drugs both suggest that there may be a ceiling on the degree of improvement that can be produced. This may in part be a result of the fact that memory-enhancing drugs often act on substrates with competing effects. It is therefore possible (but not certain) that the relatively small effects reported represent the limits of cognitive enhancement possible through pharmacological manipulation.

C. Ten Summary Points

1. Drugs influence behavior by acting on neural systems that normally function to change behavior as a result of experience. The behavioral changes mediated by these systems are usually attributed to learning and memory processes involving the storage of new information in the brain. Drugs act on the same neural systems to alter the behavior they produce.

2. Drugs can be administered peripherally or centrally. The route of administration of a drug interacts with its physical and chemical properties to determine how quickly and how much of it reaches its target.

3. Drugs act on receptors that influence synaptic transmission in the brain and periphery. Each drug acts on a specific receptor, but each type of receptor may be located in several neural systems with different, unrelated functions. Therefore, the effects of a given drug can be quite complex. Drugs can promote synaptic transmissions (agonists) or block it (antagonists).

4. The consequences of the actions of drugs on synapses can be conceptualized as responses, which are largely unobservable. These responses can be perceived subjectively as rewarding or aversive affective states. The responses can also involve activation of the neural mechanisms for approach and escape responding, but as

drugs lack external reference points, these behaviors are unidentifiable and may appear as random activity.

5. These neural responses can be subject to Pavlovian conditioning so that conditioned responses similar to those produced by drugs come to be elicited by conditioned stimuli in the absence of the drugs themselves. Conditioned affective states and approach or escape responses can act to organize behavior in the absence of the drug.

6. Two commonly used experimental paradigms for studying the affective properties of drugs are the conditioned cue preference and the conditioned taste preference. In both cases the responses produced by drugs are associated with cues— external stimuli or taste stimuli. Normally unobservable affective properties of drugs are inferred from the observable conditioned responses to the conditioned cues.

7. Another synaptic action of drugs modulates the storage of new memories during the period immediately following initial acquisition. During this posttraining period drugs can act directly on the synapses that store information, or on modulatory mechanisms that affect these synapses, either to facilitate or to impair storage and, consequently, the memory represented by the neurons that form the synapses.

8. In the most common experimental paradigm used to study modulatory actions, drugs are administered during the period immediately following the training trial of a memory task. A delayed injection, to control for proactive effects of the drug, is required to reach the conclusion that the drug influenced behavior by interacting with a memory process. These controls are required because drugs administered before acquisition (training) or expression (testing) of a memory task may alter behavior due to effects on sensory, perceptual, attentional, motivational, or motoric processes that are unrelated to memory function.

9. The particular combination of these effects produced by addictive drugs can explain why they reinforce their own self-administration to the extent of disrupting normal behavior.

10. The memory-modulating action of drugs is probably the basis of most cognitive enhancement effects. There may be real limits on the possible size of these effects.

ACKNOWLEDGMENTS

Preparation of this chapter was supported by grants from the Natural Sciences and Engineering Research Council of Canada and from Fonds FCAR, Province of Québec, to N.M.W. J. A. S. was supported by an NSF Postdoctoral Fellowship.

REFERENCES

Adolphs, R., Tranel, D., Damasio, H., & Damasio, A. R. (1995). Fear and the human amygdala. *Journal of Neuroscience, 15,* 5879–5891.

Amit, Z., Brown, Z., & Sklar, L. S. (1976). Intraventricular self-administration of morphine in naive laboratory rats. *Psychopharmacology, 48,* 291–294.

Balster, R. L., & Schuster, C. R. (1973). A comparison of *d*-amphetamine, *l*-amphetamine, and methamphetamine self-administration in rhesus monkeys. *Pharmacology, Biochemistry and Behavior, 1,* 67–71.

Beach, H. D. (1957). Morphine addiction in rats. *Canadian Journal of Psychology, 11,* 104–112.

Bechara, A., & van der Kooy, D. (1985). Opposite motivational effects of endogenous opioids in brain and periphery. *Nature, 314,* 533–534.

Bechara, A., & van der Kooy, D. (1992). A single brain stem substrate mediates the motivational effects of both opiates and food in nondeprived rats but not in deprived rats. *Behavioral Neuroscience, 106,* 351–363.

Benet, L. Z., Mitchell, J. R., & Sheiner, L. B. (1990a). Pharmacokinetics: The dynamics of drug absorption, distribution and elimination. In A. G. Gilman, T. W. Rall, A. S. Nies, & P. Taylor (Eds.), *Goodman and Gilman's The pharmacological basis of therapeutics* (pp. 3–32). New York: Pergamon.

Benet, L. Z., Mitchell, J. R., & Sheiner, L. B. (1990b). Pharmacodynamics: Mechanisms of drug action and the relationship between drug concentration and effect. In A. G. Gilman, T. W. Rall, A. S. Nies, & P. Taylor (Eds.), *Goodman and Gilman's The pharmacological basis of therapeutics* (pp. 33–48). New York: Pergamon.

Benton, D., Owens, D. S., & Parker, P. Y. (1994). Blood glucose influences memory and attention in young adults. *Neuropsychologia, 32,* 595–607.

Biel, J. H., & Bopp, B. A. (1978). Amphetamines: Structure–activity relationships. In L. L. Iversen, S. D. Iversen, & S. H. Snyder (Eds.), Handbook of psychopharmacology (Vol. 11, pp. 1–39). New York: Plenum Press.

Bloch, V. (1970). Facts and hypotheses concerning memory consolidation processes. *Brain Research, 24,* 561–575.

Bloom, F. E., Rossier, J., Battenberg, E. L., Bayon, A., French, E., Henriksen, S. J., Siggins, G. R., Segal, D., Browne, R., Ling, N., & Guillemin, R. (1978). Beta-endorphin: Cellular localization, electrophysiological and behavioral effects. *Advances in Biochemical Psychopharmacology, 18,* 89–109,

Boring, E. G. (1950). A history of experimental psychology (2nd ed.). New York: Appleton-Century-Crofts.

Bozarth, M. A., & Wise, R. A. (1988). Anatomically distinct opiate receptor fields mediate reward and physical dependence. *Science, 224,* 516–517.

Breen, R. A., & McGaugh, J. L. (1961). Facilitation of maze learning with posttrial injections of picrotoxin. *Journal of Comparative and Physiological Psychology, 54,* 498–501.

Carr, G. D., Phillips, A. G., & Fibiger, H. C. (1988). Independence of amphetamine reward from locomotor stimulation demonstrated by conditioned place preference. *Psychopharmacology, 94,* 221–226.

Carr, G. D., & White, N. M. (1984). The relationship between stereotypy and memory improvement produced by amphetamine. *Psychopharmacology, 82,* 203–209.

Carr, G. D., & White, N. M. (1986). Anatomical dissociation of amphetamine's rewarding and aversive effects: An intracranial microinjection study. *Psychopharmacology, 89,* 340–346.

Castellano, C. (1975). Effects of morphine and heroin on discrimination learning and consolidation in mice. *Psychopharmacology, 42,* 235–242.

Castellano, C. (1976). Effects of caffeine on discrimination learning, consolidation, and learned behavior in mice. *Psychopharmacology, 48,* 255–260.

Castellano, C. (1981). Strain-dependent effects of naloxone on discrimination learning in mice. *Psychopharmacology, 73,* 152–156.

Castellano, C., Cestari, V., Cabib, S., & Puglisi-Allegra, S. (1994). The effects of morphine on memory consolidation in mice involve both D1 and D2 dopamine receptors. *Behavioral and Neural Biology, 61,* 156–161.

Cavalheiro, E. A., & Izquierdo, I. (1977). Effect of hippocampal and neocortical spreading depression on rat shuttle behavior in four different experimental paradigms. *Physiology and Behavior, 18,* 1011–1016.

Classen, W., & Mondadori, C. (1984). Facilitation or inhibition of memory by morphine: A question of experimental parameters. *Experientia, 40,* 506–509.

Cohen, N. J. (1984). Preserved learning capacity in amnesia: Evidence for multiple memory systems. In N. Butters & L. R. Squire (Eds.), *Neuronal plasticity and memory formation* (pp. 83–103). New York: Guilford Press.

Cohen, N. J., & Squire, L. R. (1980). Preserved learning and retention of pattern-analyzing skill in amnesia: Dissociation of knowing how and knowing what. *Science, 210,* 207–209.

Conway, P. G., & Uretsky, N. J. (1982). Role of striatal dopaminergic receptors in amphetamine-induced behavioral facilitation. *Journal of Pharmacology and Experimental Therapeutics, 221,* 650–655.

Cooper, J. R., Bloom, F., & Roth, R. H. (1982). *The biochemical basis of neuropharmacology* (4th ed.). New York: Oxford.

Corrigall, W. A., & Linseman, M. A. (1988). Conditioned place preference produced by intra-hippocampal morphine. *Pharmacology, Biochemistry and Behavior, 30,* 787–789.

Coulombe, D., & White, N. M. (1980). The effect of post-training lateral hypothalamic self-stimulation on aversive and appetitive classical conditioning. *Physiology and Behavior, 25,* 267–272.

Dohanich, G. P., Fader, A. J., & Javorsky, D. J. (1994). Estrogen and estrogen–progesterone treatments counteract the effect of scopolamine on reinforced T-maze alternation in female rats. *Behavioral Neuroscience, 108,* 988–992.

Doty, B., & Doty, L. (1966). Facilitating effects of amphetamine on avoidance conditioning in relation to age and problem difficulty. *Psychopharmacology, 9,* 234–241.

Duncan, C. P. (1949). The retroactive effect of electroshock on learning. *Journal of Comparative and Physiological Psychology, 42,* 32–44.

Dworkin, S. I., Guerin, G. F., Goeders, N. E., & Smith, J. E. (1988). Kainic acid lesions of the nucleus accumbens selectively attenuate morphine self-administration. *Pharmacology, Biochemistry and Behavior, 29,* 175–181.

Evangelista, A. M., Gattoni, R. C., & Izquierdo, I. (1970). Effect of amphetamine, nicotine and hexa-methonium on performance of a conditioned response during acquisition and retention trials. *Psychopharmacology, 3,* 91–96.

Everitt, B. J. (1990). Sexual motivation: A neural and behavioural analysis of the mechanisms underlying appetitive and copulatory responses of male rats. *Neuroscience and Biobehavioral Reviews, 14,* 217–232.

Everitt, B. J., Morris, K. A., O'Brien, A., & Robbins, T. W. (1991). The basolateral amygdala-ventral striatal system and conditioned place preference: Further evidence of limbic-striatal interactions underlying reward-related processes. *Neuroscience, 42,* 1–18.

Faust, I. M., Johnson, P. R., Stern, J. S., & Hirsch, J. (1978). Diet-induced adipocyte number increase in adult rats: A new model of obesity. *American Journal of Physiology, 235,* 279–286.

Flood, J. F., Bennett, E. L., Orme, A. E., Rosenzweig, M. R., & Jarvik, M. E. (1978). Memory: Modification of anisomycin-induced amnesia by stimulants and depressants. *Science, 199*(4326), 324–326.

Flood, J. F., Jarvik, M. E., Bennett, E. L., Orme, A. E., & Rosenzweig, M. R. (1977). The effect of stimulants, depressants, and protein synthesis inhibition on retention. *Behavioral Biology, 20,* 168–183.

Gallagher, M., Fanelli, R. J., & Bostock, E. (1985). Opioid peptides: Their position among other neuroregulators of memory. In J. L. McGaugh (Ed.), *Contemporary psychology: Biological processes and theoretical issues* (pp. 69–93). Amsterdam: Elsevier.

Gallagher, M., & Holland, P. C. (1994). The amygdala complex: Multiple roles in associative learning and attention. *Proceedings of the National Academy of Sciences U.S.A., 91,* 11771–11776.

Gallagher, M., & Kapp, B. S. (1978). Manipulation of opiate activity in the amygdala alters memory processes. *Life Sciences, 23,* 1973–1978.

Gallagher, M., Kapp, B. S., Pascoe, J. P., & Rapp, P. R. (1981). A neuropharmacology of amygdaloid systems which contribute to learning and memory. In Y. Ben-Ari (Ed.), *The amygdaloid complex* (pp. 343–354). Amsterdam: Elsevier.

Gallagher, M., King, R. A., & Young, N. B. (1983). Opiate antagonists improve spatial memory. *Science, 221*, 975–976.

Garg, M., & Holland, H. C. (1968). Consolidation and maze learning: A further study of post-trial injections of a stimulant drug (nicotine). *International Journal of Neuropharmacology, 7*, 55–59.

Glick, S. D., Cox, R. D., & Crane, A. M. (1975). Changes in morphine self-administration and morphine dependence after lesions of the caudate nucleus in rats. *Psychopharmacology, 41*, 219–224.

Gold, P. E. (1995). Role of glucose in regulating the brain and cognition. *American Journal of Clinical Nutrition, 61* (Suppl. 4), 987S–995S.

Gold, P. E., & van Buskirk, R. (1975). Facilitation of time-dependent memory processes with posttrial epinephrine injections. *Behavioral Biology, 13*, 145–153.

Gold, P. E., & van Buskirk, R. B. (1976). Effects of post-trial hormone injections on memory processes. *Hormones and Behavior, 7*, 509–517.

Gold, P. E., Vogt, J., & Hall, J. L. (1986). Glucose effects on memory: Behavioral and pharmacological characteristics. *Behavioral and Neural Biology, 46*, 145–155.

Goldstein, G. W., & Betz, A. L. (1986). The blood–brain barrier. *Scientific American, 255*(3), 74–83.

Grossman, S. P. (1969). Facilitation of learning following intracranial injections of pentylenetetrazol. *Physiology and Behavior, 4*, 625–628.

Guix, T., Hurd, Y. L., & Ungerstedt, U. (1992). Amphetamine enhances extracellular concentrations of dopamine and acetylcholine in dorsolateral striatum and nucleus accumbens of freely moving rats. *Neuroscience Letters, 138*, 137–140.

Hebb, D. O. (1949). *The organization of behavior.* New York: Wiley.

Hebb, D. O. (1956). *A textbook of psychology.* Philadelphia: Wiley.

Hiroi, N., & White, N. M. (1990). The reserpine-sensitive dopamine pool mediates (+)-amphetamine-conditioned reward in the place preference paradigm. *Brain Research, 510*, 33–42.

Hiroi, N., & White, N. M. (1991). The amphetamine conditioned place preference: Differential involvement of dopamine receptor subtypes and two dopaminergic terminal areas. *Brain Researrch, 552*, 141–152.

Hoebel, B. G., Monaco, A. P., Hernandez, L., Aulisi, E. F., Stanley, B. G., & Lenard, L. G. (1983). Self-injection of amphetamine directly into the brain. *Psychopharmacology, 81*, 158–163.

Holaday, J. W., & Loh, H. H. (1979). Endorphin–opiate interactions with neuroendocrine systems. *Advances in Biochemical Psychopharmacology, 20*, 227–258.

Hudspeth, W. J. (1964). Strychnine: Its facilitating effect on the solution of a simple oddity problem by the rat. *Science, 145*, 1331–1333.

Huston, J. P., Mondadori, C., & Waser, P. G. (1974). Facilitation of learning by reward of post-trial memory processes. *Experientia, 30*, 1038–1040.

Huston, J. P., Mueller, C. C., & Mondadori, C. (1977). Memory facilitation by posttrial hypothalamic stimulation and other reinforcers: A central theory of reinforcement. *Biobehavioral Reviews, 1*, 143–150.

Imperato, A., & Di Chiara, G. (1988). Effects of locally applied D-1 and D-2 receptor agonists and antagonists studied with brain dialysis. *European Journal of Pharmacology, 156*, 385–393.

Introini-Collison, I. B., & McGaugh, J. L. (1986). Epinephrine modulates long-term retention of an aversively motivated discrimination. *Behavioral and Neural Biology, 45*, 358–365.

Introini-Collison, I. B., Miyazaki, B., & McGaugh, J. L. (1991). Involvement of the amygdala in the memory-enhancing effects of clenbuterol. *Psychopharmacology, 104*, 541–544.

Introini-Collison, I. B., Nagahara, A. H., & McGaugh, J. L. (1989). Memory enhancement with intra-amygdala post-training naloxone is blocked by concurrent administration of propranolo. *Brain Reseach, 476*, 94–101.

Izquierdo, I. (1979). Effect of naloxone and morphine on various forms of memory in the rat: Possible role of endogenous opiate mechanisms in memory consolidation. *Psychopharmacology, 66*, 199–203.

Izquierdo, J. A. (1982). The effects of pre- and post-trial caffeine on one trial passive avoidance behaviour in mice. *IRCS Medical Science, 10*, 387.

Jackson, D. M., Ross, S. B., & Larsson, L.-G. (1989). Dopamine D-2 receptor agonist-induced behavioural depression: Critical dependence upon postsynaptic dopamine D-1 function. A behavioural and biochemical study. *Naunyn–Scmiedeberg's Archives of Pharmacology, 340,* 355–365.

Jarvis, M. J. (1993). Does caffeine intake enhance absolute levels of cognitive performance? *Psychopharmacology, 110,* 45–52.

Kampen, D. L., & Sherwin, B. B. (1994). Estrogen use and verbal memory in healthy postmenopausal women. *Obstetrics and Gynecology, 83,* 979–983.

Katz, B. (1966). *Nerve, muscle and synapse.* New York: McGraw-Hill.

Kelly, P. H. (1991). Drug induced motor behavior. In L. L. Iverson, S. D. Iversen, & S. H. Snyder (Eds.), *Handbook of pharmacology.* New York: Plenum Press.

Kliner, D. J., & Pickens, R. (1982). Indicated preference for drugs of abuse. *The International Journal of the Addictions, 17,* 543–547.

Krivanek, J., & McGaugh, J. L. (1969). Facilitating effects of pre- and post-training amphetamine administration on discrimination learning in mice. *Agents and Actions, 1,* 36–42.

LeBlanc, A. E., & Cappell, H. (1974). Attenuation of punishing effects of morphine and amphetamine by chronic prior treatment. *Journal of Comparative and Physiological Psychology, 87,* 691–698.

LeDoux, J. E. (1993). Emotional memory systems in the brain. *Behavioural Brain Research, 58,* 69–79.

Levitan, I. B., & Kaczmarek, L. K. (1991). *The neuron: Cell and molecular biology.* New York: Oxford.

Liang, K. C., Juler, R. G., & McGaugh, J. L. (1986). Modulating effects of post-training epinephrine on memory: Involvement of the amygdala noradrenergic system. *Brain Research, 368,* 125–133.

Liang, K. C., McGaugh, J. L., & Yao, H.-Y. (1990). Involvement of amygdala pathways in the influence of post-training intra-amygdala norepinephrine and peripheral epinephrine on memory storage. *Brain Research, 508,* 225–233.

Libet, B. (1986). Nonclassical synaptic functions of transmitters. *Federation Proceedings, 45,* 2678–2686.

Lyness, W. H., Friedle, N. M., & Moore, K. E. (1979). Destruction of dopaminergic nerve terminals in nucleus accumbens: Effect on *d*-amphetamine self-administration. *Pharmacology, Biochemistry and Behavior, 11,* 553–556.

Major, R., & White, N. M. (1978). Memory facilitation by self-stimulation reinforcement mediated by the nigro-neostriatal bundle. *Physiology & Behavior, 20,* 723–733.

Martinez, J. L., Ishikawa, K., Liang, K. C., Jensen, R. A., Bennett, C., Sternberg, D. B., & McGaugh, J. L. (1983). 4-OH amphetamine enhances retention of an active avoidance response in rats and decreases regional brain concentrations of norepinephrine and dopamine. *Behavioral Neuroscience, 97,* 962–969.

Martinez, J. L., Jensen, R. A., Messing, R. B., Vasquez, B. J., Soumireu-Mourat, B., Geddes, D., Liang, K. C., & McGaugh, J. L. (1980). Central and peripheral actions of amphetamine on memory storage. *Brain Research, 182,* 157–166.

Martinez, J. L., Vasquez, B. J., Rigter, H., Messing, R. B., Jensen, R. A., Liang, K. C., & McGaugh, J. L. (1980). Attenuation of amphetamine-induced enhancement of learning by adrenal demedullation. *Brain Research, 195,* 433–443.

McDonald, R. J., & White, N. M. (1993). A triple dissociation of memory systems: Hippocampus, amygdala and dorsal striatum. *Behavioral Neuroscience, 107,* 3–22.

McDonald, R. J., & White, N. M. (1994). Parallel information processing in the water maze: Evidence for independent memory systems involving dorsal striatum and hippocampus. *Behavioral and Neural Biology, 61,* 260–270.

McGaugh, J. L. (1988). Modulation of memory storage processes. In P. R. Solomon, G. R. Goethals, C. M. Kelley, & B. R. Stephens (Eds.), *Memory—An interdisciplinary approach.* New York: Springer-Verlag.

McGaugh, J. L. (1989). Involvement of hormonal and neuromodulatory systems in the regulation of memory storage. *Annual Review of Neuroscience, 12,* 255–287.

McGaugh, J. L., & Gold, P. E. (1989). Hormonal modulation of memory. In R. B. Brush & S. Levine (Eds.), *Psychoendocrinology* (pp. 305–339). New York: Academic.

McGaugh, J. L., & Herz, M. J. (1972). *Memory consolidation.* San Francisco: Albion.

McGaugh, J. L., Introini-Collison, I. B., & Nagahara, A. H. (1988). Memory enhancing effects of post-training naloxone: Involvement of B noradrenergic influences in the amygdaloid complex. *Brain Research, 446,* 37–49.

McGaugh, J. L., & Petrinovitch, L. F. (1965). Effects of drugs on learning and memory. *International Review of Neurobiology, 8,* 139–196.

McGaugh, J. L., & Thomson, C. W. (1962). Facilitation of simultaneous discrimination learning with strychnine sulphate. *Psychopharmacology, 3,* 166–172.

Mehrara, B. J., & Baum, M. J. (1990). Naloxone disrupts the expression but not the acquisition by male rats of a conditioned place preference response for an oestrous female. *Psychopharmacology, 101,* 118–125.

Messier, C., & Gagnon, M. (1996). Glucose regulation and cognitive functions: Relation to Alzheimer's disease and diabetes. *Behavioural Brain Research, 75,* 1–10.

Messier, C., & White, N. M. (1984). Contingent and non-contingent actions of sucrose and saccharin reinforcers: Effects on taste preference and memory. *Physiology and Behavior, 32,* 195–203.

Moscovitch, M. (1994). Memory and working with memory: Evaluation of a component process model and comparisons with other models. In D. L. Schacter & E. Tulving (Eds.), *Memory systems 1994* (pp. 269–310). Cambridge, MA: MIT Press.

Mucha, R. F., van der Kooy, D., O'Shaughnessy, M., & Bucenieks, P. (1982). Drug reinforcement studied by the use of place conditioning in rat. *Brain Research, 243,* 91–105.

Muller, G. E., & Pilzecker, A. (1900). Experimentelle Beitrage zur Lehre vom Gedachtnis. *Zeitschrift fur Psychologie und Physiologie der Sennesorgane ergamzungsband, 1,* 1–288.

Nachman, M., & Ashe, J. H. (1973). Learned taste aversions in rats as a function of dosage, concentration, and route of administration of LiCl. *Physiology and Behavior, 10,* 73–78.

Ninkovic, M., Hunt, S. P., & Gleave, J. R. (1982). Localization of opiate and histamine H1-receptors in the primate sensory ganglia and spinal cord. *Brain Research, 241,* 197–206.

Packard, M. G., Cahill, L., & McGaugh, J. L. (1993). Effects of post-training *d*-amphetamine injections into hippocampus, amygdala and caudate nucleus on retention in spatial and cued water maze tasks. *Society for Neuroscience Abstracts, 19,* 1226.

Packard, M. G., Hirsh, R., & White, N. M. (1989). Differential effects of fornix and caudate nucleus lesions on two radial maze tasks: Evidence for multiple memory systems. *Journal of Neuroscience, 9,* 1465–1472.

Packard, M. G., & White, N. M. (1989). Memory facilitation produced by dopamine receptor agonists: Role of receptor subtype and mnemonic requirements. *Pharmacology, Biochemistry and Behavior, 33,* 511–518.

Packard, M. G., & White, N. M. (1991). Dissociation of hippocampal and caudate nucleus memory systems by post-training intracerebral injection of dopamine agonists. *Behavioral Neuroscience, 105,* 295–306.

Packard, M. G., Williams, C. L., & McGaugh, J. L. (1992). Enhancement of win-shift radial maze retention by peripheral posttraining administration of *d*-amphetamine and 4-OH amphetamine. *Psychobiology, 20,* 280–285.

Parsons, M. W., & Gold, P. E. (1992). Glucose enhancement of memory in elderly humans: An inverted-U dose–response curve. *Neurobiology of Aging, 13,* 401–404.

Pavlov, I. P. (1927). *Conditioned reflexes.* Oxford: Oxford University Press.

Pert, C. B., Kuhar, M. J., & Snyder, S. H. (1976). Opiate receptor: Autoradiographic localization in rat brian. *Proceedings of the National Academy of Sciences U.S.A. 73,* 3729–3733.

Pert, C. B., Pasternak, G., & Snyder, S. H. (1973). Opiate agonists and antagonists discriminated by receptor binding in brain. *Science, 182,* 1359–1361.

Phillips, A. G., Spyraki, C., & Fibiger, H. C. (1982). Conditioned place preference with amphetamine and opiates as reward stimuli: Attenuation by haloperidol. In B. G. Hoebel & D. Novin (Eds.), *The neural basis of feeding and reward* (pp. 455–464). Brunswick, ME: Haer Institute.

Reicher, M. A., & Holman, E. W. (1977). Location preference and flavor aversion reinforced by amphetamine in rats. *Animal Learning and Behavior, 5,* 343–346.

Revusky, S., Taukulis, H. K., & Peddle, C. (1979). Learned associations between drug states: Attempted analysis in Pavlovian terms. *Physiological Psychology, 7,* 352–363.

Robinson, D., Friedman, L., Marcus, R., Tinklenberg, J., & Yesavage, J. (1994). Estrogen replacement therapy and memory in older women. *Journal of the American Geriatrics Society, 42,* 919–922.

Robinson, T. E., & Camp, D. M. (1990). Does amphetamine *preferentially* increase the extracellular concentration of dopamine in the mesolimbic system of freely moving rats? *Neuropsychopharmacology, 3,* 163–173.

Romo, R., Cheramy, A., Godeheu, G., & Glowinski, J. (1986). In vivo presynaptic control of dopamine release in the cat caudate nucleus: III. Further evidence for the implications of corticostriatal glutamatergic neurons. *Neuroscience, 19,* 1091–1099.

Russell, W. R., & Nathan, P. W. (1946). Traumatic amnesia. *Brain, 69,* 280–300.

Sherman, J. E., Pickman, C., Rice, A., Liebeskind, J. C., & Holman, E. W. (1980). Rewarding and aversive effects of morphine: Temporal and pharmacological properties. *Pharmacology, Biochemistry and Behavior, 13,* 501–515.

Smith, J. E., Guerin, G. F., Co, C., Barr, T. S., & Lane, J. D. (1985). Effects of 6-OHDA lesions of the central medial nucleus accumbens on rat intravenous morphine self-administration. *Pharmacology, Biochemistry and Behavior, 23,* 843–849.

Smolders, I., De Klippel, N., Sarre, S., Ebinger, G., & Michotte, Y. (1995). Tonic GABA-ergic modulation of striatal dopamine release studied by in vivo microdialysis in the freely moving rat. *European Journal of Pharmacology, 284,* 83–91.

Soetens, E., Casaer, S., D'Hooge, R., & Hueting, J. E. (1995). Effect of amphetamine on long-term retention of verbal material. *Psychopharmacology, 119,* 155–162.

Squire, L. R., Knowlton, B., & Musen, G. (1993). The structure and organization of memory. *Annual Review of Psychology, 44,* 453–495.

Squire, L. R., & Zola-Morgan, S. (1991). The medial temporal lobe memory system. *Science, 253,* 1380–1386.

Stahle, L., & Ungerstedt, U. (1989). Yawning and suppression of exploration in amphetamine-treated rats, incompatibility with the autoreceptor hypothesis. *Psychopharmacology, 97,* 553–560.

Staubli, U., & Huston, J. P. (1980). Avoidance learning enhanced by post-trial morphine injection. *Behavioral and Neural Biology, 28,* 487–490.

Stein, L., Belluzzi, J. D., & Wise, C. D. (1975). Memory enhancement by central administration of norepinephrine. *Brain Research, 84,* 329–335.

Sternberg, D. B., Isaacs, K., Gold, P. E., & McGaugh, J. L. (1985). Epinephrine facilitation of appetitive learning: Attenuation with adrenergic receptor antagonists. *Behavioral and Neural Biology, 44,* 447–453.

Stolerman, I. P., & D'Mello, G. D. (1978). Amphetamine-induced taste aversion demonstrated with operant behaviour. *Pharmacology, Biochemistry and Behavior, 8,* 107–111.

Swerdlow, N. R., Amalric, M., & Koob, G. F. (1987). Nucleus accumbens opiate–dopamine interactions and locomotor activation in the rat: Evidence for a pre-synaptic locus. *Pharmacology, Biochemistry and Behavior, 26,* 765–769.

Thorndike, E. L. (1911). *Animal intelligence.* New York: Macmillan.

Tranel, D., & Hyman, B. T. (1990). Neuropsychological correlates of bilateral amygdala damage. *Archives of Neurology, 47,* 349–355.

van der Kooy, D., Mucha, R. F., O'Shaughnessy, M., & Bucenieks, P. (1982). Reinforcing effects of brain microinjections of morphine revealed by conditioned place preference. *Brain Research, 243,* 107–117.

Viaud, M. D., & White, N. M. (1987). Disassociation of visual and olfactory conditioning in the neostriatum of rats. *Society for Neuroscience Abstracts, 13,* 645.

Weeks, J. R. (1962). Experimental morphine addiction: Method for automatic intravenous injections in unrestrained rats. *Science, 138,* 143–144.

Weiner, N. (1980). Norepinephrine, epinephrine and the sympathomimetic amines. In L. S. Goodman & A. Gilman (Eds.), *The pharmacological basis of therapeutics* (pp. 138–176). New York: Macmillan.

White, N. M. (1988). Effect of nigrostriatal dopamine depletion on the post-training, memory improving action of amphetamine. *Life Sciences, 43,* 7–12.

White, N. M. (1996). Addictive drugs as reinforcers: Multiple partial actions on memory systems. *Addiction, 91,* 921–949.

White, N. M., & Carr, G. D. (1985). The conditioned place preference is affected by two independent reinforcement processes. *Pharmacology, Biochemistry and Behavior, 23,* 37–42.

White, N. M., & Hiroi, N. (1993). Amphetamine conditioned cue preference and the neurobiology of drug seeking. *Seminars in the Neurosciences, 5,* 329–336.

White, N. M., Major, R., & Siegel, J. (1978). Effect of morphine on one-trial appetitive learning. *Life Sciences, 23,* 1967–1972.

White, N. M., & McDonald, R. J. (1993). Acquisition of a spatial conditioned place preference is impaired by amygdala lesions and improved by fornix lesions. *Behavioural Brain Research, 55,* 269–281.

White, N. M., Messier, C., & Carr, G. D. (1987). Operationalizing and measuring the organizing influence of drugs on behavior. In M. A. Bozarth (Ed.), *Methods of measuring the reinforcing properties of abused drugs* (pp. 591–618). New York: Springer-Verlag.

White, N. M., Packard, M. G., & Seamans, J. (1993). Memory enhancement by post-training peripheral administration of low doses of dopamine agonists: Possible autoreceptor effect. *Behavioral and Neural Biology, 59,* 230–241.

White, N. M., Sklar, L., & Amit, Z. (1977). The reinforcing action of morphine and its paradoxical side effect. *Psychopharmacology, 52,* 63–66.

White, N. M., & Viaud, M. D. (1991). Localized intracaudate dopamine D2 receptor activation during the post-training period improves memory for visual or olfactory conditioned emotional responses in rats. *Behavioral and Neural Biology, 55,* 255–269.

Williams, C. L., & Jensen, R. A. (1991). Vagal afferents: A possible mechanism for the modulation of peripherally acting agents. In R. C. A. Frederickson, J. L. McGaugh, & D. L. Felten (Eds.), *Peripheral signalling of the brain: Neural, immune and cognitive function.* Toronto: Hogrefe and Huber.

Williams, C. L., Packard, M. G., & McGaugh, J. L. (1994). Amphetamine facilitation of win-shift radial-arm maze retention: The involvement of peripheral adrenergic and central dopaminergic systems. *Psychobiology, 22,* 141–148.

Wilson, M. C., & Schuster, C. R. (1972). The effects of chlorpromazine on psychomotor stimulant self-administration in the rhesus monkey. *Psychopharmacology, 26,* 115–126.

Wise, R. A., & Hoffman, D. C. (1992). Localization of drug reward mechanisms by intracranial injections. *Synapse, 10,* 274–263.

Yokel, R. A., & Wise, R. A. (1975). Increased lever pressing for amphetamine after pimozide in rats: Implications for a dopamine theory of reward. *Science, 187,* 547–549.

Yokel, R. A., & Wise, R. A. (1978). Amphetamine-type reinforcement by dopaminergic agonists in the rat. *Psychopharmacology, 58,* 289–296.

Young, P. T. (1959). The role of affective processes in learning and motivation. *Psychological Review, 66,* 104–125.

Young, P. T., & Christensen, K. R. (1962). Algebraic summation of hedonic processes. *Journal of Comparative and Physiological Psychology, 55,* 332–336.

Young, P. T., & Shuford, E. H. (1955). Quantitative control of motivation through sucrose solutions of different concentrations. *Journal of Comparative and Physiological Psychology, 48,* 114–118.

Zola-Morgan, S., & Squire, L. R. (1993). Neuroanatomy of memory. *Annual Review of Neuroscience, 16,* 547–563.

Zola-Morgan, S., Squire, L. R., Alvarez-Royo, P., & Clower, R. P. (1991). Independence of memory functions and emotional behavior: Separate contributions of the hippocampal formations and the amygdala. *Hippocampus, 1,* 207–220.

Zubin, J., & Barrera, S. E. (1941). Effect of electric convulsive therapy on memory. *Proceedings of the Society for Experimental Biology and Medicine, 48,* 596–597.

CHAPTER 5

Invertebrate Learning: Current Perspectives

Christine Sahley

Department of Biological Sciences, Purdue University, West Lafayette, Indiana 47907

Terry Crow

Department of Neurobiology and Anatomy, University of Texas Medical School, Houston, Texas 77225

I. INTRODUCTION

Invertebrates have been useful in the study of learning and memory because of the relative simplicity of their nervous systems. The nervous systems of many invertebrates contain only several thousand neurons, and some of the cells are relatively large and identifiable. This feature has resulted in the application of powerful analytical tools to the examination of mechanisms of learning and memory. A goal of studies of invertebrate learning is to establish a causal relationship between changes in the nervous system and the generation of learned behavior. Historically, learning in invertebrates has been studied on several levels from behavior to neural circuits to individual neurons to subcellular changes. The challenge is to establish the relationships among these different levels and to assess their contribution to the learned change in behavior of the intact animal. In this chapter we review work on nonassociative and associative learning from several invertebrate systems in which both behavioral and cellular analyses have been conducted.

Neurobiology of Learning and Memory

II. HABITUATION AND SENSITIZATION

A. Behavioral Studies

1. Aplysia californica

Nonassociative learning in Aplysia has been studied primarily using three reflexes: (1) the gill-withdrawal reflex in response to siphon stimulation, (2) the tail-withdrawal reflex in response to tail stimulation, and (3) the siphon-withdrawal reflex in response to tail stimulation. The reflex is elicited by a light tactile stimulus to the siphon, which evokes a withdrawal of these organs. If a noxious stimulus is presented to a naive animal, most often applied to the tail and sometimes the head, the subsequent reflex elicited by the light tactile stimulus will be enhanced (sensitization). Habituation as a result of repeated presentations of the light tactile stimulus results in a decrease in responding to the stimulus (Pinsker, Kupfermann, Castellucci, & Kandel, 1970). Following habituation training, a strong stimulus anywhere on the body can restore responding to the tactile stimulus and is termed dishabituation. Repeated training sessions over several days transform habituation and sensitization into a long-term form lasting weeks (Carew, Pinsker, & Kandel, 1972; Pinsker, Hening, Carew, & Kandel, 1973).

2. Crayfish (Procambarus clarkii)

The lateral giant fiber escape reflex (LG reflex), a type of tail flip escape response used to propel animals through the water away from danger, has been used to study the neural mechanisms of nonassociative learning in the crayfish (Krasne & Glanzman, 1986; Krasne & Stirling, 1972; Wine, Krasne, & Chen, 1975; Zucker, 1972; Zucker, Kennedy, & Selverston, 1971). The reflex is activated by a sudden tactile stimulus applied to the abdomen of the animal. When tactile stimuli are repeated, the reflex habituates and after a rest period of 3 hr shows spontaneous recovery (Wine et al., 1975). The tail flip responses are mediated by the lateral giant fibers. The LG reflex also can be sensitized by ac shocks applied to the head or abdomen and lasts for approximately 24 hr (Krasne & Glanzman, 1986).

3. Nematode (Caenorhabditis elegans)

The nematode, a simple multicellular organism consisting of approximately 1000 somatic cells (Sulston, 1983), has long been used as a model system to study the genetics of nervous system development (Brenner, 1974; Wood, 1988). Recently, several groups have also used the nematode to study the cellular and genetic correlates of habituation, dishabituation, and sensitization on three separate behavioral responses: (1) the tap withdrawal reflex (Rankin, Beck, & Chiba, 1990; Wicks & Rankin, 1995), (2) responses to chemical stimuli (Ward, 1973), and (3) responses to tactile stimuli (Chalfie & Sulston, 1981). The most extensive analysis of nonassociative learning has been done using the response to a vibrational stimulus produced by a mechanical tap on a Petri dish (Rankin et al., 1990). Basically a worm's response to vibration is usually the reversal of forward locomotion, with occasional accelerations. The distance worms traveled backward following a tap and the number of accelerations were analyzed. Repeated vibrational stimulation results in a decrease in the distance traveled backward and an increase in the acceleration. The degree of habituation is dependent on the interstimulus interval (Rankin & Broster, 1992). Habituation is retained for over 24 hr (Rankin et al., 1990). The administration of a stimulus such as a mild electric shock or head touch with a hair results in the dishabituation of the reflex (Rankin et al., 1990). In addition, the reflex is sensitized following presentation of a strong vibrational stimulus (Rankin et al., 1990).

4. Leech (Hirudo medicinalis)

In the leech, several behaviors of intact animals can be modulated by nonassociative learning, including movement in response to light and water currents (Ratner, 1972), swimming (Debski & Friesen, 1985; 1986), local bending (Lockery & Kristan, 1991; Lockery, Rawlins, & Gray, 1985), and defensive shortening (Boulis & Sahley, 1988). In all of these behaviors, repeated stimuli result in habituation as seen by a decrease in the stimulus-elicited behavior as compared to control animals. A rest interval produces spontaneous recovery, and presentation of a noxious stimulus produces dishabituation.

The effect of sensitizing stimuli has been studied predominantly within the touch-elicited shortening reflex. A noxious stimulus presented to the tail of the leech results in a change in behavior that ranges from prevention of habituation of the shortening reflex to a subsequent repeated tactile stimulus to the increase in magnitude of the reflex, depending on the intensity of the sensitizing stimulus.

B. Cellular Analysis

1. Aplysia californica

In *Aplysia* neural modifications at loci in both the central nervous system (CNS) and peripheral nervous system (PNS) contribute to the expression of nonassociative learning (Lukowiak & Jacklet, 1972, 1975; Peretz, 1970; Peretz & Moller, 1974).

Work in the CNS has focused on the synaptic connections between the siphon and tail sensory neurons and their targets. Habituation and sensitization–dishabituation are correlated with homosynaptic depression and heterosynaptic facilitation, respectively, at the synaptic connections between the siphon sensory neurons and their targets (Byrne, Castellucci, & Kandel, 1978; Castellucci, Pinsker, Kupfermann, &

Kandel, 1970; Cohen, Kaplan, Kandel, & Hawkins, 1997; Frost et al., 1997). As seen in the behavioral work, depression and facilitation can exist in both short- and long-term forms (Carew, Castellucci, & Kandel, 1979; Castellucci, Carew, & Kandel, 1978; Frost & Kandel, 1984). In cellular experiments, short-term facilitation is produced via stimulation of a peripheral nerve in the semi-intact preparation. In the isolated ganglia preparations and cells in culture, a single pulse of serotonin (5-HT) is used to produce short-term facilitation.

Work in the PNS has focused on the peripheral input into the CNS and on the gill ganglion, a cluster of approximately 200 neurons located on the branchial nerve (Peretz & Estes, 1974; Peretz & Moller, 1974). Lesions that disrupt the PNS input to the CNS result in a facilitation of the reflex during habituation training, whereas the synaptic input to gill motor neurons in the abdominal ganglion decrements. This dissociation indicates that habituation of the reflex is dependent solely on the changes in the synaptic efficacy to the gill motor neurons in the abdominal ganglion. More recent experiments demonstrate that adaptive changes occur at an additional locus, the gill ganglion. The gill ganglion neurons may provide one of the links between the CNS and PNS in the mediation of adaptive behavior (Colebrook, Bulloch, & Lukowiak, 1991; Lukowiak & Jacklet, 1972, 1975; Peretz, Jacklet, & Lukowiak, 1976). It has been suggested that habituation is the result of modifications that occur together in the abdominal ganglion, the PNS, and the peripheral terminations of the central motor pathways to the gill (gill ganglion) (Colebrook et al., 1991; Lukowiak, 1977).

a. Short Term: Cellular Mechanisms

For habituation, the decrease in the behavioral response is associated with a decrease in synaptic efficacy at the sensory to motor synapse (Byrne et al., 1978; Castellucci et al., 1970; Cohen et al., 1997; Frost et al., 1997). For sensitization and dishabituation, the increase in the behavioral response is associated with changes in synaptic efficacy at the sensory to motor synapse and an increase in excitability of the sensory neuron itself as well as an enhancement in the periphery and modulation of excitatory and inhibitory motor neurons (Cohen et al., 1997). Changes in synaptic efficacy are accompanied by changes in the action potential duration recorded in the sensory neurons. Action potential duration is reduced during repeated activation of the synapse, the analog procedure used for studying habituation, and prolonged as a result of stimulation of a peripheral nerve, the analog procedure used for studying dishabituation (Klein & Kandel, 1978). Presentation of the noxious stimulus is thought to activate a group of neurons that release a facilitatory transmitter onto the terminals of the sensory neurons mediating the reflex. Facilitatory transmitters modulate the sensory neurons, resulting in an increase in excitability of the sensory neurons themselves and an increase in transmitter release at the monosynaptic connection between the sensory neurons and their postsynaptic targets. This increase in synaptic efficacy is thought to be the result of both presynaptic action potential broadening and an action potential duration independent process.

Byrne and Kandel (1996) suggest that the spike broadening independent process is the basic mechanism of synaptic facilitation at the sensory to motor synapse, whereas spike broadening is thought of as a mechanism that amplifies and augments the spike-independent processes.

Short-term facilitation can occur as a result of two distinct training situations: (1) dishabituation training, the presentation of a noxious stimulus following the repeated presentation of a nonnoxious stimulus dishabituation, or (2) sensitization training, the presentation of a noxious stimulus to a naive animal. Although several neural modifications are thought to be shared by these and were originally thought to be due to a unitary process, with dishabituation a special instance of sensitization (Carew, Castellucci, & Kandel, 1971), itself once thought to be due to a two-behavioral phenomenon, differences have begun to emerge at the cellular (see review by Byrne and Kandel, 1996) and behavioral levels (Byrne & Kandel, 1996; Rankin & Carew, 1988) which suggest that dishabituation and sensitization probably are the result of separate processes that are activated in parallel.

A progressive decrease in a voltage-sensitive Ca^{2+} current is thought to mediate at least part of the decrease in synaptic efficacy associated with habituation of the reflex (Klein, Shapiro, & Kandel, 1980a). Gingrich and Byrne (1985) demonstrated that depletion of neurotransmitter may also play a significant role in the decrease in synaptic efficacy thought to mediate habituation.

The increase in action potential duration and excitability of the sensory neurons is due, in part, to the modulation of ion channels, specifically a decrease in two K^+ currents, I_{KV} and I_{KS} (Klein, Camardo, & Kandel, 1982; Pollock, Bernier, & Camardo, 1985; Siegelbaum, 1982). The effects of the modulation of each of these currents is complementary. I_{KV} is important for the repolarization of the action potential and thus its modulation contributes to action potential duration (Baxter & Byrne, 1989; Baxter & Byrne, 1990a; Braha, Edmonds, Sacktor, Kandel, & Klein, 1993; Critz, Baxter, & Byrne, 1991; Goldsmith & Abrams, 1992; Hochner & Kandel, 1992; Sugita, BAxter, & Byrne, 1994a; Sugita, Goldsmith, Baxter, & Byrne, 1992; Walsh & Byrne, 1989; White, Baxter, & Byrne, 1994). Decreases in I_{KS} play an important role in enhancing the excitability of the sensory neurons (Baxter & Byrne, 1990b; Belkin, Goldstein, Goldsmith, & Abrams, 1992; Byrne, Baxter, Buonomano, & Raymond, 1990; Canavier, Baxter, Clark, & Byrne, 1991). It has also been suggested that the modulation of a nifedipine-sensitive Ca^{2+} current could contribute to the 5HT-induced increase in sensory neuron excitability (Braha et al., 1993; Edmonds, Klein, Dale, & Kandel, 1990).

The mechanisms mediating the action potential broadening independent modulation of transmitter release remain unclear. Possibilities include the facilitation of vesicle mobilization or exocytosis (Braha et al., 1990; Hochner, Schacher, Klein, & Kandel, 1985) and the modulation of uncharacterized Ca^{2+} channels important for transmitter release (Klein, 1994b).

The neural model of the behavioral phenomenon of dishabituation is synaptic facilitation of depressed synapses. Facilitation of depressed synapses is effected predominantly by manipulations of protein kinase C (PKC), with only a small effect of protein kinase A (PKA) inhibition (Braha, 1990; Ghirardi et al., 1992; Hochner, Klein, Schacher, & Kandel, 1986a, 1986b). Modeling and simulation studies have supported the idea that additional processes would be necessary to produce pre-synaptic facilitation at a decremented synapse (Gingrich, Baxter, & Byrne, 1988; Gingrich & Byrne, 1984; Gingrich & Byrne, 1985; Gingrich & Byrne, 1987).

The neural analog often used to study sensitization is the facilitation of a non-decremented synapse by the application of short pulses of 5HT. Studies using non-decremented postsynaptic potential (PSP) amplitudes as baseline measures suggest that facilitation at the nondecremented synapse, and by analogy sensitization, is mediated by a cAMP/PKA pathway (Ghirardi et al., 1992; Sugita, Baxter, & Byrne, 1994c). Facilitation at the nondecremented synapse is simulated by activators of PKA and analogs of cAMP (Ghirardi et al., 1992; Klein, 1993) and is blocked by inhibitors of PKA, with only a small effect by inhibitors of PKC (Braha et al., 1990; Ghirardi et al., 1992; Goldsmith & Abrams, 1991). The PKA-dependent induction of synaptic facilitation at a nondepressed synapse is due to both an action potential duration dependent process and an action potential duration independent process (Gingrich & Byrne, 1984, 1985; Klein, 1993, 1994a; Sugita et al., 1992).

Application of 5-HT is often substituted in cellular experiments for the presen-tation of the noxious stimulus (Bailey, Hawkins, Chen, & Kandel, 1981; Brunelli, Castellucci, & Kandel, 1976; Kistler et al., 1985; Kistler, Hawkins, Koester, Kandel, & Schwartz, 1983; Klein & Kandel, 1978; Klein, Shapiro, & Kandel, 1980b). Several lines of research are consistent with the hypothesis that 5-HT acts as a facilitatory transmitter in this system. Although the neuromodulators (SCPA and SCPB) also mimic facilitation (Abrams, Castellucci, Camardo, Kandel, & Lloyd, 1984b), the preponderance of the studies have focused on the analyses of 5-HT-induced facili-tation. Immunocytochemical studies indicate that 5-HT-containing varicosities contact the sensory neurons mediating the reflex (Kistler et al., 1985). Serotonin applied to the sensory neurons mimics heterosynaptic facilitation in several ways, including broadening of the presynaptic action potential and increasing the excita-bility of the presynaptic sensory neuron in response to injected current (Baxter & Byrne, 1990a; Klein, Hochner, & Kandel, 1986; Klein & Kandel, 1978, 1980; Walters & Byrne, 1983). Furthermore, 5,7-dihydroxytryptamine-induced reduc-tion of 5-HT within the *Aplysia* CNS impairs the normal dishabituation produced by a tail stimulation (Glanzman et al., 1989).

The 5-HT-induced modulation occurs as the result of the activation of two second-messenger pathways: the cAMP-dependent protein kinase pathway via PKA and the calcium-dependent protein kinase pathway via PKC. Both of these contrib-ute to enhancement of transmitter release (Braha et al., 1990; Braha et al., 1993; Sugita et al., 1992). Two pharmacologically distinct 5-HT receptors have been found on sensory neurons (Mercer, Emptage, & Carew, 1991), and it is thought that each receptor type mediates the activation of a distinct second-messenger pathway.

At the subcellular level, 5-HT has been shown to increase adenylate cyclase activity in sensory neuron terminals (Bernier, Castellucci, Kandel, & Schwartz,

1982), resulting in a rapid (peaks in 2–3 min) increase in the intracellular concentration of cAMP (Bacskai et al., 1993). cAMP in turn binds to the regulatory subunit of the enzyme PKA, releasing and activating the catalytic subunit, which results in the stimulation of PKA. PKA is thought to phosphorylate its target proteins, including the S channel. Phosphorylation of the S channel results in its closure, leading to an increase in the duration of the action potential. This in turn allows more Ca^{2+} influx, which leads to an increase in transmitter release. Both cAMP (applied to a cell-attached membrane (Siegelbaum, 1982)), and the catalytic subunit of cAMP-dependent protein kinase (cell-free membrane patches) close S channels, suggesting that the kinase acts at the internal membrane surface to phosphorylate either the S channel itself or an associated protein that regulates the channel. Further support comes from the finding that injection of the catalytic subunit of the cAMP-dependent protein kinase into the sensory neuron broadened its action potential and increased its transmitter release (Castellucci et al., 1980) and that 5-HT-induced facilitation can be blocked by injection of the Walsh inhibitor (Castellucci, Kandel, Schwartz, & Kandel, 1982).

b. Long Term: Cellular Mechanisms

As with the behavior, cellular changes can be present in a short- or long-term form (Carew et al., 1979; Castellucci et al., 1978; Frost, Castellucci, Hawkins, & Kandel, 1985; Frost & Kandel, 1984). Synaptic transmission from sensory neurons of the siphon to motor neurons of the gill or siphon in the abdominal ganglion is decreased in animals that receive long-term habituation training and is increased in animals that receive long-term sensitization training (Frost et al., 1985; Pinsker et al., 1973). Using a semi-intact preparation, Castellucci, Blumenfeld, Goelet, and Kandel (1989) showed that the induction of long-term sensitization is dependent on new protein synthesis. Morphological changes also accompany habituation and sensitization of the reflex. Bailey and Chen (1983, 1984, 1988a, 1988b, 1988c, 1989) found that both the number, size, and vesicle complement of active zones of sensory neuron terminals and the total number of varicosities per sensory neuron were significantly reduced in long-term habituated animals and significantly increased in long-term sensitized animals as compared to control animals. This increase in growth of presynaptic contacts was evident as an increase in the frequency, size, and vesicle complement of presynaptic targets onto postsynaptic L7 processes in sensitized compared to control animals (Bailey & Chen, 1988b). The change in number of varicosites and active zones is protein synthesis dependent and persists for more than a week (Bailey, Montarolo, Chen, Kandel, & Schacher, 1992). Several steps underlying the growth process have been described. These changes are thought to be induced presynaptically by PKA-dependent activation of cAMP response element binding (CREB) transcription factors, leading to modifications of the transcription of genes such as other transcription factors, cell adhesion molecules, or structural proteins. Application of 5-HT and cAMP, for example, results in a loss of

N-CAM-related cell adhesion molecules (apCAMS) from the surface membrane of sensory neurons by means of receptor-mediated endocytosis (Bailey et al., 1992), an increase in the density of coated pits and coated vesicles, and an increase in the expression of the light chain of *Aplysia* clathrin (apClathrin) (Hu, Barzilai, Chen, Bailey, & Kandel, 1993). Clathrin-related endocytosis could function to internalize and redistribute apCAMS and other surface membrane proteins in the sensory neurons, which might play a role in the growth of new synaptic connections.

Although 5-HT produces both action potential broadening and synaptic facilitation in sensory neurons, a time dissociation between these events has been observed. Sugita, Baxter, and Byrne (1994b) report that 5-HT-induced facilitation reaches a peak within 3 min, whereas 5-HT-induced spike broadening did not reach its peak until 12 min after application, suggesting that facilitation might be more relevant to the short-term behavioral changes.

In culture, repeated applications of 5-HT can produce an increase in EPSP amplitude lasting more than 24 hr. This effect is blocked by inhibitors of translation and transcription (Montarolo, Goelet, Castellucci, Morgan, & Kandel, 1986). It has been hypothesized that long-term synaptic facilitation (LTF) is induced presynaptically by a PKA-dependent activation of CREB transcription factors, leading to modifications of the transcription of a variety of genes such as other transcription factors, cell adhesion molecules, or structurel proteins. Kaang, Kandel, and Grant (1993) reported that 5-HT induces the transcriptional activation of a *lacZ* reporter gene driven by the cAMP response element (CRE) and requiring CRE binding proteins (CREBS). The induction becomes progressively more effective following two or more pulses and is thought to be due to PKA-induced phosphorylation of CREB. Likewise, injection of the CRE into the nucleus of cultured sensory neurons blocks th 5HT-induced long-term increase in synaptic strength (Dash, Hochner, & Kandel, 1990), and APCREB 2 antibodies injected into *Aplysia* sensory neurons cause a single pulse of 5HT which on its own only induces short-term facilitation (lasting minutes), to evoke facilitation lasting more than 1 day (Bartsch et al., 1995).

Differences in procedures and protocols used for the behavioral, biochemical, and molecular studies, however, have made the direct test of the relationship between the cellular events and the behavioral expression of learning difficult. Recent experiments using semi-intact preparations, which provide a means of simultaneously monitoring cellular and behavioral responses, have questioned the extent of the contribution of the monosynaptic sensory-motor neuron to the learned change in behavior for both sensitization (Trudeau & Castellucci, 1992, 1993a, 1993b) and classical conditioning (Lukowiak & Colebrook, 1988a, 1988b). Moreover, recent work suggests that additional components of the circuit mediating the behavior need to be identified (Frost et al., 1997; Hickie, Cohen, & Balaban, 1997). Results from a semi-intact preparation using siphon stimulation identical to that used in the behavioral experiments suggest that several as yet unidentified sensory neurons contribute to the behavior (Frost et al., 1997). Optical recording methods (Zecevic et al., 1989) revealed that hundreds of neurons in the *Aplysia* abdominal ganglion are active during the gill-withdrawal reflex, suggesting that sites other than the sensory to motor synapse could participate in mediating the reflex and its modulation. Indeed, multiple sites which show experience-dependent changes in activity have been described (Falk, Wu, Cohen, & Tang, 1993; Kanz, Eberly, Cobbs, & Pinsker, 1979; Peretz et al., 1976). Sensitization-related changes, for example, have been reported in interneurons and motor neurons involved in the siphon- and gill-withdrawal reflexes (Frost et al., 1985; Frost & Kandel, 1984; Hawkins, Castellucci, & Kandel, 1981). The normal feedback inhibition onto excitatory interneurons is diminished as a result of sensitization training (Trudeau & Castellucci, 1992) and this diminution can account for a large percentage of the heterosynaptic facilitation produced by sensitization (Trudeau & Castellucci, 1993b). In addition, several studies have emphasized the coordination of pre- and postsynaptic modifications at individual synapses as important for the long-term facilitation. Application of 5-HT to both the pre- and postsynaptic neurons including the soma, synaptic terminals of the presynaptic sensory neuron, and the postsynaptic target produces more facilitation than its application solely to the soma of the presynaptic sensory neuron (Clark & Kandel, 1993; Emptage & Carew, 1993). 5-HT-induced changes in the postsynaptic neuron are dependent on protein synthesis in the postsynaptic cell and have been hypothesized to be due to the upregulation of postsynaptic receptor synthesis. Finally, Illich and Walters (1997) suggest that the previously characterized LE sensory cells studied in many of the foregoing learning experiments are not activated by weak von Frey hair, water jet, or near-field vibratory stimuli applied to the unrestrained siphon, even though these same stimuli reliably evoke behavioral and neural responses.

2. Crayfish (Procambarus clarkii)

The lateral giant fiber escape reflex, a type of tail flip escape response, has been used to study the neural mechanisms of nonassociative learning in the crayfish (Krasne & Glanzman, 1986; Krasne & Stirling, 1972; Wine et al., 1975; Zucker, 1972; Zucker et al., 1971). The reflex is activated by a sudden tactile stimulus applied to the abdomen of the animal. When tactile stimuli are repeated, the reflex habituates and after a rest period of 3 hr shows spontaneous recovery (Wine et al., 1975). The tail flip responses are mediated by the lateral giant fibers (LGs). Early cellular work using an analog preparation with the repeated activation of the mechanosensitive primary afferents substituted for the abdominal stimulus suggested that habituation of the reflex was due to synaptic depression at the chemical synapses of the reflex arc. The depression was suggested to be due to a reduction of transmitter release from the presynaptic terminals of the first-order interneurons interposed between the afferents and LG (Krasne, 1969; Zucker, 1972). Recent work on freely moving crayfish has demonstrated that habituation training causes the onset of descending inhibition (Krasne & Teshiba, 1995). Lesions which severed cords between the thorax and abdomen to remove the influence of descending inhibition reduced the tendency of the LG threshold to rise during habituation (Krasne & Teshiba, 1995). Application of pertussis toxin (PTX) reversed habituation with no effect on LG threshold, which the authors suggest demonstrates that habituation is due to the development of inhibition during habituation training. This set of experiments shows that habituation of the LG escape reflex in intact crayfish is dependent on an increase of inhibition and that although the synaptic depression reported earlier also contributes to habituation of the reflex, the descending inhibition from higher centers plays a more important role in the habituation of the reflex (Krasne & Teshiba, 1995).

The LG reflex is also modulated by sensitization. Following presentation of a sensitizing stimulus, the threshold for eliciting an LG escape is significantly reduced (Krasne & Glanzman, 1986). If the nerve cord is severed between the thorax and abdomen, aversive stimuli are no longer capable of sensitizing the abdominal LG reflex, suggesting that sensitization of the reflex depends on signals originating in the rostral half of the animal. Octopamine perfused into the isolated abdominal nerve cord mimics the effects of sensitizing stimuli (Glanzman & Krasne, 1983).

3. Nematode (Caenorhabditis elegans)

The nervous system of the nematode contains approximately 302 neurons in the adult (Krasne & Glanzman, 1986; Sulston, Schierenberg, White, & Thomson, 1983). In wild-type animals the number and types of neurons as well as the neurons they connect with are largely invariant (White, Southgate, Thomson, & Brenner, 1986). All neurons and their synaptic connections have been anatomically mapped (Chalfie, 1984; White et al., 1986). Each neuron has been described in terms of location and morphology (Hall & Russell, 1991; Ward, Thomson, White, & Brenner, 1975; White et al., 1986) and the circuitry mediating the reflex has been identified (Chalfie et al., 1985; Rankin et al., 1990). Using single-cell ablations, Wicks and Rankin (1996) suggest that important changes associated with habituation of the tap withdrawal reflex are upstream of the interneurons and motor neurons that control locomotion and are probably in sensory neurons. Moreover, lesion experiments also revealed that the contribution of chemical synapses from the touch cells onto the interneurons of the tap withdrawal circuit differs depending on the interstimulus interval (ISI) used during training, suggesting that distinct processes may be recruited during habituation at long and short ISIs (Wicks & Rankin, 1996).

4. Leech (Hirudo medicinalis)

a. Neural Analog

A neural analog system consisting of an isolated chain of ganglia with associated connectives has been developed to investigate cellular events underlying response habituation and sensitization (Bagnoli, Brunelli, Magni, & Pellegrino, 1975). Experiments using this analog preparation have implicated the fast-conducting system (FCS), a chain of electrically coupled neurons (S cells), is the mediation of nonassociative learning. Repeated tactile stimulation of the skin produces habituation of the FCS response and noxious stimulation produces dishabituation (Bagnoli et al., 1975). Bath-applied serotonin also dishabituates the FCS response, and the facilitation is blocked by both preincubation with imidazole, a cAMP-phosphodiesterase activator, and the serotonin receptor blocker methysergide (Belardetti et al., 1982). Consistent with the pharmacological effects, increases in the synthesis of cAMP in the segmental ganglia of the leech following sensitization training have been observed (Biondi, Belardetti, Brunelli, & Trevissani, 1982). Taken together, these results suggest that the facilitatory cellular changes within the FCS may be due to a 5HT-mediated increase in cAMP (Biondi et al., 1982).

b. Semi-intact Preparation

Recording and lesion studies of the S cell in a semi-intact preparation in which sensor input and motor output pathways remain intact have shown that the S cell is necessary for sensitization and normal dishabituation of the shortening reflex (Sahley, Modney, Boulis, & Muller, 1994). Intracellular recordings of the S cell during habituation and sensitization training show stimulus-elicited S-cell activity is significantly correlated with the sensitized reflex but not with the habituated reflex. Lesions of the S cell eliminated sensitization completely but only partially impaired dishabituation of the reflex. Neither the normal baseline reflex nor habituation of the reflex was changed as a result of S-cell lesions. The dissociation of dishabituation and sensitization suggests that the neural changes mediating the two types of learning could be distinct. The results of 5-HT depletion experiments were virtually identical to the results obtained following S-cell ablations: sensitization of the reflex was eliminated, dishabituation was reduced but not eliminated, and baseline measures of the reflex were unaffected. Taken together, these data suggest that the sensitization and dishabituation of the shortening reflex require an interaction between serotonergic neurons and the S cell. 5-HT immunoreactive neurons have been identified in the leech and appear to synapse on the S cell (Muller & Carbonetto, 1979) but which specific neurons are required have not been identified. Ehrlich, Boulis, Karrer, and Sahley (1992) speculated that the Retzius cells are important, for they appear to be most affected histologically after 5-HT depletion. Lockery and Kristan (1990) suggested that two other pairs of serotonergic neurons, DL and VL, are important for sensitization of local bending, a related behavior.

III. PAVLOVIAN CONDITIONING

A. Behavioral Studies

1. *Aplysia*

Classical conditioning of the gill- and siphon-withdrawal reflexes of *Aplysia* has been examined in both intact and semi-intact animals. Weak tactile stimulation of the siphon, the CS, when paired repeatedly with strong electrical shocks applied to the tail, the US, produces an increase in the duration of the withdrawal response elicited by subsequent presentations of the CS (Carew, Walters, & Kandel, 1981). Using a reduced siphon, mantle, gill, and abdominal ganglion semi-intact preparation, Lukowiak and Sahley (1981) reported that pairing a light tactile CS with a train (6/sec for 1 sec) of tactile stimuli delivered to the gill resulted in an increase in responding to the CS as compared to controls. In these examples of conditioning in *Aplysia,* the response to the CS occurs from the onset of training and is the same as the response elicited by the US. Therefore, conditioning does not result in a new response to the CS. As discussed in several reviews and analyses of learning, this is consistent with what historically has been defined as alpha conditioning or reflex potentiation since the response to the CS before conditioning is the same as the response to the US, and CS–US pairings enhance the initial CS-elicited response (Schreurs, 1989). It has been proposed that there is no fundamental distinction between an alpha response and a CR (Carew, Abrams, Hawkins, & Kandel, 1984; Hawkins & Kandel, 1984). However, counterarguments have been proposed based on both behavioral and electrophysiological studies of classical conditioning (see Schreurs, 1989).

2. Drosophila

The nervous system in *Drosophila* is complex and relatively inaccessible, and thus many cellular approaches to the study of learning are difficult to conduct in this species. However, genetic analyses of learning and memory can be carried out with ease in *Drosophila*. A number of conditioning procedures have been used; however, the primary emphasis has been on the study of conditioned odor avoidance. In this paradigm, conditioning consists of a two-stage differential odor–shock avoidance procedure where one of the odors (CS^+) is paired with shock (US) and the other is unpaired (CS^-). An odor-choice procedure is used to test the differences of conditioning (Tully, 1987; Tully & Quinn, 1985). However, both odors are aversive when tested prior to conditioning and thus the conditioning procedure may be similar to alpha conditioning where a preconditioning aversive response to the CS is enhanced (Dudai, Jan, Byers, Quinn, & Benzer, 1976).

3. Hermissenda

Pavlovian conditioning of *Hermissenda* involves changes in locomotion and foot length produced by paired stimulation of the visual and vestibular systems with light and rotation (Crow & Alkon, 1978; Lederhendler, Gart, & Alkon, 1986). *Hermissenda* normally exhibits a positive phototaxis when stimulated with light. In *Hermissenda* the phototactic response is expressed in behavior by various measures of visually influenced locomotion. Light also elicits a lengthening of the foot. Stimulation of the gravity receptors (hair cells) with rotation produces both an inhibition of locomotion and foot-shortening, the unconditioned responses (UR). The conditioning procedure consists of light, the CS, paired with high-speed rotation, the US, which produces a CS-elicited suppression of the normal positive phototactic response and foot-shortening (CR) lasting days to weeks depending on the number of conditioning trials (Alkon, 1989). The response to the CS before conditioning is different from the UR and CR. Since a new response (CR) is elicited by the CS after training, conditioning in *Hermissenda* is not an example of reflex potentiation (alpha conditioning) described earlier in this chapter.

4. Leech (Hirudo medicinalis)

Classical conditioning in the leech has been demonstrated both as the acquisition of a new response to the CS in a toxicosis conditioning paradigm (Karrer & Sahley, 1988) and as the potentiation of a response elicited prior to conditioning. Henderson and Strong (1972) found that paired presentations of light (CS) and an electric shock (US) resulted in an enhanced shortening response to the CS. More recently, Sahley and Ready (1988) reported conditioning of the shortening reflex produced by pairing a tactile stimulus with shock. Conditioning in the leech is another example of CS–US pairings enhancing a response that is elicited by the CS from the beginning of training, for example, alpha conditioning.

5. Limax maximus

Gelperin (1975) reported that the consumption of one food paired with CO_2 toxicosis significantly and specifically decreased the animal's preference for that food. This initial finding was followed up with a series of experiments that indicated that classical conditioning can modify a slug's preference for a particular odor. For example, Sahley, Rudy, and Gelperin (1981) found that slugs learn to avoid odors paired with the bitter taste of quinidine sulfate when given a choice between the odor paired with the quinine and their normal diet odor. The learned aversion was retained for approximately 3 days. Likewise, it has been shown that *Limax* is capable of appetitive conditioning; that is, an initially aversive odor can be made attractive if that odor is repeatedly paired with an appetitive US (Sahley, Martin, & Gelperin, 1990). Conditioning in *Limax* involves the acquisition of a new response and is thus not an example of associative reflex potentiation.

6. Characteristic Features of Pavlovian Conditioning

Many important variables influence the acquisition of an assocaition and the study of these variables has a long history within experimental psychology. Current cellular models of associative learning in invertebrates have focused primarily on the contiguity aspects of learning and have only recently begun to address other variables important for the acquisition of associative learning such as contingency, or the predictive relationship between the CS and US (Kamin, 1969; Rescorla, 1968, 1969). A comprehensive analysis of the cellular basis of associative learning will need to account for other phenomena in addition to providing an understanding of the mechanisms of temporal contiguity if it is to provide insights into the nature of the associative process.

Characteristics of Pavlovian conditioning including complex features have been examined in several invertebrates. Studies of context learning in *Aplysia* have reported that context can modulate the expression of a CS–US assocaition (Colwill, Absher, & Roberts, 1988). They reported that in *Aplysia* responding to a CS was greater in the context in which the CS had been paired with the US as compared with the context in which it was unpaired. Farley, Reasoner, and Janssen (1997) reported that compound conditioning potentiated phototactic suppression in *Hermissenda* (in both overshadowing and blocking paradigms), whereas second-order conditioning and sensory preconditioning of phototactic suppression were not observed. In contrast, Rogers and Matzel (1995) reported that contextual conditioning can block the expression of conditioned foot contractions in *Hermissenda*. Evidence for a role of contingency in conditioning in *Hermissenda* is provided by a study by Farley (1987) showing that extra CS and US presentations to a sequence of CS–US pairings resulted in an attenuation of conditioning.

Using the leech semi-intact preparation, Sahley, Boulis, and Schumann (1994) found that conditioning is dependent on both the contiguity and contingency between the CS and US stimuli. Learning is degraded by the introduction of unpredicted USs as well as by unreinforced presentations of the CS (latent inhibition), both manipulations reduce the contingency between the CS and US, and it is the relationship between these events, the interevent relationship, that determines if learning occurs.

In *Limax,* prior conditioning to carrot odor impaired learning to potato odor when a compound presentation of carrot and potato odor was paired with a quinine US. In contrast, animals without prior training to carrot learned to avoid both carrot and potato odor when the compound was paired with the US. These results demonstrate that, as is true for vertebrate species, in *Limax* the temporal pairing of potato odor and quinine was not the sole condition for associative learning. Rather, the predictive relationship between the odor (CS) and the quinine (US) is important. The importance of the predictive relationship has been further studied.

Inhibitory learning is characterized by a negative relationship between a CS and a US (Domjan & Burkhardt, 1982). That is, the CS is correlated with the absence of the US. For a CS to become inhibitory it must be nonreinforced in an excitatory context, in which the nonpresence of the US is surprising (Rescorla & Wagner, 1972). Studies on inhibitory learning have expanded further the role of predictability in conditioning in *Limax* (Martin & Sahley, 1986). To establish an excitatory condition, garlic odor (CS+) was paired with the onset of the US, and potato odor (CS−) was paired with the termination of the US to establish a negative relationship between the CS and US. The effect of these procedures was evaluated several times during training to determine the rate of acquisition of both types of learning. Retention of excitatory conditioning and inhibitory learning was measured on Days 5 and 6 following training. Odor-preference tests were used to evaluate the influence of conditioning. Excitatory conditioning was evaluated in a garlic versus rat chow odor test and conditioned inhibition was evaluated in a potato versus rat chow test. The performance of these animals was compared to that of animals that experienced random presentation of the stimuli.

The results indicated *Limax* could simultaneously learn both an excitatory and inhibitory relationship to two distinct odor cues. Excitatory learning was indicated by the increase in the mean percentage of time animals in the paired group spent over the garlic odor. There was no change in the time control animals spent over garlic from the pretest. Inhibitory conditioning was indicated as a reliable reduction from the pretest in the mean percentage of time paired animals spent over potato odor. Both inhibitory learning and excitatory learning were retained for at least 5 days, after which the inhibitory conditioning diminished while the excitatory conditioning effect showed little sign of decay.

This experiment suggests not only that *Limax* can learn both positive and negative CS–US relationships but that it can learn the positive association of one odor to food while simultaneously learning a negative association of another odor with the same food. Interestingly, the time course of acquisition of each of these types of learning appears to be different. A significant difference from baseline in the appetitive conditioning to garlic was observed after 25 pairings, whereas inhibitory learning was not observed until after 30 pairings.

Second-order conditioning in *Limax* was demonstrated by Sahley et al. (1981) by exposing animals to two phases of training. In Phase I, animals experienced pairings of carrot odor and quinidine (S1–US pairings), and in Phase 2 they received potato odor–carrot odor pairings (S2–S1 pairings). Animals in the experimental group displayed a reduced preference for potato odor in comparison to the animals in the control groups. The same interevent relationships that produce second-order conditioning in vertebrates produce second-order conditioning in *Limax*.

B. Cellular Analysis

1. *Aplysia*

The cellular model that has been applied to *Aplysia* conditioning is an elaboration of the basic mechanism proposed for sensitization, termed activity-dependent neuromodulation. The general cellular scheme of activity-dependent neuromodulation has evolved from studies of analogues of conditioning (Hawkins, Abrams, Carew, & Kandel, 1983; Walters & Byrne, 1983). According to this model, sensory neurons that contribute to the pathways mediating the CS make weak subthreshold connections to motor neurons. Delivering a reinforcing stimulus, shock, or US alone has two known affects. First, the US activates the motor system and produces the UR. Second, the US activates a diffuse modulatory or facilitatory system that nonselectively enhances transmitter release from all the sensory neurons. This nonselective enhancement of transmitter release contributes to sensitization in *Aplysia*. According to the proposed model, temporal specificity, characteristic of classical conditioning, occurs when there is pairing of the CS, action potentials in one of the sensory neurons, with the US, causing a selective amplification of the modulatory effects in that specific sensory neuron. Unpaired activity does not amplify the effects of the CS in other nonactivated sensory neurons. The amplification of the modulatory effects in the paired sensory neuron leads to an enhancement of the ability of the sensory neuron to activate the motor neurons and produce the CR (see previous section on cellular analysis of sensitization).

Experimental analyses of sensitization of defensive reflexes in *Aplysia* showed that the neuromodulator released by the reinforcing stimulus (shock) acts by reducing several diverse K^+ currents in the sensory neurons (Baxter & Byrne, 1989; Klein & Kandel, 1978, 1980; Klein et al., 1980a). Consequently, action potentials elicited after the shock are broader (due to less repolarizing K^+ current), causing an enhanced influx of Ca^{2+}. Enhanced influx of Ca^{2+} triggers greater release of transmitter from the sensory neurons, which causes increased activation of motor neurons and, thus, sensitization of the reflex. The second-messenger system underlying activity-dependent neuromodulation in the cellular analogue of conditioning has been examined in detail. The pairing specificity in conditioning is due, at least in part, to an enhancement of cAMP levels in the sensory neuron beyond that produced by the modulator alone (Abrams et al., 1984; Ocorr, Walters, & Byrne, 1985). Furthermore, influx of Ca^{2+} associated with the CS (spike activity) may amplify the US-mediated modulatory effect by interacting with a Ca^{2+}-sensitive component of the adenylate cyclase, which leads to enhanced synthesis of cAMP (Abrams, Eliot, Dudai, & Kandel, 1985; Schwartz et al., 1983; Weiss & Drummond, 1985).

Since the evidence for activity-dependent neuromodulation as a mechanism underlying conditioning in *Aplysia* is derived from studies of conditioning analogues, there is no direct experimental link between the proposed mechanism and the behavior of conditioned animals. It has not been shown that activity-dependent neuromodulation of sensorimotor connections is a correlate of classical conditioning and occurs during behavioral conditioning. Indeed, recent evidence suggests that facilitation of the sensorimotor EPSP and enhancement of the gill-withdrawal reflex with conditioning may be dissociated (Colebrook & Lukowiak, 1988). These investigators reported that facilitation could occur without an increase in the reflex and enhancement of the reflex without facilitation of the EPSP. Thus, although changes in the strength of the sensorimotor connections may contribute to the CR, other mechanisms must also be proposed to explain classical conditioning in *Aplysia*. Recent studies of LTP induction in *Aplysia* have suggested that a postsynaptic mechanism may contribute to plasticity in the withdrawal reflex pathway (Glanzman, 1995). A general conclusion from studies of the conditioning analogue in *Aplysia* is that mechanisms of associative learning are extensions of elaborations of the non-associative mechanism found in sensitization. Thus, it has been proposed that examples of associative learning may be the result of utilizing the mechanism of nonassociative learning as basis building blocks (Byrne & Kandel, 1996; Hawkins & Kandel, 1984). However, studies of associative and nonassociative learning in other invertebrate preparations have suggested that different mechanisms support associative and nonassociative learning in these diverse species (see sections on *Hermissenda* and the leech).

2. Drosophila

Several mutants have been identified that exhibit specific deficiencies in their ability to learn and remember (for review, see Aceves-Pina et al., 1983; Dudai, 1985, 1988, 1989; Tully, 1987). The striking feature of these mutations is that they appear to affect some aspect of a monoamine pathway and its associated intracellular biochemical cascade. Two of the mutants affect specific aspects of the cAMP cascade, involving cAMP metabolism and cAMP-dependent protein kinase A.

The analysis of memory formation after olfactory conditioning in *Drosophila* learning mutants dunce and rutabaga indicates that distinct memory phases are involved. These studies have reported that memory after olfactory conditioning consists of a protein synthesis dependent long-term stage or phase and an anesthesia-resistant phase not dependent upon protein synthesis. Interestingly, studies using an inducible transgene that expresses a dominant negative member of the fly CREB family blocked long-term memory (Yin et al., 1994). The anesthesia-resistant phase of memory was unaffected after induction. It is believed that a subset of genes from the CREB family support or mediate cAMP-responsive transcription. The recent evidence suggests that long-term memory for olfactory conditioning in *Drosophila* requires *de novo* gene expression that may be mediated by CREB family genes (DeZazzo & Tully, 1995).

3. Hermissenda

An essential step in the physiological analysis of conditioning is the identification of the loci in the animal's nervous system where the memory of the associative experience is stored. One site in the *Hermissenda* nervous system is the primary sensory neurons (photoreceptors) of the pathway mediating the CS. Each non-image-forming eye of *Hermissenda* is relatively simple, consisting of three type B photoreceptors and two type A photoreceptors (Alkon & Fuortes, 1972).

Cellular correlates of conditioning in identified cells in the CS pathway (type B photoreceptors) are expressed by a significant increase in CS-elicited spike frequency, enhanced excitability to extrinsic current, an increase in the input resistance of type B photoreceptors, both increased and decreased amplitudes of light-elicited generator potentials, a decrease in spike frequency accommodation, reductions in the peak amplitudes of several diverse K^+ currents, and enhancement of identified synaptic connections (Alkon, Lederhendler, & Shoukimas, 1982; Alkon et al., 1985; Crow, 1985; Crow & Alkon, 1980; Farley & Alkon, 1982; Farley, Richards, & Grover, 1990; Frysztak & Crow, 1993, 1994, 1997; West, Barnes, & Alkon, 1982). A second site of cellular plasticity in conditioned animals is the type A photoreceptors (Farley et al., 1990). Lateral type A photoreceptors of conditioned animals exhibit a significant increase in CS-elicited spike frequency, a decrease in generator potential amplitude, and enhanced excitability and decreased spike frequency accommodation to extrinsic current (Frysztak & Crow, 1993). In addition to enhanced excitability of identified type B and type A photoreceptors detected following conditioning, changes in the strength of synaptic connections between identified sensory neurons in the CS pathway have been reported. The amplitude of monosynaptic inhibitory postsynaptic potentials (IPSPs) recorded from medial type A photoreceptors elicited by action potentials in the medial type B photoreceptor is enhanced by conditioning (Frysztak & Crow, 1994, 1997). However, the amplitude of IPSPs recorded from lateral type A photoreceptors that are elicited by action potentials in the lateral type B photoreceptor is not enhanced in conditioned animals. Taken collectively, the evidence indicates that multiple sites of plasticity involving changes in excitability and synaptic strength can be detected in the CS pathway of conditioned animals.

Voltage-clamp studies of type B photoreceptors have identified two K^+ currents, I_A and $I_{K,CA}$, that are reduced following conditioning (Alkon et al., 1982; Alkon et al., 1985). Reductions in several diverse K^+ conductances could account for both the enhanced excitability and the enhancement of IPSPs observed in conditioned animals.

Studies of the mechanisms responsible for the reduction in the K^+ currents of type B photoreceptors have implicated several second-messenger systems. Recent evidence suggests that the phosphoinositide system may contribute to reductions in K^+ currents observed in conditioned *Hermissenda* (Farley & Auerbach, 1986; Farley & Schuman, 1991; Matzel, Lederhendler, & Alkon, 1990). Activation of PKC by phorbol esters and diacylglycerol analogues and intracellular injection of PKC into type B photoreceptors reduced both the A-type K^+ current (I_A) and $I_{K,Ca}$. It has been proposed that activation of PKC is initiated by the actions of an agonist released by stimulation of the US pathway (Crow, 1988). Recent evidence suggests that 5-HT and/or GABA may be released by stimulation of statocyst hair cells by rotation (US). Immunocytochemistry studies have identified several 5-HT immunoreactive neurons that provide serotonergic input to the visual system (Land & Crow, 1985). These serotonergic neurons may provide postsynaptic input to the photoreceptors from stimulation of the US pathway. In addition, the monosynaptic inhibitory input to photoreceptors from statocyst hair cells is presumed to be GABAergic and may contribute to the induction of cellular correlates produced by conditioning (Alkon et al., 1993; Matzel & Alkon, 1991). However, neither agonist has been shown to be both necessary and sufficient for producing the physiological changes associated with conditioning.

Studies of one-trial conditioning have provided insights into potential mechanisms for the time-dependent development of different stages of memory. The one-trial conditioning procedure produces both CS-elicited short- and long-term enhancement (STE, LTE) of generator potentials recorded from identified type B photoreceptors and enhanced excitability to extrinsic current (Crow & Forrester, 1991). LTE depends upon protein and mRNA synthesis, is expressed only in lateral B photoreceptors and is dependent upon the contiguity of the CS and US (Crow & Forrester, 1986, 1990, 1991; Crow, Siddiqi, & Dash, 1997). A cellular model for associative memory in the type B photoreceptors produced by one-trial conditioning suggests that activation of PKC by stimulation of the US pathway occurs together with elevated intracellular Ca^{2+} produced by the presentation of the CS. The consequences of activation of PKC associated with elevated intracellular Ca^{2+} may result in phosphorylation of channel proteins.

The induction of STE by one-trial conditioning is due to activation of PKC since the broad spectrum protein kinase inhibitors H-7 and sphingosine and a reduction in the activity of PKC produced by prolonged exposure to phorbol esters (downregulation) block STE (Crow, Forrester, Williams, Waxham, & Neary, 1991). Moreover, recent evidence indicates that STE and LTE may be parallel processes. The conditions that are sufficient to block STE—downregulation of PKC and kinase inhibition—do not block LTE (Crow & Forrester, 1993). These results suggest that STE and LTE are not sequential processes but are parallel processes that involve independent mechanisms.

Biochemical mechanisms underlying one-trial conditioning have been studied using an *in vitro* procedure. Stimulating the isolated eyes and proximal optic nerve with light (CS) paired with 5-HT produced an increase in five phosphoproteins detected at differnet times following *in vitro* conditioning (Crow, Siddiqi, Zhu, & Neary, 1996). The five phosphoproteins range in apparent molecular weight from 22 to 55 kDa. In addition, the increase in phosphorylation detected 2 hr postconditioning is dependent upon CS–US pairing since an unpaired control group exhibited significantly less phosphorylation. Interestingly, the pairing-specific change in phosphorylation detected 2 hr postconditioning is expressed when electrophysiological studies have revealed pairing-specific changes in type B cell excitability. The 46- and 55-kDa phosphoproteins identified in these studies are putative structural proteins and the 22-kDa phosphoprotein may be a PKC substrate previously identified in *Hermissenda* following multitrial Pavlovian conditioning (Neary, Crow, & Alkon, 1981).

4. Leech (Hirudo medicinalis)

Serotonin (5HT) has an important role in the behavioral expression of associative learning in the leech (Sahley, 1994). Using injections of the neurotoxin

5,7-dihydroxytryptamine to reduce levels of 5-HT in the CNS of the leech (Ehrlich et al., 1992; Lent, 1982) significantly impairs the expression of conditioned responding. However, depleted leeches experiencing paired CS–US pairings still performed significantly better than depleted leeches experiencing unpaired CS–US presentations, suggesting that the actions of 5-HT do not account fully for learning. This toxin-resistant paired effect appears to be associative in nature since (a) it is not present in the unpaired group and (b) an extinction procedure consisting of explicitly unpaired CS and US presentations, which also destroys the pairing and predictive interevent relationships between the stimuli, produced a decrement in performance when the paired-toxin group was shifted to extinction training, just as it did for leeches in the paired-control group. No significant differences in performance were observed between depleted and nondepleted leeches in the unpaired, CS-alone group, suggesting that the level of 5-HT in the CNS plays only a negligible, if any, role in baseline responding and habituation of the reflex.

Neither the specific neurons nor the cellular mechanisms involved in this toxin-resistant learning have been identified. However, there is at least one additional pathway that is activated by the US (strong shock). The nociceptive mechanosensory cell (N cell) fires a barrage of action potentials in response to the US. The N cell makes a monosynaptic connection to the P cell, which is one of the primary mechanosensory cells that transduces the CS (Muller, Nicholls, & Stent, 1981). The synapse between the P and N cells is a site of convergence between the CS and US pathways (French & Muller, 1986) and, therefore, a potential anatomical site for a pairing mechanism requiring coincident firing such as activity-dependent facilitation. Recent evidence suggests that sensory neurons, including N cells, may use glutamate as a transmitter (Dierkes, Hochstrate, & Schlue, 1996).

The cellular basis of the predictive relationship between the CS and US is now being investigated in the leech. Preliminary evidence indicates that a neural correlate of predictability in the leech can be observed in the serotonergic Retzius (R) cell (Sahley, 1988). Intracellular recordings from the R cell during conditioning indicate that when the CS and US are presented in a paired relationship, the R cell continues to respond to the US throughout training. In contrast, when an animal experiences unpaired CS–US presentations or unpredicted US presentations, the R cell response to the US diminishes and can eventually drop out (Sahley, 1988). Both of these procedures disrupt the acquisition of associative learning (Rescorla, 1968). This dropping out, or "habituation," of the US is one of the mechanisms suggested by Hawkins, Carew, and Kandel (1986) and modeled (Hawkins & Kandel, 1984) to account for predictability in *Aplysia*.

The evidence from conditioning in the leech suggests that classical conditioning involves more than the elaboration of sensitization. Sensitization is a central element of the activity-dependent facilitation model of classical conditioning proposed for *Aplysia*. In the leech, a residual toxin-resistant component of learning is demonstrated in the absence of sensitization. This suggests that the model needs to be extended to include a mechanism mediating some of the associative aspects of

classical conditioning that is both 5-HT independent and sensitization independent. One likely locus for additional mechanisms would be in the US pathway.

5. Limax maximus

Cellular events underlying associative learning have been studied in *Limax,* using a
semi-intact preparation consisting of cerebral ganglion, buccal ganglion, and lips
(Sokolove, Beiswanger, Prior, & Gelperin, 1977). Buccal ganglion nerve roots reliably elicited a neural correlate of feeding, coordinated rhythmic patter of moto-
neuron activity (feeding motor program) (Gelperin, Chang, & Reingold, 1978).
Training procedures similar to those originally used by Gelperin (1975) in the intact
slug have been successfully used to demonstrate associative learning in the semi-
intact preparation (Chang & Gelperin, 1980). Paired presentation of a food stimulus
(CS) and a bitter taste (US) to the lips of the preparation result in a rapid and
selective suppression of the feeding motor program to the taste paired with the US.
The neurons mediating this learning appear to be centrally rather than peripherally
located, since learning can be obtained when training is done on one lip and testing
is done on the other (Culligan & Gelperin, 1983).

Several neurons that have been identified appear to have a role in the sequence
of actions associated with the ingestion of food, the "feeding motor program." The
metacerebral giant cell has a modulatory influence on the feeding motor program
(Gelperin, 1980). Retrograde filling of the connectives from the buccal ganglia to
the cerebral ganglion has revealed a cluster of about 12 neurons that are likely to be
command-like neurons (Wieland & Gelperin, 1983).

Although associative learning has been demonstrated in *Limax* in both the whole
animal and the isolated nervous system, there are several important differences between the two preparations. In the whole animal an odor–taste association modifies
an appetitive behavior (locomotion). In contrast, in the semi-intact preparation a
taste–taste association modifies consummatory behavior (feeding). Results from
several experiments suggest that both the whole-animal and the isolated-brain
learning involve similar neural events. Gelperin and Culligan (1984) and Culligan
and Gelperin (1983) reported that following food taste–quinine pairings in the
whole animal, which result in odor avoidance, selective suppression of the feeding
motor program is evident in the isolated brain. In addition, appetitive conditioning
procedures produce both increased approach responses to the specific odor paired
with sugar and an odor-induced feeding response to the same odor (Sahley, Martin, &
Gelperin, 1992). This suggests that odor–taste associations can modify the olfactory-
guided search for food as well as the taste-guided consummatory response.

Of particular interest is the network of local interneurons in the PC lobe of
Limax. This network has complex dynamics that are responsive to input elicited by
natural odors applied to the olfactory neuroepithelium at the tip of the superior
tentacle (Gelperin & Tank, 1990). Neurons within the PC lobe have been found to
be immunoreactive for dopamine, serotonin, glutamate, and FMRFamide (Cooke &

Gelperin, 1988; Gelperin, Rhines, Flores, & Tank, 1993). Five members of the FMRFamide-related peptide family have been isolated from extracts of whole *Limax* (Krajniak, Greenber, Price, Doble, & Lee, 1989); thus all five are candidate neurotransmitters in the pro-cerebral (PC) lobe. FMRFamide and SCPB affect rhythmic motor networks in the *Limax* feeding system (Cooke & Gelperin, 1988; Prior & Watson, 1988), suggesting that some members of these two peptide families have modulatory effects on the PC lobe network.

Recently, Gelperin (1994) has demonstrated that NO synthase is present within the PC lobe and that NO has an effect on oscillators within the PC lobe. If synaptic plasticity in the PC lobe plays a role in odor learning, NO communication among PC cells could be relevant to implementing learning-dependent synaptic plasticity (Gelperin, 1994). Given that odor memories in *Limax* can last more than 120 days (Delaney & Gelperin, 1986), NO action via augmented cGMP synthesis may lead to long-term changes in gene expression in PC cells.

IV. CONCLUSION

The field of invertebrate learning has generated a number of general features that appear to be characteristic of learning in both vertebrate and invertebrate systems. As an example, changes in both synaptic efficacy and cellular excitability have been detected following nonassociative and associative conditioning. Moreover, long-term memory requires protein synthesis and gene expression whereas short-term memory does not. Another important shared feature is that changes associated with learning involve not only multiple cellular mechanisms within single neurons but multiple loci of plasticity in different neural systems. Finally, the activation of second messengers is essential in supporting the induction of cellular changes associated with learning.

An important trend in the study of invertebrate learning has been the focus on broader behavioral questions that have long been central to the study of learning in vertebrates. In the nematode, for example, experiments have addressed the effect(s) of interstimulus intervals on habituation and dishabituation. In addition, in several systems the role of contingency as well as contiguity in associative learning and their underlying mechanisms have been explored. As discussed earlier (see section on characteristic features of Pavlovian conditioning), for an animal to successfully learn the relationship between a cue (CS) and a consequence (US), the cue must reliably predict the second; temporal contiguity of the stimuli is insufficient to produce learning if the first is a poor predictor of the second (Kamin, 1969; Rescorla, 1968). Mechanisms based on more than simple coincidence detection must operate in the formation of these associations. Moreover, both excitatory and inhibitory associations can be formed (Rescorla, 1969; Bitterman et al., 1983; Martin and Sahley, 1986). A stimulus may come to predict the occurrence of another stimulus (excitatory learning) or its absence. As illustrated herein, the operation of multiple mechanisms for both nonassociative and associative learning for many species, at both the cellular and the subcellular levels, is consistent with the richness and complexity of behavior. This broader approach necessitates the identification and characterization of interacting neural networks and the assessment of the contribution of each mechanisms to the learned change in behavior. The study of neural networks opens new possibilities for the mechanisms that may mediate these fundamental properties of the associative process.

REFERENCES

Abrams, T. W., Castellucci, V. F., Camardo, J. S., Kandel, E. R., & Lloyd, P. E. (1984). Two endogenous neuropeptides modulate the gill and siphon withdrawal reflex in *Aplysia* by presynaptic facilitation involving cAMP-dependent closure of a serotonin-sensitive potassium channel. *Proceedings of the National Academy of Sciences, U.S.A., 81,* 7956–7960.

Abrams, T. W., Eliot, L., Dudai, Y., & Kandel, E. R. (1985). Activation of adenylate cyclase in *Aplysia* neural tissue by Ca^{2+}/calmodulin, a candidate for an associative mechanism during conditioning. *Society for Neuroscience Abstracts, 11,* 797.

Aceves-Pina, E. O., Booker, R., Duerr, J. S., Livingston, M. S., Quinn, W. G., Smith, R. F., Sziber, P. P., Tempel, B. L., & Tully, T. P. (1983). Learning and memory in *Drosophila*, studied with mutants. *Cold Spring Harbor Symposium on Quantitative Biology, 48,* 831–840.

Alkon, D. L. (1989). Memory storage and neural systems. *Scientific American, 261,* 42–50.

Alkon, D. L., Anderson, M. J., Kuzirian, D. J., Rogers, D. F., Fass, D. M., Collin, C., Nelson, T. J., Kapetanovic, I. M., & Matzel, L. D. (1993). GABA-mediated synaptic interaction between the visual and vestibular pathways of *Hermissenda*. *Journal of Neurochemistry, 61,* 556–566.

Alkon, D. L., & Fuortes, M. G. F. (1972). Responses of photoreceptors in *Hermissenda*. *Journal of General Physics, 60,* 631–649.

Alkon, D. L., Lederhendler, I., & Shoukimas, J. J. (1982). Primary changes of membrane currents during retention of associative learning. *Science, 215,* 693–695.

Alkon, D. L., Sakakibara, M., Forman, R., Harrigan, J., Lederhendler, I., & Farley, J. (1985). Reduction of two voltage-dependent K^+ currents mediates serotonin of a learned association. *Behavioral and Neural Biology, 44,* 278–300.

Bacskai, B. J., Hochner, B., Mahaut-Smith, M., Adams, S. R., Kaang, B. K., & Kandel, E. R. (1993). Spatially resolved dynamics of cAMP and protein kinase A subunits in *Aplysia* sensory neurons. *Science, 260,* 222–226.

Bagnoli, P., Brunelli, M., Magni, F., & Pellegrino, M. (1975). The neuron of the fast conducting system in *Hirudo medicinalis*: Identification and synaptic connections with primary afferent neurons. *Archives Italiennes de Biologie, 113,* 21–43.

Bailey, C. H., & Chen, M. (1983). Morphological basis of long-term habituation and sensitization in *Aplysia*. *Science, 220,* 91–93.

Bailey, C. H., & Chen, M. (1984). Further studies on the morphological basis of long-term habituation in *Aplysia*. *Society for Neuroscience Abstracts, 10,* 131.

Bailey, C. H., & Chen, M. (1988a). Long-term memory in *Aplysia* modulates the total number of varicosities of single identified sensory neurons. *Proceedings of the National Academy of Sciences U.S.A., 85,* 2372–2377.

Bailey, C. H., & Chen, M. (1988b). Long-term sensitization in *Aplysia* increases the number of pre-synaptic contacts onto the identified gill motor neuron L7. *Proceedings of the National Academy of Sciences U.S.A., 85,* 9356–9359.

Bailey, C. H., & Chen, M. (1988c). Morphological basis of short-term habituation in *Aplysia. Journal of Neuroscience, 8,* 2452–2459.

Bailey, C. H., & Chen, M. (1989). Time course of structural changes at identified sensory neuron synapses during long-term sensitization in *Aplysia. Journal of Neuroscience, 9,* 1774–1780.

Bailey, C. H., Hawkins, R. D., Chen, M., & Kandel, E. R. (1981). Interneurons involved in mediation and modulation of gill-withdrawal reflex in *Aplysia.* IV. Morphological basis of presynaptic facilitation. *Journal of Neurophysiology, 45,* 340–360.

Bailey, C. H., Montarolo, P., Chen, M., Kandel, E. R., & Schacher, S. (1992). Inhibitors of protein and RNA synthesis block structural changes that accompany long-term heterosynaptic plasticity in *Aplysia. Neuron, 9,* 749–758.

Bartsch, D., Ghirardi, M., Skehel, P. A., Karl, K. A., Herder, S. P., Chen, M., Bailey, C. H., & Kandel, E. R. (1995). *Aplysia* CREB2 represses long-term facilitation: Relief of repression converts transient facilitation into long-term functional and structural change. *Cell, 83,* 979–992.

Baxter, D. A., & Byrne, J. H. (1989). Serotonergic modulation of two potassium channels in the pleural sensory neurons of *Aplysia. Journal of Neurophysiology, 62,* 665–679.

Baxter, D. A., & Byrne, J. H. (1990a). Differential effects of cAMP and serotonin on membrane current, action potential duration, and excitability in somata of pleural sensory neurons of *Aplysia. Journal of Neurophysiology, 64,* 978–990.

Baxter, D. A., & Byrne, J. H. (1990b). Mathematical modeling of the serotonergic modulation of electrophysiological properties of sensory neurons in *Aplysia. Society for Neuroscience Abstracts, 16,* 1297.

Belardetti, P., Bondi, C., Colombaioni, L., Brunelli, M., Trevisani, A., & Zavagno, C. (1982). Role of serotonin and cyclic AMP on facilitation of the fast conducting system activity in the leech, *Hirudo. Brain Research, 246,* 89–103.

Belkin, K. J., Goldstein, M. I., Goldsmith, B. A., & Abrams, T. W. (1992). A simulation approach to evaluating relative contributions of multiple 5-H-modulated K^+ currents to spike broadening in *Aplysia* sensory neurons. *Society for Neuroscience Abstracts, 18,* 713.

Bernier, L., Castellucci, V. F., Kandel, E. R., & Schwartz, J. H. (1982). Facilitatory transmitter causes a selective and prolonged increase in adenosine 3':5'-monophosphate in sensory neurons mediating the gill and siphon withdrawal reflex in *Aplysia. Journal of Neuroscience, 2,* 1682–1691.

Biondi, C., Belardetti, F., Brunelli, M., & Trevissani, A. (1982). Increased synthesis of cyclic AMP and short-term plastic changes in the segmental ganglia of the leech, *Hirudo medicinalis. Cellular and Molecular Neurobiology, 2,* 81–91.

Bitterman, M. E., Menzel, R., Fietz, A., & Schafer, S. (1983). Classical conditioning of proboscis extension in honeybees (*Apis mellifera*). *J. Comp. Psychol., 97,* 107–119.

Boulis, N., & Sahley, C. (1988). A behavioral analysis of habituation and sensitization of shortening in the semi-intact leech. *Journal of Neuroscience, 8,* 4621–4627.

Braha, O. (1990). *Possible involvement of protein kinase C in presynaptic facilitation of the sensory-motor synapse of Aplysia.* Unpublished Ph.D. thesis, Columbia University.

Braha, O., Dale, N., Hochner, B., Klein, M., Abrams, T. W., & Kandel, E. R. (1990). Second messengers involved in the two processes of presynaptic facilitation that contribute to sensitization and dishabituation in *Aplysia* sensory neurons. *Proceedings of the National Academy of Sciences U.S.A., 87,* 2040–2044.

Braha, O., Edmonds, T., Sacktor, T., Kandel, E. R., & Klein, M. (1993). The contributions of protein kinase A and protein kinase C to the actions of 5-HT on the L-type Ca^{2+} current of the sensory neurons in *Aplysia. Journal of Neuroscience, 13,* 1839–1851.

Brenner, S. T. (1974). The genetics of *Caenorhabditis elegans. Genetics, 77,* 71–94.

Brunelli, M., Castellucci, V. F., & Kandel, E. R. (1976). Synaptic facilitation and behavioral sensitization in *Aplysia:* Possible role of serotonin and cAMP. *Science, 194,* 1178–1181.

Byrne, J. H., Baxter, D. A., Buonomano, D. V., & Raymond, J. L. (1990). Neuronal and network determinants of simple and higher-order features of associative learning: Experimental and modeling approaches. *Cold Spring Harbor Symposium on Quantitative Biology, 55,* 175–186.

Byrne, J. H., Castellucci, V. F., & Kandel, E. R. (1978). Contribution of individual mechanoreceptor sensory neurons to defensive gill-withdrawal reflex in *Aplysia. Journal of Neurophysiology, 41,* 418–431.

Byrne, J. H., & Kandel, E. R. (1996). Presynaptic facilitation revisited: State and time dependence. *Journal of Neuroscience, 16,* 425–435.

Canavier, C. C., Baxter, D. A., Clark, J. W., & Byrne, J. H. (1991). Simulations of action potentials, transmitter release, and plasticity of sensorimotor synapses in *Aplysia. Society for Neuroscience Abstracts, 17,* 1590.

Carew, T. J., Abrams, T. W., Hawkins, R. D., & Kandel, E. R. (1984). The use of simple invertebrate systems to explore psychological issues related to associative learning. In D. L. Alkon & J. Farley (Eds.), *Primary neural substrates of learning and behavioral change* (pp. 169–183). New York: Cambridge University Press.

Carew, T. J., Castellucci, V. F., & Kandel, E. R. (1971). An analysis of dishabituation and sensitization of the gill-withdrawl reflex in *Aplysia. International Journal of Neuroscience, 2,* 79–98.

Carew, T. J., Castellucci, V. F., & Kandel, E. R. (1979). Sensitization in *Aplysia*: Restoration of transmission in synapses inactivated by long-term habituation. *Science, 205,* 417–419.

Carew, T. J., Pinsker, H. M., & Kandel, E. R. (1972). Long-term habituation of a defensive withdrawal reflex in *Aplysia. Science, 175,* 451–454.

Carew, T. J., Walters, E. T., & Kandel, E. R. (1981). Classical conditioning in a simple withdrawal reflex in *Aplysia californica. Journal of Neuroscience, 1,* 1426–1437.

Castellucci, V. F., Blumenfeld, H., Goelet, P., & Kandel, E. R. (1989). Inhibitor of protein synthesis blocks long-term behavioral sensitization in the isolated gill-withdrawal reflex of *Aplysia. Journal of Neurobiology, 20,* 1–9.

Castellucci, V. F., Carew, T. J., & Kandel, E. R. (1978). Cellular analysis of long-term habituation of the gill-withdrawal reflex in *Aplysia californica. Science, 202,* 1306–1308.

Castellucci, V. F., Nairn, A., Greengard, P., Schwartz, J. H., & Kandel, E. R. (1982). Inhibitor of adenosine 3':5'-monophosphate-dependent protein kinase blocks presynaptic facilitation in *Aplysia. Journal of Neuroscience, 2,* 1673–1681.

Castellucci, V. F., Kandel, E. R., Schwartz, J. H., Wilson, F. D., Nairin, A. C., & Greengard, P. (1980). Intracellular injection of the catalytic subunit of cyclic AMP-dependent protein kinase simulates facilitation of transmitter release underlying behavioral sensitization in *Aplysia. Proceedings of the National Academy of Sciences U.S.A., 77,* 7492–7496.

Castellucci, V. F., Pinsker, H., Kupfermann, I., & Kandel, E. R. (1970). Neuronal mechanisms of habituation and dishabituation of the gill-withdrawal reflex in *Aplysia. Science, 167,* 1745–1748.

Chalfie, M. (1984). Neuronal development in *Caenorhabditis elegans. Trends in Neuroscience, 7,* 197–202.

Chalfie, M., & Sulston, J. (1981). Developmental genetics of the mechanosensory neurons of *Caenorhabditis elegans. Developmental Biology, 82,* 358–370.

Chalfie, M., Sulston, J. E., White, J. G., Southgate, E., Thomson, J. N., & Brenner, S. (1985). The neural circuit for touch sensitivity in *Caenorhabditis elegans. Journal of Neuroscience, 5,* 956–964.

Chang, J. J., & Gelperin, A. (1980). Rapid taste-aversion learning by an isolated molluscan central nervous system. *Proceedings of the National Academy of Sciences U.S.A., 77,* 6204–6206.

Clark, G. A., & Kandel, E. R. (1993). Induction of long-term facilitation in *Aplysia* sensory neurons by local application of serotonin to remote synapses. *Proceedings of the National Academy of Sciences U.S.A., 90,* 11411–11415.

Cohen, T. E., Kaplan, S., W., Kandel, E. R., & Hawkins, R. D. (1997). A simplified preparation for relating cellular events to behavior: Mechanisms contributing to habituation, dishabituation, and sensitization of the *Aplysia* gill-withdrawal reflex. *Journal of Neuroscience, 17,* 2886–2899.

Colebrook, E., Bulloch, A., & Lukowiak, K. (1991). Electrophysiological studies of the gill ganglion in *Aplysia californica. Cellular and Molecular Neurobiology, 11,* 305–320.

Colebrook, E., & Lukowiak, K. (1988). Learning by the *Aplysia* model system: Lack of correlation between gill and gill motor neurone responses. *Journal of Experimental Biology, 135,* 411–429.

Colwill, R. M., Absher, R. A., & Roberts, M. L. (1988). Context-US learning in *Aplysia californica. Journal of Neuroscience, 8,* 4440–4444.

Cooke, I., & Gelperin, A. (1988). Distribution of FMRFamide-like immunoreactivity in the nervous system of the slug *Limax maximus*. *Cell Tissue Research, 253,* 69–76.

Critz, S. D., Baxter, D. A., & Byrne, J. H. (1991). Modulatory effects of serotonin, FMRFamide, and myomodulin on the duration of action pote tials, excitability, and membrane currents in tail sensory neurons of *Aplysia*. *Journal of Neurophysiology, 66,* 1912–1926.

Crow, T. (1985). Conditioned modification of phototactic behavior in *Hermissenda*. II. Differential adaptation of B-photoreceptors. *Journal of Neuroscience, 5,* 215–223.

Crow, T. (1988). Cellular and molecular analysis of associative learning and memory in *Hermissenda*. *Trends in Neurosciences, 11,* 136–142.

Crow, T., & Alkon, D. L. (1978). Retention of an associative behavioral change in *Hermissenda*. *Science, 201,* 1239–1241.

Crow, T., & Alkon, D. L. (1980). Associative behavioral modification in *Hermissenda:* Cellular correlates. *Science, 209,* 412–414.

Crow, T., & Forrester, J. (1986). Light paired with serotonin mimics the effects of conditioning on phototactic behavior in *Hermissenda*. *Proceedings of the National Academy of Sciences U.S.A., 83,* 7975–7978.

Crow, T., & Forrester, J. (1990). Inhibition of protein synthesis blocks long-term enhancement of generator potentials produced by one-trial in vivo conditioning in *Hermissenda*. *Proceedings of the National Academy of Sciences U.S.A., 87,* 4490–4494.

Crow, T., & Forrester, J. (1991). Light paired with serotonin in vivo produces both short and long-term enhancement of generator potentials of identified B-photoreceptors in *Hermissenda*. *Journal of Neuroscience, 11,* 608–617.

Crow, T., & Forrester, J. (1993). Down-regulation of protein kinase C and kinase inhibitors dissociate short- and long-term enhancement produced by one-trial conditioning of *Hermissenda*. *Journal of Neurophysiology, 69,* 636–641.

Crow, T., Forrester, J., Williams, M., Waxham, M. N., & Neary, J. T. (1991). Down-regulation of protein kinase C blocks 5-HT-induced enhancement in *Hermissenda* B-photoreceptors. *Neuroscience Letters, 12,* 107–110.

Crow, T., Siddiqi, V., & Dash, P. K. (1997). Long-term enhancement but not short-term in *Hermissenda* is dependent upon mRNA synthesis. *Neurobiology of Learning and Memory, 68,* 343–350.

Crow, T., Siddiqi, V., Zhu, Q., & Neary, J. T. (1996). Time-dependent increase in protein phosphorylation following one-trial enhancement in *Hermissenda*. *Journal of Neurochemistry, 66,* 1736–1741.

Culligan, N., & Gelperin, A. (1983). One-trial associative learning by an isolated molluscan CNS: Use of different chemoreceptors for training and testing. *Brain Research, 266,* 319–327.

Dash, P. K., Hochner, B., & Kandel, E. R. (1990). Injection of the cAMP-responsive element into the nucleus of *Aplysia* sensory neurons blocks long-term facilitation. *Nature, 345,* 718–721.

Debski, E. A., & Friesen, W. O. (1985). Habituation of swimming activity in the medicinal leech. *Journal of Experimental Biology, 116,* 169–188.

Debski, E. A., & Friesen, W. O. (1986). Role of central interneurons in habituation of swimming activity in the medicinal leech. *Journal of Neurophysiology, 55,* 977–994.

Delaney, K., & Gelperin, A. (1986). Post-ingestive food-aversion learning to amino acid deficient diets by the terrestrial slug *Limax maximus*. *Journal of Comparative Physiology [A], 159,* 281–295.

DeZazzo, J., & Tully, J. (1995). Dissection of memory formation: From behavioral pharmacology to molecular genetics. *Trends in Neurosciences, 18,* 212–218.

Dierkes, P. W., Hochstrate, P., & Schlue, W. R. (1996). Distribution and functional properties of glutamate receptors in the leech central nervous system. *Journal of Neurophysiology, 75,* 2312–2321.

Domjan, M., & Burkhardt, B. (1982). *The principles of learning and behavior.* Monterey, CA: Brooks/Cole.

Dudai, Y. (1985). Genes, enzymes and learning in *Drosophila*. *Trends in Neurosciences, 8,* 18–21.

Dudai, Y. (1988). Neurogenetic dissection of learning and short-term memory in *Drosophila*. *Annual Review of Neuroscience, 11,* 537–563.

Dudai, Y. (1989). *The neurobiology of memory.* New York: Oxford University Press.

Dudai, Y., Jan, Y., Byers, D., Quinn, W., and Benzer, S. (1976). Dunce, a mutant of *Drosophila* deficient in learning. *Proceedings of the National Academy of Science, 73,* 1684–1688.

Edmonds, B., Klein, M., Dale, N., & Kandel, E. (1990). Contributions of two types of calcium channels to synaptic transmission and plasticity. *Science, 250,* 1142–1147.

Ehrlich, J., Boulis, N., Karrer, T., & Sahley, C. L. (1992). Differential effects of serotonin depletion on sensitization and dishabituation. *Journal of Neurobiology, 23,* 270–279.

Emptage, N. J., & Carew, T. J. (1993). Long-term synaptic facilitation in the absence of short-term facilitation in *Aplysia* neurons. *Science, 262,* 253–256.

Falk, C. X., Wu, J.-Y., Cohen, L. B., & Tang, A. C. (1993). Nonuniform expression of habituation in the activity of distinct classes of neurons in the *Aplysia* abdominal ganglion. *Journal of Neuroscience, 13,* 4072–4081.

Farley, J. (1987). Contingency learning and causal detection in *Hermissenda*: I. Behavior. *Behavioral Neuroscience, 101,* 13–27.

Farley, J., & Alkon, D. L. (1982). Associative neural and behavioral change in *Hermissenda*: Consequences of nervous system orientation for light- and pairing-specificity. *Journal of Neurophysiology, 48,* 785–807.

Farley, J., & Auerbach, S. (1986). Protein kinase C activation induces conductance changes in *Hermissenda* photoreceptors like those seen in associative learning. *Nature, 319,* 220–223.

Farley, J., Reasoner, H., & Janssen, M. (1997). Potentiation of phototactic suppression in *Hermissenda* by a chemosensory stimulus during compound conditioning. *Behavioral Neuroscience, 111,* 1–22.

Farley, J., Richards, W. G., & Grover, L. M. (1990). Associative learning causes changes intrinsic to *Hermissenda* type A photoreceptors. *Behavioral Neuroscience, 104,* 135–152.

Farley, J., & Schuman, E. (1991). Protein kinase C inhibitors prevent induction and continued expression of cell memory in *Hermissenda* type B photoreceptors. *Proceedings of the National Academy of Sciences U.S.A., 88,* 2016–2020.

French, K. A., & Muller, K. J. (1986). Regeneration of a distinctive set of axosomatic contacts in the leech central nervous system. *Journal of Neuroscience, 6,* 318–324.

Frost, L., Kaplan, S. W., Cohen, T. E., Henzi, V., Kandel, E. R., & Hawkins, R. D. (1997). A simplified preparation for relating cellular events to behavior: Contribution of LE and unidentified siphon sensory neurons to mediation and habituation of the *Aplysia* gill- and siphon-withdrawl reflex. *Journal of Neuroscience, 17,* 2900–2913.

Frost, W. N., Castellucci, V. F., Hawkins, R. D., & Kandel, E. R. (1985). Monosynaptic connections made by the sensory neurons of the gill- and siphon-withdrawal reflex in *Aplysia* participate in the storage of long-term memory for sensitization. *Proceedings of the National Academy of Sciences U.S.A., 82,* 8266–8269.

Frost, W. N., & Kandel, E. R. (1984). Sensitizing stimuli reduce the effectiveness of the L30 inhibitory interneurons in the siphon withdrawal reflex circuit of *Aplysia*. *Society for Neuroscience Abstracts, 10,* 510.

Frysztak, R. J., & Crow, T. (1993). Differential expression of correlates of classical conditioning in identified medial and lateral type A photoreceptors of *Hermissenda*. *Journal of Neuroscience, 13,* 2889–2897.

Frysztak, R. J., & Crow, T. (1994). Enhancement of type B and A photoreceptor inhibitory synaptic connections in conditioned *Hermissenda*. *Journal of Neuroscience, 14,* 1245–1250.

Frysztak, R. J., & Crow, T. (1997). Synaptic enhancement and enhanced excitability in presynaptic and postsynaptic neurons in the conditioned stimulus pathway of *Hermissenda*. *Journal of Neuroscience, 17,* 4426–4433.

Gelperin, A. (1975). Rapid food-aversion learning by a terrestrial mollusk. *Science, 189,* 567–570.

Gelperin, A. (1980). Synaptic modulation by identified serotonin neurons. In B. Jacobs & A. Gelperin (Eds.), *Serotonin neurotransmission and behavior.* Cambridge, MA: MIT Press.

Gelperin, A. (1994). Nitric oxide mediates network oscillations of olfactory interneurons in a terrestrial mollusc. *Nature, 369,* 61–63.

Gelperin, A., Chang, J. J., & Reingold, S. C. (1978). Feeding motor program in *Limax*. I. Neuromuscular correlates and control by chemosensory input. *Journal of Neurobiology, 9,* 285–300.

Gelperin, A., & Culligan, N. (1984). *In vitro* expression of in vivo learning by an isolated molluscan CNS. *Brain Research, 304,* 207–213.

Gelperin, A., Rhines, L. D., Flores, J., & Tank, D. W. (1993). Coherent network oscillations by olfactory interneurons: Modulation by endogenous amines. *Journal of Neurophysiology, 69,* 1930–1939.

Gelperin, A., & Tank, D. W. (1990). Odor-modulated collective network oscillations of olfactory interneurons in a terrestrial mollusc. *Nature, 345,* 437–440.

Ghirardi, M., Braha, O., Hochner, B., Montarolo, P. G., Kandel, E. R., & Dale, N. (1992). Roles of PKA and PKC in facilitation of evoked and spontaneous transmitter release at depressed and non-depressed synapses in *Aplysia* sensory neurons. *Neuron, 9,* 479–489.

Gingrich, K. J., Baxter, D. A., & Byrne, J. H. (1988). Mathematical model of cellular mechanisms contributing to presynaptic facilitation. *Brain Research Bulletin, 21,* 513–520.

Gingrich, K. J., & Byrne, J. H. (1984). Simulation of nonassociative and associative neuronal modifications in *Aplysia*. *Society for Neuroscience Abstracts, 10,* 270.

Gingrich, K. J., & Byrne, J. H. (1985). Simulation of synaptic depression, posttetanic potentiation, and presynaptic facilitation of synaptic potentials from sensory neurons mediating gill-withdrawal reflex in *Aplysia*. *Journal of Neurophysiology, 53,* 652–669.

Gingrich, K. J., & Byrne, J. H. (1987). Single-cell neuronal model for associative learning. *Journal of Neurophysiology, 57,* 1705–1715.

Glanzman, D. L. (1995). The cellular basis of classical conditioning in *Aplysia californica*—it's less simple than you think. *Trends in Neurosciences, 18,* 30–36.

Glanzman, D., & Krasne, F. B. (1983). Serotonin and octopamine have opposite modulatory effects on the crayfish's LG escape reaction. *Journal of Neuroscience, 3,* 2263–2269.

Glanzman, D. L., Mackey, S. L., Hawkins, R. D., Dyke, A. M., Lloyd, P. E., & Kandel, E. R. (1989). Depletion of serotonin in the nervous system of *Aplysia* reduces the behavioral enhancement of gill withdrawal as well as the heterosynaptic facilitation produced by tail shock. *Journal of Neuroscience, 9,* 4200–4213.

Goldsmith, B. A., & Abrams, T. W. (1991). Reversal of synaptic depression by serotonin at *Aplysia* sensory neuron synapses involves activation of adenylyl cyclase. *Proceedings of the National Academy of Sciences U.S.A., 88,* 9021–9025.

Goldsmith, B. A., & Abrams, T. W. (1992). cAMP modulates multiple K^+ currents, increasing spike duration and excitability in *Aplysia* sensory neurons. *Proceedings of the National Academy of Sciences U.S.A., 89,* 11481–11485.

Hall, D. H., & Russell, R. L. (1991). The posterior nervous system of the nematode *Caenorhabditis elegans:* Serial reconstruction of identified neurons and complete pattern of synaptic interactions. *Journal of Neuroscience, 11,* 1–22.

Hawkins, R. D., Abrams, T. W., Carew, T. J., & Kandel, E. R. (1983). A cellular mechanism of classical conditioning in *Aplysia*: Activity-dependent amplification of presynaptic facilitation. *Science, 219,* 400–405.

Hawkins, R. D., Carew, T. J., & Kandel, E. R. (1986). Effects of interstimulus interval and contingency on classical conditioning of the *Aplysia* siphon withdrawal reflex. *Journal of Neuroscience, 6,* 1659–1701.

Hawkins, R. D., Castellucci, V. F., & Kandel, E. R. (1981). Interneurons involved in mediation and modulation of gill-withdrawal reflex in *Aplysia*. I. Identification and characterization. *Journal of Neurophysiology, 45,* 304–314.

Hawkins, R. D., & Kandel, E. R. (1984). Is there a cell-biological alphabet for simple forms of learning? *Psychological Review, 91,* 375–391.

Henderson, T. B., & Strong, P. N. (1972). Classical conditioning in the leech, *Macrobdella dititra* as a function of CS and US intensity. *Conditioned Reflex, 7,* 210–215.

Hickie, C., Cohen, L. B., & Balaban, P. M. (1997). The synapse between LE sensory neurons and gill motoneurons makes only a small contribution to the *Aplysia* gill-withdrawal reflex. *European Journal of Neurosceince, 9,* 627–636.

Hochner, B., & Kandel, E. R. (1992). Modulation of a transient K⁺ current in the pleural sensory neurons of *Aplysia* by serotonin and cAMP: Implications for spike broadening. *Proceedings of the National Academy of Sciences U.S.A., 89,* 11476–11480.

Hochner, B., Klein, M., Schacher, S., & Kandel, E. R. (1986a). Action potential duration and the modulation of transmitter release from the sensory neurons of *Aplysia* in presynaptic facilitation and behavioral sensitization. *Proceedings of the National Academy of Sciences U.S.A., 83,* 8410–8414.

Hochner, B., Klein, M., Schacher, S., & Kandel, E. R. (1986b). Additional component in the cellular mechanism of presynaptic facilitation contributes to behavioral dishabituation in *Aplysia. Proceedings of the National Academy of Sciences U.S.A., 83,* 8794–8798.

Hochner, B., Schacher, S., Klein, M., & Kandel, E. R. (1985). Presynaptic facilitation in *Aplysia* sensory neurons: A process independent of K⁺ current modulation becomes important when transmitter release is depressed. *Society for Neuroscience Abstracts, 11,* 29.

Hu, Y., Barzilai, A., Chen, M., Bailey, C. H., & Kandel, E. R. (1993). 5-HT and cAMP induce the formation of coated pits and vesicles and increase the expression of clathrin light chain in sensory neurons of *Aplysia. Neuron, 10,* 921–929.

Illich, P. A., & Walters, E. T. (1997). Mechanosensory neurons innervating *Aplysia* siphon encode noxious stimuli and display nociceptive sensitization. *Journal of Neuroscience, 17,* 459–469.

Kaang, B. K., Kandel, E. R., & Grant, S. G. (1993). Activation of cAMP-responsive genes by stimuli that produce long-term facilitation in *Aplysia* sensory neurons. *Neuron, 10,* 427–435.

Kamin, L. J. (1969). Predictability, surprise, attention and conditioning. In R. Church & B. A. Campbell (Eds.), *Punishment and aversive behavior* (pp. 279–296). New York: Appleton-Century-Crofts.

Kanz, J. E., Eberly, L. B., Cobbs, J. S., & Pinsker, H. M. (1979). Neuronal correlates of siphon withdrawal in freely behaving *Aplysia. Journal of Neurophysiology, 42,* 1538–1556.

Karrer, T., & Sahley, C. L. (1988). Discriminative conditioning alters food preferences in the leech, *Haemopis marmorata. Behavioral and Neural Biology, 50,* 311–324.

Kistler, H. B. J., Hawkins, R. D., Koester, J., Kandel, E. R., & Schwartz, J. H. (1983). Immunocyto-chemical studies of neurons producing facilitation in the abdominal ganglion of *Aplysia. Society for Neuroscience Abstracts, 9,* 915.

Kistler, H. B. Jr., Hawkins, R. D., Koester, J., Steinbusch, H. W., Kandel, E. R., & Schwartz, J. H. (1985). Distribution of serotonin-immunoreactive cell bodies and processes in the abdominal ganglion of mature *Aplysia. Journal of Neuroscience, 5,* 72–80.

Klein, M. (1993). Differential cyclic AMP dependence of facilitation at *Aplysia* sensorimotor synapses as a function of prior stimulation: Augmentation versus restoration of transmitter release. *Journal of Neuroscience, 13,* 3793–3801.

Klein, M. (1994a). Synaptic augmentation by 5-HT at rested *Aplysia* sensorimotor synapses: Independence of action potential prolongation. *Neuron, 13,* 159–166.

Klein, M. (1994b). Distinct component of presynaptic calcium current is increased by cyclic AMP at *Aplysia* sensorimotor synapses in culture. *Society for Neuroscience Abstracts, 20,* 1073.

Klein, M., Camardo, J., & Kandel, E. R. (1982). Serotonin modulates a specific potassium current in the sensory neurons that show presynaptic facilitation in *Aplysia. Proceedings of the National Academy of Sciences U.S.A., 79,* 5713–5717.

Klein, M., Hochner, B., & Kandel, E. R. (1986). Facilitatory transmitters and cAMP can modulate accommodation as well as transmitter release in *Aplysia* sensory neurons: Evidence for parallel processing in a single cell. *Proceedings of the National Academy of Sciences U.S.A., 83,* 7994–7998.

Klein, M., & Kandel, E. R. (1978). Presynaptic modulation of voltage-dependent Ca⁺⁺ current: Mechanism for behavioral sensitization in *Aplysia californica. Proceedings of the National Academy of Sciences U.S.A., 75,* 3512–3516.

Klein, M., & Kandel, E. R. (1980). Mechanism of calcium current modulation underlying presynaptic facilitation and behavioral sensitization in *Aplysia. Proceedings of the National Academy of Sciences U.S.A., 77,* 6912–6916.

Klein, M., Shapiro, E., & Kandel, E. R. (1980a). Synaptic plasticity and the modulation of the Ca^{++} current. *Journal of Experimental Biology, 89,* 117–157.

Klein, M., Shapiro, E., & Kandel, E. R. (1980b). Synaptic plasticity and the modulation of the calcium current. *Journal of Experimental Biology, 89,* 117–157.

Krajniak, K. G., Greenber, M. J., Price, D. A., Doble, K. E., & Lee, T. D. (1989). The identification, localization and pharmacology of FMR Famide-related peptides and SCPB in the penis and crop of the terrestrial slug, *Limax maximus. Comparative Biochemistry and Physiology, C: Comparative Pharmacology, 94,* 485–492.

Krasne, F. B. (1969). Excitation and habituation of the crayfish escape reflex: The depolarizing response in lateral giant fibers. *Journal of Experimental Biology, 50,* 29–46.

Krasne, F. B., & Glanzman, D. L. (1986). Sensitization of the crayfish lateral giant escape reaction. *Journal of Neuroscience, 6,* 1013–1020.

Krasne, F. B., & Stirling, C. A. (1972). Synapses of crayfish abdominal ganglia with special attention to afferent and efferent connections of the lateral giant fibers. *Zeitschrift fuer Zellforschung Mikroskopische Anatomie, 127,* 526–544.

Krasne, F. B., & Teshiba, T. M. (1995). Habituation of an invertebrate escape reflex due to modulation by higher centers rather than local events. *Proceedings of the National Academy of Sciences U.S.A., 92,* 3362–3366.

Land, P. W., & Crow, T. (1985). Serotonin immunoreactivity in the circumesophageal nervous system of *Hermissenda crassicornis. Neuroscience Letters, 3,* 199–205.

Lederhendler, I., Gart, S., & Alkon, D. L. (1986). Classical conditioning of *Hermissenda*. Origin of a new response. *Journal of Neuroscience, 6,* 1325–1331.

Lent, C. M. (1982). Fluorescent properties of monoamine neurons following glyoxylic acid treatment of intact leech ganglia. *Histochemistry, 75,* 77–89.

Lockery, S. R., & Kristan, W. B. J. (1990). Distributed processing of sensory information in the leech. II. Identification of interneurons contributing to the local bending reflex. *Journal of Neuroscience, 10,* 1816–1829.

Lockery, S. R., & Kristan, W. B. J. (1991). Two forms of sensitization of the local bending reflex of the medicinal leech. *Journal of Comparative Physiology [A], 168,* 165–177.

Lockery, S. R., Rawlins, J. N., & Gray, J. A. (1985). Habituation of the shortening reflex in the medicinal leech. *Behavioral Neuroscience, 99,* 333–341.

Lukowiak, K. (1977). CNS control of the PNS-mediated gill withdrawal reflex and its habituation. *Canadian Journal of Physiology and Pharmacology, 55,* 1252–1262.

Lukowiak, K., & Colebrook, E. (1988a). Neuronal mechanisms of learning in an in vitro *Aplysia* preparation: Sites other than the sensory-motor neuron synapse are involved. *Journal of Physiology (Paris), 83,* 198–206.

Lukowiak, K., & Colebrook, E. (1988b). Classical conditioning alters the efficacy of identified gill motor neurones in producing gill withdrawal movements in *Aplysia. Journal of Experimental Biology, 140,* 273–285.

Lukowiak, K., & Jacklet, J. W. (1972). Habituation and dishabituation: Interactions between peripheral and central nervous systems in *Aplysia. Science, 67,* 1306–1308.

Lukowiak, K., & Jacklet, J. (1975). Habituation and dishabituation mediated by the peripheral and central neural circuits of the siphon of *Aplysia. Journal of Neurobiology, 6,* 183–200.

Lukowiak, K., & Sahley, C. (1981). The in vitro classical conditioning of the gill withdrawal reflex in *Aplysia californica. Science, 212,* 1516–1518.

Martin, K., & Sahley, C. L. (1986). Analysis of associative learning in *Limax maximus:* Excitatory and inhibitory conditioning. *Society for Neuroscience Abstracts, 12,* 39.

Matzel, L. D., & Alkon, D. L. (1991). GABA-induced potentiation of neuronal excitability occurs during contiguous pairings with intracellular calcium elevation. *Brain Research, 554,* 77–84.

Matzel, L. D., Lederhendler, I. I., & Alkon, D. L. (1990). Regulation of short-term associative memory by calcium-dependent protein kinase. *Journal of Neuroscience, 7,* 1198–1206.

Mercer, A. R., Emptage, N. J., & Carew, T. J. (1991). Pharmacological dissociation of modulatory effects of serotonin in *Aplysia* sensory neurons. *Science, 254,* 1811–1813.

Montarolo, P. G., Goelet, P., Castellucci, V. F., Morgan, J., & Kandel, E. R. (1986). A critical period of macromolecular synthesis in long-term heterosynaptic facilitation in *Aplysia*. *Science, 234,* 1249–1254.

Muller, K. J., & Carbonetto, S. (1979). The morphological and physiological properties of a regenerating synapse in the C.N.S. of the leech. *Journal of Comparative Neurology, 185,* 485–516.

Muller, K. J., Nicholls, J. G., & Stent, G. S. (1981). *Neurobiology of the leech*. Cold Spring Habor, NY: Cold Spring Harbor Laboratory.

Neary, J. T., Crow, T., & Alkon, D. L. (1981). Change in a specific phosphoprotein band following associative learning in *Hermissenda*. *Nature, 293,* 658–660.

Ocorr, K. A., Walters, E. T., & Byrne, J. H. (1985). Associative conditioning analog selectively increases cAMP levels of tail sensory neurons in *Aplysia*. *Proceedings of the National Academy of Sciences U.S.A., 82,* 2548–2552.

Peretz, B. (1970). Habituation and dishabituation in the absence of a central nervous system. *Science, 169,* 379–381.

Peretz, B., & Estes, J. (1974). Histology and histochemistry of the peripheral neural plexus in the *Aplysia* gill. *Journal of Neurobiology, 5,* 3–19.

Peretz, B., Jacklet, J. W., & Lukowiak, K. (1976). Habituation of reflexes in *Aplysia*: Contribution of the peripheral and central nervous systems. *Science, 191,* 396–399.

Peretz, B., & Moller, R. (1974). Control of habituation of the withdrawal reflex by the gill ganglion in *Aplysia. Journal of Neurobiology, 5,* 191–212.

Pinsker, H. M., Hening, W. A., Carew, T. J., & Kandel, E. R. (1973). Long-term sensitization of a defensive withdrawal reflex in *Aplysia. Science, 182,* 1039–1042.

Pinsker, H. M., Kupfermann, I., Castellucci, V. F., & Kandel, E. R. (1970). Habituation and dishabituation of the gill-withdrawal reflex in *Aplysia. Science, 167,* 1740–1742.

Pollock, J. D., Bernier, L., & Camardo, J. S. (1985). Serotonin and cyclic adenosine 3':5'-monophosphate modulate the potassium current in tail sensory neurons in the pleural ganglion of *Aplysia. Journal of Neuroscience, 5,* 1862–1871.

Prior, D. J., & Watson, W. H. (1988). The molluscan neuropeptide, SCPB, increases the responsiveness of the feeding motor program of *Limax maximus. Journal of Neurobiology, 19,* 87–105.

Rankin, C. H., Beck, C. D. O., & Chiba, C. M. (1990). *Caenorhabditis elegans:* A new model system for the study of learning and memory. *Behavioral Brain Research, 37,* 89–92.

Rankin, C. H., & Broster, B. S. (1992). Factors affecting habituation and recovery from habituation in the nematode *Caenorhabditis elegans. Behavioral Neuroscience, 106,* 239–249.

Rankin, C. H., & Carew, T. J. (1988). Dishabituation and sensitization emerge as separate processes during development in *Aplysia. Journal of Neuroscience, 8,* 197–211.

Rescorla, R. A. (1968). Probability of shock in the presence and absence of the CS in fear conditioning. *Journal of Comparative Physiological Psychology, 66,* 1–5.

Rescorla, R. A. (1969). Conditioned inhibition of fear resulting from negative CS–US contingencies. *Journal of Comparative Physiological Psychology, 67,* 504–509.

Rescorla, R. A., & Wagner, A. R. (1972). A theory of Pavlovian conditioning: Variations in the effectiveness of reinforcement and nonreinforcement. In A. H. Black & W. F. Prokasy (Eds.), *Classical conditioning II: Current theory and research* (pp. 64–99). New York: Appleeton-Century-Crofts.

Rogers, R. F., & Matzel, L. (1995). Higher-order associative processing in *Hermissenda* suggests multiple sites of neuronal modulation. *Learning and Memory, 2,* 279–298.

Sahley, C. L. (1988). Behavioral and cellular analysis of predictability in a semi-intact leech. *Society for Neuroscience Abstracts, 14,* 838.

Sahley, C. L. (1994). Serotonin depletion impairs but does not eliminate classical conditioning in the leech. *Hirudo medicinalis. Behavioral Neuroscience, 108,* 1043–1052.

Sahley, C. L., Boulis, N., & Schurmann, B. (1994). Associative learning in the semi-intact preparation: Effects of pairing and contingency. *Behavioral Neuroscience, 108,* 1–7.

Sahley, C. L., Martin, K. A., & Gelperin, A. (1990). Analysis of associative learning in a terrestrial mollusc *Limax maximus*. II. Appetitive learning. *Journal of Comparative Physiology [A], 167,* 339–345.

Sahley, C. L., Martin, K. A., & Gelperin, A. (1992). Odors can induce feeding motor responses in the terrestrial mollusc *Limax maximus. Behavioral Neuroscience, 106,* 563–568.

Sahley, C. L., Modney, B. K., Boulis, N. M., & Muller, K. J. (1994). The S cell: An interneuron essential for sensitization and full dishabituation of leech shortening. *Journal of Neuroscience, 14,* 6715–6721.

Sahley, C. L., & Ready, D. F. (1988). Associative learning modifies two behaviors in the leech, *Hirudo medicinalis. Journal of Neuroscience, 8,* 4612–4620.

Sahley, C. L., Rudy, J. W., & Gelperin, A. (1981). An analysis of associative learning in a terrestrial mollusc. I. Higher-order conditioning, blocking, and a US-pre-exposure effect. *Journal of Comparative Physiology, 144,* 1–8.

Schreurs, B. G. (1989). Classical conditioning of model systems: A behavioral review. *Psychobiology, 17,* 145–155.

Schwartz, J. H., Bernier, L., Castellucci, V. F., Polazzolo, M., Saitoh, T., Stapleton, A., & Kandel, E. R. (1983). What molecular steps determine the time course of the memory for short-term sensitization in *Aplysia? Cold Spring Harbor Symposium on Quantitative Biology, 48,* 811–819.

Siegelbaum, S. A. (1982). Serotonin and cyclic AMP close single K^+ channels in *Aplysia* sensory neurones. *Nature, 299,* 413–417.

Sokolove, P. G., Beiswanger, C. M., Prior, D. J., & Gelperin, A. (1977). A circadian rhythm in the locomotive behaviour of the giant garden slug *Limax maximus. Journal of Experimental Biology, 66,* 47–64.

Sugita, S., Baxter, D. A., & Byrne, J. H. (1994a). Activators of protein kinase C mimic serotonin-induced modulation of a voltage-dependent potassium current in pleural sensory neurons of *Aplysia. Journal of Neurophysiology, 72,* 1240–1249.

Sugita, S., Baxter, D. A., & Byrne, J. H. (1994b). cAMP-independent effects of 8-(4-paracholorophenylthio)-cyclic AMP on spike duration and membrane currents in pleural sensory neurons of *Aplysia. Journal of Neurophysiology, 72,* 1250–1259.

Sugita, S., Baxter, D. A., & Byrne, J. H. (1994c). Spike duration-independent processes may contribute to the rapidly developing component of serotonin- and PKC-induced facilitation of nondepressed tail sensorimotor connections in *Aplysia. Society for Neuroscience Abstracts, 20,* 815.

Sugita, S., Goldsmith, J. R., Baxter, D. A., & Byrne, J. H. (1992). Involvement of protein kinase C in serotonin-induced spike broadening and synaptic facilitation of sensorimotor connections in *Aplysia. Journal of Neurophysiology, 68,* 643–651.

Sulston, E. (1983). Neuronal cell lineages in the nematode *Caenorhabditis elegans. Cold Spring Harbor Symposia on Quantitative Biology, 2,* 443–452.

Sulston, E., Schierenberg, E., White, J. G., & Thomson, J. N. (1983). The embryonic cell lineage of the nematode *Caenorhabditis elegans. Developmental Biology, 100,* 64–119.

Trudeau, L. E., & Castellucci, V. F. (1992). Contribution of polysynaptic pathways in the mediation and plasticity of *Aplysia* gill and siphon withdrawal reflex: Evidence for differential modulation. *Journal of Neuroscience, 12,* 3838–3848.

Trudeau, L. E., & Castellucci, V. F. (1993a). Functional uncoupling of inhibitory interneurons plays an important role in short-term sensitization of *Aplysia* gill and siphon withdrawal reflex. *Journal of Neuroscience, 13,* 2126–2135.

Trudeau, L. E., & Castellucci, V. F. (1993b). Sensitization of the gill and siphon withdrawal reflex of *Aplysia*: Multiple sites of change in the neural network. *Journal of Neurophysiology, 70,* 1210–1220.

Tully, T. (1987). *Drosophila* learning and memory revisited. *Trends in Neurosciences, 10,* 330–335.

Tully, T., & Quinn, W. G. (1985). Classical conditioning and retention in normal and mutant *Drosophila melanogaster. Journal of Comparative Physiology, 157,* 263–277.

Walsh, J. P., & Byrne, J. H. (1989). Modulation of a steady-state Ca^{2+}-activated, K^+ current in tail sensory neurons of *Aplysia*: Role of serotonin and cAMP. *Journal of Neurophysiology, 61,* 32–44.

Walters, E. T., & Byrne, J. H. (1983). Associative conditioning of single sensory neurons suggests a cellular mechanism for learning. *Science, 219,* 405–408.

Ward, S. (1973). Chemotaxis by the nematode *Caenorhabditis elegans*: Identification of attractants and analysis of the response by use of mutants. *Proceedings of the National Academy of Sciences U.S.A., 70,* 817–821.

Ward, S., Thomson, N., White, J. G., & Brenner, S. (1975). Electron microscopical reconstruction of the anterior sensory anatomy of the nematode *Caenorhabditis elegans. Journal of Comparative Neurology, 160,* 313–338.

Weiss, S., & Drummond, G. I. (1985). Biochemical properties of adenylate cyclase in the gill of *Aplysia californica. Comparative Biochemistry and Physiology B: Comparative Biochemistry, 80,* 251–255.

West, A., Barnes, E. S., & Alkon, D. L. (1982). Primary changes of voltage responses during retention of associative learning. *Journal of Neurophysiology 48,* 1243–1255.

White, J. A., Baxter, D. A., & Byrne, J. H. (1994). Analysis of the modulation by serotonin of a voltage-dependent potassium current in sensory neurons of *Aplysia. Biophysical Journal, 66,* 710–718.

White, J. E., Southgate, E., Thomson, J. N., & Brenner, S. (1986). The structure of the nervous system of the nematode *Caenorhabditis elegans. Philosophical Transactions of the Royal Society of London, Series B: Biological Sciences, 314,* 1–340.

Wicks, S. R., & Rankin, C. H. (1995). Integration of mechanosensory stimuli in *Caenorhabditis elegans. Journal of Neuroscience, 15,* 2434–2444.

Wicks, S. R., & Rankin, C. H. (1996). Recovery from habituation in *Caenorhabditis elegans* is dependent on interstimulus interval and not habituation kinetics. *Behavioral Neuroscience, 110,* 840–844.

Wieland, S. J., & Gelperin, A. (1983). Dopamine elicits feeding motor program in *Limax maximus. Journal of Neuroscience, 3,* 1735–1745.

Wine, J. J., Krasne, F. B., & Chen, L. (1975). Habituation and inhibition of the crayfish lateral giant fibre escape response. *Journal of Experimental Biology, 62,* 771–782.

Wood, W. B. (1988). Introduction to *C. elegans* biology. In W. B. Wood (Ed.), *The nematode Caenorhabditis elegans* (pp. 1–16). Cold Spring Harbor, NY: Cold Spring Harbor Laboratory.

Yin, J. C., Wallach, J. S., Del Vecchio, M., Wilder, E. L., Zhou, H., Quinn, W. G., & Tully, T. (1994). Induction of a dominant negative CREB transgene specifically blocks long-term memory in *Drosophila. Cell, 79,* 49–58.

Zecevic, D., Wu, J. Y., Cohen, L. B., London, J. A., Hopp, H. P., & Falk, C. X. (1989). Hundreds of neurons in the *Aplysia* abdominal ganglion are active during the gill-withdrawal reflex. *Journal of Neuroscience, 9,* 3681–3689.

Zucker, R. S. (1972). Crayfish escape behavior and central synapses. II. Physiological mechanisms underlying behavioral habituation. *Journal of Neurophysiology, 35,* 621–637.

Zucker, R. S., Kennedy, D., & Selverston, A. I. (1971). Neuronal circuit mediating escape responses in crayfish. *Science, 173,* 645–650.

CHAPTER 6

Long-Term Potentiation, Long-Term Depression, and Learning

Joe L. Martinez, Jr., Edwin J. Barea-Rodriguez, and Brian E. Derrick

The University of Texas, San Antonio, Texas 78249

Most everyone agrees that information is acquired, stored, and retrieved by the brain. Memory is a thing in a place in a brain. However, the complexity of the brain precludes our complete understanding of how a memory trace, or an "engram," is formed. All brains consist of individual cellular elements. Most neurons have the same parts: a dendritic tree, cell body, axon, and synaptic boutons. The majority of neurons communicate with each other across a synaptic space via neurotransmitters and neuromodulators. In human brains, billions of neurons interconnect in vast networks via even more billions of synapses. The brain accomplishes all of its remarkable activity through networks of neurons. A single neuron is unlikely to encode a specific memory. Hebb (1949) increased our understanding of how networks of neurons might store information with the provocative theory that memories are represented by reverberating assemblies of neurons. Hebb recognized that a memory so represented cannot reverberate forever and that some alteration in the network must occur to provide integrity both to make the assembly a permanent trace and to make it more likely that the trace could be reconstructed as a remembrance. Because neurons communicate with each other only at synapses, the activity of the assembly or network is most easily (perhaps only) altered by changes in synaptic function. Hebb (1949) formalized this idea in what is know as Hebb's

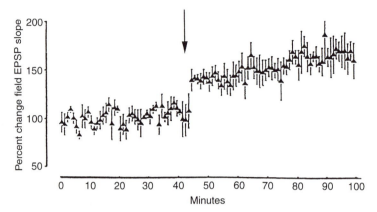

FIGURE 1   Long-term potentiation in the mossy fiber–CA3 synapse.

Postulate: "When an axon of cell A is near enough to excite cell B and repeatedly or persistently takes part in firing it, some growth process or metabolic change takes place in one or both cells such that A's efficiency, as one of the cells firing B, is increased."

Hebb's Postulate is very close to a modern-day definition of long-term potentiation (LTP). Bliss and Lomo (1973) first reported that tetanic stimulation of the perforant path in anesthetized rabbits increased the slope of the population excitatory postsynaptic potential (EPSP) recorded extracellularly in the dentate gyrus and reduced the threshold for eliciting a population action potential (population spike). They defined LTP as potentiation that lasted longer than 30 min, although they observed LTP for several hours. An example of LTP recorded from the hippocampus may be found in Fig. 1.

Later studies showed that LTP recorded in animals with permanent indwelling electrodes lasted from weeks to months (Barnes, 1979). Moreover, LTP is found in many areas of the neocortex (Bear & Kirkwood, 1993; Racine, Milgram, & Hafner, 1983). The activity-dependent induction of LTP and its longevity remain compelling reasons why LTP may be one of the mechanisms by which networks of neurons store information.

Another line of reasoning that leads to the conclusion that LTP may be a mechanism of memory is derived from theoretical studies on neural networks. Marr (1971) described an associative network in area CA3 of the hippocampus in which distributed patterns of activity were imposed on principal cells; the trace became established as a result of strengthening synaptic connections. Since the work of Hebb (1949) and the discovery of LTP (Bliss & Lomo, 1973), these theoretical connections among neurons that strengthen as a result of activity are referred to as Hebb synapses. Synaptic strengthening as described by the Hebb Rule could increase without bound. Because such a Hebbian mechanism would lead to saturation, anti-Hebb processes were suggested (Sejnowski, 1977; Stent, 1973). Recently,

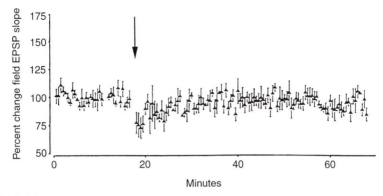

FIGURE 2   Long-term depression in the mossy fiber–CA3 synapse. Reprinted with permission from *Nature,* Derrick and Martinez (1996). Copyright 1996 Macmillan Magazines Limited.

there has been a surge of interest in long-term depression (LTD) both as a memory mechanism (homosynaptic or associative LTD) and as a process that normalizes synaptic weights in networks (homosynaptic and heterosynaptic LTD; cf. Derrick & Martinez, 1995; Linden & Connor, 1995; Morris, 1989; Rolls, 1989). LTD was first described by Dunwiddie and Lynch (1978) and results from persistent low-frequency stimulation. More recently, Dudek and Bear (1993) showed that 900 pulses of 1-Hz stimulation can reliably induce homosynaptic (restricted to stimulated fibers) LTD. Figure 2 reproduces a figure from Derrick and Martinez (1996) showing LTD in the mossy fiber–CA3 synapse.

The use of the Hebb Rule in a distributed memory system can lead to efficient storage of a number of representations within the same network (also called correlation matrix memories; see McNaughton & Morris, 1997), which can be regenerated with partial input (pattern completion). The notion of correlation matrix memories resolves the seeming paradox of how specific memories or representations are stored in nonspecific (distributed) stores. Moreover, any particular node of the network is not essential for pattern completion; the performance of the entire network deteriorates gradually as more and more units are damaged or eliminated. This feature, referred to as graceful degradation, is a natural byproduct of distributed memory (Rolls, 1989; Rumelhart & McClelland, 1986) and is characteristic of deterioration of neural systems (see Rumelhart & McClelland, 1986). Moreover, storage of memory within distributed systems rests on the ability of neurons to form synapse-specific alterations in synaptic strength. If memory is stored in networks of neurons and if network efficiency is mediated by persistent activity (Hebb's Postulate), then either LTP or LTD resulting from persistent activity at specific synapses is an efficient and plausible mechanism by which the brain stores information.

As may be expected, identification of a memory trace in a distributed system is problematic, but it could be achieved by recording from a large number of neurons (see, for example, Wilson & McNaughton, 1994). However, no one has isolated a memory trace, and neither LTP nor LTD can easily be studied in a known memory network. Thus the evidence reviewed in this chapter is correlational and inferential. Before we consider the evidence, we discuss three other similarities between LTP and learning that some consider support the notion that LTP is a memory mechanism: LTP is specific to tetanized inputs, it is associative, and it lasts a long time. Many of the early studies relating LTP to learning unfortunately focused on the aforementioned features of LTP with respect to classical conditioning, which may involve different mechanisms of plasticity such as LTD (see Ito, 1989) as well as different neural structures (e.g., see Thompson & Krupa, 1994). Nevertheless, even more recent studies relating LTP to particular types of learning in structures that display LTP and are involved in a particular type of learning (such as the hippocampus and spatial learning) still remain correlational and inferential.

Since the time of Pavlov (1927), conditioned reflexes have been thought to involve specific neural pathways. In fact, simple neural reflexes may be incorporated into conditioned reflexes (Thompson & Krupa, 1994). LTP is specific in this way in that only tetanized afferents show potentiation, so-called homosynaptic LTP. Unfortunately, the idea of specificity of tetanized afferents has become clouded with reports that the induction of LTP may affect neighboring neurons (Bonhoeffer, Staiger, & Aertsen, 1989), an effect that may arise from the effects of retrograde messengers. Currently, a plausible retrograde messenger associated with LTP might involve gases, such as nitrous oxide (NO), that can affect adjacent coactive synapses (O'Dell, Kandel, & Grant, 1991; Schuman & Madison, 1991). Such a mechanism could permit inadvertent potentiation of synapses that are active but that do not contribute to postsynaptic depolarization. However, this lack of specificity has advantages over a strict Hebb Rule in that diffuse alterations in presynaptic elements (referred to as volume learning) may permit the storage of the temporal order of inputs (Montague & Sejnowski, 1994).

Another interesting property of LTP, which led some researchers to suggest that it is a memory mechanism, is associativity. If weak non-LTP-inducing stimulation in one afferent is paired with strong LTP-inducing stimulation in another afferent to the same cell population, then the weakly stimulated afferent exhibits LTP (Levy & Steward, 1979; McNaughton et al., 1978). The property of associativity is reminiscent of classical conditioning, in which a neutral CS is associated with a strong UCS to induce conditioning (Makintosh, 1974). As the argument goes, because neural afferents in associative LTP act in a way similar to neural activity in classical conditioning and because the mechanism of associative LTP is the same as in LTP, at least in N-methyl-D-aspartate (NMDA) receptor dependent systems, LTP is a memory mechanism. This proposition has been roundly criticized. The critics' view (Gallistel, 1995) is that the temporal constraints of associative LTP are dissimilar to those of classical conditioning. In addition, the necessary ordering of CS and UCS is absent in associative LTP, and a mechanism as simple as associative LTP cannot account for the behavioral complexity observed in classical conditioning.

Today most researchers would agree that associative LTP is not classical conditioning (Diamond & Rose, 1994). LTP does, however, bear comparison to a psychological example of learning. Associative LTP is more similar to sensory preconditioning than classical conditioning (Makintosh, 1974). In this type of associative learning there is the bonding of stimuli so that presentation of one elicits the representation of the other. This form of sensory–sensory learning is very common in humans. For example, in one contemporary movie there is a large *Tyrannosaurus rex* that terrorizes people on an island. In one scene before the dinosaur appears a little boy is holding a glass of water and puzzling over the fact that it is rippling at the surface. In a few moments the dinosaur appears and there is much carnage. In a later scene the little boy is again holding a glass of water and it again begins to ripple, and each theatergoer knows exactly what will appear next—the dinosaur. Thus, the water was associated with the dinosaur and its presentation recalls the associatively presented *Tyrannosaurus rex*. Understanding of this form of associativity was anticipated by Hebb (1949) who said, ". . . any two cells or systems of cells that are repeatedly active at the same time will tend to become 'associated,' so that activity in one facilitates activity in the other." A great deal of learning in humans is sensory–sensory learning. In the field of LTP associativity is operationally defined as LTP observed in an afferent when a subthreshold stimulus is used when a suprathreshold stimulus is simultaneously delivered to a separate afferent that projects to the same cell population (McNaughton et al., 1978).

The CA3 region of the hippocampus is a good place to observe associativity, because it receives five major separate afferent projections. Interestingly, one projection is from itself, the recurrent collaterals, and provides this region with the ability to form autoassociations (Marr, 1971). The CA3 also receives a major commissural projection from the opposite CA3 region, the mossy fiber projection from the granule cells, and medial and lateral perforant path projections from the entorhinal cortex. Figure 3 shows these projections and an example of associative LTP. The data presented in this figure show associativity of the mossy fiber to commissural afferents. In this experiment the commissural fibers are first stimulated at a suprathreshold intensity. LTP is observed in this pathway, but no increase in responsiveness is seen in the mossy fiber pathway, demonstrating independence of the two afferent pathways to area CA3. Next a stimulation that is only 25% of the intensity required to elicit LTP in the mossy fiber pathway is delivered simultaneously with a suprathreshold stimulation to the commissural pathway. It can be observed that further augmentation of LTP is seen in the commissural pathway and now, because of the association of activity in the two pathways, LTP is observed in the mossy fiber pathway as well.

The comparison of LTD and habituation has not been made, but a parametric analysis of habituation is available (Thompson & Spencer, 1966). Habituation and sensitization were recognized quite early to be separate processes, and dishabituation was viewed as sensitization induced simultaneously with habituation (Thompson & Spencer, 1966). An analogous contemporary conundrum is whether depotentiation represents the addition of separate and oppositely signed processes, or the cellular reversal of LTP. The current view is that LTP is produced by phosphorylation of proteins that increase ion conductance, whereas LTD is produced by

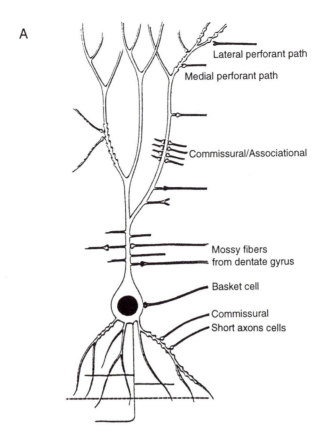

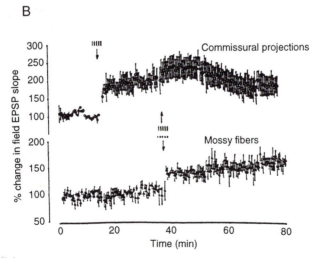

FIGURE 3 (A) Hippocampal CA3 cell field receives afferents from the contralateral commissural/association fibers, dentate gyrus mossy fibers, and lateral and medial perforant path. (B) Associativity between the commissural and mossy fiber projections to area CA3.

dephosphorylation of proteins that decrease ion conductance (Bear & Malenka, 1994; Hrabetova & Sacktor, 1996; Neveu & Zucker, 1996).

The lasting nature of LTP has been used as an argument both for (Barnes, 1979) and against (Gallistel, 1995) LTP as a memory mechanism; the latter is supported by the fact that LTP does not last a lifetime, as do some memories (Squire, 1987). However, any number of properties of networks, for example, reactivation (Hebb, 1949), may extend the biological integrity of a memory. Moreover, most studies characterizing LTP longevity observed LTP at hippocampal sites. Because the hippocampus is viewed as having a temporally restricted role in memory in both animals and humans (Barnes, 1988; Zola-Morgan & Squire, 1993), there is no *a priori* reason to expect permanent changes within the hippocampus. Thus, longevity comparisons between hippocampal LTP and long-term memories are not meaningful. Memory is not a unitary phenomenon. There are likely many memory systems, each of which encodes a different type of memory and each of which involves anatomically distinct structures and perhaps distinct cellular mechanisms (Shacter & Tulving, 1994; Squire, 1987). Perhaps synaptic plasticity within other parts of the brain—in neocortical regions, for example—may prove to be more long lasting than hippocampal LTP (Racine et al., 1983).

In our view the assertions discussed to this point offer compelling reasons to consider LTP and LTD as likely biological mechanisms of memory. However, the evidence supporting LTP and LTD as memory mechanisms is not convincing to some (Gallistel, 1995; Keith & Rudy, 1990). Because each set of studies supporting this view carries interpretational difficulties and because more and more dissociations between LTP and learning are being reported, we now turn to a discussion of the evidence. First, we briefly list the known cellular mechanisms for LTP and LTD; for more extensive reviews of cellular mechanisms, see Bliss and Collingridge (1993), Bramham (1992), Johnston, Williams, Jaffe, and Gray (1992), and Larkman and Jack (1995). Then we discuss electrophysiological correlates between LTP and learning, induction of LTP and its effect on learning, the pharmacological properties of learning and LTP, and new studies that attempt to determine simultaneously the genetic basis of LTP and learning, which have provided contradictory evidence in that some positive findings and dissociations are reported in which animals that are capable of LTP do not learn (Silva et al., 1996) and animals that learn do not show LTP (Huang et al., 1995). Finally, we will focus on LTD as a memory mechanism and highlight some recent studies in this area.

I. CELLULAR MECHANISMS OF LTP AND LTD INDUCTION

Several different forms of LTP have been described (Bliss & Collingridge, 1993). In the hippocampus, two major forms of LTP are NMDA-receptor-dependent (Collingridge, Kehl, & McLennan, 1983) and opioid-receptor-dependent (Bramham,

1992). LTD is studied primarily in the cerebellum and hippocampus, and as with LTP there are several forms.

A. NMDA-Receptor-Dependent LTP and Associative LTP

NMDA is a voltage-dependent glutamate receptor subtype. For induction, the NMDA receptor must be activated by the neurotransmitter glutamate and simultaneously there must be sufficient depolarization of the postsynaptic membrane to relieve a Mg^{2+} block in the NMDA-associated ion channel, which allows the entry of Ca^{2+} into the postsynaptic terminal. Ca^{2+} activates any number of Ca^{2+}-sensitive second-messenger processes. Because NMDA receptors are sensitive to both presynaptic transmitter release and postsynaptic depolarization, they act as Hebbian coincidence detectors. This property can explain associativity through temporal and spatial summation. Thus, activated NMDA receptors at synapses that are proximal to active sites of depolarization may be depolarized sufficiently to relieve the Mg^{2+} block and initiate the cascade of events that leads to LTP induction. This cascade may occur even though the activity of that particular synapse alone was not sufficient to induce LTP. Thus, NMDA receptors can account for the association of two separate afferent projections to the same cell, one strongly and the other weakly active (Kelso & Brown, 1986; Levy & Steward, 1979), and for the cooperative requirement that a threshold number of fibers be active. Recently, Bashir et al. (1993) suggested that other glutamate receptors, particularly the metabotropic subtype, may contribute to the induction of LTP. However, the requirement for metabotropic glutamate receptor activation remains disputed, and evidence for a role for these receptors in LTP induction is not as clear-cut as the data implicating NMDA receptors (see Larkman & Jack, 1995).

The maintenance of NMDA-receptor-dependent LTP is less well understood. In a contemporary review a distinction was suggested between short-term potentiation (STP), which decays in about 1 hr, followed by three stages of LTP (LTP1–3) requiring (a) protein kinase activation and protein phosphorylation [sometimes this is called the early phase] and (b) protein synthesis from existing mRNAs and gene expression (Bliss & Collingridge, 1993) [sometimes this is referred to as the late phase (Nguyen, Abel, & Kandel, 1994)]. Importantly, behavioral studies of learning implicate these same cellular processes in the establishment of long-term memory (Brinton, 1991).

B. NMDA-Receptor-Independent or Opioid-Receptor-Dependent LTP and Associative LTP

Although less well known and less completely studied (Bramham, Milgram, & Srebro, 1991a, 1991b; Breindl, Derrick, Rodriguez, & Martinez, 1994; Derrick,

Weinberger, & Martinez, 1991; Martin, 1983; Ishihara, Katsuki, Sugimura, Kaneko, & Satoh, 1990), this form of LTP is the predominant form of plasticity within extrinsic afferents to the hippocampal formation (mossy-fiber CA3, lateral-perforant-path dentate gyrus, and lateral-perforant-path CA3) and is present in more afferent projections to the hippocampal formation than is NMDA-receptor-dependent LTP (medial-perforant-path projections to the dentate gyrus and area CA3). Thus if the hippocampus is important in memory formation, as much data suggest, then opioid-receptor-dependent LTP and its relationship to NMDA-receptor-dependent LTP need to be understood.

LTP induction in the mossy-fiber CA3 and lateral-perforant-path CA3 pathways depends on the activation of μ, but not δ, opioid receptors (Derrick, Rodriguez, Lieberman, & Martinez, 1992; Weisskopf, Zalutsky, & Nicoll, 1993), whereas induction in the perforant-path dentate pathway depends on both μ- and δ-opioid receptors (Bramham, 1992; Bramham et al., 1991a). Therefore, it is likely that at least two mechanisms of opioid-receptor-dependent LTP induction exist in the hippocampus.

Associative opioid-receptor-dependent LTP in the mossy-fiber CA3 system appears to have constraints regulating induction that are different from those regulating associative NMDA-receptor-dependent LTP. The mossy fibers show cooperativity in that a sufficient number of fibers have to be activated to observe LTP (Derrick & Martinez, 1994a; McNaughton et al., 1978; but see Weisskopf & Nicoll, 1995). Induction of LTP in the mossy fibers also is dependent on a sufficient number of tetanizing pulses, presumably to ensure the release of opioid peptides (Derrick & Martinez, 1994b); peptides in general are only released after trains of impulses (Peng & Horn, 1991). Associative LTP of mossy-fiber responses can be observed with stimulation of the convergent commissural pathway only when trains of mossy-fiber pulses are used (Derrick & Martinez, 1994a). The commissural–CA3 system expresses NMDA-receptor-dependent LTP (Derrick & Martinez, 1994a), and the induction of associative mossy-fiber LTP is blocked by both opioid- and NMDA-receptor antagonists (Derrick & Martinez, 1994a).

Research findings in the area of mossy-fiber LTP are controversial. Although it is generally agreed that LTP in this pathway depends on trains of pulses and the presence of extracellular Ca^{2+}, the site of Ca^{2+} entry, either pre- or postsynaptically, is in dispute (Williams & Johnston, 1989; Zaslutky & Nicoll, 1990), as is the necessity of postsynaptic depolarization (Jaffe & Johnston, 1990). One group of researchers even refuses to ascribe the lofty title of LTP to the phenomenon of synaptic enhancement in mossy fibers and refers to LTP in this pathway as mossy-fiber potentiation because according to them it is nonassociative and rapidly decremental (Staubli, 1992; Staubli, Larson, & Lynch, 1990). The locus of mossy-fiber LTP induction remains controversial. One current view suggests that the induction of mossy-fiber LTP may involve exclusively presynaptic mechanisms (Zalutsky & Nicoll, 1990). However, recent studies suggest a more complex process. First, studies of mossy-fiber LTP *in vitro* suggest that LTP induced by burst stimulation of mossy fibers is blocked by both postsynaptic dialysis of calcium chelators and hyper-polarization of CA3 pyramidal cells (Jaffe & Johnston, 1990; Williams & Johnston, 1989). Moreover, studies using the associativity paradigm indicate that associativity is blocked by NMDA-receptor antagonists, further supporting a postsynaptic con-tribution to mossy-fiber LTP induction. However, studies by others (Langdon, Johnson, & Barrionuevo, 1995; Zalutsky & Nicoll, 1990) suggest that mossy-fiber LTP is completely independent of the postsynaptic element and therefore non-associative (Zalutsky & Nicoll, 1992). Moreover, mossy-fiber LTP observed by these investigators is not dependent on opioid-receptor activation (Weisskopf & Nicoll, 1995).

A resolution of these apparently contradictory findings can be found in more recent studies (Urban & Barrionuevo, 1996) suggesting two distinct potentiation processes at the mossy-fiber synapse, a non-Hebbian form that is presynaptic and does not involve the postsynaptic element, and a Hebbian form that is dependent on postsynaptic depolarization (Williams & Johnston, 1989) and postsynaptic cal-cium (Jaffe & Johnston, 1990) and requires the activation of opioid receptors (Derrick & Martinez, 1994b, 1995). The induction of either form of LTP *in vitro* is dependent on stimulation parameters, with sustained presynaptic activity producing preferentially the presynaptic, non-Hebbian form, whereas patterned, theta-like stimulation produces the associative, Hebbian form involving the postsynaptic element (Urban & Barrionuevo, 1996). The role of each form of mossy-fiber LTP in normal hippocampal function remains unknown. However, it is known that the Hebbian form exists *in vivo*. To date, there has been no demonstration of the non-Hebbian form in living animals.

C. Mechanisms of LTD Induction in the Hippocampus

Although LTD has only recently been a subject of avid research, much insight has been gained into the cellular mechanisms of induction (see Bear & Malenka, 1994, for review). LTD is classified according to the nature of synaptic activity involved with its induction. Homosynaptic LTD is defined as LTD occurring in active stim-ulated afferent systems, whereas heterosynaptic LTD is observed in nonstimulated fibers as a result of activity in other, usually neighboring, afferents. Associative LTD is somewhat of a hybrid of homo- and heterosynaptic LTD, where LTD is observed in active fibers contingent on the activity of other convergent afferents, much like associative LTP. In the cerebellum, where LTD requires the simultaneous activity of parallel and climbing fibers, associative LTD is referred to as "in phase" (Linden & Connor, 1995). "Out-of-phase" LTD is reported in hippocampal synapses that are active in between bursts of stimuli to convergent afferents (Stanton & Sejnowski, 1989). Although the finding of out-of-phase associative LTD has not been easily replicated, it appears that failures to observe this phenomenon can be attributed to the tight temporal constraints imposed on the induction of out-of-phase LTD (Debanne, Gahwiler, & Thompson, 1994). However, it is important to note that in-phase LTD also is observed at mossy fiber–CA3 synapses (Derrick & Martinez, 1996).

Today the studies investigating the mechanisms of LTD induction in the hippo-campus focus on homosynaptic LTD in the CA1 region. Interestingly, the mecha-nisms of LTD induction are somewhat similar to those underlying homosynaptic LTP in that both postsynaptic Ca^{2+} influx and NMDA-receptor activation are nec-essary. These findings were first reported by Mulkey and Malenka (1992), who found that intercellular injection of BAPTA, a calcium chelator, or suppression of NMDA currents by intracellular hyperpolarization both block LTD induction. Al-though both Ca^{2+} and NMDA receptor are necessary for LTD induction in CA1, it seems that intracellular Ca^{2+} concentration determines whether LTP or LTD is induced. According to Lisman (1989), a small influx of Ca^{2+}, which produces a low intracellular Ca^{2+} concentration, may activate selective protein phosphatases whose actions lead to the induction of LTD. Selective inhibitors of protein phosphatases block the induction of LTD in CA1 (Mulkey, Herron, & Malenka, 1993). Thus, LTD induction, at least in CA1, may require the activation of protein phosphatases.

The relationship between LTP and LTD with respect to information storage is not known, although it is suggested that LTD could serve as a mechanism of depo-tentiation, whereby newly acquired information may be "erased" by more recent information. In this view, LTD may serve as a mechanism of forgetting. LTD also could serve as a means to enforce sparse, and therefore efficient, representations by depressing synapses that are less active and therefore sharpen sparsely encoded mem-ories. However, the existence of associative forms of LTD and the dependence of LTD on postsynaptic factors (Abraham, Christie, Logan, Lawlor, & Dragunow, 1994), including NMDA-receptor activation, suggest a more direct role for LTD in information storage. The existence of both LTP and LTD at a given synapse increases the dynamic range of synapse modification, thus increasing the capacity of a neural network. Bear, Cooper, and colleagues (see Intrator, Bear, Cooper, & Paradiso, 1993) suggest that each form of LTD occurs when conditions approach, but do not meet, the requirements for LTP induction. As mentioned earlier, such a mechanism may serve as a mechanism of contrast enhancement, and that ensures a minimum number of synapses contribute to a given representation. In fact, mech-anisms of LTD in conjunction with LTP in which LTD occurs at synapses that are nearby and inactive or active at time points that are not precisely coincident with other potentiating synapses can greatly increase the capacity of a distributed mem-ory system (Mulkey & Malenka, 1992). Such bidirectional rules have been observed with NMDA-receptor-dependent plasticity in the hippocampus and visual cortex (Kirkwood & Bear, 1995) as well as with NMDA-receptor-independent forms of plasticity within the hippocampus (Derrick & Martinez, 1996), suggesting that bidirectional rules employing LTP and LTD may be a fundamental property of cortical plasticity (Intrator et al., 1993).

II. ELECTROPHYSIOLOGICAL APPROACHES TO RELATING LTP TO LEARNING

Studies addressing the contribution of LTP to learning have been approached at an electrophysiological level to answer two major questions: Does learning induce changes in synaptic responses that are similar to LTP? Does the induction of LTP alter learning?

A. Does Learning Produce LTP-like Changes?

We limit our discussion to those studies that measured changes in the population EPSP rather than the population spike, owing to general agreement that EPSP changes reflect changes in synaptic function, whereas changes in the population spike amplitude may reflect other mechanisms (Bliss & Lynch, 1988).

Changes in population EPSPs can be observed in perforant-path dentate gyrus responses during exploratory behaviors. The phenomenon was initially named short-term exploratory modulation, or STEM (Sharp, McNaughton, & Barnes, 1985). This initial study demonstrated that exploration produced increases in perforant-path synaptic responses over the course of exploration and that the increases persisted for short periods of time after exploration. The initial and subsequent studies (Green, McNaughton, & Barnes, 1990) revealed that STEM was not dependent on handling, novelty, repeated stimulation, or increased locomotion. Like LTP, STEM results in an apparent increase in the field EPSP and can be blocked by the NMDA-receptor antagonist MK 801 (Erickson, McNaughton, & Barnes, 1990). However, unlike LTP, STEM is relatively short-lived; it lasts only 20–40 min (Sharp et al., 1985).

A different approach to the problem of detecting electrophysiological changes in evoked responsiveness following learning is to record responses from *in vitro* hippocampal slices removed from animals exposed to an enriched environment and compare them with responses of slices from animals exposed to a standard laboratory environment (Green & Greenough, 1986). Rearing animals in complex environments produces anatomical changes in the cortex that are thought to be a result of learning (Bennett, Diamond, Krech, & Rosenzweig, 1964; Greenough, Volkmar, & Juraska, 1973; Rosenzweig, Krech, Bennett, & Diamond, 1962). In this study, the slope of perforant-path dentate responses was assessed. The magnitude of field EPSP slopes was larger in rats raised in a complex environment than in rats housed in standard laboratory conditions, effects that are similar to those observed after LTP induction in this pathway (Bliss & Lomo, 1973). Electrophysiological measures of antidromic (nonsynaptic) volleys and of the presynaptic-fiber volley (number of fibers activated) revealed no differences between the rearing conditions. Thus the field EPSP slopes elicited by equivalent volleys were significantly larger, which suggests that the differences arise from an enhancement of perforant-path synaptic transmission. The increased dentate responsiveness was not observed in animals that were removed from complex housing 3–4 weeks prior to testing, which suggests the effects were transient, as is LTP (Barnes, 1979).

More recently, one group of researchers recorded responses in another hippocampal system, the mossy-fiber projections, as animals learned a radial arm maze (Mitsuno, Sasa, Ishihara, Ishikawa, & Kikuchi, 1994). Incremental increases were observed in mossy-fiber field EPSPs over the course of learning. Changes in evoked responsiveness were evident 3 days after learning. Taken together, these studies show that learning induces changes in hippocampal responsiveness that resemble those observed following LTP induction.

Why should changes in amplitudes of responses evoked from random stimulation of mossy fibers be detectable? According to the view of distributed memory systems, changes underlying learning should occur in a very small fraction of the available synapses, and there is no reason to expect that such sparse changes would be evident in synaptic activation evoked by the stimulation of thousands of afferent fibers activated by a stimulating electrode. However, the hippocampal memory system could have a small capacity and utilize most synapses when storing information. In such a system an evoked response might reveal the existence of a stored memory. However, for new information to be stored, the information in this low-capacity system would either have to be erased or have to decay rapidly. Some researchers suggest that the mossy-fiber projections to CA3 represent a low-capacity store, because LTP in mossy fibers can decay quite rapidly (within hours) *in vitro* (Lynch & Granger, 1986). However, learning-induced LTP-like changes in evoked mossy-fiber responses are observed 3 days after the cessation of training (Mitsuno et al., 1994), arguing against the idea that neural changes represent a transient, low-capacity store.

One clever strategy eliminates this problem of "looking for a needle in a haystack." Synapse-specific changes in responses mediated by a large number of afferents need not be observed. Rather, the evoked response is employed as an integral part of the learning task. Detection of salient, learning-induced changes in a large number of randomly stimulated fibers is not employed; instead, the activity of the fibers is incorporated into the learning task. This strategy was employed by several laboratories and provides consistent and convincing electrophysiological evidence for a role of LTP in learning.

In one set of studies, a shuttle avoidance task with a footshock as an unconditioned stimulus was employed (Matthies, Ruethrich, Ott, Matthies, & Matthies, 1986; Ott, Ruthrich, Reymann, Lindenau, & Matthies, 1982; Reymann, Ruthrich, Lindenau, Ott, & Matthies, 1982). High-frequency perforant-path stimulation was the conditioned stimulus. Low-frequency evoked responses were recorded in the dentate gyrus before, during, and after 10 daily training sessions. Overall daily changes of the field EPSP slope roughly corresponded to changes in learned behavior. However, the relationships among the measures each day were more complex; improved performance was not correlated with response magnitude within the daily trials. The LTP-like increase in responses was apparent only at the start of the second day of training, which suggests that a consolidation process occurs after the training and prior to the session the following day. Nevertheless, the increases in the field EPSP paralleled learning across days, with asymptotic performance occurring on the days of asymptotic LTP. An important observation was that animals that were poor learners and did not acquire the task also failed to show an increase in dentate responses. The stimulation may have induced LTP that was independent of any learning-induced changes in neural function. However, the stimulation trains used as a CS did not produce any changes in the EPSP during the initial 40 trials on the first day of training. Thus, the CS stimulation alone could not induce LTP.

An interpretational difficulty of the foregoing study is that the hippocampus is not necessary for learning of the active-avoidance task; in fact, hippocampal lesions or NMDA-receptor antagonists can facilitate active- or passive-avoidance learning, respectively (Mondadori, Weiskrantz, Buerki, Petschke, & Fagg, 1989; Nadel, 1968; Ohki, 1982; Shimai & Ohki, 1980). Thus increases observed in perforant-path responses that parallel learning may reflect ancillary learning of other aspects of the conditioning situation, such as context (Kim, Fanselow, DeCola, & Landeira-Fernandez, 1992). However, in a subsequent study, colchicine lesions of the dentate gyrus eliminated both the evoked responses and the ability of perforant-path stimulation to serve as a CS (Ruthrich, Dorochow, Pohle, Ruthrich, & Matthies, 1987). These lesions did not alter conditioning to other CSs nor did they alter conditioned emotional response to the footshock. Together, these data suggest that the increases in responses of activated perforant-path dentate synapses contributed to the learning of the CS aspects of an active-avoidance response.

In a similar study (Laroche, Doyere, & Bloch, 1989), high-frequency stimulation served as a CS for a footshock that elicited behavioral suppression. Learning of the perforant-path stimulation–shock association occurred only when the trains were of an intensity sufficient to elicit LTP. Moreover, inhibition of LTP induction by prior tetanization of commissural afferents, which inhibits LTP induction by engaging inhibitory mechanisms, produced substantial deficits in learning. Furthermore, chronic infusion of AP5, a selective NMDA antagonist, blocked both LTP induction and the ability of the stimulation to serve as a CS. A significant correlation existed between the magnitude of LTP produced by these various treatments and the acquisition of the conditioned response. The decay of LTP induced in this behavioral paradigm was observed in the following 31-day period and correlated with retention of the conditioned response (Laroche, Doyere, & Redini, 1991).

In the aforementioned experiments, it was assumed that stimulation of the perforant path can serve as a sensory-like conditioning stimulus. However, the degree to which the perforant path is normally involved in representing a sensory CS is unknown. Moreover, because the stimulation produced a potentiated synaptic response, the correlation between LTP and learning may reflect merely an increase in the salience of the perforant-path stimulation. For this reason such an approach may be of limited utility.

Taken together, these studies provide positive support for the idea that LTP may be involved in conditioning because LTP-like increases in evoked potentials exist following learning in CS pathways that are chosen for experimental convenience. A more direct experimental approach to the question of whether LTP is a mechanism of learning is to induce LTP and then determine whether it influences later learning.

B. Does the Induction of LTP Influence Learning?

LTP induced prior to learning might impair learning by saturating LTP processes that normally participate in the learning; LTP induced after learning might obscure prior learning by occluding any distributed pattern of synaptic changes that were formed as a result of learning. Alternatively, LTP may enhance or impair learning by activating modulatory mechanisms (Martinez, Schulteis, & Weinberger, 1991).

In one study the effects of LTP induction on the acquisition of classically conditioned nictitating membrane response (NMR) were assessed (Berger, 1984). The rationale for this study arose from the observation that changes in hippocampal pyramidal-cell activity parallel changes in the acquisition of the conditioned behavioral response (Berger, 1984; Berger, Rinaldi, Weisz, & Thompson, 1983) as well as from the possibility that the increase in hippocampal unit firing resulted from plastic events within the hippocampus. LTP induced unilaterally in the perforant path facilitated the subsequent acquisition of a classically conditioned NMR in rabbits (Berger, 1984). Given that the hippocampus is not essential for learning of simultaneous classical conditioning of the NMR (although it appears to be important in the acquisition of more complex aspects of classical conditioning; see Berger & Orr, 1983), this effect may be of a modulatory nature, rather than a direct effect on an essential learning mechanism.

An opposite effect was observed using spatial learning in a circular maze (McNaughton, Barnes, Rao, Baldwin, & Rasmuss, 1986). Bilateral, supposedly saturating LTP stimulation of the angular bundle, which carries both the lateral and medial aspects of the perforant-path projections, disrupted performance either prior to or immediately after learning. In an important control procedure, LTP that was induced after the task was well learned did not disrupt performance. Subsequent studies (Castro, Silbert, McNaughton, & Barnes, 1989) expanded this initial observation. The strategy was to saturate LTP by stimulating rats every day for a 19-day period. Rats that received LTP-inducing stimulation displayed deficits in spatial learning, whereas rats that received only low-frequency non-LTP-inducing stimulation acquired the task. If LTP was allowed to decay, the animals displayed normal performance on a spatial task and did not show any learning deficits. Taken together, these data suggest that LTP itself, rather than nonspecific effects of stimulation, is essential for learning because saturation-impaired acquisition of the spatial learning task and the ability to learn returned with the decay of the LTP.

Several laboratories, including the laboratory of origin, reported difficulties in replicating the LTP saturation effect (Jeffery & Morris, 1993; Robinson, 1992; Sutherland, Dringenberg, & Hoesing, 1993). A number of reasons may explain the failure to replicate: the stimulation parameters used may have resulted in the saturation of LTP only in those afferents stimulated, for stimulation of the angular bundle with a single stimulation electrode may not sufficiently tetanize all fibers within the angular bundle. Because saturation of all perforant-path afferents was not likely achieved and because information stored in a distributed memory system is quite resistant to degradation, the partial saturation of LTP or even the preservation of other processes, such as LTD, may be sufficient to permit substantial learning.

Although the enhancement of classical conditioning (Berger, 1984) and the impairment of spatial maze learning (Baines et al., 1994; Castro et al., 1989; McNaughton et al., 1986) apparently are contradictory effects, the differences in the findings of these studies reflect, in our view, a differential contribution of the hippocampus, and therefore hippocampal LTP, to classical conditioning of the NMR and spatial learning, which are distinctly different memory tasks that appear to require distinct memory systems (Thompson, 1992). Because the hippocampus is not required for acquisition of the NMR response unless trace conditioning procedures are employed (see Moyer, Deyo, & Disterhoft, 1990) but is required for spatial learning, the roles of LTP in these two kinds of learning are likely different, and thus the studies cannot be compared directly.

III. PHARMACOLOGICAL APPROACHES RELATING LTP TO LEARNING

Subsequent to the demonstration of the important role for the NMDA-type glutamate receptors in LTP induction, a number of behavioral researchers rushed to characterize the effects of NMDA-receptor antagonists on learning. As in all pharmacological studies attempting to study learning, the inference of causality from a specific action of a drug is problematic (Martinez et al., 1991). Drug-related side effects and determination of the drug's specific site of action are always issues. Moreover, in the studies reviewed in the following, the drug has to be administered before the initiation of conditioning if it is to block the induction of any LTP that might contribute to the learning. Being thus present early, the drug might induce an effect on learning through a sensory, motor, motivational, attentional, or other variable (Martinez et al., 1991). As noted in the following, these concerns complicate the interpretation of studies using this strategy.

Many studies examined the effect of selective NMDA-receptor antagonists on a variety of learning tasks (Kim, DeCola, Landeira-Fernandez, & Fanselow, 1991; Walker & Gold, 1991), including tasks thought to depend on hippocampal function (Robinson, Crooks, Shinkman, & Gallager, 1990; Walker & Gold, 1991). Here we limit our discussion to pharmacological studies that address both hippocampus-based learning and LTP induction and that use relatively localized, or at least intra-CNS, administration of drugs, so that as far as possible the effects described are the result of an action of the drug in a circumscribed area of the brain. The most comprehensive studies (Morris, Anderson, Lynch, & Baudry, 1986) examined intracerebroventricular (ICV) administration of AP5, the selective NMDA antagonist, on learning in a Morris water maze task. Prior research indicated that the hippocampus is important in the acquisition of this task, that is, when the rats are required to learn the location of the platform with respect to distal clues in the environment (Morris, Garrud, Rawlins, & O'Keefe, 1982). In the initial studies (Morris et al., 1986) a significant impairment was observed in the animals infused with AP5. Potential sensorimotor impairments induced by the drug were assessed with a visual discrimination task using the same water maze apparatus, with NMDA antagonist having no apparent effect. The effect of AP5 on LTP induction also was assessed in these studies to compare the behavior-impairing and LTP-induction-impairing action of AP5. The drug had no effect on the low-frequency-evoked responses; however, AP5 impaired acquisition of the maze and AP5 completely blocked LTP induced by stimulation of the perforant-path afferents to the dentate gyrus. In reversal tests, where the platform is moved to a location different from that of the original training, the degree of the animals' learning is reflected by the persistence of the animals in returning to the place of original learning as well as the acquisition of the new platform location. The animals that received AP5 showed no acquisition of the new location of the escape platform, whereas the control groups showed substantial preference for the quadrant of original training and readily learned the new location of the platform. The interpretational problem with this study is that the AP5-treated animals' performance at the beginning of reversal training was as poor as the control animals', which suggests a negative transfer effect of some original learning.

Some critics of these studies noted that some rats fell off the platform during training and suggested that the impairment produced by AP5 was due to motor deficits (Keith & Rudy, 1990). Further control experiments suggest that falling off the platform did not have an aversive effect on performance in water maze learning (Morris, 1990). As an added measure, pretraining, within the water maze using the visual discrimination task prior to ICV infusion demonstrated that the apparent sensorimotor deficit revealed by platform instability could be overcome by pretraining. Spatial learning impairments resulting from AP5 administration were still observed in these pretrained rats. It has been noted (Keith & Rudy, 1990) that the rats receiving AP5 showed performance deficits on the first trials before learning had occurred and that this deficit may reflect a side effect of the drug on sensorimotor function. However, later studies that more closely examined learning in the early trials showed no effect of moderate doses of AP5 on performance in the first trial (Davis, Butcher, & Morris, 1992). The discrimination learning experiment may not be a good test of sensorimotor impairment because ICV administration of AP5 probably results in lower concentrations of AP5 at sites important for visual discrimination. However, actual measurement of the dispersion of AP5 following ICV administration showed that it was evenly distributed within the brain (Butcher, Davis, & Morris, 1990). Subsequent studies indicated that localized infusion of AP5 within the visual cortex did not produce impairments in the visual discrimination task (Butcher, Hamberger, & Morris, 1991). Taken together, these results suggest that the impairment of performance in the water maze produced by AP5 is the result of the effects mediated by the actions of this drug at hippocampal sites.

As noted by the embattled originators of these NMDA-antagonist studies, it would be erroneous to conclude that AP5 causes the learning deficit because AP5 blocked LTP (Morris, 1989). AP5 may affect learning, for example, because AP5 has an effect on hippocampal theta rhythm, and treatments that disrupt theta rhythm can block acquisition of learning tasks (Winson, 1978). Thus, as discussed earlier, many factors impede the interpretation of a drug effect, including the selectivity of the drug's actions, side effects, drug dispersion, and the site of drug action.

Once convincing test of whether two separate drug effects, such as impaired spatial learning and impaired induction of LTP, are related is to compare dose–response curves of the drug's separate effects. Different dose–response functions may show that the drug is acting on different processes, and identical dose–response functions are evidence in support of the notion that the drug is acting on common processes. In subsequent studies (Davis et al., 1992) identical dose–response curves were observed for both impairment of spatial learning and blocking of LTP induction. Furthermore, concentrations of AP5, measured in the brain using high-performance liquid chromatography (HPLC) microdialysis, that impaired learning and that blocked LTP were the same; no concentration of AP5 was observed to block LTP without affecting learning (Butcher et al., 1991). Lastly, the extracellular concentrations that were measured during the block of LTP induction *in vivo* matched the concentrations that were effective in blocking LTP induction *in vitro*.

Further studies (Morris, 1989) addressed the question of the effect of AP5 on both the acquisition and retrieval of a spatial learning task. NMDA-receptor activation is essential only for LTP induction but is not essential for either the expression or the maintenance of LTP. IF AP5 alters memory by locking LTP induction, then any deleterious effects of AP5 should be limited to the acquisition period, and AP5 should not impair performance on a spatial learning task when administered following training. This strategy also addresses to some degree, the possible sensorimotor and LTP-independent effects of NMDA-receptor antagonists, because any performance deficit seen in these conditions could not be due to any effect on acquisition. AP5, when infused into rats by ICV administration following asymptotic acquisition of the water maze task, has no effect on the retrieval of learned spatial information, as assessed using probe trials. Moreover, in these same rats, the doses of AP5 that had no effect on performance following training effectively blocked new learning in a subsequent reversal test. The lack of effects on performance of an already learned task suggests that the AP5 is not producing sensorimotor impairment that interferes with performance of the task. Taken together, these studies provide striking evidence that AP5 may impair learning through blocking the induction of LTP.

The data implicating metabotropic glutamate receptors in the induction of LTP prompted assessment of the role of these glutamate receptors in spatial learning. Richter-Levin, Errington, Maegawa, & Bliss (1994) reported that perfusion of the metabotropic antagonist (RS)-α-methyl-4-carboxyphenylglycine (MCPG) did not produce deficits in animals during acquisition of a Morris water maze, although a significant deficit was observed in probe trials given 24 hr after the last training trial. In these same animals, equivalent quantities of MCPG attenuated the magnitude but did not block the induction of perforant-path dentate LTP. Thus antagonism of metabotropic glutamate receptors produces some deficit in both LTP and spatial learning.

Recent studies challenge the notion that NMDA-receptor LTP is the underlying mechanism mediating hippocampally dependent spatial learning. In one study Morris and colleagues (Bannerman, Good, Butcher, Ramsay, & Morris, 1995) found that spatial learning in one room containing its own distinct cue prevented any AP5-induced impairment of spatial learning in another room with a different set of spatial cues and using a different platform location. Here the AP5 was administered ICV via implanted osmotic minipumps. Interestingly, AP5 did impair learning in naive animals that did not receive any prior training and also blocked the induction of dentate gyrus LTP in animals that received prior spatial training, suggesting that LTP and learning of the spatial task are differentially affected by NMDA receptor antagonists. Bannerman et al. suggested that the water maze task required cognitive processes that are independent of the NMDA-receptor function. An important finding in this study was that learning in the second water maze problem was dependent on the hippocampus, because ibotenic lesions, which destroyed the hippocampus, abolished learning in the second problem. Thus, the hippocampus is necessary for acquisition of the second water maze response, but NMDA receptors and by extension NMDA-receptor-dependent LTP are not required for the acquisition of the second learning problem.

The question of what effect initial learning may have on subsequent spatial learning was unfortunately not answered by conflicting results from Bannerman et al. (1995) and Saucier and Cain (1995). In both studies a curtain was placed around the maze so that the animals learned how to find the platform using nonspatial strategies. In one case this nonspatial pretraining did not block AP5-induced impairment of learning of the second spatial maze response (Bannerman et al., 1995), whereas in the second case it did block the NMDA receptor antagonist (NPC17742) impaired spatial learning. Saucier and Cain (1995) administered their drug i.p. and like Bannerman et al. they blocked the induction of LTP in the dentate gyrus.

The studies employing NMDA-receptor antagonists to assess the contribution of hippocampal LTP to learning have been the subject of particularly intense scrutiny (see Keith & Rudy, 1990). However, in our view, the fact that spatial learning is not blocked completely by NMDA-receptor antagonists is not surprising. Several pathways in the hippocampus, including the mossy-fiber pathway (Derrick et al., 1992), the lateral perforant path to area CA3 (Breindl et al., 1994), and the lateral perforant path to dentate (Bramham et al., 1991a, 1991b; but see Zhang & Levy, 1992), display opioid-receptor-dependent LTP. In addition, both NMDA-receptor-dependent and NMDA-receptor-independent mechanisms of LTP induction are observed within the CA1 region (Teyler & Grover, 1993). As mentioned earlier with respect to the saturation experiments of McNaughton and colleagues, when viewed from the perspective of distributed memories, partial sparing of function may be sufficient to permit learning. Such reasoning leads to the conclusion that the alteration of any one of the LTP systems within the hippocampus may not be sufficient to produce a total or even a profound deficit in spatial learning. That localized NMDA-receptor blockade does produce observable deficits and that these deficits are similar to, although less severe than, those observed with extensive hippocampal lesions suggest that NMDA-receptor-dependent mechanisms, and perhaps LTP, contribute to spatial learning. The recent studies by Bannerman et al. (1995) and Saucier and Cain (1995) do seriously question the assertion that LTP and NMDA-receptor function are involved in the acquisition of a water maze response following previous training in a water maze. What is unclear is how the first learning experience affects the NMDA dependence of subsequent learning. The first learning experience is sensitive to NMDA receptor function whereas the second is not. Therefore, they are not equivalent learning tasks at either a cognitive or pharmacological level, but both require a hippocampus. As noted earlier, many forms of NMDA-receptor-independent LTP exist in the hippocampus that could subserve such learning.

Does Learning of a Spatial Task Involve Hippocampal Opioid Systems?

Given that opioid-receptor antagonists impair the induction of LTP in opioidergic afferents, opioid-receptor antagonists would be expected to impair spatial learning. However, systemic administration of naloxone is reported to facilitate acquisition of a spatial water maze as measured by latency to find the platform (Decker, Introini-Collison, & McGaugh, 1989). These studies employed intraperitoneal administration of naloxone 3 mg/kg prior to training, which may be insufficient time for intraperitoneally administered naloxone to block sufficiently opioid receptors at central sites. For example, intraperitoneal naloxone effects on evoked hippocampal responses are observed only 10–15 min following intraperitoneal naloxone administration (Martinez & Derrick, 1994). Thus training may not have been given at an optimum time following drug administration. In addition, opioid antagonists exert effects on opioid systems that influence learning that may be independent of hippocampal opioid systems (Martinez et al., 1991). and alterations in these opioid

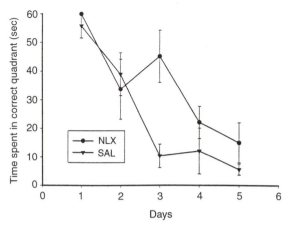

FIGURE 4   Naloxone (10 mg/kg, i.p.) impairs spatial memory on Day 3 of Morris water maze training. On this day the animals begin to reach asymptotic performance.

systems by systemic administration of opioid-receptor antagonists may also alter learning. In support of this conclusion Barea-Rodriguez et al. (in preparation) as depicted in Fig. 4 found that naloxone administered intraperitoneally to rats 30 min prior to training impaired retention of spatial maze escape responses on Day 3 of training, which is the day that the rats begin to reach asymptotic performance. Additional evidence implicating opioid systems in spatial learning and LTP induction is found in studies employing local application of opioids into the hippocampus in which an impairment of spatial learning is produced. For example, local administration of dynorphins impairs spatial learning (McDaniel, Mundy, & Tilson, 1990). Dynorphins also impair LTP induction in both the mossy-fiber CA3 and perforant-path dentate synapses via actions on kappa receptors (Wagner, Terman, & Chavkin, 1993; Weisskopf et al., 1993). Thus, there is evidence supporting a role for opioids in both the induction of LTP and acquisition of spatial learning.

IV. KNOCKOUT MUTANTS, LTP, AND HIPPOCAMPALLY DEPENDENT LEARNING

The molecular biological revolution has arrived in force in the area of LTP and learning. A paradox of learning is that it is expressed as activity among neurons, though the biological changes that underlie memories are stored within neurons. The molecular biological revolution taught us that enduring alterations of cell function, as must occur in long-term memory storage, are controlled by gene expression and resultant protein production. Thus, for every sustained memory there is likely a chain of events leading from the initiation of activity at a synaptic receptor, to the activity of second-messenger systems, to intermediate-early gene induction, to secondary gene induction in every cell that participates in the memory network. The same is likely true for LTP (Lisman, 1989).

A number of research groups are endeavoring to trace the chain of cellular events that underlie induction and maintenance of LTP (Grant et al., 1992; Silva, Paylor, Wehner, & Tonegawa, 1992; Silva, Stevens, Tonegawa, & Wang, 1992). In these studies single genes, controlling what are hoped to be specific events within cells, can be eliminated and the resultant effect can be studied simultaneously in whole animals minus one gene, so-called knockouts, for LTP and learning. In this method the gene of interest, usually a well-characterized gene, is cloned and in most cases altered so that important regulatory regions of the gene are nonfunctional. This altered DNA is introduced into embryonic stem cells derived from blastocysts. The gene combines with the DNA of the stem cells, and those cells in which the gene is inserted at appropriate regions of the DNA (via homologous recombination) can be isolated and inserted into developing blastocysts. Subsequent cells arising from these altered cells all lack the knockout gene. The resulting animal is a heterozygous chimera (combination of normal and mutant cells) that, with cross breeding, can generate progeny that are homozygous for the knocked-out targeted gene.

One reason to target genes is that these genetic procedures have the potential to overcome the current limitations of pharmacology. In studies of genes related to LTP, an area of focus in the study of transgenes has been kinases. Although data strongly suggest LTP induction involves a variety of kinases, including protein kinase C (Malinow, Schulman, & Tsien, 1989), calmodulin kinase (Malenka et al., 1989), and tyrosine kinases (O'Dell et al., 1991), these studies are limited by the fact that currently available kinase inhibitors lack a high degree of selectivity. Moreover, for a given kinase, the kinase family to which it belongs is composed of a number of subtypes, which appear to have varied functions. It would be of great utility to selectively impair the function of specific kinase isoforms, a feat that is achieved by the use of knockout mutants.

One study that attempted to trace the events underlying induction and maintenance of LTP (Grant et al., 1992) compared various knockouts of genes coding for particular tyrosine kinases. Deletion of one specific tyrosine kinase found in the *fyn* gene altered the amount of current necessary to induce LTP in area CA1. Traditional measures of synaptic function appeared normal, such as the maximal EPSP amplitudes and measures of paired-pulse facilitation, a short-term augmentation of synaptic response that appears to depend on residual presynaptic CA^{2+}. The *fyn*-knockout rats appeared to be incapable of learning the location of a hidden platform in a Morris water maze.

Unfortunately, this study is difficult to interpret. First, the hippocampus displayed obvious anatomical abnormalities, including an increase in granule and pyramidal cells. The dendrites of pyramidal cells in stratum radiatum showed disorganization and were less tightly packed, as were the cell bodies. Given the altered neural architecture, the synaptic volume might have been reduced, which may explain the reduced ability of high-intensity stimulation to produce LTP, although this is perhaps unlikely because low-frequency evoked EPSP amplitudes in the *fyn* knockouts are not different from those of wild-type controls. There were impairments in visual function because *fyn* knockouts were initially poor at performing a visual discrimination where the platform was visible, although they eventually reached latencies comparable to wild-type controls. The authors also noted that "overtraining in spatial tasks masked the *fyn* learning deficit." Apparently then, the animals learn, and the deletion of the *fyn* gene only altered the sensitivity of the knockout animals to such parametric aspects of training as the number of training trials needed to evidence learning. Because the *fyn* knockouts could express LTP, these data do not support a conclusion that LTP is a substrate of memory, because LTP and learning clearly do not depend on the presence of the *fyn* gene (Deutsch, 1993).

Other researchers (Silva, Stevens, Tonegawa, & Wang, 1992) engineered knockout mice that were deficient in α-calcium-calmodulin-dependent kinase II (α-CaMKII). The kinase α-CaMKII, in contrast with tyrosine kinase FYN, is localized to the brain and is neuron specific. The α-CaMKII mutants showed no overt physical or neuroanatomical abnormalities. Measures of postsynaptic function, such as the maximal EPSP amplitudes, in Schaffer-CA1 responses appeared normal, but paired-pulse potentiation was reduced in mutant mice. Activation of NMDA receptors appeared to elicit normal responses. Although the probability of induction of LTP was greatly reduced in the mutants, LTP in some animals was virtually indistinguishable from LTP observed in wild-type controls.

A subsequent study (Silva, Paylor, Wehner, & Tonegawa, 1992) assessed the ability of α-CaMKII mutants to learn the Morris water maze. These mutants apparently had a defect in their visual function, because they showed an initial deficit in the visual discrimination task. However, these mutant mice eventually matched the wild-type animals in performance. The α-CaMKII mutants were also impaired in their ability to find the hidden platform on the first session of training in the Morris water maze and were always slower than the wild-type control mice; that the mutants did learn is shown by the fact that their latencies to find the platform decreased over sessions. For the probe trial, the mutant mice took roughly twice as long to find the platform. An additional test employed a randomly located platform. Some trials were conducted with the hidden platform randomly located at other sites. Mutant mice took as long to find refuge at the random sites as to find refuge at the original location, whereas wild-type mice took less time to find the original location and longer times to find the random platforms, which indicates negative transfer. The results of the random probe test therefore suggest that the mutant mice did not know the spatial location of the hidden platform, although they apparently were able to use some strategy to escape the maze. Mutant animals were the equal of their wild-type cousins in learning a +-maze, which does not exact any spatial ability from its students. The α-CaMKII mutants showed greater activity in open field and did not evidence habituation of activity. Thus the evidence suggests that the α–CaMKII mutants did have a deficit in the ability to learn the spatial maze. What is not so clear is whether this spatial deficit is related to LTP. In the mutant mice only the probability of LTP induction was altered; LTP induction was not abolished. If a mutant did show LTP, then the LTP was indistinguishable from that observed in wild-type controls. The deficit in paired-pulse facilitation in the mutant mice is also problematic. Such an alteration could be important for hippocampal function that is unrelated to LTP but that is manifested as a spatial deficit. Indeed recent studies demonstrate that mutant mice with decrease paired-pulse facilitation have an impairment in spatial learning (Silva et al., 1996).

The role of CaM kinase II in learning and memory was recently investigated using single-unit recording in awake freely moving CaMKII mutant mice (Rotenberg, Mayford, Hawkins, Kandel, & Muller, 1996). These mutant mice expressed a CaM kinase II whose function was independent of Ca^{2+}. These animals showed LTP when 100-Hz high-frequency stimulation was used but did not show LTP when a 5- to 10-Hz, theta frequency stimulation was used. These mice also showed differences in place cell properties when compared with wild-type mice and they were impaired in spatial learning (Bach, Hawkins, Osman, Kandel, & Mayford, 1995). The number of place cells that can be recorded in these mutant mice were fewer as compared to wild-type controls and when present the place fields were more scattered and less stable. These investigators speculated that a relationship may exist between synaptic plasticity mediated by hippocampal theta activity and the encoding of information by place cells. Curiously, even though LTP induced by theta-type stimulation was blocked, theta activity was present. Thus according to these investigators, it is theta activity induced synaptic plasticity that is important in learning and memory processes, even though a connection between place cells and spatial learning has yet to be demonstrated (see the following).

Another group targeted protein kinase C (Abeliovich et al., 1993) and selected the PKC_γ isoform, both because inhibitors of PKC prevent induction of NMDA-receptor-dependent LTP in CA1 (Malinow et al., 1989) and because PKC_γ is specific to neurons in the CNS and is expressed postnatally. The probability of LTP induction was reduced in the mutants much as it had been in previous studies employing knockouts; but if the mutant mice were first treated with low-frequency stimulation, then the LTP was indistinguishable from that observed in wild-type controls. An interesting finding, however, was that expression of LTD was not impaired. In spite of coordination deficits, the mutant mice learned the Morris water maze at the same rate as did the wild-type controls and performed similarly in the probe and random probe tests. The authors believe the mutant mice did exhibit a mild spatial deficit, because during the probe test the mutants crossed the hidden-platform site less often than the controls, even though they were searching the correct quadrant. In contrast with their behavior in the spatial maze, the PKC_γ mutants did show deficits in contextual-fear conditioning in that they froze significantly less after return to a chamber where they experienced footshock. There is evidence that acquisition of a contextual-fear task depends on both the hippocampus and NMDA receptors (Kim & Fanselow, 1992; Kim et al., 1991, 1992). Conditioned fear (measured by observing freezing in response to a tone in a novel environment), which is thought to be independent of hippocampal function, was not impaired. The results do not support a role for PKC$_\gamma$ in either LTP or spatial learning because the mutant mice could learn the Morris water maze and, if stimulated appropriately, displayed LTP.

Departing from the study of the kinases, other groups targeted genes specific for subtypes of the glutamate receptor. One group (Sakimura et al., 1995) created mice with a mutation of the GluRϵ subunit of the NMDA-receptor channel. No obvious morphological brain abnormalities were observed, probably because this gene is expressed after development. However, the mutants appeared jumpy and had an apparently enhanced startle response. LTP could be induced in the mutants but at a reduced magnitude (smaller percentage increase from baseline). As in the case of the PKCγ, mutants, low-frequency stimulation prior to LTP restored some function but not the level of the wild-type controls. During training in the Morris water maze the mutants showed an initial latency deficit that disappeared by the end of training. During the probe trial the mutants searched the previously correct quadrant, crossed the trained site—though not at the same level of efficiency as the wild-type mice—and were less precise in their crossings. The authors consider their findings positive evidence for the participation of the mGluR1 subunit of the NMDA receptor in both LTP and the acquisition of spatial learning. Yet, as in the other studies reviewed, the gene mutation did not abolish either LTP or spatial learning, in which case this gene cannot be necessary for either.

The metabotropic glutamate receptor (mGlu) is implicated in LTP induction, though this conclusion remains controversial (Bashir et al., 1993; Manzoni, Weisskopf, & Nicoll, 1994). Activation of the metabotropic glutamate receptor 1 (mGluR) may activate G-protein-coupled second-messenger processes, and these processes may play an important role in LTP induction, acting like a metabolic switch that enables the induction of LTP. Recently, one research group created an mGluR1 mutant to test involvement of mGluR1 in LTP and contextual-fear conditioning (Aiba, Chen et al., 1994). This receptor subtype is plentiful in the dentate gyrus and CA3 areas and is apparently restricted to the presynaptic side of the Schaffer collateral projection to area CA1. These mGluR1 mutants had ataxia and were poor breeders but had brains that appeared normal. Synaptic transmission, STP, and paired-pulse potentiation were normal. LTP was observed in the mGluR1 mutants, but as in the GluRϵ mutants its magnitude was reduced. Low-frequency priming had no effect. The mGluR1 mutants were impaired in the hippocampus-dependent contextual-fear conditioning task and exhibited less freezing than did the wild-type controls in the cage where they were shocked. By contrast, the mutants learned as well as the wild-type animals to freeze in response to the tone and thus showed normal learning in response to this hippocampus-independent form of fear conditioning. The authors concluded that the mGluR1 receptor is not necessary for induction of LTP but that it modulates neural plasticity, apparently expressed as the magnitude of LTP. Because the mutant animals were moderately impaired in their learning, Aiba, Chen et al. posited that the mGluR1 receptor is not necessary for learning of the contextual-fear response but perhaps participates in some way.

A quite different set of results was found by another group who created an mGluR1 mutant (Conquet et al., 1994). These mutants exhibited ataxia as well. A neurological exam of the mutants revealed a complete loss of the righting reflex and reduced locomotor activity. LTD in cerebellar slices was severely reduced. Synaptic transmission appeared normal in the Schaffer collateral and commissural pathways to CA1, medial and lateral perforant pathways to dentate, and mossy-fiber and associational pathways in CA3. LTP was normal in all pathways except the mossy-fiber CA3 pathway, where it was greatly reduced. In the visible-platform version of the Morris water maze, the mutant mice were initially slower than the wild-type mice, but after three sessions they were indistinguishable from controls. However, in the hidden-platform version of the maze, the mGluR1 mutants could not find the platform and evidenced no learning. Because the mutant mice did learn the visually guided maze, the authors concluded that the deficit observed with respect to the hidden platform was due to an impairment of spatial ability mediated by mGluR1 receptors and probably in the mossy-fiber CA3 system, because LTP was reduced only in the mossy-fiber CA3 system. If the authors' interpretation of the data is correct, then deficits in the mossy-fiber system cannot be compensated by correctly functioning NMDA-receptor-dependent systems in other hippocampal pathways. This suggests an important role for both the dentate gyrus and opioid-receptor-dependent LTP in its mossy-fiber projections to area CA3 in learning (Marr, 1971; McNaughton, Barnes, Meltzer, & Sutherland, 1989).

Recently, the selectivity of gene knockouts has increased and it is possible to inactivate the glutaminergic NMDAR1 gene in neurons only in the hippocampal CA1 region. This localized gene deletion allows the investigation of the role of a specific hippocampal cell field in learning and memory processes. Tonegawa's group (Tsien et al., 1996) reported that mice with this restricted gene deletion had impaired spatial memory and they did not show induction of LTP in area CA1. These mice, however, did show a learning curve, demonstrated as a decrease in escape latencies over days, but they did not know the exact location of the platform as demonstrated by performing at chance level during a probe trial. Tonegawa's group (McHugh, Blum, Tsien, Tonegawa, & Wilson, 1996) also investigated place cells in NMDAR1 knockout mice. Place cells did exist in the CA1 region; however, they coded for larger areas and cells with overlapping fields lacked correlated activity.

The complexity of the mechanisms underlying learning and memory processes at the molecular level may also be appreciated in studies addressing the effect of spaced versus massed trials in learning. Previous studies indicated that better learning occurs when spaced trials are given as opposed to massed trials (Greene, 1989). Silva's group (Kogan, et al., 1997) addressed this issue by studying cAMP responsive binding protein (CREB) mutants. CREB has been associated with long-term memory in a number of species including invertebrates and vertebrates (Bourtchuladze et al., 1994; Dash, Hochner, & Kandel, 1990; Yin et al., 1994). Unique to these mutants is the finding that long- but not short-term memory is impaired in these animals. In this elegant study Kogan et al (1997) found that in a number of behavioral tasks including contextual conditioning, socially transmitted food preferences, and spatial learning, there was no impairment in learning when the animals were trained using spaced trials. The impairment observed with massed trials is explained by the fact that there is insufficient CREB to activate the long-term regulatory genes whose proteins are essential for long-term memory. The use of spaced trials allows a limited amount of CREB to initiate sufficient transcription to allow long-term memory.

Taken together, the studies utilizing the knockout strategy have provided some evidence that LTP and LTD are substrates of learning. What the knockout gains in specificity of elimination is lessened by the complexity of the mutant creature that develops without a particular gene. For example, is synaptic transmission in the mutant normal? In both the knockout studies and studies using selective drugs, it is assumed that if low-frequency synaptic transmission is not altered, then synaptic transmission is normal. However, there is no reason to believe that normal hippocampal function involves exclusively low-frequency activity; rather, high-frequency information is important for aspects of hippocampal function independent of its potential involvement in LTP induction. Such activity may be greatly influenced by the absence of a gene, as evidenced by the alterations in facilitation in one study (Silva, Stevens, Tonegawa, & Wang, 1992). Other basic questions concern whether an animal's motor system is competent to perform what is required and whether the animal can see the elevated platform. The development of a mutant that shows a restricted effect, as in the case of the NMDAR1 CA1 knockout, is a vast improvement. In the future it will be possible to knock out genes in adult animals in specific brain areas using inducible promoters. We find it curious in these mutant studies that learning is measured *in vivo* and induction of LTP is measured *in vitro* in the hippocampal slice. This strategy is based on the as-yet-uncertain assumption that LTP observed in the slice is identical to that observed *in vivo*.

V. KNOCKOUT MUTANTS, LTD, AND CEREBELLAR-DEPENDENT LEARNING

Evidence today indicates that the cerebellum is important in eyeblink classical conditioning (Thompson & Kim, 1996). Indeed the memory trace of this form of learning is localized in the cerebellum (Thompson & Kim, 1996). Although LTP may be induced in the cerebellum (Racine, Wilson, Gingell, & Sunderland, 1986), the predominant form of plasticity observed in this structure is LTD (Ito, 1989). Recent studies indicate that LTD may be a neural substrate for conditioned eyeblink response in the cerebellum. As described earlier, the metabotropic receptors have been implicated in learning and synaptic plasticity in the hippocampus (Conquet et al., 1994). One research group investigated mGluR1 mutant mice in both LTD and conditioned eyeblink response (Aiba, Kano, et al., 1994). These investigators found that in these mice short-term plasticity, as measured by paired-pulse facilitation, was normal as well as voltage-gated Ca^{2+} channel currents. This last measure was important because Ca^{2+} is required to induce LTD. LTD was impaired in these mice and they also show a deficit in eyeblink conditioning as measured by conditioned response (CR) amplitudes. Interestingly, although there was a deficit in cerebellar-dependent learning, these animals did show learning as demonstrated by an increase in CR amplitude over trials; however, in these mutants CR amplitudes were significantly less by the fourth and fifth paired session. Thus, just as in the hippocampus, other forms of synaptic plasticity may exist in the cerebellum and may be involved in learning and memory.

Generally, the knockout studies do demonstrate deficits in hippocampal LTP that mirror some deficits of hippocampus-dependent learning. If we apply the same explanation of graceful degradation as we have previously, then it is not surprising that some memory is evident in this distributed neural system even with the removal of a primary form of LTP. However, it remains disquieting that, even within a discrete afferent system, no single specific form of plasticity appears essential for learning. Even within a given cellular form of plasticity, no single kinase appears essential for the induction of NMDA-receptor-dependent LTP. Such findings, suggesting as they do the existence of parallel intracellular cascades, are problematic for reductionists trying to delineate the essential components of a successive molecular cascade. Nonetheless, from a larger view, these results emphasize that no single approach will be sufficient to elucidate the role of LTP and LTD in memory. In this context, the knockout approach is powerful and in conjunction with other techniques (which also have limitations) is likely to increase our understanding of the relationship between LTP, LTD, and learning.

VI. CONCLUSION

Although definitive proof that LTP and LTD are involved with learning has defied research efforts, proof that LTP and LTD have nothing to do with memory is even weaker. Thus the rationale for considering LTP and LTD as memory mechanisms remains viable. The absence of proof that LTP and LTD are involved in memory results from our current uncertainties about what memory is and how we should observe it. In addition, the occurrence of multiple forms of LTP together with the distributed nature of hippocampal information storage makes it difficult to identify the processes necessary for hippocampal memory and to implicate specific cellular processes in behavioral measures of memory. Thus we should proceed cautiously in interpreting negative findings. Might LTP emerge as an epiphenomenon unrelated to learning or memory? If it does, then the focus of research would shift to such other potential neural mechanisms of memory storage as population spike potentiation and presynaptic facilitation. LTP and LTD remain the best candidates for a cellular process of synaptic change that underlies learning and memory in the vertebrate brain.

VII. SUMMARY POINTS

1. Memory is a thing in a place in a brain.

2. Experience-dependent increases in synaptic strength underlie memory formation in networks of neurons and are known as Hebb's Postulate and long-term potentiation (LTP).

3. There are two fundamental types of LTP: one that is NMDA-receptor-dependent and one that is NMDA-receptor-independent, here called opioid-receptor-dependent LTP.

4. Experience-dependent decreases in synaptic strength are known as long-term depression and may code for information storage in neural networks.

5. The property of neurons to exhibit associative LTP may underlie particular forms of learning such as sensory preconditioning.

6. Learning does produce LTP-like changes in measures of evoked activity in the brain.

7. The induction of LTP prior to learning may influence later learning, but the experiments bearing on this point are not conclusive.

8. NMDA-receptor-dependent processes appear to underlie both LTP in the hippocampus and acquisition of a hippocampally dependent learning task, although there are important exceptions.

9. Opioid receptors appear to play a role in the induction of both opioid-receptor-dependent LTP in the hippocampus and the acquisition of a hippocampally dependent learning task.

10. Knockout mutant mice revealed the importance of several gene products in LTP induction and learning of a hippocampally dependent learning task, including α-CaMKII, PKCγ, GluRϵ subunit, mGluR1 receptor subtype, and NMDAR1 receptor subtype.

ACKNOWLEDGMENTS

The writing of this review was supported by DA 04195, NSF 3389, GM08194, and the Ewing Halsell Endowment of The University of Texas at San Antonio. Portions of the text of this chapter were reproduced with permission from the *Annual Review of Psychology*, Volume 47, © 1996, by Annual Reviews Inc.

REFERENCES

Abeliovich, A., Paylor, R., Chen, C., Kim, J. J., Wehner, J. M., & Tonegawa, S. (1993). PKC gamma mutant mice exhibit mild deficits in spatial and contextual learning. *Cell, 75,* 1263–1271.

Abraham, W. C., Christie, B. R., Logan, B., Lawlor, P., & Dragunow, M. (1994). Immediate early gene expression association with the persistence of heterosynaptic long-term depression in the hippocampus. *Proc. Natl. Acad. Sci. U.S.A., 91,* 10049–10053.

Aiba, A., Chen, C., Herrup, K., Rosenmund, C., Stevens, C. F., & Tonegawa, S. (1994). Reduced hippocampal long-term potentiation and context-specific deficit in associative learning in mGluR1 mutant mice. *Cell, 79,* 365–375.

Aiba, A., Kano, M., Chen, C., Stanton, M. E., Fox, G. D., Herrup, K., Zwingman, T. A., & Tonegawa, S. (1994). Deficient cerebellar long-term depression and impaired motor learning in mGluR1 mutant mice. *Cell, 79,* 377–388.

Bach, M. E., Hawkins, R. D., Osman, M., Kandel, E. R., & Mayford, M. (1995). Impairment of spatial but not contextual memory in CaMKII mutant mice with a selective loss of hippocampal LTP in the range of the theta frequency. *Cell, 81,* 905–915.

Bannerman, D. M., Good, M. A., Butcher, S. P., Ramsay, M., & Morris, R. G. (1995). Distinct components of spatial learning revealed by prior training and NMDA receptor blockade. *Nature, 378,* 182–186.

Barnes, C. A. (1979). Memory deficits associated with senescence: A neurophysiological and behavioral study in the rat. *J. Comp. Physiol. Psychol., 93,* 74–104.

Barnes, C. A. (1988). Spatial learning and memory processes: The search for their neurobiological mechanisms in the rat. *Trends Neurosci., 11,* 163–169.

Barnes, C. A., Jung, M. W., McNaughton, B. L., Korol, D. L., Andreasson, K., & Worley, P. F. (1994). LTP saturation and spatial learning disruption: Effects of task variables and saturation levels. *J. Neurosci., 14,* 5793–5806.

Bashir, Z. I., Bortolotto, Z. A., Davies, C. H., Berretta, N., Irving, A. J., Seal, A. J., Henley, J. M., Jane, D. E., Watkins, J. C., & Collingridge, G. L. (1993). Induction of LTP in the hippocampus needs synaptic activation of glutamate metabotropic receptors. *Nature, 363,* 347–350.

Bear, M. F., & Kirkwood, A. (1993). Neocortical long-term potentiation. *Curr. Opin. Neurobiol., 3,* 197–202.

Bear, M. F., & Malenka, R. C. (1994). Synaptic plasticity: LTP and LTD. *Curr. Opin. Neurobiol., 4,* 389–399.

Bennett, E. L., Diamond, M. C., Krech, D., & Rosenzweig, M. R. (1964). Chemical and anatomical plasticity of brain. *Science, 146,* 610–619.

Berger, T. W. (1984). Long-term potentiation of hippocampal synaptic transmission affects rate of behavioral learning. *Science, 224,* 627–630.

Berger, T. W., & Orr, W. B. (1983). Hippocampectomy selectively disrupts discrimination reversal conditioning of the rabbit nictitating membrane response. *Behav. Brain Res., 8,* 49–68.

Berger, T. W., Rinaldo, P. C., Weisz, D. J., & Thompson, R. F. (1983). Single-unit analysis of different hippocampal cell types during classical conditioning of rabbit nictitating membrane response. *J. Neurophysiol., 50,* 1197–1219.

Bliss, T. V., & Collingridge, G. L. (1993). A synaptic model of memory: Long-term potentiation in the hippocampus. *Nature, 361,* 31–39.

Bliss, T. V., & Lomo, T. (1973). Long-lasting potentiation of synaptic transmission in the dentate area of the anaesthetized rabbit following stimulation of the perforant path. *J. Physiol. (Lond.), 232,* 331–356.

Bliss, T. V., & Lynch, M. A. (1988). Long-term potentiation of synaptic transmission in the hippocampus: Properties and mechanisms. In P. Landfield & S. A. Deadwyler (Eds.), *LTP: From biophysics to behavior* (pp. 3–72). New York: Liss.

Bonhoeffer, T., Staiger, V., & Aertsen, A. (1989). Synaptic plasticity in rat hippocampal slice cultures: Local "Hebbian" conjunction of pre- and postsynaptic stimulation leads to distributed synaptic enhancement. *Proc. Natl. Acad. Sci. U.S.A., 86*, 8113–8117.

Bourtchuladze, R., Frenguelli, B., Blendy, J., Cioffi, D., Schutz, G., & Silva, A. J. (1994). Deficient long-term memory in mice with a targeted mutation of the cAMP-responsive element-binding protein. *Cell, 79*, 59–68.

Bramham, C. R. (1992). Opioid receptor dependent long-term potentiation: Peptidergic regulation of synaptic plasticity in the hippocampus. *Neurochem. Int., 20*, 441–455.

Bramham, C. R., Milgram, N. W., & Srebro, B. (1991a). Delta opioid receptor activation is required to induce LTP of synaptic transmission in the lateral perforant path in vivo. *Brain Res., 567*, 42–50.

Bramham, C. R., Milgram, N. W., & Srebro, B. (1991b). Activation of AP5-sensitive NMDA receptors is not required to induce LTP of synaptic transmission in the lateral perforant path. *Eur. J. Neurosci., 3*, 1300–1308.

Breindl, A., Derrick, B. E., Rodriguez, S. B., & Martinez, J. L., Jr. (1994). Opioid receptor-dependent long-term potentiation at the lateral perforant path-CA3 synapse in rat hippocampus. *Brain Res. Bull., 33*, 17–24.

Brinton, R. E. (1991). Biochemical correlates of learning and memory. In J. L. Martinez, Jr., & R. Kesner (Eds.), *Learning and memory: A biological view* (pp. 199–257). San Diego: Academic Press.

Butcher, S. P., Davis, S., & Morris, R. G. (1990). A dose-related impairment of spatial learning by the NMDA receptor antagonist, 2-amino-5-phosphonovalerate (AP5). *Eur. Neuropsychopharmacol., 1*, 15–20.

Butcher, S. P., Hamberger, A., & Morris, R. G. (1991). Intracerebral distribution of DL-2-amino-phosphonopentanoic acid (AP5) and the dissociation of different types of learning. *Exp. Brain. Res., 83*, 521–526.

Castro, C. A., Silbert, L. H., McNaughton, B. L., & Barnes, C. A. (1989). Recovery of spatial learning deficits after decay of electrically induced synaptic enhancement in the hippocampus. *Nature, 342*, 545–548.

Collingridge, G. L., Kehl, S. J., & McLennan, H. (1983). Excitatory amino acids in synaptic transmission in the Schaffer collateral-commissural pathway of the rat hippocampus. *J. Physiol. (Lond.), 334*, 33–46.

Conquet, F., Bashir, Z. I., Davies, C. H., Daniel, H., Ferraguti, F., Bordi, F., Franz-Bacon, K., Reggiani, A., Matarese, V., Conde, F., et al. (1994). Motor deficit and impairment of synaptic plasticity in mice lacking mGluR1. *Nature, 372*, 237–243.

Dash, P. K., Hochner, B., & Kandel, E. R. (1990). Injection of the cAMP-responsive element into the nucleus of *Aplysia* sensory neurons blocks long-term facilitation. *Nature, 345*, 718–721.

Davis, S., Butcher, S. P., & Morris, R. G. (1992). The NMDA receptor antagonist D-2-amino-5-phosphonopentanoate (D-AP5) impairs spatial learning and LTP in vivo at intracerebral concentrations comparable to those that block LTP in vitro. *J. Neurosci., 12*, 21–34.

Debanne, D., Gahwiler, B. H., & Thompson, S. M. (1994). Asynchronous pre- and postsynaptic activity induces associative long-term depression in area CA1 of the rat hippocampus in vitro. *Proc. Natl. Acad. Sci. U.S.A., 91*, 1148–1152.

Decker, M. W., Introini-Collison, I. B., & McGaugh, J. L. (1989). Effects of naloxone on Morris water maze learning in the rat-enhanced acquisition with pretraining but not posttraining administration. *Psychobiology, 17*, 270–275.

Derrick, B. E., & Martinez, J. L., Jr. (1994a). Frequency-dependent associative long-term potentiation at the hippocampal mossy fiber-CA3 synapse. *Proc. Natl. Acad. Sci. U.S.A., 91*, 10290–10294.

Derrick, B. E., & Martinez, J. L., Jr. (1994b). Opioid receptor activation is one factor underlying the frequency dependence of mossy fiber LTP induction. *J. Neurosci., 14*, 4359–4367.

Derrick, B. E., & Martinez, J. L., Jr. (1995). Associative LTD at the hippocampal mossy fiber-CA3 synapse. *Soc. Neurosci. Abst., 21*, 603.

Derrick, B. E., & Martinez, J. L., Jr. (1996). Associative, bidirectional modifications at the hippocampal mossy fibre-CA3 synapse. *Nature, 381*, 429–434.

Derrick, B. E., Rodriguez, S. B., Lieberman, D. N., & Martinez, J. L., Jr. (1992). Mu opioid receptors are associated with the induction of hippocampal mossy fiber long-term potentiation. *J. Pharmacol. Exp. Ther., 263,* 725–733.

Derrick, B. E., Weinberger, S. B., & Martinez, J. L., Jr. (1991). Opioid receptors are involved in an NMDA receptor-independent mechanism of LTP induction at hippocampal mossy fiber-CA3 synapses. *Brain Res. Bull., 27,* 219–223.

Deutsch, J. A. (1993). Spatial learning in mutant mice. *Science, 262,* 760–763.

Diamond, D. M., & Rose, G. M. (1994). Does associative LTP underlie classical conditioning? *Psychobiology, 22,* 263–269.

Dudek, S. M., & Bear, M. F. (1993). Bidirectional long-term modification of synaptic effectiveness in the adult and immature hippocampus. *J. Neurosci., 13,* 2910–2918.

Dunwiddie, T., & Lynch, G. (1978). Long-term potentiation and depression of synaptic responses in the rat hippocampus: Localization and frequency dependency. *J. Physiol. (Lond.), 276,* 353–367.

Erickson, C. A., McNaughton, B. L., & Barnes, C. A. (1990). Exploration-dependent enhancement of synaptic responses in rat fascia dentate is blocked by MK801. *Soc. Neurosci. Abstr., 16,* 442.

Gallistel, R. (1995). Is long-term potentiation a plausible basis for memory? In J. L. McGaugh, G. Weinberger, & G. Lynch (Eds.), *Brain and memory: Modulation and mediation of plasticity* (pp. 328–337). New York: Oxford University Press.

Grant, S. G., O'Dell, T. J., Karl, K. A., Stein, P. L., Soriano, P., & Kandel, E. R. (1992). Impaired long-term potentiation, spatial learning, and hippocampal development in *fyn* mutant mice. *Science, 258,* 1903–1910.

Green, E. J., & Greenough, W. T. (1986). Altered synaptic transmission in dentate gyrus of rats reared in complex environments: Evidence from hippocampal slices maintained in vitro. *J. Neurophysiol., 55,* 739–750.

Green, E. J., McNaughton, B. L., & Barnes, C. A. (1990). Exploration-dependent modulation of evoked responses in fascia dentate: Dissociation of motor, EEG, and sensory factors and evidence for a synaptic efficacy change. *J. Neurosci., 10,* 1455–1471.

Greene, R. L. (1989). Spacing effects in memory: Evidence for a two process account. *J. Exp. Psychol.: Learn., Mem., Cogn., 15,* 371–377.

Greenough, W. T., Volkmar, F. R., & Juraska, J. M. (1973). Effects of rearing complexity on dendritic branching in frontolateral and temporal cortex of the rat. *Exp. Neurol., 41,* 371–378.

Hebb, D. O. (1949). *The organization behavior.* New York: John Wiley and Sons.

Hrabetova, S., & Sacktor, T. C. (1996). Bidirecetional regulation of protein kinase M sigma in the maintenance of long-term potentiation and long-term depression. *J. Neurosci., 16,* 5324–5333.

Huang, Y. Y., Kandel, E. R., Varshavsky, L., Brandon, E. P., Qi, M., Idzerda, R. L., McKnight, G. S., & Bourtchouladze, R. (1995). A genetic test of the effects of mutations in PKA on mossy fiber LTP and its relation to spatial and contextual learning. *Cell, 83,* 1211–1222.

Intrator, N., Bear, M. F., Cooper, L. N., & Paradiso, M. A. (1993). Theory of synaptic plasticity in visual cortex. In M. Baudry, R. F. Thompson, & J. L. Davis (Eds.), *Synaptic plasticity: Molecular, cellular, and functional aspects* (pp. 147–167). Cambridge, MA: MIT Press.

Ishihara, K., Katsuki, H., Sugimura, M., Kaneko, S., & Satoh, M. (1990). Different drug-susceptibilities of long-term potentiation in three input systems to the CA3 region of the guinea pig hippocampus in vitro. *Neuropharmacology, 29,* 487–492.

Ito, M. (1989). Long-term depression. *Annu. Rev., Neurosci., 12,* 85–102.

Jaffe, D., & Johnson, D. (1990). Induction of long-term potentiation at hippocampal mossy-fiber synapses follows a Hebbian rule. *J. Neurophysiol, 64,* 948–960.

Jeffery, K. J., & Morris, R. G. (1993). Cumulative long-term potentiation in the rat dentate gyrus correlates with, but does not modify, performance in the water maze. *Hippocampus, 3,* 133–140.

Johnson, D., Williams, S., Jaffe, D., & Gray, R. (1992). NMDA-receptor-independent long-term potentiation. *Annu. Rev. Physiol., 54,* 489–505.

Keith, J. R., & Judy, J. W. (1990). Why NMDA receptor-dependent long-term potentiation may not be a mechanism of learning and memory: A reappraisal of the NMDA receptor blockade strategy. *Psychobiology, 18,* 251–257.

Kelso, S. R., & Brown, T. H. (1986). Differential conditioning of associative synaptic enhancement in hippocampal brain slices. *Science, 232,* 85–87.

Kim, J. J., DeCola, J. P., Landeira-Fernandez, J., & Fanselow, M. S. (1991). N-Methyl-D-aspartate receptor antagonist APV blocks acquisition but not expression of fear conditioning. *Behav. Neurosci., 105,* 126–133.

Kim, J. J., & Fanselow, M. S. (1992). Modality-specific retrograde amnesia of fear. *Science, 256,* 675–677.

Kim, J. J., Fanselow, M. S., DeCola, J. P., & Landeira-Fernandez, J. (1992). Selective impairment of long-term but not short-term conditional fear by the N-methyl-D-aspartate antagonist APV. *Behav. Neurosci., 106,* 591–596.

Kirkwood, A., & Bear, M. F. (1995). Elementary forms of synaptic plasticity in the visual cortex. *Biol. Res., 28,* 73–80.

Kogan, J. H., Frankland, P. W., Blendy, J. A., Coblentz, J., Marowitz, Z., Schutz, G., & Silva, A. J. (1997). Spaced training induces normal long-term memory in CREB mutant mice. *Curr. Biol., 7,* 1–11.

Langdon, R. B., Johnson, J. W., & Barrionuevo, G. (1995). Posttetanic potentiation and presynaptically induced long-term potentiation at the mossy fiber synapse in rat hippocampus. *Nature, 376,* 256–259.

Larkman, A. U., & Jack, J. J. (1995). Synaptic plasticity: Hippocampal LTP. *Curr. Opin. Neurobiol., 5,* 324–334.

Laroche, S., Doyere, V., & Bloch, V. (1989). Linear relation between the magnitude of long-term potentiation in the dentate gyrus and associative learning in the rat. A demonstration using commissural inhibition and local infusion of an N-methyl-D-aspartate receptor antagonist. *Neuroscience, 28,* 375–386.

Laroche, S., Doyere, V., & Redini, D. N. (1991). What role for LTP in learning and the maintenance of memories? In M. Baudry & J. L. Davis (Eds.), *LTP: A debate of the current issues* (pp. 301–316). London: MIT Press.

Levy, W. B., & Steward, O. (1979). Synapses as associative memory elements in the hippocampal formation. *Brain Res., 175,* 233–245.

Linden, D. J., & Connor, J. A. (1995). Long-term synaptic depression. *Annu. Rev. Neurosci., 18,* 319–357.

Lisman, J. (1989). A mechanism for the Hebb and the anti-Hebb processes underlying learning and memory. *Proc. Natl. Acad. Sci. U.S.A., 86,* 9574–9578.

Lynch, G., & Granger, R. (1986). Variations in synaptic plasticity and types of memory in corticohippocampal networks. *J. Cogn. Neurosci., 4,* 189–199.

Makintosh, N. J. (1974). *The psychology of animal learning.* London: Academic Press.

Malenka, R. C., Kauer, J. A., Perkel, D. J., Mauk, M D., Kelly, P. T., Nicoll, R. A., & Waxham, M. N. (1989). An essential role for postsynaptic calmodulin and protein kinase activity in long-term potentiation. *Nature, 340,* 554–557.

Malinow, R., Schulman, H., & Tsien, R. W. (1989). Inhibition of postsynaptic PKC or CaMKII blocks induction but not expression of LTP. *Science, 245,* 862–866.

Manzoni, O. J., Weisskopf, M. G., & Nicoll, R. A. (1994). MCPG antagonizes metabotropic glutamate receptors but not long-term potentiation in the hippocampus. *Eur. J. Neurosci., 6,* 1050–1054.

Marr, D. (1971). Simple memory: A theory for archicortex. *Philos. Trans. R. Soc. Lond., B: Biol. Sci., 262,* 23–81.

Martin, M. R. (1983). Naloxone and long term potentiation of hippocampal CA3 field potentials in vitro. *Neuropeptides, 4,* 45–50.

Martinez, J. L., Jr., & Derrick, B. E. (1994). Opioid receptors contribute to lateral perforant path-CA3 responses days, but not hours, following LTP induction. *Soc. Neurosci. Abstr., 20,* 897.

Martinez, J. L., Jr., Schulteis, C., & Weinberger, S. B. (1991). How to increase and decrease the strength of memory traces: The effects of drugs and hormones. In J. L. Martinez, Jr., & R. Kesner (Eds.), *Learning and memory: A biological view* (pp. 149–287). San Diego: Academic Press.

Matthies, H., Ruethrich, H., Ott, T., Matthies, H. K., & Matthies, R. (1986). Low frequency perforant path stimulation as a conditioned stimulus demonstrates correlations between long-term synaptic potentiation and learning. *Physiol. Behav., 36,* 811–821.

McDaniel, K. L., Mundy, W. R., & Tilson, H. A. (1990). Microinjection of dynorphin into the hippocampus impairs spatial learning in rats. *Pharmacol. Biochem. Behav., 35,* 429–435.

McHugh, T. J., Blum, K. I., Tsien, J. Z., Tonegawa, S., & Wilson, M. A. (1996). Impaired hippocampal representation of space in CA1-specific NMDAR1 knockout mice. *Cell, 87,* 1339–1349.

McNaughton, B. L., Barnes, C. A., Meltzer, J., & Sutherland, R. J. (1989). Hippocampal granule cells are necessary for normal spatial learning but not for spatially-selective pyramidal cell discharge. *Exp. Brain Res., 76,* 485–496.

McNaughton, B. L., Barnes, C. A., Rao, G., Baldwin, J., & Rasmussen, M. (1986). Long-term enhancement of hippocampal synaptic transmission and the acquisition of spatial information. *J. Neurosci., 6,* 563–571.

McNaughton, B. L., Douglas, R. M., & Goddard, G. V. (1978). Synaptic enhancement in fascia dentata: Cooperativity among coactive afferents. *Brain Res., 157,* 277–293.

McNaughton, B. L., & Morris, R. G. (1987). Hippocampal synaptic enhancement and information storage within a distributed memory system. *Trends Neurosci., 10,* 408–415.

Mitsuno, K., Sasa, M., Ishihara, K., Ishikawa, M., & Kikuchi, H. (1994). LTP of mossy fiber-stimulated potentials in CA3 during learning in rats. *Physiol. Behav., 55,* 633–638.

Mondadori, C., Weiskrantz, L., Buerki, H., Petschke, F., & Fagg, G. E. (1989). NMDA receptor antagonists can enhance or impair learning performance in animals. *Exp. Brain Res., 75,* 449–456.

Montague, P. R., & Sejnowski, T. J. (1994). The predictive brain: Temporal coincidence and temporal order in synaptic learning mechanisms. *Learn. Mem., 1,* 1–33.

Morris, R. G. (1989). Synaptic plasticity and learning: Selective impairment of learning rats and blockade of long-term potentiation in vivo by the *N*-methyl-D-aspartate receptor antagonist AP5. *J. Neurosci., 9,* 3040–3057.

Morris, R. G. (1990). It's heads they win, tails I lose. *Psychobiology, 18,* 261–266.

Morris, R. G., Anderson, E., Lynch, G. S., & Baudry, M. (1986). Selective impairment of learning and blockade of long-term potentiation by an *N*-methyl-D-aspartate receptor antagonist, AP5. *Nature, 319,* 774–776.

Morris, R. G., Garrud, P., Rawlins, J. N., & O'Keefe, J. (1982). Place navigation impaired in rats with hippocampal lesions. *Nature, 297,* 681–683.

Morris, R. G. M. (1989). Does synaptic plasticity play a role in information storage in the vertebrate brain? In R. G. M. Morris (Ed.), *Parallel distributed processing: Implications for psychology and neurobiology* (pp. 248–285). Oxford, England: Clarendon Press/Oxford University Press.

Moyer, J. R., Jr., Deyo, R. A., & Disterhoft, J. F. (1990). Hippocampectomy disrupts trace eye-blink conditioning in rabbits. *Behav. Neurosci., 104,* 243–252.

Mulkey, R. M., Herron, C. E., & Malenka, R. C. (1993). An essential role for protein phosphatases in hippocampal long-term depression. *Science, 261,* 1051–1055.

Mulkey, R. M., & Malenka, R. C. (1992). Mechanisms underlying induction of homosynaptic long-term depression in area CA1 of the hippocampus. *Neuron, 9,* 967–975.

Nadel, L. (1968). Dorsal and ventral hippocampal lesions and behavior. *Physiol. Behav., 3,* 891–900.

Neveu, D., & Zucker, R. S. (1996). Postsynaptic levels of [CA^{2+}]i needed to trigger LTD and LTP. *Neuron, 16,* 619–629.

Nguyen, P. V., Abel, T., & Kandel, E. R. (1994). Requirement of a critical period of transcription for induction of a late phase of LTP. *Science, 265,* 1104–1107.

O'Dell, T. J., Kandel, E. R., & Grant, S. G. (1991). Long-term potentiation in the hippocampus is blocked by tyrosine kinase inhibitors. *Nature, 353,* 558–560.

Ohki, Y. (1982). [The effects of hippocampal lesions on two types of avoidance learning in rats: Effects on learning to be active or to be inactive]. *Shinrgaku Kenkyu, 53,* 65–71.

Ott, T., Ruthrich, K., Reymann, L., Lindenau, L., & Matthies, H. (1982). Direct evidence for the participation of changes in synaptic efficacy in the development of behavioral plasticity. In C. Marsan & H. Matthies (Eds.), *Neuronal plasticity and memory formation* (pp. 441–452). New York: Raven.

Pavlov, I. P. (1927). *Conditioned reflexes.* London: Oxford University Press.

Peng, Y. Y., & Horn, J. P. (1991). Continuous repetitive stimuli are more effective than bursts for evoking LHRH release in bullfrog sympatheteic ganglia. *J. Neurosci., 11,* 85–95.

Racine, R. J., Milgram, N. W., & Hafner, S. (1983). Long-term potentiation phenomena in the rat limbic forebrain. *Brain Res., 260,* 217–231.

Racine, R. J., Wilson, D. A., Gingell, R., & Sunderland, D. (1986). Long-term potentiation in the interpositus and vestibular nuclei in the rat. *Exp. Brain Res., 63,* 158–162.

Reymann, K. G., Ruthrich, H., Lindenau, L., Ott, T., & Matthies, H. (1982). Monosynaptic activation of the hippocampus as a conditioned stimulus: Behavioral effects. *Physiol. Behav., 29,* 1007–1012.

Richter-Levin, G., Errington, M. L., Maegawa, H., & Bliss, T. V. (1994). Activation of metabotropic glutamate receptors is necessary for long-term potentiation in the dentate gyrus and for spatial learning. *Neuropharmacology, 33,* 853–857.

Robinson, G. B. (1992). Maintained saturation of hippocampal long-term potentiation does not disrupt acquisition of the eight-arm radial maze. *Hippocampus, 2,* 389–395.

Robinson, G. S., Crooks, G. B., Shinkman, P. G., & Gallagher, M. (1989). Behavioral effects of MK-801 mimic deficits associated with hippocampal damage. *Psychobiology, 17,* 156–164.

Rolls, E. T. (1989). Parallel distributed processing in the brain: Implications of the functional architecture of neuronal networks in the hippocampus. In R. G. M. Morris (Ed.), *Parallel distributed processing: Implications for psychology and neurobiology* (pp. 286–307). Oxford: Clarendon.

Rosenzweig, M. R., Krech, D., Bennett, E. L., & Diamond, M. C. (1962). Effects of environmental complexity and training on brain chemistry and anatomy: A replication and extension. *J. Physiol. Psychol., 55,* 429–437.

Rotenberg, A., Mayford, M., Hawkins, R. D., Kandel, E. R., & Muller, R. U. (1996). Mice expressing activated CaMKII lack low frequency LTP and do not form stable place cells in the CA1 region of the hippocampus. *Cell, 87,* 1351–1361.

Rumelhart, D., & McClelland, J. (1986). *Parallel distributed processing.* Cambridge, MA: MIT Press.

Ruthrich, H., Dorochow, W., Pohle, W., Ruthrich, H. L., & Matthies, H. (1987). Colchicine-induced lesion of rat hippocampal granular cells prevents conditioned active avoidance with perforant path stimulation as conditioned stimulus, but not conditioned emotion. *Physiol. Behav., 40,* 147–154.

Sakimura, K., Kutsuwada, T., Ito, I., Manabe, T., Takayama, C., Kushiya, E., Yagi, T., Aizawa, S., Inoue, Y., Sugiyama, H., et al. (1995). Reduced hippocampal LTP and spatial learning in mice lacking NMDA receptor epsilon 1 subunit. *Nature, 373,* 151–155.

Saucier, D., & Cain, D. P. (1995). Spatial learning without NMDA receptor-dependent long-term potentiation. *Nature, 378,* 186–189.

Schuman, E. M., & Madison, D. V. (1991). A requirement for the intercellular messenger nitric oxide in long-term potentiation. *Science, 254,* 1503–1506.

Sejnowski, T. J. (1977). Storing covariance with nonlinearly interacting neurons. *J. Math. Biol., 4,* 303–321.

Shacter, D. L., & Tulving, F. (1994). What are the memory systems of 1994? In D. L. Shacter & F. Tulving (Eds.), *Memory systems 1994* (pp. 1–38). Cambridge, MA: MIT Press.

Sharp, P. E., McNaughton, B. L., & Barnes, C. A. (1985). Enhancement of hippocampal field potentials in rats exposed to a novel, complex environment. *Brain Res., 339,* 361–365.

Shimai, S., & Ohki, Y. (1980). Facilitation of discriminated rearing-avoidance in rats with hippocampal lesions. *Percept. Mot. Skills, 50,* 56–58.

Silva, A. J., Paylor, R., Wehner, J. M., & Tonegawa, S. (1992). Impaired spatial learning in alpha-calcium-calmodulin kinase II mutant mice. *Science, 257,* 206–211.

Silva, A. J., Rosahl, T. W., Chapman, P. F., Marowitz, Z., Friedman, E., Frankland, P. W., Cestari, V., Cioffi, D., Sudhof, T. C., & Bourtchuladze, R. (1996). Impaired learning in mice with abnormal short-lived plasticity. *Curr. Biol., 6,* 1509–1518.

Silva, A. J., Stevens, C. F., Tonegawa, S., & Wang, Y. (1992). Deficient hippocampal long-term potentiation in alpha-calcium-calmodulin kinase II mutant mice. *Science, 257,* 201–206.

Squire, L. R. (1987). *Memory and brain*. New York: Oxford University Press.

Stanton, P. K., & Sejnowski, T. J. (1989). Associative long-term depression in the hippocampus induced by hebbian covariance. *Nature, 339,* 215–218.

Staubli, U. (1992). A peculiar form of potentiation in mossy fiber synapses. *Epilepsy Res. Suppl., 7,* 151–157.

Staubli, U., Larson, J., & Lynch, G. (1990). Mossy fiber potentiation and long-term potentiation involve different expression mechanisms. *Synapse, 5,* 333–335.

Stent, G. S. (1973). A physiological mechanism for Hebb's postulate of learning. *Proc. Natl. Acad. Sci.U.S.A., 70,* 997–1001.

Sutherland, R. J., Dringenberg, H. C., & Hoesing, J. M. (1993). Induction of long-term potentiation at perforant path dentate synapses does not affect place learning or memory. *Hippocampus, 3,* 141–147.

Teyler, T. J., & Grover, L. (1993). Forms of long-term potentiation induced by NMDA and non-NMDA receptor activation. In M. Baudry, R. F. Thompson, & J. L. Davis (Eds.), *Synaptic plasticity: Molecular, cellular, and functional aspects* (pp. 73–86). Cambridge, MA: MIT Press.

Thompson, R. F. (1992). Memory. *Curr. Opin. Neurobiol., 2,* 203–208.

Thompson, R. F., & Kim, J. J. (1996). Memory systems in the brain and localization of a memory. *Proc. Natl. Acad. Sci. U.S.A., 93,* 13438–13444.

Thompson, R. F., & Krupa, D. J. (1994). Organization of memory traces in the mammalian brain. *Annu. Rev. Neurosci., 17,* 519–549.

Thompson, R. F., & Spencer, W. A. (1966). Habituation: A model phenomenon for the study of neuronal substrates of behavior. *Psychol. Rev., 173,* 16–43.

Tsien, J. Z., Chen, D. F., Gerber, D., Tom, C., Mercer, E. H., Anderson, D. J., Mayford, M., Kandel, E. R., & Tonegawa, S. (1996). Subregion- and cell type-restricted gene knockout in mouse brain. *Cell, 87,* 1317–1326.

Urban, N. N., & Barrionuevo, G. (1996). Induction of hebbian and non-hebbian mossy fiber long-term potentiation by distinct patterns of high-frequency stimulation. *J. Neurosci., 16,* 4293–4299.

Wagner, J. J., Terman, G. W., & Chavkin, C. (1993). Endogenous dynorphins inhibit excitatory neuro-transmission and block LTP induction in the hippocampus. *Nature, 363,* 451–454.

Walker, D. L., & Gold, P. E. (1991). Effects of the novel NMDA antagonist, NPC 12626, on long-term potentiation, learning and memory. *Brain Res., 549,* 213–221.

Weisskopf, M. G., & Nicoll, R. A. (1995). Presynaptic changes during mossy fibre LTP revealed by NMDA receptor-mediated synaptic responses. *Nature, 376,* 256–259.

Weisskopf, M. G., Zalutsky, R. A., & Nicoll, R. A. (1993). The opioid peptide dynorphin mediates heterosynaptic depression of hippocampal mossy fibre synapses and modulates long-term potentia-tion. *Nature, 365,* 188.

Williams, S., & Johnson, D. (1989). Long-term potentiation of hippocampal mossy fiber synapses is blocked by postsynaptic injection of calcium chelators. *Neuron, 3,* 583–588.

Wilson, M. A., & McNaughton, B. L. (1994). Reactivation of hippocampal ensemble memories during sleep. *Science, 265,* 676–679.

Winson, J. (1978). Loss of hippocampal theta rhythm results in spatial memory deficit in the rat. *Science, 201,* 160–163.

Yin, J. C., Wallach, J. S., Del Vecchio, M., Wilder, E. L., Zhou, H., Quinn, W. G., & Tully, T. (1994). Induction of a dominant negative CREB transgene specifically blocks long-term memory in *Drosophila. Cell, 79,* 49–58.

Zalutsky, R. A., & Nicoll, R. A. (1990). Comparison of two forms of long-term potentiation in single hippocampal neurons. *Science, 248,* 1619–1624.

Zalutsky, R. A., & Nicoll, R. A. (1992). Mossy fiber long-term potentiation shows specificity but no apparent cooperativity. *Neurosci. Lett., 138,* 193–197.

Zhang, D. X., & Levy, W. B. (1992). Ketamine blocks the induction of LTP at the lateral entorhinal cortex-dentate gyrus synapses. *Brain Res., 593,* 124–127.

Zola-Morgan, S., & Squire, L. R. (1993). Neuroanatomy of memory. *Annu. Rev. Neurosci., 16,* 547–563.

CHAPTER 7

Memory Changes during Normal Aging: Neurobiological Correlates

C. A. Barnes

Departments of Psychology and Neurology and Arizona Research Laboratories, Division of Neural Systems, Memory and Aging, University of Arizona, Tucson, Arizona 85724

I. INTRODUCTION

One approach to the study of learning and memory has as its focus the attempt to understand memory's "normal" operations in enough detail to allow abnormal conditions to be identified and properly diagnosed. A major difficulty in distinguishing normal from pathological mnemonic function arises from the fact that learning and memory processes are continually changing throughout the course of development (birth to death). While it is undoubtedly obvious that the memory of a 3-year-old child should not be held as the standard to compare memory in other age groups, it is probably not as obvious that we should not necessarily consider the memory of an 18-year-old (typically a person who has recently entered a university and is required to participate in a memory experiment as part of an introductory psychology course) to be the proper standard. That is, a performance level considered normal for a healthy 80-year-old may be abormal for an 18-year-old. Furthermore, caution must be taken in the interpretation of comparisons of young university students, who may show expert levels of test-taking skills, with individuals who have not been formally tested for 50 years or more. To measure true changes in "memory" over time, such performance variables must be carefully considered. The main point here is that normal learning and memory processes need to be considered with reference to their own developmental time course (taking care to exclude potential performance confounds) and that changes in memory function with age can be informative in their own right, highlighting the features critical to an efficient information-processing system.

Interest in memory and old age can be traced at least as far back as the first Greek and Roman memory theorists (Herrmann & Chaffin, 1988). Aristotle, for example, as well as setting forth the basic "laws" of association in his work *De Memoria et Reminiscentia* in the third century B.C., also commented on the importance of memory for the aged and the decline of memory with age, as illustrated in the following passages:

> They live by memory rather than by hope; for what is left to them of life is but little as compared with the long past; and hope is of the future, memory of the past. This, again, is the cause of their loquacity; they are continually talking of the past, because they enjoy remembering it. [Rhetorica II.1390a.10 (from the English translations of Ross, 1928)]

> Infants and very old persons have bad memories, owing to the amount of movement going on within them; for the latter are in process of rapid decay, the former in process of vigorous growth. . . . [*Parva Naturalia: De Memoria et Reminiscentia* 453b.1 (from Ross, 1928)]

Possibly the true beginning of the psychology of aging, which included an interest in how memory might change with age, began with a book by Quetelet entitled *Sur l'Homme et le developpement de ses Facultes* published in 1835 (published in English in 1842). In this book Quetelet emphasized how the progressive development of intellectual processes over the life span was virtually ignored at that time and that the science of the psychology of aging was going to require the collaboration of psychologists and biologists for its full expression (Birren, 1961). Although this view was stated in the nineteenth century, and perhaps ignored for many years, it is certainly characteristic of current experimental approaches to the study of aging memory. In fact, the field of gerontology encompasses the study of the biological, psychological, and social issues surrounding organisms of advanced age and, as such, is particularly interdisciplinary in nature.

In the following, I will discuss selected evidence that supports the ideas that learning and memory changes do occur over the life span in humans and other animals, that an understanding of these behavioral changes has helped to narrow the focus of study onto certain accessible brain structures, and that the ability to relate such behavioral change to neural change in aged organisms has aided in a more complete understanding of the neurobiological processes involved in learning and memory. Finally, because the aim of most scientists studying the neurobiology of aging is to understand memory processes well enough to be able to attenuate their deterioration with age, the final portion will describe certain interventive strategies that are now being taken. Because these topics could fill a book rather than just a chapter, in the following I will limit the number of illustrations in the discussion concerning both the type of learning and memory and the brain structures that may underlie these age-related changes. Other perspectives on the problem of relating learning and memory changes with age to brain changes can be found elsewhere (e.g., Bartus & Dean, 1987; Gage, Chen, Buzsáki, & Armstrong, 1988; Gold & Stone, 1988; Ingram, 1985; Kesner, 1988; Martinez, Schulteis, Janak, & Weinberger, 1988; Olton & Wenk, 1987; Rapp & Amaral, 1992; Solomon, Beal, & Pendlebury, 1988; Zornetzer, 1986; Zyzak, Otto, Eichenbaum & Gallagher, 1995).

II. EFFECT OF AGING ON MEMORY IN HUMANS: POTENTIAL CONTRIBUTION OF ANIMAL MODELS

> Aging is a natural process that must be studied intensively, for it remains one of the most agonizing problems in all biology. Not only must the gerontologists continue to concentrate on performing the research necessary to understand aging, but they must assume an increasing role in the application of their knowledge for betterment of the status of the aged. (Lawton, 1965, p. 31)

Although Lawton made this statement several decades ago, the ultimate goal of much of the current work on normal age-related memory changes in nonhuman species is to build a foundation of knowledge both about memory and about the aging process itself. The hope is that such information can be used, eventually, to improve the life quality of our ever growing elderly population. There has been a remarkable demographic shift in the population with regard to the percentage of people over 65 years of age, not only in the United States but in most countries of the world (e.g., Kinsella & Gist, 1995; Martin, 1988). For example, in the first half of this century many Western industrial nations added 20 or more years to the average life expectancies at birth. In the United States, 75 million babies were born between 1946 and 1964. In the year 2011, this "baby boom" generation will begin to reach age 65, and by the year 2030 one in every five people will be over the age of 65 in this country. The baby boom generation will place a tremendous strain on specialized services and programs required for the elderly. It is essential that policy-makers begin now to prepare for these increased demands. Although demographers do not all agree on the exact statistics, approximately 10% of the people in the United States currently over 65 have clear symptoms of dementia or disorientation, and probably half of these have Alzheimer's disease. This is an enormous absolute number of people for our health care systems to contend with, and these numbers will clearly rise as we reach the twenty-first century. For this reason there has been a large increase in biomedical research directed toward understanding and attenuating or preventing the devastating, dementing illnesses that occur with increasing frequency as we age.

The full expression of cognitive change and underlying neurobiological hallmarks that characterize Alzheimer's disease apparently are observed together only in humans. Although an identical disease pattern is not found in other animals, contributions to the understanding of Alzheimer's disease can be made by their study in a number of ways. For example, one of the clearest and most consistent signs of the disease manifests itself in profound changes in cognition. Thus one approach has been to damage selectively different brain systems known to be important for mnemonic and attentional functions (e.g., medial temporal lobe structures and the basal forebrain cholinergic system) and to study the resultant deficits observed in these animals with an eye toward development of possible repair or treatment strategies. In fact, the use of animal models has played an important role in the overall development of experimental approaches to understanding Alzheimer's disease and normal aging, as discussed in a number of other places (e.g., Bartus, 1988; Bartus, Dean, Pontecorvo, & Flicker, 1985; Greenberg et al., 1996; Hazzard, Bronson, McClearn, & Strong, 1992; Kesner, 1988; Kesner, Crutcher, & Measom, 1986; Kotula & Wisniewski, 1995; Masoro, 1991; Mohs, 1988; Morgan & Finch, 1987; Olton & Wenk, 1987). A very exciting new avenue of investigation has been inspired by recent advances in our understanding of the genetic determinants of Alzheimer's disease (reviewed in Greenberg et al., 1996) and has been implemented through the introduction of a number of human genomic transgenes in an attempt to reproduce Alzheimer's disease pathological symptoms in rodents (Loring et al., 1996). The rationale behind these kinds of experiments is that overexpression of various genetic markers, such as the amyloid precursor protein (APP) or the E4 isoform of apolipoprotein E (apoE4), which are highly correlated with the disease in humans, should produce an animal that will bear the neurologic and cognitive defects that are caused by this genetic makeup in humans.

A parallel and important effort has also been made toward understanding the majority of the population of elderly who are thought to be aging "normally." In fact, most of us will *not* become demented but will experience changes throughout the life span that might be considered to be a natural result of the course of development. One outstanding problem that remains in the empirical domain in gerontology concerns the proper diagnosis of early symptoms of pathological states such as Alzheimer's disease. This issue has been particularly clearly expressed by Albert in her discussion of current attempts to separate disease-related from disease-free states of the elderly: ". . . one is also likely to be able to understand any disease process better if the substrate upon which it is based is well understood. Normal aging changes influence the presentation of illness, its response to treatment, and its potential complications" (Albert, 1988a, p. 5). Therefore the challenge is to distinguish changes that occur as a normal result of the aging process from those that occur as a result of a pathological condition.

A decade ago, a National Institute of Mental Health (NIMH) work group outlined a proposed set of diagnostic criteria designed to detect changes in memory in healthy individuals during the latter decades of adult life (Crook et al., 1986). An example of a major problem that arises for experiments conducted using older humans is the inadvertent inclusion of a subgroup of elderly individuals with early dementia symptoms. This, of course, would magnify unfairly the observed differences between the young and old groups. The NIMH work group concluded, even at that time, that there was a large enough number of studies in which the elderly participants received extensive medical, neurological, and psychiatric evaluations to confidently state that memory function is altered with age, even in unusually healthy individuals (for reviews of cognitive change with normal aging, see Albert, 1988b; Craik, 1984; Crook & Larrabee, 1989; Flicker, Ferris, Crook, Bartus, & Reisberg, 1985; Light, 1991; Poon, 1985; Swihart & Pirozzolo, 1988). They called the kind of change in memory that can be normally expected to occur as one ages "age-associated memory impairment" (AAMI). The development of criteria to diagnose AAMI was an important step in the facilitation of communication between investigators that study later-life memory loss. Numerous experiments conducted in the ensuing years have validated the need for consistent AAMI diagnostic criteria across laboratories. Consistent criteria are particularly critical when constructing groups for studies that test the efficacy of therapeutic intervention, in which judgments must be made as to whether individuals deviate from the norm enough to suspect a disease process.

The benefits from defining normal memory change with age goes beyond just the diagnosis of disease. The accuracy of such evaluations can be expected to have a major impact on our elderly As retirement age becomes more flexible and judgments concerning competence are separated from chronological age (e.g., Palmore, Fillenbaum, & George, 1984), the need to prevent inaccurate stereotypes grows ("ageism," Butler, 1969). A balanced, realistic appraisal both of the kinds of memory changes that can be expected and of the benefits to be gained from older persons' experience should work against these negative stereotypes. These positive assessments may arise in part from the necessity to keep more older persons in the work force to maintain an economically competitive and productive nation. This will not occur, however, without the confidence of the elderly in their own competence.

While it is true that certain individuals react to AAMI by developing strategies for coping with these memory changes (such as making lists of important things to remember for the day), to other people age-related memory impairment goes beyond inconvenience. To these people such memory loss is greatly distressing and can lead to unwarranted fears about becoming senile. The large number of people who are truly disturbed by this normal developmental change in memory underscores the importance of developing effective means of understanding and treating this problem. This is the context in which animal models of *normal* age-related memory deficits can become very important. Some advantages in using animals rather than directly studying humans include the facts that the experimenter can much more easily have control over the genotype, past experience, disease, diet, contact with environmental toxins, and social interactions than would ever be possible with humans. Furthermore, it is possible to use invasive strategies in animals to gain deeper understanding of the neurobiological processes that might be responsible for these changes.

Numerous approaches have been taken to the study of behavior in old animals, with the goal of gaining a deeper understanding of the information-processing changes that occur during aging in humans. Such experiments have been conducted using a variety of species, including rats, mice, guinea pigs, cats, rabbits, birds, mollusks, and nonhuman primates. Examples of the kinds of behaviors that have been examined in old organisms as a function of age are general *activity* and exploratory behaviors (e.g., Bailey, Castellucci, Hoister, & Chen, 1983; Bickford, Heron, Young, Gerhardt, & de la Garza, 1992; Davis, 1978; Elias, Elias, & Eleftheriou, 1975; Fletcher & Mowbray, 1962; Gage, Dunnett, & Björklund, 1989; Goodrick, 1971; Markowska et al., 1989, 1990; Slonaker, 1907; Soffié & Lejeune, 1991; Spangler et al., 1994; Wallace, Krauter, & Campbell, 1980b; Winocur, 1991), *appetitively motivated* behaviors such as operant tasks (e.g., Campbell & Haroutunian, 1981; Corke, 1964; Desroches, Kimbrell, & Allison, 1964; Goodrick, 1975a; Pontecorvo, Clissold, & Conti, 1988) or 2- to 14-choice discrimination problems (e.g., Barnes et al., 1990; Barnes, Nadel, & Honig, 1980; Bartus & Dean, 1979; Beatty, Bierley, & Boyd, 1985; Beatty, Clouse, & Bierley, 1987; Bierley, Rixen, Troster, & Beatty, 1986; Campbell, Krauter, & Wallace, 1980; Caprioli, Ghirardi, Giuliani, Ramacci, & Angelucci, 1991; de Toledo-Morrell & Morrell, 1985; de Toledo-Morrell, Morrell, & Fleming, 1984a; de Toledo-Morrell, Morrell, Fleming, & Cohen, 1984b; Fields, 1953; Gallagher, Bostock, & King, 1985; Geinisman, de Toledo-Morrell, & Morrell, 1986a, 1986b; Goodrick, 1968; Huidobro et al., 1993; Ingram, London, & Goodrick, 1981; Kay & Sime, 1962; Lebrun, Durkin, Marighetto, & Jaffard, 1990; Lowy et al., 1985; Moss, Rosene, & Peters, 1988; Munn, 1950; Ohta, Matsumoto, & Watanabe, 1993; Presty et al., 1987; Roman, Alescio-Lautier, & Soumireu-Mourat, 1996; Spangler, Chachich, Curtis, & Ingram, 1989; Spangler et al., 1994, 1995; Stone, 1929a, 1929b; Tanila, Taira, Piepponen, & Honkanen, 1994; van der Staay, Blokland, & Raaijmakers, 1990; van Gool, Mirmiran, & van Haaren, 1985; Verzar-McDougall, 1957; Wallace, Krauter, & Campbell, 1980a; Wenk, Stoehr, Mobley, Gurney, & Morris, 1996; Winocur, 1984), and *aversively motivated* behaviors such as water escape tasks (e.g., Abdulla, Abu-Bakra, Calaminici, Stephenson, & Sinden, 1995; Aitken & Meaney, 1989; Barnes, Rao, Foster, & McNaughton, 1992; Beigon, Greenberger, & Segal, 1986; Burwell & Gallagher, 1993; Chouinard, Gallagher, Yasuda, Wolfe, & McKinney, 1995; Clarke, Gage, Nilsson, & Björklund, 1986; Decker, Pelleymounter, & Gallagher, 1988; Fischer, Chen, Gage, & Björklund, 1991; Fordyce & Wehner, 1993; Foster, Barnes, Rao, & McNaughton, 1991; Frick, Baxter, Markowska, Olton, & Price, 1995; Gage & Björklund, 1986; Gage, Dunnett, & Björklund, 1984; Gage, Kelly, & Björklund, 1984; Gallagher & Burwell, 1989; Gallagher et al., 1990; Jordon & Sokoloff, 1959; Lindner & Schallert, 1988; Markowska et al., 1989; Nilsson & Gage, 1993; Pelleymounter, Smith, & Gallagher, 1987; Pitsikas, Brambilla, & Borsini, 1993; Port, Murphy, Magee, & Seybold, 1996; Rapp, Rosenberg, & Gallagher, 1987; Shen & Barnes, 1996; Smith, Gallagher, & Leslie, 1995; Turner & Deupree, 1991; Vasquez et al., 1983), classical conditioning (e.g., Buchanan & Powell, 1988; Graves & Solomon, 1985; Harrison & Buchwald, 1983; Weiss & Thompson, 1991; Woodruff-Pak, Lavond, Logan, & Thompson, 1987), or other shock-motivated tasks (e.g., Doty &

Doty, 1964; Gold, McGaugh, Hankins, Rose, & Vasquez, 1981; Martinez & Rigter, 1983; McNamara, Benignus, Benignus, & Miller, 1977; Normile & Altman, 1992; Port et al., 1996; Spangler et al., 1995; Sprott, 1978; Yerkes, 1909; Zornetzer, Thompson, & Rogers, 1982). Depending on complex sets of interacting variables, old animals' behavioral performance can be either similar to or very different from the behavior of young animals when tested in these situations. Instead of cataloging all behavioral changes that have been demonstrated with age and contrasting these with the behaviors that are preserved in aging (for such a review, see Barnes, 1990), the focus herein is on one subset of the animal work that is illustrative of the kinds of nonhuman data that can be obtained and applied to the human condition.

III. EXAMPLE OF CORRESPONDENCE BETWEEN AGE-RELATED MEMORY CHANGE IN HUMANS AND IN RODENTS

One approach to the study of animal models of memory aging is to choose a behavior in the species of study that has some analog in human behavior. If this behavior changes in an age-dependent manner in both the animal model and the human case, then the task of making inferences from the nonhuman model is simplified. Along with this behavioral requirement, it is also important to determine whether the same neural structures are responsible for the production of these similar behaviors between these species. It is only when evidence that such a brain and behavior relationship exists in both species that one can strongly argue for extending potential treatment strategies from one animal to another. As an example of such a correspondence, I will outline the evidence that spatial memory deficits occur in elderly humans and in old rats, and, in the next section, that age-related changes in the hippocampal formation may be responsible for the observed behavioral change in both species.

The kind of learning and memory that will be referred to as "spatial" involves the ability to navigate effectively through an environment, integrating self-motion with landmarks or prominent features of the space. In rats, for example, a consistent sense of direction appears to be essential for associating landmark information with reward locations (Dudchenko, Goodridge, Seiterle, & Taube, 1997; Martin, Harley, Smith, Hoyles, & Hynes, 1997). The first suggestions that elderly humans may experience difficulty with remembering spatial environmental relationships were anecdotal. For example, it was noted that the elderly would express feeling less confident than they once had been in finding new places. This included the observation that older individuals might depend more on maps and detailed procedural instructions for directions rather than using internal representations ("cognitive maps," reviewed in O'Keefe & Nadel, 1978) of the environment to understand where the new place was located. Also, family members of persons with Alzheimer's disease as well as nursing home staff frequently complain that patients often get lost even in very familiar environments. Especially in recent experiments, this idea has been more systematically assessed in "healthy" older adults. The general pattern of results confirms that older individuals do not have as effective spatial representations of their environments as do young adults (Bruce & Herman, 1983; Caplan & Lipman, 1995; Cherry & Park, 1989; Evans, Brennan, Skorpanich, & Held, 1984; Flicker, Bartus, Crook, & Ferris, 1984; Kirasic, 1991; Kirasic & Allen, 1985; Kirasic, Allen, & Haggerty, 1992; Kirasic & Bernicki, 1990; Light & Zelinski, 1983; Lipman & Caplan, 1992; Ohta & Kirasic, 1983; Ohta, Walsh, & Krauss, 1981; Park, Cherry, Smith, & Lafronza, 1990; Park, Puglisi, & Lutz, 1982; Perlmutter, Metzger, Nezworski, & Miller, 1981; Pezdek, 1983; Sharps & Gollin, 1987; Thomas, 1985; Uttl & Graf, 1993; Waddell & Rogoff, 1981; Walsh, Krauss, & Regnier, 1981; Weber, Brown, & Weldon, 1978; Zelinski & Light, 1988).

A good example of changes in spatial memory performance in older people comes from an experiment conducted by Uttl and Graf (1993), who tested people of six different "decade categories" from 20s to 70s. In this experiment, participants attended an exhibit at a science center that was held in a single large room which included paintings, displays, diagrams, and various tables of exhibit material. Half of the participants in the experiment were instructed to attend to the detailed arrangement of the items in the exhibit and were informed that they would be asked about it later. The other half were not given those instructions, nor were they told that they would be tested later. All subjects were tested individually. After navigating through the exhibit, each subject was given a copy of the floor plan and a book of photographs of the exhibit and was asked to match the photographs with the position in the exhibit hall. There was no effect of instruction type on performance across age. Performance on this task was similar among persons tested in their 20s, 30s, 40s, and 50s; however, the number of correctly located items dropped sharply for people in their 60s and 70s. This suggests an age-related difference in spatial memory performance, in a real-life situation, that can be detected in the sixth decade.

There are a number of ways in which to test spatial memory in rats, and because these animals are excellent foragers, they tend to learn these kinds of problems relatively easily. The first animal experiments that involved a systematic battery of tests of memory in rats of different ages are those of Stone (1929a, 1929b). Although his results concerning the effect of aging on memory, particularly spatial memory in the 14–unit T-maze (see Fig. 1A), were somewhat unclear (see Ingram, 1988), it is important to understand the reasons that lead to the ambiguity for the critical evaluation of other experiments using aged animals. Stone concluded that, overall, his older animals did not show striking cognitive impairments compared with his younger animals. A small proportion of his oldest animals, however, did appear to show some deficits. The rats that Stone used for his aging experiments were a relatively long-lived strain (3-year average life span), and he tested them at 2 years of age. This means that Stone's findings probably reflect the behavior of rats through late maturity but not old age. This is especially likely since more recent studies using

A

B

C

D

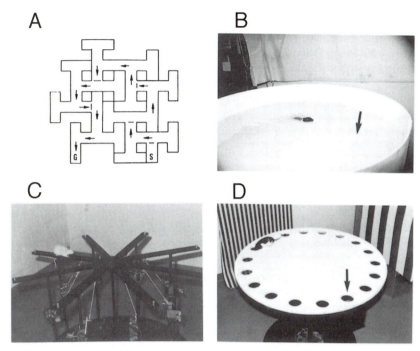

FIGURE 1   (A) Diagram of the 14-unit T-maze, or stone maze. The start box is indicated by an "S," and the arrows show the direction in which the animals must travel to find the goal box correctly (indicated by "G"). Guillotine doors are used to divide the maze into five segments (indicated by lines at choice points) so that animals are not allowed to go backward through the maze. Motivation for performance can be either food or water reward at the goal or footshock. (After Ingram, 1988.) (B) Photograph of a rat swimming in the spatial version of the Morris water task. The water is made opaque so that the submerged platform is not visible to the animal. The rat must use the cues distal to the pool to locate the escape platform. The arrow indicates the location of the hidden platform. (C) Photograph of a radial eight-arm maze, with a rat prepared for and attached to electrophysiological recording equipment. Food reward is available at the ends of each of the arms in aluminum cups, and on any given trial the cup is baited only once. (D) Photograph of a circular platform task, illustrating the rat making an "error" by looking into a hole that is not over the dark escape chamber. The arrow points to the correct location of the hole over the goal, which the rat must find on the basis of the features of the environment distal to the platform. [Reprinted with permission from *Learning and memory: A biological view* (J. L. Martinez and R. P. Kesner, Eds.), 2nd Ed., pp. 259–296. Academic Press, San Diego.]

multiple-unit T-mazes *and* shorter-lived rat strains consistently find age-related deficits on this problem (Barnes et al., 1990; Goldman, Berman, Gershon, Murphy, & Altman, 1987; Goodrick, 1968, 1972, 1973a, 1973b, 1975b; Ingram, 1985; Klein & Michel, 1977; Skalicky, Bubna-Littitz, & Hofecker, 1984; Spangler et al., 1989, 1994, 1995; Verzar-McDougall, 1957). Thus, it is particularly important that the answer to the question What constitutes an old animal? in the species of interest be established. It is clear that chronological age may not be the only important factor determining the true age of an organism (e.g., Bourliere, 1970; Ingram, 1983), as can clearly be seen in the extent of individual differences between humans of a similar age and even animals of the same genetic stock. Chronological age, however, is probably still the best overall predictor of the functional or biological age of the organism (Costa & McCrae, 1980). For humans old age is most often considered those ages past 65, whereas for rats it is those ages past the point of 50% mortality for the strain in question, which is about 2 years for rats commonly used today (approximately 1 year less than the strain used by Stone).

Several other tasks have been used to assess the spatial memory of rats of different ages. One such task is the radial maze (Olton & Samuelson, 1976). In its most common configuration, there are eight arms radiating from a central platform, with the end of each arm containing reward (Fig. 1C). The solution to the problem posed by this task is to obtain a reward at each arm end without reentering any of the arms where reward has previously been obtained. Thus the animal must remember which spatial location it has recently visited and go next only to locations not yet visited on that particular trial. The animal's memory for where it has been and where to go next on any given trial utilizing visual cues external to the maze has been called "spatial working memory." Perhaps one of the best replicated results in the animal memory literature in gerontology is that old rats take more trials to reach a given "criterion" or proficiency of performance on the radial maze than do young animals (Barnes et al., 1980, 1990; Beatty et al., 1985, 1987; Campbell et al., 1980; Caprioli et al., 1991; de Toledo-Morrell & Morrell, 1985; de Toledo-Morrell et al., 1984a, 1984b; Gallagher et al., 1985; Geinisman et al., 1986a, 1986b; Huidobro et al., 1993; Ingram et al., 1981; Lebrun et al., 1990; van Gool et al., 1985; Wallace et al., 1980a). A number of lines of evidence suggest that the older rats' difficulty with this maze is a cognitive one. These include the facts that (i) there are no correlations between the recovery cycles of visually evoked potentials and maze performance between age groups, indicating that changes in visual system sensitivity measured by this method cannot account for the behavioral change observed in old rats (van Gool et al., 1985); (ii) overtraining the motor procedural aspects of the task does not eliminate the age difference when a new environment must be learned (Gallagher et al., 1985); and (iii) nonspatial working memory tasks on the radial maze, where the solution depends on maze arm cues that are made independent of place, are performed equally well by young and old rats even though the nonspatial version tends to be more difficult than the more typically used spatial one (Barnes, Green, Baldwin, & Johnson, 1987).

The circular platform task (see Fig. 1D) was first developed for age comparisons of spatial memory and does not require food deprivation, shock, motor dexterity, speed, or stamina. This task utilizes the fact that rats naturally prefer small dark places to bright open spaces. Of the 18 holes that line the periphery of the brightly lit platform, the rat is required to find the one leading to a dark escape chamber. The escape hole is always in the same location with respect to the distal cues in the environment, and the most effective strategy for task solution is a spatial one. The general results are that the old animals are worse at remembering the spatial location of the escape chamber from day to day than are the younger rats (Barnes, 1979; Barnes & McNaughton, 1985; Barnes et al., 1980, 1990; Markowska et al., 1989). The Morris water task (Fig. 1B) has also been used to test spatial memory of young and old rats. In this task water is used to motivate the animal to find a hidden escape platform in a large pool (Morris, 1981). Older animals consistently show poorer retention of the hidden platform location from day to day than do younger animals (Abdulla et al., 1995; Aitken & Meaney, 1989; Barnes at al., 1992; Beigon et al., 1986; Burwell & Gallagher, 1993; Chouinard et al., 1995; Clarke et al., 1986; Fischer et al., 1991; Foster et al., 1991; Frick et al., 1995; Gage & Björklund, 1986; Gage, Dunnett, & Björklund, 1984; Gage, Kelly, & Björklund, 1984; Gallagher & Burwell, 1989; Gallagher et al., 1990; Lindner & Schallert, 1988; Markowska et al., 1989; Nilsson & Gage, 1993; Pelleymounter et al., 1987; Pitsikas et al., 1993; Rapp et al., 1987; Smith et al., 1995; Turner & Deupree, 1991). If, however, the escape platform is raised above the surface of the water so that the task becomes a visual discrimination problem, then the older rats' performance is just as good as the younger rats' performance (Rapp et al., 1987). Taken in conjunction with the other spatial tasks discussed, it appears safe to conclude that spatial information processing poses particular problems for older rats, just as it appears to do for older humans.

IV. INVOLVEMENT OF THE HIPPOCAMPUS IN LEARNING AND MEMORY

Although disagreements exist on the details of the scope of information processing accomplished by the rodent hippocampus (e.g., Cohen & Eichenbaum, 1993; Gabriel, Sparenborg, & Stolar, 1986; Hirsh, 1980; Kesner & DiMattia, 1984; McNaughton et al., 1996; McNaughton & Morris, 1987; Mishkin, Malamut, & Bachevalier, 1984; O'Keefe & Nadel, 1978; Olton, 1983; Rawlins, 1985; Rupniak & Gaffan, 1987; Squire, 1992; Sutherland & Rudy, 1989; Teylor & DiScenna, 1986), there is little disagreement from those investigators as to the importance of the hippocampus for spatial learning (e.g., Barnes, 1988; Barnes et al., 1994). Animals with lesions of the hippocampus or its major inputs show striking impairments in their ability to acquire the 14-unit T-maze task (Bresnahan et al., 1988), the radial maze task (e.g., Jarrard, 1978; Olton, Walker, & Gage, 1978), the circular platform task (McNaughton, Barnes, Meltzer, & Sutherland, 1989), and the Morris water task (e.g., Morris, Garrud, Rawlins, & O'Keefe, 1982; Sutherland, Whishaw, & Kolb, 1983). Thus, the hippocampus is a clear candidate for a brain structure that contributes to age-related spatial memory deficits in rats.

The hippocampus has been implicated in the normal operation of learning and memory in humans since the discovery that bilateral surgical removal of the medial temporal lobes results in profound amnesia (Scoville & Milner, 1957). Patient H.M., who underwent this surgery, has not recovered his ability to acquire many kinds of new information and certainly shows an inability to navigate normally in new environments (Corkin, 1984). Although H.M. is significantly more impaired in the

A

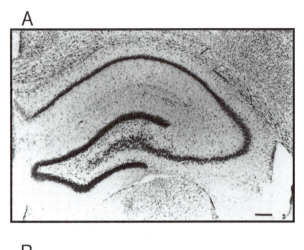

B

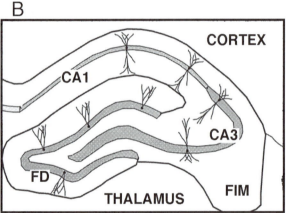

FIGURE 2   (A) Photomicrograph of a frontal section of the rat hippocampal formation. Calibration bar: 200 μm. (B) Outline of the section in part A labeling the subareas of the hippocampal formation. CA1, CA3 = hippocampus proper, pyramidal cell fields; FD = fascia dentata, granule cell fields; FIM = fimbria, a bundle of fibers the contains some of the afferents to and efferents from the hippocampus. [Reprinted with permission from *Learning and memory: A biological view* (J. L. Martinez and R. P. Kesner, Eds.), 2nd Ed., pp. 259–296. Academic Press, San Diego.]

recall of absolute and relative locations of objects than are patients with hippocampal damage restricted to the right temporal lobe (Smith & Milner, 1981), impairments have been observed in patients with right hippocampal damage in learning a correct path through a stylus maze (Corkin, 1965; Milner, 1965) and in spatial object recognition (Pigott & Milner, 1993). Furthermore, memory deficits have been observed even in a case in which an ischemic episode resulted in restricted bilateral damage to area CA1 (see Fig. 2) of the hippocampus (Zola-Morgan, Squire, &

Amaral, 1986). Taken together, these findings strongly indicate hippocampal involvement in normal human memory. The hippocampal formation also shows early signs of age-related change in the brains of normal humans (Ball, 1977, 1978; Hasan & Glees, 1973; Tomlinson & Henderson, 1976). Recently, age differences in hippocampal volume have been observed in healthy humans with the use of structural brain-imaging methods (de Toledo-Morrell, Sullivan, Morrell, Spanovic, & Spencer, 1995). Furthermore, the hippocampus and associated medial temporal lobe structures certainly play a role in the etiology of Alzheimer's disease (Eberling, Jagust, Reed, & Baker, 1992; Hyman, Van Hoesen, Damasio, & Barnes, 1984; Hyman, Van Hoesen, Kromer, & Damasio, 1986; Khachaturian, 1985; Killiany et al., 1993; Lippa, Hamos, Pulaski-Salo, Degennaro, & Drachman, 1992; Rossor, Emson, Mountjoy, Roth, & Iversen, 1980; Scheff & Price, 1993; Van Hoesen, Solodkin, & Hyman, 1995).

The study of the hippocampus of the rat has provided important information concerning the function of this structure in humans. Although certain cell fields within the hippocampal formation have greatly expanded in the human brain (Rosene & Van Hoesen, 1987), the general patterns of cell connections are remarkably conserved throughout the evolution of mammals. The neural circuit diagrams of the hippocampus of humans and rats are fundamentally the same, and this structure is important for memory in both of these species. Finally, age-related alterations are known to occur in the hippocampus of both humans and rats, and both species show changes in spatial memory with age. These factors have made the use of the aged rat as an experimental model of aging human memory a productive one. It has led to a better understanding of the basic mechanisms of memory and how it is altered during the normal process of aging, as is illustrated in the examples that follow. Memory deficits have also been observed in nonhuman primates (Bachevalier, 1993; Bachevalier et al., 1991; Lai, Moss, Killiany, Rosene, & Herndon, 1995; Presty et al., 1987; Rapp & Amaral, 1991), but these experiments will not be the focus of the present selective review (for reviews, see Rapp & Amaral, 1992; Walker et al., 1988).

V. RELATION OF SPATIAL BEHAVIORAL CHANGES IN AGING TO UNDERLYING NEURAL MECHANISMS

A number of laboratories have compared age-related changes in the rat hippocampus to spatial behavior for the reasons already outlined. In the following, examples of work attempting to correlate changes in the hippocampus in aging rats with their behavior will be presented. The experiments include approaches using electrophysiological, neuroanatomical, and neurochemical methods for correlation of brain function with behavior.

A. Electrophysiological Approaches

As outlined by Martinez, Barea-Rodriguez, and Derrick in Chapter 6, the hippocampus possesses a very interesting form of neuronal plasticity (only long-term potentiation (LTP or LTE) will be discussed here; see Chapter 6 for a more complete discussion of the types of plasticity that can be found in this structure). Hebb (1949), in his influential book *The Organization of Behavior,* first proposed that if neural connections interacted in a certain manner, then lasting cellular changes (i.e., associations) would be formed and could provide the substrate of memory:

> When an axon of cell A is near enough to excite a cell B and repeatedly or persistently takes part in firing it, some growth process or metabolic change takes place in one or both cells such that A's efficiency, as one of the cells firing B, is increased. (Hebb 1949, p. 68)

Figure 3 illustrates the principles involved in such synaptic modification. The upper diagram in Fig. 3A shows three cells with their dendrites, axons, and synaptic connections. Neuron 1 is receiving information from the visual system about the existence of a clock tower on the university grounds. Initially, there is only one effective synapse, in this case from neuron 1 onto neuron 3. For descriptive purposes, the output of neuron 3 can be thought of as contributing to the mental image of this clock tower. The lower diagram in Fig. 3A shows the same three cells. However, at this point in time neuron 2 is receiving information about the sound of the chimes in the clock tower. Initially, the synapse from neuron 2 onto neuron 3 is ineffective so that no image is elicited by hearing the chimes. The upper diagram in Fig. 3B illustrates the situation in which the chimes are heard simultaneously with the visual image of the clock tower. Pairing of information from neuron 1 and neuron 2 occurs as their activities converge onto neuron 3. Hebb's rule implies that such pairing will result in the strengthening of the synapse from neuron 2 onto neuron 3. After this pairing, the previously weak synapse from neuron 2 becomes strengthened. The result of this can be seen in the lower diagram of Fig. 3B. Now the sound of the chimes *alone* leads to the mental image of the clock tower, without neuron 1 being active and without the real clock tower being present. This, after all, is the essence of associative learning, and it is this kind of associative property that has been demonstrated to occur in neurons in the hippocampus (through LTP) that will be described in the following.

Before 1973, the changes that could be induced in synaptic transmission in the mammalian central nervous system were much too short-lived to be able to underlie more enduring forms of learning and memory. Bliss, Lømo, and Gardner-Medwin were able to modify the strength of synaptic connections for longer periods of time by applying stimulus patterns to the input axons of the hippocampal cells (Bliss & Gardner-Medwin, 1973; Bliss & Lømo, 1973). They called this phenomenon long-lasting potentiation [it was later called long-term potentiation (LTP) by Douglas

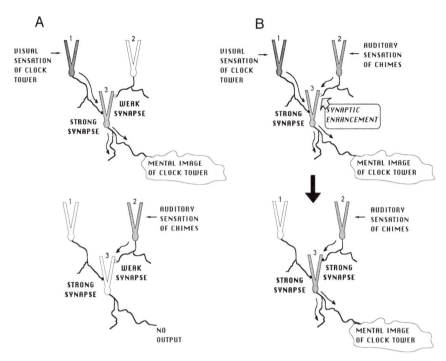

FIGURE 3   Schematic diagram illustrating the fundamental principle of associative memory resulting from synaptic enhancement according to Hebb's rule. (A) In the initial conditions, neuron 1 is imagined to begin with a strong connection to neuron 3 (see upper diagram), whereas neuron 2 has a weak, ineffective connection to neuron 3 (see lower diagram). (B) As a result of pairing the activation of neuron 1 and neuron 2 (upper diagram), an "association" process takes place that results in the enhancement of the connection from neuron 2 to neuron 3. Neuron 2 is now able to transmit information to neuron 3 (bottom diagram). See text for more description of this association process. [Reprinted from *Learning and memory: A biological view* (J. L. Martinez and R. P. Kesner, Eds.), 2nd Ed., pp. 259–296. Academic Press, San Diego.]

and Goddard (1975) and long-term enhancement (LTE) by McNaughton, Douglas, and Goddard (1978) and will be referred to here as LTP]. One of the primary reasons for the interest in LTP, of course, is that it shows the kind of associative property that was illustrated in Fig. 3. This associativity was originally demonstrated by McNaughton et al. (1978). Its durability (e.g., Barnes, 1979) and specificity for the synaptic elements involved in the information storage event (Levy & Steward, 1979; McNaughton & Barnes, 1977) are also features that make this kind of change at the synapse a very good candidate mechanism for the way in which memory is constructed in the nervous system (see Chapter 6). Furthermore, LTP can be observed in human hippocampal tissue (Haas, 1987) as well as in other mammals.

The hippocampus, of course, is not the only place in the brain capable of undergoing this type of synaptic plasticity (e.g., Lee, 1983; Racine & Milgram, 1983; for review, see Barnes et al., 1994).

Landfield and his colleagues were the first to report changes in the plastic properties of hippocampal synapses in aged, memory-deficient rats (e.g., Landfield, 1988). These experiments were carried out in the hippocampal area CA1 (Fig. 2), both in intact anesthetized rats (Landfield, McGaugh, & Lynch, 1978) and in the hippocampal slice preparation (Landfield & Lynch, 1977). They found that the time course of frequency potentiation, a shorter-lasting process than LTP, was significantly reduced in the aged animals. Furthermore, older animals took longer to reach asymptotic levels of LTP. They did, however, eventually reach the same magnitude of synaptic change as did the young animals and were able to maintain LTP over the 30-min experimental test interval. In these initial experiments, the animal's behavior was not individually related to its potential for synaptic change. In 1979, Barnes published an experiment in which the spatial memory of young and old animals was assessed on the circular platform and later compared to the plasticity of their perforant path–granule cell synapses (Fig. 2). Following behavioral testing, the rats were implanted with chronically indwelling recording electrodes below the granule cell layer of the hippocampus (fascia dentata, FD) and with stimulating electrodes in the major afferent input pathway from the entorhinal cortex (Fig. 2). In this manner, the behavioral performance of an individual rat could be related to the induction and maintenance of LTP at that rat's hippocampal synapses. Following repetitive application of LTP-inducing stimulation in FD (in the present case at intervals of once every 24 hr), the same magnitude of LTP was eventually reached in both the young and old rats (Barnes, 1979; Barnes & McNaughton, 1980), reminiscent of Landfield's results in area CA1.

Because the animals were chronically prepared, the synaptic responses could be monitored over days (Barnes, 1979) or weeks (Barnes & McNaughton, 1980) following the cessation of the LTP-inducing stimulation. Such measurement revealed that the decay of the synaptic strength back to baseline levels was much faster in the old rats than it was in the young rats (time constant of decay in young = 37 days, old = 17 days). More importantly, when the level of accuracy of spatial behavior in individual rats was related to the maintenance of LTP, a statistically significant correlation was found between how fast the change in synaptic strength decayed back to baseline levels and how good the rat's spatial memory had been. For example, the old rat with the poorest spatial memory also had the fastest decaying LTP. These experiments thus provided the first correlational evidence that LTP and spatial memory processes might be related, and further experiments suggested that there was a rather striking correspondence between forgetting rates of young and old animals on the circular platform task and the decay rates of LTP (Barnes & McNaughton, 1985). Moreover, using the radial eight-arm maze spatial memory task, de Toledo-Morrell and her colleagues showed that old animals deficient in spatial memory as assessed by this task *also* showed faster decay of hippocampal LTP (de Toledo-Morrell & Morrell, 1985; de Toledo-Morrell, Geinisman, & Morrell, 1988; Geinisman, de Toledo-Morrell, Morrell, Persina, & Rossi, 1992b) and were slower to develop hippocampal "kindling" (de Toledo-Morrell et al., 1984a, 1988; de Toledo-Morrell & Morrell, 1991). This latter phenomenon (Goddard, 1967) represents another long-lasting form of synaptic plasticity that can be induced by repeated stimulation of hippocampal afferents and, once induced, mimics spontaneous epileptiform activity. Again, the critical finding includes observations that there were significant correlations between good spatial memory and the speed of the kindling process. Although more of the old animals showed poorer spatial memory compared with the young animals, the old animals that did not show behavioral deficits also did not show impaired hippocampal kindling.

Taken together, these data suggest that the biological processes involved in frequency potentiation, LTP, and kindling in the hippocampus are compromised in aged animals, and the changes in the latter two phenomena are correlated with an animal's ability to learn and remember a spatial problem.

B. Neuroanatomical Approaches

Neuroanatomical approaches to the study of memory are outlined in more detail by Black and Greenough in Chapter 2. For the purpose of the present chapter, the work of Geinisman and his colleagues is described, who have conducted quantitative analyses of the structure of the aged hippocampal formation in relation to spatial behavior in rats (for a review, see Geinisman, de Toledo-Morrell, Morrell, & Heller, 1995). Geinisman et al. (1986a, 1986b) took advantage of the fact that during normal aging, variability occurs in the severity of the memory deficits observed in any given old rat. They tested old animals on the radial eight-arm maze (Fig. 1C) and constructed experimental groups of rats on the basis of memory scores *before* they quantified the number of synapses in the middle third of the molecular layer of the fascia dentata. The three groups ($n = 6$ in each group) used were (1) young rats that reached the behavioral criterion, (2) old rats that reached the behavioral criterion, and (3) old rats that could not reach the behavioral criterion set on the radial maze. Criterion performance consisted of three consecutive trials with no errors, and the rats were tested for a maximum of 30 trials. Although none of the old rats in the "memory-intact" group performed as well as the two best young animals and four of the six old animals in this group took more trials to criterion than the worst young animal, the means between the young and memory-intact old group did not differ statistically. None of the old animals in the "memory-impaired" group were able to reach the behavioral criterion in the 30-day testing period, and, of course, they differed significantly in their behavior from both the young and memory-intact old animals.

The number of synapses per granule cell in the FD of young and old animals was estimated using a serial section synapse reconstruction method. All brain sections were coded to ensure that anatomical judgments were made in a blind fashion with respect to age and behavioral group. The results indicated that there was a 17% decrease in the number of axospinous synapses per neuron in the memory-impaired old animals [these data have also been confirmed using modern stereological methods (e.g., West, 1993) that allow unbiased estimates of the number of synapses per neuron (Geinisman, de Toledo-Morrell, Morrell, Persina, & Rossi, 1992a)]. They were also able to distinguish between synaptic contacts that were perforated and those that were nonperforated with the serial section methods. Selection into these two synaptic types were based on whether the postsynaptic density was continuous (nonperforated) or whether it showed discontinuity in any section (perforated). Using a rank-order correlation for the number of trials to criterion and choice accuracy, it was only the number of perforated synapses (not nonperforated) in the two groups of old animals that were significantly correlated with the behavioral performance on the radial maze (the fewer the number of perforated synapses, the poorer the performance on the maze). These findings suggest that perforated synapses may play a particularly important role in spatial learning (Geinisman et al., 1995; Geinisman, Morrell, & de Toledo-Morrell, 1987). The loss of this perforated subtype of synapses with aging may therefore contribute to the deterioration of efficient memory storage mechanisms that is particularly pronounced in some old animals.

C. Neurochemical Approaches

One line of research on the possible relationship between age-related behavioral change and neurochemical systems involves the study of the neurotransmitter acetylcholine (e.g., Bartus, Dean, Beer, & Lippa, 1982). It is, of course, clear that there are multiple transmitter systems involved both in normal aging and in Alzheimer's disease (e.g., Altman & Normile, 1986; Chan-Palay, 1988; Delfs, 1985; Rossor et al., 1980; Zornetzer, 1986). There has been, however, a strong rationale for examining changes in cholinergic activity with age in relation to the hippocampus and spatial learning and memory, because lesions of the cholinergic projection to the hippocampus produce profound deficits in spatial behavior (Hepler, Olton, Wenk, & Coyle, 1985) and because deficits in this neurotransmitter system have been found to occur during aging (e.g., Decker et al., 1988; Gallagher et al., 1990; Ingram et al., 1981; Potier, Rascol, Jazat, Lamour, & Dutar, 1992; Shen & Barnes, 1996; Taylor & Griffith, 1993; Wenk, Hepler, & Olton, 1984). The actual contribution that the cholinergic system makes to specific learning and memory processes, however, has been a matter of heated debate recently (e.g., Gallagher & Colombo, 1995), as outlined in the following paragraphs.

Recently, a promising new tool has become available for selectively lesioning cholinergic basal forebrain neurons (Wiley, 1992), which takes advantage of the fact that cholinergic neurons that project to the hippocampus and neocortex also express high levels of the low-affinity p75 NGF receptor. When a monoclonal antibody to the p75 NGF receptor (192 IgG) is coupled to the ribosomal-inactivating protein saporin, it selectively destroys neurons bearing the NGF receptor. Thus, for the first time, it has become possible to kill selectively cholinergic cells but spare noncholinergic neurons that project to the hippocampus (Baxter, Gorman, Bucci, Wiley, & Gallagher, 1995; Berger-Sweeney, Heckers, Mesulam, Wiley, & Lappi, 1994; Shen, Barnes, Wenk, & McNaughton, 1996; Wenk, Stoehr, Quintana, Mobley, & Wiley, 1994). Taken together, the results of experiments using this toxin in young rats demonstrate that performance on the spatial version of the Morris water task or reference memory aspects of the radial maze task are not disrupted following this selective loss of cholinergic cells. On the other hand, tasks that require attention, or short-term working memory, are disrupted. Thus, it appears that the cholinergic system may facilitate acquisition of a task when vigilance, or short-term memory, is required but is probably not involved in retention of this information. This may explain why it has been difficult to find significant correlations across age groups when retention of a spatial memory task is used as the behavioral variable for relation to functional cholinergic transmission (Shen & Barnes, 1996). These data underscore the importance of examining the interactions of multiple neurotransmitter systems during aging for relation to cognitive function (e.g., Decker & McGaugh, 1991) and considering how each may contribute to memory and attentional variables that determine performance.

Another approach to understanding age-related declines in learning and memory examines the role of hormones. It is well known that neural–endocrine interactions can profoundly modulate the durability of memory (e.g., Martinez et al., 1988) and that the rat hippocampus has a high concentration of one class of hormonal receptors, the glucocorticoids (McEwen, Weiss, & Schwartz, 1968). An examination of the integrity of glucocorticoid function in the aged hippocampus has led to a number of important discoveries. For example, the hippocampus is known to participate in the negative feedback regulation of the secretion of glucocorticoids in response to stress, and it is known that there is a decrease in the numbers of these receptors in the hippocampus with aging (Sapolsky, Krey, & McEwen, 1985). Because of this decrease in receptor numbers, old animals are unable to terminate the stress response as quickly as young animals. It has been proposed that one possible outcome of having sluggish negative feedback regulation, and therefore sustained high levels of circulating glucocorticoids, is a disruption of cell metabolism, which could potentially lead to cell hyperexcitability and death (e.g., Sapolsky, 1987).

Landfield and his colleagues demonstrated that the anatomical appearance of brains of animals that were adrenalectomized at 12 months of age and examined at 24 months resembled younger brains compared with old animals that had intact adrenal glands (Landfield, Baskin, & Pitler, 1981). The rats that were free of glucocorticoids for the last year of life showed a particularly striking decrease in the numbers of glial clusters and astrocytes in the hippocampus. Considering the observation that stress in early life leads to an increased number of glucocorticoid receptors in the hippocampus (Meaney et al., 1985), Meaney and colleagues tested the following hypothesis: if stress induced in early life results in an increased number of receptors in the hippocampus, then animals with early handling (or stress) should show reduced signs of aging in the hippocampus, if levels of circulating glucocorticoids were actually responsible for some of the age-related changes observed in that structure (Meaney, Aitken, van Berkel, Bhatnagar, & Sapolsky, 1988). In fact, old (24 month) animals that had been handled (stressed) in early life were shown to terminate the hormonal response to stress sooner than nonhandled (nonstressed) old animals. Furthermore, the handled rats showed less hippocampal neuronal cell loss than the nonhandled old rats and showed no memory impairments on the spatial version of the Morris water task at 24 months of age. These findings suggest that the change in feedback regulation of the adrenocortical axis with age may contribute substantially to the neural alterations that occur in the hippocampus during the course of normal aging.

It should be pointed out that there is some controversy concerning the extent to which the older methods of counting cells can lead to biased results (Wickelgren, 1996) and whether, in fact, there is detectable death of hippocampal principal cells in normal aged humans or rats when using the new stereological methods such as the optical fractionator technique (Rasmussen, Schliemann, Sørensen, Zimmer, & West, 1996; West, 1993). Although more experiments will be needed to clarify these issues to the satisfaction of all concerned, the current general consensus on this methodological question is that the unbiased stereological methods should certainly be used in any new experiment that wishes to address the question of cell loss in the aging brain. What is not clear, however, is what proportion of the older studies will be found to be incorrect in their cell count estimates. Even if it turns out in the end that all agree that there is no loss of principal cells in the hippocampus during normal aging, glucocorticoids could still play a critical role in cellular dysfunction that could profoundly change the information-processing characteristics of the system.

VI. THERAPEUTIC APPROACHES TO MEMORY LOSS WITH AGING

> Acquire learning in youth which restores the damage of old age; and if you understand that old age has wisdom for its food, you will so conduct yourself in youth that your old age will not lack sustenance. [Leonardo da Vinci, 1452–1519 (Literary Works II.1176, from translations by Richter, 1981, compiled from notebooks after his death)]

Prescriptions for successful aging have a long history, as illustrated in the foregoing quote from Leonardo da Vinci's Literary Works. More modern gerontologists have also emphasized the importance of understanding the conditions that allow certain people to maintain the highest quality of life, so that others may benefit, as stated in the following.

> One of the major aims of gerontology is to provide society and individuals with advice on the making of societal and individual choices. In order to provide good advice, it is essential that gerontology have a theory of successful aging. (Havighurst, 1961 p. 8)

Because it has been possible to establish certain correlations between changes in the psychology, chemistry, or anatomy of the aging hippocampus and performance of old animals on spatial tasks, it is now important to attempt to establish stronger potential causal links between the neural changes observed and behavior. The rationale is that if a treatment can be found that prevents a common neural change in the aged brain, and if this change is truly responsible for the behavioral deficit that is concurrently observed, then both a stronger case for this brain–behavior relationship has been established and a potential therapeutic device may have been discovered. Again, increasing numbers of promising approaches are being tested, from which certain examples will be chosen. The categories of therapeutic approach that have been selected to be discussed here include nondrug approaches, drug replacement therapies, and neural grafting methods.

A. Manipulations Not Using Drugs

Beatty and his colleagues (Beatty et al., 1985, 1987; Bierley et al., 1986) first noted that if rats were trained on the radial eight-arm maze (see Fig. 1C) for most of their lives, then their performance did not deteriorate with age (somewhat reminiscent of the foregoing quote from da Vinci). This is in striking contrast to the large deficits shown by rats that are trained in the radial maze for the first time when they are old. Furthermore, Beatty's results held even though the procedure used to test rats on the radial maze imposed a 5-hr delay between the animal's fourth and fifth choices. In addition to continuously training animals from 3 to 26 months of age on this task, Beatty and his colleagues gave some of the old rats either a 3-month break in training (Beatty et al., 1985) or a 10-month break in training (Bierley et al., 1986) before retesting their spatial memory. This allowed an assessment of whether the training experience needed to be uninterrupted and whether the effects of early training would last into old age. The results indicated that accurate spatial memory could survive at least a 10-month period without intervening training. It was also demonstrated that these old animals were not solving the task by simply traversing arms in sequential order around the maze and that they were not using other nonspatial strategies to perform accurately. The older rats were exceptional at remembering where they had been and where to go next to receive reward on any given trial.

One possible explanation of the mechanism by which maze training preserves spatial memory on the radial maze is that during the long periods of training, the animals were food restricted to approximately 80% of their normal free-feeding weights. Although there is by no means universal agreement that dietary restriction results in preserved cognition in older rats (e.g., Bond, Everitt, & Walton, 1989;

Stewart, Mitchell, & Kalant, 1989), some investigators have found consistent beneficial effects (e.g., Pitsikas, Carli, Fidecka, & Algeri, 1990). To investigate whether it was the food restriction or the radial maze training that resulted in preserved spatial memory, Beatty et al. (1987) compared the performance of three groups of rats: (1) old rats that had been fully fed (22 months), (2) old rats that had been fed every other day from 3 to 21 months, and (3) a young (3 month) control group. Neither the freely fed nor the food-restricted old rats in Groups 1 and 2, however, reached behavioral criterion as quickly as did the young rats, nor did they differ from one another. This finding suggests the *training* rather than the food restriction accounts for the preservation of spatial memory in old rats in the earlier studies.

Another possible interpretation of the experiments conducted by Beatty and his colleagues is that training acts as a form of enrichment treatment. It is well known that rats allowed to live in environments with many objects to explore and other rats to interact with often show improved learning ability over controls (e.g., Hebb, 1949). This type of living condition is frequently referred to as an enrichment treatment, whereas solitary housing in a cage with no extra objects is considered a control or an impoverished living condition. By exposing the rats to a daily memory challenge on the radial maze, Beatty may have essentially created an enrichment treatment for these rats. Although there are no studies that directly assess this question, by comparing maze training and enriched housing conditions in old animals, an experiment by Goldman et al. (1987) comes close to doing so. These investigators found that with a 60-day enriched housing treatment, memory impairments on the multiple-unit T-maze were attenuated in their old enriched animals compared to controls. Although improvements were observed, these old rats never reached the levels of performance typically reached by young rats on this task. Perhaps if longer periods of enrichment were implemented, then the older rats would perform even more like young control rats. The interesting question that remains from studies such as these is whether spatial experience such as maze training or enriched housing conditions can act to preserve neural mechanisms that would otherwise be compromised by the normal process of aging. If this were true, then it may be possible to detect a change in some property of the hippocampus that reflects this preservation.

There are, in fact, interesting data on the impact of being mentally active throughout the life span on cognitive abilities in aging humans. When university professors were given a test battery that assessed cognitive performance, the declines typically expected in performance during the sixth and seventh decades of life were attenuated compared to persons of the same age that were not engaged in such activities throughout life (Shimamura, Berry, Mangels, Rusting, & Jurica, 1995). Furthermore, the prevalence Alzheimer's disease appears to be higher in individuals with fewer years of education, and Mayeux and his colleagues have proposed that increased educational and occupational attainment may reduce the risk of the disease by giving those individuals a reserve that delays the clinical onset or reduces the ease of clinical detection (Stern et al., 1994). The line of investigation into the factors that contribute to "successful aging" (e.g., Glass, Seeman, Herzog, Kahn, & Berkman, 1995) should be extremely interesting to follow over the next decade.

B. Drug Treatment Approaches

Drachman and Leavitt (1974) first suggested that the cognitive changes observed in aging humans are similar to those changes produced by anticholinergic drugs in younger adults. These ideas have been supported and extended by many other investigators using humans with Alzheimer's disease, normal elderly controls, non-human primates, and other mammals (e.g., Bartus & Johnson, 1976; Bowen, Smith, White, & Davison, 1976; Ingram et al., 1994; Lippa et al., 1980). Therefore, it is not surprising that a number of approaches have been taken to improve aged rat's memory on spatial problems that involve manipulations of acetylcholine and other putative neurotransmitters. An example of such an approach is the attempt to give treatments that might specifically aid in the restoration of calcium homeostatic mechanisms that change in old animals and that could lead to a disruption of cholinergic activity (e.g., Gibson & Peterson, 1987; Peterson, 1992). One such agent is 3,4-diaminopyridine (3,4-DAP), which stimulates the release of acetylcholine by promoting clacium influx into the cells (e.g., Glover, 1982). Daily administration of 3,4-DAP improves short-term spatial working memory of old rats on the radial eight-arm maze (Fig. 1C; Barnes, Eppich, & Rao, 1989; Davis, Idowu, & Gibson, 1983) but does not improve performance of animals on the circular platform task (Fig. 1D) in which rats must remember the spatial location of the escape tunnel from day to day (Barnes et al., 1989). These data are reminiscent of the newer findings from experiments in which selective lesions of the cholinergic system (discussed earlier) result in a similar pattern of results (i.e., cholinergic depletion results in deficits on short-term but not long-term memory components of spatial tasks).

Another method that has been used to improve calcium homeostasis in aged rat brains is to increase levels of magnesium in diets of old animals. Landfield and Morgan (1984) fed old rats control or high-magnesium diets for 4 days before training on a T-maze reversal task and were able to show that elevation of plasma magnesium levels could both effect reversal performance in old animals and also reduce the deficits in frequency potentiation of hippocampal CA1 cells typically observed in old rats (as discussed under the Electrophysiological Approaches). Although it is not clear whether elevated magnesium improved synaptic transmission in the hippocampus in a general way or was more selective to cholinergic transmission, the observation that dietary alterations can have clear effects on brain function and behavior is a critical step in the development of treatment strategies for memory dysfunction.

Another very interesting way in which calcium regulation has been manipulated to improve memory in aged organisms is through the use of the calcium channel blocker nimodipine. Disterhoft and his colleagues first reported that nimodipine improved the acquisition of a conditioned eye-blink task in old rabbits to within the range of young rabbit performance (Deyo, Straube, & Disterhoft, 1989). Moreover, these improvements in conditioning were correlated with reductions in afterhyperpolarizations elecited in hippocampal pyramidal cells in the old rabbits. Nimodipine presumably has its effect on pyramidal cell after hyperpolarizations by affecting the calcium-activated potassium currents responsible for their production. Furthermore, the improvement in learning abilities of old rabbits can be induced by oral administration of nimodipine (Straube, Deyo, Moyer, & Disterhoft, 1990). Nimodipine also affects long-term retention of these types of associative tasks as well as their initial acquisition (Solomon et al., 1995). The beneficial effect of nimodipine also extends to other species, as it has been shown to improve performance of old monkeys on a delayed-response task (Sandin, Jasmin, & Levere, 1990) and improves old rats' performance of a 14-unit T-maze (Fig. 1A; Ingram et al., 1994). Because deficits in classical conditioning have been observed in normal aged humans and in patients with Alzheimer's disease (e.g. Solomon, Levine, Bein, & Pendlebury, 1991; Woodruff-Pak, 1988), the beneficial effects of nimodipine in these animal models suggests a high likelihood of successful applications to humans.

Another interesting approach to changing the brain's neurochemical composition, and therefore potentially altering behavior in old animals, is through chronic intraventricular cannulation and administration of some agent. This strategy is illustrated in an experiment by Fischer et al. (1987). In this experiment nerve growth factor (NGF) was administered to old animals that were categorized as either impaired in their performance on the spatial version of the Morris water task or unimpaired on this task. NGF was chosen because of its potential to stimulate regenerative and plastic events in cholinergic neurons and therfore to reverse the deterioration that might occur in these neurons. The rats that were impaired on the spatial memory problem were divided into two groups, one that received an infusion of NGF into one lateral ventricle for a 1-month period, and one that did not receive NGF. During this time the rats were retested on the water task either after 2 weeks of NGF treatment or at the end of the 4-week interval. The performance of the rats that received NGF did not differ significantly from their previous performance levels at the 2-wk interval or from the performance of the rats that were impaired and did not receive NGF. At the four week interval, however, the NGF-treated old rats improved to the level of the old unimpaired rats. Furthermore, at the end of the infusion period, the NGF-treated rats showed larger cholinergic cell bodies on the side of the brain that received the drug than on the contralateral side. The investigators suggest that NGF reverses the cell shrinkage that would normally occur with age and that this may act to improve spatial memory.

Because of findings such as the foregoing, clinical trials using NGF have been suggested for patients with Alzheimer's disease (Phelps et al., 1989), and positive results have been reported in one patient (Olson et al., 1992). Because neurotrophic factors, such as NGF, are not able to cross the blood–brain barrier, they must be administered intracerebrally. This has been accomplished by mechanical pump devices that can deliver substances directly to the cerebral ventricles and can be refilled through the skin. Such treatment would not be appropriate for normal aged persons, but more effective drug delivery (noninvasive) systems are being sought quite actively, and such efforts may lead to methods for altering the substances chemically or packaging them in a way that allows them to cross the blood–brain barrier. Such routes of administration would be more amenable to nonpatient populations. A caveat that must be raised, of course, is the possibility that NGF might have negative as well as positive effects, and caution is certainly warranted (e.g., Olson, 1993). A very exciting new approach for administration of therapeutic factors has arisen in the area of gene therapy. With such methods specific agents can be administered in a region-specific, sustained manner. For example, a single unilateral injection of a recombinant adenovirus encoding NGF caused an increase in size of cholinergic neurons in the nucleus basalis magnocellularis in old rats, with no significant tissue damage or inflammatory response (Castel-Barthe et al., 1996). Approaches such as this one are likely to lead to important advances in treatment.

C. Tissue Transplantation

As reviewed by Gage and Björklund (1987), there were approximately a dozen articles published by 1987 addressing issues of how transplant technology might benefit the aging brain. First, it was important to establish whether the grafts of fetal central nervous system tissue would survive in older animals, and second whether these transplants could lead to improved behavioral performance in memory-deficient old animals. It is now clear that fetal tissue not only can survive in old rodent brain but can also cause functional recovery. The two kinds of grafting methods involve either grafts from intact tissue or grafts of neural cells that have been dissociated from one another, called suspension grafts. Two groups report encouraging results of grafting with respect to learning and memory. Gash, Collier, and Sladek (1985) found that, in old rats, grafts from the locus coeruleus improved 24-hr retention of a passive avoidance task in old rats. The object of the task is to remember not to go into a dark box, where shock is given, but to stay in a brightly lit compartment. The behavioral improvement of the old animals was to levels equivalent with young animal performance. Gage, Dunnett, and Björklund (1984) and Gage and Björklund (1986) found that suspension grafts prepared from the septal-diagonal band area improved spatial memory on the Morris water task. Gage and his colleagues implanted these suspensions bilaterally in several areas of the hippocampus in a group of animals that showed clear behavioral impairments on the water task. The control group consisted of similarly impaired old animals that were left unoperated. Several months after the grafts were implanted, these two groups of animals' again underwent behavioral testing. The old animals with the grafts performed significantly better than the control old animals without grafts and also better than their previous performance. Although invasive surgery is not likely to be a viable alternative for normal age-related memory problems in the near future, for devastating illnesses such as Alzheimer's or Parkinson's disease, such therapeutic strategies may be welcomed in the attempt to prolong the time periods where reasonable levels of functioning are possible in these individuals.

VII. CONCLUDING REMARKS

The primary reasons for studying the normal changes in learning and memory that occur with age have been reviewed, and a number of approaches to this problem have been presented. These themes of the chapter include the following:

1. One main rationale for studying normal changes in learning and memory with age involves the attempt to understand the neural mechanisms that underlie learning and memory in enough detail that memory loss in aging might be prevented or attenuated.

2. The importance of carefully choosing the appropriate behavior and the neural structure for study has been emphasized, because it is easier to relate the findings between mammals when correspondences are sought between the nonhuman and human cases from the beginning. In this regard, most of the examples given in the present chapter have revolved around the theme of spatial memory and hippocampal function. As the foregoing sections suggested, this has been a productive line of investigation that has, indeed, led to the development of therapeutic interventive approaches to age-related memory declines.

3. The emphasis on the hippocampus and spatial memory is meant to be illustrative and to provide focus for this chapter rather than to imply that other memory functions or brain areas are not equally well-suited for such an analysis. In fact, it is critical that similar approaches be taken to the study of forms of memory for which the hippocampus is not involved, so that more global treatment strategies may be designed.

4. Another major rationale for studying the aging process in relation to learning and memory operations is to direct the investigator's attention to those mechanisms that are altered in aging organisms and, by inference, are critical for the most efficient processing of information.

Particularly salient examples from the literature using old animals that illustrate the foregoing points include the following observations:

5. Old memory-deficient animals' ability to maintain elevated synaptic strength (LTP) or to reach synaptic modification levels that produce epileptiform activity (kindling) are defective compared with the ability of young rats, suggesting that the mechanisms involved in maintaining synaptic communication strength may be important for the durability of memories at the electrophysiological level.

6. Comparison of young and old animals' morphologically distinct "perforated" synaptic contacts, which are reduced in old memory-deficient animals, suggests that this anatomical component and the change in connectivity may be critically involved in effective information-processing mechanisms.

7. Recently developed methods for producing selective neurochemical lesions, transgenic deletion methods, and new unbiased methods derived from the field of stereology for cell counting are likely to lead to important new insights into the chemical systems and morphological substrates of age-related learning and memory changes in the next decade.

8. Investigations into methods that might attenuate or delay age-related cognitive changes, such as extensive training or stimulation (enrichment treatments), may provide guidance for optimizing performance in later years or for prescribing ways in which "successful aging" can be achieved.

9. Promising new therapeutic agents are on the horizon for the potential alleviation of cognitive changes during aging.

10. Direct brain delivery of trophic factors or implantation of cells that secrete these agents may have more immediate application for disease states but may lead to the development of methods that will be applicable to normal cognitive changes with age.

It is the integration of the kind of information that has been outlined herein that should lead to a better understanding of the biology of learning and memory and its changes throughout the life span.

ACKNOWLEDGMENTS

The work cited from the author's laboratory was largely supported by the National Institute on Aging (AG03376) and the National Institute of Mental Health (MH01227). I am grateful to M. Suster and K. Kenny for assistance with manuscript preparation.

REFERENCES

Abdulla, F. A., Abu-Bakra, M. A. J., Calaminici, M. R., Stephenson, J. D., & Sinden, J. D. (1995). Importance of forebrain cholinergic and GABAergic systems to the age-related deficits in water maze performance of rats. *Neurobiology of Aging, 16,* 41–52.

Aitken, D. H., & Meaney, M. J. (1989). Temporally graded, age-related impairments in spatial memory in the rat. *Neurobiology of Aging, 10,* 273–276.

Albert, M. S. (1988a). General issues in geriatric neuropsychology. In M. S. Albert & M. B. Moss (Eds.), *Geriatric neuropsychology* (pp. 3–10). New York: Guilford Press.

Albert, M. S. (1988b). Cognitive function. In M. S. Albert & M. B. Moss (Eds.), *Geriatric neuropsychology* (pp. 33–53). New York: Guilford Press.

Altman, H., & Normile, H. J. (1986). Serotonin, learning, and memory: Implications for the treatment of dementia. In T. Crook, R. T. Bartus, S. Ferris, & S. Gershon (Eds.), *Treatment development strategies for Alzheimer's disease* (pp. 361–383). Madison, CT: Mark Powley Associates.

Bachevalier, J. (1993). Behavioral changes in aged rhesus monkeys. *Neurobiology of Aging, 14,* 619–621.

Bachevalier, J., Landis, L. S., Walker, L. C., Brickson, M., Mishkin, M., Price, D. L., & Cork, L. C. (1991). Aged monkeys exhibit behavioral deficits indicative of widespread cerebral dysfunction. *Neurobiology of Aging, 12,* 99–111.

Bailey, Ch. H., Castellucci, V. F., Hoister, J., & Chen, M. (1983). Behavioral changes in aging *Aplysia*: A model system for studying the cellular basis of age-impaired learning, memory, and arousal. *Behavioral and Neural Biology, 38,* 70–81.

Ball, M. J. (1977). Neuronal loss, neurofibrillary tangles and granulovacuolar degeneration in the hippocampus with ageing and dementia. *Acta Neuropathologica (Berlin), 37,* 111–118.

Ball, M. J. (1978). Topographic distribution of neurofibrillary tangles and granulovacuolar degeneration in hippocampal cortex of aging and demented patients. *Acta Neuropathologica (Berlin), 42,* 73–80.

Barnes, C. A. (1979). Memory deficits associated with senescence: A neurophysiological and behavioral study in the rat. *Journal of Comparative and Physiological Psychology, 93,* 74–104.

Barnes, C. A. (1988). Spatial learning and memory processes: The search for their neurobiological mechanisms in the rat. *Trends in Neurosciences, 11,* 163–169.

Barnes, C. A. (1990). Animal models of age-related cognitive decline. In F. Boller & S. Corkin (Eds.), *Handbook of neuropsychology* (pp. 167–196). Amsterdam: Elsevier Science Publishers.

Barnes, C. A., Baranyi, A., Bindman, L. J., Dudai, Y., Frégnac, Y., Ito, M., Knöpfel, T., Lisberger, S. G., Morris, R. G. M., Moulins, M., Movshon, J. A., Singer, W., & Squire, L. R. (1994). Relating activity dependent modifications of neuronal function to changes in neural systems and behavior. In A. I. Selverston & P. Ascher (Eds.), *Cellular and molecular functions underlying higher neural functions.* Chichester: John Wiley and Sons Ltd.

Barnes, C. A., Eppich, C., & Rao, G. (1989). Selective improvement of aged rat short-term spatial memory by 3,4-diaminopyridine. *Neurobiology of Aging, 10,* 337–341.

Barnes, C. A., Green, E. J., Baldwin, J., & Johnson, W. E. (1987). Behavioral and neurophysiological examples of functional sparing in senescent rat. *Canadian Journal of Psychology, 41,* 131–140.

Barnes, C., Markowska, A., Ingram, D., Kametani, H., Spangler, E., Lemken, J., & Olton, D. (1990). Acetyl-*l*-carnitine. 2: Effects on learning and memory performance of aged rats in simple and complex mazes. *Neurobiology of Aging, 11,* 499–506.

Barnes, C. A., & McNaughton, B. L. (1980). Spatial memory and hippocampal synaptic plasticity in middle-aged and senescent rats. In D. G. Stein (Ed.), *The psychobiology of aging: Problems and perspectives* (pp. 253–272). New York: Elsevier, North-Holland.

Barnes, C. A., & McNaughton, B. L. (1985). An age comparison of the rates of acquisition and forgetting of spatial information in relation to long-term enhancement of hippocampal synapses. *Behavioral Neuroscience, 99,* 1040–1048.

Barnes, C. A., Nadel, L., & Honig, W. K. (1980). Spatial memory deficit in senescent rats. *Canadian Journal of Psychology, 34,* 29–39.

Barnes, C. A., Rao, G., Foster, T. C., & McNaughton, B. L. (1992). Region specific age effects on AMPA sensitivity: Electrophysiological evidence for loss of synaptic contacts in hippocampal field CA1. *Hippocampus, 2,* 457–468.

Bartus, R. T. (1988). The need for common perspectives in the development and use of animal models for age-related cognitive and neurodegenerative disorders. *Neurobiology of Aging, 9,* 445–451.

Bartus, R. T., & Dean, R. L. (1979). Recent memory in aged non-human primates: Hypersensitivity to visual interference during retention. *Experimental Aging Research, 5,* 385–400.

Bartus, R. T., & Dean, R. L. (1987). Animal models for age-related memory disturbances. In J. T. Coyle (Ed.), *Animal models of dementia: A synaptic neurochemical perspective* (pp. 69–79). New York: Alan R. Liss.

Bartus, R. T., Dean, R. L., Beer, B., & Lippa, A. S. (1982). The cholinergic hypothesis of geriatric memory dysfunction. *Science, 217,* 408–417.

Bartus, R. T., Dean, R. L., Pontecorvo, M. J., & Flicker, C. (1985). The cholinergic hypothesis: A historical overview, current perspective and future directions. In D. Olton, E. Gamzu, & S. Corkin (Eds.), *Memory dysfunctions: An integration of animal and human research from clinical and preclinical perspectives* (Vol. 44, pp. 332–358). New York: New York Academy of Sciences.

Bartus, R. T., & Johnson, H. R. (1976). Short-term memory in the rhesus monkey: Disruption from the anticholinergic scopolamine. *Pharmacology, Biochemistry, and Behavior, 5,* 39–46.

Baxter, M. G., Bucci, D. J., Gorman, L. K., Wiley, R. G., & Gallagher, M. (1995). Selective immuno-toxic lesions of basal forebrain cholinergic cells: Effects on learning and memory in rats. *Behavioral Neuroscience, 109,* 714–722.

Beatty, W. W., Bierley, R. A., & Boyd, J. G. (1985). Preservation of accurate spatial memory in aged rats. *Neurobiology of Aging, 6,* 219–225.

Beatty, W. W., Clouse, B. A., & Bierley, R. A. (1987). The effects of long-term restricted feeding on radial maze performance by aged rats. *Neurobiology of Aging, 8,* 325–327.

Beigon, A., Greenberger, V., & Segal, M. (1986). Quantitative histochemistry of brain acetylcholinesterase and learning rate in the aged rat. *Neurobiology of Aging, 7,* 215–217.

Berger-Sweeney, J., Heckers, S., Mesulam, M.-M., Wiley, R. G., & Lappi, D. A. (1994). Differential effects on spatial navigation of immunotoxin-induced cholinergic lesions of the medial septal area and nucleus basalis magnocellularis. *Journal of Neuroscience, 14,* 4507–4519.

Bickford, P., Heron, C., Young, D. A., Gerhardt, G. A., & de la Garza, R. (1992). Impaired acquisition of novel locomotor tasks in aged and norepinephrine-depleted F344 rats. *Neurobiology of Aging, 13,* 475–481.

Bierley, R. A., Rixen, G. J., Troster, A. I., & Beatty, W. W. (1986). Preserved spatial memory in old rats survives 10 months without training. *Behavioral and Neural Biology, 45,* 223–229.

Birren, J. E. (1961). A brief history of the psychology of aging. *Gerontologist, 1,* 69–77.

Bliss, T. V. P., & Gardner-Medwin, A. R. (1973). Long-lasting potentiation of synaptic transmission in the dentate area of unanaesthetized rabbit following stimulation of the perforant path. *Journal of Physiology (London), 22,* 357–374.

Bliss, T. V. P., & Lømo, T. (1973). Long-lasting potentiation of synaptic transmission in the dentate area of the anaesthetized rabbit following stimulation of the perforant path. *Journal of Physiology (London), 232,* 331–356.

Bond, N. W., Everitt, A. V., & Walton, J. (1989). Effects of dietary restriction on radial-arm maze performance and flavor memory in aged rats. *Neurobiology of Aging, 10,* 27–30.

Bourliere, F. (1970). *The assessment of biological age in man* (World Health Organization Publication No. 37, pp. 1–67). Geneva: World Health Organization.

Bowen, D. M., Smith, C. B., White, P., & Davison, A. N. (1976). Neurotransmitter-related enzymes and indices of hypoxia in senile dementia and other abiotrophies. *Brain, 99,* 459–496.

Bresnahan, E., Kametani, E., Spangler, M., Chachich, M., Wiser, P., & Ingram, D. (1988). Fimbria-fornix lesions impair acquisition performance in a 14-unit T maze similar to prior observed performance deficits in aged rats. *Psychobiology, 16,* 243–250.

Bruce, P. P., & Herman, J. F. (1983). Spatial knowledge of young and elderly adults: Scene recognition from familiar and novel perspectives. *Experimental Aging Research, 9,* 196–173.

Buchanan, S. L., & Powell, D. A. (1988). Age-related changes in associative learning: Studies in rabbits and rats. *Neurobiology of Aging, 9,* 523–534.

Burwell, R. D., & Gallagher, M. (1993). A longitudinal study of reaction time performance in Long–Evans rats. *Neurobiology of Aging, 14,* 57–64.

Butler, R. N. (1969). Age-ism: Another form of bigotry. *Gerontologist, 9,* 243–246.

Campbell, B. A., & Haroutunian, V. (1981). Effects of age on long-term memory: Retention of fixed interval responding. *Journal of Gerontology, 36,* 338–341.

Campbell, B. A., Krauter, E. E., & Wallace, J. E. (1980). Animal models of aging: Sensory-motor and cognitive function in the aged rat. In D. G. Stein (Ed.), *Psychobiology of aging: Problems and perspectives* (pp. 201–226). New York: Elsevier/North-Holland.

Caplan, L. J., & Lipman, P. D. (1995). Age and gender differences in the effectiveness of map-like learning aids in memory for routes. *Journal of Gerontology, 50B,* 126–133.

Caprioli, A., Ghirardi, O., Giuliani, A., Ramacci, M. T., & Angelucci, L. (1991). Spatial learning and memory in the radial maze: A longitudinal study in rats from 4 to 25 months of age. *Neurobiology of Aging, 12,* 605–607.

Castel-Barthe, M. N., Jazat-Poindessous, F., Barneoud, P., Vigne, E., Revah, F., Mallet, J., & Lamour, Y. (1996). Direct intracerebral nerve growth factor gene transfer using a recombinant adenovirus: Effect on basal forebrain cholinergic neurons during aging. *Neurobiology of Disease, 3,* 76–86.

Chan-Palay, V. (1988). Somatostatin and neuropeptide Y: Alterations and coexistence in the Alzheimer's Dementia hippocampus. In J. Ulrich (Ed.), *Histology and histopathology of the aging brain. Interdisciplinary topics in gerontology* (Vol. 25, pp. 38–58). New York: Karger.

Cherry, K. E., & Park, D. C. (1989). Age-related differences in three-dimensional spatial memory. *Journal of Gerontology, 44,* 16–22.

Chouinard, M. L., Gallagher, M., Yasuda, R. P., Wolfe, B. B., & McKinney, M. (1995). Hippocampal muscarinic receptor function in spatial learning-impaired aged rats. *Neurobiology of Aging, 16,* 955–963.

Clarke, D. J., Gage, F. H., Nilsson, O. G. & Björklund, A. (1986). Grafted septal neurons from cholinergic synaptic connections in the dentate gyrus of behaviorally impaired aged rats. *Journal of Comparative Neurology, 252,* 483–492.

Cohen, N. J., & Eichenbaum, H. (1993). *Memory, amnesia, and the hippocampal System.* Cambridge, MA: MIT Press.

Corke, P. P. (1964). Complex behavior in "old" and "young" rats. *Psychological Reports, 15,* 371–376.

Corkin, S. (1965). Tactually-guided maze-learning in man: Effects of bilateral hippocampal, bilateral frontal, and unilateral cerebral lesions. *Neuropsychologia, 3,* 339–351.

Corkin, S. (1984). Lasting consequences of bilateral medial temporal lobectomy: Clinical course and experimental finds in H. M. *Seminars in Neurology, 4,* 249–259.

Costa, P. T., Jr., & McCrae, R. R. (1980). Functional age: A conceptual and empirical critique. In S. G. Haynes & M. Feinlab (Eds.), *Epidemiology of aging* (NIH Publication No. 80-969, pp. 23–46). Washington, DC: U.S. Government Printing Office.

Craik, R. I. M. (1984). Age difference in remembering. In L. R. Squire & N. Butters (Eds.), *Handbook of the psychology of aging* (pp. 3–12). New York: Guilford Press.

Crook, T., Bartus, R. T., Ferris, S. H., Whitehouse, P., Cohen, G. D., & Gershon, S. (1986). Age-associated memory impairment: Proposed diagnostic criteria and measures of clinical change. Report of a National Institute of Mental Health Work Group. *Developmental Neuropsychology, 2,* 261–276.

Crook, T. H., & Larrabee, G. J. (1989). Clinical assessment procedures for distinguishing age-associated memory impairment from dementia. In H. J. Altman & B. N. Altman (Eds.), *Alzheimer's and Parkinson's diseases: Recent advances in research and clinical management* (pp. 39–56). New York: Plenum Press.

Davis, H. P., Idowu, A., & Gibson, G. E. (1983). Improvement of 8-arm maze performance in aged Fischer 344 rats with 3,4-diaminopyridine. *Experimental Aging Research, 9,* 211–214.

Davis, R. T. (1978). Old monkey behavior. *Experimental Gerontology, 13,* 237–250.

Decker, M. W., & McGaugh, J. L. (1991). The role of interactions between the cholinergic system and other neuromodulatory systems in learning and memory. *Synapse, 7,* 151–168.

Decker, M. W., Pelleymounter, M. A., & Gallagher, M. (1988). Effects of training on a spatial memory task on high affinity choline uptake in hippocampus and cortex in young adult and aged rats. *Journal of Neuroscience, 8,* 90–99.

Delfs, J. R. (1985). Somatostatin and Alzheimer's disease: Possible pathophysiological associations. *Neurology and Neurobiology, 18,* 243–262.

Desroches, H. F., Kimbrell, G. M., & Allison, J. T. (1964). Effect of age and experience of bar pressing and activity in the rat. *Journal of Gerontology, 19,* 168–172.

de Toledo-Morrell, L., Geinisman, Y., & Morrell, F. (1988). Age-dependent alterations in hippocampal synaptic plasticity: Relation to memory disorders, *Neurobiology of Aging, 9,* 581–590.

de Toledo-Morrell, L., & Morrell, F. (1985). Electrophysiological markers of aging and memory loss in rats. *Annals of the New York Academy of Sciences, 444,* 296–311.

de Toledo-Morrell, L., & Morrell, F. (1991). Age-related alterations in long-term potentiation and susceptibility to kindling. In F. Morrell (Ed.), *Kindling and synaptic plasticity: The legacy of Graham Goddard* (pp. 160–175). Boston: Birkhäuser.

de Toledo-Morrell, L., Morrell, F., & Fleming, S. (1984a). Age dependent deficits in spatial memory are related to impaired hippocampal kindling. *Behavioral Neuroscience, 98,* 902–907.

de Toledo-Morrell, L., Morrell, F., Fleming, S., & Cohen, M. (1984b). Pentoxifylline reverses age-related deficits in spatial memory. *Behavioral and Neural Biology, 42,* 1–8.

de Toledo-Morrell, L., Sullivan, M. P., Morrell, F., Spanovic, C., & Spencer, S. (1995). Gender differences in the vulnerability of the hippocampal formation during aging. *Society for Neuroscience Abstracts, 21,* 1708 (abstract 668.4).

Deyo, R. A., Straube, K. T., & Disterhoft, J. F. (1989). Nimodipine facilitates associative learning in aging rabbits. *Science, 243,* 809–811.

Doty, B. A., & Doty, L. A. (1964). Effect of age and chlorpromazine on memory consolidation. *Journal of Comparative and Physiological Psychology, 57,* 331–334.

Douglas, R. M., & Goddard, G. V. (1975). Long-term potentiation of the perforant path-granule cell synapse in the rat hippocampus. *Brain Research, 86,* 205–215.

Drachman, D. A., & Leavitt, J. (1974). Human memory and the cholinergic system: A relationship to aging? *Archives of Neurology, 30,* 113–121.

Dudchenko, P. A., Goodridge, J. P., Seiterle, D. A., & Taube, J. S. (1997). Effects of repeated disorientation on the acquisition of spatial tasks in rats: Dissociation between the appetitive radial arm maze and aversive water maze. *Journal of Experimental Psychology: Animal Behavior Processes, 23,* 194–210.

Eberling, J. L., Jagust, W. J., Reed, B. R., & Baker, M. G. (1992). Reduced temporal lobe blood flow in Alzheimer's disease. *Neurobiology of Aging, 13,* 483–491.

Elias, P. K., Elias, M. F., & Eleftheriou, B. E. (1975). Emotionality, exploratory behavior, and locomotion in aging inbred strains of mice. *Gerontologia, 21,* 46–55.

Evans, G., Brennan, P., Skorpanich, M. A., & Held, D. (1984). Cognitive mapping and elderly adults: Verbal and location memory for urban landmarks. *Journal of Gerontology, 39,* 452–457.

Fields, P. E. (1953). The age factor in multiple-discrimination learning by white rats. *Journal of Comparative Physiological Psychology, 46,* 387–389.

Fischer, W., Chen, K. S., Gage, F. H., & Björklund, A. (1991). Progressive decline in spatial learning and integrity of forebrain cholinergic neurons in rats during aging. *Neurobiology of Aging, 13,* 9–23.

Fischer, W., Wictorin, K., Björklund, A., Williams, L. R., Varon, S., & Gage, F. H. (1987). Amelioration of cholinergic neuron atrophy and spatial memory impairment in aged rats by nerve growth factor. *Nature, 329,* 65–68.

Fletcher, H. J., & Mowbray, J. B. (1962). Note on learning in an aged monkey. *Psychological Reports, 10,* 11–13.

Flicker, C., Bartus, R. T., Crook, T. H., & Ferris, S. H. (1984). Effects of aging and dementia upon recent visuospatial memory. *Neurobiology of Aging, 5,* 275–283.

Flicker, C., Ferris, S. H., Crook, T., Bartus, R. T., & Reisberg, B. (1985). Cognitive function in normal aging and early dementia. In J. Traber & W. H. Gispen (Eds.), *Senile dementia of the Alzheimer type* (pp. 2–17). New York: Springer-Verlag.

Fordyce, D. E., & Wehner, J. M. (1993). Effects of aging on spatial learning and hippocampal protein kinase C in mice. *Neurobiology of Aging, 14,* 309–317.

Foster, T. C., Barnes, C. A., Rao, G., & McNaughton, B. L. (1991). Increase in perforant path quantal size in aged F-344 rats. *Neurobiology of Aging, 12,* 441–448.

Frick, K. M., Baxter, M. G., Markowska, A. L., Olton, D. S., & Price, D. L. (1995). Age-related spatial reference and working memory deficits assessed in the water maze. *Neurobiology of Aging, 16,* 149–160.

Gabriel, M., Sparenborg, S. P., & Stolar, N. (1986). An executive function of the hippocampus: Pathway selection for thalamic neuronal significance code. In R. Isaacson & K. H. Pribram (Eds.), *The hippocampus* (Vol. 3, pp. 1–39). New York: Plenum Publishers.

Gage, F. H., & Björklund, A. (1986). Cholinergic septal grafts into the hippocampal formation improve spatial learning and memory in aged rats by an atropine-sensitive mechanism. *Journal of Neuroscience, 6,* 2837–2847.

Gage, F. H., & Björklund, A. (1987). Intracerebral grafting of identified cell types in aging brain. In P. Davies & C. E. Finch (Eds.), *Molecular neuropathology of aging* (pp. 55–66). New York: Cold Spring Harbor Laboratory.

Gage, F. H., Chen, K. S., Buzsaki, G., & Armstrong, D. (1988). Experimental approaches to age-related cognitive impairments. *Neurobiology of Aging, 9,* 645–655.

Gage, F. H., Dunnett, S. B., & Björklund, A. (1989). Age-related impairments in spatial memory are independent of those in sensorimotor skills. *Neurobiology of Aging, 10,* 347–352.

Gage, F. H., Dunnett, S. B., & Björklund, A. (1984). Spatial learning and motor deficits in aged rats. *Neurobiology of Aging, 5,* 43–48.

Gage, F. H., Kelly, P. A., & Björklund, A. (1984). Regional changes in brain glucose metabolism reflect cognitive impairments in aged rats. *Journal of Neuroscience, 4,* 2856–2865.

Gallagher, M., Bostock, E., & King, R. (1985). Effects of opiate antagonists on spatial memory in young and aged rats. *Behavioral and Neural Biology, 44,* 374–385.

Gallagher, M., & Burwell, R. D. (1989). Relationship of age-related decline across several behavioral domains. *Neurobiology of Aging, 10,* 691–708.

Gallagher, M., Burwell, R. D., Kodsi, M. H., McKinney, M., Southerland, S., Vella-Rountree, L., & Lewis, M. H. (1990). Markers for biogenic amines in the aged rat brain: Relationship to decline in spatial learning ability. *Neurobiology of Aging, 11,* 507–514.

Gallagher, M., & Colombo, P. J. (1995). Ageing: The cholinergic hypothesis of cognitive decline. *Current Opinion in Neurobiology, 5,* 161–168.

Gash, D. M., Collier, T. J., & Sladek, J. R., Jr. (1985). Neural transplantation: A review of recent developments and potential applications to the aged brain. *Neurobiology of Aging, 6,* 131–150.

Geinisman, Y., de Toledo-Morrell, L., & Morrell, F. (1986a). Loss of perforated synapses in the dentate gyrus: Morphological substrate of memory deficit in aged rats. *Proceedings of the National Academy of Sciences U.S.A., 83,* 3027–3031.

Geinisman, Y., de Toledo-Morrell, L., & Morrell, F. (1986b). Aged rats need a preserved complement of perforated axospinous synapses per hippocampal neuron to maintain good spatial memory. *Brain Research, 398,* 266–275.

Geinisman, Y., de Toledo-Morrell, L., Morrell, F., & Heller, R. E. (1995). Hippocampal markers of age-related memory dysfunction: Behavioral, eletrophysiological and morphological perspectives. *Progress in Neurobiology, 45,* 222–252.

Geinisman, Y., de Toledo-Morrell, L., Morrell, F., Persina, I. S., & Rossi, M. (1992a). Age-related loss of axospinous synapses formed by two afferent systems in the rat dentate gyrus as revealed by the unbiased stereological dissector technique. *Hippocampus, 2,* 445–456.

Geinisman, Y., de Toledo-Morrell, L., Morrell, F., Persina, I. S., & Rossi, M. (1992b). Structural synaptic plasticity associated with the induction of long-term potentiation is preserved in the dentate gyrus of aged rats. *Hippocampus, 2,* 437–444.

Geinisman, Y., Morrell, F., & de Toledo-Morrell, L. (1987). Axospinous synapses with segmented postsynaptic densities: A morphologically distinct synaptic subtype contribution to the number of profiles of "perforated" synapses visualized in random sections. *Brain Research, 423,* 179–188.

Gibson, G. E., & Peterson, C. (1987). Consideration of neurotransmitters and calcium metabolism in therapeutic design. In T. Crook, R. T. Bartus, S. Ferris, & S. Gershon (Eds.), *Treatment development strategies for Alzheimer's disease* (pp. 499–577). Madison, CT: Mark Powley Associates.

Glass, T. A., Seeman, T. E., Herzog, R. A., Kahn, R., & Berkman, L. F. (1995). Changes in productive activity in late adulthood: MacArthur studies of successful aging. *Journal of Gerontology: Social Sciences, 50B,* 65–76.

Glover, W. E. (1982). The aminopyridines. *General Pharmacology, 13,* 259–285.

Goddard, G. V. (1967). The development of epileptic seizures through brain stimulation at low intensity. *Nature, 214,* 1020–1021.

Gold, P. E., McGaugh, J. L., Hankins, L. L., Rose, R. P., & Vasquez, B. J. (1981). Age dependent changes in retention in rats. *Experimental Aging Research, 8,* 53–58.

Gold, P. E., & Stone, W. S. (1988). Neuroendocrine effects on memory in aged rodents and humans. *Neurobiology of Aging, 9,* 709–717.

Goldman, H., Berman, R. F., Gershon, S., Murphy, S. L., & Altman, H. J. (1987). Correlation of behavioral and cerebrovascular functions in the aging rat. *Neurobiology of Aging, 8,* 409–416.

Goodrick, C. L. (1968). Learning, retention, and extinction of a complex maze habit for mature-young and senescent Wistar albino rats. *Journal of Gerontology, 23,* 298–304.

Goodrick, C. L. (1971). Free exploration and adaptation within an open field as a function of trials and between-trial-interval for mature-young, mature-old, and senescent Wistar rats. *Journal of Gerontology, 26,* 58–62.

Goodrick, C. L. (1972). Learning by mature-young and aged Wistar albino rats as a function of test complexity. *Journal of Gerontology, 8,* 75–83.

Goodrick, C. L. (1973a). Maze learning of mature-young and aged rats as a function of distribution of practice. *Journal of Experimental Psychology, 98,* 344–349.

Goodrick, C. L. (1973b). Error goal-gradients of mature-young and aged rats during training in a 14-unit spatial maze. *Psychological Reports, 32,* 359–362.

Goodrick, C. L. (1975a). Behavioral differences in young and aged mice: Strain differences for activity measures, operant learning, sensory discrimination, and alcohol preference. *Experimental Aging Research, 1,* 191–207.

Goodrick, C. L. (1975b). Behavioral rigidity as a mechanism for facilitation of problem solving for aged rats. *Journal of Gerontology, 30,* 181–184.

Graves, C. A., & Solomon, P. R. (1985). Age-related disruption of trace but not delay classical conditioning of the rabbit's nictitating membrane responses. *Behavioral Neuroscience, 99,* 88–96.

Greenberg, B. D., Savage, M. J., Howland, D. S., Ali, S. M., Siedlak, S. L., Perry, G., Siman, R., & Scott, R. W. (1996). APP transgenesis: Approaches toward the development of animal models for Alzheimer disease neuropathology. *Neurobiology of Aging, 17,* 153–171.

Haas, H. L. (1987). Recording from human hippocampus *in vitro. Neuroscience Letters Supplement, 29,* 13.

Harrison, J., & Buchwald, J. (1983). Eyeblink conditioning deficits in the old cat. *Neurobiology of Aging, 4,* 45–51.

Hasan, M., & Glees, P. (1973). Ultrastructural age changes in hippocampal neurons, synapses and neuroglia. *Experimental Gerontology, 8,* 75–83.

Havighurst, R. J. (1961). Successful aging. *Gerontologist, 1,* 8–13.

Hazzard, D. G., Bronson, R. T., McClearn, G. E., & Strong, R. (1992). Selection of an appropriate animal model to study aging processes with special emphasis on the use of rat strains. *Journal of Gerontology, 47,* 63–64.

Hebb, D. O. (1949). *The organization of behavior.* New York: John Wiley & Sons.

Hepler, D. J., Olton, D. S., Wenk, G. L., & Coyle, J. T. (1985). Lesions in nucleus basalis magnocellularis and medial septal area of rats produce qualitatively similar memory impairments. *Journal of Neuroscience, 5,* 866–873.

Herrmann, D. J., & Chaffin, R. (1988). *Memory in historical perspective: The literature before Effinghaus.* New York: Springer-Verlag.

Hirsh, R. (1980). The hippocampus, conditional operations and cognition. *Physiological Psychology, 8,* 175–182.

Huidobro, A., Blanco, P., Villalba, M., Gómez-Puertas, P., Villa, A., Pereira, R., Bogónez, E., Martínez-Serrano, A., Aparicio, J. J., & Satrústegui, J. (1993). Age-related changes in calcium homeostatic mechanisms in synaptosomes in relation with working memory deficiency. *Neurobiology of Aging, 14,* 479–486.

Hyman, B. T., Van Hoesen, G. W., Damasio, A. R., & Barnes, C. L. (1984). Alzheimer's disease: Cell-specific pathology isolates the hippocampal formation. *Science, 225,* 1168–1170.

Hyman, B. T., Van Hoesen, G. W., & Kromer, L. J., & Damasio, A. R. (1986). Perforant pathway changes and the memory impairment of Alzheimer's disease. *Annals of Neurology, 20,* 472–481.

Ingram, D. K. (1983). Toward the behavioral assessment of biological aging in the laboratory mouse: Concepts, terminology, and objectives. *Experimental Aging Research, 9,* 225–238.

Ingram, D. K. (1985). Analysis of age-related impairments in learning and memory in rodent models. *Annals of the New York Academy of Sciences, 444,* 312–331.

Ingram, D. K. (1988). Complex maze learning in rodents as a model of age-related memory impairment. *Neurobiology of Aging, 9,* 475–485.

Ingram, D. K., Joseph, J. A., Spangler, E. L., Roberts, D., Hengemihle, J., & Fanelli, J. (1994). Chronic nimodipine treatment in aged rats: Analysis of motor and cognitive effects and muscarinic-induced striatal dopamine release. *Neurobiology of Aging, 15,* 55–61.

Ingram, D. K., London, E. D., & Goodrick, C. L. (1981). Age and neurochemical correlates of radial maze performance in rats. *Neurobiology of Aging, 2,* 41–47.

Ingram, D. K., Spangler, E. L., Iijima, S., Kuo, H., Bresnanan, E. L., Greig, H. H., & London, E. D. (1994). New pharmacological strategies for cognitive enhancement using a rat model of age-related memory impairment. *Annals of the New York Academy of Sciences, 717,* 16–32.

Jarrard, L. E. (1978). Selective hippocampal lesions: Differential effects on performance by rats of a spatial task with preoperative versus postoperative training. *Journal of Comparative and Physiological Psychology, 92,* 1119–1127.

Jordon, J., & Sokoloff, B. (1959). Air ionization, age, and maze learning of rats. *Journal of Gerontology, 14,* 344–348.

Kay, H., & Sime, M. E. (1962). Discrimination learning with old and young rats. *Journal of Gerontology, 17,* 75–80.

Kesner, R. P. (1988). Reevaluation of the contribution of the basal forebrain cholinergic system to memory. *Neurobiology of Aging, 9,* 609–616.

Kesner, R. P., Crutcher, K. A., & Measom, M. O. (1986). Medial septal and vulceus basalis magnocellularis lesions produce order memory deficits in rats which mimic symptomatology of Alzheimer's disease. *Neurobiology of Aging, 7,* 287–295.

Kesner, R. P., & DiMattia, B. V. (1984). Posterior parietal association cortex and hippocampus: Equivalency of mnemonic function in animals and humans. In L. P. Squire & N. Butters (Eds.), *Neuropsychology of memory* (pp. 385–398). New York: Guilford Press.

Khachaturian, Z. (1985). Diagnosis of Alzheimer's disease. *Archives of Neurology, 42,* 1097–1105.

Killiany, R. J., Moss, M. B., Albert, M. S., Sandor, T., Tieman, J., & Josesz, F. (1993). Temporal lobe regions on magnetic resonance imaging identify patients with early Alzheimer's disease. *Archives of Neurology, 50,* 949–954.

Kinsella, K., & Gist, Y. J. (1995). *Older workers, retirement, and pensions*: Washington, DC: Department of Commerce.

Kirasic, K. C. (1991). Spatial cognition and behavior in young and elderly adults: Implication for learning new environments. *Psychology and Aging, 6,* 10–18.

Kirasic, K. C., & Allen, G. C. (1985). Aging, spatial performance and competence. In N. Charness (Ed.), *Aging and human performance* (pp. 191–224). New York: Wiley.

Kirasic, K. C., Allen, G. L., & Haggarty, D. (1992). Age-related differences in adults' marospatial cognitive processes. *Experimental Aging Research, 18,* 33–39.

Kirasic, K. C., & Bernicki, M. R. (1990). Acquisition of spatial knowledge under conditions of temporo-spatial discontinuity in young and elderly adults. *Psychological Research, 52,* 76–79.

Klein, Q. W., & Michel, M. E. (1977). A morphometric study of the neocortex of young adult and old maze-differentiated rats. *Mechanisms of Ageing and Development, 6,* 441–452.

Kotula, L., & Wisniewski, H. M. (1995). New hopes arise with the transgenic model for Alzheimer's disease. *Neurobiology of Aging, 16,* 701–703.

Lai, Z. C., Moss, M. B., Killiany, R. J., Rosene, D. L., & Herndon, J. G. (1995). Executive system dysfunction in the aged monkey: Spatial and object reversal learning. *Neurobiology of Aging, 16,* 947–954.

Landfield, P. W. (1988). Hippocampal neurobiological mechanisms of age-related memory dysfunction. *Neurobiology of Aging, 9,* 571–579.

Landfield, P. W., Baskin, R., & Pitler, T. (1981). Brain–aging correlates: Retardation by hormonal–pharmacological treatments. *Science, 214,* 581.

Landfield, P. W., & Lynch, G. (1977). Impaired monosynaptic potentiation in *in vitro* hippocampal slices from aged, memory-deficient rats. *Journal of Gerontology, 32,* 523–533.

Landfield, P. W., McGaugh, J. L., & Lynch, G. (1978). Impaired synaptic potentiation processes in the hippocampus of aged, memory-deficient rats. *Brain Research, 150,* 85–101.

Landfield, P. W., & Morgan, G. A. (1984). Chronically elevating plasma MG²⁺ improves hippocampal frequency potentiation and reversal learning in aged and young rats. *Brain Research, 322,* 167–171.

Lawton, A. H. (1965). The historical developments in the biological aspects of aging and the aged. *Gerontologist, 5,* 25–32.

Lebrun, C., Durkin, T. P., Marighetto, A., & Jaffard, R. (1990). A comparison of the working memory performances of young and aged mice combined with parallel measures of testing and drug-induced activations of septo-hippocampal and nbm-cortical cholinergic neurones. *Neurobiology of Aging, 11,* 515–521.

Lee, K. S. (1983). Sustained modification of neuronal activity in the hippocampus and neocortex. In W. Seifert (Ed.), *Neurobiology of the hippocampus* (pp. 265–272). New York: Academic Press.

Levy, W. B., & Steward, O. (1979). Synapses as associative memory elements in the hippocampal formation. *Brain Research, 175,* 233–245.

Light, L. L. (1991). Memory and aging: Four hypotheses in search of data. *Annual Review of Psychology, 42,* 333–376.

Light, L. L., & Zelinski, E. M. (1983). Memory for spatial information in young and old adults. *Developmental Psychology, 19,* 901–906.

Lindner, M. D., & Schallert, T. (1988). Aging and atropine effects on spatial navigation in the Morris water task. *Behavioral Neuroscience, 102,* 621–634.

Lipman, P. D., & Caplan, L. J. (1992). Adult age differences in memory for routes: Effects of instruction and spatial diagram. *Psychology and Aging, 7,* 435–442.

Lippa, A. S., Pelham, R. W., Beer, B., Critchett, D. J., Dean, R. L., & Bartus, R. T. (1980). Brain cholinergic dysfunction and memory in aged rats. *Neurobiology of Aging, 1,* 13–19.

Lippa, C. F., Hamos, J. E., Pulaski-Salo, D., Degennaro, L. J., & Drachman, D. A. (1992). Alzheimer's disease and aging: Effects on perforant pathway perikarya and synapses. *Neurobiology of Aging, 13,* 405–411.

Loring, J. F., Paszty, C., Rose, A., McIntosh, T. K., Murai, H., Pierce, J. E. S., Schramm, S. R., Wymore, K., Lee, V.M.-L., Trojanowski, J. Q., & Peterson, K. R. (1996). Rational design of an animal model for Alzheimer's disease: Introduction of multiple human genomic transgenes to reproduce AD pathology in a rodent. *Neurobiology of Aging, 17,* 173–182.

Lowy, A. M., Ingram, D. K., Olton, D. S., Waller, S. B., Reynolds, M. A., & London, E. D. (1985). Discrimination learning requiring different memory components in rats: Age and neurochemical comparisons. *Behavioral Neuroscience, 99,* 638–651.

Markowska, A. L., Ingram, D. K., Barnes, C. A., Spangler, E. L., Lemken, V. J., Kametani, H., Yee, W., & Olton, D. S. (1990). Acetyl-*l*-carnitine. 1: Effects on mortality, pathology, and sensory-motor performance in aging rats. *Neurobiology of Aging, 11,* 491–498.

Markowska, A. L., Stone, W. S., Ingram, D. K., Reynolds, J., Gold, P. E., Conti, L. H., Pontecorvo, M. J., Wenk, G. L., & Olton, D. S. (1989). Individual differences in aging: Behavioral and neurobiological correlates. *Neurobiology of Aging, 10,* 31–43.

Martin, L. G. (1988). The aging of Asia. *Journal of Gerontology, 43,* S99–S113.

Martin, G. M., Harley, C. W., Smith, A. R., Hoyles, E. S., & Hynes, C. A. (1997). Spatial disorientation blocks reliable goal location in the Morris maze. *Journal of Experimental Psychology: Animal Behavior Processes, 23,* 183–193.

Martinez, J. L., Jr., & Rigter, H. (1983). Assessment of retention capacities in old rats. *Behavioral and Neural Biology, 39,* 181–191.

Martinez, J. L., Jr., Schulteis, G., Janak, P. H., & Weinberger, S. B. (1988). *Neurobiology of Aging, 9,* 697–708.

Masoro, E. J. (1991). Use of rodents as models for the study of "normal aging": Conceptual and practical issues. *Neurobiology of Aging, 12,* 639–643.

McEwen, B., Weiss, J., & Schwartz, L. (1968). Selective retention of corticosterone by limbic structures in rat brain. *Nature, 220,* 911.

McNamara, M. C., Benignus, G., Benignus, V. A., Miller, A. T., Jr. (1977). Active and passive avoidance in rats as a function of age. *Experimental Aging Research, 3,* 3–16.

McNaughton, B. L., & Barnes, C. A. (1977). Physiological identification and analysis of dentate granule cell response to stimulation of the medial and lateral perforant pathways in the rat. *Journal of Comparative Neurology, 175,* 439–454.

McNaughton, B. L., Barnes, C. A., Gothard, K. M., Jung, M. W., Knierim, J. J., Kudrimoti, H. K., Qin, Y.-L., Skaggs, W. E., Gerrard, J. L., Suster, M., & Weaver, K. L. (1996). Deciphering the hippocampal polyglot: The hippocampus as a path integration system. *Journal of Experimental Biology, 199,* 173–185.

McNaughton, B. L., Barnes, C. A., Meltzer, J., & Sutherland, R. J. (1989). Hippocampal granule cells are necessary for normal spatial learning but not for spatially-selective pyramidal cell discharge. *Experimental Brain Research, 76,* 485–496.

McNaughton, B. L., Douglas, R. M., & Goddard, G. V. (1978). Synaptic enhancement in fascia dentata: Cooperativity among coactive afferents. *Brain Research, 157,* 277–293.

McNaughton, B. L., & Morris, R. G. M. (1987). Hippocampal synaptic enhancement and information storage within a distributed memory system. *Trends in Neurosciences, 10,* 408–415.

Meaney, M. J., Aitken, D. H., Bodnoff, S. R., Iny, L. J., Tatarewicz, J. E., & Sapolsky, R. M. (1985). Early postnatal handling alters glucocorticoid receptor concentration in selected brain regions. *Behavioral Neuroscience, 99,* 765–770.

Meaney, M. J., Aitken, D. H., van Berkel, C., Bhatnagar, S., & Sapolsky, R. M. (1988). Effect of neonatal handling on age-related impairments associated with the hippocampus. *Science, 239,* 766–768.

Milner, B. (1965). Visually-guided maze-learning in man: Effects of bilateral hippocampal, bilateral frontal, and unilateral cerebral lesions. *Neuropsychologia, 3,* 317–338.

Mushkin, M., Malamut, B. L., & Bachevalier, J. (1984). Memories and habits: Two neural systems. In J. L. McGaugh, G. Lynch, & N. M. Weinberger (Eds.), *Neurobiology of learning and memory* (pp. 65–77). New York: Guilford Press.

Mohs, R. C. (1988). Memory impairment in amnesia and dementia: Implications for the use of animal models. *Neurobiology of Aging, 9,* 465–468.

Morgan, D. G., & Finch, C. E. (1987). Neurotransmitter receptors in Alzheimer's disease and nonpathological aging. In P. Davies & C. E. Finch (Eds.), *Molecular neuropathology of aging* (pp. 21–35). New York: Cold Spring Harbor Laboratory.

Morris, R. G. M. (1981). Spatial localization does not require the presence of local cues. *Learning and Motivation, 12,* 239–261.

Morris, R. G. M., Garrud, P., Rawlins, J. N. P., & O'Keefe, J. (1982). Place navigation impaired in rats with hippocampal lesions. *Nature, 297,* 681–683.

Moss, M. B., Rosene, D. L., & Peters, A. (1988). Effects of aging on visual recognition memory in the rhesus monkey. *Neurobiology of Aging, 9,* 495–502.

Munn, N. L. (1950). *Handbook of psychological research on the rat.* Boston: Houghton Mifflin Co.

Nilsson, O. G., & Gage, F. H. (1993). Anticholinergic sensitivity in the aging rat septohippocampal system as assessed in a spatial memory task. *Neurobiology of Aging, 14,* 487–497.

Normile, H. J., & Altman, H. J. (1992). Effect of combined acetylcholinesterase inhibition and serotonergic receptor blockade on age-associated memory impairments in rats. *Neurobiology of Aging, 13,* 735–740.

Ohta, H., Matsumoto, K., & Watanabe, H. (1993). Impairment of acquisition but not retention of a simple operant discrimination performance in aged Fischer 344 rats. *Physiology and Behavior, 54,* 443–448.

Ohta, R. J., & Kirasic, K. C. (1983). The investigation of environmental learning in the elderly. In G. D. Rowles & R. J. Ohta (Eds.), *Aging and milieu* (pp. 83–95). New York: Academic Press.

Ohta, R. J., Walsh, D. A., & Krauss, I. K. (1981). Spatial perspective-taking in young and elderly adults. *Experimental Aging Research, 7,* 45–63.

O'Keefe, J., & Nadel, L. (1978). *The hippocampus as a cognitive map.* Oxford: Clarendon Press.

Olson, L. (1993). NGF and the treatment of Alzheimer's diseases. *Experimental Neurology, 124,* 5–15.

Olson, L., Nordberg, A., Von Holst, H., Backman, L., Ebendahl, T., Alafuzoff, I., Amberla, K., Hartvig, P., Herlitz, A., Lilja, A., Lundquist, H., Langstron, B., Meyerson, B., Persson, A., Viitanen, M., Winblad, B., & Seiger, A. (1992). Nerve growth factor affects 11 C-nicotine binding, blood flow, EEG and verbal episodic memory in an Alzheimer patient. *Journal of Neurological transmission, 4,* 79–95.

Olton, D. S. (1983). Memory functions and the hippocampus. In W. Seifert (Ed.), *Neurobiology of the hippocampus* (pp. 335–373). New York: Academic Press.

Olton, D. S., & Samuelson, R. J. (1976). Remembrance of places passed: Spatial memory in rats. *Journal of Experimental Psychology, Animal Behavior Processes, 2,* 97–116.

Olton, D. S., Walker, J. A., & Gage, F. H. (1978). Hippocampal connections and spatial discrimination. *Brain Research, 139,* 295–308.

Olton, D. S., & Wenk, G. (1987). Dementia: Animal models of the cognitive impairments produced by degeneration of the basal forebrain cholinergic system. In H. Y. Meltzer (Ed.), *Psychopharmacology: The third generation of progress* (pp. 941–953). New York: Raven Press.

Palmore, E. B., Fillenbaum, G. G., & George, L. K. (1984). Consequences of retirement. *Journal of Gerontology, 39,* 109–116.

Park, D. C., Cherry, K. E., Smith, A. D., & Lafronza, V. N. (1990). Effect of distinctive context on memory for objects and their locations in young and elderly adults. *Psychology and Aging, 5,* 250–255.

Park, D. C., Puglisi, J., & Lutz, R. R. (1982). Spatial memory in older adults: Effects of intentionality. *Journal of Gerontology, 37,* 330–335.

Pelleymounter, M. A., Smith, M. Y., & Gallagher, M. (1987). Spatial learning impairments in aged rats trained with a salient configuration of stimuli. *Psychobiology, 15,* 248–254.

Perlmutter, M., Metzger, R., Nezworski, T., & Miller, K. (1981). Spatial and temporal memory in 20 and 60 year olds. *Journal of Gerontology, 36,* 59–65.

Peterson, C. (1992). Changes in calcium's role as a messenger during aging in neuronal and nonneuronal cells. *Annals of the New York Academy of Sciences, 663,* 279–293.

Pezdek, K. (1983). Memory for items and their spatial locations by young and elderly adults. *Developmental Psychology, 19,* 895–900.

Phelps, C. H., Gage, F. H., Growdon, J. H., Hefti, F., Harbaugh, R., Johnston, M. V., Khachaturian, Z. S., Mobley, W. C., Price, D. L., Raskind, M., Simpkin, J., Thal, L. J., & Woodcock, J. (1989). Potential use of nerve growth factor to treat Alzheimer's disease. *Neurobiology of Aging, 10,* 205–207.

Pigott, S., & Milner, B. (1993). Memory for different aspects of complex visual scenes after unilateral temporal- or frontal-lobe resection. *Neuropsychologia, 31,* 1–15.

Pitsikas, N., Brambilla, A., & Borsini, F. (1993). DAU 6215, a novel 5-HT3 receptor antagonist, improves performance in the aged rat in the Morris water maze task. *Neurobiology of Aging, 14,* 561–564.

Pitsikas, N., Carli, M., Fidecka, S., & Algeri, S. (1990). Effect of life-long hypocaloric diet on age-related changes in motor and cognitive behavior in a rat population. *Neurobiology of Aging, 11,* 417–423.

Pontecorvo, M., Clissold, D. B., & Conti, L. H. (1988). Automated repeated measures tests for age related cognitive impairments. *Neurobiology of Aging, 9,* 617–625.

Poon, L. W. (1985). Differences in human memory with aging: Nature, causes, and clinical implications. In J. E. Birren & K. W. Schaie (Eds.), *The handbook of the psychology of aging* (pp. 427–462). New York: Van Nostrand Reinhold.

Port, R. L., Murphy, H. A., Magee, R. A., & Seybold, K. S. (1996). Prior instrumental conditioning improves spatial cognition and attenuated changes in hippocampal function in aged rats. *Journal of Gerontology: Biological Sciences, 51A,* 17–20.

Potier, B., Rascol, O., Jazat, F., Lamour, Y., & Dutar, P. (1992). Alterations in the properties of hippocampal pyramidal neurons in the aged rat. *Neuroscience, 48,* 793–806.

Presty, S. K., Bachevalier, J., Walker, L. C., Struble, R. G., Price, D. L., Mishkin, M., & Cork, L. C. (1987). Age differences in recognition memory of the rhesus monkey (*Macaca mulatta*). *Neurobiology of Aging, 8,* 435–440.

Quetelet, A. (1842). *A treatise on man and the development of his faculties.* Edinburgh: William and Robert Chambers.

Racine, R. J., & Milgram, N. W. (1983). Long-term potentiation phenomenon in the rat limbic forebrain. *Brain Research, 260,* 217–231.

Rapp, P. R., & Amaral, D. G. (1991). Recognition memory deficits in a subpopulation of aged monkeys resemble the effects of medial temporal lobe damage. *Neurobiology of Aging, 12,* 481–486.

Rapp, P. R., & Amaral, D. G. (1992). Individual differences in the cognitive and neurobiological consequences of normal aging. *Trends in Neurosciences, 15,* 340–345.

Rapp, P. R., Rosenberg, R. A., & Gallagher, M. (1987). An evaluation of spatial information processing in aged rats. *Behavioral Neuroscience, 103,* 3–12.

Rasmussen, T., Schliemann, T., Sørensen, J. C., Zimmer, J., & West, M. J. (1996). Memory impaired aged rats: No loss of principal hippocampal and subicular neurons. *Neurobiology of Aging, 17,* 143–147.

Rawlins, J. N. P. (1985). Associations across time: The hippocampus as a temporary memory store. *Behavioral and Brain Sciences, 8,* 479–496.

Richter, P. (1981). *The literary works of Leonardo da Vinci.* London: Phaidon Press.

Roman, F. S., Alescio-Lautier, B., & Soumireu-Mourat, B. (1996). Age-related learning and memory deficits in odor-reward association in rats. *Neurobiology of Aging, 17,* 31–40.

Rosene, D. L., & Van Hoesen, G. W. (1987). The hippocampal formation of the primate brain: A review of some comparative aspects of cytoarchitecture and connections. In E. G. Jones & A. Peters (Eds.), *Cerebral cortex: Vol. 6: Further aspects of cortical function, including hippocampus* (pp. 345–456). New York: Plenum Press.

Ross, W. D. (Ed.). (1928). *The works of Aristotle translated into English.* Oxford: Oxford University Press.

Rossor, M. N., Emson, P. C., Montjoy, C. Q., Roth, M., Iversen, L. L. (1980). Reduced amounts of immunoreactive somatostatin in the temporal cortex in senile dementia of Alzheimer type. *Neuroscience Letters, 20,* 373–377.

Rupniak, N. M. J., & Gaffan, D. (1987). Monkey hippocampus and learning about spatially directed movements. *Journal of Neuroscience, 7,* 2331–2337.

Sandin, M., Jasmin, S., & Levere, T. E. (1990). Aging and cognition: Facilitation of recent memory in aged nonhuman primates by nimodpinine. *Neurobiology of Aging, 11,* 573–575.

Sapolsky, R. M. (1987). Protecting the injured hippocampus by attenuating glucocorticoid secretion. In P. Davies & C. E. Finch (Eds.), *Molecular neuropathology of aging* (pp. 191–204). New York: Cold Spring Harbor Laboratory.

Sapolsky, R. M., Frey, L., & McEwen, B. (1985). Prolonged glucocorticoid exposure reduces hippocampal neuron number: Implications for aging. *Journal of Neuroscience, 5,* 1222–1227.

Scheff, S. W., & Price, D. A. (1993). Synapse loss in the temporal lobe in Alzheimer's disease. *Annals of Neurology, 33,* 190–199.

Scoville, W. B., & Milner, B. (1957). Loss of recent memory after bilateral hippocampal lesions. *Journal of Neurology, Neurosurgery, andPsychiatry, 20,* 11–21.

Sharps, M. J., & Gollin, E. S. (1987). Memory for object locations in young and elderly adults. *Journal of Gerontology, 42,* 336–341.

Shen, J., & Barnes, C. A. (1996). Age-related decrease in cholinergic synaptic transmission in three hippocampal subfields. *Neurobiology of Aging, 17,* 439–451.

Shen, J., Barnes, C. A., Wenk, G. L., & McNaughton, B. L. (1996). Differential effects of selective immunotoxic lesions of medial septal cholinergic cells on spatial working and reference memory. *Behavioral Neuroscience, 110,* 1181–1186.

Shimamura, A. P., Berry, J. M., Mangels, J. A., Rusting, C. L., & Jurica, P. J. (1995). Memory and cognitive abilities in university professors: Evidence for successful aging. *Psychological Science, 6,* 271–275.

Skalicky, M., Bubna-Littitz, H., & Hofecker, G. (1984). The influence of persistent crowding on the age changes of behavioral parameters and survival characteristics of rats. *Mechanisms of Ageing and Development, 28,* 325–336.

Slonaker, J. R. (1907). The normal activity of the white rat at different ages. *Journal of Comparative Neurology and Psychology, 17,* 342–359.

Smith, M. L., & Milner, B. (1981). The role of the right hippocampus in the recall of spatial location. *Neuropsychologia, 19,* 781–793.

Smith, T. D., Gallagher, M., & Leslie, F. M. (1995). Cholinergic binding sites in rat brain: Analysis by age and cognitive status. *Neurobiology of Aging, 16,* 161–173.

Soffié, M., & Lejeune, H. (1991). Acquisition and long-term retention of a two-level DRL schedule: Comparison between mature and aged rats. *Neurobiology of Aging, 12,* 25–30.

Solomon, P. R., Beal, M. F., & Pendlebury, W. W. (1988). Age-related disruption of classical conditioning: A model systems approach to memory disorders. *Neurobiology of Aging, 9,* 535–546.

Solomon, P. R., Levine, E., Bein, T., & Pendlebury, W. W. (1991). Disruption of classical conditioning in patients with Alzheimer's disease. *Neurobiology of Aging, 12,* 283–287.

Solomon, P. R., Wood, M. S., Groccia-Ellison, M. E., Yang, B., & Fanelli, R. J. (1995). Nimodipine facilitates retention of the classically conditioned nictitating membrane response in aged rabbits over long retention intervals. *Neurobiology of Aging, 16,* 791–796.

Spangler, E. L., Chachich, M. E., Curtis, N. J., & Ingram, D. K. (1989). Age-related impairment in complex maze learning in rats: Relationship to neophobia and cholinergic antagonism. *Neurobiology of Aging, 10,* 131–141.

Spangler, E. L., Waggie, K. S., Hengemihle, J., Roberts, D., Hess, B., & Ingram, D. K. (1994). Behavioral assessment of aging in male Fischer 344 and brown Norway rat strains and their F1 hybrid. *Neurobiology of Aging, 15,* 319–328.

Spangler, E. L., Waggie, K. S., Rea, W., Roberts, D., Hengemihle, J., Danon, D., & Ingram, D. K. (1995). Relationship of hematological variables to learning performance in aged Fischer-344 rats. *Neurobiology of Aging, 16,* 85–89.

Sprott, R. L. (1978). The interaction of genotype and environment in the determination of avoidance behavior of aging inbred mice. In *The National Foundation–March of Dimes genetic effects on aging* (Vol. 14, pp. 109–120). New York: Alan R. Liss.

Squire, L. R. (1992). Memory and the hippocampus: A synthesis from findings with rats, monkeys, and humans. *Psychological Review, 99,* 195–231.

Stern, Y., Gurland, B., Tatemichi, T. K., Tang, M. X., Wilder, D., & Mayeux, R. (1994). Influence of education and occupation on the incidence of Alzheimer's disease. *Journal of the American Medical Association, 27,* 1004–1010.

Stewart, J., Mitchell, J., & Kalant, N. (1989). The effects of life-long food restriction on spatial memory in young and aged Fischer 344 rats measured in the eight-arm radial and the Morris water mazes. *Neurobiology of Aging, 10,* 669–675.

Stone, C. P. (1929a). The age factor in animal learning: I. Rats in the problem box and the maze. *Genetic Psychology Monographs, 5,* 1–130.

Stone, C. P. (1929b). The age factor in animal learning: II. Rats on a multiple light discrimination box and a difficult maze. *Genetic Psychology Monographs, 6,* 125–201.

Straube, K. T., Deyo, R. A., Moyer, J. R., & Disterhoft, J. P. (1990). Dietary nimodipine improves associative learning in aging rabbits. *Neurobiology of Aging, 11,* 659–661.

Sutherland, R. J., & Rudy, J. W. (1989). Configural association theory: The role of the hippocampal formation in learning, memory, and amnesia. *Psychobiology, 17,* 129–144.

Sutherland, R. J., Whishaw, I. Q., & Kolb, B. (1983). A behavioral analysis of spatial localization following electrolytic kainate- or colchicine-induced damage to the hippocampal formation in the rat. *Behavioral Brain Research, 7,* 133–153.

Swihart, A. A., & Pirozzolo, F. J. (1988). The neuropsychology of aging and dementia: Clinical issues. In H. A. Whitaker (Ed.), *Neuropsychological studies of nonfocal brain damage: Dementia and Trauma* (pp. 1–60). New York: Springer-Verlag.

Tanila, H., Taira, T., Piepponen, T. P., & Honkanen, A. (1994). Effect of sex and age on brain monoamines and spatial learning in rats. *Neurobiology, 15,* 733–741.

Taylor, L., & Griffith, W. H. (1993). Age-related decline in cholinergic synaptic transmission in hippocampus. *Neurobiology of Aging, 14,* 509–515.

Teyler, T. J., & DiScenna, P. (1986). The hippocampal memory indexing theory. *Behavioral Neuroscience, 100,* 147–154.

Thomas, J.-L. (1985). Visual memory: Adult age difference in map recall and learning strategies. *Experimental Aging Research, 11,* 93–95.

Tomlinson, B. E., & Henderson, G. (1976). Some quantitative cerebral findings in normal and demented old people. In R. D. Terry and S. Gershon (Eds.), *Neurobiology of Aging* (pp. 183–204). New York: Raven Press.

Turner, D. A., & Deupree, D. L. (1991). Functional elongation of CA1 hippocampal neurons with aging in Fischer 344 rats.

Uttl, B., & Graf, P. (1993). Episodic spatial memory in adulthood. *Psychology and Aging, 8,* 257–273.

van der Staay, F. J., Blokland, A., & Raaijmakers, W. (1990). Different time course for age-related changes of behavior in a complex spatial cone-field discrimination task in Lewis rats. *Psychobiology, 18,* 305–311.

van Gool, W. A., Mirmiran, M., & van Haaren, F. (1985). Spatial memory and visual evoked potentials in young and old rats after housing in an enriched environment. *Behavioral and Neural Biology, 44,* 454–469.

Van Hoesen, G. W., Solodkin, A., & Hyman, B. T. (1995). Neuroanatomy of Alzheimer's disease: Hierarchical vulnerability and neural system compromise. *Neurobiology of Aging, 16,* 278–280.

Vasquez, B. J., Martinez, J. L., Jensen, R. A., Messing, R. B., Rigter, J., & McGaugh, J. L. (1983). Learning and memory in young and aged Fischer 344 rats. *Archives of Gerontology and Geriatrics, 2,* 279–291.

Verzar-McDougall, E. (1957). Studies in learning and memory in ageing rats. *Gerontologia, 1,* 65–85.

Waddell, K. J., & Rogoff, B. (1981). Effect of contextual organization on spatial memory of middle-aged and older women. *Developmental Psychology, 17,* 878–885.

Walker, L. C., Kitt, C. A., Struble, R. G., Wagster, M. V., Price, D. L., & Cork, L. C. (1988). The neural basis of memory decline in aged monkeys. *Neurobiology of Aging, 9,* 657–666.

Wallace, J. E., Krauter, E. E., & Campbell, B. A. (1980a). Animal models of declining memory in the aged: Short-term spatial memory in the aged rat. *Journal of Gerontology, 353,* 355–363.

Wallace, J. E., Krauter, E. E., & Campbell, B. A. (1980b). Motor and reflexive behavior in the aging rat. *Journal of Gerontology, 35,* 364–370.

Walsh, D., Krauss, I., & Regnier, V. (1981). Spatial ability, environmental knowledge and environmental use. In L. Liben, A. H. Patterson, & N. Newcombe (Eds.), *Spatial representation and behavior across the life span* (pp. 321–357). New York: Academic Press.

Weber, R., Brown, L., & Weldon, J. (1978). Cognitive maps of environmental knowledge and preference in nursing home patients. *Experimental Aging Research, 4,* 157–174.

Weiss, C., & Thompson, R. F. (1991). The effects of age on eyeblink conditioning in the freely moving Fischer-344 rat. *Neurobiology of Aging, 12,* 249–254.

Wenk, G. L., Hepler, D., & Olton, D. (1984). Behavior alters the uptake of [3H]choline into acetylcholinergic neurons of the nucleus basalis magnocellularis and medial septal area. *Behavioral Brain Research, 13,* 129–138.

Wenk, G. L., Stoehr, J. D., Mobley, S. L., Gurney, J., & Morris, R. J. (1996). Age-related decrease in vulnerability to excitatory amino acids in the nucleus basalis. *Neurobiology of Aging, 17,* 1–7.

Wenk, G. L., Stoehr, J. D., Quintana, G., Mobley, S., & Wiley, R. G. (1994). Behavioral, biochemical, histological, and electrophysiological effects of 192 IgG-saporin injections into the basal forebrain of rats. *Journal of Neuroscience, 14,* 5986–5995.

West, M. J. (1993). New stereological methods for counting neurons. *Neurobiology of Aging, 14,* 275–285.

Wickelgren, I. (1996). Is hippocampal cell death a myth? *Science, 271,* 1229–1230.

Wiley, R. G. (1992). Neural lesioning with ribosome-inactivating proteins: Suicide transport and immunolesioning. *Trends in Neurosciences, 15,* 285–290.

Winocur, G. (1984). The effects of retroactive and proactive interference on leaerning and memory in old and young rats. *Developmental Psychobiology, 17,* 537–545.

Winocur, G. (1991). Conditional learning in aged rats: Evidence of hippocampal and prefrontal cortex impairment. *Neurobiology of Aging, 13,* 131–135.

Woodruff-Pak, D. S. (1988). Aging and classical conditioning: Parallel studies in rabbits and humans. *Neurobiology of Aging, 9,* 511–522.

Woodruff-Pak, D. S., Lavond, D. G., Logan, C. G., & Thompson, R. F. (1987). Classical conditioning in 3-, 30-, and 45-month-old rabbits: Behavioral learning and hippocampal unit activity. *Neurobiology of Aging, 8,* 101–108.

Yerkes, R. M. (1909). Modifiability of behavior in its relations to the age and sex of the dancing mouse. *Journal of Comparative Neurology and Psycholoogy, 19,* 237–271.

Zelinski, E. M., & Light, L. L. (1988). Young and older adults' use of context in spatial memory. *Psychology and Aging, 3,* 99–101.

Zola-Morgan, S., Squire, L. R., & Amaral, D. G. (1986). Human amnesia and the medial temporal region: Enduring memory impairment following a bilateral lesion limited to field CA1 of the hippocampus. *Journal of Neuroscience, 6,* 2950–2967.

Zornetzer, S. F. (1986). The noradrenergic locus coeruleus and senescent memory dysfunction. In T. Crook, S. H. Ferris, & R. T. Bartus (Eds.), *Assessment in geriatric psychopharmacology* (pp. 201–322). Madison, CT: Mark Powley Associates.

Zornetzer, S. F., Thompson, R., & Rogers, J. (1982). Rapid forgetting in aged rats. *Behavioral and Neural Biology, 36,* 49–60.

Zyzak, D. R., Otto, T., Eichenbaum, H., & Gallagher, M. (1995). Cognitive decline associated with normal aging in rats: A neuropsychological approach. *Learning and Memory, 2,* 1–16.

CHAPTER 8

Vertebrate Models of Learning and Memory

Bruce S. Kapp, Amy J. Silvestri, and Fay A. Guarraci

Department of Psychology, The University of Vermont, Burlington, Vermont 05405

I. INTRODUCTION

To achieve a more complete understanding of the neural substrates of learning and memory, several goals must be attained. Clearly, identifying critical brain areas that participate in the acquisition, storage, and retrieval of information would be necessary. Having identified these areas, it would then be necessary to determine the exact manner in which each contributes to learning and memory processes. For example, does a particular area represent a sensory input or motor output channel, or is it actually a site of information storage? Ultimately, it would be necessary to provide a precise description of the synaptic and intracellular mechanisms that are the substrates for learning and memory, including possible alterations in synaptic efficacy, the synthesis of new proteins, and changes in neural membrane structure.

To advanced students of behavioral neuroscience, it should come as no surprise that many of these goals have yet to be realized. Nevertheless, substantial progress is being made toward achieving these goals by using a variety of research strategies, including the use of neural analogue and intact invertebrate model systems (see Chapters 5 and 6). The rationale for the use of these models is obvious, and the importance of the results arising from their use cannot be overemphasized. However,

Neurobiology of Learning and Memory
289

the degree to which the neural substrates of learning and memory in these models are similar or identical to the analogous neural substrates in the intact vertebrate nervous system is a matter for speculation.

The analysis of the neural substrates of learning and memory in a nervous system as complex as that of the vertebrate has benefited greatly from the use of well-characterized vertebrate models. In this chapter, we review selected examples of current research efforts using vertebrate models in this analysis. We begin with a discussion of the desirable characteristics of a vertebrate model with which to study the neural substrates of learning and memory.

II. CHARACTERISTICS OF A VERTEBRATE MODEL

Although scientists investigating the neural substrates of vertebrate learning and memory have adopted behavioral paradigms that promote both nonassociative (e.g., habituation and sensitization) and associative (e.g., Pavlovian and instrumental conditioning) forms of learning, much current research employs Pavlovian defensive conditioning procedures. There are a variety of reasons for this. First, the procedures involved in this form of associative learning provide the investigator with a great deal of control over the stimulus environment during learning. Second, behavioral scientists have made great strides in understanding precisely what is learned during Pavlovian conditioning. It is generally accepted that Pavlovian conditioning involves the learning of relationships among many different events (Rescorla, 1988). For example, an animal learns that one event, the occurrence of the conditioned stimulus (CS), provides information about the occurrence of another event, the unconditioned stimulus (US). This associative information is stored in the nervous system such that subsequent presentations of the CS will elicit expectations regarding the occurrence of the US, expectations that are associated with emotional, motivational, and behavioral (somatic and/or autonomic) responses. Behavioral responses to the CS are measured, and those that are a specific consequence of the associative relationship between the CS and US are called conditioned responses (CRs). Hence, the probability of the occurrence of a CR can reflect the extent to which learning has taken place. Third, several Pavlovian CRs have been investigated extensively, and a large amount of data exists concerning their characteristics under a variety of experimental conditions (Gormezano, Kehoe, & Marshall, 1983; LeDoux, Sakaguchi, & Reis, 1984; Schneiderman, 1972). Fourth, instrumental conditioning typically incorporates procedures that promote Pavlovian conditioning. The analysis of learning in instrumental conditioning paradigms is therefore more complex, as are attempts to specify relationships between this form of learning and neurophysiological events. Thus, Pavlovian conditioning procedures generally have been preferred.

A variety of CRs have been used to assess associative learning using Pavlovian conditioning procedures. Lennartz and Weinberger (1992) have classified these CRs into two categories based on their rate of development over the course of conditioning: rapidly versus slowly acquired CRs. They, as others before them (Konorski, 1967; Mowrer, 1947), noted several additional distinguishing characteristics of these two categories. For example, slowly acquired CRs generally are somatic responses [e.g., nictitating membrane (NM) extension, eyelid closure, and limb flexion]. Further, they are specific to the nature of the CS. For example, the limb flexion CR develops when paw shock is used as a US, whereas the eyelid closure CR develops when a puff of air directed at the cornea is used as a US. Rapidly acquired CRs, on the other hand, include autonomic (e.g., heart rate, blood pressure, and pupillary dilation) and diffuse somatic (e.g., behavioral immobility or freezing) responses. These CRs are not specific to the nature of the US because they can be conditioned using many different types of stimuli as the US. Furthermore, many rapidly acquired CRs may emerge simultaneously during conditioning using but a single US.

These rapidly and slowly acquired CRs have been interpreted to reflect the engagement of two associative processes during conditioning, forming the basis for two-process theories of Pavlovian conditioning (e.g., Konorski, 1967; Mowrer, 1947; Wagner & Brandon, 1989). The first, reflected in the emergence of rapidly acquired CRs, results in a learned change in the central motivational state of the organism. This is generally referred to as an early emotional stage of learning. In situations utilizing an aversive US, this state is commonly referred to as conditioned fear. The second, reflected in more slowly acquired CRs, results in the learning of a specific CR that is directed at the US to lesson its noxious impact if, for example, it is aversive.

With the emergence of well-defined behavioral paradigms that promote Pavlovian defensive conditioning came the recognition of their usefulness as models in the analysis of the neural substrates of learning and memory (Table I). Among these, two in particular deserve special recognition, since they were among the first to be used in such an analysis and underscored the benefits of the model system approach in vertebrates. The first, Pavlovian conditioning of the NM, or third eyelid, in the rabbit was developed by Gormezano and colleagues (Gormezano et al., 1983), who extensively defined the conditions under which the NM CR emerged. This paradigm was initially adopted by Thompson and colleagues (Thompson, 1976) in their search for the neural sites of information storage. The second, Pavlovian conditioning of heart rate in the pigeon, was developed by Cohen and colleagues (Cohen, 1974) in their attempt to identify the entire neural circuit, from sensory input to motor output, essential for the conditioning of this response. Although the latter paradigm is no longer actively being used, its initial use, along with the NM model, emphasized several important characteristics that are essential for the successful use of vertebrate models in the analysis of the neural substrates of learning and memory (Cohen, 1974; Thompson, 1976). Perhaps the most important of these is the amenability of the model to the identification of the sensory and motor pathways that

TABLE I   Examples of Vertebrate Models That Have Been Commonly Used in Analyses of the Neural Substrates of Learning and Memory

Response	Species	Conditioning procedure	Investigators
Heart rate	Pigeon	Pavlovian	Cohen (1974)
	Rabbit	Pavlovian	Schneiderman (1972) Powell and Levine-Bryce (1988) Kapp *et al.* (1992)
Blood pressure and freezing	Rat	Pavlovian	LeDoux (1995)
Pupillary dilation	Cat	Pavlovian	Weinberger (1982)
Eyeblink	Cat	Pavlovian	Woody (1982)
Potentiated startle	Rat	Pavlovian	Davis (1992)
Nictitating membrane Extension/eyelid Closure	Rabbit	Pavlovian	Thompson (1976) Moore, Desmond, and Berthier (1982) Berger and Weisz (1987) Disterhoft, Shipley, and Kraus (1982) Solomon *et al.* (1986)
Locomotor avoidance	Rabbit	Instrumental	Gabriel and Schmaijuk (1990)

contribute to the acquisition and expression of the CR. Once the sensory pathways that convey CS and US information into the brain have been identified, additional experiments can be performed to identify brain areas that receive these sensory projections and, therefore, may function in the storage of information. Similarly, identification of the motor neurons that mediate the expression of a CR will suggest the details of additional experiments that might lead to the identification of brain areas that project to these motor neurons and thus may also function in information storage. As will soon become apparent, this characteristic, or variants thereof, is inherent in current analyses using well-defined vertebrate models.

III. ANALYSES OF NEURAL CIRCUITRY MEDIATING THE ACQUISITION OF RAPIDLY ACQUIRED CRs

The most commonly followed strategy used with the model system approach has been to initially localize and identify brain areas and pathways that participate in the development of the learned response under study. The identification of this critical circuitry then provides the opportunity to (a) investigate further the functional contributions of its various components, (b) determine the nature of synaptic and intracellular changes that occur in these components during conditioning, and (c) determine the degree to which their development may correlate in time with the development of associative CRs. This strategy was used by Cohen and his colleagues in their analysis of the neural changes that form the substrate for the development of the Pavlovian heart rate CR in the pigeon, a rapidly acquired CR (Cohen, 1974, 1980). Cohen's strategy placed particular emphasis on the identification of sensory, motor, and central neuroanatomical pathways and structures that convey information that is necessary to the acquisition of the CR. His strategy was based on the idea that a systematic analysis of the flow of information, from sensory input to behavioral response output, should eventually reveal sites of afferent and efferent convergence where conditioning-induced neuronal modifications occur. As stated previously, heart rate conditioning in the pigeon is no longer being used as a model. Nevertheless, the strategy used by Cohen proved highly successful and has been adopted by others with the use of other models. Further, his analysis revealed a potential site where the neural changes responsible for the formation of the association reflected in the development of the avian heart rate CR were located. This site, the posteromedial archistriatum, is the avian homologue of the mammalian amygdala. Cohen's finding (Cohen, 1975) that its destruction produced severe conditioning deficits played an important role in guiding research, including our own, concerning the contribution of the mammalian amygdala and its anatomically related structures to learning and memory using the rapidly acquired heart rate CR in the rabbit as a model response.

A. Conditioned Bradycardia in the Rabbit

The complexity of the mammalian amygdala dictated that a thorough investigation be undertaken to identify the exact amygdaloid components that contribute to associative learning. If a component that is essential for CR acquisition could be found, then an analysis of its afferent and efferent projection systems would eventually lead to the identification of an entire circuit, from sensory input to motor output, essential for CR acquisition. This identification would then set the stage for functional analyses of the various components of the circuit. As described in the following subsections, an essential component of the amygdala has been identified and has led to additional analyses designed to elucidate the circuitry responsible for the acquisition of the model bradycardic CR.

1. The Model

The Pavlovian conditioned heart rate response in the rabbit was a suitable model for our analysis for several reasons. First, the parameters of this rapidly acquired CR, a cardiodecelerative response (bradycardia), are well defined (Fredericks, Moore, Metcalf, Schwaber, & Schneiderman, 1974; Powell & Kazis, 1976; Schneiderman, 1972). Typically, the CR emerges within 5–10 conditioning trials in which the offset of a 5-sec tone CS is coincident with the onset of a 0.5-sec shock US. Second, the final motor pathway for CR expression is known. It is carried by cardioinhibitory neurons of the vagus nerve (Fredericks et al., 1974), the cell bodies of which are located within the nucleus ambiguus and dorsal motor nucleus of the vagus in this species (Jordan, Khalid, Schneiderman, & Spyer, 1982). Third, electrical stimulation of the mammalian amygdala produces cardiovascular responses (Hilton & Zbrozyna, 1963). These observations, together with Cohen's research demonstrating a contribution of the avian amygdaloid homologue to acquisition of the heart rate CR in the pigeon, suggested that Pavlovian-conditioned bradycardia in the rabbit would be an appropriate model.

2. Contributions of the Amygdala: Essential Component of the CR Pathway

Focusing on the amygdaloid central nucleus (ACe), we and others demonstrated that a variety of manipulations of this nucleus administered prior to conditioning essentially prevented the development of the CR. These included radiofrequency lesions and microinjections of β-receptor antagonists, opioid agonists, and ibotenic acid (Gallagher, Kapp, Frysinger, & Rapp, 1980; Gallagher, Kapp, & Pascoe, 1982; Kapp, Frysinger, Gallagher, & Haselton, 1979; McCabe, Gentile, Markgraf, Teich, & Schneiderman, 1992). These effects were selective to the CR and could not be attributed to any effect on CS or US sensitivity (Fig. 1). Furthermore, that electrolytic lesions of the ACe administered after conditioning essentially abolished the CR during subsequent CS presentations (Gentile, Jarrell, Teich, McCabe, & Schneiderman, 1986) suggested that the integrity of this nucleus was also essential for the expression of this CR.

Although these experiments indicated a contribution of the ACe to CR acquisition, the specific nature of this contribution remained unknown. Important anatomical findings, however, yielded an insight: Projections that extend directly from the ACe to sites of vagal cardioinhibitory neurons, including the dorsal motor nucleus of the vagus and nucleus ambiguus in the dorsal medulla, were found to exist in the rat, cat, rabbit, and primate (Higgins & Schwaber, 1983; Hopkins & Holstege, 1978; Price & Amaral, 1981; Schwaber, Kapp, Higgins, & Rapp, 1982). In the rabbit, these neurons form the final motor pathway for the expression of the bradycardic CR.

These behavioral and anatomical findings suggested the hypothesis that the ACe may contribute to the motoric expression of the CR via either direct or perhaps indirect excitation of vagal cardioinhibitory neurons (Fig. 2). This does not exclude the possibility that the ACe also contributes to associative processes nor exclude a contribution of other brain areas to CR expression.

Additional results are consistent with this working hypothesis. First, electrical stimulation of the ACe in the rabbit produced short-latency, vagus-mediated bradycardia accompanied by a decrease in arterial blood pressure (Applegate, Kapp, Underwood, & McNall, 1983; Cox, Jordan, Paton, Spyer, & Wood, 1987; Kapp, Gallagher, Underwood, McNall, & Whitehorn, 1982), responses identical to the

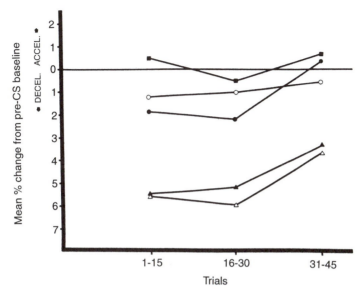

FIGURE 1   Percentage change in heart rate to the 5-sec CS from the immediately preceding 5-sec baseline period over the course of 45 conditioning trials. Data points represent group means (n = 8) for 15 trial blocks: (▲) unoperated; (△) surgical control groups; groups with (●) small (>50% damage) and (○) large (>50% damage) lesions of the central nucleus; (■) unoperated control group that received 45 unpaired presentations of the CS and US. [Reprinted with permission from Kapp, Gallagher, Applegate, & Frysinger (1982).]

CR (Powell & Kazis, 1976; Yehle, Dauth, & Schneidermann, 1967). Second, recordings obtained from small populations of neurons in the rabbit ACe during conditioning revealed that neuronal responses to the CS emerged during early conditioning trials, often in parallel with the emergence of the bradycardic CR (Applegate, Frysinger, Kapp, & Gallagher, 1982).

The activity of single ACe neurons also supported our working hypothesis (Pascoe & Kapp, 1985). For these experiments a Pavlovian discriminative conditioning paradigm was used in which two tones of different frequencies were presented, one that was always followed by the US, the CS+, and another that was never followed by the US, the CS−. During conditioning, the CS+ effected the bradycardic CR, whereas the CS− resulted in little or no heart rate change. After the discriminative heart rate CR was well established, the majority of ACe neurons responded differently to the CS+ and CS− just as the heart rate did. Furthermore, the magnitude of the neuronal response to the CS+ in some neurons correlated significantly with the magnitude of the bradycardic CR (Fig. 3). A study by McEchron, McCabe, Green, Llabre, and Schneiderman (1995) extended these earlier observations by demonstrating that, similar to the development of the bradycardic CR, discriminative responding developed in a subpopulation of ACe neurons

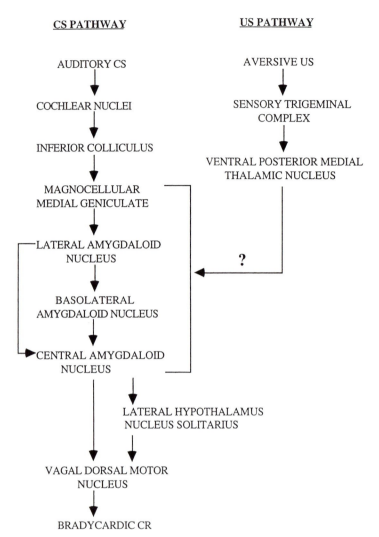

FIGURE 2   Putative pathways and structures comprising the essential circuit for the acquisition of the bradycardic CR in the rabbit (see text for details).

in less than six conditioning trials and that the latency of the response to CS+ presentations decreased over conditioning.

Although many ACe neurons demonstrate associative responding, the topography of that response varies among neurons. Whereas some neurons show enhanced activity to the CS+ versus the CS−, others show more inhibition to the CS+ than to the CS−. The extent to which these different populations exert their influence

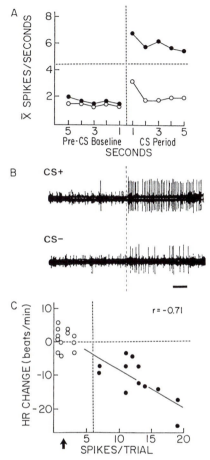

FIGURE 3   Characteristics of amygdaloid central nucleus neurons that show differentially increased activity to the CS+ and CS− during the expression of the bradycardic CR. (A) Mean activity in 13 neurons before and during presentations of the CS+ (●) and CS− (O). Points above the dashed horizontal line are significantly different from the pre-CS baseline rate ($p < 0.05$). (B) Recordings of the activity of one such neuron during presentations of the CS+ and CS−. Dashed vertical line indicates the onset of each 5-sec CS. (C) Relationship between CR magnitude and the activity of the neuron shown in (B) during 12 presentations each of the CS+ (●) and CS− (O). The arrow indicates the spontaneous rate, and the dashed vertical line indicates the rate beyond which activity is significantly elevated over baseline ($p < 0.05$). The correlation coefficient and regression line are based on the 12 CS+ trials only. HR, heart rate. [Adapted from *Behav. Brain Res., 16,* J. P. Pascoe and B. S. Kapp; Electrophysiological characteristics of amygdaloid central nucleus neurons during Pavlovian fear conditioning in the rabbit; 117–133; copyright 1985 with kind permission of Elsevier Science-NL, Sara Burgerhartstraat 25, 1055 KV Amsterdam, The Netherlands.]

on medullary cardioinhibitory neurons and to which that influence is exerted via direct and/or indirect projections has yet to be determined. However, the projection of the nucleus to the ventral midbrain periaqueductal gray (PAG) does not appear to be a component of the CR pathway because lesions of this region do not affect the expression of the CR (Wilson & Kapp, 1994).

In summary, CS information alters neuronal activity within the ACe in a manner that often is related to both CR acquisition and CR magnitude. This neuronal activity in turn may, via direct and/or indirect projections, increase activity in vagal cardioinhibitory neurons, leading to CR expression.

3. Sensory Pathways That Convey CS Information

Given that ACe activity is altered during CS presentations, the question arises concerning the pathway(s) by which auditory CS information might access the nucleus. Figure 2 shows some major areas that send projections to the nucleus based on neuroanatomical research across a variety of species. Concerning the auditory CS pathway(s), analyses have been directed primarily at the magnocellular component of the medial geniculate nucleus (MGm) of the thalamus. Recent research has provided evidence that the MGm is an essential component of the CS pathway to the ACe. First, neurons within the MGm project to the lateral nucleus of the amygdala (LeDoux, Farb, & Ruggiero, 1990) which in turn sends both direct and indirect projections to the ACe (Pitkänen et al., 1995). Second, lesions of the MGm administered prior to conditioning produce deficits in the acquisition of the bradycardic CR (Jarrell, Romanski, Gentile, McCabe, & Schneiderman, 1986; McCabe, McEchron, Green, & Schneiderman, 1993). Third, associative changes in CS-evoked MGm neuronal activity rapidly develop in several species during Pavlovian conditioning (McEchron et al., 1995; Ryugo & Weinberger, 1978; Supple & Kapp, 1989). For example, McEchron et al. (1995) recorded simultaneously from single neurons of both the ACe and MGm or the adjacent thalamic posterior intralaminar nucleus (PIN) of the rabbit over the course of conditioning trials. They observed that (a) discriminative neuronal responding in neurons of the MGm/PIN emerged within six conditioning trials, similar to that observed in ACe neurons and (b) the response latencies of MGm/PIN neurons to CS presentations were shorter than those of ACe neurons. These combined observations are consistent with the hypothesis that neurons in the MGm/PIN are components of the CS pathway and that CS information is relayed by them to the lateral amygdaloid nucleus and from there either directly or via intra-amygdaloid projections to the ACe.

4. Sites of Plasticity: The Convergence of CS and US Information

The evidence reviewed in the previous section points to a circuit by which CS information can access the ACe which in turn may contribute to the motoric expression of the bradycardic CR via either direct or indirect projections to cardioinhibitory neurons. But which of these circuit component(s) is responsible for the plasticity or changes that form the substrate for the development of the newly learned bradycardic CR? One can initially address this question by identifying components that demonstrate associative neuronal responses. Our discussion has pointed to two such areas, the ACe and the MGm. A necessary prerequisite for such associative responses to actually develop within a site requires the convergence of CS and US information at that site, a prerequisite that represents a basic tenet of neuronal theories of Pavlovian conditioning. Does CS and US information converge onto ACe and MGm neurons? As McEchron et al. (1995) have shown, the answer is yes; a population of CS-responsive neurons were encountered in both areas that also responded to US presentations. It is yet to be shown, however, that such convergence is essential for the emergence of the associative neuronal changes in these regions.

That associative neuronal responses are observed in ACe neurons is not conclusive evidence that it is the site where the associative responses actually develop. Such responses may simply reflect the relay of responses from the MGm where the necessary plasticity occurs, and recent evidence by McEchron, Green, et al., (1996) is consistent with the hypothesis that the MGm is at least one site of plasticity during conditioning of the rabbit bradycardic CR. They analyzed auditory inputs from the inferior colliculus onto MGm neurons for changes in synaptic strength as a function of conditioning. This was accomplished by examining the response of MGm neurons to electrical stimulation of the input pathway from the inferior colliculus (i.e., the brachium of the inferior colliculus, or BIC) before, immediately after, and 1 hr after conditioning using an auditory CS. The results demonstrated that compared to stimulation before conditioning, stimulation of the BIC immediately after conditioning elicited more reliable and more numerous responses at shorter latencies in MGm neurons (Fig. 4). Stimulation of the superior colliculus (SC), which sends nonauditory projections to the MGm, elicited no such increase in synaptic strength onto these same neurons. These changes were observed only in animals receiving paired conditioning trials and not in animals receiving random CS and US presentations, which did not develop the CR. The results suggest that learning-specific increases in synaptic strength occur at synapses that carry auditory CS information onto MGm neurons. In contrast to the bradycardic CR, many of these neuronal changes were markedly diminished 1 hr after conditioning. Nevertheless, as suggested by McEchron, Green, et al. (1996), a transient change in synaptic strength in the MGm could serve to promote more long-lasting changes in other structures of the essential circuit, for example, the amygdala. The extent to which changes in synaptic strength occur in the amygdala is a matter for future research.

The mechanism(s) by which changes in MGm synaptic strength is induced during conditioning has yet to be determined. However, long-term potentiation (LTP) is a likely candidate. LTP, a long-lasting increase in the excitability of neurons caused by high-frequency stimulation of their input pathways, is believed to be one mechanism responsible for the synaptic plasticity that forms the substrate for learning (see

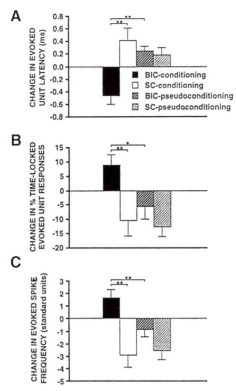

FIGURE 4   Mean change in stimulus-evoked neuronal response latency (A), reliability (B; percentage of time-locked neuronal responses), and spike frequency (C) immediately after training. Values obtained during pretraining stimulation are subtracted from those during posttraining stimulation. Groups BIC-conditioning and SC-conditioning received stimulation to either the BIC or SC prior to and following conditioning trials comprised of paired CS–US presentations. Groups BIC-pseudoconditioning and SC-pseudoconditioning received stimulation to either the BIC or SC prior to and following pseudo-conditioning trials in which the CS and US were randomly presented. Asterisks show significant comparisons among groups ($\star p < 0.05$; $\star\star p < 0.01$). Comparison of the BIC-conditioning group with control groups suggests that conditioning resulted in enhanced synaptic strength at synapses carrying auditory CS information to the MGm. Bars indicate SE. [Reprinted with permission from McEchron, Green, et al. (1996).]

Chapter 6). That LTP in MGm neurons occurs following high-frequency stimulation of the BIC has been demonstrated by Gerren and Weinberger (1983). Importantly, LTP can occur in neurons following temporally contiguous stimulation of two spatially different inputs (Kelso & Brown, 1986), endowing it with an associative characteristic analogous to Pavlovian conditioning (Fanselow, 1993). Since convergence of CS and US input onto MGm neurons has been demonstrated as described earlier, a mechanism is provided by which converging inputs carrying CS and US information could result in enhanced responses to one input (e.g., the CS) in MGm neurons. It will be of interest to determine if blockade of LTP in the MGm during conditioning results in CR acquisition deficits.

Do conditioned changes in the activity of neurons in sensory or more central structures simply reflect a general change in the excitability of these neurons, rendering them more responsive to all stimuli in the CS modality? Alternatively, might paired presentations of a CS and US somehow alter the manner in which sensory systems process information such that responsiveness to the particular stimulus used as a CS is increased? Evidence that distinguishes between these alternatives derives from an elegant series of experiments by Weinberger and colleagues detailing the changes in excitability of sensory neurons before and after conditioning (Diamond & Weinberger, 1986; Edeline & Weinberger, 1992). For example, Edeline and Weinberger (1992) measured neuronal responses in the MGm to tones of various frequencies, both before and after Pavlovian conditioning of bradycardia in the guinea pig using an auditory CS. In naive animals, the MGm neurons typically respond more robustly to sounds within a particular range of frequencies. Measurements of the response of a neuron to tones of various frequencies provide a description of the frequency receptive field (FRF) of that neuron. If conditioned changes in the response of a neuron to a CS are solely a consequence of a general change in that neuron's excitability, then responses to all frequencies within the FRF of the neuron should be modified. If, however, conditioned changes are a consequence of altered processing of CS-specific information, then the neuron's FRF should be altered such that the neuron specifically becomes more responsive to the particular frequency of the auditory stimulus used as the CS.

Edeline and Weinberger's (1992) results demonstrated that the effect of paired presentations of the CS and US during conditioning was a shift in the FRFs of 48% of the recorded neurons toward the specific frequency of the CS, a result not observed in animals that received unpaired presentations of the CS and US. These conditioned FRF shifts are known to occur in the auditory cortex as well (Diamond & Weinberger, 1986) and to persist for at least 1 hr. In conclusion, conditioning appears to alter the manner in which sensory systems process information so as to specifically favor or enhance processing of the CS.

5. Sensory Pathways That Convey US Information

Recall that convergence of CS and US information is believed to be a prerequisite for the plasticity underlying Pavlovian conditioning. Some progress has been made concerning the pathways by which US information gains access to structures where convergence occurs. For example, McEchron, McCabe, et al. (1996) presented a series of corneal airpuffs, which they have used as USs in the rabbit bradycardic model, to rabbits. Shortly thereafter the brains were processed using immunohistological techniques for identification of Fos, a protein that is synthesized in active neurons and presumably would be contained in neurons activated by the US. The protein was observed in the areas of the spinal trigeminal complex which are recipients of sensory information from the head region. In an additional experiment, neurotoxic lesions of the thalamic projection field of the trigeminal complex prevented the acquisition of the bradycardic CR (McCabe, McEchron, Green, & Schneiderman, 1995). The pathway(s) by which US information from the thalamus reaches critical structures of the essential circuit as described earlier awaits further research. In this regard, however, multiple pathways may exist, since US information can access multiple sites in the essential circuit.

6. Other Central Circuitry That Contributes to CR Acquisition

Research using the rabbit model implicates two other central structures in the acquisition of the bradycardic CR: Area 32 of the medial prefrontal cortex (Maxwell, Powell, & Buchanan, 1994; Powell, 1994) and the cerebellar vermis (Supple & Kapp, 1993; Supple & Leaton, 1990; Supple, Sebastiani, & Kapp, 1993). For example, lesions of both areas severely retard the aquisition of the bradycardic CR, and associative neuronal activity that correlates with the magnitude of the CR occurs in both areas as a function of Pavlovian conditioning. Investigations of the interactions between these two brain structures and the MGm and amygdala during Pavlovian conditioning will be an integral component of further efforts to identify the entire circuitry that is critical for CR acquisition and to determine the functional contributions of each of its components.

B. Conditioned Freezing and Blood Pressure Responses in the Rat

Heart rate CRs represent only one category of a constellation of rapidly acquired responses that can develop during the course of Pavlovian conditioning. For example, alterations in blood pressure and regional blood flow, hormone release, and diffuse somatic adjustments (e.g., freezing or immobility) also develop. As stated earlier, many of these rapidly acquired responses may be considered as manifestations of a conditioned change in the central state of the organism. In paradigms utilizing an aversive CS, many of these responses are considered indices of conditioned fear. Our discussion now turns to the research of LeDoux and his colleagues, who have been analyzing structures that participate in the acquisition and expression of two additional CRs that develop during Pavlovian aversive conditioning: conditioned blood pressure and freezing in the rat (LeDoux, 1995). These two responses have served not only to identify the neural pathways of associative learning but also to identify the neural structures that contribute to the acquisition and expression of the emotion of fear. LeDoux's strategy has been to identify and establish whether or not projections between various brain areas contribute to the expression of these two CRs, with the aim of eventually identifying the flow of information through the brain during the conditioning of fear as well as the critical sites where the plasticity required for conditioned fear occurs. Furthermore, by studying more than a single CR, it is sometimes possible to distinguish between the circuitry that may contribute to the development of an association between the CS and US versus that which contributes primarily to motor output; that is, if a lesion disrupts one CR, but not another, by implication the lesion has not prevented the development of an association but has merely disrupted the motoric expression of a particular CR. During our discussion particular emphasis will be placed on similarities and differences between the circuitry of LeDoux's model and that of the conditioned bradycardic model discussed earlier.

1. The Model

The CRs in the model developed by LeDoux are a Pavlovian-conditioned increase in blood pressure and conditioned freezing (a cessation of ongoing motor activity). Typically, rats first receive 10 trials during which a 10-sec tone is presented. These trials serve to habituate orienting responses that may occur to the presentation of this novel stimulus. During 30 subsequent trials, a footshock US is delivered during the final 0.5-msec of the tone CS. Animals in a control group are given random presentations of the CS and US (pseudoconditioned group), so that the responses of conditioned animals can be compared with responses that occur to the CS as a result of nonassociative processes such as sensitization or pseudoconditioning.

On the following day, the CS is presented alone three times while blood pressure is recorded. Presentations of the CS to animals in the conditioned group elicit a reliable blood pressure increase, and this response can readily be distinguished from the smaller responses evoked by the CS in animals in the pseudoconditioned group. Two hours later, the CS is presented for 120 sec and the amount of time spent freezing during this period is recorded. Animals that previously had received paired as opposed to random presentations of the CS and US spend significantly more time freezing during this CS presentation. While LeDoux's original research had focused on both freezing and blood pressure responses, his more recent research has focused solely on the freezing response.

2. Sensory Pathways That Convey CS Information

In examining the effects of lesions placed along pathways that convey auditory information to the forebrain, LeDoux and colleagues found that lesions of the inferior colliculus, as well as the medial geniculate nucleus (MG), prevented the acquisition of the freezing and blood pressure CRs (LeDoux et al., 1984) (Fig. 5). These lesions did not affect URs to the CS (measured prior to conditioning) or US. The results suggested that the inferior colliculus and MG are essential relays in the

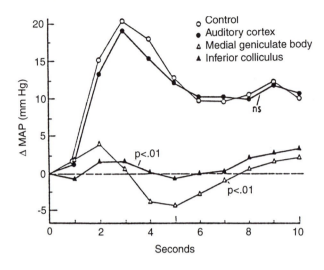

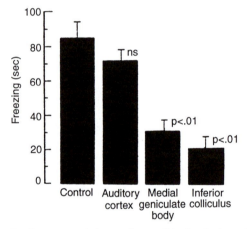

FIGURE 5   Effects of auditory-system lesions on fear conditioning. Lesions of the auditory cortex had no significant effect on blood pressure and freezing responses, but lesions of the medial geniculate or inferior colliculus significantly reduced both CRs. Blood pressure was measured during three 10-sec CS presentations and freezing during a subsequent 120-sec CS presentation. [Reprinted from LeDoux (1990), *Learning and computational neuroscience: Foundations of adaptive networks*, pp. 3–51. Copyright 1990 MIT Press.]

pathway that conveys auditory CS information necessary for the acquisition of freezing and blood pressure CRs, similar to their role in the acquisition of the bradycardic CR as previously described.

3. Central Circuitry That Contributes to Response Acquisition

Having identified the MG as an essential relay in the CS pathway, anatomical studies were conducted to identify areas that receive projections from the MG and that might also be critical components of the learning circuit. Areas recipient of MG projections included the perirhinal and auditory neocortex and a subcortical area that included portions of the caudate-putamen and the dorsal amygdala (LeDoux et al., 1984; LeDoux, Ruggiero, & Reis, 1985). In subsequent experiments, large lesions of the neocortical areas that receive MG efferents had no consistent effect on CR acquisition (Romanski, Xagoraris, Reis, & LeDoux, 1988). However, destruction of the projections from the magnocellular component of the MG (MGm) to the subcortical region, or lesions of this subcortical region itself, prevented acquisition of both CRs (Iwata, LeDoux, Meeley, Arneric, & Reis, 1986; LeDoux, Sakaguchi, Iwata, & Reis, 1986). These results suggested that learning in LeDoux's model can be supported entirely by CS information that diverges from the auditory pathway at the level of the MGm and is relayed to the subcortical region.

More recent experiments have revealed the details of the essential learning circuit. For example, the MGm and the adjacent posterior intralaminar nucleus (PIN) send a dense, direct projection to the lateral amygdaloid nucleus (AL) (LeDoux, Farb, & Ruggiero, 1990), and electrolytic lesions of the AL administered prior to conditioning disrupted the development of the blood pressure and freezing CRs (LeDoux, Cicchetti, Xagoraris, & Romanski, 1990) (Fig. 6). Lesions of the striatum located dorsal to the AL and lesions of the cortex lying lateral to the AL were without effect.

Collectively, these data support the hypothesis that information critical to the acquisition of CRs in LeDoux's model is relayed from the inferior colliculus to the MGm/PIN and from the MGm/PIN to the AL. The AL projects both directly and indirectly (via the amygdaloid basolateral nucleus) to the ACe, and LeDoux has gathered evidence that the ACe contributes to the acquisition of both CRs (Iwata et al., 1986). Further observations demonstrating that lesions of the ACe disrupt both freezing and bradycardic CRs in the rat in a markedly different Pavlovian conditioning paradigm (Roozendaal, Koolhaus, & Bohus, 1991a, 1991b) provide additional support for the contribution of the ACe. Importantly, the latter results are consistent with the results in the rabbit and suggest that the ACe may contribute to the expression of a variety of CRs via its extensive descending projections to the brainstem (Hopkins & Holstege, 1978; Price & Amaral, 1981).

4. The CR Pathways

Following the identification of the CS pathway from the inferior colliculus to the amygdala, LeDoux and colleagues sought to determine whether or not several areas that receive efferent projections from the ACe, including the bed nucleus of the

Lateral amygdala lesions

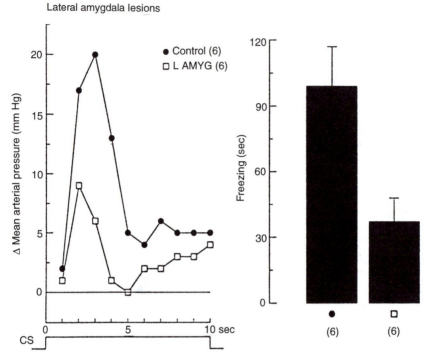

FIGURE 6   Bilateral destruction of the lateral amygdaloid nucleus significantly reduced both blood pressure and freezing CRs during CS presentations. Numbers in parentheses indicate number of rats in each group. [Reprinted with permission from LeDoux, Cicchetti, et al. (1990).]

stria terminalis, the lateral hypothalamus (LH), and the midbrain periaqueductal gray (PAG), might also be critical to the acquisition of these CRs (LeDoux, Iwata, Cicchetti, & Reis, 1988). His analysis demonstrated that lesions of the bed nucleus were without effect. Lesions of the LH, however, had no effect on the freezing CR but abolished the blood pressure CR. Complementary data were obtained from animals with lesions of the PAG: these lesions had no effect on the blood pressure CR but disrupted acquisition of the freezing CR. By implication, neither structure is essential to the formation of an association between the CS and US because rats with lesions of the LH or PAG do, in fact, acquire at least one of the two CRs.

The research of LeDoux and colleagues has identified essential elements of the circuitry that contributes to the acquisition of Pavlovian freezing and blood pressure CRs in the rat. It is obvious that several of the structures so identified (e.g., the MGm/PIN and the ACe) also appear to play an important role in the acquisition of other nonspecific Pavlovian CRs, as discussed previously and as will be discussed in the sections to follow. These converging data have set the stage for further analyses, including those that will extend these findings to the synaptic and intracellular

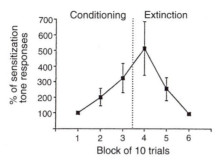

FIGURE 7   A learning curve showing the development of enhanced neuronal responding in the lateral amygdaloid nucleus over conditioning and extinction trials. Data from only those neurons showing statistically significant increases in responding during extinction trials (CS only) when compared to sensitization trials (impaired CS and US presentations) presented prior to conditioning trials are shown. Tone responses at all points in the experiment are expressed as a percentage of the tone response during sensitization trials (Block 1). [Reprinted with permission from Quirk et al. (1995). Copyright 1995 Cell Press.]

levels and will eventually provide a description of the events that are the basis of associative learning. As will soon become apparent, some of these analyses are now in progress.

5. Sites of Plasticity: The Convergence of CS and US Information

With the identification of the essential circuit for the establishment of Pavlovian-conditioned blood pressure and freezing CRs, the question arises concerning the location of the plasticity within this circuit that forms the substrate for their acquisition. Recall that sites that demonstrate associative neuronal responses are likely candidates. With respect to the MGm/PIN, although LeDoux has not recorded from MGm neurons during conditioning in his model, the development of associative responses in the MGm has been demonstrated in the rat in an aversive Pavlovian conditioning paradigm similar to his (Edeline, Dutrieux, & Neuenschwander-El Massioui, 1988). These results, together with those demonstrating such changes in the MGm of other species as described earlier, provide compelling evidence that the MGm is a potential site of plasticity.

With respect to the AL, LeDoux and colleagues have observed associative responding in these neurons (Quirk, Repa, & LeDoux, 1995). In this experiment, responses of neurons to the CS during conditioning and extinction trials were compared to those during sensitization trials in which the CS and US were presented in an unpaired manner prior to conditioning trials. Twenty-seven percent of recorded neurons showed greater responses to the CS during extinction than during sensitization, thereby demonstrating associative responding in AL neurons as a result of conditioning (Fig. 7).

In our discussion of the bradycardic CR we emphasized that convergence of CS and US information is a necessary prerequisite for the development of associative responses within a particular site. Bordi and LeDoux (1994) and Romanski, Clugnet, Bordi, and LeDoux (1993) have demonstrated convergence of CS and US information onto single neurons of the MGm/PIN and AL of rats. In the MGm/PIN 26% of the neurons from which recordings were made responded to both stimuli whereas 88% of those in the AL demonstrated such convergence. The substantial incidence of convergence in the AL suggests that it may represent a critical site in the circuit for the plasticity that forms the substrate for Pavlovian conditioning.

6. Mechanisms of Plasticity within the Circuit

Identification of the essential learning circuit and potential sites of convergence creates the opportunity to examine the cellular mechanisms of plasticity within these sites. Recall that LTP is thought to be one mechanism of synaptic plasticity that forms the substrate for learning. As described previously, LTP has been demonstrated to occur across inferior colliculus–MGm synapses (Gerren & Weinberger, 1983), suggesting that the enhanced transmission across these synapses following Pavlovian conditioning may be a function of LTP. LeDoux's research has also revealed the existence of LTP in the AL following high-frequency stimulation of the MGm/PIN (Clugnet & LeDoux, 1990; Rogan & LeDoux, 1995). Of particular importance was the finding that high-frequency stimulation of the MGm/PIN elicited an enhanced neuronal response in AL not only to a subsequent stimulus pulse applied to the MGm/PIN but also to an auditory stimulus as well (Fig. 8). Thus, the enhanced neuronal responding in AL to the CS following Pavlovian conditioning, like that observed in the MGm, may be a function of an LTP mechanism. However, as emphasized previously, the extent to which the enhanced neuronal responding in AL during conditioning is a reflection of plasticity occurring in the AL or simply the reflection of the relay of responses from the MGm, for example, has yet to be determined. Experiments of a design similar to that conducted by McEchron, Green, et al. (1996) in demonstrating enhanced synaptic strength in the MGm will aid in this determination.

Clearly, the overall results raise the possibility that there may be multiple sites of plasticity in the essential circuit (e.g., the MGm, AL, and ACe). What is the functional significance of the existence of multiple sites in terms of the development of a CR during Pavlovian conditioning? The answer is far from clear, but LeDoux (1995) has raised the possibility that plasticity in different locations might serve different functions: "plasticity in sensory structures could make stimulus processing more efficient; plasticity in motor systems could make the execution of the responses more efficient; and plasticity in the amygdala could represent the integrative (stimulus- and response-independent) aspects of learning" (LeDoux, 1995, p. 217). Future research will bear importantly on the validity of this possibility.

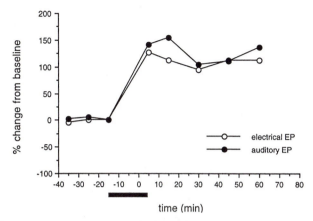

FIGURE 8   Group data showing percentage change from baseline of the slope of either electrical stimulation-induced or auditory stimulus-induced evoked potentials (EP) from a population of AL neurons before and after high-frequency stimulation of the MGm. An increased slope is indicative of LTP. Baseline was calculated as the mean slope of three stimulus pulses applied to the MGm prior to a high-frequency stimulus train applied to the MGm as indicated by the horizontal bar. The percentage change was calculated for each time point following the high-frequency stimulus train. Filled circles show changes in slope of the auditory-evoked potentials following stimulation and unfilled circles show changes in slope of potentials evoked by an electrical stimulus pulse applied to the MGm. All measurement points following high-frequency stimulation were significantly different from baseline for both evoked potentials. [Adapted with permission from Rogan and LeDoux (1995). Copyright 1995 Cell Press.]

C. Conditioned Modulation of the Acoustic Startle Reflex in the Rat

By now it has become evident that common elements exist in the circuits that contribute to the acquisition of the bradycardic CR in the rabbit and the blood pressure and freezing CRs in the rat using an auditory CS. In fact, the main difference in these circuits may reside in different CR pathways that arise in the ACe. But are there other circuits that contribute to the acquisition of other CRs during Pavlovian fear conditioning to CSs of different modalities, for example, a visual CS? As a final example of a rapidly acquired CR we turn to the research of Davis and colleagues, who have used a different measure of fear conditioned to a visual CS (Davis, 1992).

1. The Model

The model used by Davis is atypical in terms of the CR used to assess conditioning. Rather than directly measuring the development of a CR such as freezing, Davis and colleagues have identified structures and pathways that contribute to Pavlovian conditioned fear by analyzing the pathways by which a fear-arousing visual CS potentiates the acoustic startle reflex that normally occurs in response to an intense auditory stimulus. The potentiation of the reflex occurs when the visual CS (e.g., a light), which previously has been paired with an aversive event during conditioning (e.g., footshock), is presented immediately prior to the presentation of the startle stimulus. Importantly, the visual CS itself does not elicit the reflex, nor does it potentiate the reflex when previously presented with the US in an unpaired manner. Therefore, the reflex circuit that mediates the acoustic startle reflex is modulated at some point along its course by associative information. The identification of the startle reflex pathway and the point along its course where it is modulated by the CS creates the opportunity to identify the pathway by which associative information accesses the reflex, ultimately resulting in the identification of the entire conditioning circuit.

The primary components of the acoustic startle reflex circuit have been identified (Lee, Lopez, Meloni, & Davis, 1996). The circuit consists of cochlear root neurons in the auditory nerve that receive auditory input from the cochlea. These neurons project to the ventrolateral aspects of the nucleus reticularis pontis caudalis (PnC) in the brain stem, which projects to motor neurons in the spinal cord responsible for the startle response (Fig. 9). Additional experiments have determined that a fear-arousing CS modulates the flow of information in the circuit at the level of the PnC (Berg & Davis, 1985; Lee et al., 1996).

2. Central Circuitry Involved in Modulation of the Reflex

The identification of the site in the circuit at which the CS potentiates the reflex led to additional experiments designed to identify the pathways by which the CS accessed the circuit. Converging evidence has led to the conclusion that the pathway originates in the ACe. First, this nucleus projects both directly and indirectly (e.g., via the PAG) to the PnC (Fendt, Koch, & Schnitzler, 1994; Rosen, Hitchcock, Sananes, Miserendino, & Davis, 1991). Second, lesions of the ACe blocked the acquisition and expression of fear-potentiated startle using either a visual or auditory CS (Campeau & Davis, 1995; Hitchcock & Davis, 1986) (Fig. 10). In addition, lesions along the pathway by which ACe neurons project toward the startle circuit completely blocked fear-potentiated startle, as did lesions of the PAG (Fendt, Koch, & Schnitzler, 1996; Hitchcock & Davis, 1991). Third, electrical or chemical stimulation of the ACe potentiated the startle reflex (Koch & Ebert, 1993; Rosen & Davis, 1988). Importantly, this stimulation-induced facilitation appears to occur at the level of the PnC, since it facilitated the tone-evoked response of auditory responsive neurons in this nucleus (Koch & Ebert, 1993). These combined observations suggest that CS information accesses the startle circuit via a projection from the ACe to the PAG, which in turn projects to the PnC (Fendt et al., 1994).

Recall that an auditory CS predictive of an aversive event activates neurons in the ACe (Pascoe & Kapp, 1985). On the basis of the work of Davis and others, one

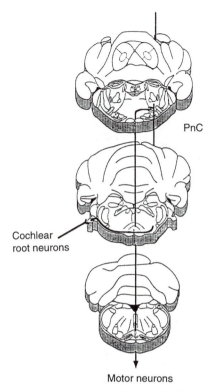

PnC

Cochlear
root neurons

Motor neurons

FIGURE 9   Diagram illustrating the primary acoustic startle circuit in the model used by Davis and colleagues. It consists of cochlear root neurons, the ventrolateral part of the PnC, and axons projecting to motor neurons of the spinal cord. [Reprinted with permission from Lee et al. (1996).]

would predict that these neurons should also be activated by a visual CS predictive of such an event. Although this has not been demonstrated with the conditioning parameters used in the potentiated startle paradigm, neurons in the ACe of the monkey are responsive to visual stimuli that predict an aversive event (Ono & Nishijo, 1992). What pathways convey visual CS information to the nucleus? A likely candidate is the AL, which projects both directly and indirectly to the ACe (Pitkanen et al., 1995) and contains neurons that also respond to visual stimuli predictive of an aversive event (Ono & Nishijo, 1992).

In additional experiments, lesions confined to the AL and basolateral amygdaloid nuclei and administered prior to conditioning trials blocked the acquisition of fear-potentiated startle conditioned to either visual or auditory CSs. Likewise, when administered following the conditioning trials, these lesions blocked the expression of potentiated startle to subsequent presentations of these CSs (Fig. 11; Campeau & Davis, 1995; Sananes & Davis, 1992). However, direct infusions of

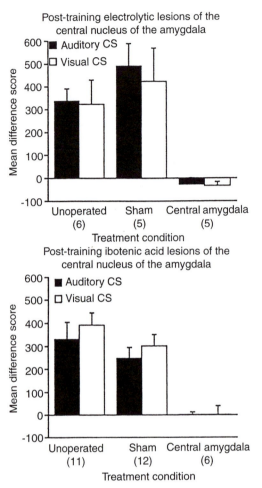

FIGURE 10   Effects of post conditioning electrolytic or ibotenic acid lesions of the central amygdaloid nucleus on the subsequent expression of the acoustic startle response during the presentation of
either a visual CS or an auditory CS. Mean difference scores (±SEM) are calculated by subtracting the
magnitude of the startle response to the startle stimulus when presented alone from the magnitude of the
response when elicited in the presence of either the visual or auditory CS. A positive score reflects
potentiated startle during CS presentation. Data are shown for unoperated and sham-lesioned control
groups and for groups receiving lesions. Numbers in parentheses indicate number of rats in each group.
[Reprinted with permission from Campeau and Davis (1995).]

AP5, an antagonist of the glutaminergic NMDA receptor, aimed at the lateral
aspects of the amygdala blocked the acquisition but not the expression of fear-
potentiated startle to visual or auditory CSs. (Campeau, Miserendino, & Davis,
1992; Miserendino, Sananes, Melia, & Davis, 1990). Of importance here are the

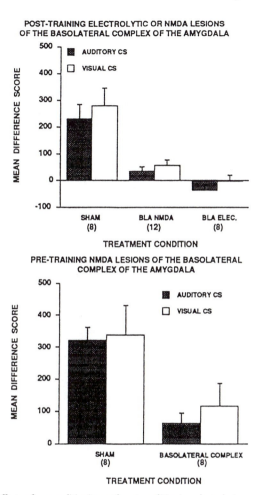

POST-TRAINING ELECTROLYTIC OR NMDA LESIONS
OF THE BASOLATERAL COMPLEX OF THE AMYGDALA

PRE-TRAINING NMDA LESIONS OF THE BASOLATERAL
COMPLEX OF THE AMYGDALA

FIGURE 11   Effects of preconditioning and postconditioning electrolytic or neurotoxic (NMDA) lesions of the amygdaloid basolateral nuclear complex on the acquisition or expression of the acoustic startle response during the presentation of either a visual or auditory CS. Numbers in parentheses indicate number of rats in each group. [Reprinted with permission from Campeau and Davis (1995).]

findings that AP5 blocks the induction but not the expression of LTP in other neural systems, thereby implicating this receptor in the mechanism for the plasticity responsible for the establishment of LTP. Overall, these results suggest that LTP in the lateral aspects of the amygdala may contribute, at least in part, to the plasticity responsible for associative modulation of the acoustic startle reflex. The results are consistent with Fanselow's (1993) suggestion that LTP can provide an adequate substrate for the plasticity underlying Pavlovian fear conditioning.

Finally, we are left with the question of the route by which visual CS information originating from the retina gains access to the amygdala. Earlier research by Tischler and Davis (1983) demonstrated that lesions of the lateral geniculate nucleus block potentiated startle. However, complete removal of the visual cortex, to which the lateral geniculate projects, exerts no significant effect (Rosen et al., 1992) and currently the pathway(s) by which visual CS information reaches the amygdala has yet to be elucidated.

IV. ANALYSES OF NEURAL CIRCUITRY MEDIATING THE ACQUISITION OF SLOWLY ACQUIRED CRs

Thus far, we have focused on research designed to identify the neural circuitry that contributes to rapidly acquired CRs, those CRs that are not specific to the nature of the US and are considered to reflect a conditioned change in the central psychological state of the organism. We turn now to a discussion of slowly acquired CRs, those CRs that are specific to the nature of the US. Many other differences between slowly and rapidly acquired CRs will become apparent as well. Some of these differences are procedural: For example, optimal acquisition of slowly acquired CRs often requires a shorter CS duration. Other differences are quite fundamental: For example, very different brain areas participate in the acquisition of slowly versus rapidly acquired CRs.

A. Conditioned Nictitating Membrane Response in the Rabbit

Over the past 35 years, the Pavlovian-conditioned nictitating membrane (NM) response in the rabbit has been the focus of intensive behavioral and neurophysiological analysis, in part because this CR satisfies many of the requirements of an ideal vertebrate model of learning (Gormezano et al., 1983; Thompson, 1976). Although other models of slowly acquired CRs have been used (see Table I), far less data have accumulated due to the infrequency of their use. Thus, our discussion will focus on the NM model.

1. The Model

The NM is a sheet of tissue located under the inner canthus (where the upper and lower eyelids meet). This tissue sweeps across the cornea (the UR) when the eye is stimulated sufficiently and, after conditioning, during a CS that predicts stimulation of the eye (the CR). The NM CR actually is part of a coordinated defensive movement that also includes retraction of the eyeball, eyelid closure (i.e., eyeblink), and contraction of periorbital facial musculature. All of these CRs are essentially perfectly correlated in amplitude and latency both within and across conditioning trials (McCormick, Lavond, & Thompson, 1982). Most often, however, only the NM or eyeblink CR is measured because these responses are discrete and simple to quantify. During typical procedures that promote acquisition of these CRs, a noxious US (a puff of air directed toward the cornea or a brief electric shock to the periorbital region) is presented during the final 100 msec of a 350-msec auditory CS. After 50–200 such trials, the CRs occur during most (e.g., 80%) CS presentations.

2. Central Circuitry That Contributes to Response Acquisition: The Essential Role of the Cerebellum

In searching for central sites that play an essential role in the acquisition of the NM CR, Thompson and colleagues, the leading researchers using this model, identified two structures that developed striking associative neuronal changes over the course of conditioning: the hippocampus and the cerebellum (Berger & Thompson, 1978; McCormick & Thompson, 1984). The hippocampus, however, did not appear to be essential for the acquisition of the NM CR since lesions of this structure did not retard the development of the CR using a standard delay conditioning procedure in which the CS and US coterminate as described earlier (Solomon & Moore, 1975). Only under conditions that place increased demands on the animal's learning ability (Solomon, Vander Schaaf, Thompson, & Weisz, 1986) do lesions retard CR acquisition, leading to the suggestion that the hippocampus plays a modulatory role in acquisition, exerting its influence only under specific conditions (Penick & Solomon, 1991). An entirely different picture emerged in the cerebellum. Of special interest were recordings from the interpositus nucleus (IP), a deep cerebellar nucleus. Prior to CR acquisition, neuronal activity at sites within IP increased briefly to the CS *and* US but was not changed in relation to the UR. As learning developed, the NM CR developed together with neuronal activity that modeled the amplitude and time course of the CR both within and over conditioning trials (McCormick & Thompson, 1984) (Fig. 12).

Thompson and his colleagues then demonstrated that the IP is an essential component of the circuit for CR acquisition and retention. For example, lesions of IP administered either before or after conditioning permanently abolished the CR. They had no effect on the UR, and unilateral lesions did not prevent CR acquisition by the contralateral eye (Clark, McCormick, Lavond, & Thompson, 1984; Steinmetz, Lavond, Ivkovich, Logan, & Thompson, 1992) (Fig. 13). These effects were observed under all conditioning parameters and CR measurement techniques (Steinmetz et al., 1992) and generalized to a variety of CS modalities (e.g., light and white noise) and USs (e.g., corneal airpuff or periorbital shock) as well as to different slowly acquired CRs, such as the leg-flexion CR using pawshock as a US (Thompson et al., 1987).

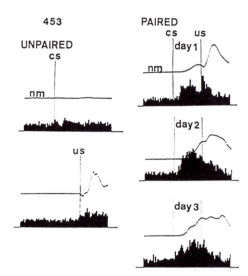

FIGURE 12   Example of change in neuronal activity within the lateral IP during unpaired and paired CS and US presentations. The animal was first given pseudorandomly unpaired presentations of the tone and corneal airpuff to which the neurons responded very little to either stimulus. However, when the stimuli were paired together in time, the cells began responding within the CS period as the animal learned the eyeblink response. The onset of this unit activity preceded the behavioral NM response within a trial by 36–58 msec. Stimulation through this recording site yielded ipsilateral eyelid closure and NM extension. Each histogram bar is 9 msec in duration. The upper trace of each histogram represents the movements of the NM, with up being extension across the eyeball. [Reprinted with permission from McCormick and Thompson (1984).]

Lesions of the cerebellar cortex, which projects to the IP, produced more variable results. According to Thompson and Krupa (1994), the degree of impairment may be a function of the amount of tissue destroyed, for it appears that the more extensive the damage, the greater the acquisition and/or retention deficits observed, with very large lesions preventing acquisition in some animals. Consistent with this interpretation are findings demonstrating that mutant mice completely devoid of Purkinje cells, the sole output neurons of the cerebellar cortex, are profoundly impaired in acquisition of the eyeblink CR (Chen, Bao, Lockard, Kim, & Thompson, 1996). These observations and those showing that associative neuronal responses develop in Purkinje cells during conditioning (Berthier & Moore, 1986; Foy & Thompson, 1986) indicate that the cerebellar cortex, like the IP, plays an essential role in eyeblink conditioning.

Finally, evidence indicates that the contribution of the cerebellum to eyeblink conditioning generalizes to humans: Acquisition of the eyeblink CR by an individual who had sustained unilateral cerebellar damage occurred rapidly on the side contralateral to the lesion but was impaired severely on the ipsilateral side (Lye, O'Boyle, Ramsden, & Schady, 1988). Together, these findings indicate that the cerebellum plays an essential role in the acquisition of slowly acquired CRs.

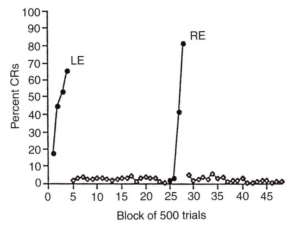

FIGURE 13   Percentage of CRs elicited by the CS during paired CS–US conditioning trials from a representative rabbit given extensive training after an IP lesion. Each data point is the average of five training sessions (500 CS–US trials). The rabbit received 20 prelesion sessions in which the left eyeblink was conditioned followed by a left IP lesion. After the lesion, the rabbit received 100 left-eye training sessions, 20 right-eye training sessions, and then an additional 100 left-eye training sessions. LE, left eye; RE, right eye. [Reprinted with permission from Steinmetz et al. (1992).]

3. The CR Pathway

That a coordinated pattern of CRs emerges during conditioning suggests that a variety of cranial nerve motor nuclei serve as the final common pathways for their expression. This has been supported by the observations that (a) learning-specific increases in neuronal activity occurred over conditioning trials in cranial motor nuclei innervating the facial musculature, including the accessory abducens nucleus, which produces eyeball retraction leading to the passive extension of the NM over the eye, and (b) cooling-induced inactivation of these nuclei abolished eyeblink CRs (Cegavske, Patterson, & Thompson, 1979; Zhang & Lavond, 1991).

The identification of the motor nuclei essential for CR expression raises the question of the pathway(s) by which the IP influences them. Research has demonstrated that this pathway involves a projection from the IP to the contralateral red nucleus and a projection from the latter to the cranial nerve motor nuclei (Fig. 14). For example, McCormick and Thompson (1984) have shown that electrical stimulation of the IP elicits a variety of short latency movements, including the coordinated eyeblink response pattern. Lesions of the superior cerebellar peduncle, which carries axons of IP neurons to the red nucleus, abolished the stimulation-induced response. Stimulation of the red nucleus also elicits eyeblink responses (Chapman, Steinmetz, & Thompson, 1988), associative neuronal responses develop in this nucleus during conditioning (Chapman, Steinmetz, Sears, & Thompson, 1990), and lesions of this nucleus contralateral to the conditioned eye abolish the eyeblink CR with no effect on the UR (Chapman et al., 1988).

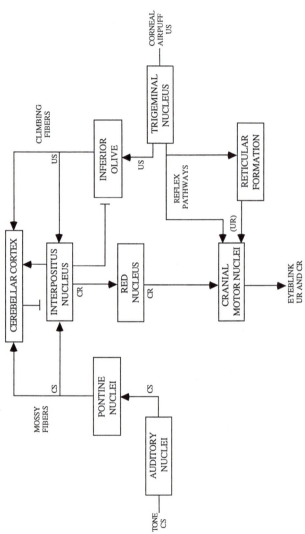

FIGURE 14 Diagram of the brain circuitry essential for classical conditioning of the NM/eyeblink CR. [From: THE BRAIN: A Neuroscience Primer by Thompson 2/e. Copyright © 1993 by W. H. Freeman and Company. Used with permission.]

4. Sensory Pathways That Convey CS Information

Removal of all brain tissue rostral to the caudal thalamus does not prevent CR expression in well-trained animals (Mauk & Thompson, 1987), suggesting that the CS pathway differs significantly from that for rapidly acquired CRs and diverges from sensory relay nuclei at subthalamic levels to gain access to the cerebellum. Indeed, neurons of the cochlear nucleus project to neurons in the lateral pontine region (Thompson, Thompson, Weiss, & Lavond, 1988) which in turn project to the IP and cerebellar cortex (Steinmetz & Sengelaub, 1992), providing a rather direct route by which CS information can reach the cerebellum. Lesions of this lateral pontine region abolished the CR to a tone CS (Steinmetz, Logan, Rosen, Thompson, Lavond, & Thompson, 1987), and electrical stimulation of this region can serve as an effective CS for conditioning of the CR, which can be abolished by subsequent lesions of the IP (Steinmetz, Rosen, Chapman, Lavond, & Thompson, 1986). In summary, CS information gains access to the cerebellum via a projection from the cochlear nucleus to the lateral pontine region which in turn projects directly to the cerebellum.

5. Sensory Pathways That Convey US Information

Analyses have revealed a critical region of the inferior olive, the dorsal accessory olive (DAO), which appears to convey US information to the cerebellum. Presentations of the airpuff US elicit neuronal responses in the face representation area of the DAO, and lesions administered prior to conditioning trials completely prevent CR acquisition without affecting the UR (Sears & Steinmetz, 1991). Furthermore, electrical stimulation of the DAO is an effective US for the acquisition of a variety of somatic CRs, including the eyeblink CR (Mauk, Steinmetz, & Thompson, 1986). In fact, CR acquisition can occur when using pontine stimulation as the CS and DAO stimulation as the US (Steinmetz, Lavond, & Thompson, 1989). If the DAO is a component of the US pathway, then lesions of the DAO in the well-trained animal should result in extinction of the CR over additional conditioning trials. Evidence for this has been presented (McCormick, Steinmetz, & Thompson, 1985). It appears, then, that US information reaches the cerebellum via the DAO, which ultimately receives US information from the sensory trigeminal complex. Recall that neurons in the trigeminal complex are activated by airpuff presentations to the cornea (McEchron, McCabe, et al., 1996).

Figure 14 summarizes the fundamental circuit essential for the acquisition of the coordinated NM/eyeblink CR pattern. With slight modifications of the US pathway, this same circuit is believed to be essential for the acquisition of other, slowly acquired CRs such as conditioned leg flexion. It is important to note that additional components of this essential circuit are continually being identified; for example, projections from the red nucleus to the cerebellar cortex (Rosenfield & Moore, 1995). The functional significance of these additional components is unknown and will most likely be a focus of future research.

6. Sites of Plasticity: The Convergence of CS and US Information

Recall that a prerequisite for the plasticity that forms the substrate for associative learning is the convergence of CS and US information onto individual neurons at a site in the essential circuitry. Although such convergence does not appear to occur in pontine and DAO neurons that project to the cerebellum, it does occur in the cerebellar cortex (Foy, Krupa, Tracy, & Thompson, 1992) and IP (Yang & Weisz, 1992). Compelling evidence that the IP is a site of plasticity has been provided by reversible lesion techniques. For example, cooling-induced inactivation of the IP during acquisition trials resulted in no evidence of learning (Clark, Zhang, & Lavond, 1992). Upon termination of cooling, learning progressed at a rate similar to that observed in naive animals, and no signs of behavioral savings from conditioning trials presented during the inactivation period were observed. Further, cooling-induced inactivation of the IP in well-trained animals abolished the NM CR. These responses, however, reappeared upon termination of cooling (Clark et al., 1992) (Fig. 15).

A different picture emerged when the red nucleus was inactivated. During acquisition trials, inactivation produced no signs of learning. Following inactivation, however, animals showed near-asymptotic performance, demonstrating that learning occurred during inactivation (Clark & Lavond, 1993; Krupa, Thompson, & Thompson, 1993). A similar result was observed with inactivation of the appropriate cranial nerve motor nuclei (Krupa, Weng, & Thompson, 1996; Zhang & Lavond, 1991). The results, taken together, strongly suggest that the IP is one cerebellar site where plasticity essential for the Pavlovian conditioning of the NM response occurs and that sites efferent to it are not.

The compelling evidence implicating the cerebellum as a site of plasticity raises the question of the cellular mechanisms that form the substrate for this plasticity. With respect to the IP, little research has been directed at this question, although it has been demonstrated that LTP can be induced in the nucleus by stimulation of its afferents (Racine, Wilson, Gingell, & Sutherland, 1986). Some research addressing this question has been directed at the cerebellar cortex. Although Purkinje neurons develop associative responses over conditioning (Berthier & Moore, 1986; Foy & Thompson, 1986) unlike IP neurons, the majority show decreased activity during CS presentations. This leads to disinhibition of IP neurons. A possible mechanism for this decrease is long-term depression (LTD), or the depression of synaptic input from fibers carrying CS information onto these Purkinje neurons. To determine if LTD appears in Purkinje cells under the conditioning parameters that promote acquisition of NM CRs, Chen and Thompson (1995) used a cerebellar slice preparation. They presented paired electrical pulses to fibers known to carry CS and US information to Purkinje cells using temporal parameters that promote eyeblink conditioning. LTD was observed when stimulation of the CS input pathway preceded stimulation of the US input pathway and was maximal at interstimulus intervals that are optimal for eyeblink conditioning. These results, together with

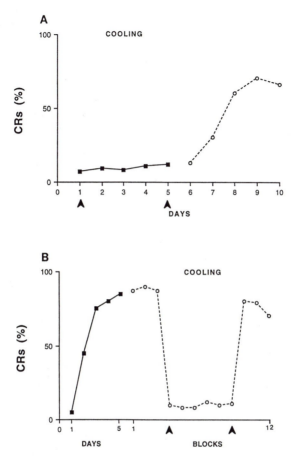

FIGURE 15   Mean percentage of CRs elicited by the CS during cooling-induced inactivation of the IP. (A) Cooling was induced in six animals during each day of five acquisition days during which paired conditioning trials were given. Five additional conditioning days without cooling were then given. (B) Cooling was induced in nine animals during six 10-trial blocks on Day 6 following five acquisition training days during which asymptotic acquisition of the CR was achieved. Termination of cooling occurred during the last three trial blocks of Day 6. [From R. E. Clark, A. A. Zhang, & D. G. Lavond (1992). Reversible lesions of the cerebellar interpositus nucleus during acquisition and retention of a classically conditioned behavior. *Behav. Neurosci.*, *106*, 879–888. Copyright © 1992 by the American Psychological Association. Adapted with permission.]

evidence demonstrating that mutant mice deficient in cerebellar LTD are impaired in eyeblink conditioning (Aiba et al., 1994), suggest that LTD of CS synaptic input onto Purkinje neurons may represent a mechanism for the associative plasticity observed in these neurons during conditioning.

V. RAPIDLY AND SLOWLY ACQUIRED CRs: RELATIONSHIPS AT THE BEHAVIORAL AND NEURAL LEVELS AND IMPLICATIONS FOR TWO-PROCESS LEARNING THEORIES

Thus far, we have considered rapidly and slowly acquired CRs simply as indices of learning in our search for the brain circuits and mechanisms that form the substrates of associative processes. Yet recall that these two categories of CRs reflect two different associative processes, support for which is obviously derived from the fact that they engage different brain circuits. Furthermore, over the course of conditioning, these CRs, and the associative processes they represent, occur sequentially (Lennartz & Weinberger, 1992). For example, during conditioning of the NM CR, bradycardic and other CRs (e.g., pupillary dilation) develop prior to the emergence of the NM CR (Powell & Levine-Bryce, 1988). The final issue to be addressed in our discussion is the relationship between these associative processes over the course of conditioning. Specifically, might the early developing associative process responsible for the emotional stage of learning modulate or affect the later developing associative process representing the learning of a specific CR directed at a US? If so, what comprises the neural substrate(s) for this modulatory relationship?

An analysis by Brandon and Wagner (1991) bears directly on this issue. They found that the magnitude of the eyeblink CR conditioned to a visual CS was enhanced when elicited in the presence of a Pavlovian-conditioned, fear-eliciting auditory stimulus. These results suggest that activation of the circuit representing the associative process for emotional learning is capable of modulating the circuit representing the associative process for the eyeblink CR. It follows that manipulations of the circuit components essential for the rapidly acquired associative process should affect the expression, or perhaps even the development, of more slowly acquired CRs. In terms of the circuitry essential for the acquisition of rapidly acquired CRs, lesions of the amygdala, a primary component of that circuit as described previously, might be predicted to affect the acquisition of the NM CR in the rabbit. Evidence consistent with this prediction has been provided by Weisz, Harden, and Xiang (1992), who have demonstrated that lesions in the ACe region significantly retard the acquisition of the NM CR. This retardation, however, occurred only when a lower intensity tone was used as the CS; no effects were observed with the use of a higher intensity. The intensity-specific effects reported by Weisz et al. (1992) might appear puzzling. However, when taken in concert with a wealth of additional observations concerning the ACe as described in the following paragraphs, they make a great deal of sense.

Although our previous discussion concentrated on the projections of the ACe that contribute to the expression of various rapidly acquired CRs (e.g., to the dorsal medulla, PAG, and lateral hypothalamus), these projections represent only a small contingent of the vast efferent projection system of this nucleus (Hopkins & Holstege, 1978; Price & Amaral, 1981). Indeed, many of these additional projections would appear to represent substrates for the numerous responses that are elicited upon stimulation of the ACe, including pupillary dilation, reflex enhancement, bradycardia, pinna orientation electroencephalographic (EEG) arousal, and an arrest of ongoing behavior (Applegate et al., 1983; Kapp, Supple, & Whalen, 1994; Whalen & Kapp, 1991). As we have reviewed elsewhere (Kapp, Whalen, Supple, & Pascoe, 1992), a feature common to most of these responses is that they all appear to function in enhancing the ability of the organism to detect and process sensory information from the environment. (In the case of reflex enhancement, the increased reflex magnitude could reflect a stimulation-induced increase in sensory flow through the reflex, leading to enhanced motor output.) In essence, then, they contribute to a heightened state of arousal or vigilance.

Importantly, most all of these responses can be rapidly conditioned (see Kapp et al., 1992), resulting in a rapidly acquired conditioned enhancement of vigilance. Of equal importance are the findings that lesions of the ACe severely retard the conditioning of many of them (Hitchcock & Davis, 1986; Kapp et al., 1979; Kapp, Whalen, Silvestri, Jordan, & Fechter, 1993; Weisz et al., 1992), thereby impairing conditioned vigilance early on in the conditioning process and compromising the ability of the animal to detect and efficiently process sensory information. How might this lesion-induced compromise affect the formation of the associations responsible for the acquisition of slowly acquired CRs? The answer is straightforward: Without the most efficient detection and processing of sensory information, CS information, for example, would have less of an impact on the organism and enter into an association less readily, thereby retarding the formation of the association and the acquisition of the CR. This retardation would be particularly prominent with the use of a low-intensity or near-threshold CS but perhaps would not occur at high CS intensities, exactly what was observed by Weisz et al. (1992) following lesions of the ACe region.

Two important questions remain. First, if ACe activation enhances the detection and processing of sensory information and thereby creates optimal conditions for the formation of the association that mediates NM/eyeblink conditioning, then it must do so at the level of the essential cerebellar circuit. Are there ACe projections to that circuit, perhaps to the pontine nuclei, which represent the source of auditory CS input to the cerebellum? A detailed analysis has yet to be undertaken, but recall that the ACe does project to the PnC located in the lateral pons (Rosen et al., 1992) as well as to other lateral pontine regions (Hopkins & Holstege, 1978). Furthermore, that electrical stimulation of the ACe enhances the response of neurons in the PnC to an acoustic stimulus (Koch & Ebert, 1993) may be an indication that ACe activation is capable of modulating the activity of other auditory responsive pontine neurons that convey CS information to the cerebellum. Second, given that components of the circuit essential for the acquisition of rapidly acquired CRs are capable of modulating components of the circuit essential for the acquisition of slowly acquired CRs, might not the opposite be true? For now, the answer is no; lesions of the IP do not affect the acquisition of conditioned bradycardia (Lavond,

Lincoln, McCormick, & Thompson, 1984), nor do they affect conditioned potentiation of reflexes (Hitchcock & Davis, 1986; Weisz & LoTurco, 1988).

In summary, the available data suggest that the amygdala, and in particular the ACe, is an important component of an essential circuit that functions, at least in part, in conditioned vigilance, manifested in a variety of rapidly acquired CRs that serve to enhance the detection and processing of sensory information. By creating the optimal conditions for sensory processing, this circuit may influence the development of the association responsible for the acquisition of more slowly acquired CRs. This influence may be mediated by direct projections from the ACe to components of the essential cerebellar circuitry. Elucidation of the interactions between these circuits should greatly aid in clarifying important issues relating to two-process theories of learning and provide a fertile ground for future research.

VI. SUMMARY

1. Substantial progress is being realized in our efforts to understand the neural substrates of vertebrate learning and memory. Much of this progress has been achieved using carefully designed animal models of learning that most often incorporate Pavlovian conditioning procedures.

2. Pavlovian CRs can be separated into two general categories: slowly and rapidly acquired CRs. Slowly acquired CRs are somatic responses that are specific to the nature of the US and are discrete defensive responses. Rapidly acquired CRs include autonomic and diffuse somatic CRs that are not specific to the nature of the US and are considered to be manifestations of an early emotional stage of learning.

3. We have reviewed examples of research demonstrating the integrated use of a variety of neurobiological techniques within the context of four well-characterized vertebrate models of learning, three that involve the measurement of rapidly acquired CRs and one that involves the measurement of a slowly acquired CR.

4. The amygdaloid complex is a structure common to all circuits essential for the acquisition of rapidly acquired CRs, whereas the cerebellum is a structure common to the essential circuit for the acquisition of slowly acquired CRs during Pavlovian defensive conditioning.

5. As a result of the use of vertebrate models, potential sites have been identified where the plasticity necessary for learning occurs. Among these are the MGm, amygdala, and cerebellum.

6. The identification of sites of plasticity within these essential circuits has prompted investigations of the mechanisms that form the substrate(s) for this plasticity. Most notably, LTP and LTD have been implicated as possible mechanisms.

7. That different brain circuits contribute to rapidly and slowly acquired CRs suggests that different associative processes are engaged during Pavlovian defensive conditioning, supporting two-process learning theory.

8. Evidence has been reviewed that suggests that many rapidly acquired CRs function to enhance the detection and processing of sensory information, thereby implicating components of this circuit, in particular the amygdala, in the enhancement of vigilance.

9. The activation of the essential circuit that contributes to rapidly acquired CRs, by functioning to enhance vigilance, may influence the cerebellar circuit responsible for the associative process mediating the development of slowly acquired CRs.

10. The identification of two vastly different circuits for the acquisition of Pavlovian CRs provides the opportunity for additional analyses designed to elucidate the interactions between these circuits during Pavlovian defensive conditioning, with the goal of furthering our understanding of a variety of learning phenomena.

REFERENCES

Aiba, A., Kano, M., Chen, C., Stanton, M. E., Fox, G. D., Herrup, K., Zwingman, T. A., & Tonegawa, S. (1994). Deficient cerebellar long-term depression and impaired motor learning in mGlu R1 mutant mice. *Cell, 79,* 377–388.

Applegate, C. D., Frysinger, R. C., Kapp, B. S., & Gallagher, M. (1982). Multiple unit activity recorded from amygdala central nucleus during Pavlovian heart rate conditioning in rabbit. *Brain Res., 238,* 457–462.

Applegate, C. D., Kapp, B. S., Underwood, M. D., & McNall, C. L. (1983). Autonomic and somato-motor effects of amygdala central N. stimulatin in awake rabbits. *Physiol. Behav., 31,* 353–360.

Berg, W. K., & Davis, M. (1985). Associative learning modifies startle reflexes at the lateral lemniscus. *Behav. Neurosci., 99,* 191–199.

Berger, T. W., & Thompson, R. F. (1978). Neuronal plasticity in the limbic system during classical conditioning of the rabbit nictitating membrane response. I. The hippocampus. *Brain Res., 145,* 323–346.

Berger, T. W., & Weisz, D. J. (1987). Single unit analysis of hippocampal pyramidal and granule cells and their role in classical conditioning of the rabbit nictitating membrane response. In I. Gormezano, W. F. Prokasy, & R. F. Thompson (Eds.), *Classical conditioning* (pp. 217–253). Hillsdale, NJ: Lawrence Erlbaum.

Berthier, N. E., Moore, J. W. (1986). Cerebellar Purkinje cell activity related to the classically conditioned nictitating membrane response. *Exp. Brain Res., 63,* 341–350.

Bordi, F., & LeDoux, J. E. (1994). Response properties of single units in areas of rat auditory thalamus that project to the amygdala. II. Cells receiving convergent auditory and somatosensory inputs and cells antidromically activated by amygdala stimulation. *Exp. Brain Res., 98,* 275–286.

Brandon, S. E., & Wagner, A. R. (1991). Modulation of a discrete Pavlovian conditioned reflex by a putative emotive Pavlovian conditioned stimulus. *J. Exp. Psychol., 13,* 299–311.

Campeau, S., & Davis, M. (1995). Involvement of the central nucleus and basolateral complex of the amygdala in fear conditioning measured with fear-potentiated startle in rats trained concurrently with auditory and visual conditioned stimuli. *J. Neurosci., 15,* 2301–2311.

Campeau, S., Miserendino, M. J. D., & Davis, M. (1992). Intra-amygdala infusion of the *N*-methyl-*D*-aspartate receptor antagonist AP5 blocks acquisition but not expression of fear-potentiated startle to an auditory conditioned stimulus. *Behav. Neurosci., 106,* 569–574.

Cegavske, C. F., Patterson, M. M., & Thompson, R. F. (1979). Neuronal unit activity in the abducens nucleus during classical conditioning of the nictitating membrane response in the rabbit, *Oryctolagus cuniculus. J. Comp. Physiol. Psychol., 93,* 595–609.

Chapman, P. F., Steinmetz, J. E., & Thompson, R. F. (1988). Classical conditioning does not occur when direct stimulation of the red nucleus or cerebellar nuclei is the unconditioned stimulus. *Brain Res., 442,* 97–104.

Chapman, P. F., Steinmetz, J. E., Sears, L. L., & Thompson, R. F. (1990). Effects of lidocaine injection in the interpositus nucleus and red nucleus on conditioned behavioral and neuronal responses. *Brain Res., 537,* 140–156.

Chen, C., & Thompson, R. F. (1995). Temporal specificity of long-term depression in parallel fiber-Purkinje synapses in rat cerebellar slice. *Learn. Mem., 2,* 185–198.

Chen, L., Bao, S., Lockard, J. M., Kim. J. J., & Thompson, R. F. (1996). Impaired classical eyeblink conditioning in cerebellar-lesioned and Purkinje cell degeneration (pcd) mutant mice. *J. Neurosci., 16,* 2829–2838.

Clark, G. A., McCormick, D. A., Lavond, D. G., & Thompson, R. F. (1984). Effects of lesions of cerebellar nuclei on conditioned behavioral and hippocampal neuronal responses. *Brain Res., 291,* 125–136.

Clark, R. E., & Lavond, D. G. (1993). Reversible lesions of the red nucleus during acquisition and retention of a classically conditioned behavior in rabbit. *Behav. Neurosci., 107,* 264–270.

Clark, R. E., Zhang, A. A., & Lavond, D. G. (1992). Reversible lesions of the cerebellar interpositus nucleus during acquisition and retention of a classically conditioned behavior. *Behav. Neurosci., 106,* 879–888.

Clugnet, M. C., & LeDoux, J. E. (1990). Synaptic plasticity in fear conditioning circuits: Induction of LTP in the lateral nucleus of the amygdala by stimulation of the medial geniculate body. *J. Neurosci., 10,* 2818–2824.

Cohen, D. H. (1974). The neural pathways and informational flow mediating a conditioned autonomic response. In L. V. DiCara (Ed.), *Limbic and autonomic nervous systems research* (pp. 223–275). New York: Plenum Press.

Cohen, D. H. (1975). Involvement of the avian amygdalar-homologue (archistriatum posterior and mediale) in defensively conditioned heart rate change. *J. Comp. Neurol., 160,* 13–36.

Cohen, D. H. (1980). The functional neuroanatomy of a conditioned response. In R. F. Thompson, L. H. Hicks, & V. B. Shvyrkov (Eds.), *Neural mechanisms of goal directed behavior and learning* (pp. 283–302). New York: Academic Press.

Cox, G. E., Jordan, D., Paton, J. F., Spyer, K. M., & Wood, L. M. (1987). Cardiovascular and phrenic nerve responses to stimulation of the amygdala central nucleus in the anaesthetized rabbit. *J. Physiol. (London), 389,* 541–556.

Davis, M. (1992). The role of the amygdala in conditioned fear. In J. P. Aggleton (Ed.), *The amygdala: Neurobiological aspects of emotion, memory, and mental dysfunction* (pp. 255–306). New York: Wiley-Liss.

Diamond, D. M., & Weinberger, N. M. (1986). Classical conditioning rapidly induces specific changes in frequency receptive fields of single neurons in secondary and ventral ectosylvian auditory cortical fields. *Brain Res., 372,* 357–360.

Disterhoft, J. E., Shipley, M. T., & Kraus, N. (1982). Analyzing the rabbit NM conditioned reflex arc. In C. D. Woody (Ed.), *Conditioning: Representation of involved neural functions* (pp. 433–449). New York: Plenum Press.

Edeline, J. M., Dutrieux, G., & Neuenschwander-El Massioui, N. (1988). Multiunit changes in hippocampus and medial geniculate body in free-behaving rats during acquisition and retention of a conditioned response to a tone. *Behav. Neural Biol., 50,* 61–79.

Edeline, J.-M., & Weinberger, N. M. (1992). Associative retuning of the thalamic source of input to the amygdala and auditory cortex: Receptive field plasticity in the medial division of the medial geniculate body. *Behav. Neurosci., 106,* 81–105.

Fanselow, M. S. (1993). Associations and memories: The role of NMDA receptors and long-term potentiation. *Curr. Dir. Physiol. Sci., 2,* 152–156.

Fendt, M., Koch, M., & Schnitzler, H.-U. (1994). Lesions of the central gray block the sensitization of the acoustic startle response in rats. *Brain Res. 74,* 127–134.

Fendt, M., Koch, M., & Schnitzler, H.-U. (1996). Lesions of the central gray block conditioned fear as measured with the potentiated startle paradigm. *Behav. Brain Res., 661,* 163–173.

Foy, M. R., Krupa, D. J., Tracy, J., & Thompson, R. F. (1992). Analysis of single unit recordings from cerebellar cortex of classically conditioned rabbits. *Soc. Neurosci. Abstr., 18,* 1215.

Foy, M. R., & Thompson, R. F. (1986). Single unit analysis of Purkinje cell discharge in classically conditioned and untrained rabbits. *Soc. Neurosci. Abstr., 12,* 518.

Fredericks, A., Moore, J. W., Metcalf, F. U., Schwaber, J. S., & Schneiderman, N. (1974). Selective autonomic blockage of conditioned and unconditioned heart rate changes in rabbits. *Pharmacol. Biochem. Behav., 2,* 493–501.

Gabriel, M., & Schmajuk, N. A. (1990). Neural and computational models of avoidance learning. In M. Gabriel & J. Moore (Eds.), *Learning and computational neuroscience: Foundations of adaptive networks* (pp. 143–170). Cambridge, MA: MIT Press.

Gallagher, M., Kapp, B. S., Frysinger, R. C., & Rapp, P. R. (1980). Beta-adrenergic manipulation in amygdala central n. alters rabbit heart rate conditioning. *Pharmacol. Biochem Behav., 12,* 419–426.

Gallagher, M., Kapp, B. S., & Pascoe, J. P. (1982). Enkephalin analogue effects in the amygdala central nucleus on conditioned heart rate. *Pharmacol. Biochem. Behav., 17,* 217–222.

Gentile, C. G., Jarrell, T. W., Teich, A. H., McCabe, P. M., & Schneiderman, N. (1986). The role of amygdaloid central nucleus in differential Pavlovian conditioning of bradycardia in rabbits. *Behav. Brain Res., 20,* 263–276.

Gerren, R., & Weinberger, N. M. (1983). Long term potentiation in the magnaellular medial geniculate nucleus of the anesthetized cat. *Brain Res., 265,* 138–142.

Gormezano, I., Kehoe, E. I., & Marshall, B. S. (1983). Twenty years of classical conditioning research with the rabbit. In A. N. Epstein (Ed.), *Progress in psychobiology and physiological psychology* (pp. 197–275). New York: Academic Press.

Higgins, G. A., & Schwaber, J. S. (1983). Somatostatinergic projections from the central nucleus of the amygdala to vagal nuclei. *Peptides, 4,* 1–6.

Hilton, S. M., & Zbrozyna, A. W. (1963). Amygdaloid region for defense reactions and its efferent pathway to the brainstem. *J. Physiol. (London) 165,* 160–173.

Hitchcock, J., & Davis, M. (1986). Lesions of the amygdala, but not of the cerebellum or red nucleus, block conditioned fear as measured with the potentiated startle paradigm. *Behav. Neurosci. 100,* 11–22.

Hitchcock, J., & Davis, M. (1991). Efferent pathway of the amygdala involved in conditioned fear as measured with the fear-potentiated startle paradigm. *Behav. Neurosci., 105,* 826–842.

Hopkins, D. A., & Holstege, G. (1978). Amygdaloid projections to the mesencephalon, pons and medulla oblongata in the cat. *Exp. Brain Res., 32,* 529–547.

Iwata, J., LeDoux, J. E., Meeley, M. P., Arneric, S., & Reis, D. J. (1986). Intrinsic neurons in the amygdaloid field projected to by the medial geniculate body mediate emotional responses conditioned to acoustic stimuli. *Brain Res., 383,* 195–214.

Jarrell, T. W., Romanski, L. M., Gentile, C. G., McCabe, P. M., & Schneiderman, N. (1986). Ibotenic acid lesions in the medial geniculate region prevent the acquisition of differential Pavlovian conditioning of bradycardia to acoustic stimuli in rabbits. *Brain Res., 382,* 199–203.

Jordan, D., Khalid, M. E. M., Schneiderman, N., & Spyer, K. M. (1982). The location and properties of preganglionic vagal cardiomotor neurons in the rabbit. *Pflügers Arch., 395,* 244–250.

Kapp, B. S., Frysinger, R., Gallagher, M., & Haselton, J. R. (1979). Amygdala central nucleus lesions: Effects on heart rate conditioning in the rabbit. *Physiol. Behav., 23,* 1109–1117.

Kapp, B. S., Gallagher, M., Applegate, C. D., & Frysinger, R. C. (1982). The amygdala central nucleus: Contributions to conditioned cardiovascular responding during aversive Pavlovian conditioning in the rabbit. In C. D. Woody (Ed.), *Conditioning: Representation of involved neural functions* (pp. 581–600). New York: Plenum Press.

Kapp, B. S., Gallagher, M., Underwood, M. D., McNall, C. L., & Whitehorn, D. (1982). Cardiovascular responses elicited by electrical stimulation of the amygdala central nucleus in the rabbit. *Brain Res., 360,* 355–361.

Kapp, B. S., Supple, W. F., Jr., & Whalen, P. J. (1994). Effects of electrical stimulation of the amygdaloid central nucleus on neocortical arousal in the rabbit. *Behav. Neurosci., 108,* 81–93.

Kapp, B. S., Whalen, P. J., Silvestri, A. J., Jordan, M. P., & Fechter, J. H. (1993). The effect of amygdaloid lesions on the acquisition of EEG and heart rate conditioned responses (CRs) in the rabbit. *Soc. Neurosci. Abstr., 19,* 1230.

Kapp, B. S., Whalen, P. J., Supple, W. F., & Pascoe, J. P. (1992). Amygdaloid contributions to conditioned arousal and sensory information processing. In J. P. Aggleton (Ed.), *The amygdala: Neurobiological aspects of emotion, memory, and mental dysfunction* (pp. 229–254). New York: Wiley-Liss.

Kelso, S. R., & Brown, T. H. (1986). Differential conditioning of associative synaptic enhancement in hippocampal brain slices. *Science, 232,* 85–87.

Koch, M., & Ebert, U. (1993). Enhancement of the acoustic startle response by stimulation of an excitatory pathway from the central amygdala/basal nucleus of Meynert to the pontine reticular formation. *Exp. Brain Res., 93,* 231–241.

Konorski, J. (1967). *Integrative activity of the brain: An interdisciplinary approach.* Chicago: University of Chicago Press.

Krupa, D. J., Thompson, J. K., & Thompson, R. F. (1993). Localization of a memory trace in the mammalian brain. *Science, 260,* 989–991.

Krupa, D. J., Weng, J., & Thompson, R. F. (1996). Inactivation of brainstem motor nuclei blocks expression but not acquisition of the rabbit's classically conditioned eyeblink response. *Behav. Neurosci., 110,* 219–227.

Lavond, D. G., Lincoln, J. S., McCormick, D. A., & Thompson, R. F. (1984). Effects of bilateral lesions of the dentate and interpositus cerebellar nuclei on conditioning of heart-rate and nictitating membrane/eyelid responses in the rabbit. *Brain Res., 305,* 323–330.

LeDoux, J. E. (1990). Information flow from sensation to emotion: Plasticity in the neural computation of stimulus value. In M. Gabriel & J. Moore (Eds.), *Learning and computational neuroscience: Foundations of adaptive networks* (pp. 3–51). Cambridge, MA: MIT Press.

LeDoux, J. E. (1995). Emotion: Clues from the brain. *Annu. Rev. Psychol., 46,* 209–235.

LeDoux, J. E., Cicchetti, P., Xagoraris, A., & Romanski, L. M. (1990). The lateral amygdaloid nucleus: Sensory interface of the amygdala in fear conditioning. *J. Neurosci., 10,* 1062–1069.

LeDoux, J. E., Farb, C., & Ruggiero, D. A. (1990). Topographic organization of neurons in the acoustic thalamus that project to the amygdala. *J. Neurosci., 10,* 1043–1054.

LeDoux, J. E., Iwata, J., Cicchetti, P., & Reis, D. J. (1988). Different projections of the central amygdaloid nucleus mediate autonomic and behavioral correlates of conditioned fear. *J. Neurosci., 8,* 2517–2529.

LeDoux, J. E., Ruggiero, D. A., & Reis, D. J. (1985). Projections to the subcortical forebrain from anatomically defined regions of the medial geniculate body in the rat. *J. Comp. Neurol., 242,* 182–213.

LeDoux, J. E., Sakaguchi, A., Iwata, J., & Reis, D. J. (1986). Interruption of projections from the medial geniculate body to an archi-neostriatal field disrupts the classical conditioning of emotional responses to acoustic stimuli. *Neuroscience, 17,* 615–627.

LeDoux, J. E., Sakaguchi, A., & Reis, D. J. (1984). Subcortical efferent projections of the medial geniculate nucleus mediate emotional responses conditioned to acoustic stimuli. *J. Neurosci., 4,* 683–698.

Lee, Y., Lopez, D. E., Meloni, E. G., & Davis, M. (1996). A primary acoustic startle pathway: Obligatory role of cochlear root neurons and the nucleus reticularis pontis caudalis. *J. Neurosci., 16,* 3775–3789.

Lennartz, R. C., & Weinberger, N. M. (1992). Analysis of response systems in Pavlovian conditioning reveals rapidly versus slowly acquired conditioned responses: Support for two factors, implications for behavior and neurobiology. *Psychobiology, 20,* 93–119.

Lye, R. H., O'Boyle, D. J., Ramsden, R. T., & Schady, W. (1988). Effects of a unilateral cerebellar lesion on the acquisition of eye-blink conditioning in man. *J. Physiol. (London), 403,* 58P.

Mauk, M. D., Steinmetz, J. E., & Thompson, R. F. (1986). Classical conditioning using stimulation of the inferior olive as the unconditioned sitmulus. *Proc. Natl. Acad. Sci. U.S.A., 83,* 5349–5353.

Mauk, M. D., & Thompson, R. F. (1987). Retention of classically conditioned eyelid responses following acute decerebration. *Brain Res., 403,* 89–95.

Maxwell, B., Powell, D. A., & Buchanan, S. L. (1994). Multiple- and single-unit activity in area 32 (prelimbic region) of the medial prefrontal cortex during Pavlovian heart rate conditioning in rabbits. *Cerebral Cortex, 4,* 230–246.

McCabe, P. M., Gentile, C. G., Markgraf, C. G., Teich, A. H., & Schneiderman, N. (1992). Ibotenic acid lesions in the amygdaloid central nucleus but not in the lateral subthalamic area prevent the acquisition of differential Pavlovian conditioning of bradycardia in rabbits. *Brain Res., 580,* 155–163.

McCabe, P. M., McEchron, M. D., Green, E. J., & Schneiderman, N. (1993). Effects of electrolytic and ibotenic acid lesions of the medial nucleus of the medial geniculate nucleus on single tone heart rate conditioning. *Brain Res., 69,* 291–298.

McCabe, P. M., McEchron, M. D., Green, E. J., & Schneiderman, N. (1995). Destruction of neurons in the VPM thalamus prevents rabbit heart rate conditioning. *Physiol. Behav., 57,* 159–163.

McCormick, D. A., Lavond, D. G., & Thompson, R. F. (1982). Concomitant classical conditioning of the rabbit nictitating membrane and eyelid responses: Correlations and implications. *Physiol. Behav., 28,* 769–775.

McCormick, D. A., Steinmetz, J. E., & Thompson, R. F. (1985). Lesions of the inferior olivary complex cause extinction of the classically conditioned eyeblink response. *Brain Res., 359,* 120–130.

McCormick, D. A., & Thompson, R. F. (1984). Neuronal responses of the rabbit cerebellum during acquisition and performance of a classically conditioned nictitating membrane–eyelid response. *J. Neurosci., 4,* 2811–2822.

McEchron, M. D., Green, E. J., Winters, R. W., Nolen, T. G., Schneiderman, N., & McCabe, P. M. (1996). Changes of synaptic efficacy in the medial geniculate nucleus as a result of auditory classical conditioning. *J. Neurosci., 16,* 1273–1283.

McEchron, M. D., McCabe, P. M., Green, E. J., Llabre, M. M., & Schneiderman, N. (1995). Simultaneous single unit recording in the medial nucleus of the medial geniculate nucleus and amygdaloid central nucleus throughout habituation, acquisition, and extinction of the rabbit's classically conditioned heart rate. *Brain Res., 682,* 157–166.

McEchron, M. D., McCabe, P. M., Green, E. J., Hitchcock, J. M., & Schneiderman, N. (1996). Immunohistochemical expression of the *c*-Fos protein in the spinal trigeminal nucleus following presentation of a corneal airpuff stimulus. *Brain Res., 710,* 112–120.

Miserendino, M. J. D., Sananes, C. B., Melia, K. R., & Davis, M. (1990). Blocking of acquisition but not expression of conditioned fear-potentiated startle by NMDA antagonists in the amygdala. *Nature, 345,* 716–718.

Moore, J. W., Desmond, J. E., & Berthier, N. E. (1982). The metencephalic basis of the conditioned nictitating membrane response. In C. D. Woody (Ed.), *Conditioning: Representation of involved neural functions* (pp. 459–482). New York: Plenum Press.

Mowrer, O. H. (1947). On the dual nature of learning: A reinterpretation of "conditioning" and "problem-solving." *Harvard Educ. Rev., 17,* 102–148.

Ono, T., & Nishijo, H. (1992). Neurophysiological basis of the Klüver–Bucy syndrome: Responses of monkey amygdaloid neurons to biologically significant objects. In J. P. Applegate (Ed.), *The amygdala: Neurobiological aspects of emotion, memory, and mental dysfunction* (pp. 167–190). New York: Wiley-Liss.

Pascoe, J. P., & Kapp, B. S. (1985). Electrophysiological characteristics of amygdaloid central nucleus neurons during Pavlovian fear conditioning in the rabbit. *Behav. Brain Res., 16,* 117–133.

Penick, S., & Solomon, P. R. (1991). Hippocampus, context, and conditioning. *Behav. Neurosci., 105,* 611–617.

Pitkänen, A., Stefanacci, L., Farb, C. R., Go, G. G., LeDoux, J. E., & Amaral, D. G. (1995). Intrinsic connections of the rat amygdaloid complex: Projections originating in the lateral nucleus. *J. Comp. Neurol., 356,* 288–310.

Powell, D. A. (1994). Rapid associative learning: Conditioned bradycardia and its central nervous system substrates. *Integr. Physiol. Behav. Sci., 29,* 109–133.

Powell, D. A., & Kazis, E. (1976). Blood pressure and heart rate changes accompanying classical eyeblink conditioning in the rabbit (*Oryctolagus cuniculus*). *Psychophysiology, 13,* 441–448.

Powell, D. A., & Levine-Bryce, D. (1988). A comparison of two model systems of associative learning: Heart rate and eyeblink conditioning in the rabbit. *Psychophysiology, 25,* 672–682.

Price, J. L., & Amaral, D. G. (1981). An autoradiographic study of the projections of the amygdala central nucleus of the monkey amygdala. *J. Neurosci., 1,* 1242–1259.

Quirk, G. J., Repa, J. C., & LeDoux, J. E. (1995). Fear conditioning enhances short-latency auditory responses of lateral amygdala neurons: Parallel recordings in the freely behaving rat. *Neuron, 15,* 1029–1039.

Racine, R. J., Wilson, D. A., Gingell, R., & Sutherland, D. (1986). Long-term potentiation in the interpositus and vestibular nuclei in the rat. *Exp. Brain Res., 63,* 158–162.

Rescorla, R. A. (1988). Pavlovian conditioning: It's not what you think it is. *Am. Psychol., 43,* 151–160.

Rogan, M. T., & LeDoux, J. E. (1995). LTP is accompanied by commensurate enhancement of auditory-evoked responses in a fear conditioning circuit. *Neuron, 15,* 127–136.

Romanski, L. M., Clugnet, M. C., Bordi, F., & LeDoux, J. E. (1993). Somatosensory and auditory convergence in the lateral nucleus of the amygdala. *Behav. Neurosci., 107,* 444–450.

Romanski, L. M., Xagoraris, A. E., Reis, D. J., & LeDoux, J. E. (1988). Destruction of perirhinal and neocortical projection targets of the acoustic thalamus does not disrupt fear conditioning. *Soc. Neurosci. Abstr., 14,* 1227.

Roozendaal, B., Koolhaas, J. M., & Bohus, B. (1991a). Attenuated cardiovascular, neuroendocrine, and behavioral responses after a single footshock in central amygdaloid lesioned male rats. *Physiol. Behav. 50,* 771–775.

Roozendaal, B., Koolhaas, J. M., & Bohus, B. (1991b). Central amygdala lesions affect behavioral and autonomic balance during stress in rats. *Physiol. Behav., 50,* 777–781.

Rosen, J. B., & Davis, M. (1988). Enhancement of acoustic startle by electrical stimulation of the amygdala. *Behav. Neurosci., 102,* 195–202.

Rosen, J. B., Hitchcock, J. M., Miserendino, M. J., Falls, W. A., Campeau, S., & Davis, M. (1992). Lesions of the perirhinal cortex but not of the frontal, medial prefrontal, visual, or insular cortex block fear-potentiated startle using a visual conditioned stimulus. *J. Neurosci., 12,* 4624–4633.

Rosen, J. B., Hitchcock, J. M., Sananes, C. B., Miserendino, M. J., & Davis, M. (1991). A direct projection from the central nucleus of the amygdala to the acoustic startle pathway: Anterograde and retrograde tracing studies. *Behav. Neurosci., 105,* 817–825.

Rosenfield, M. E., & Moore, J. N. (1995). Connections to cerebellar cortex (Larsell's HVI) in the rabbit: A WGA-HRP study with implications for classical eyeblink conditioning. *Behav. Neurosci., 109,* 1106–1118.

Ryugo, D. K., & Weinberger, N. M. (1978). Differential plasticity of morphologically distinct neuron populations in the medial geniculate body of the cat during classical conditioning. *Behav. Biol., 22,* 275–301.

Sananes, C. B., & Davis, M. (1992). *N*-Methyl-*D*-aspartate lesions of the lateral and basolateral nuclei of the amygdala block fear-potentiated startle and shock sensitization of startle. *Behav. Neurosci., 106,* 72–80.

Schneiderman, N. (1972). Response system divergencies in aversive classical conditioning. In A. H. Black & W. F. Prokasy (Eds.), *Classical conditioning, Vol. II: Current research and theory* (pp. 341–378). New York: Appleton-Century-Crofts.

Schwaber, J. S., Kapp, B. S., Higgins, G. A., & Rapp, P. R. (1982). Amygdaloid and basal forebrain direct connections with the nucleus of the solitary tract and the dorsal motor nucleus. *J. Neurosci., 2,* 1424–1438.

Sears, L. L., & Steinmetz, J. E. (1991). Dorsal accessory inferior olive activity diminishes during acquisition of the rabbit classically conditioned eyelid response. *Brain Res., 545,* 114–122.

Solomon, P. R., & Moore, J. W. (1975). Latent inhibition and stimulus generalization for the classically conditioned nictitating membrane response in rabbits (*Oryctolagus cuniculus*) following dorsal hippocampal ablation. *J. Comp. Physiol. Psychol., 89,* 1192–1203.

Solomon, P. R., Vander Schaaf, E. R., Thompson, R. F., & Weisz, D. J. (1986). Hippocampus and trace conditioning of the rabbit's classically conditioned nictitating membrane response. *Behav. Neurosci., 100,* 729–744.

Steinmetz, J. E., Lavond, D. G., Ivkovich, D., Logan, C. G., & Thompson, R. F. (1992). Disruption of classical eyelid conditioning after cerebellar lesions: Damage to a memory trace system or a simple performance deficit? *J. Neurosci., 12,* 4403–4426.

Steinmetz, J. E., Lavond, D. G., & Thompson, R. F. (1989). Classical conditioning in rabbits using pontine nucleus stimulation as a conditioned stimulus and inferior olive stimulation as an unconditioned stimulus. *Synapse, 3,* 225–232.

Steinmetz, J. E., Logan, C. G., Rosen, D. J., Thompson, J. K., Lavond, D. G., & Thompson, R. F. (1987). Initial localization of the acoustic conditioned stimulus projection system to the cerebellum essential for classical eyelid conditioning. *Proc. Natl. Acad. Sci. 84,* 3531–3535.

Steinmetz, J. E., Rosen, D. J., Chapman, P. F., Lavond, D. G., & Thompson, R. F. (1986). Classical conditioning of the rabbit eyelid response with a mossy fiber stimulation CS. I. Pontine nuclei and middle cerebellar peduncle stimulation. *Behav. Neurosci., 100,* 871–880.

Steinmetz, J. E., & Sengelaub, D. R. (1992). Possible conditioned stimulus pathway for classical eyelid conditioning in rabbits. I. Anatomical evidence for direct projections from the pontine nuclei to the cerebellar interpositus nucleus. *Behav. Neural Biol., 57,* 103–115.

Supple, W. F., & Kapp, B. S. (1989). Response characteristics of neurons in the medial component of the medial geniculate nucleus during Pavlovian differential fear conditioning in the rabbit. *Behav. Neurosci., 103,* 1276–1286.

Supple, W. F., Jr., & Kapp, B. S. (1993). The anterior cerebellar vermis: Essential involvement in classically conditioned bradycardia in the rabbit. *J. Neuroscience, 13,* 3705–3711.

Supple, W. F., Jr., & Leaton, R. N. (1990). Cerebellar vermis: Essential for classically conditioned bradycardia in the rat. *Brain Res., 509,* 17–23.

Supple, W. F., Jr., Sebastiani, L., & Kapp, B. S. (1993). Purkinje cell responses in the anterior cerebellar vermis during Pavlovian fear conditioning in the rabbit. *NeuroReport, 4,* 975–978.

Thompson, J. K., Thompson, R. F., Weiss, C., & Lavond, D. G. (1988). Pontine projections of cochlear nuclei using anterograde HRP or PHA-L. *Soc. Neurosci. Abstr., 14,* 782.

Thompson, R. F. (1976). The search for the engram. *Am. Psychol., 31,* 209–227.

Thompson, R. F. (1993). *The brain, a neuroscience primer.* New York: W. H. Freeman and Company.

Thompson, R. F., Donegan, N. H., Clark, G. A., Lavond, D. G., Lincoln, J. S., Madden, J., Mamounas, L. A., Mauk, M. D., & McCormick, D. A. (1987). Neuronal substrates of discrete, defensive conditioned reflexes, conditioned fear states, and their interactions in the rabbit. In I. Gormezano, W. F. Prokasy, & R. F. Thompson (Eds.), *Classical conditioning* (pp. 371–399). Hillsdale, NJ: Lawrence Erlbaum.

Thompson, R. F., & Krupa, D. J. (1994). Organization of memory traces in the mammalian brain. *Annu. Rev. Neurosci., 17,* 519–549.

Tischler, M. D., & Davis, M. (1983). A visual pathway that mediates fear-conditioned enhancement of acoustic startle. *Brain Res., 276,* 55–71.

Wagner, A. R., & Brandon, S. E. (1989). Evolution of a structured connectionist model of Pavlovian conditioning (AESOP). In S. B. Klein & R. R. Mowrer (Eds.), *Contemporary learning theories: Pavlovian conditioning and the status of traditional learning theory* (pp. 149–190). Hillsdale, NJ: Lawrence Erlbaum.

Weinberger, N. M. (1982). Effects of conditioned arousal on the auditory system. In A. L. Beckman (Ed.), *The neural basis of behavior* (pp. 63–91). Jamaica, NY: Spectrum Publications, Inc.

Weisz, D. J., Harden, D. G., & Xiang, Z. (1992). Effects of amygdala lesions on reflex facilitation and conditioned response acquisition during nictitating membrane response conditioning in rabbit. *Behav. Neurosci., 106,* 262–273.

Weisz, D. J., & LoTurco, J. J. (1988). Reflex facilitation of the nictitating membrane response remains after cerebellar lesions. *Behav. Neurosci., 103,* 203–209.

Whalen, P. J., & Kapp, B. S. (1991). Contributions of the amygdaloid central nucleus to the modulation of the nictitating membrane reflex in the rabbit. *Behav. Neurosci., 105,* 141–153.

Wilson, A., & Kapp, B. S. (1994). Effects of lesions of the ventrolateral periacqueductal gray on the Pavlovian conditioned heart rate response in the rabbit. *Behav. Neural Biol., 62,* 73–76.

Woody, C. D. (1982). Acquisition of conditioned facial reflexes in the cat: Cortical control of different facial movements. *Fed. Proc., 41,* 2160–2168.

Yang, B.-Y., & Weisz, D. J. (1992). An auditory conditioned stimulus modulates unconditioned stimulus-elicited neuronal activity in the cerebellar anterior interpositus and dentate nuclei during nictitating membrane response conditioning in rabbits. *Behav. Neurosci., 106,* 889–899.

Yehle, A., Dauth, G., & Schneiderman, N. (1967). Correlates of heart-rate classical conditioning in curarized rabbits. *J. Comp. Physiol. Psychol., 64,* 98–104.

Zhang, A. A., & Lavond, D. G. (1991). Effects of reversible lesion of reticular or facial neurons during eyeblink conditioning. *Soc. Neurosci. Abstr., 17,* 869.

CHAPTER 9

The Neuropsychology of Human Learning and Memory

Felicia B. Gershberg

Memory Disorders Research Center, Boston University School of Medicine and Department of Veterans Affairs Medical Center, Boston, Massachusetts 02130

Arthur P. Shimamura

Department of Psychology, University of California, Berkeley, California 94720

I. INTRODUCTION

Neuropsychological descriptions of memory disorders date back to the late nineteenth century, the same era as the beginning of psychology as a science (e.g., Korsakoff, 1889/1955; Ribot, 1881). Yet it has been only in the past few decades that cognitive psychologists have joined neuropsychologists in exploring the realm of memory dysfunction as a means to understanding normal memory function. This effort has been characterized by tension between two theoretical approaches. Cognitive psychologists, who study mental abilities in normal individuals, have generally characterized memory in terms of the *processes* that operate within a general cognitive system. In contrast, neuropsychologists, who study the effects of brain damage, have characterized memory in terms of multiple brain *systems,* with each system playing a specific role in memory functioning. In this chapter, we will trace the progress that has been made toward the goal of understanding human learning and memory through the integration of these two approaches.

Neurobiology of Learning and Memory

II. THE AMNESIC SYNDROME

One of the richest sources of insight into memory dysfunction in humans has been the study of patients with organic amnesia. This neurological disorder is characterized by a striking impairment in the ability to form new memories in the context of otherwise preserved intellectual function (for review, see Mayes, 1988; Shimamura & Gershberg, 1992; Squire, 1987). Amnesia is associated with damage to either medial temporal or diencephalic midline structures. The importance of the medial temporal region in human memory was dramatically illustrated by the famous case H.M., who, to relieve severe epilepsy, underwent bilateral excision of the hippocampal gyrus, amygdala, and anterior two-thirds of the hippocampus (Scoville & Milner, 1957). Since his surgery, H.M. has exhibited severe amnesia. In daily life, events are forgotten as soon as they pass from immediate awareness (Milner, 1966). On formal memory tests, such as free recall, paired-associate learning, and recognition, H.M.'s performance is severely impaired. H.M.'s memory deficit is selective in that other cognitive functions, including IQ score and language, were unaffected by the surgery (Corkin, 1984; Milner, Corkin, & Teuber, 1968).

Other neurological disorders that involve bilateral damage to the medial temporal region, such as viral encephalitis and hypoxia, can also result in a selective memory deficit. A particularly striking example is patient S.S., in whom viral encephalitis resulted in severely impaired memory function but preserved above-average intelligence (Cermak, 1976; Cermak & O'Connor, 1983). Another important case study was that of patient R.B., who became amnesic due to a hypoxic episode. After his death, examination of R.B.'s brain revealed a lesion limited to the CA1 subfield of the hippocampus, bilaterally (Zola-Morgan, Squire, & Amaral, 1986). Additional neuropathological and imaging studies have confirmed the crucial role of the medial temporal region in human memory (Press, Amaral, & Squire, 1989; Rempel-Clower, Zola, Squire, & Amaral, 1996; Squire, Amaral, & Press, 1990).

Amnesia can also result from damage to diencephalic midline structures. The central role of the diencephalic midline in memory function has been demonstrated in amnesic patients with direct damage to this area. For example, patient N.A. acquired a selective amnesia for verbal information following a penetrating head injury that damaged the midline thalamic nuclei and mammillary nuclei on the left side (Squire & Moore, 1979; Squire, Amaral, Zola-Morgan, Kritchevsky, & Press, 1989). In addition, amnesia can result from bilateral thalamic infarct (e.g., Graff-Radford, Tranel, Van Hoesen, & Brandt, 1990; Mori, Yamadori, & Mitani, 1986; von Cramon, Hebel, & Schuri, 1985). However, the best known etiology of amnesia related to diencephalic damage is Korsakoff's syndrome. Korsakoff (1889/1955) explained that a patient with this syndrome "gives the impression of a person in complete possession of his faculties" and yet "remembers absolutely nothing of what goes on around him" (Korsakoff, 1889/1955, p. 398). In Korsakoff's time, the cause of the syndrome was not understood, its etiology was highly varied, and the resulting pathology was unknown. Today, most cases of Korsakoff's amnesia occur as a result of long-term alcohol abuse, with neurological damage caused by a severe thiamine deficiency. Pathological studies have revealed bilateral lesions along the walls of the third and fourth ventricles, involving midline thalamic nuclei and the mammillary bodies, as well as cortical and cerebellar atrophy (Mair, Warrington, & Weiskrantz, 1979; Mayes, Meudell, Mann, & Pickering, 1988; Victor, Adams, & Collins, 1971). The patterns of memory impairment and cognitive function in Korsakoff's amnesia differ somewhat from those of medial temporal amnesia, at least in part because of the additional damage that goes beyond the diencephalic midline (Squire, 1982; Squire & Shimamura, 1986). Yet, all of these etiological variants of amnesia share in common the essential characteristics of severely impaired new memory ability in the face of otherwise generally preserved cognitive function.

III. EARLY VIEWS OF AMNESIA

The primary focus of early amnesia research up to the 1970s was to characterize the nature and extent of the memory disorder. In an early systems view, amnesia was related to a dual store model of memory described by cognitive psychologists (e.g., Atkinson & Shiffrin, 1968). This model distinguished between two different memory storage systems: short-term memory, which holds a small amount of information for about 2 sec, and long-term memory, which holds a large amount of information more permanently. The observation that amnesic patients could retain information only as long as it was held in mind without interruption led to the suggestion that amnesic patients had intact short-term memory but impaired transfer of information to long-term memory (Atkinson & Shiffrin, 1968; Baddeley & Warrington, 1970).

Evidence from cognitive psychology supported the distinction between long-term and short-term memory in normal memory. In particular, findings of functional dissociations between free-recall memory for items from the beginning of a list, or primacy items, and items from the end of a list, or recency items, suggested that primacy and recency items were retrieved from two different memory stores. For example, faster presentation of study items reduced memory for primacy items but not recency items, whereas a delay between study and test reduced memory for recency items but not primacy items (Murdock, 1962; Postman & Phillips, 1965). These findings were interpreted as reflecting, on the one hand, reduced transfer of primacy items into long-term memory due to limited rehearsal and, on the other hand, the elimination of recency items from short-term memory due to the delay before the test (e.g., Atkinson & Shiffrin, 1968; Glanzer & Cunitz, 1966). A study of free recall with amnesic patients revealed impaired recall of primacy items but intact recall of recency items (Baddeley & Warrington, 1970). Thus, amnesia was seen as an illustration—or, more strongly, a validation—of the dissociation between two memory systems, long-term memory and short-term memory (e.g., Baddeley & Warrington, 1970).

During this early period, however, the focus of cognitive psychology shifted from models of multiple memory stores to models of multiple forms of processing. This approach influenced the focus of theories of amnesia, which moved toward attempting to understand amnesia in terms of impaired memory processes rather than as an impaired memory system. This effort utilized theoretical constructs developed by cognitive psychologists, such as the distinction between encoding and retrieval (Tulving & Pearlstone, 1966). Specifically, one debate centered around the issue of whether amnesia involved a specific impairment in encoding processes or a specific impairment in retrieval processes. "Encoding" refers to the processes that occur when information is perceived and stored; "retrieval" refers to the processes that occur when information is accessed from memory. The retrieval view of amnesia suggested that the memory deficit in amnesia was due to increased susceptibility to interference, which blocked successful retrieval of information from memory. This view drew support from findings that amnesic patients exhibited relatively less impaired performance on tests of recall in which cues were provided. It was suggested that the test cues, which narrowed the range of possible responses, ameliorated amnesic patients' retrieval deficit by reducing interference from competing alternative responses (Warrington & Weiskrantz, 1968, 1970, 1974).

The encoding view of amnesia focused on the concept of levels of processing. That is, in normal memory, "deep" processing of the meaning of an item results in better memory than does "shallow" processing of perceptual characteristics of the item (Craik & Lockhart, 1972; Craik & Tulving, 1975). The encoding view of amnesia drew support from the observation that, left to their own devices, amnesic patients performed only shallow encoding (Cermak & Butters, 1972; Cermak, Butters, & Gerrein, 1973; Cermak, Butters, & Moreines, 1974). Also, amnesic patients' memory performance improved when they were required to process items deeply or meaningfully (Cermak & Reale, 1978). The debate between encoding and retrieval impairments was resolved to some extent by the sides coming to agree that both encoding and retrieval were disrupted. Yet, these processing approaches did not fully account for the patterns of memory performance in amnesia, such as findings of situations in which amnesic patients could exhibit preserved learning. This state of affairs set the stage for a move back to a systems view of memory.

IV. A SYSTEMS VIEW OF MEMORY

Another line of research, which was conducted over the same time period as the research discussed in the preceding section, focused on preserved memory function in amnesia rather than memory impairments. This line of research provided the foundation for the new systems view that was to emerge. These studies investigated procedural learning—that is, gradual learning of skills over the course of many practice trials (see Squire, 1987). For example, studies of procedural learning in the amnesic patient H.M. examined his ability to acquire various perceptuomotor skills such as copying an image reflected in a mirror, following a tactile maze, and manually tracking a point on a rotating disk (rotary pursuit). In these tasks, H.M. exhibited greatly improved performance over trials and across testing sessions, despite his lack of recollection of the learning experiences (Corkin, 1965, 1968; Milner, 1962, 1966; Milner et al., 1968). In other studies, groups of amnesic patients exhibited significant and often normal degrees of learning of these same tasks as well as other perceptuomotor skills, such as jigsaw puzzle assembly and tool use, and a nonmotor, perceptual skill of reading mirror-reversed text (Brooks & Baddeley, 1976; Cermak, Lewis, Butters, & Goodglass, 1973; Cohen & Squire, 1980; Talland, 1965). Even at this early stage, it was suggested that preserved skill learning in the face of otherwise impaired memory function in amnesia supported a systems view of memory, in that this dissociation indicated "more than one set of neural structures concerned with memory" (Corkin, 1968, p. 264).

In light of these findings of preserved learning of motor and perceptual skills, a new look was taken at the findings of relatively preserved cued recall performance in amnesic patients, which had previously been seen as evidence for a retrieval impairment in amnesia (i.e., Warrington & Weiskrantz, 1968, 1970). Specifically, in those studies, test cues consisted of fragmented or incomplete versions of studied pictures and words. It was suggested that identification or completion of those test stimuli could reflect a form of perceptual skill learning (e.g., Parkin, 1982)—that is, increased efficiency in processing or retrieving a particular representation of an individual word or picture as a result of prior exposure (see also Jacoby & Dallas, 1981). Furthermore, it was observed that the common element linking skill learning tasks and the word and picture completion tasks used in the cued recall studies was that performance did not necessarily depend upon explicit reference to the study episode (e.g., Graf, Squire, & Mandler, 1984; Jacoby & Witherspoon, 1982; Parkin, 1982).

The manner in which memory was tested was identified as a key factor in determining whether amnesic patients performed normally. In one study, subjects studied a list of words and then were asked to complete three-letter word stems with the first word to come to mind. Amnesic patients exhibited normal performance on the word-stem completion task—that is, they produced as many more studied items than unstudied, baseline items as did controls (Graf et al., 1984). This sort of test has been called implicit or indirect, in that subjects are not explicitly or directly instructed to refer back to the study episode, and the increased tendency to use previously presented items in implicit tests is called priming (for review, see Richardson-Klavehn & Bjork, 1988; Roediger & McDermott, 1993; Schacter, 1987). Thus, amnesic patients were shown to exhibit normal priming on this implicit test of memory. In contrast, when subjects were given a test of word-stem-cued recall, in which they were explicitly asked to try to recall studied words to complete word stems, amnesic patients exhibited impaired performance (Graf et al., 1984).

Initial demonstrations of a dissociation between implicit and explicit tests of memory in amnesic patients caused a watershed in amnesia research. The focus of research turned from the study of what is impaired in amnesia to the study of what is spared in amnesia (for review, see Moscovitch, Vriezen, & Goshen-Gottstein, 1993; Shimamura, 1986, 1993). Amnesic patients were shown to exhibit normal priming on many implicit tests of memory, including word identification, word-stem completion, word association, and production of category exemplars (Cermak, O'Connor, & Talbot, 1986; Cermak, Talbot, Chandler, & Wolbarst, 1985; Gardner, Boller, Moreines, & Butters, 1973; Graf, Shimamura, & Squire, 1985; Graf et al., 1984; Shimamura & Squire, 1984). Furthermore, their implicit test performance showed normal patterns of effects of variables such as level of processing at study, change in modality between study and test, and retention interval (Graf et al., 1984, 1985; Squire, Shimamura, & Graf, 1987).

An early view of priming was that it was a result of activation of preexisting memory representations (Graf & Mandler, 1984; Morton, 1970) and that this activation process was spared in amnesia (Graf et al., 1984; Rozin, 1976; Warrington & Weiskrantz, 1982). The idea that activation from recent exposure made memory representations more accessible was challenged by cognitive psychologists who found evidence of priming of novel stimuli, such as nonwords and novel patterns and objects, in normal subjects (e.g., Feustel, Shiffrin, & Salasoo, 1983; Kirsner & Smith, 1974; Musen & Treisman, 1990; Rueckl, 1990; Schacter, Cooper, & Delaney, 1990). Subsequently, it was shown that amnesic patients also could exhibit normal priming of novel stimuli, including nonwords (Gabrieli & Keane, 1988; Haist, Musen, & Squire, 1991; Keane, Gabrieli, Mapstone, Johnson, & Corkin, 1995; Keane, Gabrieli, Noland, & McNealy, 1995; Musen & Squire, 1991), novel line patterns (Gabrieli, Milberg, Keane, & Corkin, 1990; Musen & Squire, 1992), and novel three-dimensional objects (Schacter, Cooper, Tharan, & Rubens, 1991). The straightforward activation view of priming was undermined by these findings of priming of novel stimuli. A fairly well accepted alternative view is that priming of both novel and familiar stimuli reflects enhanced efficiency of processing resulting from accessing representations of procedures that were engaged at encoding (e.g., Schacter, 1994; Shimamura, 1993; Squire, 1987).

Findings of dissociations between the performance of amnesic patients on implicit and explicit tests of memory suggested that priming effects depend on processing that occurs in a brain system that is not damaged in amnesia. Thus, consensus began to move toward a systems view of memory, with one system contributing to performance on implicit tests of memory and another system contributing to performance on explicit tests. One such view made a distinction between procedural and declarative memory (Cohen & Squire, 1980; Squire, 1987). Procedural memory, the form of memory that is intact in amnesia, was described as an incremental form of learning that could be expressed only by activating the "particular processing structures engaged by learning tasks" (Squire, 1987, p. 162). In contrast, declarative memory, which is disrupted in amnesia, was described as the basis for one-trial learning of information bound to a specific context and accessible in a flexible manner.

The procedural–declarative distinction was clearly expressed as a systems view. Procedural memory and declarative memory were described as different forms of memory, not as different means of gaining access to the same underlying memory representation (Squire, 1987). Declarative memory was seen as depending on the structures damaged in amnesia, whereas procedural memory is independent of those structures. As the boundaries of preserved memory performance in amnesia were extended, this systems view of memory evolved. Most notably, the concept of procedural memory was broadened and renamed nondeclarative memory to encompass the multiple forms of memory that do not depend on the medial temporal and diencephalic structures that are damaged in amnesia (Squire & Zola-Morgan, 1988). A distinction similar to the declarative–nondeclarative view was made between explicit memory, which is responsible for intentional or conscious recollection and is impaired in amnesia, and implicit memory, which is responsible for effects of memory on performance in the absence of intentional recollection and is intact in amnesia (Schacter, 1987).

V. A PROCESSING VIEW OF MEMORY

Over the same period during which this systems view of memory took hold in neuropsychology, implicit tests of memory were also being explored in cognitive psychology. Cognitive psychologists demonstrated a number of functional dissociations between implicit and explicit tests of memory. In one study, it was shown that performance on an explicit recognition test was significantly better following a study task that required processing the meanings of words, compared to study tasks that focused attention on the letters or sounds of words. In contrast, in an implicit word identification task, in which studied words were identified more quickly than unstudied words, all of the study tasks produced the same level of priming (Jacoby & Dallas, 1981). This differential sensitivity to levels of processing was demonstrated in many subsequent studies. Explicit tests, including free recall, word-stem-cued recall, word-fragment-cued recall, and recognition, have generally been found to be affected by level of processing, whereas implicit tests, including word-stem completion, word-fragment completion, and word identification, have not (Graf & Mandler, 1984; Roediger, Weldon, Stadler, & Riegler, 1992; for review, see Richardson-Klavehn & Bjork, 1988; Roediger & McDermott, 1993; Schacter, 1987). On the other hand, implicit tests have been found to be sensitive to manipulations of the perceptual characteristics of stimuli between study and test. For example, changing the modality of presentation (visual or auditory) of stimuli

between study and test reduces priming on implicit tests such as word-stem completion, word-fragment completion, and word identification (Graf et al., 1985;
Jacoby & Dallas, 1981; Roediger & Blaxton, 1987; Weldon, 1991).

These functional dissociations between implicit and explicit tests of memory
were the basis for processing views of memory. One prominent view, the transfer-
appropriate processing view, proposed that memory performance varies with the
extent to which the processes required by the test are like the processes performed
during study (Roediger, Rajaram, & Srinivas, 1990; Roediger, Srinivas, & Weldon,
1989; Roediger, Weldon, & Challis, 1989). Proponents of this view have pointed
out that the implicit tests that have been studied the most, such as word-stem
completion and word identification, provide cues that orient subjects toward perceptual information. Therefore, such tests are affected by manipulations of the
perceptual characteristics of stimuli, such as presentation modality, but not by manipulations of the degree to which meaning is processed. In contrast, many explicit
tests, such as free recall and category-cued recall, provide cues that are not perceptually similar to studied items. These tests are not affected by perceptual manipulations but are affected by levels of processing manipulations. Thus, it was suggested
that functional dissociations between implicit and explicit tests result from the confound that most implicit tests that have been studied are perceptual tests, and most
explicit tests are conceptual tests (Roediger et al., 1990; Roediger, Srinivas, &
Weldon, 1989; Roediger, Weldon, & Challis, 1989). This idea was supported by
findings of dissociations within the realm of implicit tests—that is, by demonstrations that implicit tests that provide perceptual cues (such as word fragments) are
sensitive to perceptual manipulations, whereas implicit tests that provide conceptual
cues (such as category names) are sensitive to conceptual manipulations (e.g.,
Hamann, 1990; Roediger & Blaxton, 1987; for review, see Roediger, Weldon, &
Challis, 1989).

A strong statement of the transfer-appropriate processing view suggested that
confounding of the implicit–explicit dimension and the perceptual–conceptual
dimension could explain the dissociation in the performance of amnesic patients on
implicit and explicit tests (Blaxton, 1992). Similar to the earlier encoding view of
amnesia (Cermak, Butters, & Gerrein, 1973; Cermak et al., 1974), this view hypothesized that the memory deficit in amnesia was a result of impaired conceptual
processing. Intact implicit test performance in amnesia was attributed to intact
perceptual processing. By this view, amnesic patients should exhibit impairment on
implicit conceptual tests (Blaxton, 1992). A study to test this hypothesis examined
the performance of memory-impaired patients with medial temporal lobe damage
related to temporal lobe epilepsy (Blaxton, 1992). In one experiment, subjects
studied a categorized list of words, with items from each category either randomly
intermixed or blocked by category. For the implicit category exemplar production
test, subjects were given category names and were asked to give the first several
category members that came to mind. Priming was reflected in the subjects' increased tendency to give studied items from studied categories compared to baseline

items from categories that were not on the studied list. Control subjects exhibited greater priming after studying the blocked list, but the memory-impaired patients failed to show this effect. This finding was seen as supporting the hypothesized impairment in conceptual processing (Blaxton, 1992).

The conceptual processing deficit hypothesis has been weakened, however, by the many findings of normal performance by amnesic patients on a variety of conceptual implicit tests. Two early studies demonstrated normal performance by amnesic patients on implicit category exemplar production (Gardner et al., 1973; Graf et al., 1985). Indeed, even in Blaxton's study (1992), the performance of the memory-impaired patients appeared to be normal on the implicit test of memory for the random categorized list. On another type of conceptual test, in which subjects are asked to free associate to cues that are meaningfully related to studied words, several studies have demonstrated normal priming in amnesic patients (Carlesimo, 1994; Cermak, Verfaellie, & Chase, 1995; Shimamura & Squire, 1984; Vaidya, Gabrieli, Keane, & Monti, 1995). Furthermore, amnesic patients can exhibit normal effects of conceptual manipulations, such as level of processing and generation effects, on implicit conceptual tests (Carlesimo, 1994; Cermak et al., 1995; Keane et al., 1997). The conceptual processing deficit view of amnesia has also been undermined by findings that amnesic patients are impaired on explicit tests even if they are designed to tap perceptual processing, such as word-fragment-cued recall and graphemic-cued recall, which uses as test cues words that look similar to studied words (Cermak et al., 1995; Vaidya et al., 1995). Thus, for amnesic patients, performance consistently dissociates along the implicit–explicit dimension and not along the perceptual–conceptual dimension.

VI. CONTEMPORARY VIEWS: INTEGRATING SYSTEMS AND PROCESSING

Given the findings of functional dissociations between perceptual and conceptual tests as well as a neurological dissociation between implicit and explicit tests, many researchers have come to agree that both processes and systems must be considered to successfully explain memory function in the brain (e.g., Roediger & McDermott, 1993; Schacter, Chiu, & Ochsner, 1993; Shimamura, 1993; Squire, 1992). The approach of recent years has been to integrate systems and processing views in an attempt to determine what brain systems contribute to the various processes that underlie learning and memory. As already discussed, amnesia research identified memory processes, such as skill learning and priming, that could not be subserved by the medial temporal or diencephalic structures damaged in amnesia. Thus, recent research has sought to identify the brain systems that subserve these memory functions. Furthermore, because normal memory research identified functional dissociations between perceptual and conceptual implicit tests of memory, the search for the systems underlying priming effects has been able to proceed at a finer grain. An even more recent development has been the effort to analyze explicit memory at a finer grain to understand the specific processes subserved by the system damaged in amnesia as well as processes contributed by other brain systems. The remainder of this chapter will discuss the associations between brain systems and memory processes that have been revealed by two approaches: the study of neurological patients, particularly those with damage to brain systems other than those involved in amnesia, and the use of functional imaging techniques such as positron emission tomography (PET) and functional magnetic resonance imaging (fMRI), which can reveal brain activity associated with task performance in normal subjects.

A. Skill Learning

Early findings of normal performance by amnesic patients on skill learning tasks suggested that the medial temporal and diencephalic midline structures damaged in amnesia do not play a critical role in skill learning (e.g., Brooks & Baddeley, 1976; Cermak, Lewis, Butters, & Goodglass, 1973; Cohen & Squire, 1980; Corkin, 1968). A number of more recent studies of skill learning in other patient groups have suggested that the basal ganglia may play a central role in this memory function. Specifically, patients with basal ganglia dysfunction due to Parkinson's disease or Huntington's disease exhibit impaired learning of skills such as the rotary pursuit task and reading mirror-reversed text (Harrington, Haaland, Yeo, & Marder, 1990; Heindel, Butters, & Salmon, 1988; Heindel, Salmon, Shults, Walicke, & Butters, 1989; Martone, Butters, Payne, Becker, & Sax, 1984). Furthermore, two of these studies demonstrated a double dissociation between skill learning and explicit tests of memory (free recall, recognition), with Huntington's patients showing impaired skill learning but normal explicit memory performance and amnesic patients showing the reverse pattern of effects (Heindel et al., 1988; Martone et al., 1984). Based on these data, it has been suggested that at least some forms of skill learning, which are not dependent on the structures damaged in amnesia, are dependent on the basal ganglia.

Functional imaging studies have provided some additional support for the participation of the basal ganglia in motor skill learning. In one study, subjects underwent PET scanning while learning a finger-tapping skill. Comparisons between activations seen during initial stages of learning and skilled performance revealed reductions in basal ganglia activation over the course of learning (Seitz, Roland, Bohm, Greitz, & Stone-Elander, 1990), perhaps reflecting increased processing efficiency. Changes in activation over the course of motor skill learning have also been observed in motor cortex, somatosensory processing areas of the thalamus and cortex, and the cerebellum—indeed, in all areas thought to be involved in motor behavior (e.g., Friston, Frith, Passingham, Liddle, & Frackowiak, 1992; Grafton et al., 1992; Seitz et al., 1990). These findings suggest that the products of skill learning are represented in widely distributed networks involving many, if not all, of the brain areas that contribute to performance of the skill.

B. Implicit Memory

As with skill learning, earlier findings of normal performance by amnesic patients on implicit tests of memory suggested that the structures damaged in amnesia do not play a critical role in priming (e.g., Cermak et al., 1985, 1986; Graf et al., 1984, 1985). Yet cognitive studies indicated that implicit memory is not a unitary phenomenon but rather that different processes contribute to perceptually and conceptually based priming (e.g., Roediger et al., 1990; Roediger, Srinivas, & Weldon, 1989; Roediger, Weldon, & Challis, 1989). Thus, recent research has been aimed at identifying the different brain systems that contribute to different forms of priming (e.g., Schacter, 1994).

Evidence for the neurological locus of perceptual word priming has come from study of patients with occipital or temporal–occipital cortex lesions. These patients can perform normally on explicit tests of memory on which amnesic patients are impaired, such as recognition memory (e.g., Fleischman et al., 1995). However, they exhibit impaired performance on implicit tests of word-stem completion and word identification priming on which amnesic patients perform normally (Fleischman et al., 1995; Keane, Gabrieli, Mapstone, Johnson, & Corkin, 1995; Nielsen-Bohlman, Ciranni, Shimamura, & Knight, 1997). These findings suggest that these forms of word priming depend on perceptual processing that occurs in temporal–occipital cortex, whereas explicit memory depends on the medial temporal structures that are damaged in amnesia.

The dependence of perceptual word priming on occipital cortex has also been indicated by functional imaging studies. In a number of studies, perceptual processing of visually presented words has been associated with activation in occipital cortex (Howard et al., 1992; Petersen, Fox, Posner, Mintun, & Raichle, 1988; Petersen, Fox, Snyder, & Raichle, 1990). In other studies, word priming has been associated with reduced activation in the very same areas of occipital cortex (Buckner et al., 1995; Schacter, Alpert, Savage, Rauch, & Albert, 1996; Squire et al., 1992). Specifically, performance of a word-stem completion task after having seen target words that can be used to complete the stems results in less activation of visual word processing areas of cortex than does performance of the same task without having seen target words. These findings support the idea that priming effects reflect increased efficiency of processing resulting from repetition of encoding processes and, further, that these effects take place in brain areas that are not compromised in amnesia (i.e., occipital cortex).

Research regarding the identification of a specific brain area associated with conceptual priming has been more limited. Studies of conceptual priming in patient populations have revealed impaired performance in patients with widespread cortical damage due to Alzheimer's disease. Specifically, Alzheimer's patients have exhibited impaired priming on tests of free association to cue words related to studied words and tests of production of category members (Monti et al., 1996; Salmon, Shimamura, Butters, & Smith, 1988). However, these patients have also exhibited impaired performance on some perceptual priming tasks, such as word-stem completion and fragmented picture identification (Heindel, Salmon, & Butters, 1990; Heindel et al., 1989; Keane, Gabrieli, Fennema, Growdon, & Corkin, 1991; Shimamura, Salmon, Squire, & Butters, 1987). Furthermore, recent studies have revealed that Alzheimer's patients can exhibit intact priming on some conceptual tasks, such as repeated verification that an item is a member of a particular category and generation of items from strongly associated cue words (Thompson-Schill, Gabrieli, Vaidya, Grinnell, & Fleischman, 1994; Vaidya, Gabrieli, Lange, & Fleischman, 1996). These findings suggest that instances of impaired conceptual priming in Alzheimer's patients are not related to the conceptual processing component alone. Thus, patient studies have not yet identified a key brain area that contributes to conceptual forms of priming.

In contrast, functional imaging studies have implicated a specific area of left inferior prefrontal cortex in conceptual processing of word stimuli (Demb et al., 1995; Kapur, Craik, et al., 1994; Kapur, Rose, et al., 1994; Petersen et al., 1988, 1990; Tulving, Kapur, Craik, Moscovitch, & Houle, 1994). In addition, one study has revealed reduced activation in the same frontal area in a conceptual priming task (Demb et al., 1995). As with the perceptual priming findings, this finding suggests that conceptual priming effects reflect increased efficiency of processing in the frontal area in which conceptual processing of words occurs.

C. Explicit Memory

As specific processes underlying implicit memory have been associated with specific brain systems, recent research has endeavored to characterize more precisely the processes underlying explicit memory and the brain systems associated with those processes. The study of patients with amnesia has revealed an association between explicit memory in general and the medial temporal region. Functional imaging studies have provided some support for this relationship. Comparisons of certain memory tasks to nonmemory control tasks have revealed increased hippocampal activation in the memory tasks. Specifically, greater hippocampal activation was found in the memory task of judging whether pictures of faces have been seen before compared to the nonmemory task of juding the gender of the faces (Kapur, Friston, Young, Frith, & Frackowiak, 1995) and in the memory task of word-stem-cued recall compared to the nonmemory task of completing word stems without retrieving items from memory (Squire et al., 1992; Buckner et al., 1995). Greater hippocampal activation has also been observed when the level of recall in stem-cued recall was high, after meaningful encoding of studied words, than when the level of recall was low, after superficial encoding (Schacter et al., 1996). Such findings suggest that the medial temporal region is particularly involved in retrieval of items from memory. In addition, both PET and fMRI studies of memory have revealed increased hippocampal activation during viewing of scenes or objects that had not been seen before compared to items that were repeated (Schacter et al., 1995; Stern et al., 1996; Tulving, Markowitsch, Craik, Habib, & Houle, 1996; Tulving, Markowitsch, Kapur, Habib, & Houle, 1994). These findings suggest that another role of the medial temporal region may be to selectively process novel items for memory encoding and storage.

Although functional imaging studies have suggested some specific processes underlying explicit memory that may be subserved by the medial temporal region, such as memory retrieval and encoding of novel items, these findings have not been consistent. In a number of studies, no differential activation of the medial temporal region has been observed in memory tasks. These tasks have included judging whether words or sentences had been seen before, with presentation of many items that were seen before compared to presentation of few such items (Kapur, S., et al., 1995; Tulving, Kapur, Markowitsch, et al., 1994); judging whether words had been seen before compared to judging whether they were living or nonliving things (Kapur, N., et al., 1995); category-cued recall compared to baseline generation of members of unstudied categories (Fletcher et al., 1995; Shallice et al., 1994); and stem-cued recall compared to baseline stem completion when the format or modality of the word stems differed from that of the studied words (Buckner et al., 1995).

One possible explanation of the inconsistency in functional imaging findings in memory studies is that the key processes that the medial temporal region contributes to learning and memory have not been identified or isolated by the tasks that have been compared. Recent neuropsychological studies have begun to characterize some of the essential components of explicit memory. One candidate for the specific process that is mediated by the brain system that is damaged in amnesia is the formation, storage, and retrieval of new associations that support conscious or effortful recollection. This function, sometimes called "binding," has been associated with the medial temporal region by researchers who study memory in animals and computational models as well as those who study humans with memory disorders (e.g., Cohen, Poldrack, & Eichenbaum, 1997; Johnson & Chalfonte, 1994; Metcalfe, Mencl, & Cottrell, 1994; Rudy & Sutherland, 1994; Squire, 1992). Binding allows the various components of a complex memory for an event—including perceptual, conceptual, and contextual information—to be linked and to be accessed with conscious awareness.

Evidence for a deficit in memory for new associations in amnesic patients has been explored in implicit tests of memory. In one type of implicit test of memory for new associations, subjects study word pairs and then are tested with a context word and a word stem. Priming of new associations is reflected in greater completion of stems with studied words when they are presented with the same context word as in the studied word pairs compared to when they are presented with a different context word. Cognitive studies have demonstrated that priming of new associations in this task depends upon rich, meaningful encoding that relates the members of the word pairs at study (Graf & Schacter, 1985; Schacter & Graf, 1986a). These findings suggest that the task taps the sort of binding function that has been attributed to the medial temporal region. Amnesic patients not only have exhibited impaired priming of new associations in this task (Cermak, Bleich, & Blackford, 1988; Mayes & Gooding, 1989; Schacter & Graf, 1986b; Shimamura & Squire, 1989) but also have exhibited a relationship between the degree of priming and the severity of the memory disorder (Schacter & Graf, 1986b; Shimamura & Squire, 1989). These findings of impaired implicit memory for new associations in amnesic patients support the hypothesis of a deficit in binding, which could contribute to the explicit memory deficit in amnesia.

Amnesic patients have also exhibited impaired binding in explicit tests of memory. In one study, subjects studied a categorized list of words that was presented either in a random order or with the items blocked by category. Category cues were provided in a cued recall test. To benefit from being given a blocked list at study, one must be able to store associations between the studied category members. Control subjects recalled more category members when they had been studied in a blocked list. Amnesic patients, however, did not benefit from studying a blocked list, suggesting a deficit in storing the organizing associations between the items (Gershberg, Verfaellie, & Cermak, 1995). In another study, subjects studied two-syllable words and were given a test of recognition memory that included new words made up of syllables that had been part of the studied words (e.g., study "snowman" and "baseball," test "snowball"). Patients with hippocampal damage were more likely to incorrectly classify these new conjunction words as having been studied, suggesting that they had less successfully bound together the parts of each word at study (Kroll, Knight, Metcalfe, Wolf, & Tulving, 1996). Taken together, these findings of impaired binding in implicit and explicit tests of memory support the hypothesis that the specific process underlying explicit memory that is mediated by the brain system that is damaged in amnesia is the formation, storage, and retrieval of new associations.

On the other hand, amnesic patients have shown preserved memory for new associations when priming of these associations could be supported by implicit memory processes. For example, amnesic patients showed normal priming of new associations when the components to be associated formed an integrated perceptual unit in the form of a word and the color of ink in which it was printed (Musen & Squire, 1993). In another task, pairs of words were presented simultaneously at study and at test, so that each word pair could be processed as a perceptual unit, and the test task was to determine whether both items in the pair were real words. In cognitive studies, priming of new associations in this task was found to be perceptually based, in that the amount of priming was not increased by meaningful processing at study compared to superficial processing, but associative priming was reduced or eliminated when the words were presented in different formats at study and test (Goshen-Gottstein & Moscovitch, 1995b, 1995c). Amnesic patients have shown preserved priming of new associations in this task (Goshen-Gottstein & Moscovitch, 1995a). Priming of new associations in both the colored word and word pair tasks could be based on speeded perceptual processing of the stimulus configuration as a whole.

D. Control of Memory

Another component process contributing to explicit memory is the use of organizational memory strategies. This component has been associated with prefrontal cortex. Patients with frontal lobe lesions exhibit impaired strategy use in cognition in general, in the form of impaired planning and problem solving in both laboratory tasks and everyday life (Mayes, 1988; Milner, 1964; Shallice, 1982). The role of prefrontal cortex in strategy use in explicit memory was suggested by a finding of disproportionately impaired free recall compared to recognition in patients with frontal lobe lesions (Janowsky, Shimamura, Kritchevsky, & Squire, 1989). Use of organizational strategies is particularly important in free recall because this type of test provides few external cues or constraints to guide memory. In direct examinations of the use of memory strategies in tests of free recall, patients with frontal lobe lesions have exhibited reduced consistency of organization across trials in recall of unrelated lists (subjective organization) and reduced grouping of category members in recall of categorized lists (category clustering), indicating reduced use of organizational strategies (Eslinger & Grattan, 1994; Gershberg & Shimamura, 1995; Stuss et al., 1994).

Functional imaging studies have provided further insights into the role of prefrontal cortex in learning and memory. A number of studies have implicated an area of left inferior prefrontal cortex in encoding information for memory. Some of these studies have suggested that this area plays a broad role in conceptual processing of items, regardless of whether they are presented in the context of a memory task. For example, this area showed greater activation when subjects processed the meanings of words, such as judging whether they were abstract versus concrete or determining category membership, compared to when they processed the perceptual characteristics of words, such as judging whether they were printed in upper case versus lower case or if they contained the letter "a" (Demb et al., 1995; Fletcher et al., 1995; Kapur, Craik, et al., 1994; Kapur, Rose et al., 1994; Shallice et al., 1994; Tulving, Kapur, Craik, Moscovitch, & Houle, 1994). These tasks did not require or instruct subjects to try to remember the words.

Although findings of left inferior prefrontal cortex activation in conceptual processing tasks with no stated memory demands suggest that this area may play a central role in conceptual processing in general, other findings suggest that the area may play a more specific role in meaningfully encoding information for the purpose of memory storage. In particular, functional imaging studies have compared conditions that hold constant the need for conceptual processing but vary the degree to which effortful and strategic memory processes are engaged. Subjects studied word pairs for a memory test at the same time as they performed either a difficult distractor task, which allowed conceptual processing of the word pairs but precluded more effortful use of memory strategies, or an easy distractor task, which allowed both conceptual and strategic processing. Increased left prefrontal activation was revealed only in the easy distractor task condition (Fletcher et al., 1995; Shallice et al., 1994). Similarly, a study of patients with frontal lobe lesions revealed normal performance on implicit conceptual tests of memory, such as category production priming, which benefit from meaningful processing of study items, but impaired performance on parallel explicit tests, such as category-cued recall, which additionally benefit from effortful use of memory strategies (Gershberg, 1997). These functional imaging and patient studies suggest that the frontal lobes may play a specific role in the effortful, organizational, and strategic aspects of processing items for memory storage rather than a more general role in conceptual processing.

In addition to the identification of the role of left prefrontal cortex in encoding for memory, an area in right prefrontal cortex has been associated with retrieval of memories. In recognition memory tasks, increased activation in right prefrontal cortex was observed when subjects viewed pictures or sentences that had been seen before compared to new items (Tulving, Kapur, Craik, Moscovitch, & Houle, 1994; Tulving, Kapur, Markowitsch, et al., 1994; Tulving et al., 1996). These findings suggest that right prefrontal cortex may play a general role in recognizing that information is familiar. Other findings, however, suggest that the area may play a more specific role in the effortful attempt to retrieve information from memory. For example, increased right prefrontal activation was observed when explicit category-cued recall tests, which require effortful retrieval, were compared to baseline category exemplar generation tasks (Fletcher et al., 1995; Shallice et al., 1994). Furthermore, this area showed increased activation when tasks that involved a high degree of retrieval effort but little successful recollection were compared to control tasks that required no retrieval effort at all, thus separating the role of right prefrontal cortex in retrieval effort from its role in recollection. These tasks included a recognition memory test with a low proportion of studied items compared to a non-memory control task (Kapur, S., et al., 1995) and an explicit word-stem-cued recall test with a low level of recall success, due to superficial processing of items at study, compared to baseline stem completion (Schacter et al., 1996). Taken together, the functional imaging findings regarding the functions of left and right prefrontal cortex converge with findings from patient studies in suggesting that the role of the frontal lobes in learning and memory may be to control the processes involved in effortful, strategic encoding and retrieval.

The contributions of the frontal lobes to effortful, strategic processes in memory may be related to a more basic role in working memory—that is, holding items in mind to meaningfully process and organize them at encoding and to strategically guide retrieval. A relationship between working memory and memory strategy use has been suggested by findings that the performance of frontal patients improved when the working memory load required for using organizational strategies was reduced. Specifically, in tests of memory for categorized lists of words, when category names were provided as cues at study or test, the use of category clustering by frontal patients increased, sometimes to normal levels (Gershberg & Shimamura, 1995).

In addition, patient studies have provided some direct evidence that the frontal lobes play a role in tasks that place demands on working memory. Patients with frontal lobe lesions perform poorly on tasks that involve passively holding information in mind and on tasks that involve holding and manipulating information. Tasks in which frontal patients have exhibited deficits in passively holding information have included tests of digit span (e.g., Janowsky et al., 1989) and tests that required retaining spatial locations or natural sounds during a brief period of interfering activity (Baldo & Shimamura, 1996; Chao & Knight, 1995; Ptito, Crane, Leonard, Amsel, & Caramanos, 1995). Tasks in which frontal patients have exhibited deficits in both holding and manipulating information have included a flanker task and self-ordered pointing tasks. In the flanker task, subjects were required to press a button to indicate the color of a central square while ignoring the color of a flanking square. Frontal patients showed reduced interference from the presence of a flanking square relative to control subjects, suggesting a disruption in the storage of stimulus–response mappings in working memory (Rafal et al., 1996). In self-ordered pointing tasks, subjects were shown an array of words or abstract designs and were asked to point to a different item in the array on each of a series of trials, with the items placed in different positions on each trial. The impaired performance exhibited by frontal patients suggested a disruption of the ability to hold in mind throughout the task the items that they had already selected in earlier trials (Petrides & Milner, 1982).

Functional imaging studies have contributed additional evidence that the frontal lobes play a role in working memory. Such studies have revealed increased activation of prefrontal cortex during performance of working memory tasks—again, both tasks that involve passively holding information in mind and tasks that involve holding and manipulating information. Tasks that revealed prefrontal cortex activation while subjects passively held information have included holding five words over the course of a 40-sec scan (Fiez et al., 1996) and holding the spatial locations of several objects for 3 sec (Smith et al., 1995).

A number of tasks have revealed prefrontal cortex activation while subjects both held and manipulated information. These tasks have included both the same self-ordered pointing task that has been found to be impaired in frontal patients and a task of generating random sequences of digits, which similarly requires retaining previous responses over the course of a number of trials (Petrides, Alivisatos, Evans, & Meyer, 1993; Petrides, Alivisatos, Meyer, & Evans, 1993). Another task requiring holding and manipulating information is the two-back task. In this task, subjects were required to monitor a sequence of stimuli to detect matches between an item and the item presented two items previously. The two-back task requires subjects to continuously hold and update several items in working memory. Compared to a task of monitoring sequences of stimuli for a single target item, which places little demand on working memory, performance of the two-back task has revealed increased activation in prefrontal cortex in both PET and fMRI studies and across a variety of types of stimuli, including letters, symbols, faces, and abstract patterns (Awh et al., 1996; D'Esposito, Shin, et al., 1995). Prefrontal cortex activation has also been demonstrated when working memory was taxed by requiring subjects to perform two tasks simultaneously. Separately, the two tasks, monitoring a sequence of words for members of a target category and judging which of two images matched a rotated version of one of the images, placed little demand on working memory and failed to activate prefrontal cortex. Thus, the prefrontal cortex activation revealed in the dual-task situation was interpreted as reflecting the working memory load involved in allocating attention and coordinating performance of the two tasks (D'Esposito, Detre, et al., 1995).

VII. CONCLUSIONS

The study of learning and memory in humans over the past several decades has been characterized by both tension and synergy between different methodological approaches. Neuropsychology research, focusing on exploring the nature of memory systems of the brain, has contributed evidence of dissociations in the performance of patient groups, illuminating key distinctions between different forms of memory, such as implicit and explicit memory. Cognitive psychology, focusing on exploring the nature of the processes contributing to learning and memory, has contributed evidence of functional dissociations in the performance of normal subjects, illuminating distinctions between different types of memory tasks, such as conceptual and perceptual tests. Research using new functional imaging techniques, revealing brain activity during memory task performance, has contributed converging evidence regarding the relationships between the brain systems and cognitive processes involved in learning and memory.

Together, these approaches have revealed that the entire brain participates in learning and memory. Different brain systems contribute to different forms of memory, with the common principle that memories are stored in the brain areas that process the information that constitutes the contents of the memories. Thus, skill learning occurs in areas involved in the performance of the particular skill, such as motor cortex and the basal ganglia. Perceptual memories are stored in areas involved in perceptual processing, such as occipital cortex. Conceptual memories are stored in association areas involved in conceptual processing, such as prefrontal cortex. Implicit tests of memory reveal the presence of such memories by demonstrating increased processing efficiency that results from having access to the traces of prior processing stored in these areas. Explicit tests of memory depend upon access to additional information—associations that bind together the various perceptual, conceptual, and contextual components of a memory for an event. These associations are stored and retrieved with the participation of the medial temporal and diencephalic structures that are involved in amnesia. Additional contributions are made to performance on explicit tests of memory by prefrontal cortex, through its role in the control of working memory and the effortful use of memory strategies in encoding and retrieval.

VIII. KEY POINTS

1. Human organic amnesia, which is associated with damage to either medial temporal or diencephalic midline structures, is characterized by a striking impairment in the ability to form new memories in the context of otherwise preserved intellectual function.

2. Dissociations between the form of memory that is impaired in amnesia, explicit memory for past events, and forms of memory that are preserved in amnesia, including priming and skill learning, suggested that memory is not a unitary phenomenon but rather is subserved by multiple brain systems.

3. Functional dissociations between tests of memory that tap the products of perceptual processing and tests that tap the products of conceptual processing have allowed a finer grained analysis of the processes that underlie human learning and memory and the brain systems that subserve those processes.

4. Findings that patients with basal ganglia dysfunction exhibit impaired skill learning and that structures including the basal ganglia, motor cortex, and cerebellum show changes in activation in functional imaging studies of motor skill learning suggest that such learning occurs in the same brain areas that are involved in the performance of the skill.

5. Findings of impaired perceptual priming in patients with lesions in occipital cortex and of reduced activity in occipital cortex in functional imaging studies of perceptual priming suggest that perceptual priming effects reflect increased processing efficiency resulting from repetition of encoding procedures that took place in perceptual processing areas of cortex.

6. Some functional imaging studies have provided converging evidence of the role of medial temporal structures in memory, revealing increased hippocampal activation associated with encoding new information and retrieving information from memory.

7. A candidate process contributed to explicit memory by the medial temporal and diencephalic structures involved in amnesia is binding—the formation, storage, and retrieval of new associations that allow the various components of a complex memory for an event to be linked and to be accessed with conscious awareness.

8. Patients with lesions in prefrontal cortex exhibit impaired use of organizational strategies in memory, suggesting that the frontal lobes contribute to effortful strategy use in explicit memory tasks.

9. Findings from functional imaging studies, which have revealed increased activation in prefrontal cortex when subjects engage in meaningful memory encoding and effortful memory retrieval, provide further evidence of the role of the frontal lobes in strategic aspects of memory.

10. Findings that patients with frontal lobe lesions exhibit impaired performance on tasks that tax working memory and that functional imaging studies reveal increased activation in prefrontal cortex when subjects perform working memory tasks suggest that the contributions of the frontal lobes to effortful, strategic processes in memory may be related to a more basic role of the frontal lobes in the control of working memory.

REFERENCES

Atkinson, R. C., & Shiffrin, R. M. (1968). Human memory: A proposed system and its control processes. In K. W. Spence & J. T. Spence (Eds.), *The psychology of learning and motivation: Vol. 2. Advances in research and theory* (pp. 89–195). New York: Academic Press.

Awh, E., Jonides, J., Smith, E. E., Schumacher, E. H., Koeppe, R. A., & Katz, S. (1996). Dissociation of storage and rehearsal in verbal working memory: Evidence from positron emission tomography. *Psychological Science, 7,* 25–31.

Baddeley, A. D., & Warrington, E. K. (1970). Amnesia and the distinction between long- and short-term memory. *Journal of Verbal Learning and Verbal Behavior, 9,* 176–189.

Baldo, J. V., & Shimamura, A. P. (1996). Spatial working memory in patients with frontal lobe lesions. *Society for Neuroscience Abstracts, 22,* 1108.

Blaxton, T. A. (1992). Dissociations among memory measures in memory-impaired subjects: Evidence for a processing account of memory. *Memory and Cognition, 20,* 549–562.

Brooks, D. N., & Baddeley, A. D. (1976). What can amnesic patients learn? *Neuropsychologia, 14,* 111–122.

Buckner, R. L., Petersen, S. E., Ojemann, J. G., Miezen, F. M., Squire, L. R., & Raichle, M. E. (1995). Functional anatomical studies of explicit and implicit memory retrieval tasks. *Journal of Neuroscience, 15,* 12–29.

Carlesimo, G. A. (1994). Perceptual and conceptual priming in amnesic and alcoholic patients. *Neuropsychologia, 32,* 903–921.

Cermak, L. S. (1976). The encoding capacity of a patient with amnesia due to encephalitis. *Neuropsychologia, 14,* 311–326.

Cermak, L. S., Bleich, R. P., & Blackford, S. P. (1988). Deficits in the implicit retention of new associations by alcoholic Korsakoff patients. *Brain and Cognition, 7,* 312–323.

Cermak, L. S., & Butters, N. (1972). The role of interference and encoding in the short-term memory deficits of Korsakoff patients. *Neuropsychologia, 10,* 89–96.

Cermak, L. S., Butters, N., & Gerrein, J. (1973). The extent of verbal encoding ability of Korsakoff patients. *Neuropsychologia, 11,* 85–94.

Cermak, L. S., Butters, N., & Moreines, J. (1974). Some analyses of the verbal encoding deficit of alcoholic Korsakoff patients. *Brain and Language, 1,* 141–150.

Cermak, L. S., Lewis, R., Butters, N., & Goodglass, H. (1973). Role of verbal mediation in performance of motor tasks by Korsakoff patients. *Perceptual and Motor Skills, 37,* 259–262.

Cermak, L. S., & O'Connor, M. (1983). The retrieval capacity of a patient with amnesia due to encephalitis. *Neuropsychologia, 21,* 213–234.

Cermak, L. S., O'Connor, M., & Talbot, N. (1986). The semantic biasing of alcoholic Korsakoff patients. *Journal of Clinical and Experimental Neuropsychology, 8,* 543–555.

Cermak, L. S., & Reale, L. (1978). Depth of processing and retention of words by alcoholic Korsakoff patients. *Journal of Experimental Psychology: Human Learning and Memory, 4,* 165–174.

Cermak, L. S., Talbot, N., Chandler, K., & Wolbarst, L. R. (1985). The perceptual priming phenomenon in amnesia. *Neuropsychologia, 23,* 615–622.

Cermak, L. S., Verfaellie, M., & Chase, K. A. (1995). Implicit and explicit memory in amnesia: An analysis of data-driven and conceptually driven processes. *Neuropsychology, 9,* 281–290.

Chao, L. L., & Knight, R. T. (1995). Human prefrontal lesions increase distractibility to irrelevant sensory inputs. *NeuroReport, 6,* 1605–1610.

Cohen, N. J., Poldrack, R. A., & Eichenbaum, H. (1997). Memory for items and memory for relations in the procedural/declarative memory framework. *Memory, 5,* 131–178.

Cohen, N. J., & Squire, L. R. (1980). Preserved learning and retention of pattern analyzing skill in amnesia: Association of knowing how and knowing that. *Science, 210,* 207–209.

Corkin, S. (1965). Tactually-guided maze learning in man: Effects of unilateral cortical excisions and bilateral hippocampal lesions. *Neuropsychologia, 3,* 339–351.

Corkin, S. (1968). Acquisition of motor skill after bilateral medial temporal lobe excision. *Neuropsychologia, 6,* 225–265.

Corkin, S. (1984). Lasting consequences of bilateral medial temporal lobectomy: Clinical course and experimental findings in H. M. *Seminars in Neurology, 4,* 249–259.

Craik, F. I. M., & Lockhart, R. S. (1972). Levels of processing: A framework for memory research. *Journal of Verbal Learning and Verbal Behavior, 11,* 671–684.

Craik, F. I. M., & Tulving, E. (1975). Depth of processing and retention of words in episodic memory. *Journal of Experimental Psychology: General, 104,* 268–294.

Demb, J. B., Desmond, J. E., Wagner, A. D., Vaidya, C. J., Glover, G. H., & Gabrieli, J. D. E. (1995). Semantic encoding and retrieval in the left inferior prefrontal cortex: A functional MRI study of task difficulty and process specificity. *Journal of Neuroscience, 15,* 5870–5878.

D'Esposito, M., Detre, J. A., Alsop, D. C., Shin, R. K., Atlas, S., & Grossman, M. (1995). The neural basis of the central executive system of working memory. *Nature, 378,* 279–281.

D'Esposito, M., Shin, R. K., Detre, J. A., Incledon, S., Annis, D., Aguirre, G. K., Grossman, M., & Alsop, D. C. (1995). Object and spatial working memory activates dorsolateral prefrontal cortex: A functional MRI study. *Society for Neuroscience Abstracts, 21,* 1498.

Eslinger, P. J., & Grattan, L. M. (1994). Altered serial position learning after frontal lobe lesion. *Neuropsychologia, 32,* 729–739.

Feustel, T. C., Shiffrin, R. M., & Salasoo, M. A. (1983). Episodic and lexical contributions to the repetition effect in word identification. *Journal of Experimental Psychology: General, 112,* 309–346.

Fiez, J. A., Raife, E. A., Balota, D. A., Schwarz, J. P., Raichle, M. E., & Petersen, S. E. (1996). A positron emission tomography study of the short-term maintenance of verbal information. *Journal of Neuroscience, 16,* 808–822.

Fleischman, D. A., Gabrieli, J. D. E., Reminger, S., Rinaldi, J., Morrell, F., & Wilson, R. (1995). Conceptual priming in perceptual identification for patients with Alzheimer's disease and a patient with right occipital lobectomy. *Neuropsychology, 9,* 187–197.

Fletcher, P. C., Frith, C. D., Grasby, P. M., Shallice, T., Frackowiak, R. S. J., & Dolan, R. J. (1995). Brain systems for encoding and retrieval of auditory–verbal memory. *Brain, 118,* 401–416.

Friston, K. J., Frith, C. D., Passingham, R. E., Liddle, P. F., & Frackowiak, R. S. J. (1992). Motor practice and neurophysiological adaptation in the cerebellum: A positron emission tomographic study. *Proceedings of the Royal Society of London, Series B, 248,* 223–228.

Gabrieli, J. D. E., & Keane, M. M. (1988). Priming in the amnesic patient H. M.: New findings and a theory of intact and impaired priming in patients with memory disorders. *Society for Neuroscience Abstracts, 14,* 1290.

Gabrieli, J. D. E., Milberg, W., Keane, M. M., & Corkin, S. (1990). Intact priming of patterns despite impaired memory. *Neuropsychologia, 28,* 417–427.

Gardner, H., Boller, F., Moreines, J., & Butters, N. (1973). Retrieving information from Korsakoff patients: Effects of categorical cues and reference to the task. *Cortex, 9,* 165–175.

Gershberg, F. B. (1997). Implicit and explicit conceptual memory following frontal lobe damage. *Journal of Cognitive Neuroscience, 9,* 105–116.

Gershberg, F. B., & Shimamura, A. P. (1995). Impaired use of organizational strategies in free recall following frontal lobe damage. *Neuropsychologia, 33,* 1305–1333.

Gershberg, F. B., Verfaellie, M., & Cermak, L. S. (1995). Blocking effects in implicit and explicit memory for categorized lists in amnesia. *Society for Neuroscience Abstracts, 21,* 754.

Glanzer, M., & Cunitz, A. R. (1966). Two storage mechanisms in free recall. *Journal of Verbal Learning and Verbal Behavior, 5,* 351–360.

Goshen-Gottstein, Y., & Moscovitch, M. (1995a). Intact implicit memory for newly-formed verbal associations in amnesic patients. *Society for Neuroscience Abstracts, 21,* 1446.

Goshen-Gottstein, Y., & Moscovitch, M. (1995b). Repetition priming for newly formed and preexisting associations: Perceptual and conceptual influences. *Journal of Experimental Psychology: Learning, Memory, and Cognition, 21,* 1229–1248.

Goshen-Gottstein, Y., & Moscovitch, M. (1995c). Repetition priming for newly formed associations are perceptually based: Evidence from shallow encoding and format specificity. *Journal of Experimental Psychology: Learning, Memory, and Cognition, 21,* 1249–1262.

Graf, P., & Mandler, G. (1984). Activation makes words more accessible, but not necessarily more retrievable. *Journal of Verbal Learning and Verbal Behavior, 25,* 553–568.

Graf, P., & Schacter, D. L. (1985). Implicit and explicit memory for new associations in normal and amnesic subjects. *Journal of Experimental Psychology: Learning, Memory, and Cognition, 11,* 501–518.

Graf, P., Shimamura, A. P., & Squire, L. R. (1985). Priming across modalities and priming across category levels: Extending the domain of preserved function in amnesia. *Journal of Experimental Psychology: Learning, Memory, and Cognition, 11,* 386–396.

Graf, P., Squire, L. R., & Mandler, G. (1984). The information that amnesic patients do not forget. *Journal of Experimental Psychology: Learning, Memory, and Cognition, 10,* 164–178.

Graff-Radford, N. R., Tranel, D., Van Hoesen, G. W., & Brandt, J. P. (1990). Diencephalic amnesia. *Brain, 113,* 1–25.

Grafton, S. T., Mazziotta, J. C., Presty, S., Friston, K. J., Frackowiak, R. S. J., & Phelps, M. E. (1992). Functional anatomy of human procedural learning determined with regional cerebral blood flow and PET. *Journal of Neuroscience, 12,* 2542–2548.

Haist, F., Musen, G., & Squire, L. R. (1991). Intact priming of words and nonwords in amnesia. *Psychobiology, 19,* 275–285.

Hamann, S. B. (1990). Level-of-processing effects in conceptually driven implicit tasks. *Journal of Experimental Psychology: Learning, Memory, and Cognition, 16,* 970–977.

Harrington, D. L., Haaland, K. Y., Yeo, R. A., & Marder, E. (1990). Procedural memory in Parkinson's disease: Impaired motor but not visuoperceptual learning. *Journal of Clinical and Experimental Neuropsychology, 12,* 323–339.

Heindel, W. C., Butters, N., & Salmon, D. P. (1988). Impaired learning of a motor skill in patients with Huntington's disease. *Behavioral Neuroscience, 102,* 141–147.

Heindel, W. C., Salmon, D. P., & Butters, N. (1990). Pictorial priming and cued recall in Alzheimer's and Huntington's disease. *Brain and Cognition, 13,* 282–295.

Heindel, W. C., Salmon, D. P., Shults, C. W., Walicke, P. A., & Butters, N. (1989). Neuropsychological evidence for multiple implicit memory systems: A comparison of Alzheimer's, Huntington's, and Parkinson's disease patients. *Journal of Neuroscience, 9,* 582–587.

Howard, D., Patterson, K., Wise, R., Brown, W. D., Friston, K., Weiller, C., & Frackowiak, R. (1992). The cortical localization of the lexicons. *Brain, 115,* 1769–1782.

Jacoby, L. L., & Dallas, M. (1981). On the relationship between autobiographical memory and perceptual learning. *Journal of Experimental Psychology: General, 110,* 306–340.

Jacoby, L. L., & Witherspoon, D. (1982). Remembering without awareness. *Canadian Journal of Psychology, 36,* 300–324.

Janowsky, J. S., Shimamura, A. P., Kritchevsky, M., & Squire, L. R. (1989). Cognitive impairment following frontal lobe damage and its relevance to human amnesia. *Behavioral Neuroscience, 103,* 548–560.

Johnson, M. K., & Chalfonte, B. L. (1994). Binding complex memories: The role of reactivation and the hippocampus. In D. L. Schacter & E. Tulving (Eds.), *Memory systems 1994* (pp. 311–350). Cambridge, MA: MIT Press.

Kapur, N., Friston, K. J., Young, A., Frith, C. D., & Frackowiak, R. S. J. (1995). Activation of human hippocampal formation during memory for faces: A PET study. *Cortex, 31,* 99–108.

Kapur, S., Craik, F. I. M., Jones, C., Brown, G. M., Houle, S., & Tulving, E. (1995). Functional role of the prefrontal cortex in retrieval of memories: A PET study. *NeuroReport, 6,* 1880–1884.

Kapur, S., Craik, F. I. M., Tulving, E., Wilson, A. A., Houle, S., & Brown, G. M. (1994). Neuroanatomical correlates of encoding in episodic memory: Levels of processing effect. *Proceedings of the National Academy of Sciences U.S.A., 91,* 2008–2011.

Kapur, S., Rose, R., Liddle, P. F., Zipursky, R. B., Brown, G. M., Stuss, D., Houle, S., & Tulving, E. (1994). The role of the left prefrontal cortex in verbal processing: Semantic processing or willed action? *NeuroReport, 5,* 2193–2196.

Keane, M. M., Gabrieli, J. D. E., Fennema, A. C., Growdon, J. H., & Corkin, S. (1991). Evidence for a dissociation between perceptual and conceptual priming in Alzheimer's disease. *Behavioral Neuroscience, 105,* 326–342.

Keane, M. M., Gabrieli, J. D. E., Mapstone, H. C., Johnson, K. A., & Corkin, S. (1995). Double dissociation of memory capacities after bilateral occipital-lobe or medial temporal-lobe lesions. *Brain, 118,* 1129–1148.

Keane, M. M., Gabrieli, J. D. E., Monti, L. A., Fleischman, D. A., Cantor, J. M., & Noland, J. S. (1997). Intact and impaired conceptual memory processes in amnesia. *Neuropsychology, 11,* 59–69.

Keane, M. M., Gabrieli, J. D. E., Noland, J. S., & McNealy, S. I. (1995). Normal perceptual priming of orthographically illegal nonwords in amnesia. *Journal of the International Neuropsychological Society, 1,* 424–433.

Kirsner, K., & Smith, M. C. (1974). Modality effects in word identification. *Memory and Cognition, 2,* 637–640.

Korsakoff, S. S. (1889/1955). Psychic disorder in conjunction with multiple neuritis (M. Victor & V. M. Yakovlev, Trans.). *Neurology, 5,* 394–406.

Kroll, N. E. A., Knight, R. T., Metcalfe, J., Wolf, E. S., & Tulving, E. (1996). Cohesion failure as a source of memory illusions. *Journal of Memory and Language, 35,* 176–196.

Mair, W. G. P., Warrington, E. K., & Weiskrantz, L. (1979). Memory disorder in Korsakoff's psychosis: A neuropathological and neuropsychological investigation of two cases. *Brain, 102,* 749–783.

Martone, M., Butters, N., Payne, M., Becker, J. T., & Sax, S. (1984). Dissociations between skill learning and verbal recognition in amnesia and dementia. *Archives of Neurology, 41,* 965–970.

Mayes, A. R. (1988). *Human organic memory disorders.* Cambridge, U.K.: Cambridge University Press.

Mayes, A. R., & Gooding, P. (1989). Enhancement of word completion priming in amnesics by cueing with previously novel associates. *Neuropsychologia, 27,* 1057–1072.

Mayes, A. R., Meudell, P. R., Mann, D., Pickering, A. (1988). Location of lesions in Korsakoff's syndrome: Neuropsychological and neuropathological data on two patients. *Cortex, 24,* 367–388.

Metcalfe, J., Mencl, W. E., & Cottrell, G. W. (1994). Cognitive binding. In D. L. Schacter & E. Tulving (Eds.), *Memory systems 1994* (pp. 369–394). Cambridge, MA: MIT Press.

Milner, B. (1962). Les troubles de la memoire accompagnant des lesions hippocampiques bilaterales. In *Physiologie de l'hippocampe* (pp. 257–272). Paris: Centre National de la Recherche Scientifique.

Milner, B. (1964). Some effects of frontal lobectomy in man. In J. M. Warren & K. Akert (Eds.), *The frontal granular cortex and behavior* (pp. 313–334). New York: McGraw-Hill.

Milner, B. (1966). Amnesia following operation on the temporal lobes. In C. W. M. Whitty & O. L. Zangwill (Eds.), *Amnesia* (1st ed., pp. 109–133). London: Butterworths.

Milner, B., Corkin, S., & Teuber, H. (1968). Further analysis of the hippocampal amnesic syndrome: 14-year follow-up study of H. M. *Neuropsychologia, 6,* 215–234.

Monti, L. A., Gabrieli, J. D. E., Reminger, S. L., Rinaldi, J. A., Wilson, R. S., & Fleischman, D. A. (1996). Differential effects of aging and Alzheimer's disease on conceptual implicit and explicit memory. *Neuropsychology, 10,* 101–112.

Mori, E., Yamadori, A., & Mitani, Y. (1986). Left thalamic infarction and disturbance of verbal memory: A clinicoanatomical study with a new method of computed tomographic stereotaxic lesion localization. *Annals of Neurology, 20,* 671–676.

Morton, J. (1970). A functional model for memory. In D. A. Norman (Ed.), *Models of human memory* (pp. 203–254). New York: Academic Press.

Moscovitch, M., Vriezen, E., & Goshen-Gottstein, Y. (1993). Implicit tests of memory in patients with focal lesions and degenerative brain disorders. In H. Spinnler & F. Boller (Eds.), *Handbook of neuropsychology* (Vol. 8, pp. 133–173). Amsterdam: Elsevier.

Murdock, B. B. (1962). The serial position effect of free recall. *Journal of Experimental Psychology, 64,* 482–488.

Musen, G., & Squire, L. R. (1991). Normal acquisition of novel verbal information in amnesia. *Journal of Experimental Psychology: Learning, Memory, and Cognition, 17,* 1095–1104.

Musen, G., & Squire, L. R. (1992). Nonverbal priming in amnesia. *Memory and Cognition, 20,* 441–448.

Musen, G., & Squire, L. R. (1993). Implicit learning of color–word associations using a Stroop paradigm. *Journal of Experimental Psychology: Learning, Memory, and Cognition, 19,* 789–798.

Musen, G., & Treisman, A. (1990). Implicit and explicit memory for visual patterns. *Journal of Experimental Psychology: Learning, Memory, and Cognition, 16,* 127–137.

Nielsen-Bohlman, L., Ciranni, M., Shimamura, A. P., & Knight, R. T. (1997). Impaired word-stem priming in patients with temporal-occipital lesions. *Neuropsychologia, 35,* 1087–1092.

Parkin, A. J. (1982). Residual learning capability in organic amnesia. *Cortex, 18,* 417–440.

Petersen, S. E., Fox, P. T., Posner, M. I., Mintun, M., & Raichle, M. E. (1988). Positron emission tomographic studies of the cortical anatomy of single-word processing. *Nature, 331,* 585–589.

Petersen, S. E., Fox, P. T., Snyder, A. Z., & Raichle, M. E. (1990). Activation of extrastriate and frontal cortical areas by visual words and word-like stimuli. *Science, 249,* 1041–1044.

Petrides, M., Alivisatos, B., Evans, A. C., & Meyer, E. (1993). Dissociation of human mid-dorsolateral from posterior dorsolateral frontal cortex in memory processing. *Proceedings of the National Academy of Sciences U.S.A., 90,* 873–877.

Petrides, M., Alivisatos, B., Meyer, E., & Evans, A. C. (1993). Functional activation of the human frontal cortex during the performance of verbal working memory tasks. *Proceedings of the National Academy of Sciences U.S.A., 90,* 878–882.

Petrides, M., & Milner, B. (1982). Deficits in subject-ordered tasks after frontal- and temporal-lobe lesions in man. *Neuropsychologia, 20,* 249–262.

Postman, L., & Phillips, L. W. (1965). Short term temporal changes in free recall. *Quarterly Journal of Experimental Psychology, 17,* 132–138.

Press, G. A., Amaral, D. G., & Squire, L. R. (1989). Hippocampal abnormalities in amnesic patients revealed by high-resolution magnetic resonance imaging. *Nature, 341,* 45–57.

Ptito, A., Crane, J., Leonard, G., Amsel, R., & Caramanos, Z. (1995). Visual-spatial localization by patients with frontal-lobe lesions invading or sparing area 46. *NeuroReport, 6,* 1781–1784.

Rafal, R., Gershberg, F., Egly, R., Ivry, R., Kingstone, A., & Ro, T. (1996). Response channel activation and the lateral prefrontal cortex. *Neuropsychologia, 34,* 1197–1202.

Rempel-Clower, N. L., Zola, S. M., Squire, L. R., & Amaral, D. G. (1996). Three cases of enduring memory impairment after bilateral damage limited to the hippocampal formation. *Journal of Neuroscience, 16,* 5233–5255.

Ribot, T. (1881). *Diseases of memory.* New York: Appleton.

Richardson-Klavehn, A., & Bjork, R. A. (1988). Measures of memory. *Annual Review of Psychology, 39,* 475–543.

Roediger, H. L., & Blaxton, T. A. (1987). Effects of varying modality, surface features, and retention interval on priming in word-fragment completion. *Memory and Cognition, 15,* 379–388.

Roediger, H. L., & McDermott, K. B. (1993). Implicit memory in normal human subjects. In H. Spinnler & F. Boller (Eds.). *Handbook of neuropsychology* (Vol. 8, pp. 63–131). Amsterdam: Elsevier.

Roediger, H. L., Rajaram, S., & Srinivas, K. (1990). Specifying criteria for postulating memory systems. *Annals of the New York Academy of Sciences, 608,* 572–595.

Roediger, H. L., Srinivas, K., & Weldon, M. S. (1989). Dissociations between implicit measures of retention. In S. Lewandowsky, J. C. Dunn, & K. Kirsner (Eds.), *Implicit memory: Theoretical issues* (pp. 67–84). Hillsdale, NJ: Erlbaum.

Roediger, H. L., Weldon, M. S., & Challis, B. H. (1989). Explaining dissociations between implicit and explicit measures of retention: A processing account. In H. L. Roediger & F. I. M. Craik (Eds.), *Varieties of memory and consciousness: Essays in honour of Endel Tulving* (pp. 3–41). Hillsdale, NJ: Erlbaum.

Roediger, H. L., Weldon, M. S., Stadler, M. A., & Riegler, G. H. (1992). Direct comparison of word stems and word fragments in implicit and explicit retention tests. *Journal of Experimental Psychology: Learning, Memory, and Cognition, 18,* 1251–1269.

Rozin, P. (1976). The psychobiological approach to human memory. In M. R. Rosenzweig & E. L. Bennett (Eds.), *Neural mechanisms of learning and memory* (pp. 3–46). Cambridge, MA: MIT Press.

Rudy, J. W., & Sutherland, R. J. (1994). The memory-coherence problem, configural associations, and the hippocampal system. In D. L. Schacter & E. Tulving (Eds.), *Memory systems 1994* (pp. 119–146). Cambridge, MA: MIT Press.

Rueckl, J. G. (1990). Similarity effects in word and pseudoword repetition priming. *Journal of Experimental Psychology: Learning, Memory, and Cognition, 16,* 374–391.

Salmon, D. P., Shimamura, A. P., Butters, N., & Smith, S. (1988). Lexical and semantic priming deficits in patients with Alzheimer's disease. *Journal of Clinical and Experimental Neuropsychology, 10,* 477–494.

Schacter, D. L. (1987). Implicit memory: History and current status. *Journal of Experimental Psychology: Learning, Memory, and Cognition, 13,* 501–518.

Schacter, D. L. (1994). Priming and multiple memory systems: Perceptual mechanisms of implicit memory. In D. L. Schacter & E. Tulving (Eds.), *Memory systems 1994* (pp. 233–268). Cambridge, MA: MIT Press.

Schacter, D. L., Alpert, N. M., Savage, C. R., Rauch, S. L., & Albert, M. S. (1996). Conscious recollection and the human hippocampal formation: Evidence from positron emission tomography. *Proceedings of the National Academy of Sciences U.S.A., 93,* 321–325.

Schacter, D. L., Chiu, C. Y. P., & Ochsner, K. N. (1993). Implicit memory: A selective review. *Annual Review of Neuroscience, 16,* 159–182.

Schacter, D. L., Cooper, L. A., & Delaney, S. M. (1990). Implicit memory for unfamiliar objects depends on access to structural descriptions. *Journal of Experimental Psychology: General, 119,* 5–24.

Schacter, D. L., Cooper, L. A., Tharan, M., & Rubens, A. (1991). Preserved priming of novel objects in patients with memory disorders. *Journal of Cognitive Neuroscience, 3,* 117–130.

Schacter, D. L., & Graf, P. (1986a). Effects of elaborative processing on implicit and explicit memory for new associations. *Journal of Experimental Psychology: Learning, Memory, and Cognition, 12,* 432–444.

Schacter, D. L., & Graf, P. (1986b). Preserved learning in amnesic patients: Perspectives from research on direct priming. *Journal of Clinical and Experimental Neuropsychology, 6,* 727–743.

Schacter, D. L., Reiman, E., Uecker, A., Polster, M. R., Yun, L. S., & Cooper, L. A. (1995). Brain regions associated with retrieval of structurally coherent visual information. *Nature, 376,* 587–590.

Scoville, W. B., & Milner, B. (1957). Loss of recent memory after bilateral hippocampal lesions. *Journal of Neurology, Neurosurgery, and Psychiatry, 20,* 11–21.

Seitz, R. J., Roland, P. E., Bohm, C., Greitz, T., & Stone-Elander, S. (1990). Motor learning in man: A positron emission tomographic study. *NeuroReport, 1,* 17–20.

Shallice, T. (1982). Specific impairments of planning. *Philosophical Transactions of the Royal Society of London (Biology), 298,* 199–209.

Shallice, T., Fletcher, P., Frith, C. D., Grasby, P., Frackowiak, R. S. J., & Dolan, R. J. (1994). Brain regions associated with acquisition and retrieval of verbal episodic memory. *Nature, 368,* 633–635.

Shimamura, A. P. (1986). Priming in amnesia: Evidence for a dissociable memory function. *Quarterly Journal of Experimental Psychology, 38,* 619–644.

Shimamura, A. P. (1993). Neuropsychological analyses of implicit memory: History, methodology, and theoretical interpretations. In P. Graf & M. E. J. Masson (Eds.), *Implicit memory: New directions in cognition, development, and neuropsychology* (pp. 265–285). Hillsdale, NJ: Erlbaum.

Shimamura, A. P., & Gershberg, F. B. (1992). Neuropsychiatric aspects of memory and amnesia. In S. C. Yudofsky & R. E. Hales (Eds.), *American Psychiatric Press textbook of neuropsychiatry* (pp. 345–362). Washington, DC: American Psychiatric Press.

Shimamura, A. P., Salmon, D. P., Squire, L. R., & Butters, N. (1987). Memory dysfunction and word priming in dementia and amnesia. *Behavioral Neuroscience, 101,* 347–351.

Shimamura, A. P., & Squire, L. R. (1984). Paired-associate learning and priming effects in amnesia: A neuropsychological study. *Journal of Experimental Psychology: General, 113,* 556–570.

Shimamura, A. P., & Squire, L. R. (1989). Impaired priming of new associations in amnesia. *Journal of Experimental Psychology: Learning, Memory, and Cognition, 15,* 721–728.

Smith, E. E., Jonides, J., Koeppe, R. A., Awh, E., Schumacher, E. H., & Minoshima, S. (1995). Spatial versus object working memory: PET investigations. *Journal of Cognitive Neuroscience, 7,* 337–356.

Squire, L. R. (1982). Comparisons between forms of amnesia: Some deficits are unique to Korsakoff's syndrome. *Journal of Experimental Psychology: Learning, Memory, and Cognition, 8,* 560–571.

Squire, L. R. (1987). *Memory and brain.* New York: Oxford University Press.

Squire, L. R. (1992). Memory and the hippocampus: Synthesis of findings with rats, monkeys, and humans. *Psychological Review, 99,* 195–231.

Squire, L. R., Amaral, D. G., & Press, G. A. (1990). Magnetic resonance imaging of the hippocampal formation and mammillary nuclei distinguish medial temporal lobe and diencephalic amnesia. *Journal of Neuroscience, 10,* 3106–3117.

Squire, L. R., Amaral, D. G., Zola-Morgan, S., Kritchevsky, M., & Press, G. (1989). Description of the brain injury in the amnesic patient N. A. based on magnetic resonance imaging. *Experimental Neurology, 105,* 23–35.

Squire, L. R., & Moore, R. Y. (1979). Dorsal thalamic lesion in a noted case of human memory dysfunction. *Annals of Neurology, 6,* 503–506.

Squire, L. R., Ojemann, J. G., Miezen, F. M., Petersen, S. E., Videen, T. O., & Raichle, M. E. (1992). Activation of the hippocampus in normal humans: A functional anatomic study of memory. *Proceedings of the National Academy of Sciences U.S.A., 89,* 1837–1841.

Squire, L. R., & Shimamura, A. P. (1986). Characterizing amnesic patients for neurobehavioral study. *Behavioral Neuroscience, 100,* 866–877.

Squire, L. R., Shimamura, A. P., & Graf, P. (1987). Strength and duration of priming effects in normal subjects and amnesic patients. *Neuropsychologia, 25,* 195–210.

Squire, L. R., & Zola-Morgan, S. (1988). Memory: Brain systems and behavior. *Trends in Neurosciences, 11,* 170–175.

Stern, C. E., Corkin, S., González, R. G., Guimaraes, A. R., Baker, J. R., Jennings, P. J., Carr, C. A., Sugiura, R. M., Vendantham, V., & Rosen, B. R. (1996). The hippocampal formation participates in novel picture encoding: Evidence from functional magnetic resonance imaging. *Proceedings of the National Academy of Sciences U.S.A., 93,* 8660–8665.

Stuss, D. T., Alexander, M. P., Palumbo, C. L., Buckle, L., Sayer, L., & Pogue, J. (1994). Organizational strategies of patients with unilateral or bilateral frontal lobe injury in word list learning tasks. *Neuropsychology, 8,* 355–373.

Talland, G. A. (1965). *Deranged memory.* New York: Academic Press.

Thompson-Schill, S. L., Gabrieli, J. D. E., Vaidya, C. J., Grinnell, E., & Fleischman, D. A. (1994). Preserved identification but impaired generation of repeated stimuli in conceptual priming tasks in patients with Alzheimer's disease. *Society for Neuroscience Abstracts, 20,* 430.

Tulving, E., Kapur, S., Craik, F. I. M., Moscovitch, M., & Houle, S. (1994). Hemispheric encoding/retrieval asymmetry in episodic memory: Positron emission tomography findings. *Proceedings of the National Academy of Sciences U.S.A., 91,* 2016–2020.

Tulving, E., Kapur, S., Markowitsch, H. J., Craik, F. I. M., Habib, R., & Houle, S. (1994). Neuroanatomical correlates of retrieval in episodic memory: Auditory sentence recognition. *Proceedings of the National Academy of Sciences U.S.A., 91,* 2012–2015.

Tulving, E., Markowitsch, H. J., Craik, F. I. M., Habib, R., & Houle, S. (1996). Novelty and familiarity activations in PET studies of memory encoding and retrieval. *Cerebral Cortex, 6,* 71–79.

Tulving, E., Markowitsch, H. J., Kapur, S., Habib, R., & Houle, S. (1994). Novelty encoding networks in the human brain: Positron emission tomography data. *NeuroReport, 5,* 2525–2528.

Tulving, E., & Pearlstone, Z. (1966). Availability versus accessibility of information in memory for words. *Journal of Verbal Learning and Verbal Behavior, 5,* 381–391.

Vaidya, C. J., Gabrieli, J. D. E., Keane, M. M., & Monti, L. A. (1995). Perceptual and conceptual memory processes in global amnesia. *Neuropsychology, 9,* 580–591.

Vaidya, C. J., Gabrieli, J. D. E., Lange, K. L., & Fleischman, D. A. (1996). Dissociable conceptual priming processes: Evidence from Alzheimer's disease. *Society for Neuroscience Abstracts, 22,* 1449.

Victor, M., Adams, R. D., & Collins, G. H. (1971). *The Wernicke–Korsakoff syndrome.* Philadelphia: Davis Company.

von Cramon, D. Y., Hebel, N., & Schuri, U. (1985). A contribution to the anatomical basis of thalamic amnesia. *Brain, 108,* 993–1008.

Warrington, E. K., & Weiskrantz, L. (1968). New method of testing long-term retention with special reference to amnesic patients. *Nature, 217,* 972–974.

Warrington, E. K., & Weiskrantz, L. (1970). Amnesic syndrome: Consolidation or retrieval? *Nature, 228,* 628–630.

Warrington, E. K., & Weiskrantz, L. (1974). The effect of prior learning on subsequent retention in amnesic patients. *Neuropsychologia, 12,* 419–428.

Warrington, E. K., & Weiskrantz, L. (1982). Amnesia: A disconnection syndrome? *Neuropsychologia, 20,* 233–248.

Weldon, M. S. (1991). Mechanisms underlying priming on perceptual tests. *Journal of Experimental Psychology: Learning, Memory, and Cognition, 17,* 526–541.

Zola-Morgan, S., Squire, L. R., & Amaral, D. G. (1986). Human amnesia and the medial temporal region: Enduring memory impairment following a bilateral lesion limited to field CA1 of the hippocampus. *Journal of Neuroscience, 6,* 2950–2967.

CHAPTER 10

Neurobiological Views of Memory

Raymond P. Kesner

Department of Psychology, University of Utah, Salt Lake City, Utah 84112

I. INTRODUCTION

The structure and utilization of memory are central to one's knowledge of the past, interpretation of the present, and prediction of the future. Therefore, the understanding of the structural and process components of memory systems at the psychological levels is of paramount importance. In recent years, there have been a number of attempts to divide learning and memory into multiple memory systems. Schacter and Tulving (1994) suggested that one needs to define memory systems in terms of the kind of information to be represented, the processes associated with the operation of each system, and the neurobiological substrates including neural structures and mechanisms that subserve each system. Furthermore, it is likely that there are multiple forms or subsystems associated with each memory system and there are likely to be multiple processes that define the operation of each system. Finally, there are probably multiple neural structures that form the overall substrate of a memory system.

Currently, the most established models of memory can be characterized as dual memory system models, with an emphasis on the hippocampus for one component of the model and a composite of other brain structures as the other component. For example, Squire (1994) proposed that memory can be divided into a hippocampal-dependent declarative memory which provides for conscious recollection of facts and events and a nonhippocampal-dependent nondeclarative memory which provides for memory without conscious access for skills, habits, priming, simple classical conditioning, and nonassociative learning. Others have used different terms to reflect the same type of distinction, including a hippocampal-dependent explicit memory versus a nonhippocampal-dependent implicit memory (Schacter, 1987) and a hippocampal-dependent declarative memory based on the representation of relationships among stimuli versus a nonhippocampal-dependent procedural memory based on the representation of a single stimulus or configuration of stimuli (Cohen & Eichenbaum, 1993). Olton (1983) suggested a different dual memory system in which memory can be divided into a hippocampal-dependent working memory, defined as memory for the specific, personal, and temporal context of a situation, and a nonhippocampal-dependent reference memory, defined as memory for rules and procedures (general knowledge) of specific situations. Different terms have been used to reflect the same distinction, including episodic versus semantic memory (Tulving, 1983).

However, memory is more complex and involves many neural systems in addition to the hippocampus. To remedy this situation, Kesner and DiMattia (1987) proposed a neurobiology of a dual-system model organized into a data-based memory system and a knowledge-based memory system and composed of multiple attributes or forms of memory. Based on extensive research aimed at testing this dual-system model, the model has been refined to include a set of operating characteristics and updated. In this chapter I will first present my own comprehensive dual memory system model, followed by a presentation of other dual-system neurobiological models, including the locale–taxon memory model (Nadel, 1994), the working–reference memory model (Olton, 1983), the declarative–nondeclarative model (Squire, 1994), and the declarative–procedural model (Cohen & Eichenbaum, 1993).

II. NEUROBIOLOGY OF A DUAL-SYSTEM, MULTIPLE-ATTRIBUTE MODEL

In this comprehensive model, it is assumed that any specific memory is organized into a data-based memory system and a knowledge-based memory system. The data-based memory system is biased in providing for temporary representations of incoming data concerning the present, with an emphasis on facts, data, and events that are usually personal or egocentric and that occur within specific external and internal contexts. The emphasis is on bottom-up processing. During initial learning great emphasis is placed on the data-based memory system, which continues to be of importance even after initial learning in situations where unique or novel trial information needs to be remembered. The data-based memory system is composed of different independently operating forms or attributes of memory. Even though there could be many attributes, the most important attributes include *space, time, response, sensory perception, and affect.* In humans a *language* attribute is also added.

A spatial attribute within this framework involves memory representations of places or relationships between places, which are usually independent of the subjects's own body schema. It is exemplified by the ability to encode and remember spatial maps and to localize stimuli in external space. Memory representations of the spatial attribute can be further subdivided into specific spatial features including allocentric spatial distance, egocentric spatial distance, allocentric direction, egocentric direction, and spatial location.

A temporal attribute within this framework involves memory representation of the duration of a stimulus, memory representation of the succession, or temporal order, of temporally separated events or stimuli, and, from a time perspective, memory representation of the past.

A response attribute within this framework involves memory representations based on feedback from motor responses (often based on kinesthetic and vestibular cues) that occur in specific situations as well as memory representations of stimulus–response associations.

A sensory-perceptual attribute within this framework involves memory representations of a set of sensory stimuli that are organized in the form of cues as part of a specific experience. Each sensory modality (touch, taste, smell, sight, and hearing) has its own memory representations and can be considered to be part of the sensory-perceptual attribute component of memory.

An affect attribute within this framework involves memory representations of reward value, positive or negative emotional experiences, and the associations between stimuli and rewards.

A language attribute within this framework involves memory representations of phonological, lexical, and morphological information.

Although the organization of these attributes within the data-based memory system can take many forms, they are probably organized hierarchically and in parallel. Some interactions between attributes are important and can aid in identifying specific neural regions that might subserve a critical interaction. For example, the interaction between spatial and temporal attributes can provide for the external context of a situation which is important in defining when and where critical events occurred. The interaction between sensory-perceptual attributes and the spatial attribute can provide for the memory representation of a spatial cognitive map.

Within the data-based memory system there are operational characteristics associated with each attribute, which include a number of processes: (a) pattern separation based on selective filtering or attenuation of interference associated with temporary memory representations of new information, (b) short-term memory, or working memory, of new information, (c) consolidation or elaborative rehearsal of new information, and (d) retrieval of new information based on flexibility and action.

Based on a series of experiments, it can be shown that within the data-based memory system different neural structures and circuits mediate different forms or attributes of memory. The most extensive data set is based on the use of paradigms that measure the short-term or working memory process, such as matching or nonmatching-to-sample, delayed conditional discrimination, or continuous recognition memory of single items or lists of items, and paradigms that measure new learning requiring a consolidation process, such as learning an inhibitory avoidance response, taste aversion learning, and water maze spatial navigation.

A. Spatial Attribute

1. Short-Term or Working Memory

With respect to spatial attribute information, it can be shown, using aforementioned paradigms to measure short-term or working memory for spatial information, that there are severe impairments for rats, monkeys, and humans with right hippocampal damage or bilateral hippocampal damage (Chiba, Kesner, Matsuo, & Heilbrun, 1990; Hopkins, Kesner, & Goldstein, 1995a; Kesner, 1990a; Olton, 1983, 1986; Parkinson, Murray, & Mishkin, 1988; Pigott & Milner, 1993; Smith & Milner, 1981).

With respect to specific spatial features, such as allocentric spatial distance, egocentric spatial distance, and spatial location, it has been shown in both rats and humans with bilateral hippocampal damage that there are severe deficits in short-term memory for these spatial features (Kesner & Hopkins, unpublished; Long & Kesner, 1994, 1996). These data are consistent with the recording of place cells (cells that increase their firing rate when an animal is located in a specific place) within the hippocampus of rats and monkeys (Kubie & Ranck, 1983; McNaughton, Barnes, & O'Keefe, 1983; O'Keefe, 1983; O'Keefe & Speakman, 1987; Rolls et al., 1989). Short-term memory for the spatial direction feature has not yet been investigated, but based on recording data indicating that head direction cells (cells that increase their firing rate as a function of the animal's head direction in the horizontal plane, independent of the animal's behavior, location, or trunk position) are not found in the hippocampus (Taube, Goodridge, Golob, Dudchenko, & Stackman, 1996), it is possible that the hippocampus does not represent spatial head direction information. The hippocampus is not the only neural region that mediates short-term memory for spatial information. Using a continuous spatial short-term recognition task, Kesner has shown that lesions of the dorsal lateral thalamus, pre- and parasubiculum, medial entorhinal cortex, and pre- and infralimbic cortex produce profound deficits similar to what has been described for hippocampal lesions, suggesting that other neural regions contribute to the spatial attribute within the data-based memory system (Kesner, unpublished; Kesner, Hunt, Williams, & Long, 1995). The exact contribution of each of these areas needs to be investigated, but it should be noted that place cells have also been recorded from the medial entorhinal cortex (Quirk, Muller, Kubie, & Ranck, 1992) and parasubiculum (Muller, Ranck, & Taube, 1996; Taube et al., 1996) and that head direction cells have been recorded from the lateral dorsal nucleus of the thalamus (Mizumori & Williams, 1993). Furthermore, it is likely that spatial short-term memory representations within the hippocampus might be important to amplify a subsequent consolidation process when necessary, and spatial short-term memory representations within the pre- and infralimbic cortex might be important to engage a retrieval, action, or strategy selection process. Thus, in general, the hippocampus represents within short-term memory some, if not all, of the spatial features associated with the spatial attribute.

2. Consolidation

The hippocampus also plays a role in the acquisition of learning of new spatial information requiring the consolidation of spatial attributes. This is readily observable in the acquisition of spatial navigation tasks in a water maze or dry-land version of the water maze and in inhibitory avoidance tasks requiring an association of a painful stimulus with a specific spatial location in that rats with hippocampal lesions are markedly impaired in these tasks (Kesner, 1990a; Morris, Garrud, Rawlins, & O'Keefe, 1982; O'Keefe & Nadel, 1978). Furthermore, it has been shown that posttrial disruption of normal hippocampal function with, for example, electrical brain stimulation results in time-dependent memory impairments (Kesner & Wilburn, 1974). These effects reveal that the hippocampus is involved in short-term consolidation processes, because the gradients are usually short, within minutes to a few hours. Long-term temporally graded functions have also been observed for previously learned spatial discriminations prior to surgery in rats and mice, but these long-term gradiens (2–4 weeks) are observed primarily following entorhinal cortex rather than hippocampal lesions (Cho, Beracochea, & Jaffard, 1993; Cho & Kesner, 1996; Cho, Kesner, & Brodale, 1995). Seizure-level electrical stimulation of the hippocampus 1 day, but not 7 days, after inhibitory avoidance training produces a temporary disruption in inhibitory avoidance memory. Subseizure-level stimulation of the hippocampus 1 or 7 days after training was ineffective (Kesner, Dixon, Pickett, & Berman, 1975). It is likely that in contrast to subseizure-level stimulation, seizure-level stimulation spread to adjacent neural regions including the entorhinal cortex, providing further support for the idea that long-term retrograde amnesia gradients might arise from entorhinal cortex dysfunction. A long-term gradient following hippocampal lesions has been reported following contextual fear conditioning (Kim & Fanselow, 1992), but recent results have questioned whether these gradients can be reliably measured (Maren, Aharonov, & Fanselow, 1996b; Weisend, Astur, & Sutherland, 1996). Thus, it is possible that short-term consolidation gradients derive from hippocampal dysfunction, whereas entorhinal cortex dysfunction is necessary to produce long-term retrograde amnesia consolidation gradients. Whether the hippocampus promotes the transfer of spatial information to the knowledge-based system or whether the hippocampus promotes the consolidation of information already processed in the knowledge-based system still needs to be resolved.

3. Pattern Separation

It can clearly be demonstrated that single cells within the hippocampus are activated by most sensory inputs, including vestibular, olfactory, visual, auditory, and somatosensory, as well as higher order integration of sensory stimuli (Cohen & Eichenbaum, 1993). The question of importance is whether these sensory inputs have a memory representation within the hippocampus. Thus far, it appears that short-term or working memory for odor or visual object information is not altered by lesions of the hippocampus (Aggleton, Hunt, & Rawlins, 1986; Jackson-Smith, Kesner, & Chiba, 1993; Kesner, Bolland, & Dakis, 1993; Mumby, Wood, & Pinel, 1992; Otto & Eichenbaum, 1992a), implying that sensory-perceptual information is not represented in memory within the hippocampus. One possible role for the hippocampus in processing all sensory information might be to provide for sensory markers to demarcate a spatial location, so that the hippocampus can more efficiently mediate spatial information. It is, thus, possible that one of the main process functions of the hippocampus is to encode and separate spatial events from each other. This would ensure that new highly processed sensory information is organized within the hippocampus and enhances the possibility of remembering and temporarily storing one place as separate from another place. It is assumed that this is accomplished via pattern separation of event information, so that spatial events can be separated from each other and spatial interference is reduced. This process is akin to the idea that the hippocampus is involved in orthogonalization of sensory input information (Rolls, 1989), in representational differentiation (Myers, Gluck, & Granger, 1995), and indirectly in the utilization of relationships (Cohen & Eichenbaum, 1993).

To assess this function rats were trained in a *spatial* order task. In this task rats were required to remember a spatial location dependent on the distance between the study phase object and an object used as a foil. More specifically, during the study phase an object covering a baited food well was randomly positioned in one of fifteen possible locations on a cheese board. Rats exited a start box and displaced the object to receive a food reward and were then returned to the start box. In the ensuing test phase rats were allowed to choose between two objects that were identical to the study phase object. One object was baited and positioned in the previous study phase location (correct choice) and the other (foil) was unbaited and placed in a different location (incorrect choice). Five distances (minimum 15 cm, maximum 105 cm) were randomly used to separate the foil from the correct object. Following the establishment of a criterion of 75% correct averaged across all separation distances, rats were given either large (dorsal and ventral) hippocampal or cortical control lesions dorsal to the dorsal hippocampus. Following recovery from

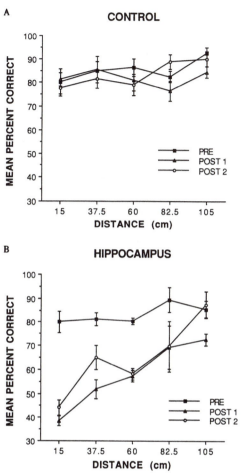

FIGURE 1   Mean percentage correct performance of the cortical control lesioned group (A) and the hippocampal lesioned group (B) on preoperative (PRE) and two blocks of postoperative (POST 1 and POST 2) trials.

surgery, the rats were retested. The results are shown in Fig. 1 and indicate that whereas control rats matched their presurgery performance for all spatial distances, hippocampal lesioned rats displayed impairments for short (15–37.5 cm) and medium (60 cm) spatial separations but performed as well as controls when the spatial separation was long (82.5–105 cm). The fact that the hippocampal lesioned group was able to perform the task well at large separations indicates that the deficits observed at the shorter separations were not the result of an inability to remember the rule. The results suggest that the hippocampus may serve to separate incoming spatial information into patterns or categories by temporarily storing one place as separate from another place. It can be shown that the ability to remember the long distances was not based on an egocentric response strategy, because if the study phase was presented on one side of the cheese board and the test originated on the opposite side, the hippocampal lesioned rats still performed the long distances without difficulty. Furthermore, the hippocampal lesioned group had no difficulty discriminating between two short distances. It is clear that in this task it is necessary to separate one spatial location from another spatial location. Hippocampal lesioned rats cannot separate these spatial locations very well, so they can perform the task only when the spatial locations are far apart (DeCoteau, Kesner, & Gilbert, 1995). Similar deficits have been observed for new geographical information in patients with hippocampal damage due to a hypoxic episode (Hopkins & Kesner, 1993).

Does spatial pattern separation based on spatial interference play a role in the acquisition (consolidation) of a variety of hippocampal-dependent tasks? A few examples will suffice. Because rats are started in different locations in the standard water maze task, there is a great potential for interference among similar and overlapping spatial patterns. Thus, the observation that hippocampal lesioned rats are impaired in learning and subsequent consolidation of important spatial information in this task could be due to difficulty in separating spatial patterns, resulting in enhanced spatial interference. Support for this idea comes from the observation of Eichenbaum, Stewart, and Morris (1990), who demonstrated that when fimbria-fornix lesioned rats are trained on the water maze task from only a single starting position (less spatial interference) there are hardly any learning deficits, whereas training from many different starting points resulted in learning difficulties. In a somewhat similar study it was shown that total hippocampal lesioned rats learned or consolidated rather readily that only one spatial location was correct on an eight-arm maze (Hunt, Kesner, & Evans, 1994). In a different study, McDonald and White (1995) used a place preference procedure in an eight-arm maze. In this procedure food is placed at the end of one arm and no food is placed at the end of another arm. In a subsequent preference test normal rats prefer the arm that contains the food. In this study fornix lesioned rats acquired the place preference task as quickly as controls if the arm locations were opposite each other but were markedly impaired if the locations were adjacent to each other. Clearly, it is likely that there would be greater spatial interference when the spatial locations are adjacent to each other rather than far apart. Thus, spatial pattern separation can play a role in the acquisition of new spatial information.

If short-term memory and consolidation processes associated with mnemonic processing of spatial information are both subserved by the hippocampus, is it possible to dissociate the two? The answer to the question is positive. It has been shown that phencyclidine (an NMDA antagonist) injections into the dentate gyrus of the hippocampus at dose levels to block electrical stimulation of the medial entorhinal cortex-induced LTP disrupts consolidation of new learning in a dry-land version of the water maze, but the same dose of phencyclidine has only a mild effect on a short-term memory task for spatial location information in an eight-arm maze (Kesner & Dakis, 1995). In contrast, naloxone (an opiate antagonist) injections into the dentate gyrus of the hippocampus at dose levels to block electrical stimulation of the lateral entorhinal cortex-induced LTP disrupts completely performance within the short-term memory task but has no effect on consolidation of new learning in the dry-land version of the water maze spatial navigation task (Dakis, Martinez, Kesner, & Jackson-Smith, 1992). These results suggest that short-term memory and consolidation processes can operate independently of each other and that perhaps each process is mediated by a different form of LTP.

4. Retrieval

Even though it has been proposed that the hippocampus also plays an important role in retrieval of new information (Hirsh, 1980), there is only a limited data base for an important retrieval function for the hippocampus. Eichenbaum and colleagues have devised a series of transitivity tasks demonstrating that rats with hippocampal lesions are impaired in retrieving novel information, suggesting an inflexibility in solving new problems (Eichenbaum, 1994, 1996). However, other studies that have tested hippocampal lesioned rats have shown normal transfer to novel tasks, suggesting flexible use of information to solve new problems (Cho & Kesner, 1995; DeCoteau & Kesner, 1996; Jackson-Smith & Kesner, 1989; Walker & Olton, 1984). In humans, it has been difficult to demonstrate PET activation of the hippocampus during retrieval of information (Tulving et al., 1994), but in a recent study Schacter et al. (1996) have shown that the hippocampus becomes active only when difficult material requiring a great deal of effort needs to be remembered within the data-based memory system. In contrast, the right and left prefrontal cortices become active in many studies that measure retrieval for all different forms of memory (Nyberg, Cabeza, & Tulving, 1996). Thus, there is some, albeit limited, support for a hippocampus-mediated retrieval function.

B. Temporal Attribute

1. Short-Term or Working Memory

With respect to temporal attribute information, it can be shown, using the aforementioned paradigms to measure short-term memory, that there are severe impairments for duration information for rats and humans with bilateral hippocampal damage (Hopkins & Kesner, 1994; Jackson-Smith, Kesner, & Amann, 1994; Meck, Church, & Olton, 1984), suggesting that the hippocampus plays an important role in short-term memory representation of duration of exposure of a stimulus as an important feature of temporal attribute information.

2. Consolidation

It has been suggesetd that trace conditioning requires memory for the duration of the conditioned stimulus. Thus, it is of importance to note that rabbits with hippocampal lesions and humans with hypoxia resulting in bilateral hippocampal damage are impaired in acquisition (consolidation) of trace but not delayed eye-blink conditioning (Disterhoft, Carrillo, Hopkins, Gabrieli, & Kesner, 1996; Moyer, Deyo, & Disterhoft, 1990).

3. Pattern Separation

Based on ample evidence that almost all sensory information is processed by hippocampal neurons perhaps to provide for sensory markers for time as well as space and that the hippocampus mediates temporal information, it is likely that one of the main process functions of the hippocampus is to encode the temporal order of events. This would ensure that new highly processed sensory information is organized within the hippocampus and enhances the possibility of remembering and temporarily storing one event as separate from another event in time.

In the *temporal* order task, rats are required to remember an event (e.g., spatial location or visual object) dependent on the temporal order of occurrence of events. More specifically, on an eight-arm maze during the study phase of each trial, rats were allowed to visit each of the eight arms once in an order randomly selected for that trial. The test phase required the rats to choose which of two arms occurred earlier in the sequence of arms visited during the study phase. The arms selected as test arms varied according to temporal lag or distance (0–6) or the number of arms that occurred between the two test arms in the study phase. After the rats reached a criterion of 75% or better performance on all distances but zero, the rats received large (dorsal and ventral) hippocampal lesions, small (dorsal) hippocampal lesions, cortical control lesions dorsal to the dorsal hippocampus, or medial prefrontal cortex (anterior cingulate and medial precentral cortex) lesions. Following recovery from surgery, the rats were retested. The results are shown in Fig. 2 and indicate that for both pre- and postsurgery tests, the control rats performed poorly at a temporal distance of zero, but their performance was excellent for the remaining temporal distances. In contrast, on postsurgery tests dorsal hippocampal lesions disrupted performance for temporal distances of 0 and 2 but did not affect performance for the longest temporal distances of 4 and 6. Furthermore, on postsurgery tests large (dorsal plus ventral) hippocampal or medial prefrontal cortex lesions produced a marked deficit for all temporal distances, with a slight improvement for the longest temporal distance. In this task it is necessary to separate one event from another. Hippocampal lesioned rats cannot separate events across time, because of an inability to inhibit interference that is likely to accompany sequential events that are similar to each other. The resultant increase in temporal interference impairs the rat's ability to remember the order of specific events. It appears that the larger the

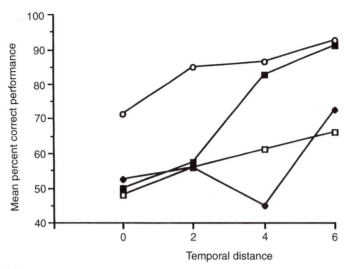

FIGURE 2   Mean percentage of correct postsurgery performance as a function of temporal distance for control (O), dorsal hippocampus (■), total (dorsal and ventral) hippocampus (□), and medial prefrontal cortex (●) lesioned rats within a short-term memory for temporal order of a spatial location task.

damage to the hippocampus, the greater the temporal interference. It is possible to reduce the presence of temporal interference by presenting the rats with a constant sequence of eight spatial locations followed by temporal distance tests and at the same time reduce the importance of the involvement of the data-based memory system while accentuating the importance of the knowledge-based memory system. The results indicate that large or small hippocampal lesions following training did not result in any significant deficits (Chiba, Johnson, & Kesner, 1992; Chiba, Kesner, & Reynolds, 1994). However, lesions of the medial prefrontal cortex produced a significant deficit.

The events do not have to be based on only spatial location information. Similar temporal distance deficits have been observed with lists of visual objects in rats and lists of spatial locations and words in patients with hippocampal damage due to a hypoxic episode or temporal lobe resection as well as early and middle DAT patients (Chiba, Kesner, Matsuo, Heilbrun, & Plumb, submitted; Johnson & Kesner, 1997; Kesner & Ragozzino, 1997). These data support the idea that the hippocampus might function to separate events from each other in time by reducing temporal interference between events.

Similar temporal interference effects can be observed during the learning of new information. In one study it was shown that hippocampal lesioned rats do not have a problem in learning (consolidating) a simple object-pair discrimination but have difficulty in learning eight-pair concurrent object discriminations (Shapiro & Olton, 1994). In contrast to the one-pair discrimination, there is a heightened temporal interference in learning eight pairs simultaneously. This increased temporal interference could account for the observed impairment in hippocampal lesioned rats. In another study, hippocampal lesioned rats learned a set of odor–odor paired associates as readily as controls. However, on transfer tests for transitivity and for symmetry they were impaired relative to controls (Bunsey & Eichenbaum, 1996). These transfer deficits could be due to the inability to separate the paired associates across time, resulting in temporal interference and, thus, poor transfer performance on tests for transitivity and tests for symmetry.

In summary, the hippocampus appears to be important in processing spatial and temporal information in terms of short-term memory representations and in terms of promoting consolidation of new information. This is accomplished in part by pattern separation, resulting in reduced interference for spatial and temporal information and thus accentuating the temporal and spatial resolution of events. It appears that the hippocampus plays a more limited role in retrieval of information.

With the use of short-term memory paradigms to measure short-term memory, it has been shown that for rats and humans with hippocampal damage there are, in contrast to deficits for spatial and temporal information, no impairments for remembering response attribute, affect attribute, and sensory-perceptual attribute information. This is based on the following observations: (a) rats with hippocampal lesions are not impaired in short-term or working memory for a right- or left-turn response (response attribute), visual object (sensory-perceptual attribute), or magnitude of reinforcement (affect attribute) information, but they are impaired for short-term or working memory for spatial location information (Kesner et al., 1993; Kesner & Williams, 1995); (b) rats with hippocampal lesions display impaired performance in a spatial continuous recognition memory task (sensory-perceptual attribute) (Jackson-Smith et al., 1993); (c) patients who have undergone resection of the right temporal lobe, which includes the hippocampus, are impaired in remembering that the location of an object was changed within a scene (spatial attribute) but have no difficulty in remembering that an object was changed for a specific location within a scene (sensory-perceptual attribute) and are impaired in short-term memory for the spatial location of an array of objects but do not have difficulty in free recall of the same objects (sensory-perceptual attribute) (Pigott & Milner, 1993; Smith & Milner, 1981); (d) patients with right or left temporal lobe resection are not impaired in short-term or working memory for the distance of a motor movement response (response attribute), in implicit sensory-perceptual priming of various stimuli, or in displaying a liking response based on the mere exposure effect (affect attribute) (Chiba, Kesner, Matsuo, & Heilbrun, 1993; Leonard & Milner, 1991; Shimamura, 1986); and finally (e) hypoxic subjects with hippocampal damage are only mildly impaired in short-term memory for a list of motor movements (response attribute) but are markedly impaired in short-term memory for a list of spatial locations (spatial attribute) or for the duration of exposure of a stimulus (temporal attribute) (Hopkins & Kesner, 1994; Hopkins et al., 1995a).

Rats and humans with hippocampal lesions are also not impaired in the acquisition (consolidation) of stimulus–response associations, motor skills (mirror reading or pursuit rotor), probability classification, and conditioned autonomic responses to visual or auditory stimuli (Bechara et al., 1995; Knowlton, Squire, & Gluck, 1994; McDonald & White, 1993; Squire, 1992).

In summary, these data suggest that the hippocampus mediates short-term memory for spatial and temporal attributes but not sensory-perceptual (object), response, or affect attribute information. Furthermore, the hippocampus does not mediate the acquisition of sensory-perceptual, response, or affect attributes. Instead, other neural regions are involved in mediating short-term memory and consolidation of sensory-perceptual, response, and affect attributes.

C. Language Attribute

With respect to language attribute information, it can be shown, using the aforementioned paradigms to measure short-term memory, that there are severe impairments for lists of words for humans with left hippocampal or bilateral hippocampal damage (Kesner, Hopkins, & Chiba, 1992), suggesting that the hippocampus plays an important role in short-term memory representation of word information as an important feature of language attribute information. There is a lot of evidence supporting the idea of important lateralization for hippocampal function in humans, with the right hippocampus representing spatial information and the left hippocampus representing linguistic information (Milner, 1971; Smith & Milner, 1981). For example, Milner (1971) tested patients who had left or right temporal lobectomies on a task of recall for a visual location. In this task subjects made a mark on an 8-in. line to reproduce as closely as possible the exact position of the previously shown circle. Subjects with right temporal lobe lesions were impaired on this task, whereas subjects with left temporal lobe lesions were not significantly different from control subjects. Smith and Milner (1981) tested patients with right and left temporal lobectomies and control subjects on a memory task involving incidental recall of the locations of the objects. Subjects were asked to estimate the prices of several objects placed in a spatial array on a test board. After a short or 24-hr delay, subjects were asked to place the objects in their appropriate locations. Left temporal lobe and control subjects performed well on this task at both the immediate and delayed recall of the object locations. Right temporal lobe subjects were impaired for both the immediate and delayed recall of the object locations. Additional support for the idea that the right hippocampus mediates memory for temporal order for novel spatial information and the left hippocampus mediates temporal order for novel linguistic information comes from a study by Chiba et al. (submitted). They demonstrated that subjects with right temporal lobe lesions were impaired relative to controls for temporal order for novel spatial location information but not for novel linguistic information. Subjects with left temporal lobe lesions were impaired relative to control subjects for novel linguistic information but not for novel spatial information. Even though hypoxic subjects or left temporal resected patients are impaired for new linguistic information, they are not impaired when they can use semantic or syntactic information to remember the order of presentation of systactically or syntactically and semantically meaningful sentences (Chiba et al., submitted; Hopkins, Kesner, & Goldstein, 1995b).

D. Response Attribute

1. Short-Term or Working Memory

With respect to response attribute information, it can be shown, using the aforementioned paradigms to measure short-term memory, that for rats with caudate-putamen lesions and humans with caudate-putamen damage due to Huntington's disease (HD) there are profound deficits for a right- or left-turn response or a list of hand motor movement responses (Cook & Kesner, 1988; Duncan-Davis, Filoteo, & Kesner, 1996; Kesner et al., 1993; Kesner & Filoteo, in press). For example, it has been shown that electrolytic-induced caudate lesions in rats impair short-term or working memory for a specific motor response (right–left turn) without any impairments in memory for a visual object or for a spatial location (Kesner et al., 1993). A similar lack of effects has been reported following medial caudate lesions in working memory performance for spatial locations on an eight-arm maze (Colombo, Davis, & Volpe, 1989; Cook & Kesner, 1988). A similar pattern of results has been reported following dysfunction of the caudate nucleus in patients with HD. For example, Duncan-Davis et al. (1996) administered tests of spatial and motor working memory to a small group of HD patients. During the study phase of the spatial memory task, subjects were shown a subset of six stimulus locations (X's) randomly selected from a set of sixteen and presented in a sequential manner. Immediately following the study phase, the test phase was presented. During the test phase, two stimulus locations (X's) were presented simultaneously. The subjects were asked to indicate which one they had seen during the study phase. During the study phase of the hand position memory task, subjects were shown sequential presentations of six hand positions randomly selected from a set of sixteen and were asked to imitate the hand position in the display. On the test phase, subjects were shown two pictures of different hand positions and were asked to determine which one they had seen in the study phase. The results of this study indicate that, relative to normal controls, the HD patients are differentially impaired in the motor memory task as compared to the spatial memory task. Interestingly, Pasquier, Van Der Linden, Lefebvre, Bruyer, and Petit (1994) demonstrated that HD patients were impaired on a task requiring them to recall the spatial displacement of a handle on the apparatus. The results of the foregoing studies suggest that patients with HD and rats with caudate lesions are impaired on working-memory tasks, particularly when the task places a heavy demand on motor information.

Furthermore, rats, monkeys, and humans with caudate lesions have deficits in tasks like delayed response, delayed alternation, and delayed matching to position (Divac, Rosvold, & Szwarcbart, 1967; Dunnett, 1990; Oberg & Divac, 1979; Partiot et al., 1996; Sanberg, Lehmann, & Fibiger, 1978). One salient feature of delayed response, delayed alternation, and delayed matching to position tasks is the maintenance of spatial orientation to the baited food well relative to the position of the subject's body, often based on proprioceptive and vestibular feedback. These data suggest that the caudate-putamen plays an important role in short-term memory representation for the feedback from a motor response feature of response attribute information. The memory impairments following caudate-putamen lesions are specific to the response attribute, because these same lesions in rats do not impair short-term memory performance for spatial location, visual object, or affect attribute information (Kesner et al., 1993; Kesner & Williams, 1995).

2. Consolidation

Based on research with animals, it has been assumed that the basal ganglia, including the caudate nucleus, mediate the consolidation and learning of stimulus–response associations or habits (Mishkin & Petri, 1984; Phillips & Carr, 1987). Support for this idea comes from the findings that visual pattern discrimination and concurrent visual object discriminations are disrupted in monkeys with lesions of either the putamen or tail of the caudate, but lesions of the hippocampus do not result in any deficits in these tasks (Mishkin, 1982; Wang, Aigner, & Mishkin, 1990). It should be noted, however, that monkeys with lesions in the tail of the caudate do not have difficulty in remembering previously learned concurrent visual object discriminations, but they are impaired only in learning a new set of concurrent visual objects.

It has been suggested in rats that the caudate is involved in sensory-motor integration including learning and consolidation of stimulus–response associations usually defined by tasks in which a particular motor response is reinforced in the presence of a single cue or tasks that require a consistent choice of direction or consistent choice to initiate or withhold responding (McDonald & White, 1993; Phillips & Carr, 1987). Support for this idea comes from a large number of studies indicating that damage to the dorsal caudate impairs brightness discrimination (Schwartzbaum & Donovick, 1968), tactile discrimination (Colombo et al., 1989), conditional visual discrimination (Reading, Dunnett, & Robbins, 1991), right–left maze discrimination (Cook & Kesner, 1988), runway learning (Kirkby, Polgar, & Coyle, 1981), eight-arm maze learning (reference memory or nonvarying component of the task) (Colombo et al., 1989; Packard & White, 1990), and cued radial arm maze and cued Morris water maze learning (Packard & White, 1990; Whishaw, Mittleman, Bunch, & Dunnett, 1987). In the last task, only an approach response to the correct visual cue location is required. Furthermore, lesions of the caudate have resulted in inappropriate selection of fixed-interval schedules (Hansing, Schwartzbaum, & Thompson, 1967). It should be noted that rats with hippocampal lesions are not impaired in the aforementioned tasks (McDonald & White, 1993). In rabbits lesions of the caudate impair classical conditioning of an eye-blink response, but not heart rate conditioning (Powell, Mankowski, & Buchanan, 1978), suggesting that the caudate is involved only in stimulus–somatic motor response associations. There is some evidence for regional specificity, since in a conditional visual discrimination (fast versus slow frequency of light flashes) task using a choice bar press response, only ibotenic acid lesions of the lateral, but not the medial, caudate resulted in an impairment in the acquisition of the task, suggesting that the lateral caudate is necessary for the acquisition of response rules to perform accurately on a conditional visual discrimination task (Reading et al., 1991). A similar impairment in learning a stimulus–response association (enter an arm on an eight-arm maze if cued by a light) following lateral caudate lesions was reported by McDonald and White (1993). Similar results have been shown to characterize HD patients with caudate lesions in that they are impaired in acquisition and learning of a variety of motor tasks (Heindel, Salmon, Shults, Walicke, & Butters, 1989; Martone, Butters, Payne, Becker, & Sax, 1984).

The major problem for interpretation of the exact involvement of the caudate in stimulus–response association learning derives from the difficulty in determining whether the impairment is due to a failure in detecting the sensory stimulus, a deficiency in learning stimulus–reward associations, or a defect in shifting an attentional set. With respect to visual information, it can be shown that caudate lesioned rats are not impaired in recognizing visual stimuli, in learning stimulus–reward associations, or in shifting attention (Kesner et al., 1993; McDonald & White, 1993; Ward & Brown, 1996). Furthermore, it is possible to demonstrate that increased firing of single cells recorded within the caudate nucleus in a learned right or left head movement to an auditory cue task is context dependent; that is, caudate cells respond when the auditory cue elicits a head movement in the task but do not respond when the auditory cue does not elicit a head movement response (Gardiner & Kitai, 1992). In general, there is overwhelming support for a caudate, probably lateral, mediation of stimulus–response learning requiring the activation of the response attribute.

The memory impairments following caudate-putamen lesions are specific to the response attribute, because these same lesions in rats do not impair acquisition of spatial location, visual object, or affect attribute information (McDonald & White, 1993).

E. Affect Attribute

1. Short-Term or Working Memory

With respect to affect attribute information, it can be shown, using the aforementioned paradigms to measure short-term memory, that for rats with amygdala lesions and humans with amygdala damage there are major deficits for reward value associated with magnitude of reinforcement or for a liking response based on the mere exposure of a novel stimulus (Chiba et al., 1993; Kesner & Williams, 1995), suggesting that the amygdala plays an important role in short-term memory representation for reward value as a critical feature of the affect attribute. Since very few studies have measured the role of the amygdala in mediating short-term memory for affect, it was necessary to develop a new task (Kesner & Williams, 1995). In the study phase of the task, rats were given one of two cereals. One cereal contained 25% sugar, the other 50% sugar. One of the two cereals was always designated as the positive stimulus and the other as the negative stimulus. This study phase was followed by the test phase in which the rat was shown an object which covered a food well. If the rat was given the negative food stimulus during the study phase, no food was placed beneath the object. If the rat was given the positive food stimulus during the study phase, another food reward was placed beneath the object. Latency to approach the object was used as the dependent measure. Rats learn to approach the objects quickly when they expect a reward and they are slow to approach the object when they expect no reward. After they reached criterion of at least a 5-sec difference between the positive and negative trials, the rats were given amygdala or control lesions. The results are shown in Fig. 3 and indicate that in contrast to controls, the amygdala lesioned rats displayed a deficit in performance as indicated by smaller latency differences between positive and negative trials on postsurgery tests. This deficit persisted at both short and long delays. In additional experiments, it was shown that the amygdala lesioned rats, like controls, had similar taste preferences and transferred readily to different cereals containing 25 or 50% sugar. It should be noted that similar deficits can be obtained with electrolytic or quinolinic acid lesions of the agranular insular cortex, suggesting that this region also plays an important part in short-term memory representation of reward value information (DeCoteau, Kesner, & Williams, 1994; Ragozzino & Kesner, 1996). In addition, it should be noted that rats with hippocampal, pre- and infralimbic or anterior cingulate cortex lesions are not impaired on this task (DeCoteau et al., 1994; Kesner & Williams, 1995). A similar result was reported by Kesner, Walser, and Winzenried (1989), who showed that amygdala lesioned rats were impaired in short-term memory performance for 1 versus 7 pieces of food associated with different spatial locations on an eight-arm maze. Thus, the amygdala appears to mediate short-term affect-laden information based on the reward value (magnitude) of reinforcement.

To what extent can one generalize from amygdala function in rats to humans with respect to affect attribute information? Previous research has shown that bilateral damage to the amygdala in humans impairs recognition of affect embedded within facial expressions (Adolphs, Tranel, Damasio, & Damasio, 1994). To elaborate further on the role of the amygdala in humans, Chiba et al. (1993) developed a liking test based on the mere exposure effect described by Zajonc (1968). Based on this principle, a computerized liking task was designed to test the presence of the mere exposure effect. The liking task consisted of eight abstract pictures and eight

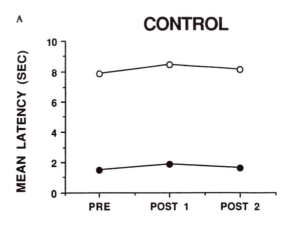

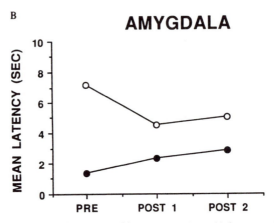

FIGURE 3   Mean positive and negative trial latency scores (seconds) for pre- and postsurgery performance in rats with cortical control lesions (A) and amygdala lesions (B).

unknown words that were sequentially presented on the computer screen. Following the individual presentation of each of these sixteen study stimuli, sixteen liking trials were presented. In each liking trial, two stimuli, one study stimulus, and a matched lure were simultaneously presented on the computer screen. Subjects were then asked which of the two stimuli they liked better. Four groups of subjects were tested on this task: college students as control subjects, subjects with partial complex epilepsy of temporal lobe origin, subjects who had undergone unilateral temporal lobe resections including the temporal cortex and the hippocampus, and subjects who had undergone unilateral temporal lobe resections including the temporal

A

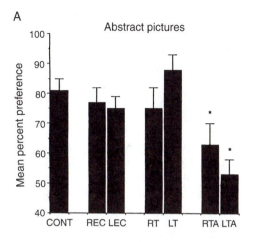

B

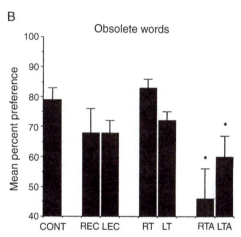

FIGURE 4   Mean percentage of preference for abstract pictures and obsolete words for CONT (control subjects), REC and LEC (seizure control subjects lateralized to the right or left side, respectively), RT and LT (temporal lobe resected patients with hippocampal damage to the right or left side, respectively), and RTA and LTA (temporal lobe resected patients with amygdala and hippocampal damage to the right or left side, respectively).

cortex, hippocampus, and amygdala. Results are shown in Fig. 4 for mean percentage of preference for abstract pictures and words and indicate that all subject groups showed a stable liking or mere exposure effect for both sets of stimuli, with the exception of those who sustained amygdala damage. It appears that the integrity of the amygdala is critical to the existence of the liking effect.

Thus, it is likely that the amygdala of animals and humans is involved in a short-term memory representation of the affective quality and quantity (reward value) of stimuli. This idea is an extension of earlier theoretical notions that the amygdala is involved in the interpretation and integration of reinforcement (Weiskrantz, 1956), serves as a reinforcement register (Douglas & Pribram, 1966), mediates stimulus-reinforcement associations (Jones & Mishkin, 1972), and serves to associate stimuli with reward value (Gaffan, 1992).

2. Consolidation

It has also been shown that amygdala lesions in the rat impair acquisition or consolidation of fear conditioning, place or cue preference, and taste aversion (McDonald & White, 1993; Nachman & Ashe, 1974; Phillips & LeDoux, 1992). Similarly, pre- or posttraining electrical stimulation or chemical stimulation produces profound memory deficits in a variety of tasks in which reinforcement contingencies of sufficiently high magnitude are used (Gold, Hankins, Edwards, Chester, & McGaugh, 1975; Hitchcock & Davis, 1986; Kesner, Berman, Burton, & Hankins, 1975; Kesner & Andrus, 1982; McDonough & Kesner, 1971; Phillips & LeDoux, 1992; Todd & Kesner, 1978), suggesting that the amygdala might also be involved in learning both positive and negative affect attribute information.

It has also been suggested that the amygdala modulates memory by promoting the consolidation of other memory attributes (McGaugh, Intrioni-Collison, Cahill, Kim, & Liang, 1992). This is likely to be accomplished by direct amygdala activation of neural circuits that mediate attention and arousal processes (Kapp, Whalen, Supple, & Pascoe, 1992). The best evidence in support of amygdala modulation of the consolidation of other forms of memory representations comes from a study by Packard, Cahill, and McGaugh (1994). They showed that posttraining intrahippocampal injections of d-amphetamine facilitated retention of a spatial task but had no facilitatory effect on a cued task. In contrast, posttraining intracaudate injections of d-amphetamine facilitated retention of the cued task but had no facilitatory effect on the spatial task. Posttraining intraamygdala injections of d-amphetamine enhanced retention of both tasks, even though amygdala lesions did not affect performance in the spatial and cued tasks. These results suggest that the amygdala might indeed modulate consolidation of attribute information that is dependent on mediation by other neural regions.

Does the amygdala represent all attribute information in memory or is it restricted to affect (reward value) attribute information? A case has been made elsewhere (Kesner, 1992) indicating that the amygdala does not contribute to short-term memory representation of spatial location, time (duration), response, or sensory-perceptual attribute information. A few explicit examples will suffice.

With respect to spatial location information, (a) Raffaele and Olton (1988) reported that rats with amygdala lesions were not impaired in performance of a delayed, left–right alternation task in a T-maze, (b) Kesner, Crutcher, and Omana (1990) reported that rats with amygdala lesions were not impaired in remembering a list of five spatial locations, and (c) Parkinson et al. (1988) showed that monkeys with amygdala lesions were not impaired in performance of a delayed nonmatching-to-sample task for object–place associations.

With respect to time (duration) information, Olton, Meck, and Church (1987) showed that rats with amygdala lesions are not impaired in remembering the duration of a stimulus across a short delay interval.

With respect to sensory-perceptual information, Sutherland and McDonald (1990) reported that rats with amygdala lesions are not impaired in memory for odor or visual information using a nonmatching-to-sample task.

With respect to the response attribute, amygdala lesions do not disrupt learning of a light–approach an arm (S–R) task in an eight-arm maze (McDonald & White, 1993).

Thus, the amygdala does not appear to mediate spatial location, temporal, response, and sensory-perceptual attribute information. The amygdala, however, does represent new affect attribute information.

3. Pattern Separation

Based on ample evidence that all sensory information, including internally generated visceral sensory and hormonal information, is processed by amygdala neurons perhaps to provide markers for experiencing reward value, it is likely that one of the main process functions of the amygdala is to encode the reward value of events. This would ensure that newly processed sensory information is organized within the amygdala and enhances the possibility of remembering and temporarily storing one event with its associated reward value as separate from another event with its associated reward value.

There is very little evidence thus far to provide for a clear evaluation of the role of the amygdala in utilizing a pattern selection process to separate values associated with magnitude of reward. It is clear that amygdala lesions disrupt short-term memory for magnitude of reward differences (Kesner & Williams, 1995), but no psychophysical experiments in which the dimension of reward is varied across a large number of values have yet been carried out.

4. Retrieval

In recent work it has been shown that excitotoxic lesions of the basolateral amygdala 6 or 30 days after training completely blocked the expression or retrievability of fear potentiated startle (Lee, Walker, & Davis, 1996). Similar lesions of the basolateral amygdala 1, 14, or 28 days after Pavlovian fear conditioning abolished conditional freezing to both the acoustical and contextual stimuli at all retention delays, suggesting this neural region plays an important role in retrieval of conditioned fear information (Maren, Aharonov, & Fanselow, 1996a).

In summary, the amygdala appears to be important in processing affect (reward value) information in terms of short-term memory representations and in terms of consolidation and retrieval of reward value information as well as modulation of consolidation of other attribute information. This is accomplished in part by pattern selection or filtering of interfering values of reward and thus acentuates the specificity of an appropriate association of reward with new events.

F. Sensory-Perceptual Attribute

1. Short-Term or Working Memory

With respect to sensory-perceptual attribute information, I will concentrate on visual object information as an exemplar of memory representation of the sensory-perceptual attribute. It can be shown, using aforementioned paradigms to measure short-term memory, that there are severe impairments for visual object information for rats and monkeys with extrastriate or perirhinal cortex lesions (Gaffan & Murray, 1992; Horel, Pytko-Joiner, Baytko & Salsbury, 1987; Kesner et al., 1993; Meunier, Hadfield, Bachevalier, & Murray, 1996; Mumby & Pinel, 1994; Ravindranathan, Jackson-Smith, & Kesner, 1992; Suzuki, Zola-Morgan, Squire, & Amaral, 1993), suggesting that the extrastriate and perirhinal cortex play an important role in short-term memory representation for visual object information as an exemplar of the sensory-perceptual attribute. Further support derives from single-unit studies in rats and monkeys which indicate that activity of neurons in the rhinal cortex reflect stimulus repetition, which is an integral part of the delayed nonmatching-to-sample tasks used to measure short-term recognition memory for objects (Brown, 1996; Zhu, Brown, & Aggleton, 1995). It should be noted that other neural regions may contribute to short-term memory for visual object information. For example, in rats lesions of the prelimbic and infralimbic subregions of the prefrontal cortex and in monkeys lesions of the ventromedial region of the prefrontal cortex impair short-term memory for visual object information using a delayed nonmatching-to-sample task, suggesting that these regions may be part of a neural circuit that mediates visual object information (Bachevalier & Mishkin, 1986; Kesner et al., 1995).

2. Consolidation

The perirhinal cortex also plays a role in the acquisition or consolidation of visual object information. It can be shown that monkeys with perirhinal cortex lesions are impaired in acquiring an object–object paired associate task (Murray, Gaffan, & Mishkin, 1993). Similarly, Higuchi and Miyashita (1996) have shown that lesions of the perirhinal cortex disrupt significant pair coding activity in area TE, an area presumed to act as a final repository for visual object long-term memory within the knowledge-based memory system. With respect to long-term consolidation, it has been shown that hippocampus plus entorhinal, parahippocampal gyrus, and perirhinal cortex lesions in monkeys can produce a 2- to 12-week retrograde amnesia gradient for visual object discrimination problems learned at different intervals prior to surgery (Zola-Morgan & Squire, 1990), suggesting that perhaps the perirhinal cortex could play a role in reorganizing information within long-term memory.

3. Pattern Separation

Eacott, Graffan, and Murray (1994) have shown that perirhinal cortex lesions in monkeys impaired performance in the delayed nonmatching-to-sample task only when many objects were used; no deficits were observed when only two objects were used. One possible explanation for this difference is that the two tasks differ in the demands they place on object classification—that is, they differ in the number of different patterns that need to be classified. Animals with perirhinal cortex lesions have difficulty in separating similar and potentially confusing patterns and thus perform poorly when many patterns are used. Further support for this idea comes from the finding that perirhinal lesions impair concurrent learning of 320 complex naturalistic scenes (Gaffan, 1994) but only mildly impair concurrent learning of 40 abstract patterns (Eacott et al., 1994).

The memory impairments following extrastriate lesions are specific to the visual object component of the sensory-perceptual attribute, because these same lesions in rats do not impair short-term memory performance of spatial location or response attribute information (Kesner et al., 1993).

In summary, the perirhinal cortex appears to be critical in mediating short-term or working memory and consolidation of visual object information as an exemplar of the sensory-perceptual attribute system. Somewhat different neural circuits are involved in representing other types of sensory-perceptual information. For example, lesions of the lateral entorhinal cortex, but not hippocampus, disrupt short-term memory for odor information as well as odor–odor paired associate learning (Bunsey & Eichenbaum, 1993; Otto & Eichenbaum, 1992a). Furthermore, single cells in the entorhinal cortex, but not hippocampus, are active during the delay of a short-term memory for odor task (Otto & Eichenbaum, 1992b; Young, Otto, Fox, & Eichenbaum, 1995). It appears that for odor information the lateral entorhinal cortex plays a parallel role to perirhinal cortex contribution to visual object information.

III. KNOWLEDGE-BASED MEMORY SYSTEM

The knowledge-based memory system is biased in providing more permanent representations of previously stored information in long-term memory and can be thought of as one's general knowledge of the world. It can operate in the abstract in the absence of incoming data. The emphasis is on top-down processing. The knowledge-based memory system would tend to be of greater importance after a task has been learned given that the situation is invariant and familiar. In most situations, however, one would expect a contribution of both systems with a varying proportion of involvement of one relative to the other.

The knowledge-based memory system is composed of the same set of different independently operating forms or attributes of memory. These attributes include *space, time, response, sensory-perception, and affect.* In humans a *language* attribute is also added. A spatial attribute within this framework involves long-term memory representations of places or relationships between places, which are usually independent of the subject's own body schema. It is exemplified by long-term storage of a spatial cognitive map based on higher order (global) organization of a number of individual spatial features.

A temporal attribute within this framework involves long-term memory representations of programs for the temporal order of temporally separated events or stimuli and, from a time perspective, memory representation of the future.

A response attribute within this framework involves long-term memory representations of motor programs based on feedback from motor responses (often based on kinesthetic and vestibular cues) that occur in specific situations as well as memory programs for representations of stimulus–response associations and selection of appropriate responses.

A sensory-perceptual attribute within this framework involves long-term memory representations of higher order organization of a set of sensory stimuli. Each sensory modality (touch, taste, smell, sight, and hearing) has its own long-term memory representations and can be considered to be part of the sensory-perceptual attribute component of memory.

An affect attribute within this framework involves long-term memory representations of reward value, positive or negative emotional experiences, and the associations between stimuli and rewards.

A language attribute within this framework involves memory representations of syntax, semantic, and lexicon information.

Although the organization of these attributes within the knowledge-based memory system can take many forms, they are assumed to be organized as a set of cognitive maps, or neural nets and their interactions, that are unique for each memory. It is assumed that long-term representations within cognitive maps are more abstract and less dependent on specific features. Some interactions between attributes are important and can aid in identifying specific neural regions that might subserve a critical interaction. For example, the interaction between sensory-perceptual attributes and the spatial attribute can provide for the long-term memory representation of a spatial cognitive map or spatial schemas, the interaction between temporal and spatial attributes can provide for the long-term memory representation of scripts, the interaction between temporal and affect attributes can provide for the long-term memory representation of moods, and the interaction between sensory-perceptual and response attributes can provide for the long-term memory of skills.

Within the knowledge-based memory system there are operational characteristics associated with each attribute, which include a number of processes: (a) selective attention and selective filtering associated with permanent memory representations of familiar information, (b) perceptual memory, (c) long-term memory storage, (d) selection of strategies and rules ("executive functions"), and (e) retrieval of familiar information based on flexibility and action.

Based on a series of experiments it can be shown that within the knowledge-based memory system, different neural structures and circuits mediate different forms or attributes of memory. The most extensive data set is based on the use of paradigms that measure repetition priming, the acquisition of new information, discrimination performance, executive functions, and strategies and rules to perform in a variety of tasks including skills and the operation of a variety of long-term memory programs.

A. Spatial Attribute

With respect to spatial attribute information, it is assumed that the parietal cortex plays an important role in perceptual and long-term memory processing of complex spatial information within the knowledge-based memory system. Support for this idea can be found in an analysis of human patients with parietal cortex damage. In addition to problems with attention, sensation, and motor control, there is often a deficit associated with spatial aspects of the patients' environment. These include an inability to draw maps or diagrams of familiar spatial locations, to use information to guide them in novel or familiar routes, to discriminate near from far objects, and to solve complex mazes. There is also spatial neglect and deficits in spatial attention (Heilman, Watson, & Valenstein, 1993; Rafal & Robertson, 1995). Furthermore, in patients with parietal lesions and spatial neglect there is a deficit in spatial repetition priming without a loss in short-term or working memory for spatial information (Ellis, Sala, & Logie, 1996). There is a general loss of "topographic sense," which may involve loss of long-term geographical knowledge as well as an inability to form cognitive maps of new environments. Using PET scan and functional MRI data, it can be shown that complex spatial information results in activation of the parietal cortex (Ungerleider, 1995). Thus, memory for complex spatial information appears to be impaired (Benton, 1969; De Renzi, 1982).

Additional support comes from studies with parietal lesioned monkeys. These animals demonstrate deficits in place reversal, landmark reversal, distance discrimination, bent wire route-finding, pattern string-finding, and maze-learning tasks (Milner, Ockleford, & DeWar, 1977; Petrides & Iversen, 1979; Pohl, 1973). Similarly, rats with parietal cortex lesions cannot perform in mazes (Thomas & Weir, 1975). Furthermore, rats with parietal cortex lesions display deficits in both the acquisition and retention of spatial navigation tasks that are presumed to measure the operation of a spatial cognitive map within a complex environment (DiMattia & Kesner, 1988b; Kesner, Farnsworth, & Kametani, 1992). They also display deficits in the acquisition and retention of spatial recognition memory for a list of five spatial locations (DiMattia & Kesner, 1988a). In a complex discrimination task in which a rat has to detect the change in location of an object in a scene, rats with parietal cortex lesions are profoundly impaired (DeCoteau & Kesner, 1996), yet on less complex tasks involving the discrimination or short-term memory for single spatial features including spatial location and allocentric and egocentric spatial distance (Long & Kesner, 1994, 1996), there are no impairments. Similarly, there are no impairments in discriminating between visual objects in terms of either new learning or performance of a previously learned visual discrimination (Long & Kesner, 1995; Long, Mellen, & Kesner, 1996). When the task is more complex, involving the association of objects and places (components of a spatial cognitive map), the parietal cortex plays an important role. Support for this comes from the finding that rats with parietal lesions are impaired in the acquisition and retention of a spatial location plus object discrimination (paired associate task) but show no deficits for only spatial or object discriminations (Long & Kesner, 1995; Long et al., 1996). Comparable deficits are found within an egocentric–allocentric distance paired associate task, but no deficit is found for an object–object paired associate task, suggesting that spatial features are essential in activating and involving the parietal cortex (unpublished observations). Finally, it should be noted that in rats neurons have been found within the parietal cortex that encode spatial location and head direction information and that many of these cells are sensitive to multiple cues including visual, proprioceptive, sensorimotor, and vestibular cue information (Chen, Lin, Barnes, & McNaughton, 1994; McNaughton, Chen, & Marcus, 1991).

In a somewhat different study, it was shown that, as for humans with parietal cortex lesions, rats with such lesions are impaired in an implicit spatial repetition priming experiment but perform without difficulty in a short-term or working memory spatial experiment (Chiba, Jackson-Smith, & Kesner, 1991), suggesting that the parietal cortex plays a role in spatial perceptual memory within the knowledge-based memory system but does not play a role in spatial memory within the data-based memory system.

Finally, there is some support to suggest that the parietal cortex may be a site for long-term representation of complex spatial information. Cho & Kesner (1996) have shown that rats with parietal cortex lesions have a nongraded retrograde amnesia for four, but not two, previously learned spatial discriminations prior to surgery, suggesting that the deficit cannot be due to a performance or anterograde amnesia problem but rather appears to be a function of the number or complexity of the spatial information to be stored and to be remembered.

The parietal cortex is probably not the only neural region that mediates long-term memory for spatial information. For example, topographical amnesia has also been reported for patients with parahippocampal lesions, and spatial navigation deficits have also been found following retrosplenial and entorhinal cortex lesions (Habib & Sirigu, 1987; Sutherland, Whishaw, & Kolb, 1988). Thus, other neural regions (e.g., the parahippocampal cortex, entorhinal cortex, and retrosplenial cortex) may also contribute to the long-term representation of a spatial cognitive map.

B. Temporal Attribute

With respect to temporal attribute information, it is assumed that the anterior cingulate in rats and dorsolateral frontal cortex in monkeys and humans play an important role in subserving the critical temporal features associated with the development of temporal programs and processing of temporal information within the knowledge-based memory system.

Support for this hypothesis can be found in the clinical literature dealing with human patients with frontal cortex lesions. In addition to problems with lack of initiative or spontaneity, poor movement programming, and reduced corollary discharge, there is often a deficit for information concerning temporal aspects of their environment. They cannot remember the order in which information was experienced, nor can they plan and create a complex set of activities. Frontal cortex damaged patients can remember that certain words or pictures have been presented but cannot discriminate the more from the less recent. Thus, memory for item information is intact, but memory for order information is impaired (Hopkins et al., 1995a; Milner, 1971).

In addition, frontal cortex damaged patients are impaired in a short-term memory task in which two stimuli had to be remembered for a 60-sec time interval (paired-comparison task) (Milner, 1964). This task requires short-term temporal memory for two events, implying that frontal cortex damaged patients cannot remember the order of stimulus presentation. In another experiment, frontal cortex damaged patients are impaired in their ability to self-order a sequence of stimuli presented one at a time (Petrides & Milner, 1982).

In monkeys, dorsolateral prefrontal cortex lesions result in deficits in the temporal ordering of events, a finding that is comparable to what has been described in humans. This temporal ordering deficit is evidenced by impairments in delayed response, delayed alternation, and delayed matching-to-sample tasks, as well as self-ordering of a sequence of responses (Petrides & Milner, 1982; Rosenkilde, 1979). In rats, lesions of the medial prefrontal cortex produce deficits in tasks in which rats emit a specific sequence of behavioral responses requiring temporal organization (Barker, 1967; Slotnick, 1967; Stamm, 1955).

To test further whether there is a correspondence in function of prefrontal cortex in rats and humans, rats were tested for item and order memory for a list of items (places on a maze) (Kesner & Holbrook, 1987). Rats were trained on an eight-arm radial maze. Each animal was allowed to visit four arms on each trial (one per day) in an order that was randomly selected for that trial (study phase). The sequencing of the four arms was accomplished by sequentially opening Plexiglas doors (one at a time) located at the entrance of each arm. Immediately after the animal had received reinforcement from the last of the four arms, the test phase began. During the test phase the animal was given two tests—one to test order memory and one to test item memory. The test for order memory consisted of opening either the first and second, second and third, or third and fourth doors that occurred in the sequence. The rule to be learned leading to an additional reinforcement was to choose the arm that occurred earlier in the sequence. The test for item memory consisted of opening a door that was previously visited for that trial and a door that was not. The rule to be learned resulting in an additional reinforcement was to choose the arm previously visited during the study phase of the trial (win–stay rule). The order of presentation of the two tests was varied randomly.

Following extensive training, animals performed better than chance for each item or order position on both tests. The animals then received medial prefrontal cortex aspiration lesions. The results indicate that medial prefrontal cortex lesioned animals had an order memory deficit for all spatial locations but had excellent item memory for the first spatial locations of the list. The possibility exists that poor performance for item information was due to the variable temporal–spatial sequences presented during the study phase. To test this possibility the lesioned animals were trained with a constant sequence (e.g., the same four arms were always selected) followed by tests of item and order memory. The results indicate that prefrontal cortex lesioned animals had excellent item memory for all spatial locations of the list but had no memory for the order of presentation of the spatial locations. In additional tests it was shown that this order deficit appeared even when the animals were allowed to self-order the spatial locations during the study phase or when the list length was only two spatial locations (Kesner & Holbrook, 1987).

The possibility exists, however, that order memory was impaired in the Kesner and Holbrook (1987) experiment, because only temporally adjacent items were selected. This is especially a problem because Estes (1986) has summarized data in humans demonstrating that order or sequential information is remembered better when more items (lag) occur between any two items to be tested. Thus, an experiment was designed to test order memory for items that were further apart temporally in the to-be-remembered sequence (Chiba et al., 1993). This experiment was described in the section on spatial attribute information within the data-based memory system. The results indicated that on postsurgery tests medial prefrontal cortex lesions produced a marked deficit for all temporal distances, with a slight improvement for the longest temporal distance. In this experiment, rats are required to remember an event (e.g., spatial location) dependent on the temporal order of occurrence of events. The data are thus consistent, indicating a marked deficit for temporal order information following medial prefrontal cortex lesions. In this task it is necessary to separate one event from another.

In the previous experiment the selected sequence to be remembered varied on each trial, emphasizing the importance of new information which is likely to be processed by the data-based memory system. An alternative procedure is based on the presentation of a single fixed or constant sequence to be remembered. After learning the temporal order of this sequence, there is high likelihood that the knowledge-based system rather than the data-based system would mediate memory for this constant order. Based on the hypothesis that the medial prefrontal cortex rather than the hippocampus mediates temporal order within the knowledge-based memory system, it should be possible to determine whether the medial prefrontal cortex plays a more important role than the hippocampus in the constant temporal distance task. To test this idea rats were presented with a constant sequence of eight spatial locations followed by temporal distance tests. The results indicate that relative to controls small and large hippocampal lesions do not result in any significant deficits, but medial prefrontal cortex lesions do produce a significant impairment (Chiba et al., 1992, 1994). Thus, these data support the importance of the medial prefrontal cortex for maintaining well-learned temporal sequences in long-term memory. It should be noted that the events do not have to be based on only spatial location information. Similar deficits have been observed with lists of visual objects in rats (unpublished observations).

Since temporal organization is required for frequency memory (repetition), it is not surprising that patients with prefrontal cortex damage are impaired in judgment for frequency of occurrence of specific items within a list (Milner, Petrides, & Smith, 1985). To elaborate further on possible correspondence in function of prefrontal cortex in rats and humans, a test was devised to study frequency memory in rats (Kesner, 1990b). After extensive training and based on at least eight observations per lag, animals showed excellent memory for the repetition with a lag of three arms between a repetition but performed poorly for a lag of one or two arms even when the data were analyzed for those trials on which the repetition with a lag occurred in the last serial position. This repetition lag effect (i.e., better retention with more items between a repetition) has also been reported for humans (Estes, 1986). The animals then received medial prefrontal cortex aspiration lesions. After recovery from surgery, animals were given an additional 24 tests with 8 tests for each lag condition. Animals with medial prefrontal cortex lesions displayed a deficit for all lag conditions. The results, thus, indicate that rats with medial prefrontal cortex lesions have, like humans with prefrontal cortex damage, a similar deficit in performance of frequency memory. Based upon the previously mentioned findings, it has been suggested that the prefrontal cortex is primarily involved in temporal structuring of information in short-term memory (Fuster, 1985).

Thus far, many studies have been presented in support of a critical role of the medial prefrontal cortex in the mediation of temporal information, but very few studies have explicitly tested whether the medial prefrontal cortex does indeed code information within the knowledge-based memory system. One recently published study was designed to test the contribution of the medial prefrontal cortex to the knowledge-based memory system.

Rats with medial prefrontal cortex lesions were tested in a task that provided them with an opportunity to utilize retrospective and prospective memory codes while rembering items (spatial locations) within short or long lists (Cook, Brown, & Riley, 1985; Kesner, 1989). More specifically, on any one trial a rat was presented with 2, 4, 6, 8, or 10 items (spatial locations) on a 12-arm radial maze followed 15 min later by two win–shift tests comprising a choice between a place previously visited and a novel place. Each animal was given a total of 20 trials with 8 tests of each list length (2, 4, 6, 8, or 10). The results indicate that sham-operated animals display an increase in errors as a function of set size for 2–8 items followed by a decrease in errors with a set size of 10 items, suggesting the use of both retrospective and prospective memory codes. In contrast, animals with medial prefrontal cortex lesions made few errors for short list lengths but a large number of errors for long list lengths, reflecting an inability to shift from a retrospective to prospective memory code.

These data suggest that the medial prefrontal cortex mediates prospective memories in a task that utilizes spatiotemporal information, providing additional support for an essential role for the medial prefrontal cortex in subserving important temporal attributes within the expectancy or knowledge-based memory system. Fuster (1985) also suggested that the dorsolateral prefrontal cortex of monkeys and humans mediates prospective functions of temporal ordering of information. Support for this possible prospective function comes from the findings that some cells in the dorsolateral frontal cortex of monkeys show a gradual increase in their firing rate during the delay in apparent anticipation of the test phase of a delayed matching to sample, delayed response, or delayed alternation task (Fuster, Bauer, & Jervey, 1982; Kojima, Matsumura, & Kubota, 1981; Niki, 1974a, 1974b). Furthermore, Shallice (1982) showed that left frontal lobe damaged patients have a difficult time solving the Tower of London problem. This task requires temporal ordering of simple moves and thus requires planning and the utilization of prospective codes. Finally, using SPECT during learning of the Tower of London task resulted in increased cerebral blood flow in the left prefrontal cortex (Morris, Ahmed, Syed, & Toone, 1993).

C. Language Attribute

With respect to language attribute information, it can be shown that humans with left parietal cortex damage have difficulty in word formation (Caramazza & Berndt, 1978), suggesting that the parietal cortex might mediate the lexicon feature of the language attribute. In other subjects, damage to Wernicke's area and Broca's area results in difficulties with semantic and syntactic processing of language information (Caramazza & Berndt, 1978), suggesting that these areas might mediate syntactic and semantic features of the language attribute.

D. Response Attribute

With respect to response attribute information, it can be shown that motor programs associated with stimulus–response associations are mediated by the premotor, supplementary, and motor cortex in conjunction with the cerebellum (Karni et al., 1995; Roland, 1985; Thompson, 1986). For example, cells in the premotor cortex of monkeys increase their responsiveness during the learning of a conditional visuomotor response task (Mitz, Godschalk, & Wise, 1991), and there is increased blood flow in these critical areas based on PET scans during the performance of conditional visuomotor tasks (Picard & Strick, 1996). Furthermore, the dorsolateral frontal cortex in humans and anterior cingulate and precentral motor cortex in rats mediate long-term memory programs associated with response feedback in the form of egocentric localization as indicated by lesion-induced deficits in tasks that measure egocentric localization (Kesner, Fransworth, & DiMattia, 1989; Passingham, 1978; Phol, 1973; Semmes, Weinstein, Ghent, & Teuber, 1963).

E. Affect Attribute

With respect to affect attribute information, it can be shown that lesions of the orbital frontal cortex in humans can result in euphoria, lack of responsibility, and lack of affect (Hecaen & Albert, 1978). In monkeys such lesions result in emotional changes such as decreased aggression and a reduced tendency to reject certain foods like meat (Butter, Snyder, & McDonald, 1970), and in rats there are also reductions in aggressive behavior (Kolb, 1974). Orbitofrontal cortex damaged animals have difficulty in changing their behavior when the value or rewards are not consistent with expectations based on prior experiences. Thus, monkeys with orbitofrontal cortex lesions display prolonged extinction of previously rewarded response (Butter, 1969), and they are impaired in visual and spatial discrimination reversal tasks (Butter, 1969; Iversen & Mishkin, 1970; Jones & Mishkin, 1972). Also, Thorpe, Rolls, and Maddison (1983) found cells in the orbitofrontal cortex that respond differentially to the expectation of a reward or a punishment. In rats orbitoprefrontal cortex lesions including the agranular insular cortex resulted in an impairment in the acquisition of a flavor preference task and a delayed nonmatching-to-sample task for odor information (Otto & Eichenbaum, 1992a; Ragozzino & Kesner, 1996). These data suggest that the orbital frontal cortex may subserve the affect attribute within the knowledge-based memory system.

F. Sensory-Perceptual Attribute

With respect to sensory-perceptual attribute information, I will concentrate on visual object information as an exemplar of memory representation of the sensory-perceptual attribute. It can be shown that lesions of the inferotemporal cortex in monkeys and humans and temporal cortex (TE2) in rats result in visual object discrimination problems (Dean, 1990; Fuster, 1995; Gross, 1973; McCarthy & Warrington, 1990; Weiskrantz & Saunders, 1984), suggesting that the inferotemporal or TE2 may play an important role in mediating long-term representations of visual object information. Additional support comes from PET scan and functional MRI data in humans, where it can be shown that visual object information results in activation of the inferotemporal cortex (Ungerleider, 1995). In a somewhat different study, Sakai and Miyashita (1991) have shown that neurons within the inferotemporal cortex responded more readily after training to a complex visual stimulus that had been paired with another complex visual stimulus across a delay, suggesting the formation of long-term representations of object–object pairs within the inferotemporal cortex.

IV. INDEPENDENCE OF THE DATA-BASED AND KNOWLEDGE-BASED MEMORY SYSTEMS

Even though the two systems are supported by neural substrates and different operating characteristics, suggesting that the two systems can operate independently of each other, there are also important interactions between the two systems, especially during the consolidation of new information and retrieval of previously stored information. It is, thus, likely to be very difficult to separate the contribution of each system in new learning tasks, since each system supports one component of the consolidation process. There are, however, a few examples especially based on tasks where the major consolidation processes have already taken place. Olton and Pappas (1979) ran animals in a seventeen-arm maze with food available in eight arms and no food available in nine arms. To solve this maze an animal should not enter unbaited arms activating knowledge-based memory, but they should enter baited arms only once utilizing data-based memory. After learning the task to criterion performance, animals were given fimbria-fornix lesions. The lesioned animals had a deficit for the data-based memory component, but not for the knowledge-based memory component, of the task. In a different study, Kesner, DiMattia, & Crutcher (1987) have shown that in an eight-arm maze parietal cortex lesions placed in rats after training on four unbaited and four baited arms resulted in a deficit in the knowledge-based, but not data-based, memory. If one assumes that the presentation of unbaited arms reflects the operation of the knowledge-based memory system and that the presentation of baited arms reflects the operation of the data-based memory system, then it appears that lesions of the hippocampus disrupt only the data-based memory system, whereas lesions of the parietal cortex only disrupt the knowledge-based memory system. These data suggest that the parietal cortex might subserve knowledge-based memory and the hippocampus might subserve data-based memory, at least for spatial information, and that the two systems can operate independently of each other.

In a different series of studies a double dissociation between implicit memory (a measure reflective of the operation of the knowledge-based memory system) and explicit memory (a measure reflective of the operation of the data-based memory system) has been reported in human subjects (Gabrieli, Fleischman, Keane, Reminger, & Morrell, 1995; Keane, Gabrieli, Mapstone, Johnson, & Corkin,

1995). They showed that patients with a right occipital and posterior parietal cortical lesion displayed impaired performance for implicit tests of visual priming for words but intact performance on explicit tests of recognition and cued recall of words. In contrast, the reverse pattern was present for amnesic subjects with hippocampal damage. Furthermore, for patients with parietal lesions resulting in spatial neglect there is a deficit in spatial repetition priming without a loss in short-term or working memory for spatial information (Ellis, et al., 1996). Thus, it appears that the knowledge-based memory system based on implicit memory representations and the data-based memory system based on explicit memory representations can operate independently of each other and can be processed by distinct neural regions. To test whether a similar double dissociation can be observed in rats, two spatial continuous recognition training procedures designed to query either implicit or explicit memory in rats were designed. A continuous recognition procedure was used to train rats on a twelve-arm radial maze. Each rat was allowed to visit a sequence of twelve arms per day in an order predetermined for that trial. Of the twelve arms visited, either three or four of the arms were repeated within the running sequence. The arms selected for repetition varied according to lag (0–6), or the number of arms which occurred between the first visit to an arm and its repetition. To gain access to each arm, the animal was required to orient to a cue on the Plexiglas door at the entrance of the arm. Once the animal oriented to the cue, the door was lowered and the latency for the animal to reach the end of the arm was measured. Two groups of rats were trained, one on an implicit training procedure and one on an explicit training procedure. The implicit group received reinforcement at the end of each arm regardless of whether the arm was a novel arm or a repeated arm. This group showed decreased latencies when visiting repeated arms (see Fig. 5). The explicit group received reinforcement only when visiting an arm for the first time in a given sequence. This group showed increased latencies for repeated arms (see Fig. 5). After training, rats received total hippocampus, parietal cortex, or sham-operated and cortical control lesions. The results are shown in Fig. 5 and indicate that following total hippocampal ablation, the performance of the rats in the implicit condition was not significantly different from preoperative performance, whereas rats in the explicit condition showed a deficit, that is, a significant decrease in latency to return to an arm. Following parietal lesions, rats in the implicit condition showed a deficit, that is, an increase in latency to return to an arm, whereas the performance of rats in the explicit condition was not significantly different from preoperative performance. The performance of sham-operated control rats and cortical control rats did not differ significantly from preoperative performance in either reinforcement condition (Chiba et al., 1991). Thus, a double dissociation appears to exist between parietal cortex and hippocampus for memory operations associated with the knowledge-based memory system versus memory operations associated with the data-based memory system for spatial location information.

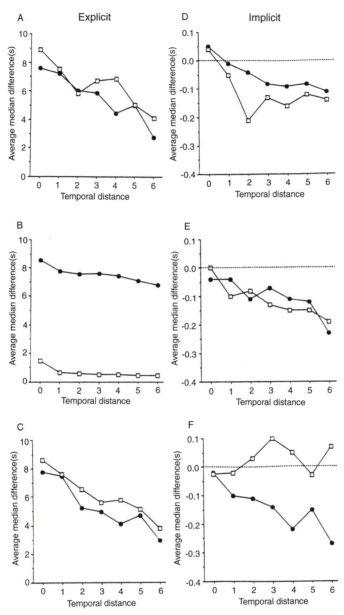

FIGURE 5 Average median difference in latency to traverse an arm of the first versus a repeated presentation of the same arm as a function of temporal lag (number of different arms presented between the first and second presentations) pre- and postsurgery for the cortical control lesioned group (A), hippocampal lesioned group (B), and parietal cortex lesioned group (C) in the explicit condition and for the cortical control lesioned group (D), hippocampal lesioned group (E), and parietal cortex lesioned group (F) in the implicit condition.

V. OTHER NEUROBIOLOGICAL MEMORY SYSTEM MODELS

A. Locale–Taxon Memory Model

O'Keefe and Nadel (1978) and Nadel (1994) concentrate on space as the critical attribute of specific memories. They further divide the spatial attribute to a locale system, which codes places in the environment into cognitive maps, and a taxon system, which codes motor responses in terms of specific orientations within a spatial environment. They suggest that the hippocampus mediates the locale system and stores a cognitive map. The cognitive map can be used for place recognition, navigation, and coding of context. They do not specify which neural regions code the taxon system. With respect to the operation of each system, it is assumed that learning based in part on consolidation processes is all-or-none in the locale system and incremental in the taxon system. Furthermore, representations within the locale system are more sensitive to interference in comparison with the taxon system. It is assumed that the hippocampus functions as a system that separates memory traces, whereas the taxon system combines memory traces based on overlapping features. With respect to retrievability of information, the locale system is assumed to be more flexible and responsive to novel information in comparison with the taxon system.

The best evidence for hippocampus mediation of space comes from the identification of specific place cells in the hippocampus (O'Keefe, 1979), the observation that hippocampal theta activity is related to movement in space (Vanderwolf, Bland, & Whitshaw, 1973), and the finding that animals with hippocampus lesions perform very poorly in tasks in which memory for spatial location is important (Olton, 1983). Furthermore, memory for response, sensory-perceptual, and affect information is not sensitive to hippocampal dysfunction (Aggleton et al., 1986; Kesner et al., 1993; Kesner & Williams, 1995; Mumby et al., 1992; Otto & Eichenbaum, 1992a).

An experiment that strongly supports hippocampus mediation of a cognitive map was carried out by Morris (1983). Rats were trained in a large circular tub filled with water, made opaque by the addition of milk. Their task was to find a platform that was hidden just below the surface of the cloudy water. Even though the starting place was varied from trial to trial, animals could learn this task rather quickly and thus appear to use the locale system. Animals with large lesions of the hippocampus were impaired in learning the task, as indicated by long latencies to find the hidden platform. However, when the platform was visible, hippocampus lesioned animals could learn the task very quickly. This latter version of the task requires cue rather than place navigation. More recent observations using the Morris task have not supported O'Keefe and Nadel's prediction. First, when one trains animals prior to removal of the hippocampus, only small deficits are found on further retests. Second, rats with removal of the parietal cortex perform even more poorly in the Morris task than hippocampus lesioned animals. Finally, there is a large deficit even when parietal lesioned animals are trained prior to the lesion (DiMattia & Kesner, 1988b; Kesner, Farnsworth, & Kametani, 1992). These latter observations suggest that the parietal cortex might also be of importance in mediating the locale system.

There are other experiments that are not totally consistent with the exclusive involvement of the hippocampus in storing a spatial map. Walker and Olton (1984) trained animals to enter a specific goal box from each of three different starting positions. After fimbria-fornix lesions the animals were given transfer tests on a new starting position and asked to go to the same goal box. Successful selection of the goal box on the transfer tests requires the utilization of a cognitive map. The task is conceptually similar to the Morris task. Controls as well as animals with fimbria-fornix lesions performed the transfer tests without any difficulty. Thus, the hippocampus does not appear to be the permanent site of a spatial cognitive map, which is not to say that a temporary spatial cognitive map representation may not exist within the hippocampus. The Walker and Olton experiment also suggests that the hippocampus does not necessarily mediate flexibility in a novel situation, since in the novel transfer task, the hippocampal lesioned rats transferred as readily as controls.

The hippocampus appears to play a role in mediating temporal information, including memory for temporal order and memory for duration of exposure of information as well as trace conditioning of the nictitating membrane response (Disterhoft et al., 1996; Hopkins & Kesner, 1994; Jackson-Smith et al., 1994; Solomon & Vander Schaaf, 1986) which cannot easily be accounted for within an exclusive hippocampus-mediated locale system based on only spatial information.

Even though the hippocampus is assumed to be the mediator to the locale system, the neural circuit subserving spatial information includes a number of neural regions including the entorhinal cortex, the retrosplenial cortex, the pre- and parapostsubiculum, the parietal cortex, and the pre- and infralimbic cortex. The focus on the hippocampus might be too limiting. The taxon system is large and needs to be differentiated. Furthermore, a genuine neurobiological system analysis requires the identification of neural regions that subserve the taxon system.

In summary, the neural system analysis of O'Keefe and Nadel (1978) and Nadel (1994) is somewhat limiting in that it only emphasizes the importance of the hippocampus in representing spatial information within the locale system, with many other neural regions subserving the taxon system. The locale system can be thought of as a component of the data-based memory system, but in the attribute model the hippocampus mediates not only spatial but also temporal and linguistic (humans) information, and the neural circuit that subserves spatial information includes neural regions other than the hippocampus. A number of proposed operating systems dealing with pattern selection, consolidation, and retrievability via flexible use of novel information are similar to what is proposed in the attribute model. The taxon system contains components of the data-based memory system, such as sensory-perceptual and response attributes, as well as all the attributes or forms of memory, including spatial, that compose the knowledge-based memory system.

B. Working–Reference Memory Model

Olton proposed a somewhat different system distinction, emphasizing more the importance of process. He suggested that within every learning task there are two types of memories that organize the critical information into two systems, labeled working and reference memory (Olton, 1983; Olton, Becker, & Handelmann, 1979). On the basis of a distinction made by Honig (1978), Olton suggested that the specific, personal, and temporal context of a situation is coded in working memory. This would translate into memory for events that occur on a specific trial in a task, biasing mnemonic coding toward the processing of incoming data. In contrast, general information concerning rules and procedures (general knowledge) of specific situations is coded in reference memory. This would translate into memory for events that happen on all trials in a task, biasing mnemonic coding toward the processing of expectancies based on the organization of the extant memory. One would expect that in any new task to be learned there would be a somewhat greater emphasis on working memory but that after learning, the emphasis would shift toward reference memory, unless the task requires the processing of new information on every trial. In this latter case both working and reference memory systems would be activated.

Olton further suggested that both working and reference memory can operate independently of each other. On the basis of a large number of experiments, Olton proposed that the hippocampus and its interconnections mediate working memory for all attributes, whereas some other system, such as the neocortex, mediates reference memory. For instance, consider one critical experiment in which food-deprived rats are placed in the center of an eight-arm maze. The ends of each arm contain food reinforcement. The animals are allowed to choose any arm freely. Normal rats learn very quickly to use an optimal strategy, which is to enter each arm once and to choose a previously visited arm. In addition to reference memory, which includes the knowledge that food can be obtained at the end of each arm and that the maze has eight arms, this task has an important working memory component, which includes the knowledge of which arms had been previously visited for that trial. Bilateral lesions placed in the medial septum, postcommissural fornix, fimbria-fornix, dorsal hippocampus, or entorhinal cortex resulted in impaired performance, with many repetitions of arms previously entered. Lesions of other neural regions, such as the caudate nucleus or amygdala complex, did not produce any deficit, suggesting some specificity of hippocampus function for working memory.

As was noted earlier, the radial arm maze also has a reference memory component, so the possibility exists that hippocampus lesions also disrupt reference memory. To test for this possibility, Olton and Pappas (1979) ran animals in a seventeen-arm maze with food available in eight arms and no food available in nine arms. To solve this maze an animal should not enter unbaited arms, activating reference memory, but they should enter baited arms only once, utilizing working memory. After learning the task to criterion performance, animals were given fimbria-fornix lesions. The lesioned animals had a deficit for the working, but not for the reference, component of the task. It should be noted, however, that during acquisition of an eight-arm maze fimbria-fornix lesioned animals often make many reference memory errors (entries into arms that do not contain food) in addition to working memory errors (entries into arms that have been visited before).

Given that working and reference memory can be dissociated, neural regions other than the hippocampus should mediate reference memory. One possible neural region might be the parietal cortex. Support for this possibility comes from a study by Kesner et al. (1987), who showed that in an eight-arm maze parietal cortex lesions placed in rats after training on four unbaited and four baited arms resulted in a deficit in reference, but not working, memory. This suggests that the parietal cortex might subserve reference memory, at least for spatial information. Together the parietal cortex and hippocampus lesion data support the possibility that, at least after training in a spatial task, reference and working memory might operate independently.

The Olton model has some limits in that the emphasis is placed only on the hippocampus and interconnected neural circuits as the neural system subserving working memory for all information. However, it is clear that the hippocampus is limited to working memory for only spatial, temporal, and linguistic information but not affect, response, and sensory-perceptual information (see previous sections). Furthermore, the hippocampus is also involved in processes other than short-term or working memory, such as pattern separation, consolidation, and retrieval of information (Kesner, 1996).

In summary, the neural system analysis of Olton is somewhat limiting in that it only emphasizes the importance of the hippocampus and interconnected neural regions in representing all information within the working system, with the cortex subserving the reference memory system. The working memory system can be thought of as a component of the data-based memory system, but in the Kesner attribute model the hippocampus mediates only spatial, temporal, and linguistic (humans) information and the hippocampus subserves pattern separation, consolidation, and retrieval processes in addition to working memory. The reference memory system is similar to the knowledge-based memory system proposed by Kesner, but differential contribution of different cortical regions and the inclusion of different operating characteristics were not included in the Olton model.

C. Declarative–Nondeclarative Memory Model

A different approach was taken by Squire and his colleagues, who suggested that there are two memory systems, which they named declarative and nondeclarative, with each characterized by a specific set of operations within or between tasks (Squire, 1983). The declarative memory system is based on explicit information that is easily accessible and is concerned with specific facts or data. It includes episodic and semantic representations of propositions and images. On the other hand, the nondeclarative memory system is based on implicit information that is not easily accessible and includes unaware representations of motor, perceptual, and cognitive skills as well as priming, simple classical conditioning, and nonassociative learning. Squire also assumes that the two memory systems are independent of each other. Furthermore, he proposes that the hippocampus and interconnected neural regions, such as the entorhinal cortex, parahippocampal gyrus, and perirhinal cortex, mediate declarative, but not nondeclarative, memory. Recently, Squire (1995) suggested that skills and habits are mediated by the striatum, priming by the neocortex, simple classical conditioning of emotional responses by the amygdala, simple classical conditioning of skeletal musculature by the cerebellum, and nonassociative learning by reflex pathways.

Support for this distinction comes from studies with human amnesic patients (Cohen & Squire, 1981). Korsakoff patients, with presumably diencephalic damage, and patients receiving electroconvulsive shock treatments, which presumably produce major disruptive effects in the temporal lobe, can acquire and retain (for at least 3 months) a mirror reading skill as easily as normal subjects (nondeclarative memory). However, when asked to remember the words they read in this task, they were severely impaired (declarative memory). In another experiment patient H.M., with bilateral medial temporal lobe damage, including the hippocampus and amygdala, was able to learn and remember a set of complicated skills associated with solving the Tower of Hanoi problem, yet this patient could not recall any contextual aspect of the task or the strategies involved in solving the task (Cohen, 1984). Thus, it appears that amnesic patients can acquire skills necessary for correct mirror reading performance or finding the appropriate solutions for the Tower of Hanoi problem but cannot remember the specific facts or data-based experiences of the experiment. Further support for a problem with conscious awareness associated with declarative information is based on a patient with bilateral damage to the hippocampus who was impaired in learning which stimuli were paired with an unconditioned response but learned very readily a conditioned autonomic response to the critical visual and auditory stimuli. In contrast, a different patient with a bilateral lesion of the amygdala was impaired in learning a conditioned autonomic response to visual or auditory stimuli but learned very readily which stimuli were paired with the unconditioned response (Bechara et al., 1995). Also, amnesic subjects with damage to the hippocampus are not impaired on a variety of tests that measure implicit memory for a variety of stimulus patterns, but they are impaired in explicitly remembering the same stimulus patterns using the declarative memory system (for a review, see Shimamura, 1986). Finally, amnesic subjects can learn a complex probability classification task but perform poorly on multiple-choice tests that attempt to measure the training experience (Knowlton et al., 1994).

In this model the temporal lobe and especially the hippocampus are directly involved in representing declarative memory. There is no place for different forms of declarative memory. Yet, many of the tasks that presumably measure short-term memory representations within declarative memory, such as matching or non-matching-to-sample, have resulted in an absence of profound deficits in both animals and humans. For example, rats with hippocampal lesions have no short-term memory deficits for a right- or left-turn response, for a visual object or an odor, or for magnitude of reinforcement information (Kesner et al., 1993; Kesner & Williams, 1995; Otto & Eichenbaum, 1992a). Patients who have undergone resection of the right temporal lobe, which includes the hippocampus, are not impaired in remembering an array of objects nor do they have difficulty in remembering that an object was changed within a scene (Pigott & Milner, 1993; Smith & Milner, 1981). Patients with right or left temporal lobe resection are not impaired in short-term or working memory for the distance of a motor movement response, implicit sensory-perceptual priming of various stimuli, or in displaying a liking response based on the mere exposure effect (Chiba et al., 1993; Leonard & Milner, 1991; Shimamura, 1986). Thus, many forms of memory that utilize declarative memory appear to be intact in temporal lobe resected patients and appear to be mediated by other neural systems (see previous sections). The declarative memory system differs from the data-based memory system in that conscious representation of information is an essential process component of the declarative system, whereas it is not an essential process that characterizes the data-based memory system. Furthermore, because there is no recognition of different forms of declarative memory, the neural representation of declarative memory is more limited in comparison with the data-based memory system. The nondeclarative memory system has a large memory representation and compared to the attribute model it includes the knowledge-based memory system as well as some components of the data-based memory system. It is, therefore, very difficult to characterize the operations that are necessary for efficient functioning of the nondeclarative system.

D. Declarative–Procedural Memory Model

This model was proposed by Cohen and Eichenbaum and represents an extension and refinement of the Squire declarative versus nondeclarative model. Cohen and Eichenbaum suggested that there are two memory systems, labeled declarative and procedural. The declarative system is dependent on the hippocampus and is characterized not only by supporting conscious processing of information but also by providing a substrate for relational representation of all items in memory as well as representational flexibility allowing for the retrieval of memories in novel situations. In contrast, the procedural system is independent of the hippocampus and is characterized by individual representations and inflexibility in retrieving memories in novel situations. These latter memories tend to emphasize the importance of neural systems that subserve sensory and motor processing of information during learning (Cohen & Eichenbaum, 1993; Eichenbaum, 1994, 1996). A number of elegant experiments have been reported in support of this model. For example, in one experiment Eichenbaum et al. (1990) and Eichenbaum (1994) demonstrated that when fimbria-fornix lesioned rats are trained in a water maze task from only a single starting position, there are hardly any learning deficits, whereas training from many different starting points resulted in learning difficulties. Furthermore, when normal rats that were trained on a fixed starting position were transferred to a novel start position, they swam directly to the correct location, whereas the fimbria-fornix lesioned rats swam in many directions and took a long time to find the correct location. These data suggest that rats with hippocampal dysfunction can learn the task if only one viewpoint needs to be learned but are impaired when many viewpoints with multiple relationships need to be learned. Furthermore, the controls that had only learned the task from one starting point were flexible and able to perform well from new starting locations, whereas rats with hippocampal dysfunction were not flexible and not able to perform well on the transfer tests. One alternative interpretation of these results is that rats with hippocampal dysfunction cannot readily separate one spatial location from another, which would explain their ability to learn the task when trained from one starting position and would explain their inability to perform well in transfer tests to new locations. Also, it is not clear why rats with hippocampal dysfunction can learn the task only slightly slower than controls in the constant start position situation given that even in this situation the rat has to learn a new set of stimulus relationships.

In another experiment rats were trained in a paired associate task for 8 pairs of odors which resulted in the presence of a water reward, facilitating a go response, but any combination of 48 possible mispairs resulted in the absence of a water reward, facilitating a no-go response. Compared to control rats, rats with hippocampal or fimbria-fornix lesions learned the task more quickly and rats with perirhinal and entorhinal cortex lesions learned the task more slowly (Bunsey & Eichenbaum, 1993). In a different study Cho and Kesner (1996) showed that hippocampal lesioned rats performed without any difficulty in a previously learned object–object (two sets) paired associate task using Bunsey and Eichenbaum's procedure. In another study Long and Kesner (1995) showed that hippocampal lesioned rats performed very poorly in a previously learned object–place (four sets) paired associate task. In a study with monkeys, Murray et al. (1993) showed that relearning or new learning of visual stimulus–stimulus paired associates was not disrupted following hippocampal lesions. In a somewhat different odor paired associate task, control rats and rats with hippocampal lesions had to learn in Set 1 across a short delay that A is associated with B and that X is associated with Y and in Set 2 that B is associated with C and that Y is associated with Z. There were no differences between the two groups in the acquisition of the task (Bunsey & Eichenbaum, 1996). In all five of these studies hippocampal lesioned rats had no difficulty learning odor–odor or object-object relationships, yet when the paired associate involved a place component there was a significant deficit.

Eichenbaum suggests that rats with hippocampal lesions learn the paired associate task by unitizing the elements, so that they do not maintain the compositionality of the components of the pair. To test this idea and to test the role of the hippocampus in mediating flexibility to novel situations in the Bunsey and Eichenbaum (1996) experiment, the rats were given after training two transfer tests, a test for transitivity between never paired items that shared a common association, such as A followed by C and X followed by Z, and a test for symmetry where the stimulus pairings were presented in the reverse order, such as C followed by B and Z followed by Y. In both cases the control rats transferred well to the new problems, whereas the hippocampal lesioned rats showed no evidence of transfer. Bunsey and Eichenbaum conclude that to test for the nominal presentation of a relationship, transfer tests are necessary to determine how the information is represented and to test the role of the hippocampus in utilizing flexible strategies in new situations. Cho and Kesner (1996) also tested for flexible use of novel information in control and hippocampal lesioned rats, in this case for spatial symmetry by reversing the location of the pairs of objects. They found the level of transfer to be the same for both the control and hippocampal lesioned rats.

An alternative interpretation to the Eichenbaum model is that the hippocampus does not mediate all relationships, but only relationships that involve space or time, since no transfer tests are necessary for demonstrating hippocampal involvement in the object–place paired associate task. Furthermore, since Set 1 was learned prior to Set 2, the transfer deficits observed for hippocampal lesioned rats could be due to the inability to separate the paired associates across time, resulting in temporal interference and, thus, poor transfer performance on tests for transitivity and tests for symmetry.

The hippocampus is not the only neural region that can mediate relationships. Clearly, the perirhinal cortex, entorhinal cortex, parietal cortex, and anterior cingulate cortex have all been shown to disrupt paired associate learning or performance for odor–odor, object–object, or object–place relationships (Bunsey & Eichenbaum, 1993; Kurzina, Granholm, & Kesner, 1995; Long & Kesner, 1995). Whether these other regions represent only a unique set of stimulus relationships and whether these relationships are based only on a unified representation need to be determined.

In the Eichenbaum model there is also no place for different forms of declarative memory. However, in the Eichenbaum model it is possible to suggest that normal performance of rats with hippocampal lesions on many of the tasks that measure short-term memory for a right- or left-turn response, for a visual object or an odor, or for magnitude of reinforcement information is due to the lack of a need to learn stimulus relationships, whereas deficits following hippocampal lesions in memory for a spatial location, for a spatial distance, and for a specific time duration are due to the importance of stimulus relationships. The major concern with the Eichenbaum model is in the difficulty of defining what is meant by a relationship. This is especially important, because Jarrard (1995) has shown that in a number of tasks that involve relationships, such as conditional discriminations, negative patterning problems, and configural learning problems, rats with hippocampal lesions do not have any problems.

In comparison with the attribute model, the same differences that were described for the declarative–nondeclarative model apply to the Eichenbaum model. The emphasis on relationships needs to be explored further, but the attribute model would predict that the hippocampus is critical only for representing spatial and temporal relationships rather than all relationships.

VI. SUMMARY

Memory is a complex phenomenon due to a large number of potential interactions that are associated with the organization of memory at the psychological and neural system levels. Most of the neurobiological models of memory postulate an organizational schema involving two systems, each supported by different neurobiological substrates and each mediated by different operating characteristics. These systems are labeled data-based versus knowledge-based memory, locale versus taxon memory, working versus reference memory, declarative versus nondeclarative memory, and declarative versus procedural memory.

In the Kesner attribute memory model (Kesner, 1996; Kesner & DeMattia, 1987; Kesner & Ragozzino, 1997), it is assumed that any specific memory is organized into a data-based memory system and a knowledge-based memory system. The data-based memory system is biased in providing for temporary representations of incoming data concerning the present, with an emphasis upon facts, data, and events that are usually personal or egocentric and that occur within specific external and internal contexts. The emphasis is on bottom-up processing. The data-based memory system is composed of different independently operating forms or attributes of memory. Even though there could be many attributes, the most important attributes include *space, time, response, sensory-perception, and affect*. In humans a *language* attribute is also added.

The knowledge-based memory system is biased in providing more permanent representations of previously stored information in long-term memory and can be thought of as one's general knowledge of the world. It can operate in the abstract in the absence of incoming data. The emphasis is on top-down processing. The knowledge-based memory system is composed of the same set of different independently operating forms or attributes of memory. These attributes include *space, time, response, sensory-perception, affect, and language*. The data-based versus knowledge-based memory model recognizes different forms or attributes of memory within each system supported by different operating neural substrates. For example, within the data-based memory system, the hippocampus and interconnected neural regions subserve spatial, temporal, and linguistic attribute information, the caudate and interconnected neural regions subserve response and stimulus–response attribute information, the amygdala and interconnected neural regions subserve affect and stimulus–reward attribute information, and the perirhinal visual cortex and interconnected neural regions subserve visual object information as an example of sensory-perceptual attribute information. Within the knowledge-based memory system, the parietal cortex and interconnected neural regions subserve spatial attribute information, the prefrontal cortex and interconnected neural regions subserve temporal and response attribute information, the orbital frontal cortex and interconnected neural regions subserve the affect attribute, the inferotemporal cortex and interconnected neural regions subserve object information as an example of the sensory-perceptual attribute, and the temporal, parietal, and frontal neural regions subserve linguistic attribute information. Furthermore, these substrates can operate independently of each other as indexed by empirical observations of double dissociations between neural regions and between attributes. Each system is also subserved by a unique set of operating process characteristics including for the data-based memory system (a) pattern separation based on selective filtering or attenuation of interference associated with temporary memory representations of new information, (b) short-term memory or working memory of new information, (c) consolidation or elaborative rehearsal of new information, and (d) retrieval of new information based on flexibility and action and for the knowledge-based memory system (a) selective attention and selective filtering associated with permanent memory representations of familiar information, (b) perceptual memory, (c) long-term memory storage, (d) selection of strategies and rules ("executive functions"), and (e) retrieval of familiar information based on flexibility and action. Empirical support based on both animal and human research was presented for each of these processes. Finally, it can be shown that the two systems can also operate independently of each other.

In the O'Keefe and Nadel (1978) and Nadel (1994) memory model, there is a concentration on space as the critical attribute of specific memories. They further divide the spatial attribute into a locale system, which codes places in the environment into cognitive maps, and a taxon system, which codes motor responses in terms of specific orientations within a spatial environment. The locale versus taxon system proposes that the hippocampus is important in mediating only one form of memory, namely spatial, within the locale system and other neural regions as important for subserving the taxon system. With respect to the operation of each system, it is assumed that learning within the locale system is based in part on consolidation processes and is (a) all-or-none, (b) sensitive to interference, (c) involved in separating traces, and (d) flexible, whereas learning in the taxon system is (a) incremental, (b) not sensitive to interference, (c) involved in combining traces, and (d) not flexible.

In the working memory model, Olton proposes a somewhat different system distinction emphasizing more the importance of process. He has suggested that within every learning task there are two types of memories that organize the critical information into two systems, labeled working memory and reference memory (Olton, 1983; Olton, Becker, and Handelmann, 1979). He suggests that the specific, personal, and temporal context of a situation is coded in working memory. This would translate into memory for events that occur on a specific trial in a task, biasing mnemonic coding toward the processing of incoming data. In contrast, general information concerning rules and procedures (general knowledge) of specific situations is coded in reference memory. This would translate into memory for events that happen on all trials in a task, biasing mnemonic coding toward the processing of expectancies based on the organization of the extant memory. The working versus reference memory system emphasizes the role of the hippocampus and interconnected neural systems as the critical substrate of memory for a single process, namely working memory, and the neocortex as the critical neural substrate within reference memory for all forms or attributes of memory. It is assumed that the two memory systems are independent of each other.

With respect to the declarative versus nondeclarative system model (Squire, 1992, 1994, 1995), it is assumed that the declarative memory system is based on explicit information that is easily accessible and is concerned with specific facts or data. It includes episodic and semantic representations of propositions and images. On the other hand, the nondeclarative memory system is based on implicit information that is not easily accessible and includes unaware representations of motor, perceptual, and cognitive skills as well as priming, simple classical conditioning, and nonassociative learning. In this model the hippocampus and interconnected neural regions are assumed to be the critical neural substrate in mediating all forms of memory within the declarative memory system and the role of different neural substrates in mediating different forms of nondeclarative memory, including the mediation of skills and habits by the striatum, priming by the neocortex, simple classical conditioning of emotional responses by the amygdala, simple classical conditioning of skeletal musculature by the cerebellum, and nonassociative learning by reflex pathways. It is assumed that the two memory systems are independent of each other.

The declarative versus procedural memory system represents an extension of the declarative versus nondeclarative model (Cohen & Eichenbaum, 1993; Eichenbaum, 1994, 1996). This model proposes that the declarative memory system is dependent on the hippocampus and is characterized not only by supporting conscious processing of information but also by providing a substrate for relational representation of all forms of memory as well as representational flexibility allowing for the retrieval of memories in novel situations. In contrast, the procedural system is independent of the hippocampus and is characterized by individual representations and inflexibility in retrieving memories in novel situations.

Even though there are many similarities among the different neurobiological views of memory in terms of the proposed memory systems, there are important differences that should stimulate the development of new paradigms and further experimentation.

REFERENCES

Adolphs, R., Tranel, D., Damasio, H., & Damasio, A. (1994). Impaired recognition of emotion in facial expressions following bilateral damage to the human amygdala. *Nature, 372,* 669–672.

Aggleton, J. P., Hunt, P. R., & Rawlins, J. N. P. (1986). The effects of hippocampal lesions upon spatial and non-spatial tests of working memory. *Behavioural Brain Research, 19.* 133–146.

Bachevalier, M., & Mishkin, M. (1986). Visual recognition impairment follows ventromedial but not dorsolateral prefrontal lesions in monkeys. *Behavioural Brain Research, 20,* 249–261.

Barker, D. J. (1967). Alterations in sequential behavior of rats following ablation of midline limbic cortex. *Journal of Comparative Physiological Psychology, 3,* 453–604.

Bechara, A., Tranel, D., Damasio, H., Adolphs, R., Rockland, C., & Damasio, A. R. (1995). Double dissociation of conditioning and declarative knowledge relative to the amygdala and hippocampus in humans. *Science, 269,* 1115–1118.

Benton, A. L. (1969). Disorders of spatial orientation. In P. J. Vinken & G. W. Bruyn (Eds.), *Handbook of clinical neurology* (Vol. 3). Amsterdam: North-Holland.

Brown, M. W. (1996). Neuronal responses and recognition memory. *Seminars in the Neurosciences, 8,* 23–32.

Bunsey, M., & Eichenbaum, H. (1993). Critical role of the parahippocampal region for paired-associate learning in rats. *Behavioral Neuroscience, 107,* 740–747.

Bunsey, M., & Eichenbaum, H. (1996). Conservation of hippocampal memory function in rats and humans. *Nature, 379,* 255–257.

Butter, C. M. (1969). Perseveration in extinction and in discrimination reversal tasks following selective frontal ablations in *Macaca mulatta*. *Physiology & Behavior, 4,* 163–171.

Butter, C. M., Snyder, D. R., & McDonald, J. A. (1970). Effects of orbitalfrontal lesions on aversive and aggressive behaviors in rhesus monkeys. *Journal of Comparative and Physiological Psychology, 72,* 132–144.

Caramazza, A., & Berndt, R. S. (1978). Semantic and syntactic processes in aphasia: A review of the literature. *Psychological Bulletin, 85,* 898–918.

Chen, L. L., Lin, L., Barnes, C. A., & McNaughton, B. L. (1994). Head-direction cells in the rat posterior cortex: II. Contributions of visual and ideothetic information to the directional firing. *Experimental Brain Research, 101,* 24–34.

Chiba, A. A., Jackson-Smith, P., & Kesner, R. P. (1991). A double dissociation between implicit and explicit spatial memory following hippocampal and parietal cortex lesions. *Society for Neuroscience Abstracts, 17,* 131.

Chiba, A. A., Johnson, D. L., & Kesner, R. P. (1992). The effects of lesions of the dorsal hippocampus or the ventral hippocampus on performance of a spatial location order recognition task. *Society for Neuroscience Abstracts, 18,* 1422.

Chiba, A. A., Kesner, R. P., Matsuo, F., & Heilbrun, M. P. (1990). A dissociation between verbal and spatial memory following unilateral temporal lobectomy. *Society for Neuroscience Abstracts, 16,* 286.

Chiba, A. A., Kesner, R. P., Matsuo, F., & Heilbrun, M. P. (1993). A dissociation between affect and recognition following unilateral temporal lobectomy including the amygdala. *Society for Neuroscience Abstracts, 19,* 792.

Chiba, A. A., Kesner, R. P., Matsuo, F., Heilbrun, M. P., & Plumb, S. (submitted). A double dissociation between the right and left hippocampus in processing the temporal order of spatial and verbal information.

Chiba, A. A., Kesner, R. P., & Reynolds, A. M. (1994). Memory for spatial location as a function of temporal lag in rats: Role of hippocampus and medial prefrontal cortex. *Behavioral and Neural Biology, 61,* 123–131.

Cho, Y. H., Beracochea, D., & Jaffard, R. (1993). Extended temporal gradient for retrograde and anterograde amnesia produced by ibotenate entorhinal cortex lesions in mice. *Journal of Neuroscience, 13,* 1759–1766.

Cho, Y. H., & Kesner, R. P. (1995). Relational object association learning in rats with hippocampal lesions. *Behavioural Brain Research, 67,* 91–98.

Cho, Y. H., & Kesner, R. P. (1996). Involvement of enthorhinal cortex or parietal cortex in long-term spatial discrimination memory in rats: Retrograde amnesia. *Behavioral Neuroscience, 110,* 436–442.

Cho, Y. H., Kesner, R. P., & Brodale, S. (1995). Retrograde and anterograde amnesia for spatial discrimination in rats: Role of hippocampus, entorhinal cortex and parietal cortex. *Psychobiology, 23,* 185–194.

Cohen, J. J., & Squire, L. R. (1981). Preserved learning and retention of pattern-analyzing skill in amnesia: Dissociation of knowing how and knowing that. *Science, 210,* 207–210.

Cohen, N. (1984). Preserved learning capacity in amnesia: Evidence for multiple memory systems. In L. R. Squire & N. Butters (Eds.), *Neuropsychology of memory.* New York: Guilford Press.

Cohen, N. J., & Eichenbaum, H. B. (1993). *Memory, amnesia, and hippocampal function.* Cambridge, MA: MIT Press.

Colombo, P. J., Davis, H. P., & Volpe, B. T. (1989). Allocentric spatial and tactile memory impairments in rats with dorsal caudate lesions are affected by preoperative behavioral training. *Behavioral Neuroscience, 103,* 1242–1250.

Cook, D., & Kesner, R. P. (1988). Caudate nucleus and memory for egocentric localization. *Behavioral Neural Biology, 49,* 332–343.

Cook, R. G., Brown, M. G., & Riley, D. A. (1985). Flexible memory processing in rats: Use of prospective and retrospective information in the radial maze. *Journal of Experimental Psychology and Animal Behavior Processes, 11,* 453–469.

Dakis, M., Martinez, J. S., Kesner, R. P., & Jackson-Smith, P. (1992). Effects of phencyclidine and naloxone on learning of a spatial navigation task and performance of a spatial delayed non-matching to sample task. *Society for Neuroscience Abstracts, 18,* 1220.

Dean, P. (1990). Sensory cortex: Visual perceptual functions. In B. Kolb & R. C. Tees (Eds.), *Cerebral cortex of the rat* (pp. 275–308). Cambridge, MA: MIT Press.

DeCoteau, W. E., & Kesner, R. P. (1996). Hippocampal and parietal cortex processing of object scenes. *Society for Neuroscience Abstracts, 22,* 1121.

DeCoteau, W. E., Kesner, R. P., & Gilbert, P. (1995). The role of the hippocampus in reducing spatial interference. *Society for Neuroscience Abstracts, 21,* 1943.

DeCoteau, W. E., Kesner, R. P., & Williams, J. M. (1994). Memory for food reward magnitude: The role of the agranular insular cortex. *Society for Neuroscience Abstracts, 20,* 1211.

De Renzi, E. (Ed.). (1982). *Disorders of space exploration and cognition.* New York: John Wiley & Sons.

DiMattia, B. V., & Kesner, R. P. (1988a). The role of the posterior parietal association cortex in the processing of spatial event information. *Behavioral Neuroscience, 102,* 397–403.

DiMattia, B. V., & Kesner, R. P. (1988b). Spatial cognitive maps: Differential role of parietal cortex and hippocampal formation. *Behavioral Neuroscience, 102,* 471–480.

Disterhoft, J. F., Carrillo, M. C., Hopkins, R. O., Gabrieli, J. D. E., & Kesner, R. P. (1996). Impaired trace eyeblink conditioning in severe medial temporal lobe amnesics. *Society for Neuroscience Abstracts, 22,* 1866.

Divac, I., Rosvold, H. E., & Szwarcbart, M. K. (1967). Behavioral effects of selective ablation of the caudate nucleus. *Journal of Comparative and Physiological Psychology, 63,* 184–190.

Douglas, R. J., & Pribram, K. H. (1966). Learning and limbic lesions. *Neuropsychology, 4,* 197–220.

Duncan-Davis, J., Filoteo, V., & Kesner, R. P. (1996, March). *Memory impairment for spatial location and motor movements in patients with Huntington's disease.* Paper presented at the Third Annual Meeting of the Cognitive Neuroscience Society, San Francisco.

Dunnett, S. B. (1990). Role of prefrontal cortex and striatal output systems in short-term memory deficits associated with ageing, basal forebrain lesions, and cholinergic-rich grafts. *Canadian Journal of Psychology, 44,* 210–232.

Eacott, M. J., Gaffan, D., & Murray, E. A. (1994). Preserved recognition memory for small sets, and impaired stimulus identification for large sets, following rhinal cortex ablations in monkeys. *European Journal of Neuroscience, 6,* 1466–1478.

Eichenbaum, H. (1994). The hippocampal system and declarative memory in humans and animals: Experimental analysis and historical origins. In D. L. Schacter & E. Tulving (Eds.), *Memory systems 1994* (pp. 147–201). Cambridge, MA: MIT Press.

Eichenbaum, H. (1996). Is the rodent hippocampus just for 'place'? *Current Opinion in Neurobiology, 6,* 187–195.

Eichenbaum, H., Stewart, C., & Morris, R. G. M. (1990). Hippocampal representation in spatial learning. *Journal of Neuroscience, 10,* 331–339.

Ellis, A. X., Della Sala, S., & Logie, R. H. (1996). The bailiwick of visuo-spatial working memory: Evidence from unilateral spatial neglect. *Brain Research. Cognitive Brain Research, 3,* 71–78.

Estes, W. K. (1986). Memory for temporal information. In J. A. Michon & J. L. Jackson (Eds.), *Time, mind and behavior* (pp. 151–168). New York: Springer-Verlag.

Fuster, J. M. (1985). The prefrontal cortex, mediator of cross-temporal contingencies. *Human Neurobiology, 4,* 169–179.

Fuster, J. M. (1995). *Memory in the cerebral cortex: An empirical approach to neural networks in the human and nonhuman primate.* Cambridge, MA: MIT Press.

Fuster, J. M., Bauer, R. H., & Jervey, J. P. (1982). Cellular discharge in the dorsolateral prefrontal cortex of the monkey in cognitive tasks. *Experimental Neurology, 77,* 679–694.

Gabrieli, J. D. E., Fleischman, D. A., Keane, M. M., Reminger, S. L., & Morrell, F. (1995). Double dissociation between memory systems underlying explicit and implicit memory in the human brain. *Psychological Science, 6,* 76–82.

Gaffan, D. (1992). Amygdala and the memory of reward. In J. P. Aggleton (Ed.), *The amygdala: Neurobiological aspects of emotion, memory, and mental dysfunction.* New York: Wiley-Liss.

Gaffan, D. (1994). Dissociated effects of perirhinal cortex ablation, fornix transection and amygdalectomy: Evidence for multiple memory systems in the primate temporal lobe. *Experimental Brain Research, 99,* 411–422.

Gaffan, D., & Murray, E. A. (1992). Monkeys (*Macaca fascicularis*) with rhinal cortex ablations succeed in object discrimination learning despite 24-hr intertrial intervals and fail at matching to sample despite double sample presentations. *Behavioral Neuroscience, 106,* 30–38.

Gardiner, T. W., & Kitai, S. T. (1992). Single-unit activity in the globus pallidus and neostriatum of the rat during performance of a trained head movement. *Experimental Brain Research, 88,* 517–530.

Gold, P. E., Hankins, L. L., Edwards, R., Chester, J., & McGaugh, J. L. (1975). Memory interference and facilitation with posttrial amygdala stimulation. Effect on memory varies with footshock level. *Brain Research, 86,* 509–513.

Gross, C. G. (1973). Inferotemporal cortex and vision. In E. Stellar & J. M. Sprague (Eds.), *Progress in physiological psychology* (Vol. 5, pp. 77–123). New York: Academic Press.

Habib, M., & Sirigu, A. (1987). Pure topographical disorientation: A definition and anatomical basis. *Cortex, 23,* 73–85.

Hansing, R. A., Schwartzbaum, J. S., & Thompson, J. B. (1967). Operant behavior following unilateral and bilateral caudate lesions in the rat. *Journal of Comparative and Physiological Psychology, 66,* 378–388.

Hecaen, H., & Albert, M. L. (1978). *Human neuropsychology.* New York: Wiley.

Heilman, K. M., Watson, R. T., & Valenstein, E. (1993). Neglect and related disorders. In K. M. Heilman & E. Valenstein (Eds.), *Clinical neuropsychology* (3rd ed.). New york: Oxford University Press.

Heindel, W. C., Salmon, D. P., Shults, C. W., Walicke, P. A., & Butters, N. (1989). Neuropsychological evidence for multiple implicit memory systems: A comparison of Alzheimer's, Huntington's, and Parkinson's disease patients. *Journal of Neuroscience, 9,* 582–587.

Higuchi, S., & Miyashita, Y. (1996). Formation of mnemonic neuronal responses to visual paried associates in inferotemporal cortex is impaired by perirhinal and entorhinal lesions. *Proceedings of the National Academy of Sciences U.S.A., 93,* 739–743.

Hirsh, R. (1980). The hippocampus, conditional operations, and cognition. *Physiological Psychology, 8,* 175–182.

Hitchcock, J., & Davis, M. (1986). Lesions of the amygdala, but not of the cerebellum or red nucleus, block conditioned fear as measured with the potentiated startle paradigm. *Behavioral Neuroscience, 100,* 11–22.

Honig, W. K. (1978). Studies of working memory in the pigeon. In W. H. Hulse, H. Fowler, & W. K. Honig (Eds.), *Cognitive process in animal behavior.* Hillsdale, NJ: Erlbaum.

Hopkins, R. O., & Kesner, R. P. (1993). Memory for temporal and spatial distances for new and previously learned geographical information in hypoxic subjects. *Society for Neuroscience Abstracts, 19,* 1284.

Hopkins, R. O., & Kesner, R. P. (1994). Short-term memory for duration in hypoxic subjects. *Society for Neuroscience Abstracts, 20,* 1075.

Hopkins, R. O., Kesner, R. P., & Goldstein, M. (1995a). Item and order recognition memory for words, pictures, abstract pictures, spatial locations, and motor responses in subjects with hypoxic brain injury. *Brain and Cognition, 27,* 180–201.

Hopkins, R. O., Kesner, R. P., & Goldstein, M. (1995b). Memory for novel and familiar spatial and linguistic temporal distance information in hypoxic subjects. *Journal of the International Neuropsychological Society, 1,* 454–468.

Horel, J. A., Pytko-Joiner, D. E., Boytko, M. L., & Salsbury, K. (1987). The performance of visual tasks while segments of the inferotemporal cortex are suppressed by cold. *Behavioural Brain Research, 23,* 29–42.

Hunt, M. E., Kesner, R. P., & Evans, R. B. (1994). Memory for spatial location: Functional dissociation of entorhinal cortex and hippocampus. *Psychobiology, 22,* 186–194.

Iversen, S. D., & Mishkin, M. (1970). Perseverative interference in monkeys following selective lesions of the inferior prefrontal convexity. *Experimental Brain Research, 11,* 376–386.

Jackson-Smith, P., & Kesner, R. P. (1989). Does the hippocampus play a role in mediating spatial and temporal configurations? *Society for Neuroscience Abstracts, 15,* 608.

Jackson-Smith, P., Kesner, R. P., & Amann, K. (1994). Effects of hippocampal and medial prefrontal lesions on discrimination of duration in rats. *Society for Neuroscience Abstracts, 20,* 1210.

Jackson-Smith, P., Kesner, R. P., & Chiba, A. A. (1993). Continuous recognition of spatial and non-spatial stimuli in hippocampal lesioned rats. *Behavioral and Neural Biology, 59,* 107–119.

Jarrard, L. E. (1995). What does the hippocampus really do? *Behavioural Brain Research, 71,* 1–10.

Johnson, D. L., & Kesner, R. P. (1997). Comparison of temporal order memory in early and middle stage Alzheimer's disease. *Journal of Clinical and Experimental Neuropsychology, 19,* 83–100.

Jones, B., & Mishkin, M. (1972). Limbic lesions and the problem of stimulus-reinforcement associations. *Experimental Neurology, 36,* 362–377.

Kapp, B. S., Whalen, P. J., Supple, W. F., & Pascoe, J. P. (1992). Amygdaloid contributions to conditioned arousal and sensory information processing. In J. P. Aggleton (Ed.), *The amygdala: Neurobiological aspects of emotion, memory, and mental dysfunction.* New York: Wiley-Liss.

Karni, A., Meyer, G., Jezzard, P., Adams, M. M., Turner, R., & Ungerleider, L. G. (1995). Functional MRI evidence for adult motor cortex plasticity during motor skill learning. *Nature, 377,* 155–158.

Keane, M. M., Gabrieli, J. D. E., Mapstone, H. C., Johnson, K. A., & Corkin, S. (1995). Double dissociation of memory capacities after bilateral occipital-lobe or medial temporal-lobe lesions. *Brain, 118,* 1129–1148.

Kesner, R. P. (1989). Retrospective and prospective coding of information: Role of the medial prefrontal cortex. *Journal of Experimental Brain Research, 74,* 163–167.

Kesner, R. P. (1990a). Learning and memory in rats with an emphasis on the role of the hippocampal formation. In R. P. Kesner & D. S. Olton (Eds.), *Neurobiology of comparative cognition.* Hillsdale, NJ: Erlbaum.

Kesner, R. P. (1990b). Memory for frequency in rats: Role of the hippocampus and medial prefrontal cortex. *Behavioral and Neural Biology, 53,* 402–410.

Kesner, R. P. (1992). Learning and memory in rats with an emphasis on the role of the amygdala. In J. P. Aggleton (Ed.), *The amygdala: Neurobiological aspects of emotion, memory, and mental dysfunction.* New York: Wiley-Liss.

Kesner, R. P. (1996). An exploration of the neural bases of memory representations of reward and context. In K. H. Pribram & J. King (Eds.), *Learning as self organization* (pp. 393–419). Mahwah, NJ: Lawrence Erlbaum Associates.

Kesner, R. P., & Andrus, R. G. (1982). Amygdala stimulation disrupts magnitude of reinforcement contribution to long-term memory. *Physiological Psychology, 10,* 55–59.

Kesner, R. P., Berman, R. F., Burton, B., & Hankins, W. G. (1975). Effects of electrical stimulation of amygdala upon neophobia and taste aversion. *Behavioral Biology, 13,* 349–358.

Kesner, R. P., Bolland, B. L., & Dakis, M. (1993). Memory for spatial locations, motor responses, and objects: Triple dissociation among the hippocampus, caudate nucleus, and extrastriate visual cortex. *Experimental Brain Research, 93,* 462–470.

Kesner, R. P., Crutcher, K. A., & Omana, H. (1990). Memory deficits following nucleus basalis magnocellularis lesions may be mediated through limbic, but not neocortical, targets. *Neuroscience, 38,* 93–102.

Kesner, R. P., & Dakis, M. (1995). Phencyclidine injections into the dorsal hippocampus disrupt long- but not short-term memory within a spatial learning task. *Psychopharmacology, 120,* 203–208.

Kesner, R. P., & DiMattia, B. V. (1987). Neurobiology of an attribute model of memory. *Progress in psychobiology and physiological psychology.* New York: Academic Press.

Kesner, R. P., DiMattia, B. V., & Crutcher, K. A. (1987). Evidence for neocortical involvement in reference memory. *Behavioral and Neural Biology, 47,* 40–53.

Kesner, R. P., Dixon, D. A., Pickett, D., & Berman, R. F. (1975). Experimental animal model of transient global amnesia: Role of the hippocampus. *Neuropsychologia, 13,* 465–480.

Kesner, R. P., Farnsworth, G., & DiMattia, B. V. (1989). Double-dissociation of egocentric and allocentric space following medial prefrontal and parietal cortex lesions in the rat. *Behavioral Neuroscience, 103,* 907–910.

Kesner, R. P., Farnsworth, G., & Kametani, H. (1992). Role of parietal cortex and hippocampus in representing spatial information. *Cerebral Cortex, 1,* 367–373.

Kesner, R. P., & Filoteo, J. V. (in press). Non-primate animal models of motor and cognitive functions associated with Huntington's disease. In A. I. Troster (Ed.), *Memory in neurodegenerative disease: Biological, cognitive and clinical perspectives.* Cambridge, MA: Cambridge University Press.

Kesner, R. P., & Holbrook, T. (1987). Dissociation of item and order spatial memory in rats following medial prefrontal cortex lesions. *Neuropsychologia, 25,* 653–664.

Kesner, R. P., Hopkins, R. O., & Chiba, A. A. (1992). Learning and memory in humans, with an emphasis on the role of the hippocampus. In L. R. Squire & N. Butters (Eds.), *Neuropsychology of memory.* New York: Guilford Press.

Kesner, R. P., Hunt, M. E., Williams, J. M., & Long, J. M. (1995). Prefrontal cortex and working memory for egocentric spatial, allocentric spatial and visual object information in the rat. *Cerebral Cortex, 6,* 311–318.

Kesner, R. P., & Ragozzino, M. (1997). Structure and dynamics of multiple memory systems in Alzheimer's disease. In J. D. Brioni & M. W. Decker (Eds.), *Pharmacological treatment of Alzheimer's disease: Molecular and neurobiological foundations* (pp. 3–36). New York: Wiley-Liss.

Kesner, R. P., Walser, R. D., & Winzenried, G. (1989). Central but not basolateral amygdala mediates memory for positive effective experiences. *Behavioural Brain Research, 33,* 189–195.

Kesner, R. P., & Wilburn, M. W. (1974). A review of electrical stimulation of the brain in context of learning and retention. *Behavioral Biology, 10,* 259–293.

Kesner, R. P., & Williams, J. M. (1995). Memory for magnitude of reinforcement: Dissociation between the amygdala and hippocampus. *Neurobiology of Learning and Memory, 64,* 237–244.

Kim, J. J., & Fanselow, M. S. (1992). Modality-specific retrograde amnesia of fear. *Science, 256,* 675–677.

Kirkby, R. J., Polgar, S., & Coyle, I. R. (1981). Caudate nucleus lesions impair the ability of rats to learn a simple straight-alley task. *Perceptions and Motor Skills, 52,* 499–502.

Knowlton, B. J., Squire, L. R., & Gluck, M. (1994). Probabilistic classification learning in amnesia. *Learning and Memory, 1,* 106–120.

Kojima, S., Matsumura, M., & Kubota, K. (1981). Prefrontal neuron activity during delayed-response performance without imperative GO signals in the monkey. *Experimental Neurology, 74,* 396–407.

Kolb, B. (1974). Social behavior of rats with chronic prefrontal lesions. *Physiological Psychology, 87,* 466–474.

Kubie, J. L., & Ranck, J. B. (1983). Sensory-behavioral correlates in individual hippocampal neurons in three situations: Space and context. In W. Seifert (Ed.), *Neurobiology of the hippocampus* (pp. 433–447). New York: Academic Press.

Kurzina, N., Granholm, M., & Kesner, R. P. (1995). Memory for object–object paired associates: Role of the prefrontal cortex. *Society for Neuroscience Abstracts, 21,* 1448.

Lee, Y., Walker, D., & Davis, M. (1996). Lack of a temporal gradient of retrograde amnesia following NMDA-induced lesions of the basolateral amygdala assessed with the fear-potentiated startle paradigm. *Behavior Neuroscience, 110,* 836–839.

Leonard, G., & Milner, B. (1991). Contribution of the right frontal lobe to the encoding and recall of kinesthetic distance information. *Neuropsychologia, 29,* 47–58.

Long, J. M., & Kesner, R. P. (1994). The effects of parietal cortex and hippocampal lesions on memory for allocentric distance, egocentric distance, and spatial location in rats. *Society for Neuroscience Abstracts, 20,* 1210.

Long, J. M., & Kesner, R. P. (1995). The effects of hippocampal and parietal cortex lesions on memory for an object/spatial location paired associate task in rats. *Society for Neuroscience Abstracts, 21,* 1215.

Long, J. M., & Kesner, R. P. (1996). The effects of dorsal vs. ventral hippocampal, total hippocampal, and parietal cortex lesions on memory for allocentric distance in rats. *Behavioral Neuroscience, 110,* 922–932.

Long, J. M., Mellen, J., & Kesner, R. P. (1996). The effects of total and partial parietal cortex lesions on memory for an object/spatial location paired associate task in rats. *Society for Neuroscience Abstracts, 22,* 682.

Maren, S., Aharonov, G., & Fanselow, M. S. (1996a). Retrograde abolition of conditional fear after excitotoxic lesions in the basolateral amygdala of rats: Absence of a temporal gradient. *Behavioral Neuroscience, 110,* 718–726.

Maren, S., Aharonov, G., & Fanselow, M. S. (1996b). Excitotoxic dorsal hippocampus lesions and Pavlovian fear conditioning in rats. *Society for Neuroscience Abstracts, 22,* 1379.

Martone, M., Butters, N., Payne, M., Becker, J., & Sax, D. S. (1984). Dissociations between skill learning and verbal recognition in amnesia and dementia. *Archives of Neurology, 41,* 965–970.

McCarthy, R. A., & Warrington, E. K. (1990). *Cognitive psychology: A clinical introduction.* London: Academic Press.

McDonald, R. J., & White, N. M. (1993). A triple dissociation of systems: Hippocampus, amygdala, and dorsal striatum. *Behavioral Neuroscience, 107,* 3–22.

McDonald, R. J., & White, N. M. (1995). Hippocampal and nonhippocampal contributions to place learning in rats. *Behavioral Neuroscience, 109,* 579–593.

McDonough, J. R., & Kesner, R. P. (1971). Amnesia produced by brief electrical stimulation of the amygdala or dorsal hippocampus in cats. *Journal of Comparative Physiological Psychology, 77,* 171–178.

McGaugh, J., Intrioni-Collison, I., Cahill, L., Kim, M., & Liang, K. (1992). Involvement of the amygdala in neuromodulatory influences on memory storage. In J. P. Aggleton (Ed.), *The amygdala. Neurobiological aspects of emotion, memory, and mental dysfunction.* New York: Wiley-Liss.

McNaughton, B. L., Barnes, C. A., & O'Keefe, J. (1983). The contributions of position, direction and velocity to single unit activity in the hippocampus of freely-moving rats. *Experimental Brain Research, 52,* 41–49.

McNaughton, B. L., Chen, L. L., & Marcus, E. J. (1991). "Dead reckoning," landmark learning, and the sense of direction: A neurophysiological and computational hypothesis. *Journal of Cognitive Neuroscience, 3,* 190–202.

Meck, W. H., Church, R. M., & Olton, D. S. (1984). Hippocampus, time and memory. *Behavioral Neuroscience, 98,* 3–22.

Meunier, M., Hadfield, W., Bachevalier, J., & Murray, E. A. (1996). Effects of rhinal cortex lesions combined with hippocampectomy on visual recognition memory in rhesus monkeys. *Journal of Neurophysiology, 75,* 1190–1205.

Milner, A. D., Ockleford, E. M., & DeWar, W. (1977). Visuo-spatial performance following posterior parietal and lateral frontal lesions in stumptail macaques. *Cortex, 13,* 170–183.

Milner, B. (1964). Some effects of frontal lobectomy in man. In J. M. Warren & K. Akert (Eds.), *The frontal granular cortex and behavior* (pp. 313–334). New York: McGraw-Hill.

Milner, B. (1971). Interhemispheric differences in the localization of psychological processes in man. *British Medical Bulletin, 27*, 272–277.

Milner, B., Petrides, M., & Smith, M. L. (1985). Frontal lobes and the temporal organization of memory. *Human Neurobiology, 4*, 137–142.

Mishkin, M. (1982). A memory system in the monkey. *Philosophical Transactions of the Royal Society of London, B, 298*, 85–95.

Mishkin, M., & Petri, H. L. (1984). Memories and habits: Some implications for the analysis of learning and retention. In L. R. Squire & N. Butters (Eds.), *Neuropsychology of memory* (pp. 287–296). New York: Guilford Press.

Mitz, A. R., Godschalk, M., & Wise, S. P. (1991). Learning-dependent neuronal activity in the premotor cortex: Activity during the acquisition of conditional motor associations. *Journal of Neuroscience, 11*, 1855–1872.

Mizumori, S. J. Y., & Williams, J. D. (1993). Directionally selective mnemonic properties of neurons in the lateral dorsal nucleus of the thalamus of rats. *Journal of Neuroscience, 13*, 4015–4028.

Morris, R. G. M. (1983). An attempt to dissociate "spatial-mapping" and "working-memory" theories of hippocampal function. In W. Seifert (Ed.), *Neurobiology of the hippocampus*. New York: Academic Press.

Morris, R. G. M., Ahmed, S., Syed, G. M., & Toone, B. K. (1993). Neural correlates of planning ability: Frontal lobe activation during the Tower of London test. *Neuropsychologia, 31*, 1367–1378.

Morris, R. G. M., Garrud, P., Rawlins, J. N., & O'Keefe, J. (1982). Place navigation impaired in rats with hippocampal lesions. *Nature, 297*, 681–683.

Moyer, J. R., Jr., Deyo, R. A., & Disterhoft, J. F. (1990). Hippocampectomy disrupts trace eye-blink conditioning in rabbits. *Behavioral Neuroscience, 104*, 243–252.

Muller, R. U., Ranck, J. B., Jr., & Taube, J. S. (1996). Head direction cells: Properties and functional significance. *Current Opinion in Neurobiology, 6*, 196–206.

Mumby, D. G., & Pinel, J. P. J. (1994). Rhinal cortex lesions and object recognition in rats. *Behavioral Neuroscience, 108*, 11–18.

Mumby, D. G., Wood, E. R., & Pinel, J. P. J. (1992). Object recognition memory is only mildly impaired in rats with lesions of the hippocampus and amygdala. *Psychobiology, 20*, 18–27.

Murray, E. A., Gaffan, D., & Mishkin, M. (1993). Neural substrates of visual stimulus–stimulus association in rhesus monkeys. *Journal of Neuroscience, 13*, 4549–4561.

Myers, C. E., Gluck, M. A., & Granger, R. (1995). Dissociation of hippocampal and entorhinal function in associative learning: A computational approach. *Psychobiology, 23*, 116–138.

Nachman, M., & Ashe, J. H. (1974). Effects of basolateral amygdala lesions on neophobia, learned taste aversions, and sodium appetite in rats. *Journal of Comparative Physiological Psychology, 87*, 622–643.

Nadel, L. (1994). Multiple memory systems: What and why, an update. In D. L. Schacter & E. Tulving (Eds.), *Memory systems 1994* (pp. 39–63). Cambridge, MA: MIT Press.

Niki, H. (1974a). Prefrontal unit activity during delayed alternation in the monkey. I. Relation to direction of response. *Brain Research, 68*, 185–196.

Niki, H. (1974b). Prefrontal unit activity during delayed alternation in the monkey. II. Relation to absolute versus relative direction of response. *Brain Research, 68*, 185–196.

Nyberg, L., Cabeza, R., & Tulving, E. (1996). PET studies of encoding and retrieval: The HERA model. *Psychonomic Bulletin and Review, 3*, 135–148.

Oberg, R. G. E., & Divac, I. (1979). "Cognitive" functions of the neostriatum. In I. Divac & R. G. E. Oberg (Eds.), *The neostriatum* (pp. 291–313). Oxford: Pergamon.

O'Keefe, J. (1979). A review of the hippocampal place cells. *Progress in neurobiology, 13*, 419–439.

O'Keefe, J. (1983). Spatial memory within and without the hippocampal system. In W. Seifert (Ed.), *Neurobiology of the hippocampus* (pp. 375–403). London: Academic Press.

O'Keefe, J., & Nadel, L. (1978). *The hippocampus as a cognitive map*. Oxford: Clarendon Press.

O'Keefe, J., & Speakman, A. (1987). Single unit activity in the rat hippocampus during a spatial memory task. *Experimental Brain Research, 68*, 1–27.

Olton, D. S. (1983). Memory functions and the hippocampus. In W. Seifert (Ed.), *Neurobiology of the hippocampus* (pp. 335–373). New York: Academic Press.

Olton, D. S. (1986). Hippocampal function and memory for temporal context. In R. L. Isaacson & K. H. Pribram (Eds.), *The hippocampus*, Vol. 3, New York: Plenum Press.

Olton, D. S., Becker, J. T., & Handelmann, G. H. (1979). Hippocampus, space, and memory. *Behavioral and Brain Sciences, 2,* 313–365.

Olton, D. S., Meck, W. H., & Church, R. M. (1987). Separation of hippocampal and amygdaloid involvement in temporal memory dysfunctions. *Brain Research, 404,* 180–188.

Olton, D. S., & Pappas, B. C. (1979). Spatial memory and hippocampal system function. *Neuropsychologia, 17,* 669–681.

Otto, T., & Eichenbaum, H. (1992a). Complementary roles of the orbital prefrontal cortex and the perirhinal–entorhinal cortices in an odor-guided delayed-nonmatching-to-sample task. *Behavioral Neuroscience, 106,* 762–775.

Otto, T., & Eichenbaum, H. (1992b). Neuronal activity in the hippocampus during delayed nonmatch to sample performance in rats: Evidence for hippocampal processing in recognition memory. *Hippocampus, 2,* 323–334.

Packard, M. G., Cahill, L., & McGaugh, J. L. (1994). Amygdala modulation of hippocampal-dependent and caudate nucleus-dependent memory processes. *Proceedings of the National Academy of Sciences U.S.A., 91,* 8477–8481.

Packard, M. G., & White, N. M. (1990). Lesions of the caudate nucleus selectively impair "reference memory" acquisition in the radial maze. *Behavioral Neural Biology, 53,* 39–50.

Parkinson, J. K., Murray, E. A., & Mishkin, M. (1988). A selective mnemonic role for the hippocampus in monkeys: Memory for the location of objects. *Journal of Neuroscience, 8,* 4159–4167.

Partiot, A., Verin, M., Pillon, B., Teixeira-Ferreira, C., Agid, Y., & Dubois, B. (1996). Delayed response tasks in basal ganglia lesions in man: Further evidence for a striato-frontal cooperation in behavioural adaptation. *Neuropsychologia, 34,* 709–721.

Pasquier, F., Van Der Linden, M., Lefebvre, C., Bruyer, R., & Petit, H. (1994)., Motor memory and the preselection effect in Huntington's and Parkinson's disease. *Neuropsychologia, 32,* 951–968.

Passingham, R. (1978). Information about movements in monkeys (*Macaca mulatta*) with lesions of dorsal prefrontal cortex. *Brain Research, 152,* 313–328.

Petrides, M., & Iversen, S. D. (1979). Restricted posterior parietal lesions in the rhesus monkey and performance on visuo-spatial tasks. *Brain Research, 161,* 63–77.

Petrides, M., & Milner, B. (1982). Deficits on subject-ordered tasks after frontal- and temporal-lobe lesions in man. *Neuropsychologia, 20,* 249–262.

Phillips, A. G., & Carr, G. D. (1987). Cognition and the basal ganglia: A possible substrate for procedural knowledge. *Canadian Journal of Neurology and Science, 14,* 381–385.

Phillips, R. G., & LeDoux, J. E. (1992). Differential contribution of amygdala and hippocampus to cued and contextual fear conditioning. *Behavioral Neuroscience, 106,* 274–285.

Picard, N., & Strick, P. L. (1996). Motor areas of the medial wall: A review of their location and functional activation. *Cerebral Cortex, 6,* 342–353.

Pigott, S., & Milner, B. (1993). Memory for different aspects of complex visual scenes after unilateral temporal- or frontal-lobe resection. *Neuropsychologia, 31,* 1–15.

Pohl, W. (1973). Dissociation of spatial discrimination deficits following frontal and parietal lesions in monkeys. *Journal of Comparative and Physiological Psychology, 82,* 227–239.

Powell, D. A., Mankowski, D., & Buchanan, S. L. (1978). Concomitant heart rate and corneoretinal potential conditioning in the rabbit (*Oryctolagus cuniculus*): Effects of caudate lesions. *Physiology & Behavior, 20,* 143–150.

Quirk, G. J., Muller, R. U., Kubie, J. L., and Ranck, J. B., Jr. (1992). The positional firing properties of medial entorhinal neurons: Description and comparison with hippocampal place cells. *Journal of Neuroscience, 12,* 1945–1963.

Rafal, R., & Roberston, L. (1995). The neurology of visual attention. In M. Gazzaniga (Ed.), *The cognitive neurosciences* (pp. 625–648). Cambridge, MA: MIT Press.

Raffaele, K. C., & Olton, D. S. (1988). Hippocampal and amygdaloid involvement in working memory for nonspatial stimuli. *Behavioral Neuroscience, 102,* 349–355.

Ragozzino, M. E., & Kesner, R. P. (1996). Learning and memory for taste information: Role of the agranular insular cortex. *Society for Neuroscience Abstracts, 22,* 1868.

Ravindranathan, A., Jackson-Smith, P., & Kesner, R. P. (1992). Effects of perirhinal cortex and medial extrastriate visual cortex lesions on memory associated with an object continuous recognition task. *Society for Neuroscience Abstracts, 18,* 1058.

Reading, P. J., Dunnett, S. B., & Robbins, T. W. (1991). Dissociable roles of the ventral, medial and lateral striatum on the acquisition and performance of a complex visual stimulus–response habit. *Behavioural Brain Research, 45,* 147–161.

Roland, P. E. (1985). Cortical organization of voluntary behavior in man. *Human Neurobiology, 4,* 155–167.

Rolls, E. (1989). Functions of neuronal networks in the hippocampus and neocortex in memory. In J. H. Byrne & W. O. Berry (Eds.), *Neural models of plasticity: Theoretical and empirical approaches.* New York: Academic Press.

Rolls, E. T., Miyashita, Y., Cahusac, P. M. B., Kesner, R. P., Niki, H., Feigenbaum, J., & Bach, L. (1989). Hippocampal neurons in the monkey with activity related to the place in which a stimulus is shown. *Journal of Neuroscience, 9,* 1835–1844.

Rosenkilde, C. E. (1979). Functional heterogeneity of the prefrontal cortex in the monkey: A review. *Behavioral Neural Biology, 25,* 301–345.

Sakai, K., & Miyashita, Y. (1991). Neural organization for the long-term memory of paired associates. *Nature, 354,* 152–155.

Sanberg, P. R., Lehmann, J., & Fibiger, H. C. (1978). Impaired learning and memory after kainic acid lesions of the striatum: A behavioral model of Huntington's disease. *Brain Research, 149,* 546–551.

Schacter, D. L. (1987). Implicit memory: History and current status. *Journal of Experimental Psychology: Learning, Memory, and Cognitition, 13,* 501–518.

Schacter, D. L., Alpert, N. M., Savage, C. R., Rauch, S. L., & Albert, M. S. (1996). Conscious recollection and the human hippocampal formation: Evidence from positron emission tomography. *Proceedings of the National Academy of Sciences U.S.A., 93,* 321–325.

Schacter, D. L., & Tulving, E. (1994). *Memory systems 1994.* Cambridge, MA: MIT Press.

Schwartzbaum, J. S., & Donovick, P. J. (1968). Discrimination reversal and spatial alternation associated with septal and caudate dysfunction in rats. *Journal of Comparative Physiological Psychology, 65,* 83–92.

Semmes, J., Weinstein, S., Ghent, L., & Teuber, H. L. (1963). Correlates of impaired orientation in personal and extrapersonal space. *Brain, 86,* 747–772.

Shallice, T. (1982). Specific impairments of planning. *Philosophical Transactions of the Royal Society of London, B, 298,* 199–209.

Shapiro, M. L., & Olton, D. S. (1994). Hippocampal function and interference. In D. L. Schacter & E. Tulving (Eds.), *Memory systems 1994* (pp. 87–117). Cambridge, MA: MIT Press.

Shimamura, A. P. (1986). Priming effects in amnesia: Evidence for a dissociable memory function. *The Quarterly Journal of Experimental Psychology, 38A,* 619–644.

Slotnick, B. M. (1967). Disturbances of maternal behavior in the rat following lesions of the cingulate cortex. *Behavior, 29,* 204–236.

Smith, M. L., & Milner, B. (1981). The role of the right hippocampus in the recall of spatial location. *Neuropsychologia, 19,* 781–793.

Solomon, P. R., & Vander Schaaf, E. R. (1986). Hippocampus and trace conditioning of the rabbit's classically conditioned nictitating membrane response. *Behavioral Neuroscience, 100,* 729–744.

Squire, L. R. (1983). The hippocampus and the neuropsychology of memory. In W. Seifert (Ed.), *Neurobiology of the hippocampus.* New York: Academic Press.

Squire, L. R. (1992). Memory and the hippocampus: A synthesis from findings with rats, monkeys, and humans. *Psychological Review, 99,* 195–231.

Squire, L. R. (1994). Declarative and nondeclarative memory: Multiple brain systems supporting learning and memory. In D. L. Schacter & E. Tulving (Eds.), *Memory systems 1994* (pp. 203–231). Cambridge, MA: MIT Press.

Squire, L. R. (1995). Biological foundation of accuracy and inaccuracy in memory. In D. L. Schacter (Ed.), *Memory distortion* (pp. 197–225). Cambridge, MA: Harvard University Press.

Stamm, J. S. (1955). The function of the median cerebral cortex in maternal behavior in rats. *Journal of Comparative Physiological Psychology, 48,* 347–356.

Sutherland, R. J., & McDonald, R. J. (1990). Hippocampus, amygdala, and memory deficits in rats. *Behavioural Brain Research, 37,* 57–79.

Sutherland, R. J., Whishaw, I. Q., & Kolb, B. (1988). Contributions of cingulate cortex to two forms of spatial learning and memory. *Journal of Neuroscience, 8,* 1863–1872.

Suzuki, W. A., Zola-Morgan, S., Squire, L. R., & Amaral, D. G. (1993). Lesions of the perirhinal and parahippocampal cortices in the monkey produce long-lasting memory impairment in the visual and tactual modalities. *Journal of Neuroscience, 13,* 2430–2451.

Taube, J. S., Goodridge, J. P., Golob, E. J., Dudchenko, P. A., & Stackman, R. W. (1996). Processing the head direction cell signal: A review and commentary. *Brain Research Bulletin, 40,* 447–486.

Thomas, R. K., & Weir, V. K. (1975). The effects of lesions in the frontal or posterior association cortex of rats on Lashley III maze. *Physiological Psychology, 3,* 210–214.

Thompson, R. F. (1986). The neurobiology of learning and memory. *Science, 233,* 941–947.

Thorpe, S. J., Rolls, E. T., & Maddison, S. (1983). The orbitofrontal cortex: Neuronal activity in the behaving monkey. *Experimental Brain Research, 49,* 93–115.

Todd, J. W., & Kesner, R. P. (1978). Effects of posttraining injection of cholinergic agonists and antagonists into the amygdala on retention of passive avoidance training in rats. *Journal of Comparative Physiological Psychology, 92,* 958–968.

Tulving, E. (1983). *Elements of episodic memory.* Oxford: Clarendon Press.

Tulving, E., Kapur, S., Markowitsch, H. J., Craik, F. I. M., Habib, R., & Houle, S. (1994). Hemispheric encoding/retrieval asymmetry in episodic memory: Positron emission tomography findings. *Proceedings of the National Academy of Sciences U.S.A., 91,* 2012–2015.

Ungerleider, L. G. (1995). Functional brain imaging studies of cortical mechanisms of memory. *Science, 270,* 769–775.

Vanderwolf, C. H., Bland, B. H., & Whishaw, I. Q. (1973). Diencephalic, hippocampal and neocortical mechanisms in voluntary movement. In J. D. Maser (Ed.), *Efferent organization and the integration of behavior* (pp. 229–263). New York: Academic Press.

Walker, J. A., & Olton, D. S. (1984). Fimbria-fornix lesions impair spatial working memory but not cognitive mapping. *Behavioral Neuroscience, 98,* 226–242.

Wang, J., Aigner, T., & Mishkin, M. (1990). Effects of neostriatal lesions on visual habit formation in rhesus monkeys. *Society for Neuroscience Abstracts, 16,* 617.

Ward, N. M., & Brown, V. J. (1996). Covert orienting of attention in the rat and the role of striatal dopamine. *Journal of Neuroscience, 16,* 3082–3088.

Weisend, M. P., Astur, R. S., & Sutherland, R. J. (1996). The specificity and temporal characteristics of retrograde amnesia after hippocampal lesions. *Society for Neuroscience Abstracts, 22,* 1118.

Weiskrantz, L. (1956). Behavioral changes with ablation of the amygdaloid complex in monkeys. *Journal of Comparative Physiological Psychology, 49,* 381–391.

Weiskrantz, L., & Saunders, C. (1984). Impairments of visual object transforms in monkeys. *Brain, 107,* 1033–1072.

Whishaw, I. Q., Mittleman, G., Bunch, S. T., & Dunnett, S. B. (1987). Impairments in the acquisition, retention and selection of spatial navigation strategies after medial caudate-putamen lesions in rats. *Behavioural Brain Research, 24,* 125–138.

Young, B. J., Otto, T., Fox, G. D., & Eichenbaum, H. (1995). Neuronal activity in the parahippocampal region of rats performing a delayed non-matching to sample task. *Society for Neuroscience Abstracts, 21*, 943.

Zajonc, R. B. (1968). Attitudinal effects of mere exposure. *Journal of Personality and Social Psychology, 9*, 1–27.

Zhu, X. O., Brown, M. W., & Aggleton, J. P. (1995). Neuronal signalling of information important to visual recognition memory in rat rhinal and neighbouring cortices. *European Journal of Neuroscience, 7*, 753–765.

Zola-Morgan, S., & Squire, L. R. (1990). The primate hippocampal formation: Evidence for a time-limited role in memory storage. *Science, 25*, 288–290.

CHAPTER 11

Psychobiological Models of Hippocampal Function in Learning and Memory[1]

Mark A. Gluck and Catherine E. Myers

Center for Molecular and Behavioral Neuroscience, Rutgers University, Newark, New Jersey 07102

I. INTRODUCTION

Many models and theories have been proposed over the past few decades that attempt to characterize the role of the hippocampal region in learning and memory. Most of these theories are qualitative, consisting of a central concept or metaphor that attempts to capture the essence of hippocampal-region function. We focus here on more formal computational network models of hippocampal function in learning and memory. Such models have an advantage in that they can be rigorously tested with computer simulations and, occasionally, formal mathematical analysis.

Given the breadth and diversity of current hippocampal models, we concentrate on just that subset of hippocampal theories that make strongest contact with psychological issues and data from behavioral studies of learning and memory. Given this psychobiological perspective, we omit more physiological models that make less contact with behavioral aspects of learning and memory. Among the theories that do address observable memory behaviors, we emphasize those that relate most strongly to traditional theories and models within the literature.

Our purpose in the first part of the review is to provide a general understanding of the aims, successes, and limitations of the computational approach to

[1] This chapter reproduced with permission from the Annual Review of Psychology, Volume 48 © 1997 by Annual Reviews.

understanding hippocampal function in learning and memory behavior. The emphasis is on describing the spirit and behavior of the models rather than on their exact mathematical underpinnings. A few mathematical equations are given where critical to this description. For a full exposition on implementation details, see the original journal articles.

The remainder of the review is organized as follows. We present a brief summary of the major points of hippocampal anatomy and a review of the empirical data on memory deficits produced by hippocampal damage in animals and human beings. We then provide some important historical background, discussing David Marr's early theories of the hippocampus as an autoassociative memory storage device. In the section entitled "Autoassociative Models of CA3 and Episodic Memory" we show how Marr's earlier theories have influenced current computational models of hippocampal region CA3 and its role in episodic memory. Next we turn to more incremental forms of associative learning, reviewing models of conditioning and hippocampus. The next two sections illustrate how some of these models, at different levels of analysis, are beginning to converge into integrated theories incorporating a wider range of behavioral and biological detail.

II. THE HIPPOCAMPAL REGION IS CRITICAL FOR LEARNING AND MEMORY

The hippocampal region (Fig. 1) consists of a group of brain structures located deep inside the brain that form part of what (in human beings) is often called the *medial-temporal lobe*. The region includes the *hippocampus* and the nearby *dentate gyrus, subiculum,* and *entorhinal cortex*. The outermost of these structures—the entorhinal cortex—receives highly processed information from the entire spectrum of sensory modalities as well as from multimodal association areas. Information flows in a roughly unidirectional fashion from the entorhinal cortex to the dentate gyrus, to the hippocampus, to the subiculum, and back to the entorhinal cortex before returning to the same sensory areas where it originally arose. In addition to this basic pathway of information flow, there are many direct connections between the structures of the region. The hippocampus also has another input and output pathway through the *fornix,* a fiber bundle connecting it with subcortical structures that provide modulation.

A. Hippocampal Damage Produces Amnesia in Human Beings

Damage to the hippocampal region in human beings produces a characteristic *anterograde amnesia* syndrome, which strongly impairs the acquisition of new information (Squire, 1987). Human hippocampal damage can result from a variety

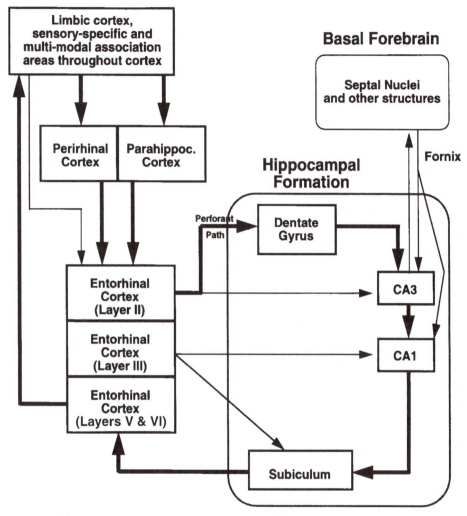

FIGURE 1   The structures of the hippocampal region. CA3, hippocampal field CA3; CA1, hippo-campal field CA1. [Adapted from Myers et al. (1996).]

of causes, including aneurysms to the arteries that vascularize the hippocampus, anoxia, and epileptic seizures (Zola-Morgan & Squire, 1993). The hippocampal region is also among the first structures to be damaged in the course of Alzheimer's disease and normal aging (de Leon et al., 1993). Damage to other related structures, such as the basal forebrain, can also cause amnesic syndromes that share features with hippocampal amnesia, presumably because such damage indirectly interferes with normal hippocampal-region processing (Volpe & Hirst, 1983).

The anterograde amnesia that follows human hippocampal-region damage is most saliently characterized by an inability to acquire new *episodic* information, the kind of information about individual events and experiences that is accessible to conscious control. Patients with this debilitation may also show some degree of retrograde amnesia—disruption of previously acquired information—but this is usually limited to information acquired shortly before the trauma and tends to lessen in a time-graded fashion for progressively older information (Squire, 1987). This relationship between hippocampal damage and anterograde amnesia led to the idea that the hippocampus is a specialized memory processor needed to lay down new episodic memories.

B. Hippocampal Damage Produces Varied Memory Deficits in Animals

Animal models of hippocampal amnesia have had an obvious difficulty in addressing this loss of episodic information in nonverbal subjects; animals are unable to tell the experimenter directly what they can remember. However, by using indirect memory tests in which the animal is challenged to use memory of specific events, hippocampal-region damage in animals has been shown to cause learning deficits broadly similar to the episodic memory loss in human hippocampal amnesics (Eichenbaum, 1992). Animal studies have also documented that certain kinds of learning capabilities do survive hippocampal-region damage. For example, the acquisition of learned responses in elementary associative conditioning tasks is largely unimpaired (Gabrieli et al., 1995). Human hippocampal amnesics show similar residual learning abilities in motor-reflex conditioning, cognitive skill learning, and simple categorization tasks (Cohen, 1984). All these tasks are learnable over many trials and do not require the formation of single episodic memories.

However, even the simple iterative tasks such as conditioning are disrupted in hippocampal-damaged animals if they involve additional complexities, such as requiring comparisons or configurations of multiple stimulus cues, or if attention to the experimental context is important (see section entitled "Stimulus Representation in Associative Learning"; Hirsh, 1974; Rudy & Sutherland, 1989, 1995).

III. MARR'S AUTOASSOCIATIVE MEMORY STORE

One of the earliest and most influential models of hippocampal-region processing was proposed by David Marr (1971). Starting with what was known then about hippocampal anatomy and physiology, Marr sought to infer an emergent information-processing capability. His ideas gave rise to a broad class of models, often termed *Hebb–Marr* models because they incorporate Hebb's (1949) ideas on how associa-

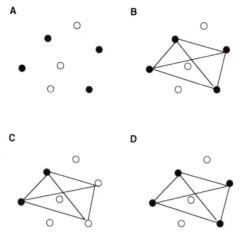

FIGURE 2   Storage of an event memory as a pattern of cell activations in the neocortex according to Marr's (1971) model. (A) Initially, the event memory simply evokes a pattern of activations (darkened circles) across a group of unrelated cells. (B) As the pattern is stored, various elements of the pattern are associated by weighted connections (lines). (C) Later, if a partial version of the original pattern is presented (darkened circles), activation spreads along the associations to activate the complete pattern (D).

tions are acquired between groups of cells in the brain (McNaughton & Nadel, 1990). Since Marr's original publication, new empirical data have shown that some aspects of his model are incomplete or incorrect (see, e.g., Willshaw & Buckingham, 1990). Nonetheless, many of the basic ideas in the Hebb–Marr model of the hippocampus have withstood continuing empirical and theoretical tests and remain the basis for many current models and theories. This section reviews a generalized version of the Hebb–Marr model. Later sections describe several more current models that build on Marr's original specification.

Marr's basic idea was to distinguish separable roles in memory for the archicortex, including the hippocampus, and for the neocortex. He assumed that the chief role of the neocortex was to store large complex *event memories*—broadly equivalent to what today are usually called *episodic memories*—composed of several integrated associations. For example, the event memory of a meal might include associations about the food eaten, the meal's location and time, and the company sharing it. In Marr's model, an event memory is defined as a pattern E of activities over a large number of neocortical cells, evoked by a particular set of sensory inputs (Fig. 2A). Such a pattern is stored by associating its elements so that activation of some of the cells representing elements in E can activate other elements in turn (Fig. 2B). Later, if a subset of E is presented to the neocortex (Fig. 2C), the neocortex should be able to retrieve the full pattern E (Fig. 2D). This ability is *pattern completion*. One difficulty in implementing this function in the neocortex is that a large number of very precise connections is required to associate each element in E

with every other element in E. Further, the associations required to store E may well disrupt preexisting associations created to store other patterns with common elements. Worse, if another stored pattern F shares common elements with E, then F may interfere with attempted retrieval of E: If a subset of E is presented, activation will spread to these common elements, which will then begin to retrieve F as well as E. At the extreme, if many overlapping patterns are stored, an attempt to retrieve any stored pattern will result in a pattern of activation that shares elements with all stored patterns but is identical to none. This situation is called *catastrophic interference* (Hetherington, 1990).

Because of this potential for interference in recall, Marr suggested that it would be useful to have a separate processor—such as the hippocampus—that could rapidly store event memories and then allow gradual transfer of this pattern to the neocortex, which would reorganize and classify this information, incorporating it with existing knowledge to reduce interference. More specifically, Marr proposed that the hippocampus is able to rapidly store new patterns, holding them in a temporary memory store, but is not able to integrate them with the larger body of existing knowledge.

Marr imagined the hippocampus as functionally consisting of two layers or groups of cells (Fig. 3A). Inputs cause activity on the first A layer of cells, which project onto the second B layer of cells. The B cells in turn project back to the A cells. All synapses between cells are modifiable, but they are simplified to allow only binary on or off values. Similarly, cell activity is assumed to be either on or off. This network is essentially the same as that shown in Fig. 2, except that cells are differentiated according to whether they directly receive external input (A cells) or not (B cells). A stored pattern can be retrieved if, when part is presented to the A cells, the evoked activity on the B cells feeds back to complete the original firing pattern on the A cells. As shown in the next section, Marr's pattern associator model forms the basis for many subsequent—and more detailed—models of hippocampal physiology and function.

IV. AUTOASSOCIATIVE MODELS OF CA3 AND EPISODIC MEMORY

The network described by Marr is a form of *autoassociator*. An autoassociator network learns to associate an input pattern with an identical output pattern (Anderson, 1977; Hinton, 1989; Kohonen, 1984). A general form of autoassociator is shown in Fig. 3B and consists of a single layer of nodes receiving excitatory connections from external sources as well as from each other. Nodes are assumed to have binary states: either active or firing (represented by an output value of 1) or quiescent (represented by an output value of 0). Node j becomes active if the sum of inputs exceeds some firing threshold (cf. Grossberg, 1976; Kohonen, 1984; McCulloch & Pitts, 1943; Rosenblatt, 1962):

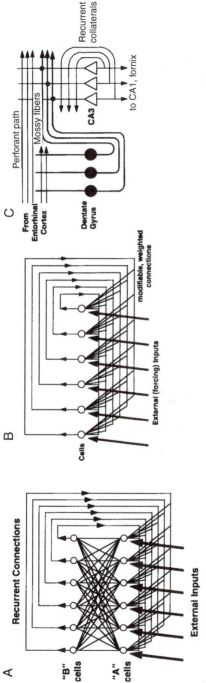

FIGURE 3 (A) Simplified schematic of Marr's (1971) model of the hippocampus. Cells are either A cells, which receive direct activation from the external input (heavy lines), or B cells, which are driven only by A cells and afferent them in turn. Learning consists of strengthening connections between B cells and the A cells that activate them. Later, if a partial version of a stored pattern is presented to the A cells, the B cells feed back and activate the remaining A cells required to complete the stored pattern. (B) A generalized form of an autoassociative network. There is a single layer of cells with outputs that ramify to provide feedback input to the cell layer. These synapses are weighted, and cells become active if the total weighted synaptic input exceeds a threshold (Eq. 1). Patterns are stored by presenting external (forcing) input to the cells; learning then consists of weighting the synapses between all pairs of coactive cells (Eq. 2). Later, if a partial version of a stored pattern is presented on the external inputs, activity spreads iteratively through the recurrent feedback connections, which activates additional cells until the entire pattern is reconstructed. (C) A schematic representation of information flow in hippocampal field CA3. Inputs to the pyramidal cells arrive directly from the entorhinal cortex as well as indirectly via the mossy fibers from the dentate gyrus. The mossy fiber afferents make sparse, presumably strong, synapses onto CA3 dendrites, and so they are putative forcing inputs to the network. CA3 pyramidal cell outputs ramify to become feedback afferents to CA3 and also exit to hippocampal field CA1 and through the fornix to other, extrahippocampal targets.

$$y_j = 1 \quad \text{if} \quad \sum_i w_{ij} y_j > \theta_j, \quad \text{else } 0. \tag{1}$$

In Eq. 1, y_j is the output or activation of cell j, w_{ij} is the weight of the synapse on j from another cell i, and θ_j is cell j's threshold. This threshold, θ_j, is then set so that j will become active if the weighted sum of its inputs exceeds some proportion of the total inputs active in the original pattern. Additional inhibitory processes, not shown in Fig. 3B, may be required to determine the threshold. More complex networks may also allow continuous (real-valued) inputs and outputs, but the central ideas are the same.

A binary pattern E is stored in this network by presenting E as an external input. The nth element of E is presented to the nth node in the network and forces that node to output the same value as that element. For this reason, the external inputs are often termed *forcing inputs,* and the one synapse each node receives from the forcing input is often called a *forcing synapse.* The network then undergoes synaptic plasticity at the feedback connections, so that synapses from active presynaptic cells have excitatory effects on other active postsynaptic cells. This can be accomplished by a Hebbian learning rule of the form

$$w_{ij} = \alpha \left(y_i y_j \right), \tag{2}$$

where y_i and y_j are the activities of presynaptic cell i and postsynaptic cell j, α is a constant term, and w_{ij} is the weight of the synapse between i and j. Note that synaptic mechanisms of long-term potentiation and depression (LTP and LTD) are Hebbian in nature (Levy, Brassel, & Moore, 1983; McNaughton & Morris, 1987). Later, if some subset of E is presented to the network, activity in the recurrent collaterals will iterate through the network and activate the cells needed to complete the missing parts of E. Thus, this network performs pattern completion.

A. Three Common Features of Autoassociators and Field CA3

Marr's important contribution was to conceptualize the hippocampus as an auto-associator network that performs pattern storage and retrieval. Many subsequent models have elaborated on this idea (Hasselmo, 1995; Hasselmo, Wyble, & Wallenstein, 1996; McNaughton & Morris, 1987; McNaughton & Nadel, 1990; Rolls, 1989; Treves & Rolls, 1992). An autoassociator such as the one shown in Fig. 3b has three basic requirements: (a) a high degree of internal recurrency among the principal cells; (b) strong, sparse synapses from external afferents, which could function as forcing synapses; and (c) plasticity at the synapses between coactive cells.

These requirements suffice to allow the functions of pattern storage, completion, and retrieval. Hippocampal field CA3 satisfies all three requirements (Fig. 3C). First, the principal neurons of CA3—pyramidal cells—are perhaps unique in the brain for their high degree of internal recurrency: Each CA3 pyramidal may receive contact from about 4% of other pyramidals in the field, a high enough contact probability to allow autoassociation (Rolls, 1989). Second, in addition to recurrent collaterals and sparse entorhinal afferents, CA3 pyramidals receive a small number of inputs from mossy fibers, containing entorhinal information that reaches CA3 via the dentate gyrus. While each CA3 pyramidal in the rat may receive 12,000 synapses from recurrent collaterals and 4000 synapses from direct entorhinal afferents, it may only receive about 50 mossy fiber synapses (Treves & Rolls, 1992). However, the mossy fiber synapses are very large and presumably also very strong, so that coincident activity on a relatively small number of mossy fiber synapses could activate a CA3 pyramidal (Rolls, 1989). The mossy fiber synapses are thus good candidates for forcing synapses in an autoassociator (Marr, 1971; McNaughton, 1991; McNaughton & Morris, 1987). Third, plasticity in the form of LTP has been demonstrated at the synapses of recurrent collaterals in CA3 (Bliss & Lomo, 1973; Kelso, Ganong, & Brown, 1986). LTP involves strengthening of synapses between coactive pre- and postsynaptic cells; this could implement Hebbian learning as defined in Eq. 2.

In summary, CA3 seems to be a likely candidate to implement autoassociative memory in the brain. Patterns would be stored by presentation over the mossy fibers, which would force CA3 pyramidal output. Recurrent collateral synapses between coactive pyramidals would then undergo LTP to store the pattern. Later, if a partial version of that pattern is presented along the weaker entorhinal afferents, some CA3 pyramidals would become active. After several iterations of activity through the recurrent collaterals, more CA3 pyramidals would be activated until the entire stored pattern is retrieved. Additional inhibitory units are also generally assumed to allow implementation of the firing thresholds.

B. Autoassociative Networks Implement Hippocampal-Dependent Memory Behaviors

This type of autoassociative network can be used to implement various forms of memory, many of which are much like those that appear to be impaired following hippocampal damage in animals and human beings. For example, autoassociative memories can create unified memories from several component features and then retrieve the entire memory from a partial input.

1. Sequence Learning

Many models of hippocampal function have drawn on the details of its anatomy and physiology to argue that it has the capacity for learning sequences of input patterns. These models are often generally based on the recurrent architectures of autoassociative networks: Given a partial input consisting of the present state, an autoassociative network can perform pattern completion and retrieve the predicted next state. Levy (1996) presented a model of hippocampal region CA3 as a sequence predictor and argued that this general sequence prediction paradigm can provide a computational unification of a variety of putative hippocampal-dependent functions, including contextual sensitivity, configuration, and cognitive mapping (see also Levy, Wu, & Baxter, 1995; Prepscius & Levy, 1994). Granger, Wiebe, Taketani, and Lynch (1996) presented a model of field CA1 incorporating an LTP learning rule in which the amount of potentiation depends on the order of arrival of afferent activity to a target neuron. They show that with this temporally dependent LTP learning, the CA1 network model can learn to store brief simulated temporal sequences of inputs. Liaw and Berger (1996) also described a model of hippocampal neurons in which they argued that the dynamic interplay of hippocampal synaptic mechanisms for facilitative and inhibitory processes results in an emergent "temporal chunking" mechanism for sequential pattern recognition. In this model, each dynamic synapse learns to respond to a small subpattern of inputs, and the postsynaptic neuron learns how to properly combine these subpatterns.

2. Spatial Memory and Navigation

This aspect of autoassociative memory systems seems ideal for implementing a spatial processor, in which the broad memory of a place should be evoked by any of several views of the area, even if some of the usual cues are missing. In fact, spatial memory is extremely hippocampal dependent in rats (e.g., O'Keefe & Nadel, 1978), and many connectionist models of hippocampal processing in spatial learning have been based on autoassociative models of the hippocampal region (Burgess, Recce, & O'Keefe, 1994; Levy, 1989; McNaughton & Morris, 1987; McNaughton & Nadel, 1990; Muller, Kubie, & Ranck, 1987; Muller & Stead, 1996; Recce & Harris, 1996; Sharp, 1991; Sharp, Blair, & Brown, 1996). One possibility is to define spatial maps as composed of sets of complex configural associations representing places (McNaughton, 1989; McNaughton & Nadel, 1990). In one place, there may be many views, depending on which way the animal is facing, the location of landmarks, etc. The hippocampal autoassociator would be able to map from one of these views to the full representation of the current place. With this interpretation, place learning need not be fundamentally different from any other kind of representational learning. However, because of the need for such complex representations in spatial tasks, these behaviors might be especially sensitive to hippocampal damage.

3. Episodic Memory and Consolidation

Perhaps most pervasive is the idea that the fast, temporary storage in an autoassociator is an important component of an episodic or declarative memory system, in which arbitrary patterns are stored (Alvarez & Squire, 1994; Hasselmo et al., 1996; McClelland & Goddard, 1996; Murre, 1996; O'Reilly & McClelland, 1994; Treves & Rolls, 1992). It is generally assumed in these models that a relatively small

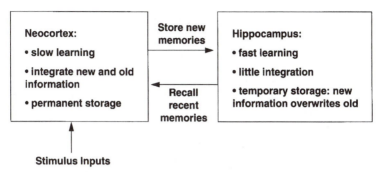

FIGURE 4   General format of many connectionist models of amnesia. The neocortex is assumed to be a large-capacity, permanent store for memory associations and to be able to integrate new information with old associations. However, learning is assumed to be slow and possibly require several iterated presentations. The hippocampus is assumed to be capable of storing memory within as little as a single exposure, but older memories are liable to be overwritten by newer ones. The hippocampus therefore captures episodic memories and iteratively allows the neocortex to integrate these memories with existing associations.

temporary store in the hippocampus interacts with a relatively large neocortical system (Fig. 4). Such an assumption was made by Marr (1971), and many connectionist models of amnesia center on similar assumptions (e.g., Alvarez & Squire, 1994; Lynch & Granger, 1992; McClelland, McNaughton, & O'Reilly, 1994; Murre, 1996; O'Reilly & McClelland, 1994; Treves & Rolls, 1992). Many preconnectionist models assume this general organization as well (e.g., Mishkin, 1982; Teyler & DiScenna, 1986; Wickelgren, 1979).

In these models, the central assumption is that a stimulus enters the neocortex via the sensory system and subsequently activates cells in the hippocampus. The hippocampus in turn feeds back to the neocortex and initiates activation patterns there. It may activate new cell populations, which are then added to the representation, or it may allow connections to form between active cells in the neocortex. The hippocampus may be required to present memories to the neocortex repeatedly, over some period, to allow the neocortex to integrate new knowledge without overwriting the old (McClelland et al., 1994). This process is termed memory *consolidation.* Over time, as this consolidation occurs, the sensory input is able to activate these cells directly, without hippocampal intervention. At this point, the hippocampus has completed its function of helping to bind together disparate cortical activities into a coherent pattern, and memories are safe from subsequent hippocampal damage. However, a more recent memory, which is not yet fully consolidated, may be disrupted. The probability of such disruption is higher for more recent memories, which have had less time to be consolidated, than older ones. This is consistent with data showing that while hippocampal damage leads to severe anterograde amnesia, there is only temporally gradated retrograde amnesia

(Squire & Alvarez, 1995). This inverse relationship between memory age and hippocampal independence is known as the *Ribot gradient* of retrograde amnesia (Ribot, 1882; see also Alvarez & Squire, 1994). Examples from animal and human experiments are shown in Figs. 5A and 5B (Kim & Fanselow, 1992; Squire & Cohen, 1979).

Note that a model consisting of an autoassociator alone would predict the opposite effect: namely, that older memories would be increasingly susceptible to interference from newer memories. The addition of a "remote" neocortical storage site allows the models of hippocampal–cortical interaction to account for both the anterograde and retrograde aspects of hippocampal amnesia. Further elaborations may be assumed on this general model scheme, such as nonspecific modulatory influences that determine the storage rates in CA3 (Grossberg, 1976; Hasselmo, Schnell, & Barkai, 1995; Murre, 1996; Treves & Rolls, 1992) or additional preprocessing in the dentate gyrus and postprocessing in CA1 (Hasselmo & Schnell, 1994; Levy, 1989; McNaughton, 1991; Treves & Rolls, 1992).

C. Open Issue: How and When Does Consolidation Take Place?

A major challenge confronting these models of anterograde amnesia is to specify in detail just how consolidation of memories from the hippocampus to neocortex might take place. One small-scale implementation is provided by Alvarez and Squire (1994), who suggested that most memory consolidation may occur during sleep (see also Buzsaki, 1989; Crick & Mitchison, 1983; McClelland et al., 1994). This is consistent with recent data showing that hippocampal activity during slow-wave sleep echoes specific patterns recorded earlier while the animal was exploring its environment (Wilson & McNaughton, 1994). Alvarez and Squire suggested that this activity reflects a process during which the hippocampus reinstates patterns it stored earlier and presents them to the neocortex for consolidation. The electrical activity in the hippocampus is markedly different during waking exploration and slow-wave sleep, which further suggests that the hippocampus is operating in two different modes (information storage and information reinstatement) during these two behavioral states (Buzsaki, 1989). Other possible mechanisms of consolidation may include conscious and unconscious rehearsal (Murre, 1996). All these hypotheses await thorough verification through combined neurophysiological and neuropsychological studies.

D. Open Issue: The Problem of Interference in Memory Networks

Another issue concerns the problem of interference. One constraint on the utility of an autoassociative network is that it has very limited capacity. A network of *n*

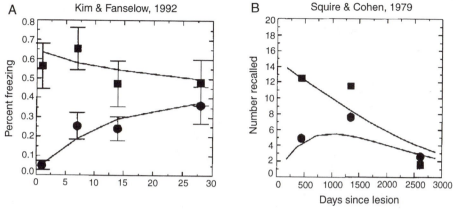

FIGURE 5   Examples of Ribot gradients, which illustrate how older memories are less likely to be disrupted by hippocampal damage than are newer memories. (A) Ribot gradient in animal data. Behavioral responses of animals receiving extensive hippocampal system lesions (circles) or control lesions (squares) as a function of the number of days elapsing between exposure to the relevant experiences and the occurrence of the lesion. Fear response (freezing) behavior shown by rats when returned to an environment in which they had experienced paired presentations of tones with footshock. Bars surrounding each data point indicate the standard error (from Kim & Fanselow, 1992). (B) Ribot gradient in human data. Recall by depressed human subjects of details of television shows aired different numbers of years before the time of test, after electroconvulsive treatment (circles) or just before treatment (squares) (from Squire & Cohen, 1979).

nodes is able to store only about $0.15n$ random patterns before they begin to interfere with one another (Hopfield, 1982). Interference refers to the likelihood that patterns overlap sufficiently such that retrieval of one will activate retrieval of part or all of additional patterns, and the resulting network output will contain elements of multiple stored patterns. In the extreme, in a net that is filled to capacity, addition of a single new pattern can disrupt the ability to correctly retrieve any previously stored pattern. As described earlier, this phenomenon is called catastrophic interference (Hetherington, 1990), and it is a general feature of all connectionist networks that perform fast storage, as the hippocampal autoassociative network is assumed to do (McClelland et al., 1994). One way to increase capacity and avoid catastrophic interference is to explicitly decrease the overlap between patterns. It has been suggested that this is one effect of the sparse connections from the dentate gyrus to CA3: Since any one mossy fiber contacts only about 14 of the 3×10^5 CA3 cells in the rat, there is very little probability that two patterns of mossy fiber activity will activate the same pattern of CA3 activity (Rolls, 1989). In addition, plasticity in the dentate gyrus may further help to sparsify CA3 inputs (Hasselmo, 1995; O'Reilly & McClelland, 1994; Treves & Rolls, 1992). Even with such *pattern separation*, a pattern stored in the hippocampus will only remain intact for a limited period before it is overwritten by storage of newer memories. This implies that memories stored in the hippocampus must be transferred elsewhere to survive for long periods.

V. STIMULUS REPRESENTATION IN ASSOCIATIVE LEARNING

The foregoing models focus on the ability of the hippocampal region to perform fast, temporary storage, and they suggest that this underlies the hippocampal region's role in episodic memory formation. This is consistent with the basic idea that episodic memory impairments are the most obvious behavioral effects in human amnesia following hippocampal-region damage. Nondeclarative learning (including procedural or implicit learning) often survives such damage. For example, animals with hippocampal-region damage can often show normal acquisition of classically conditioned responding (e.g., Solomon & Moore, 1975) or discrimination of successively presented odors (Eichenbaum, Fagan, Matthews, & Cohen, 1988). Similarly, human hippocampal-damaged amnesics are not impaired at acquiring conditioned motor reflex responses (Daum, Channon, & Canavan, 1989; Gabrieli et al., 1995; Woodruff-Pak, 1993), learning simple classification tasks (Knowlton, Squire, & Gluck, 1994), or learning new motor skills such as mirror drawing (Cohen, 1984). All these tasks can be solved by incremental formation of habits or tendencies, without requiring episodic memories of any individual learning session.

However, there are other tasks that seem superficially to be just as nondeclarative but that are impaired after hippocampal-region damage. For example, although the simplest acquisition of a classically conditioned response is not impaired by hippocampal-region damage, there may be severe impairments in classical conditioning tasks that require learning about unreinforced stimuli (Kaye & Pearce, 1987; Solomon & Moore, 1975), configurations of stimuli (Rudy & Sutherland, 1989), contextual information (Hirsh, 1974), or relationships that span short delays (Moyer, Deyo, & Disterhoft, 1990; Port, Romano, & Patterson, 1986). These findings imply that the hippocampal region does participate in information processing during procedural tasks, although this participation may not necessarily be evident in the simplest kinds of learning. These findings also indicate that a conception of the hippocampal region as a purely passive store for episodic memories is insufficient.

Several recent qualitative theories and computational models have focused on possible information-processing roles for the hippocampal region, especially in incrementally acquired (nondeclarative) learning (e.g., Eichenbaum, Cohen, Otto, & Wible, 1992; Gluck & Myers, 1993, 1995; Hirsh, 1974; Moore & Stickney, 1980; Myers, Gluck, & Granger, 1995; Myers et al., 1996; Schmajuk & DiCarlo, 1992; Sutherland & Rudy, 1989). In turn, these models are less concerned with the issues that motivate the above-described models of consolidation. A full account of hippocampal-region function would, of course, address its role in both information processing and the consolidation of declarative memories.

Most of these associative theories of incremental learning assume that whereas the hippocampus is required for some complicated forms of stimulus association, the neocortex is sufficient for simpler stimulus–response associations such as those that underlie classical conditioning (e.g., Gluck & Myers, 1993; Myers et al., 1995; Schmajuk & DiCarlo, 1990, 1992). Here we focus on one representative computational model, which incorporates some of the earlier ideas regarding hippocampal autoassociation (Gluck & Myers, 1993).

A. Hippocampal Function and Stimulus Representations

Gluck and Myers (1993) presented a computational theory of hippocampal-region function in associative learning, which argued that the hippocampal region is critical during learning for recoding neural representation to reflect environmental regularities. Central to this theory is the definition of a stimulus representation as a pattern of activities over a set of elements (neuron groups in a brain or nodes in a connectionist network) evoked by the stimulus. Learning to make a response to that stimulus involves mapping from that representation to appropriate behavioral outputs. Learning about one stimulus will transfer—or generalize—to other stimuli as a function of how similar their representations are. Therefore, the particular representations can have a great impact on how hard a task is to learn.

The key idea of Gluck and Myers' (1993) corticohippocampal model is that the hippocampal region is able to facilitate learning by adapting representations in two ways. First, it is assumed to compress, or make more similar, representations of stimuli that co-occur; second, it is assumed to differentiate, or make less similar, representations of stimuli that are to be mapped to different responses. This kind of function can be implemented in a connectionist model that is related to the autoassociators described earlier but that includes a middle (often termed hidden) layer of nodes. Such a network, termed an autoencoder (Hinton, 1989), is shown on the left in Fig. 6. It maps input activations representing stimulus inputs through weighted connections to activate the middle layer of nodes that in turn feed through weighted connections to activate the output layer of nodes. The network is trained to produce outputs that reconstruct the inputs as well as predict the behavioral response. Because the autoencoder has a narrow hidden layer of nodes, this task can only be accomplished by compressing redundant information, while preserving and differentiating enough predictive information to allow reconstruction at the output layer. Although the details of the model are not biologically realistic (especially the use of backpropagation error correction for updating the autoencoder weights), the model nevertheless is a useful tool for exploring the kinds of representations that might evolve under the constraints of the two biases described (for a more biological

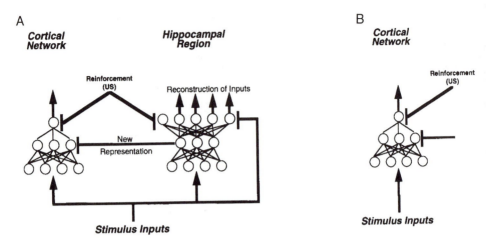

FIGURE 6   The corticohippocampal model (Gluck & Myers, 1993). (A) The intact system is assumed to include a predictive autoencoder, representing hippocampal-region processing that constructs
new stimulus representations in its internal layer that are biased to compress redundancies while differentiating predictive information. These stimulus representations are acquired by long-term storage sites
in the cortex, represented as a multilayer network that learns to predict US arrival. The cortical network
uses the Rescorla–Wagner rule to map from inputs to the hippocampal-mediated internal representations
and again to map from the internal layer to output activations. (B) Hippocampal-region lesion is assumed
to disable the hippocampal network, in which case the cortical network can no longer acquire new
internal representations but can acquire new behavioral responses based on its preexisting (and now
fixed) internal representations. [Reprinted from Gluck and Myers (1993).]

instantiation of these same ideas, see section entitled "Dissociating Parahippocampal
and Hippocampal Contributions" and Myers et al. (1995).

This network is incorporated into the full corticohippocampal model shown in
Fig. 6 (Gluck & Myers, 1993). A cortical network is shown on the left, which is
assumed to map from stimulus inputs to outputs that determine the behavioral
response. However, this network is assumed to be unable to construct hidden layer
representations on its own. Instead, it can adopt those representations formed in the
hidden layer of the hippocampal-region network. It can then learn to map from
these to the correct responses. Hippocampal lesion is simulated in this model by
disabling the hippocampal network and assuming that the hidden layer representations in the cortical network are now fixed. Those already acquired are maintained,
so little retrograde amnesia is expected after hippocampal-region damage (although
the model does not rule out the idea of an indefinitely long consolidation period
during which information is transferred, as suggested by the models of McClelland,
Murre, and others reviewed earlier). Further, the cortical network can still learn to
map from the existing representations to new behavioral responses. All that is lost is
the hippocampal-dependent ability to modify those representations.

B. Application to Behavioral Data

Gluck and Myers' (1993) model can be applied to classical conditioning by assuming that the inputs are conditioned stimuli and that the output is a conditioned response that is expected to anticipate the reinforcing unconditioned stimulus. The model then captures many aspects of the behavior of intact and hippocampal-region-damaged animals (Gluck & Myers, 1993, 1996; Myers & Gluck, 1994, 1996). For example, the model correctly expects that hippocampal-region damage causes no particular impairment—or even a slight facilitation—in learning a conditioned response. For such a simple task, new adaptive representations are probably not needed, and even the lesioned model can learn to map from its existing representations to the correct response. In fact, because the intact model is slowed by constructing new representations, it may often be slower than the lesioned model. This is consistent with similar effects often seen in animals (e.g., Eichenbaum et al., 1988; Schmaltz & Theos, 1972).

However, latent inhibition—the slower learning after unreinforced exposure to the to-be-conditioned stimulus (Lubow, 1973)—is disrupted by broad hippocampal-region damage (Fig. 7A) (Kaye & Pearce, 1987; Solomon & Moore, 1975). The model correctly shows these effects (Myers & Gluck, 1994). During the exposure phase, the stimulus is partially redundant with the background context. Neither predicts any reinforcing event, so the hippocampal-region network compresses their representations. Later, when the task is to respond to the stimulus but not the context alone, this compression must be undone, which results in slowed learning in the intact model (Fig. 7B). In contrast, the lesioned model has no compression during the exposure phase, so learning is not retarded in the subsequent learning phase (Fig. 7B).

Many of the learning deficits associated with hippocampal damage can be described as context effects (Hirsch, 1974). For example, human hippocampal-damaged amnesics may be able to remember an experience but not where or when that information was acquired—and they may even be unaware they know the information itself until indirectly prompted for it (Haist, Musen, & Squire, 1991; Weiskrantz & Warrington, 1979). Animals show related effects. For example, under some conditions, an animal trained to respond to a stimulus in one environment gives a decremented response when that stimulus is presented in another environment (Fig. 7C) (Hall & Honey, 1989). A hippocampal-lesioned animal does not show this decrement but responds just as strongly in the new environment (Honey & Good, 1993; Penick & Solomon, 1991). The corticohippocampal model implies a similar effect (Fig. 7D) (Myers & Gluck, 1994) because the hippocampal-region autoencoder is assumed to reconstruct not only the conditioned stimuli but also any background or context cues that are present during learning. Thus, as the autoencoder learns to represent a conditioned stimulus, information about the context is included in that representation. As a result, if the stimulus is presented in a new

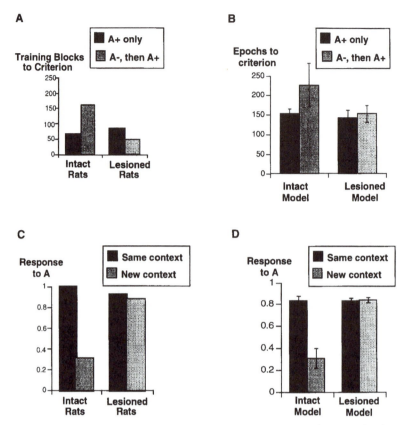

FIGURE 7   Behavioral results from intact and hippocampal-lesioned animals compared with simulation results from the intact and lesioned corticohippocampal models. (A) Latent inhibition. In intact animals, unreinforced preexposure to a cue A slows later acquisition of conditioned responding to A (Lubow, 1973). This is reflected in longer training times until criterion is reached on responding to A. Broad hippocampal-region lesion eliminates this effect (Kaye & Pearce, 1987; Solomon & Moore, 1975). [Figure plotted from data presented in Solomon and Moore (1975).] (B) The intact model correctly shows latent inhibition, whereas the lesioned model does not. [Figure reprinted from Myers et al. (1995).] (C) In normal animals, a conditioned response to A may show a decrement if A is then presented in a new context (Hall & Honey, 1989). Hippocampal-lesioned animals do not show this response decrement after a context shift (Honey & Good, 1993; Penick & Solomon, 1991). [Figure replotted from data presented in Penick and Solomon (1991).] (D) The intact but not lesioned model correctly shows this response decrement with context shift (Myers & Gluck, 1994). [Figure reprinted from Myers et al. (1995).]

context, the representation of that stimulus will be less weakly activated than usual, and in turn the conditioned response will be decremented, just as observed in intact animals. In contrast, the lesioned model does not form new, compressed representations, and so responding does not drop in a new context.

In the same way that the corticohippocampal model can account for latent inhibition and context shift phenomena, it can similarly address results from a range of conditioning studies (Gluck & Myers, 1993, 1996; Myers & Gluck, 1994, 1996). It provides a computational instantiation of several prior qualitative theories that posited hippocampal-region roles in context learning (Hirsh, 1974), configural learning (Sutherland & Rudy, 1989), and representational learning (Eichenbaum & Bunsey, 1995).

C. Open Issues and Alternative Approaches

The most obvious limitation of the corticohippocampal model, like others in the same domain, is that it does not make any particular attempt to address the episodic memory deficits that are the most obvious feature of human hippocampal amnesia. This is the converse of the limitation of models that address episodic memory but not information processing in the hippocampal region. Eventually, a complete model of hippocampal-region function will have to account for both these aspects of hippocampal-region damage. For now, though, these models should be judged on the basis of how well they account for the circumscribed set of data they attempt to address.

There are also several limitations of Gluck & Myers' corticohippocampal model. As a trial-level model, it cannot capture any of the intricacies of timing within a trial—such as the effects of varying stimulus scheduling, the latency of onset of the conditioned response, and so on. Others (e.g., Schmajuk & DiCarlo, 1990, 1992) do include real-time effects in their models, and they capture these aspects of animal learning. In the next section, we consider in more detail another model of Schmajuk and colleagues that addresses a similar body of behavioral conditioning data.

A more general limitation of this entire class of models is the restricted degree of physiological realism they involve. The network architectures and learning algorithms are determined more by functional (behavioral) considerations than by biological properties. In fact, most of these models include properties that are clearly unrealistic, for example, full or near-full connectivity between sets of nodes. Some attempts have been made to address this limitation. These are reviewed in the next section, which considers more recent attempts to take abstract theories of hippocampal-region function and clarify more precisely the functional role of the different anatomical components of this region.

VI. DISSOCIATING PARAHIPPOCAMPAL AND HIPPOCAMPAL CONTRIBUTIONS

Recent refinements in lesion techniques indicate that the extent of memory impairment often depends critically on exact lesion extent. This suggests that the different substructures of the hippocampal region have differentiable contributions to the processing of the region as a whole. However, the precise assignment of function to substructure and the ways in which they interact are as yet poorly understood. One example is the latent inhibition effect described earlier, in which prior unreinforced exposure to a stimulus retards later learning to respond to that stimulus (Lubow, 1973). Latent inhibition is attenuated by broad hippocampal-region damage (Kaye & Pearce, 1987; Solomon & Moore, 1975) but not by damage strictly limited to the hippocampus and sparing the entorhinal cortex (Honey & Good, 1993; Reilly, Harley, & Revusky, 1993). Similarly, odor discrimination reversal is impaired by hippocampal lesion but actually facilitated after entorhinal lesion (Otto, Schottler, Stanbli, Eichenbaum, & Lynch, 1991).

Although the representational theory of hippocampal function proposed by Gluck and Myers (1993) treated the hippocampal region as a single processing system, subsequent work by these researchers has suggested how their basic representational processes might be subdivided and the subfunctions localized in different anatomical sites around the region (Myers et al., 1995). In particular, Myers et al. (1995) proposed that stimulus–stimulus redundancy compression could emerge from the anatomy and physiology of superficial entorhinal cortex.

A. Parahippocampal Function in Stimulus Compression and Clustering

The Myers et al. model of entorhinal (and parahippocampal) function in learning is derived from an earlier physiologically realistic model of superficial piriform (olfactory) cortex by Ambros-Ingerson, Granger, and Lynch (1990), which argued that the anatomy and physiology of this cortical structure are sufficient to implement hierarchical clustering of odor inputs. In brief, Ambros-Ingerson et al. proposed a competitive network model in which local recurrent inhibition silences all but the most strongly responding pyramidal cells. These so-called winning cells come to respond to a family or cluster of inputs with similar features. Recurrent feedback from the piriform cortex to olfactory bulb is also assumed to allow iterative responses to odors, from which successively finer-grained (hierarchical) classifications can be constructed. One aspect of this model is that, since similar inputs tend to be clustered to similar output responses, the network performs redundancy compression of exactly the sort previously proposed by Gluck and Myers (1993) to occur in the hippocampal region (Myers et al., 1995). In particular, if two inputs co-occur, they will be treated as a single compound input. Later, if one of the inputs occurs alone, the network will tend to treat this as a degraded version of the compound input and assign it to the same cluster as the compound.

The piriform cortex and entorhinal cortex elide in the rat, and their superficial layers are closely related anatomically and physiologically, suggesting the possibility of related functionality (Price, 1973; Van Hoesen & Pandya, 1975; Woodhams,

Celio, Ulfig, & Witter, 1993). Specifically, superficial entorhinal cortex contains pyramidal cells with sparse nontopographic connections with afferents in Layer I (Van Hoesen & Pandya, 1975) and shows NMDA-dependent, theta-induced long-term potentiation (LTP) (de Curtis & Llinas, 1993). Noting this similarity, Gluck and Granger (1993) suggested that the entorhinal cortex could perform a similarity-based clustering operation similar to that proposed to occur in the piriform cortex.

In sum, then, Myers et al. (1995) have proposed that the entorhinal cortex would be sufficient to implement the redundancy compression aspect of the representational changes that Gluck and Myers (1993) ascribe to the hippocampal region as a whole (Myers et al., 1995). A model implementing these proposed processes and based on the physiologically and anatomically motivated model of Ambros-Ingerson et al. (1990) is shown in Fig. 8A. One difference between the piriform and entorhinal models is that the piriform model assumes repetitive sampling and input masking, based on recurrent connections from the piriform cortex to olfactory bulb. Myers et al. (1995) have not assumed this in the entorhinal model, and so it only performs a single-stage, similarity-based clustering or compression of its inputs. The resulting network is similar to the unsupervised, competitive-learning systems developed by Kohonen (1984), Rumelhart and Zipser (1985), Grossberg (1976), and others. A second important difference between the piriform and entorhinal cortices is that, while the piriform cortex is primarily an olfactory area, the entorhinal cortex receives input from a broad spectrum of polymodal cortices, as well as from the piriform cortex. Thus, Myers et al. (1995) have suggested that whereas the piriform cortex might be sufficient to implement redundancy compression within the olfactory domain, the entorhinal cortex might be required to implement redundancy compression between stimuli from different modalities or across the polymodal featurs of a single stimulus (Myers et al., 1995).

This model can be compared with a lesion that selectively damages the hippocampus and dentate gyrus but that leaves intact the entorhinal cortex. As already noted, such lesions often produce different results from lesions of the entire hippocampal region. For example, such a restricted lesion does not disrupt latent inhibition, although, as already described, a larger lesion does (Honey & Good, 1993; Reilly et al., 1993). The selectively lesioned model produces the same effect (Fig. 8B). The redundancy compression in the entorhinal network is sufficient to mediate latent inhibition. The model accounts for several other selective-lesion effects (Myers et al., 1995) as well as makes specific novel predictions that other behaviors, which are interpreted as reflecting stimulus compression, are likely to depend more on the entorhinal cortex than on the hippocampus proper, and so should survive such a localized lesion.

The idea that the entorhinal cortex is involved in stimulus compression also relates to a suggestion by Eichenbaum and Bunsey (1995) that the entorhinal cortex performs "fusion" of coincident or nearly coincident stimuli, based on the tendency of animals with selective hippocampal (but not entorhinal) damage to overcompress stimulus information.

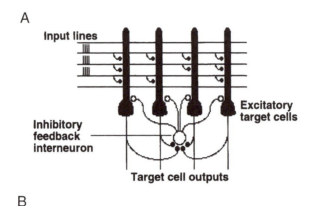

FIGURE 8 (A) In the entorhinal model, target cells are excited by sparse afferents, and in turn activate local inhibitory feedback interneurons. Feedback silences all but the most strongly activated target cells. Synaptic plasticity makes these "winning" target cells more likely to "win" in response to similar inputs in the future. The resulting network activity is constrained by stimulus–stimulus redundancy compression. (B) The H-lesioned model, in which an entorhinal cortex network provides new compressed representations to the internal layer of a long-term memory network. [Adapted from Myers et al. (1995).]

This hypothesis regarding the selective contribution of entorhinal processing to hippocampal-region function assumes that the remaining subfunction of predictive differentiation could be implemented elsewhere in the hippocampal region. One possibility is that the dentate gyrus or hippocampus proper could perform this subfunction. This idea is consistent with several suggestions that the hippocampus is involved in predicting future events (such as US arrival) given current inputs (e.g.,

Gray, 1985; Levy, 1985; Lynch & Granger, 1992; McNaughton & Nadel, 1990; Treves & Rolls, 1992).

B. Parahippocampal Function in Configural Associations

In an alternative approach to modeling entorhinal function, Schmajuk and Blair (Schmajuk, 1994; Schmajuk & Blair, 1993) have suggested the particular contribution of the entorhinal cortex to the Schmajuk–DiCarlo (Schmajuk & DiCarlo, 1992) model of hippocampal-region function is stimulus competition, whereas the hippocampus proper is responsible for configural association. They therefore predict that localized hippocampal lesion, which does not otherwise damage the entorhinal cortex, should eliminate the configural but not the stimulus competition function. Empirical data are somewhat consistent with this idea (see Schmajuk, 1994), although further empirical studies are certainly indicated, as mentioned earlier in the context of testing our own model of entorhinal function. The stimulus competition function proposed by Schmajuk and Blair is quite distinct from the stimulus–stimulus clustering we have proposed as an entorhinal function. In fact, our entorhinal stimulus–stimulus clustering is probably more closely related to the configural function that Schmajuk and Blair assign not to the entorhinal cortex but to the hippocampus proper. Until such time as more empirical data become available, it may be difficult to provide a definitive discrimination between these two accounts. However, future experiments that address the selective role of the entorhinal cortex in stimulus competition and in stimulus–stimulus clustering are required to properly evaluate these two models.

In a more recent paper, Buhusi and Schmajuk (1996) presented a different model of hippocampal function in conditioning that attributes both attentional and configural mechanisms to specific components of the hippocampal region. Buhusi and Schmajuk proposed that the entorhinal and parahippocampal cortices have a unique role in error correction in which expected reinforcement is compared with actual reinforcement. In contrast, we have argued that these same overlying cortices are essential for stimulus–stimulus redundancy compression. This is consistent with studies showing that latent inhibition, a result Myers et al. (1995) have interpreted as being mediated by stimulus compression, is spared after hippocampal lesions that do not extend to the entorhinal cortex (Honey & Good, 1993; Reilly et al., 1993).

VII. INCORPORATING SUBCORTICAL CHOLINERGIC MODULATION

The models of episodic memory and consolidation reviewed in the section "Autoassociative Models of CA3 and Episodic Memory" are fairly abstract in that there is no particular mapping of nodes and connections to neurons and synapses. As

Hasselmo and colleagues have shown, however, it is possible to construct autoassociative models that are much more physiologically realistic. In this view, Hasselmo and Schnell (1994; see also Hasselmo et al., 1995) have developed a model of laminar connections in the hippocampus to study the possible function of the strong cholinergic input from the medial septum. These authors have suggested that the function of this cholinergic input is to allow the hippocampus to switch between pattern storage and pattern retrieval states. When a new pattern is presented to an autoassociative network as a forcing input, it will activate some of the nodes in the network. Activation from these nodes will travel through the recurrent feedback connections to activate other nodes, and after several iterations, this runaway excitation may result in the entire network becoming active, rather than just those nodes associated with the pattern to be stored. To avoid this runaway excitation, an autoassociative network is usually assumed to operate in two modes, a storage mode during which forcing inputs are present but feedback collaterals are suppressed, and a recall mode during which there is no forcing input and recurrent collaterals are allowed to activate nodes. In the context of a network model, it is easy to define two such disparate states.

If hippocampal field CA3 is assumed to operate as an autoassociative network, with mossy fiber afferents providing the forcing inputs, there must be a physiological mechanism to suppress activity on the recurrent collaterals during storage. Hasselmo (Hasselmo, 1995; Hasselmo & Schnell, 1994) proposed that the septal cholinergic input can provide this switch. Briefly, he suggested that cholinergic input suppresses the recurrent collaterals to allow storage of the new pattern without runaway excitation. When cholinergic input is absent and entorhinal inputs activate a few CA3 cells, feedback connections recruit more cells to activity, until a stored pattern is recalled and instated on the CA3 nodes. Hasselmo (Hasselmo, 1995; Hasselmo & Schnell, 1994) further proposed a scheme whereby CA3 can self-regulate this cholinergic input, allowing the hippocampus to recognize when a new pattern should be stored, and signal the septum to send the cholinergic input that allows storage to proceed. In model simulations, such self-regulated suppression of recurrent collaterals does suffice to allow switching between storage and recall states in an autoassociative network (Hasselmo & Schnell, 1994). In empirical support of this hypothesis, Hasselmo et al. (1995) have shown that the cholinergic agonist carbachol does suppress activity of CA3 cells in slice more in the stratum radiatum, where the recurrent collaterals afferent CA3 dendrites, than in the stratum lucidum, where the mossy fibers afferent CA3 dendrites. Further support comes from findings of anterograde amnesia after medial septal lesion (Berry & Thompson, 1979) or pharmacological disruption through anticholinergic drugs such as scopolamine (Solomon, Solomon, Van der Schaaf, & Perry, 1983), consistent with Hasselmo's prediction that cholinergic input is necessary for storage of new information in the hippocampus (Hasselmo, 1995; Hasselmo & Schnell, 1994). In the next subsection, we discuss how this cholinergic model of Hasselmo can be related to independently developed models of hippocampal function in classical conditioning (Myers et al., 1996) reviewed earlier.

A. Septohippocampal Cholinergic Modulation in Conditioning

Myers and Gluck, in collaboration with Hasselmo and Solomon, have recently shown how a simplified version of Hasselmo's cholinergic hypothesis can be instantiated within the Gluck–Myers model, to provide an interpretation of Solomon's data on the behavioral consequences of anticholinergic drugs on classical conditioning. In brief, the integrated model assumes that the tendency of the hippocampal-region network to store new information, as opposed to simply processing it and recalling old information, is determined by the hippocampal-region network's learning rate (Myers et al., 1996). Disrupting septal input can therefore be approximated within the Gluck–Myers model by lowering this learning rate—although not the rate at which this information is transferred to the cortical network nor the rate at which cortical associations develop. The consequence of this depressed hippocampal learning rate is to prolong the initial nonresponding phase before onset of the initial conditioned responses (Fig. 9B), much as is seen in the experimental data (Fig. 9A). This computational model of cholinergic function in conditioning is broadly consistent with an earlier suggestion by Berry and Thompson (1979), who argued that the medial septum is involved primarily in early attentional stages of learning rather than subsequent associational processes.

With this interpretation of cholinergic function, Myers et al. (1996) showed that the Gluck–Myers model correctly expects that hippocampal disruption retards conditioning even though outright hippocampal lesion does not. This apparent paradox has previously been noted in the animal literature (Solomon et al., 1983), and the model provides insight into why it might be so. Further, the model predicts that if lowering hippocampal learning rates retards learning, increasing learning rates may hasten it (Myers et al., 1996). This is consistent with data showing that cholinergic agonists can improve learning in subjects with abnormally reduced levels of brain acetylcholine (for a review, see Myers et al., 1996). However, in the model, increasing hippocampal learning rates beyond some optimal level actually results in degraded learning, as the network becomes unstable (Myers et al., 1996). Therefore, the model predicts that cholinergic therapy should only be transiently effective in normal subjects. In fact, this is the case: Whereas cholinergic agonists at moderate doses tend to improve learning, higher doses may either result in no facilitation or actually impair learning (for a review, see Myers et al., 1996). The model therefore provides an account for this empirical phenomenon, which has been problematic in the clinical pharmacology literature.

An alternative approach to modeling septohippocampal cholinergic pathways is the model of Buhusi and Schmajuk (1996). These authors interpret the septohippocampal cholinergic pathways as providing an error signal that drives learning. In contrast, Myers et al. (1996) argued that these pathways can be functionally interpreted as providing modulation of learning rates, which builds on similar arguments by Hasselmo (see Hasselmo et al., 1996). Despite different functional interpretations of the medial septal inputs, both the Buhusi and Schmajuk (1996) and the Myers

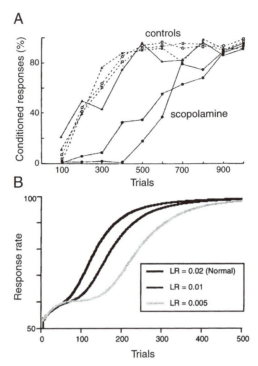

FIGURE 9   Experimental data and modeling of the effects of the anticholinergic drug scopolamine on acquisition of a conditioned eyeblink response. (A) Systemic application of scopolamine (Solomon et al., 1983) in which it is shown that the effect of scopolamine is to delay the onset of conditioning, rather than preventing it. (B) Learning curves for three different hippocampal learning rates in the Myers et al. (1996) model showing how lowered learning rates shift the acquisition curve to the right, delaying the onset of learning, much as seen in (A).

et al. (1996) models correctly expect that cholinergic antagonists (such as scopolamine) should impair acquisition, but not latent inhibition. Buhusi and Schmajuk have not, however, addressed the detailed aspects of learning curves that are analyzed by Myers et al. (1996).

VIII. SUMMARY AND GENERAL DISCUSSION

We have reviewed several computational models of hippocampal function in learning and memory, concentrating on those that make strongest contact with psychological issues and data from behavioral experiments. Many of these models can be traced to the influential early model of Marr (1971) that, in turn, built upon Hebb's (1949) ideas on how associations are acquired between groups of cell assemblies in the brain. The basic network architecture described by Marr's theory is known as an autoassociator, which learns to associate all components of an input pattern with all other components of the same pattern.

Many researchers have used Marr's basic framework for modeling episodic or event memories in the hippocampus, especially within hippocampal field CA3, which shares many of the basic connectivity requirements for an autoassociator (Hasselmo et al., 1996; McNaughton & Morris, 1987; McNaughton & Nadel, 1990; Rolls, 1989). These models focus on the ability of the hippocampal region to perform fast, temporary storage, which suggests that this underlies the hippocampal region's role in episodic memory formation. This is consistent with the neuropsychological data showing that episodic memory impairments are the most obvious behavioral effects in human amnesia following hippocampal-region damage. Variations on the hippocampal autoassociator model have been developed to explain sequential learning (for reviews, see Granger et al., 1996; Levy, 1996; Liaw & Berger, 1996), spatial navigation (Burgess et al., 1994; Levy, 1989; McNaughton & Morris, 1987; McNaughton & Nadel, 1990; Muller et al., 1987; Muller & Stead, 1996; Recce & Harris, 1996; Sharp, 1991; Sharp et al., 1996), and the consolidation of episodic memories (Alvarez & Squire, 1994; McClelland & Goddard, 1996; Murre, 1996; O'Reilly & McClelland, 1994; Treves & Rolls, 1992).

Another class of hippocampal models have focused on hippocampal involvement in incrementally learned associative habits, such as classical conditioning or probabilistic pattern classification. Many qualitative theories and several computational models have focused on possible information-processing roles for the hippocampal region that are most evident from studying complex training procedures in incrementally acquired learning (Buhusi & Schmajuk, 1996; Eichenbaum et al., 1992; Gluck & Myers, 1993, 1995, 1996; Hirsh, 1974; Moore & Stickney, 1980; Schmajuk & DiCarlo, 1992; Sutherland & Rudy, 1989). Recent modeling efforts have attempted to make closer contact with the underlying anatomy and physiology. These include models of parahippocampal function (Myers et al., 1995; Schmajuk & Blair, 1993) and models of the subcortical influences of cholinergic modulation (Buhusi & Schmajuk, 1996; Myers et al., 1996).

In reviewing these psychobiological models of hippocampal function in learning and memory, we have seen three major themes emerge. First, we have seen how computational models can provide the "glue" to bind together analysis and data at multiple levels of analysis including cellular, physiological, anatomical, and behavioral levels. In particular, we noted how some models are developed in a top-down fashion, beginning with detailed behavioral analyses and then seeking a mapping to underlying biological substrates. Other models are developed in a more bottom-up fashion, beginning with biological details and, via computational simulations, seeking to identify emergent functional properties of these substrates [for further discussion of these distinctions in learning models, see Gluck and Granger (1993)].

A second theme that emerged was the importance of models as tools to integrate data from both animal and human studies of hippocampal function in learning and memory. Although these two bodies of research have often been quite separate and disconnected, it seems clear that ultimately they must converge so that each body of literature and theory can inform the other, which should lead to a more general and broadly applicable understanding of the hippocampal region in all species.

Finally, a third theme that emerged from reviewing these models is the importance of relating current computational models to earlier traditions in memory research, especially the many earlier psychological models that capture important behavioral principles of memory. In drawing these connections between current models and earlier qualitative theories in psychology and neurobiology, one can see to what extent the models represent cumulative progress.

All the models reviewed here represent preliminary attempts to incorporate both biological data and behavioral analysis within formal computationally defined theories. The value of these models—crude approximations at best—will become most clearly apparent if they lead to important new empirical studies that will inform and constrain future generations of models and theories.

ACKNOWLEDGMENTS

We are grateful to Gyorgy Buzsaki, Michael Hasselmo, Brandon Ermita, Kari Hoffman, and Todd Allen for their helpful comments and suggestions on early drafts of the manuscript. This research was supported by grants to M.A.G. from the Office of Naval Research through the Young Investigator program, by Grant N00014-88-K-0112, and by a grant from the McDonnell–Pew Program in Cognitive Neuroscience.

REFERENCES

Alvarez P., & Squire L. (1994). Memory consolidation and the medial temporal lobe: A simple network model. *Proc. Natl. Acad. Sci. U.S.A., 91,* 7041–7045.

Ambros-Ingerson, J., Granger R., & Lynch G. (1990). Simulation of paleocortex performs hierarchical clustering. *Science, 247,* 1344–1348.

Anderson J. (1977). Neural models with cognitive implications. In D. LaBerge, & S. Samuels (Eds.), *Basic processes in reading: Perception and comprehension* (pp. 27–90). Hillsdale, NJ: Erlbaum.

Berry S., & Thompson, R. (1979). Medial septal lesions retard classical conditioning of the nictitating membrane response in rabbits. *Science, 205,* 209–211.

Bliss, T., & Lomo, T. (1973). Long-lasting potentiation of synaptic transmission in the dentate area of the anaesthetized rabbit following stimulation of the perforant path. *J. Physiol., 232,* 331–356.

Buhusi, C., & Schmajuk, N. A., (1996). Attention, configuration, and hippocampal function. *Hippocampus, 6,* 621–642.

Burgess, N., Recce, M., & O'Keefe, J. (1994). A model of hippocampal function. *Neural Networks, 17,* 1065–1081.

Buzsaki, G. (1989). Two-stage model of memmory-trace formation: A role for "noisy" brain states. *Neuroscience, 31,* 551–570.

Cohen, N. (1984). Preserved learning capacity in amnesia: Evidence for multiple learning systems. In L. Squire & N. Butters (Eds.), *Neuropsychology of memory* (pp. 83–103). New York: Guilford.

Crick, F., & Mitchison, G. (1983). The function of dream sleep. *Nature, 304,* 111–114.

Daum, I., Channon, S., & Canavan, A. (1989). Classical conditioning in patients with severe memory problems. *J. Neurol. Neurosurg. Psychiatry, 52,* 47–51.

de Curtis, M., & Llinas, R. (1993). Entorhinal cortex long-term potentiation evoked by theta-patterned stimulation of associative fibers in the isolated in vitro guinea pig brain. *Brain Res., 600,* 327–330.

de Leon, M., Golomb, J., George, A., Convit, A., Rusinek, H., et al. (1993). Hippocampal formation atrophy: Prognostic significance for Alzheimer's disease. In B. Corain, K. Iqbal, M. Nicolini, B. Winblad, H. Wisniewski, & P. Zatta (Eds.), *Alzheimer's disease: Advances in clinical and brain research* (pp. 35–46). New York: Wiley.

Eichenbaum, H. (1992). The hippocampal system and declarative memory in animals. *J. Cogn. Neurosci., 4,* 217–231.

Eichenbaum, H., & Bunsey, M. (1995). On the binding of associations in memory: Clues from studies on the role of the hippocampal region in paired associate learning. *Curr. Dir. Psychol. Sci., 4,* 19–23.

Eichenbaum, H., Cohen, N. J., Otto, T., & Wible, C. (1992). Memory representation in the hippocampus: Functional domain and functional organization. In L. R. Squire, G. Lynch, N. M. Weinberger, & J. L. McGaugh (Eds.), *Memory organization and locus of change* (pp. 163–204). Oxford: Oxford University Press.

Eichenbaum, H., Fagan, A., Mathews, P., & Cohen, N. J. (1988). Hippocampal system dysfunction and odor discrimination learning in rats: Impairment or facilitation depending on representational demands. *Behav. Neurosci., 102,* 331–339.

Gabrieli, J., McGlinchey-Berroth, R., Carrillo, M., Gluck, M., Cermack, L., & Disterhoft, J. (1995). Intact delay-eyeblink classical conditioning in amnesia. *Behav. Neurosci., 109,* 819–827.

Gluck, M. A., & Granger, R. (1993). Computational models of the neural bases of learning and memory. *Annu. Rev. Neurosci., 16,* 667–706.

Gluck, M. A., & Myers, C. (1993). Hippocampal mediation of stimulus representation: A computational theory. *Hippocampus, 3,* 491–516.

Gluck, M., & Myers, C. (1995). Representation and association in memory: A neurocomputational view of hippocampal function. *Curr. Dir. Psychol. Sci., 4,* 23–29.

Gluck, M. A., & Myers, C. E. (1996). Integrating behavioral and physiological models of hippocampal function. *Hippocampus, 6,* 643–653.

Granger, R., Wiebe, S. P., Taketani, M., & Lynch, G. (1996). District memory circuits composing the hippocampal region. *Hippocampus, 6,* 567–578.

Gray, J. A. (1985). Memory buffer and comparator can share the same circuitry. *Behav. Brain Sci., 8,* 501.

Grossberg, S. (1976). Adaptive pattern classification and recoding: Part I. *Biol. Cybern., 23,* 121–134.

Haist, F., Musen, G., & Squire, L. R. (1991). Intact priming of words and nonwords in amnesia. *Psychobiology, 19,* 275–285.

Hall, G., & Honey, R. C. (1989). Contextual effects in conditioning, latent inhibition, and habituation: Associative and retrieval functions of contextual cues. *J. Exp. Psychol.: Anim. Behav. Process, 15,* 232–241.

Hasselmo, M. E. (1995). Neuromodulation and cortical function: Modeling the physiological basis of behavior. *Behav. Brain Res., 67,* 1–27.

Hasselmo, M. E., & Schnell, E. (1994). Laminar selectivity of the cholinergic suppression of synaptic transmission in rat hippocampal region CA1: Computational modeling and brain slice physiology. *J. Neurosci., 14,* 3898–3914.

Hasselmo, M. E., Schnell, E., & Barkai, E. (1995). Dynamics of learning and recall at excitatory recurrent synapses and cholinergic modulation in rat hippocampal region CA3. *J. Neurosci., 15,* 5249–5262.

Hasselmo, M. E., Wyble, B. P., & Wallenstein, G. V. (1996). Encoding and retrieval of episodic memories: Role of cholinergic and GABAergic modulation in the hippocampus. *Hippocampus, 6,* 693–708.

Hebb, D. O. (1949). *The organization of behavior.* New York: Wiley.

Hetherington, P. (1990). The sequential learning problem in connectionist networks. MS thesis, McGill University.

Hinton, G. (1989). Connectionist learning procedures. *Artif. Intell., 40,* 185–234.

Hirsh, R. (1974). The hippocampus and contextual retrieval of information from memory: A theory. *Behav. Biol., 12,* 421–444.

Honey, R. C., & Good, M. (1993). Selective hippocampal lesions abolish the contextual specificity of latent inhibition and conditioning. *Behav. Neurosci., 107,* 23–33.

Hopfield, J. J. (1982). Neural networks and physical systems with emergent collective computational abilities. *Proc. Natl. Acad. Sci. U.S.A., 79,* 2554–2558.

Kaye, H., & Pearce, J. (1987). Hippocampal lesions attenuate latent inhibition and the decline of the orienting response in rats. *Q. J. Exp. Psychol., 39,* 107–125.

Kelso, S. R., Ganong, A. H., & Brown, T. H. (1986). Hebbian synapses in hippocampus. *Proc. Natl. Acad. Sci. U.S.A., 83,* 5326–5330.

Kim, J. J., & Fanselow, M. S. (1992). Modality-specific retrograde amnesia of fear. *Science, 256,* 675–677.

Knowlton, B., Squire, L., & Gluck, M. (1994). Probabilistic classification learning in amnesia. *Learn. Mem., 1,* 106–120.

Kohler, C. (1986). Intrinsic connections of the retrohippocampal region in the rat brain. II. The medial entorhinal area. *J. Comp. Neurol., 246,* 149–169.

Kohonen, T. (1984). *Self-organization and associative memory.* New York: Springer-Verlag.

Levy, W. (1985). An information/computation theory of hippocampal function. *Soc. Neurosci. Abstr., 11,* 493.

Levy, W. B. (1989). A computational approach to hippocampal function. In R. Hawkins & G. Bower (Eds.), *Psychology of learning and motivation* (pp. 243–304). London: Academic.

Levy, W. B. (1996). A sequence predicting CA3 is a flexible associator that learns and uses context to solve hippocampal-like tasks. *Hippocampus, 6,* 579–590.

Levy, W. B., Brassel, S. E., & Moore, S. D. (1983). Partial quantification of the associative synaptic learning rule of the dentate gyrus. *Neuroscience, 8,* 799–808.

Levy, W., Wu, X., & Baxter, R. (1995). Unifications of hippocampal function via computational/encoding considerations. *Int. J. Neur. Syst., 6,* (Suppl.), 71–80.

Liaw, J., & Berger, T. W. (1996). Dynamic synapse: A new concept of neural representation and computation. *Hippocampus, 6,* 591–600.

Lubow, R. (1973). Latent inhibition. *Psychol. Bull., 79,* 398–407.

Lynch, G., & Granger, R. (1992). Variations in synaptic plasticity and types of memory in corticohippocampal networks. *J. Cogn. Neurosci., 4,* 189–199.

Marr, D. (1971). Simple memory: A theory for archicortex. *Proc. R. Soc. London, Ser. B, 262* (No. 841), 23–81.

McClelland, J., & Goddard, N. (1996). Considerations arising from a complementary learning systems perspective on hippocampus and neocortex. *Hippocampus, 6,* 654–665.

McClelland, J., McNaughton, B., & O'Reilly, R. (1994). *Why we have complementary learning systems in the hippocampus and neocortex: Insights from the successes and failures of connectionist models of learning and memory* (Tech. Rep. No. PDP.CNS.94.1). Pittsburgh: Carnegie Mellon University.

McCulloch, W. S., & Pitts, W. (1943). A logical calculus of the ideas immanent in neural nets. *Bull. Math. Biographys., 5,* 115–137.

McNaughton, B. (1989). Neuronal mechanisms for spatial computation and information storage. L. Nadel, L. Cover, P. Culicover, & R. Harnish (Eds.), *Neural connections, mental computations.* (pp. 285–350). Cambridge, MA: MIT Press.

McNaughton, B. L. (1991). Associative pattern completion in hippocampal circuits: New evidence and new questions. *Brain Res. Rev., 16,* 202–204.

McNaughton, B. L., & Morris, R. G. M. (1987). Hippocampal synaptic enhancement and information storage. *Trends Neurosci., 10,* 408–415.

McNaughton, B. L., & Nadel, L. (1990). Hebb–Marr networks and the neurobiological representation of action in space. In M. Gluck, & D. Rumelhart (Eds.), *Neuroscience and connectionist theory* (pp. 1–63). Hillsdale, NJ: Erlbaum.

Mishkin, M. (1982). A memory system in the monkey. *Philos. Trans. R. Soc. London, 298,* 85–92.

Moore, J., & Stickney, K. (1980). Formation of attentional-associative networks in real time: Role of the hippocampus and implications for conditioning. *Physiol. Psychol., 8,* 207–217.

Moyer, J. R., Deyo, R. A., & Disterhoft, J. F. (1990). Hippocampectomy disrupts trace eye-blink conditioning in rabbits. *Behav. Neurosci., 104,* 243–252.

Muller, R. U., Kubie, J. L., & Ranck, J. B. (1987). Spatial firing patterns of hippocampal complex-spike cells in a fixed environment. *J. Neurosci., 7,* 1935–1950.

Muller, R. U., & Stead, M. (1996). Hippocampal place cells connected by Hebbian synapses can solve spatial problems. *Hippocampus, 6,* 709–719.

Murre, J. M. (1996). TraceLink: A model of amnesia and consolidation of memory. *Hippocampus, 6,* 675–684.

Myers, C., & Gluck, M. (1994). Context, conditioning and hippocampal re-representation. *Behav. Neurosci., 108,* 835–847.

Myers, C. E., & Gluck, M. A. (1996). Cortico-hippocampal representations in simultaneous odor discrimination: A computational interpretation of Eichenbaum, Mathews, and Cohen (1989). *Behav. Neurosci., 110,* 1–22.

Myers, C. E., Gluck, M. A., & Granger, R. (1995). Dissociation of hippocampal and entorhinal function in associative learning: A computational approach. *Psychobiology, 23,* 116–138.

Myers, C. M., Ermita, B. R., Harris, K., Hasselmo, M., Solomon, P., & Gluck, M. A. (1996). A computational model of cholinergic disruption of septo-hippocampal activity in classical eyeblink conditioning. *Neurobiol. Learn. Mem., 66,* 51–66.

O'Keefe, J., & Nadel, L. (1978). *The hippocampus as a cognitive map.* Oxford: Clarendon.

O'Reilly, R., & McClelland, J. (1994). Hippocampal conjunctive encoding, storage, and recall: Avoiding a tradeoff. *Hippocampus, 4,* 661–682.

Otto, T., Schottler, F., Staubli, U., Eichenbaum, H., & Lynch, G. (1991). Hippocampus and olfactory discrimination learning: Effects of entorhinal cortex lesions on olfactory learning and memory in a successive-cue, go-no-go task. *Behav. Neurosci., 105,* 111–119.

Penick, S., & Solomon, R. (1991). Hippocampus context and conditioning. *Behav. Neurosci., 105,* 611–617.

Port, R., Romano, A., & Patterson, M. (1986). Stimulus duration discrimination in the rabbit: Effects of hippocampectomy on discrimination and reversal learning. *Physiol. Psychol., 4,* 124–129.

Prepscius, C., & Levy, W. (1994). Sequence prediction and cognitive mapping by a biologically plausible neural network. *Proceedings of the World Congress on Neural Networks* (Vol. 4, p. 164; Vol. 5, p. 169). San Diego: INNS Press.

Price, J. (1973). An autoradiographic study of complementary laminar patterns of termination of afferent fiber to the olfactory cortex. *J. Compar. Neurol., 150,* 87–108.

Recce, M., & Harris, K. D. (1996). Memory for places: A navigational model in support of Marr's theory of hippocampal function. *Hippocampus, 6,* 735–748.

Reilly, S., Harley, C., & Revusky, S. (1993). Ibotenate lesions of the hippocampus enhance latent inhibition in conditioned taste aversion and increase resistance to extinction in conditioned taste preference. *Behav. Neurosci., 107,* 996–1004.

Ribot, T. (1882). *The diseases of memory.* New York: Appleton.

Rolls, E. (1989). The representation and storage of information in neural networks in the primate cerebral cortex and hippocampus. In R. Durbin, C. Miall, & G. Mitchison, (Eds.), *The computing neuron* (pp. 125–159). Wokingham, UK: Addison-Wesley.

Rosenblatt, F. (1962). *Principles of neurodynamics.* New York: Spartan.

Rudy, J. W., & Sutherland, R. J. (1989). The hippocampal formation is necessary for rats to learn and remember configural discriminations. *Behav. Brain Res., 34,* 97–109.

Rudy, J. W., & Sutherland, R. J. (1995). Configural association theory and the hippocampal formation: An appraisal and reconfiguration. *Hippocampus, 5,* 375–389.

Rumelhart, D., & Zipser, D. (1985). Feature discovery by competitive learning. *Cogn. Sci., 9,* 75–112.

Schmajuk, N. A. (1994). Stimulus configuration, classical conditioning, and spatial learning: Role of the hippocampus. *Proceedings of the World Congress on Neural Networks* (Vol. 2, pp. 723–728). San Diego: INNS Press.

Schmajuk, N. A., & Blair, H. T. (1993). Stimulus configuration spatial learning and hippocampal function. *Behav. Brain Res., 59,* 103–117.

Schmajuk, N. A., & DiCarlo, J. J. (1990). *Backpropagation, classical conditioning and hippocampal function* (Tech. Rep.). Evanston, IL: Northwestern University.

Schmajuk, N. A., & DiCarlo, J. J. (1991). A neural network approach to hippocampal function in classical conditioning. *Behav. Neurosci., 105,* 82–110.

Schmajuk, N. A., & DiCarlo, J. J. (1992). Stimulus configuration, classical conditioning and hippocampal function. *Psychol. Rev., 99,* 268–305.

Schmaltz, l. W., & Theios, J. (1972). Acquisition and extinction of a classically conditioned response in hippocampectomized rabbits (*Oryctolagus cuniculus*). *J. Comp. Physiol. Psychol., 79,* 328–333.

Sharp, P. (1991). Computer simulation of hippocampal place cells. *Psychobiology, 19,* 103–115.

Sharp, P. E., Blair, H. T., & Brown, M. (1996). Neural network modeling of the hippocampal formation spatial signals and their possible role in navigation: A modular approach. *Hippocampus, 6,* 720–734.

Solomon, P. R., & Moore, J. (1975). Latent inhibition and stimulus generalization of the classically conditioned nictitating membrane response in rabbits (*Oryctolagus cuniculus*) following dorsal hippocampal ablation. *J. Comp. Physiol. Psychol., 89,* 1192–1203.

Solomon, P. R., Solomon, S. D., Van der Schaaf, E., & Perry, H. E. (1983). Altered activity in the hippocampus is more detrimental to classical conditioning than removing the structure. *Science, 220,* 329–331.

Squire, L. (1987). *Memory and brain.* New York: Oxford University Press.

Squire, L. R., & Alvarez, P. (1995). Retrograde amnesia and memory consolidation: A neurobiological perspective. *Curr. Opin. Neurobiol., 5,* 169–177.

Squire, L., & Butters, N. (Eds.). (1984). *Neuropsychology of memory.* New York: Guilford.

Squire, L., & Cohen, N. (1979). Memory and amnesia: Resistance to disruption develops for years after learning. *Behav. Neur. Biol., 25,* 115–125.

Sutherland, R., & Rudy, J. (1989). Configural association theory: The role of the hippocampal formation in learning, memory and amnesia. *Psychobiology, 17,* 129–144.

Teyler, T., & DiScenna, P. (1986). The hippocampal memory indexing theory. *Behav. Neurosci., 100,* 147–154.

Treves, A., & Rolls, E. (1992). Computational constraints suggest the need for two distinct input systems to the hippocampal CA3 network. *Hippocampus, 2,* 189–200.

Van Hoesen, G., & Pandya, D. (1975). Some connections of the entorhinal (area 28) and perirhinal (area 35) cortices of the rhesus monkey. I. Temporal lobe afferents. *Brain Res., 95,* 1–24.

Volpe, B. T., & Hirst, W. (1983). Amnesia following the rupture and repair of an anterior communicating artery aneurysm. *J. Neurol. Neurosurg. Psychiatry, 46,* 704–709.

Weiskrantz, L., & Warrington, E. K. (1979). Conditioning in amnesic patients. *Neuropsychologia, 17,* 187–194.

Wickelgren, W. (1979). Chunking and consolidation: A theoretical synthesis of semantic networks, configuring in conditioning, S–R versus cognitive learning, normal forgetting, the amnesic syndrome, and the hippocampal arousal system. *Psychol. Rev., 86,* 44–60.

Willshaw, D., & Buckingham, J. (1990). An assessment of Marr's theory of the hippocampus as a temporary memory store. *Philos. Trans. R. Soc. London, Ser. B, 329,* 205–215.

Wilson, M. A., & McNaughton, B. A. (1994). Reactivation of hippocampal ensemble memories during sleep. *Science, 265,* 676–679.

Woodhams, P. L. L., Celio, M. R., Ulfig, N., & Witter, M. P. (1993). Morphological and functional correlates of borders in the entorhinal cortex and hippocampus. *Hippocampus, 3,* 303–311.

Woodruff-Pak, D. (1993). Eyeblink classical conditioning in HM: Delay and trace paradigms. *Behav. Neurosci., 107,* 911–925.

Zola-Morgan, & Squire, L. R. (1993). Neuroanatomy of memory. *Annu. Rev. Neurosci., 16,* 547–563.

Index

A